Royal Air Force &
Australian Flying Corps

Squadron Losses

12th November 1918 – 31st December 1920

W.R. Chorley and P.J. McMillan

AVIATION
BOOKS
LIMITED

First published in the United Kingdom in 2021 by Mention the War Ltd., 25 Cromwell Street, Merthyr Tydfil, CF47 8RY.

Cover design: Topics – The Creative Partnership www.topicdesign.co.uk

Front cover image: RAF war grave headstone (Gosnold family).

A CIP catalogue reference for this book is available from the British Library

ISBN 9781911255574

"He Lived And Died A Good Lad And A Gallant Soldier"

Inscription on the headstone of Lieutenant Lyell Keith Swann MM 4 Squadron

Australian Flying Corps, buried in Ascq Communal Cemetery, France

BOOKS by W R CHORLEY

Squadron Histories

In Brave Company - 158 Squadron [With R N Benwell]
To See The Dawn Breaking - 76 Squadron Operations
In Brave Company - 158 Squadron Operations [Revision]

Royal Air Force Bomber Command Losses of the Second World War

Volume 1 1939-1940
Volume 2 1941
Volume 3 1942
Volume 4 1943
Volume 5 1944
Volume 6 1945
Volume 7 Operational Training Units 1940-1947
Volume 8 Heavy Conversion Units and Miscellaneous Units 1939-1947
Volume 9 Roll of Honour 1939-1947
Volume 1 1939-1940 2nd Edition Including Prewar Losses July 1936-September 1939

Royal Air Force & Australian Flying Corps Squadron Losses 1st April-30th June 1918
Royal Air Force & Australian Flying Corps Squadron Losses 1st July-11th November 1918

ARTICLES by W R CHORLEY

Sixpenny Handley War Memorial
Biographies of the twenty-six servicemen named on the Memorial
Published in village journal, *The Downsman*

Table of Contents

GLOSSARY of TERMS

ACM	Air Chief Marshal		Kt	Knight
ADC	Aide de Camp			
AFC	Air Force Cross		LAC	Leading Aircraftman
AM	Air Marshal		LG	London Gazette
ANZAC	Australian and New Zealand Army Corps		LRCP	Licentiate of the Royal College of Physicians
AusFC	Australian Flying Corps			
A/Cmdr	Air Commodore		Lt-Col	Lieutenant Colonel
AV-M	Air Vice-Marshal			
			MA	Master of Arts
BA	Bachelor of Arts		MB	Medicinae Baccalaureus
BDAC	Boscombe Down Aviation Collection [Old Sarum]		MC	Military Cross
			MM	Military Medal
BEF	British Expeditionary Force		MRAF	Marshal of the Royal Air Force
BEM	British Empire Medal		MRCP	Membership of the Royal College of Physicians
BSc	Batchelor of Science			
			MVO	Member of the Victorian Order
CAF	Canadian Air Force			
CB	Companion of the Order of the Bath		NCO	Non-Commissioned Officer
CBE	Commander of the Most Excellent Order of the British Empire		OBE	Order of the Most Excellent Order of the British Empire
CCS	Casualty Clearing Station			
CFS	Central Flying School		OTU	Operational Training Unit
CIE	Companion of the Indian Empire			
CMG	Companion [of the Order Of] St. Michael and St. George		RAAF	Royal Australian Air Force
			RAFM	Royal Air Force Museum
CVO	Commander of the Royal Victorian Order		RAMC	Royal Army Medical Corps
CWGC	Commonwealth War Graves Commission		RASC	Royal Army Service Corps
			RCAF	Royal Canadian Air Force
DCM	Distinguished Conduct Medal		RFC	Royal Flying Corps
DFC	Distinguished Flying Cross		RMS	Royal Mail Ship
DFM	Distinguished Flying Medal		RNAS	Royal Naval Air Service
DSC	Distinguished Service Cross			
DSO	Distinguished Service Order		SHAEF	Supreme Headquarters Allied Expeditionary Force
EG	Edinburgh Gazette		SS	Steam Ship
			S/Ldr	Squadron Leader
FRCS	Fellow of the Royal College of Surgeons			
F/L	Flight Lieutenant		TNA	The National Archives
GCB	Grand Commander of the Bath		UK	United Kingdom
GCVO	Grand Cross of the Royal Victorian Order		US	United States
GM	George Medal		USA	United States of America
G/Capt	Group Captain		USAS	United States Air Service
			USS	United States Ship
HMA	His Majesty's Airship			
HMHS	His Majesty's Hospital Ship		VC	Victoria Cross
HMS	His Majesty's Ship			
HMT	His Majesty's Transport		W/Cdr	Wing Commander
HMY	His Majesty's Yacht			
HS	Hospital Ship		2Lt	2nd Lieutenant
IWM	Imperial War Museum		*	When attached to an award indicates a First Bar; a double asterisk indicates a Second Bar
KBE	Knight Commander of the Most Excellent Order of the British Empire			
KCB	Knight Commander of the Bath			

BIBLIOGRAPHY & SOURCES

BOOKS

Air-Britain [Historians] Limited
Always Prepared : The Story of 207 Squadron Royal Air Force John F Hamlin, 1999
Flat Out : The story of 30 Squadron Royal Air Force John F Hamlin, 2002
Hawks Rising : The story of 25 Squadron Royal Air Force Francis K Mason, 2001
The Camel File Ray Sturtivant & Gordon Page, 1993
The DH.4/DH.9 File Ray Sturtivant & Gordon Page, 1999
The SE.5a File Ray Sturtivant & Gordon Page, 1996
The Squadrons of the Royal Air Force & Commonwealth 1918-1988 James J Halley MBE, 1988

Air-Britain [Historians] Limited in association with Cross & Cockade International
Bristol Fighter : Frank Barnwell's Ubiquitous Multirole Masterpiece Ray Sturtivant, Gordon Page,
                                     James I Halley & Philip Jarrett, 2020
Allen Lane
The Birth of the RAF 1918 Richard Overy, 2018

Fetubi Books
The Sky Their Battlefield II - Air Fighting and Air Casualties of the Trevor Henshaw, 2014
  Great War - British Commonwealth and United States Air Services
  1912 to 1919

Hayward
The Distinguished Flying Medal : A Record of Courage 1918-1982 I T T Tavender, 1990

Macdonald
Fighter Squadrons Of The RAF And Their Aircraft John Rawlings, 1969

Mention The War Publications
Trusty to the End - The History of 148 [Special Duties] Squadron Oliver Clutton-Brock,
  2017 *1918-1945*

Pen & Sword Aviation
Fallen Eagles - Airmen who survived the Great War Norman Franks, 2017
  Only to die in Peacetime

Volplane Press
For Your Tomorrow : Volume One - Fates 1915-1942 Errol W Martyn, 1998
Sweeping the Skies - A History of No 40 Squadron RFC and RAF David Gunby, 1995

Weidenfeld & Nicholson
The War Behind The Wire John Lewis-Stempel, 2014

William Kimber
For Valour : The Air VCs Chaz Bowyer, 1978
RAF Operations 1918-1938 Chaz Bowyer, 1988

OFFICIAL SOURCES, MAGAZINES & JOURNALS

Air Historical Branch [RAF]
Australian War Memorial
Commonwealth War Graves Commission
The National Archives, Kew
Bulletin
Flight
Stand To! - The Journal of the Western Front Association
The London & Edinburgh Gazettes

PRIVATE PUBLICATION
The Flying Camels - The History of No 45 Sqn RAF C G Jefford, Wg Cdr MBE BA RAF
                                     [Retd], 1995

INTRODUCTION

It gives me great pleasure to welcome Paul J McMillan as my co-author for this the third volume and I look forward to continuing this partnership in all future volumes. Paul's input centres on the appendices, particularly those reporting permanent and short service commissioned officers where on numerous occasions he had unearthed material that has escaped my searches in regard to officers 'out of service' dates. With the number of aircraft accidents declining in which the airframe was destroyed, or damaged beyond repair, the information recorded in the appendices takes on an importance in their own right and will have an appeal to persons pursuing research into their ancestors. The data does not cover every promotion, posting et al, but it does provide an extremely useful starting point into the service history of the officer concerned. Regretfully, it has not been possible to pursue similar searches into non-commissioned officers.

The transition from war to peace impacted on all our armed services, but particularly so where the Royal Air Force was concerned and but for Sir Hugh Trenchard in his many conversations with Winston Churchill, whom Lloyd George had given two departments to run, the outcome for this very junior service may well have been terminal; therefore, the foresight of Trenchard not only saved the air force from being absorbed into the pre-April 1918, times of a Royal Flying Corps, administered by the War Office, and the Admiralty controlling those squadrons whose remit centred upon coastal protection.

Although the day was saved, the savage reductions in manpower married to equally swinging cuts in the number of squadrons resulted in a Royal Air Force pared to the bone with most of its energies spread across the Empire, leaving the United Kingdom with a single fighter squadron at Hawkinge and a collection of research and training establishments as the backbone of the home base.

Again, it was Trenchard's vision that in time would establish a training regime that would ensure that those who served would be the finest in all fields of aviation from those who flew to the highly trained technical personnel that maintained aircraft that, in truth and to use a modern expression were *"well past their sale by date."*

And so it would be the norm until the mid-'30s when the expansion of the Royal Air Force was set in train to meet the increasing threat of German aggression.

It now remains for me to thank everyone who has encouraged me in the production of this third volume, principally Simon Hepworth, my publisher, who has waited patiently for this work to land on his desk. In this technical age and with the plethora of websites specialising in all manner of aviation related subjects I extend my grateful thanks to those most diligent researchers who have uploaded their material for inspection. Where appropriate I draw attention to these sites, an example being the Air of Authority - A History of RAF Organisation which is overseen by Malcom Barrass. Any omissions of credit can be laid at my door, and for which I sincerely apologise.

Bill Chorley,
April 2021

Part 1 - Squadron Losses 12th November 1918 - 31st December 1918

Although the guns had fallen silent for the first time in over four years, vigilance remained the 'Order of the Day' and would remain so as each phase of the armistice*agreement was closely monitored. Consequently, operational flying orders continued to be issued with patrols overflying the columns of enemy forces retreating towards the German frontier from France, Belgium, Luxembourg and Alsace-Lorraine and onwards to beyond the Rhine, as stipulated, while Allied forces, including those of the United States, prepared to occupy the Rhineland and various bridgeheads to the east. The agreed timescale for the retreat was fifteen days; to mitigate any suffering of wounded personnel, such cases could be left in the care of Allied medical facilities. An additional sixteen days was approved for the evacuation of German troops from the Rhineland.

The discipline displayed by the German during their withdrawal from territory that until the 11th had been firmly under their control varied. An illuminating article written by Sebastian Laudan and titled *Heinkehr - Coming Home : The Demobilisation and Transformation of the Germany Army 1918-1919* was published in a special edition of *Stand To! - The Journal of the Western Front Association* in October 2019. The majority of the front-line units maintained good order throughout but the same cannot be said of some of the rear echelon formations where valuable stores were discarded and barracks plundered, thereby bringing discredit upon their units. The writer quotes an almost unimaginable figure of six-million troops on the move, all heading towards a homeland gripped in civil disorder and in the mind of many officers abandoned by the rest of the world to its fate.

Appropriately, the same issue carries an equally informative piece by Peter Hart and simply titled *Back Home!* describes the process of dismantling of the British Army. Likewise, the Senior Service and the still fledgling Royal Air Force started down similar paths. The esteemed historian and author Chaz Bowyer states in the first chapter of *RAF Operations 1918-1938* that by the time of the armistice in excess of 27,000 officers and close on 300,000 airmen and airwomen were employed. Over the next fourteen months a cull of 26,087 officers, 21,259 cadets and 227,229 other ranks took place and with it [as my appendices will show] a massive reduction in squadron strength.

Although not on the scale of recent weeks, daily returns from the squadrons continued to report accidents, many being caused by the inclement weather now affecting most of the Continent of Europe. Furthermore, the state of the airfields remained poor. The winter rain reduced landing areas to glutinous mud and when the frosts arrived so undercarriages suffered from dropping into hard rutted surfaces. Maintenance facilities were little improved and the unreliability of aero engines led to many an unscheduled forced-landing in a countryside ravaged by the recent fighting. Months would elapse before the detritus of war would be cleared and the immense task of rebuilding shattered towns and communities could begin. Also to be taken into account was the physical discomfort of the airmen and in particular the aircrew as they endured the discomforts of carrying out their duties in cockpits exposed to the elements. Photographs taken at the time might show many a smiling face, but the attire that was worn to try and combat the worst of the cold must have made for difficulty in handling of the controls of aircraft that were not the easiest to fly.

When peace came, aircrew continued to fly without the reassurance of a parachute that in times of emergency might well save their lives. There were a number of factors; the early designs were bulky and unsuited for the limited cockpit space of the aircraft of the time while the mindset of those that had been responsible for directing air operations had formed the belief that airmen might readily bale out rather than in an emergency try to save his aircraft, or continue to scrap with his opponent if he thought his odds were slim. Thus, it was only artillery observers hoisted in their baskets beneath balloons that were equipped with a simple type of 'chute that if his balloon was likely to be attacked, he could save himself from becoming a fiery torch by jumping to safety. The German air force, however, did introduce para-chutes to their pilots and I make mention of this in some of my summaries of our pilots returning to report such instances. Fortunately, this 'blinkered' approach to aircrew safely would be dispelled, particularly when it was recognised by higher authority that training aircrew to high standards was a costly business and to endanger them when escape from a doomed aircraft by means of a parachute might be instrumental in saving their lives and thereby ensure their continued worth to the service was both sensible and humane.

An aspect of the armistice rarely given prominence was the repatriation of the thousands of Allied prisoners of war incarcerated in camps across Germany. According to an introduction in respect of surviving records, The National Archives [TNA] state an estimated 192,000 British and Commonwealth servicemen were captured by the enemy in the various theatres of conflict, while John Lewis-Stempel in his 2014 work published by Weidenfeld & Nicholson with the title *The War Behind The Wire* quotes a figure of 171,720 British officers and other ranks. There are no precise figures given for airmen, but the fate of some of those held are reported in his text - a few are featured in my first two volumes. In general the conditions in which the majority of prisoners were held were appalling with brutality by the guards meted out to all ranks going well beyond the parameters set by the Geneva Convention [in part this was down to the German military acceptance of traditional Prussian authority which brooked no argument against authority]. The pace of getting the men home was agonisingly slow; in some cases news of the armistice was deliberately withheld at some camps, the inmates only learning that the fighting had ceased by reading discarded German newspapers.

It is to the shame of the British Government that crimes committed against prisoners were not vigorously pursued. A case in point was the inhumane treatment of Captain William Leefe Robinson VC who was taken prisoner in April

1917, and who was so harshly treated by Karl Niemeyer, Commandant at Holzminden that by the time he returned to England in mid-December 1918 his health was completely broken. Officially, he died from heart failure and virulent influenza, but there can be no doubt the actions of Karl Niemeyer were a significant factor.

* *Flight* November 14, 1918, pages 1276 and 1277, detail the clauses of the armistice, the duration of which was set to last for 36 days, with an option of extension. During this period a breach of any of the clauses could be denounced by one of the contracting parties provided 48-hours of notice of intent had been lodged. It is no surprise when reading the various clauses that the main focus of attention was given to the surrender of artillery pieces and machine-guns, weapons that had wrought death and destruction on a unprecedented scale in four years of unrelenting war, but it was the demands made in regard to the High Seas Fleet that caused the German Delegation the greatest alarm and despondency. The pride of their navy, which had remained pretty much intact since Jutland, was about to be reduced to little more than a coastal defence force.

Tuesday 12 November 1918

| 15 Squadron | 2Lt K G Welch | Safe | Unemployed list 25 March 1919 |
| RE.8 C2787 | | | |

T/o Selvigny authorised for practice flying and on return to the airfield 2nd Lieutenant Welch had the misfortune to strike a ridge of soft earth which resulted in a total collapse of the undercarriage. Presumed struck off charge as there are no further entries for this aircraft which was taken on charge as recently as 15th September and issued to the squadron twelve days later. Kenneth Gibbs Welch, born on the 2nd of September 1896, had been seconded from the Royal Garrison Artillery with effect from 17th August 1918 [LG 17 December 1918, supplement 31076, page 14918].

| 23 Squadron | 2Lt G Whittall | + | Caudry British Cemetery |
| 5F.1 Dolphin F5961 | | | |

T/o Bertry East for a practice during which Garth Whittall dived at a steep angle of attack and in pulling out he over-stressed the wings, one of which folded. Moments later the Dolphin, which had been with the squadron since the last day of September, hit the ground and was totally destroyed. From Hyde Park in London, 2nd Lieutenant Whittall was aged 22 and is believed to have joined the squadron the day before the armistice was signed. The reverse side of Army Form B.103c indicates he embarked for France on the 30th of October. His funeral service was conducted on 20th November by the Reverend J B Simpson who was attached to 21 CCS. TNA Kew holds a number of files pertaining to Garth Whittall who was born on the 3rd of January 1896, one example being AIR 79/2741/317022.

| 48 Squadron | Captain L A Payne MC | Safe | |
| Bristol F.2b F6041 | 2Lt T L Jones | Safe | |

T/o Reckem with orders to patrol the corridor Audenarde - Renaix - Tournai in the course of which the Bristol's engine failed and in the ensuing forced-landing near Elsegem [Oost-Vlaanderen] it was damaged beyond repair. 'F6041' had been reconstructed from salvaged parts and arrived with the squadron shortly before being air tested on 10th of October. Born on the 15th of July 1894, Leonard Allan Payne joined the RFC on the 17th of February 1917, noting his next of kin as his brother who at the time was living in the Transvaal. Crossing to France on the 5th of September 1917, and initially attached to 2 Aeroplane Supply Depot, Leonard Payne reported to 48 Squadron at Bray Dunes on the 12th, going on to serve with distinction throughout the remainder of the war. His decoration had been *Gazetted* on 23 July 1918, supplement 30813, page 8832: *'For conspicuous gallantry and devotion to duty. Volunteering to proceed on a special reconnaissance under adverse weather conditions, he penetrated for a distance of nine miles behind the enemy's lines, flying at an altitude of 200 feet, despite the most intense machine-gun and rifle fire. He returned later, his machine riddled with bullets, with required information. Previous to this he had bombed and engaged with machine-gun fire bodies of hostile infantry with the most effective results. He has destroyed one hostile machine and driven down two others out of control. He has at all times displayed the greatest fearlessness and dash.'* Regarding his observer, 2nd Lieutenant Jones, two officers with the surname Jones and initials T L served with the Royal Air Force but, unfortunately, neither of their service records have any information as to the squadrons or units in which they served. One, Thomas Lewis Jones, is shown as having previously served with the 4th Welsh Regiment, joining the Royal Air Force on the 29th of April 1918. The order of his service as typed on Army Form B.103 suggests he subsequently served with the 15th Battalion Welsh Regiment.

49 Squadron	Lt L W Boland	Safe	See 17 January 1919
DH.9 E8864	Canada		
	2Lt N J Spencer	Safe	

T/o Villers-lès-Cagnicourt in the company of other DHs from the squadron to practice flying in formation. Wrecked, owing to an error of judgement, on landing. On charge since 25th September, E8864 is known to have been involved in a raid on the railway junction at Aulnoye on 9th October, 2nd Lieutenant S C Lambert returning to base with his observer, 2nd Lieutenant John Warren, suffering from wounds; he was repatriated to England three days later.

According to entries on Army Form B.103, 2nd Lieutenant Lambert was prone to severe air sickness. His time with the squadron lasted from 19th September until 18th of October, and he was posted to Home Establishment on the day the armistice came into effect. The form for Lloyd Winton Boland has no information pertaining to the units in which he served. His next of kin address is for his father, Mr A G Boland of 176 Fourth Avenue, Ottawa, Ontario and that his bankers as from 11th May 1917, were Cox & Co [common to the majority of officers].

50 Squadron   Captain W C Rowell   Injured   Wolborough [St. Mary] Churchyard
F.1 Camel F2124

T/o Bekesbourne and while making a turn at low altitude flew into the structure of a hangar and crashed. William Cecil Rowell died on the 22nd of May 1919, but I cannot say with certainty if his death was the consequence of the injuries sustained on 12th November. Formerly of the Loyal North Lancashire Regiment, he was badly wounded and was "*placed on the h.p. list on account of ill-health caused by wounds.*" [LG 14 August 1917, supplement 30321, page 8297]. The regiment's history shows a total of twenty-one battalions raised during the *Great War,* William being appointed as a Temporary Lieutenant with effect from 18th September 1914 [LG 6 April 1915, issue 29119, page 3341]. To which of the battalions he was attached is not recorded. His burial in Devonshire at Wolborough is devoid of unit and next of kin. A non-digitised record for this officer is held at TNA Kew under WO 339/8842.

74 Squadron   2Lt W T Carew   Safe   Unemployed list 24 April 1919
SE5a C9066

T/o Cuerne for an unspecified task during which the pilot became unwell and crash-landed. C9066 arrived with 1 Air Issues on 6th August, and thence to the squadron, then at Clairmarais, two days later. His training over, 2nd Lieutenant Carew was initially attached to 1 Aeroplane Supply Depot [this was common practice for pilots on arrival in France] on 2nd October, reporting to 74 Squadron on the 10th. Then, in February 1919, and eight days before the squadron returned to England and Lopcombe Corner north of Salisbury, he was posted on the 2nd to 92 Squadron [SE.5a] at Eil in the Rhineland before being repatriated on the 3rd of March.

79 Squadron   Lt K C Whitwell   Safe
5F.1 Dolphin E4652

T/o Reckem tasked for a line patrol and on return clipped the lip of a road and turned over; believed damaged beyond repair. From the 14th to the 29th of September 1918, Lieutenant Whitwell [he features in my second volume of page 330] was on the establishment of 1 Aeroplane Supply Depot, proceeding on the 29th to join 79 Squadron at Ste Marie Capel. On the 5th of April 1919, he left the squadron, now at Bickendorf, and reported to 1 Aeroplane Supply Depot, Reception Park from where on the 13th he was posted to 6 Issue Section and on the last day of the month to the Depot's headquarters. On the 2nd of May he went to the Reinforcement Park to await demobilisation. In the Second World War he served until relinquishing his commission under the Provisions of the Navy, Army and Air Force Reserves Act 1954, retaining the rank of Flight Lieutenant [LG 3 September 1954, supplement 40271, page 5138].

98 Squadron   Lt W H Whitlock   Safe   Unemployed list 9 October 1919
DH.9 E672/R   Lt McInnes   Safe

T/o Abscon for an air test during which the radiator burst. Forced-landed near Doullens [Somme] and wrecked after running into a post and turning over. With Lieutenant J Andrews as his observer, Lieutenant Whitlock participated in a hotly contested raid on Mons on 30th October, the squadron sustaining serious casualties [see page 368 of my second volume]. His name appears in *The London Gazette* 8 June 1918, issue 30736, page 6864, showing his attachment to the RFC from the 1st/4th Devons, Territorial Forces, with effect from 28th March 1918. His training over he reported to Blangemont and 98 Squadron on the 4th of October.

108 Squadron   2Lt A H Gooch   Safe
DH.9 E676   Sgt W J Jackson   Safe

T/o Bisseghem to practice formation flying. All went well until an oil pipe burst and though the emergency landing was controlled, the rough ground caused sufficient damage that it was deemed the aircraft was beyond repair. E676 had been with the squadron since the 7th of October, and with 2nd Lieutenants Edward Birbeck Thomson and Edward Leslie Chafe as its crew, it helped to drive down an enemy aircraft near Sotteghem on the 4th of November. The engagement was a spirited affair and in total it took the combined fire from seven DHs to seal the enemy's fate whose dogged resistance wounded Edward Chafe. Service and Casualty forms for these officers are quite revealing. Edward Thomson arrived with the squadron from 1 Aeroplane Supply Depot on 23rd September and remained on establishment until the 30th of January 1919, when he reported to 91st Wing at St. Omer from where he went to Alquines on the 3rd of March to join 98 Squadron. When '98' returned to the United Kingdom on the 21st of that month, Edward remained in France, posted on the 8th of April to the Reinforcement Park from where he eventually returned to England on the 1st of August. Edward Chafe, formerly of the Rifle Brigade, also joined 108 Squadron on September 23rd, and although reported as wounded seems not to have been admitted to hospital. From the 13th to the 25th of January he was detached to the Aerial Ranges for a course of instruction, after which he was posted on the 4th of February to 85 Squadron at Ascq. However, 85 Squadron was destined to return home to Lopcombe Corner on the 16th leaving Edward to report the next day to Château Borel and 9th Brigade at Morlenweltz. However, barely had he settled in than he was on the move again, this time to 49 Squadron at Bavai where he arrived on the 22nd. Here he remained until returning home in late April where he joined the growing list of officers whose services were no longer required and he left the Royal Air Force on the 26th of April 1919. Concerning 2nd Lieutenant Gooch, although I cannot be certain [his Army Form B.103 has no details of postings] it is possible he was commissioned from Flight Cadet status on the 24th of August 1918 [LG 10 September 1918, issue 30892, page 10664].

139 Squadron   Lt G A Hadley   Safe   Unemployed list 3 November 1919
Bristol F.2b C999

T/o Arcade for an air test and crashed on return. Two days later, the squadron moved to Grossa where it would remain until returning to England and Blandford [on the outskirts of Blandford Forum in Dorset] on 25th February 1919, and disband a few weeks later on the 7th of March. George Alfred Hadley returned to the service as a Flying Officer on granting of a short service commission with effect from 23rd October 1922 [LG 31 October 1922, issue 32762, page 7673] for duties in the General Duties Branch. Subsequently, and still ranked Flying Officer, he was appointed to a permanent commission, effective from the 26th of September 1925 [*Flight* October 22, 1925, quoting from the *The London Gazette* of 13th October 1925]. His name appears in the magazine on June 25, 1925, page 39, where the results of the RAF Athletic Championships, held at Uxbridge on June 20th, are reported. Representing Spittlegate in the Junior Division, George Hadley retained his title as champion of the long jump. The following month [*Flight* July 16, page 459], he was posted on the 13th to HQ Coastal Area. In the half-yearly promotions of 1927, he was promoted Flight Lieutenant and continuing to trace his postings via *Flight;* August 8, 1930 and October 31, 1930, show he went to RAF Base Gosport on 14th July, from where he was attached to 445 Flight on 6th October. His next posting, 19th July 1935, found him desk bound at the Air Ministry for duties with the Chief of the Air Staff, a position he was still holding the following year, after which his service career is yet to be traced.

203 Squadron   Sgt J A Nicholls   Injured   Valenciennes [St. Roch] Communal Cemetery
F.1 Camel E4422

T/o Bruille with orders to patrol the Valenciennes area and it was whilst so engaged that he got into a spin and crashed near Aubry-du-Hainau [Nord] on the NW side of his patrol area. From West Dulwich, London, 22 year old Sgt Nicholls died late in the day from his injuries. Although a Casualty Card exists for this non-commissioned officer, it does not identify his Christian names, or provide any information as to who conducted his funeral. However, his service number 1270 identifies him as joining the RFC in 1914.

206 Squadron   Lt A L Seddon   Safe   Unemployed list 16 May 1919
DH.9 D5838   2Lt E W Richardson   Safe
Presentation Aircraft: His Highness The Maharajah of Bikanir No 9

T/o Linselles tasked for a line patrol. On return struck a rut on landing and believed damaged beyond repair. Lieutenant Seddon had been seconded from the London Regiment, Territorial Forces, on the 5th of October 1917 [LG 14 December 1917, supplement 30430, page 13160].

And so ended the first day of peace time flying in the Royal Air Force. A dozen aircraft had been written off, eleven during duties on the Western Front and one in the United Kingdom. Two pilots had been killed and another injured, Captain Rowell's subsequent death possibly as a consequence of his crash. It is, however, worth remembering that the total of Royal Air Force casualties on this day, including those mentioned in the summaries, came to twenty-two. They ranged in age from 18 year old Flight Cadet Harry Cecil Matthews of the 24th Battalion, Training Reserve, to 40 year old Air Mechanic William Skinner attached to 14 Squadron and who rests in Grecian soil at Mikra British Cemetery, Kalamaria.

Wednesday 13 November 1918
One of the more notable of events on this day was Russia cancelling the Treaty of Brest-Litovsk, signed on 3rd March 1918, between the Bolshevik Government of Russia and the Central Powers which effectively ended Russian involvement in the *Great War,* and thereby releasing divisions from the east to the Western Front in time for the start of the German spring offensive. Also on this day the occupation by British forces of Constantinople; a photograph taken by William Joseph Brunell showing an officer and a sergeant examining solid brass gun barrels in the dockyard is among the Imperial War Museum collection of interwar photographs, catalogue number Q 14241.

23 Squadron   2Lt L Whitfield   Safe
5F.1 Dolphin D3580

T/o Bertry East for a practice flight which ended with 2nd Lieutenant Whitfield overshooting the landing area at Boussières. Arriving in France on 11th September, and briefly attached to 3 Aeroplane Supply Depot, he reported on the 26th to the squadron at Cappy. Between the 1st and 15th February 1919, he was on leave followed on the 4th of March with a posting to 79 Squadron [5F.1 Dolphin] at Bickendorf in the Rhineland. However, two days later he was cross-posted to 48 Squadron [Bristol F.2b] and, I suspect, went with the squadron to India in late May.

46 Squadron   2Lt A D MacPherson   Safe   Relinquished commission 31 May 1919
F.1 Camel H802

T/o Busigny for an air test but before becoming airborne ran onto rough ground and turned over. Recovered the next day and taken to 7 Salvage Section it seems that the damage was so extensive that after a mere five days of use it was destined for the scrap heap. A former Flight Cadet, he was granted a temporary commission as a Second Lieutenant on 9th May 1918, as reported in *Flight* June 27, 1918, repeated the *Gazette's* list published on 18th June 1918. His operational service lasted from 17th October to 1st February 1919, by which time the squadron was preparing to return to England and Rendcombe in Gloucestershire.

56 Squadron   2Lt R R MacDonald   Injured
SE.5a E1347/F6433/H7261
T/o La Targette for a practice flight only to crash with such force that 2nd Lieutenant MacDonald was unable to recall any of the events leading up to his accident. Unfortunately, his Service and Casualty Form contains no detail whatsoever in regard to his service. His aircraft was one of many that had been rebuilt following previous mishaps and it arrived with the squadron as F6433 but was soon re-numbered H7261.

72 Squadron   SE.5a B685   Reported as written off but without supporting information. By April 1918, it was on squadron charge and in the hands of Captain James Stanley Beatty accounted for an Albatros DIII on 31st May, forced down on the Allied side of the lines near Jebers [sic]. Then with Lieutenant H F C Cannel, whose service record is as yet untraced, at the controls two hostiles described as scouts, were destroyed during the morning of 27th June, near Sharjah. James Stanley Beatty's active service began on the 12th of May 1916, when he joined 5 Squadron, a reconnaissance squadron equipped with a mixture BEs and using Droglandt as its base. Then, for reasons unknown, he was attached on the 20th to 1 Aircraft Depot and thence to 1 Squadron on the 27th. Operating from Bailleul, James flew Morane Parasols and possibly Nieuport 12s before returning to Home Establishment on 27th July. During his brief sojourn in France he was detached to Paris for temporary duty between the 9th and 23rd of July. His movements over the next few years have not been recorded but for his actions in Mesopotamia he was awarded the DFC [LG 15 July 1918, supplement 31457, page 8985: *'During operations near Sheroat, 24th to 30th October, he rendered gallant service in harassing the enemy by machine-gun fire from very low altitudes, being vigorously fired upon the whole time. Captain Beatty has always been conspicuous for gallantry and devotion to duty. On the 21st April 1918, he destroyed one enemy machine and brought down another out of control.'* According to AIR 76/30/86 held at TNA Kew, James Beatty was born on the 15th of October 1890.

79 Squadron   Lt B M F Albanese   Safe   Unemployed list 26 September 1919
5F.1 Dolphin D3745
T/o Reckem briefed for a line patrol. On return, and landing, Lieutenant Albanese swerved to avoid running into a loosely filled bomb crate and in doing so he lost control and ended up inverted. Although identified in *The London Gazette* it seems his Army Form B.103 has not survived the passage of time.

105 Squadron*   2Lt J M Wilson   +   Glasgow [Sighthill] Cemetery
RE.8   Corporal T G Bradshaw   +   Northampton [Kingsthorpe] Cemetery
T/o Omagh and crashed following a midair collision with the RE summarised below, the two aircraft falling to earth near Dromore, nine miles SW from Omagh in Co Tyrone. Both airmen were brought back for burial at the request of their next of kin.

105 Squadron   2Lt L H Booth [Canada]   +   Omagh [Dublin Road] Cemetery
RE.8   Mechanic R Gaudie   Injured
T/o Omagh and destroyed in the manner described above. Lawrence Howard Booth, 20 years of age, hailed from Toronto. Their deaths were the sole casualties reported from the squadron between the armistice and the New Year. During the December, the REs were phased out and replaced by Bristol F.2bs.

* Formed at Waddington on the 23rd of September 1917, it was intended the squadron would work up as a day bomber unit but in April 1918, and now based at Andover, it received RE.8s and was re-classified as a Corps reconnaissance squadron. However, instead of heading for the Western Front, 105 Squadron crossed the Irish Sea and set up its base at Omagh where it supported army units and, in addition, flew anti-submarine patrols.

151 Squadron   Captain D V Armstrong   Injured   Tincourt New British Cemetery
F.1 Camel C6713   DFC South Africa
T/o Bancourt and while stunting over Bouvincourt went into a spinning nosedive from which he failed to recover. Norman Franks in his excellent work recording the exploits of decorated officers who had survived the recent hostilities only to perish subsequently states D'urban Victor Armstrong was alive when lifted from the wreckage but died while receiving treatment at 58 CCS, Lille. He was buried with full military honours by the unit's padre, his headstone being inscribed with the words: *"Will Ever Be Remembered For His Skill And Modesty"*. The citation for his DFC reads: *'A brilliant pilot of exceptional skill. His success in night operations has been phenomenal and the service he renders in training other pilots is of the greatest value, personally supervising their flying and demonstrating the only successful method of attack by night. On the night of 10-11th September, learning that an enemy aeroplane was over our front, he volunteered to go up. The weather conditions were such to render flying almost impossible, the wind blowing about fifty miles an hour, his machine at times being practically out of control. The foregoing is only one of many instances of this officer's remarkable skill and resolution in night operations.'* [LG 3 December 1918, supplement 31046, page 14318]. Army Form B.103 is not available; however, *Wikipedia* shows he was born in the Natal on 26th July 1897, and was educated at Hilton College [Natal]. Between 1916 and his untimely death at the age of 21, he was attached to four squadrons, 60, 44, 78 and 151. While serving with 60 Squadron he was credited with one aerial victory, and as a night fighter pilot he drove down four enemy machines between the 29th of June and 17th September. According to *The Camel File* while with 44 Squadron at Hainault Farm and flying F.1 Camel B3826 he took part in anti-Gotha patrols on 22nd August 1917, 30th September, 1st October, 31st October, 1st November, 6th, 18th and 22nd December, while at

Sutton's Farm as a Flight Commander on 78 Squadron he flew similar patrols in F.1 Camel C6713 on 29th January 1918 and 16th and 17th February. Apparently C6713 was painted overall in red, the name DORIS being added when used by Captain Armstrong, now with 151 Squadron. It was in this aircraft that he achieved his four victories and, ultimately, in which he was fatally injured.

208 Squadron	2Lt C R Curry	Safe	See 14 November 1918

F.1 Camel F1931

T/o Maretz for an unspecified task and on return touched down and promptly turned over; damaged beyond repair. Built by Boulton & Paul at Norwich, F1931 arrived at 1 Air Issues on 13th September and was assigned to the squadron on the 16th. Army Form B.103-I raised in respect of this officer has no information regarding postings but in the section for Regiment or Corps there is a barely legible note that seems to read *"16/Cam* [or Can] *7 Amb."*

210 Squadron	Lt V F Symondson	+	Caudry British Cemetery

F.1 Camel F3132

T/o Boussières authorised to carry out a practice flight during which a slow turn near the airfield resulted in the Camel spinning out of control. During patrols on 30th October, Lieutenant Symondson claimed a Fokker DVII south of Onnezies in the morning and a second over Mareke in mid-afternoon. A brief, but illuminating biography of Vernon Francis Symondson appears on the Bromly War Memorial website courtesy of Uppingham School archives, which I have pleasure in acknowledging. Entering Sandhurst in 1913, he was commissioned to the 13th Hussars from 8th August 1914 to 27th August 1916, on which date he resigned his commission, subsequently becoming a probationary Flight Officer in the Royal Naval Air Service [RNAS] gaining his aviator's certificate at Eastbourne on 12th June 1917. During his time with the Hussars he fell foul of the law and was prosecuted on two occasions in the autumn of 1915, for driving offences, the first for speeding down Egham Hill and the second, a more serious charge, for driving in a dangerous manner while drunk in Piccadilly where he skidded and knocked down a pedestrian. When questioned his manner can only be described as arrogant as if it was of little consequence that he had injured anyone. His Record of Service indicates he had been promoted to Acting Captain but apart from this it is devoid of detail.

Thursday 14 November 1918

One of the least reported actions of the *Great War* ended this day when General Paul Emil von Lettow-Vorbeck* surrendered his forces on the Chambezi river south of Kasama in what was then Northern Rhodesia. Since the outbreak of hostilities in 1914, von Lettow-Vorbeck, nicknamed *The Lion of Africa* had successfully thwarted every attempt by much superior forces to bring him to heel.

Meanwhile, it came to the attention of Marshal Foch that German troops retreating from regions occupied during the war were continuing to commit sporadic acts of violence, thereby contravening the terms of the armistice. A sharp note was immediately conveyed to the German High Command demanding immediate cessation of such practices.

In Vienna the Republic of German-Austria was proclaimed.

* Born 20th March 1870, in Saarlouis, the Rhine Province of Prussia, Paul Emil von Lettow-Vorbeck outlived nearly all his contemporaries, his death at the age of 93 being reported from Hamburg on the 9th of March 1964.

3 Squadron AusFC	Lt Fossett	Safe
RE.8 C2913	Lt C B Hanson	Safe

T/o Premont and set course for Boussières but before reaching their destination a thick fog enveloped their aircraft and soon the crew were hopelessly lost. Forced-landing at Map Reference Sheet 57 cJ11b07 from where the RE was recovered to 2 Advanced Salvage Depot and struck off charge on 12th December. By accessing the Australian War Memorial website a superb black and white photograph can be viewed, and ordered if required, showing officers and men of the squadron in front of RE.8 B2271. The accession number is P00355.026. The same website also has the history of the squadron, which includes the *Great War's* nominal roll.

4 Squadron AusFC	Lt L K Swann MM	+	Ascq Communal Cemetery

7F.1 Snipe E8052

T/o Grand Ennetières for squadron formation flying practice and crashed just beyond the aerodrome. From Parkside in South Australia his headstone has been inscribed: *"He Lived And Died A Good Lad And A Gallant Soldier".* His award of the Military Medal was *Gazetted* on 14 August 1917, supplement 30234, page 8428. A potted history of the squadron can be accessed by way of the Australian Memorial website.

82 Squadron	2Lt R S Wreathall	Injured	Tourcoing [Pont-Neuville] Communal Cemetery
FK.8 F5803	Lt H B Kennedy	Injured	
	Canada		

T/o Coucou for camera gun practice. On return, and in marginal weather, the crew undershot and crashed into a tree some 150 metres or so short of the airfield. The impact was severe and 21 year old Robert Scott Wreathall died the next day, his injuries being described as advanced compression fractures to the ribs and femur. His headstone bears the inscription: *"He Does Well Who Serves The Common Weal Than His Own Will."* Recently rebuilt and tested at 1 Air Issues, the FK had arrived on the squadron three days previously. Army Form B.103-II contains a number of notes concerning Robert Wreathall, the first entry shows he embarked for France on the 16th of October, and arrived with the squadron on the 24th. His burial at Tourcoing, possibly on or before the 28th November, was conducted by the

Reverend M P F Leonard whose parent unit at the time was 7 Squadron. The Record of Service for his observer shows he joined the squadron on the 6th of October. He was admitted to 8 CCS with an injured nose and suffering from concussion; he returned to England on the 29th of November by way of Ambulance Transport,*no doubt to continue treatment and convalesce.

* I am indebted to Sandra Gittings who answered my query regarding the abbreviation A/T which, I am advised, stands for Ambulance Transport, while HMHS which appears on some records interprets as His Majesty's Hospital Ship, a comprehensive list of these vessels can be found on the website BirtwhistleWiki. For a fuller understanding please consult John H Plumridge's *Hospital Ships & Ambulance Trains*; written in 1975, copies are available on *Amazon.* I also wish to thank the following who responded to my *Twitter* question; in no particular order - Simon Worrall, *fourteeneighteen,* David Underdown and Taff Gillingham.

92 Squadron	Lt E E Davies	Safe

SE.5a F8959

T/o from an unidentified location for a protective patrol, heading for the squadron's airfield at Betry, but *en route* he became lost and forced-landed in a field that he been put to the plough near Bohain [Aisne]. Presumed struck off charge. I can only find one Army Form B.103 with the surname Davies and the initials E E and this relates to a 2nd Lieutenant E E Davies of the Australian Flying Corps. However, this shows he was attached to 2 Squadron Australian Flying Corps on the 7th of April 1918, which at the time was equipped with SE.5a and operating from Fouquerolles. There are no further entries, so, it is possible that he subsequently ended up with 92 Squadron. I have consulted the nominal roll for 2 Squadron Australian Flying Corps but can find nothing for this officer.

102 Squadron	Lt F W Knox	Safe	Unemployed list 11 June 1919

FE.2b E7088

T/o 2 Air Issues for delivery to the squadron at Bevillers but lost his bearings in fog and while making a precautionary landing near Cambrai ran against a bank and damaged the FE beyond repair.

203 Squadron	2Lt D H Woodhouse	Safe	Unemployed list 8 July 1919

F.1 Camel F8524

T/o 1 Air Issues and set off the squadron's base at Bruille where, on landing, the Camel ran onto uneven ground and was damaged beyond repair. According to *The Camel File* it had been earmarked for the squadron on November 1st. Douglas Hogarth Woodhouse joined 203 Squadron on the first day of August. On the 26th of April 1919, he was ordered to Köln for duty at 2nd Brigade, remaining here until returning home on the 4th of July.

207 Squadron	2Lt W F A Snell	Injured	Unemployed list 6 August 1919
BE.12 C3180	Sgt J A Forsyth	Safe	

T/o Ligescourt tasked to take the BE which had been left here when the squadron moved to Estrée-en-Chaussée on 26th October, but crash-landed near Abbeville [Somme] and presumed wrecked. Taken on squadron charge on 5th September [presumably as a hack], as the squadron's main equipment was HP O/400 bombers. William Frederick Aubrey Snell arrived in France by air on the 4th of July, nominally on the roll of 215 Squadron. On the 24th he was posted to 2 Aeroplane Supply Depot, and thence to 207 Squadron on 13th August. Treated at 2 Stationary Hospital, he was discharged to duty six days later. He was posted back to the UK on the 21st of June 1919.

208 Squadron	2Lt C R Curry	Safe	See 17 November 1918

F.1 Camel E7311

T/o Maretz briefed for a line patrol. On return, and in poor visibility, he made a heavy landing, pitching the Camel onto its nose and in doing so wrote off his second aircraft in the space of 24-hours. E7311 was accepted from 2 Air Issues on the 1st of October.

Friday 15 November 1918
Admiral Sir David Beatty, Commander-in-Chief of the Grand Fleet received Rear-Admiral Hugo von Meurer on board HMS *Queen Elizabeth* in the Firth of Forth to discuss arrangements for the surrender of the German High Seas Fleet. Both admirals had been present at Jutland in May 1916, von Meurer in command of SMS *Deutschland* while Beatty commanded the 1st Battlecruiser Squadron, viewing the action from the flagship HMS *Lion* which in the course of the battle sustained serious damage in an engagement with the *Lützow.*

19 Squadron	Lt Mitchell	Safe

5F.1 Dolphin E4742

T/o Abscon for a defensive patrol and on return the engine cut resulting in a heavy landing, the Dolphin ending up on its back. Removed to 1 Advanced Salvage Dump on the 22nd and presumed struck off charge. It had been with the squadron for just six days.

35 Squadron	Lt C G Kingman	Safe	Unemployed list 19 April 1919

FK.8 F7429

T/o Elincourt ordered to try and locate FK.8 F7482 [on charge ex-Fienvillers 29th October] reported to have collided with a fence while making a forced-landing during a contact patrol on the day the armistice came into effect [see my second volume page 402] On his return to Elincourt, Lieutenant Kingman crash-landed. There are two reports regarding this incident: AIR 1/1402 states the crash occurred the collecting of an un-named observer from Sivry, while AIR 1/865 indicates; *"wrecked on landing from a travelling flight to locate AW B7482."* Cyril Gilbert Kingman was born on the 1st of December 1894, and joined the RFC on the 4th of August 1917. His first operational posting on the 23rd of March 1918, was to 82 Squadron, and it was with '82' that he saw much of his *Great War* service before joining 35 Squadron on the 9th of August, 24-hours after the start of the *Battle of Amiens*. On 24th November he returned to England.

46 Squadron   Lt H W Clarke   Safe
F.1 Camel D9431/F6269
T/o Busigny tasked for a protective patrol in the course of which a forced-landing was made on a hillside after running out of petrol. Recovered to 7 Salvage Section on 22nd November and presumed struck off charge. As D9431 it had been involved in a landing accident, probably at Vigncourt, on 16th August, Canadian born 2nd Lieutenant R E Thompson*of 80 Squadron, six days into his operational tour, escaping uninjured. Rebuilt, and with its new identity, it arrived with 46 Squadron on 26th October, and 24-hours before the armistice came into effect it was hit by enemy ground fire which wounded Captain C A Brown. Admitted to 48 CCS for treatment, he was evacuated to England by HMHS *Guildford Castle* on 13th November. He had been attached to the squadron since the 29th of September.

* Single, and born on 21st November 1899, Robert Ellerton Thompson's father was an ordained minister. Sadly, when Robert left Canada for the United Kingdom he would never see his country again for he failed to return from an offensive patrol on the 1st of October, the details of his final flight being reported in my second volume on page 278.

80 Squadron   2Lt H P Sharkey*   Safe
F.1 Camel C8335/F6287
T/o Betry West to transit to the squadron's new base at Flaumont where on arrival he blotted his copy book by an ill-judged landing. A rebuilt airframe, it had been on charge for just nine days. It was, however, no stranger to the squadron for as C8335 it was on establishment between 28th July and 10th August, on which date Lieutenant J A C Randal crashed while landing.

* An unusual surname, but no trace in *The London Gazette* for an officer of this name. Fortunately, Army Form B.103 and its derivatives [recently digitised at the RAFM Hendon] throw some light on 2nd Lieutenant Sharkey's service. On the 21st of September he crossed the Channel and was briefly attached to 2 Aeroplane Supply Depot before reporting to Assévillers and attachment to 80 Squadron on the 28th. From the 3rd to the 18th of February 1919, he was on leave and then on the 1st of May he joined 208 Squadron at Stree in Belgium. However, his time with '208' lasted for less than a month for on the 27th he was ordered to embark for Egypt, arriving in the Middle East on the 10th of June. It seems most likely he had been re-posted to 80 Squadron for the day that he landed, so '80' took up residence at Aboukir and it is here that he reported four days later. Finally, on the 2nd of October he went to Alexandria where he boarded a troopship bound for England.

84 Squadron   Sgt P J Palmer   Safe
SE.5a F5509
T/o Bertry for a defensive patrol and written off after running out of petrol and crashing near Maretz airfield. Apart from noting that this SE was Viper engined, *The SE.5a File* has no information whatsoever. Although conjecture on my part, defensive patrol suggests these sorties were flown as a precaution to counter any rogue enemy air activity.

138 Squadron   Lt T W Williamson   Injured
Bristol F.2b F4290 2Lt W L Folkard   +   Stowmarket Cemetery
T/o Chingford and crashed almost immediately. William Landels Folkard appointment as an observer officer was promulgated on 15th August 1918 [LG 24 September 1918, issue 30918, page 11350]. There are a number of websites which identify him, and I'm particularly grateful for an entry beneath the banner *Culford Remembers* instigated by his nephew, William Landels Wild who reports that 2nd Lieutenant Folkard first saw service as a private soldier with the Royal Engineers.

Saturday 16 November 1918
Many provincial newspapers that published on a once a week basis summarised in their editions celebratory reports of how the armistice was received and that appearing in the *Market Rasen Mail* was likely typical for such papers across the nation. As the news spread and flags and bunting began to festoon the streets of this small market town on the edge of the Lincolnshire Wolds an aeroplane flew over and to the delight of the crowd that had gathered performed a 'stunt' before flying away.
   In Belgium, 39 Squadron which had moved into Bavichove of the 6th of the month, disbanded.

15 Squadron   2Lt A Manders   +   Caudry British Cemetery
RE.8 E247
Presentation Aircraft: Punjab No 51 Malwa
T/o Selvigny for a practice flight which, tragically, ended in loss of control and a spinning nosedive. On impact the RE burst into flames. The entry in the register for 2nd Lieutenant Manders is devoid of his Christian name, age and next of

kin. However, I'm reasonably confident that his Christian name was Arthur and that he was born on the 1st of September 1890, and his next of kin was his wife who lived in London. E247 was in France by late September and, briefly, passed through the hands of 12 Squadron for the purpose of ferrying to the squadron, probably on, or soon after, the 25th of October.

64 Squadron	Captain D Lloyd-Evans	Safe
SE.5a E5664/E	MC DFC	

T/o Aniche and believed damaged beyond repair while making an emergency landing in a ploughed field near Estreux [Nord]. Dudley Lloyd-Evans came into the world on the 6th of November 1895, his military service commencing in 1914, when he was commissioned to the South Wales Borders. On the 10th of October 1917, he joined the RFC, his commission being on the General List, and following completion of his training he embarked for France on 17th April 1918, joining 64 Squadron on the 24th. Already he had gained the Military Cross [LG 21 December 1916, supplement 29872, page 12432] and an entry on Army Form B.103c for 22nd September 1918, states *"awarded DFC"*.

Citations for his honours are recorded on *Wikipedia* [which I gratefully acknowledge] and read as follows: *'For conspicuous gallantry in action. He wired the intermediate portion of the enemy's intermediate line which was captured that night. Later, he led a bombing attack with great courage and initiative'*. Recognition of his bravery while serving in the Royal Air Force continues thus: *'A brilliant fighting pilot who has carried out numerous offensive and low-bombing patrols with marked success. He has accounted for six enemy aeroplanes, and in these combats in the air he is conspicuous for his dash and courage.'*

Postwar he remained in the service and gained a First Bar while on operations overseas: *'For gallantry, skill and devotion to duty on 1 November 1920, while accompanying another machine on reconnaissance. Owing to engine trouble the second machine, with pilot and observer, had to make a forced-landing in hostile country. A party of mounted Arabs at once started firing at the observer, who was dismantling a Lewis gun. On seeing this, Flying Officer Evans landed with great peril to himself, took both officers in his already loaded machine, and getting off with much difficulty, returned to Headquarters.'*

Eventually attaining the rank of Wing Commander he retired on the 10th of September 1945. Dudley Lloyd-Evans died in Cheltenham on the 20th of March 1972, and was laid to rest in St. Mary Magdalene's churchyard at Boddington in Gloucestershire.

99 Squadron	Sgt C F R Hemphill	Safe
DH.9A F2737	Mechanic A T Hancock	Safe

T/o Azelot to transit to Crecy on the first stage of the squadron's move to Auxi-le-Château but the formation ran into fog and while attempting to land at Volse [sic] airfield, Sergeant Hemphill lost control and crashed. His Record of Service shows his Service No as 97803 which identifies him as joining the RFC at some time between April and October 1917, either as a direct entrant or a transfer from another of the armed services. Initially he flew as an Aerial Gunner; details of his re-mustering to pilot are absent. I am unable to trace any information regarding Mechanic Hancock. Two other crews also crash-landed but it is believed their machines were repaired and continued in service.

Sunday 17 November 1918
The first Sunday since the declaration of cessation of hostilities and across the land church services were heralded by the loud pealing of bells rung with an overriding sense of relief that the war was at an end. Under the Authority of the Archbishops of Canterbury and York an official form of thanksgiving in the name of Almighty God was issued with the prayers emphasising God's grace in giving *"victory"* to the Allies. Services of similar ilk would have been conducted by service chaplains in all theatres now under Allied occupation.

This, however, was not the official day of thanksgiving; nearly eight months would pass before at the insistence of King George V services of thanksgiving were to be held across the United Kingdom and the Empire on Sunday the 6th of July, while a National Celebration of Peace was to held later in the month on the 19th. A report on the organisation and the background to this historic day appears in *Bulletin'* August 2019, written by Mike Hally who, at the time, was in his final year as a PhD student at the University of Edinburgh.

10 Squadron	2Lt L H Proctor	+	Kortrijk [St. Jan] Communal Cemetery
FK.8 B4185	2Lt W K Salton	+	Kortrijk [St. Jan] Communal Cemetery

T/o Staceghem and reported to have stalled while stunting at low altitude, nosediving in to a house somewhere in Belgium. Formerly of the Army Service Corps, Leslie Horner Proctor's headstone bears the words: *"A Day's March Nearer Home."* The entry in the register for his observer has no information regarding his Christian name or next of kin, but Army Form B.103c shows him to be William Kenneth Salton born on the 17th of January 1897, in the West Hartlepool district. Along with his pilot William was posted to 10 Squadron as recently as the 19th of October. Both were buried on 28th November, the Reverend F S Oakly, attached to 62 CCS, officiating.

57 Squadron	2Lt S C H Biddle	Safe	Unemployed list 22 November 1919
DH.4 F5741	2Lt W G Anderson	Safe	

T/o Bethancourt and on return landed on solid ground and with virtually no headwind ran for a considerable distance before dropping into a trench which damaged the airframe beyond repair. Some documents report the incident occurring 24-hours later. Born on the 1st of September 1899, Sydney Charles Hedley Biddle of Farnham Common in Buckinghamshire, was posted to the squadron on the 29th of September, and on 27th October was wounded on duty; it is likely his wounds were minor as he appears not to have been admitted to hospital. On the 8th of December, he proceeded on leave to England where, I suspect, he fell ill for though scheduled to return on the 22nd, his leave was extended to the 12th of January. Again, conjecture on my part, I suspect he was far from well and in February illness struck and he was admitted to 57 General Hospital, finally being discharged on the 15th of April. Three days after returning to duty he was posted to 25 Squadron at Maubeuge and he remained with the squadron until it returned to South Carleton in Lincolnshire on 6th September, Sydney then being attached to the resident 46 Training Depot Squadron for the remainder of his service. Presently, 2nd Lieutenant Anderson's Record of Service is untraced.

| 110 Squadron | 2Lt R A Gardner | Safe |
| DH.9A F1011 | Mechanic E Reed | Safe |

T/o Bettencourt to transit to Auxi-le-Château ahead of the squadron's planned move on the 20th. Forced-landed and damaged beyond repair. On charge from 18th September, this DH had one hostile aircraft to its credit when early in the afternoon of 5th October, Lieutenant W Armstrong and Sergeant W G H Ambler drove down a Fokker DVII west of Kaiserslautern.

| 110 Squadron | Lt A R MacDonald | Safe |
| DH.9A F1028 | Sgt F W Hawkes | Safe |

T/o Bettencourt similarly charged and wrecked in a forced-landing near Le Grande-Paroisse [Somme] which straddles the Seine east of Fontainbleau. It is not clear on Army Form B.103 as to how long Lieutenant MacDonald had been attached to the squadron, but there are a number of entries showing he had been hospitalised at various times. What is clear is that he remained on establishment until 110 Squadron disbanded at Marquise on 27th August, after which he returned to England.

| 208 Squadron | 2Lt C R Curry | Safe | Unemployed list 11 April 1919 |
| F.1 Camel D3345/F6228 | | | |

T/o Maretz but failed to become airborne and crashed out of control, for the unfortunate Curry this was his third major accident since the armistice and it also marked the end of the Camel era for 208 Squadron, now about to convert to Sopwith Snipes . As D3345 it saw extensive service with 209 Squadron and was present at the famous encounter with Manfred von Richthofen on 21st April, flown by the late Captain E B Drake [please refer to my second volume and pages 140 and 273]. Following the encounter on the 21st, and while supporting operations over Le Hamel on the 4th of July, and with Lieutenant James Andrew Fenton at the controls, it was hit by machine-gun fire and forced-landed near Oresmaux [Somme], turning over in the process. James Fenton's death in action is reported in my second volume on page 267. He had been with '209; since the 26th of April 1918, and had been laid low with a bout of influenza which put him in hospital [55 CCS is recorded on his Record of Service] between the 14th and 19th of June.

Monday 18 November 1918
The start of the second week of the armistice. In Antwerpen and Brussels there were celebrations with the arrival of Belgian troops, while in north-eastern France the citizens of Longwy and Briey welcomed units of the United States army.

| 3 Squadron AusFC | Lt D S Dimsey | Safe |
| RE.8 C2920 | Lt H R Hillier | Safe |

T/o Premont for a mail duty sortie during which they flew into of deluge of rain which caused the engine to fail. Thoroughly soaked, the crew forced-landed on the road between Amiens and Saint-Quentin from where the RE was recovered to 2 Advanced Salvage Dump and struck off charge on 4th December. An Army Form B103 Part 1 has been raised for Lieutenant Hillier but no entries regarding postings et al have been appended.

| 61 Squadron | Lt H A Bird | Safe | Unemployed list 14 June 1919 |
| F.1 Camel C6745 | | | |

T/o Rochford for a training exercise. Crash-landed, owing to engine failure, in the grounds of Bancroft's School at Woodford Green in Essex.

| 79 Squadron | Lt W B Kelly | Safe |
| 5F.1 Dolphin E4746 | | |

T/o Reckem for a line patrol and on return finished up in a ditch; presumed damaged beyond repair. Lieutenant Kelly's service record has no entries, apart from his name. Similarly, the record card for E4746 is confined to the single entry indicating it had crashed, as here described.

Tuesday 19 November 1918
A second day of celebrations taking place in France and Belgium. At the port city of Antwerpen cheering crowds lined the streets for the State entry of King Albert and Queen Elizabeth and to show appreciation to their country's troops as they marched past the royal dais. A photograph of this auspicious event is held by IWM, catalogue number Q 7171. Across the border in France, General Henri Philippe Benoni Joseph Pétain, revered by the nation as *Le Lion de Verdun* was promoted Marshal, and with loud applause ringing in their ears French troops entered Metz, a city that had been under the heel of Germany since its annexing by the Treaty of Frankfurt of 1871, which ended the Franco-Prussian War. Also on this day, American forces crossed into recently liberated Luxembourg. In the West, in contrast to the turmoil in the East, the green shoots of peace were breaking out.

| 9 Squadron | 2Lt E W Steele | Safe |
| RE.8 B4105 | 2Lt P V Kilby | Safe |

T/o Premont for camera gun practice. On return the crew overshot their approach and ended up in a sunken road. It is possible the pilot was Ernest William Steele, but his Record of Service has no supporting information. However, the record for his observer is far more illuminating. Born of the 13th of March 1892, and having arrived in France he reported to Agenvilliers on the 12th of July 1918, for attachment to 9 Squadron. On 16th October he was granted leave until the 30th, this being extended on medical grounds to 5th November. He remained with the squadron, now at Luden-dorf until the 17th of April 1919, when he was posted to Home Establishment.

Note. Anyone wishing to research the squadron's history can do so by way of IX Squadron Association website. For the period reported here [and for years 1914 onwards] an extract of the squadron's history has been supplied by Historical Section committee of Imperial Defence and is written up in AIR 27/125. This gives an overall view by way of the Form 540 as to the squadron's work and movements but references to *Great War* losses and casualties are non-existent. The period from April 1924 to the outbreak of the Second World War is far more illuminating, and with the commencement of hostilities Form 541 has been included.

| 27 Squadron | Lt B M Bowyer-Smythe | Safe | Unemployed list 12 July 1919 |
| DH.4 B2135 | 2Lt W A Hall | Safe | |

T/o Villers-lès-Cagnicourt for a training sortie. On return ran into a loosely filled shell hole, turned over and damaged beyond repair. A squadron veteran this DH since 25th March had accounted for a Fokker DrI 'flamed' by the combined efforts of Lieutenant F W Knight and Corporal F Y McLauchlen SW of Péronne in the evening of 10th May, and during the same sortie and in the same area an unidentified aircraft sent spiralling out of control. On 8th June, again in the evening, Lieutenant Knight, accompanied this time by Lieutenant A R Shephard sent another Fokker DrI into what appeared to be an uncontrolled dive over Flavy. An uneventful few months elapsed before Lieutenant F C Crummey and 2nd Lieutenant F T McKilligin got the better of a Fokker DVII in the early morning of 27th September, smoke being seen after the engagement NW of Émerchicourt [Nord].

   The Records of Service in respect of the officers mentioned vary in content; Lieutenant Bowyer-Smythe's has no information whatsoever, apart from his name, but that for his observer shows he was attached from the 9th of August and served until the squadron commenced reducing in strength in March; thus, on the 10th he reported to Nivelles to join 22 Squadron [Bristol F.2b] and serving until returning home from Spich on the 29th of July. Frank William Knight, born on 17th May 1898, enlisted with the RFC on the 2nd of May 1917, shortly before his nineteenth birthday, and arrived with the squadron on the 10th of March. On June 15th, he proceeded home to Bognor Regis for leave during which he fell ill and was admitted to hospital. It appears his illness was serious enough for him to be struck off the strength of the British Expeditionary Force [BEF] [29th June]; subsequently, he was transferred to the Unemployed List on the 2nd of May 1919 [LG 27 May 1919, issue 31361, page 6515].

   I have not been able to find any records regarding Corporal McLauchlen or 2nd Lieutenant Shephard but in respect of Frank Charles Crummey, he he was on establishment from the 7th of June until 30th October on which date he was taken to hospital stricken with influenza from which he died on 20th November [see the Roll of Honour for further information]. No record has survived for 2nd Lieutenant McKilligin.

27 Squadron	2Lt T A Dickinson DFC	Injured	
DH.9 D2874	USA		
	Captain I H Stockwood	Injured	Unemployed list 4 May 1919

T/o Villers-lès-Cagnicourt similarly authorised and during which both officers came close to being drowned. Entering a steep dive Thomas Archibald Dickinson left it far too late to recover safely, the DH plunging into a deep pond and being completely submerged. On squadron strength since the 8th of July, it appears apart from a soaking his injuries were superficial for there are no entries regarding admittance to hospital. He had been recommended for a DFC, the citation being reported in *The Edinburgh Gazette* on 4 November 1918, issue 13346, page 4066: *'These two officers* [his observer being 2nd Lieutenant Norman Frederick Frome] *performed most excellent service on a recent occasion. Flying at a very low altitude, they bombed a couple of bridges, and then attacked large bodies of the enemy on the roads and in a town. Whilst such engaged they were attacked by four enemy machines, which were driven off. Fire was then opened on them from two machine-guns. Descending to a still lower altitude, 2nd Lieutenant Frome, engaged these guns and drove off the detachment. 2nd Lieutenant Dickinson, the Pilot, then returned over the lines, and despite the fact that his machine had been badly shot about and his petrol tanks empty, landed in safety. The height throughout this fight was never more than 400 feet. The coolness, courage and skill displayed by these two officers is deserving of the highest praise, and it is more the creditable as they had no previous experience of active service flying.'* Consulting *The DH.4/ DH.9 File,* reveals this action took place on the opening day of the *Battle of Amiens* [8th August] and their DH was D2874 now written off as recorded above. Also, it is noted Norman Frome was wounded, though this is not mentioned in the citation. He was, however, taken to 59 CCS with gunshot wounds to one of his feet and on the last day of August he returned to England by way of HS *Stad Antwerpen.** Notes on his Record of Service show he was born on the 23rd of September 1899. Subsequently he was placed on the Unemployed List on 4th March 1919 [LG 28 March 1919, issue 31255, page 4037]. Continuing with his pilot's service, he went to 49 Squadron at Bavai on the 13th of March and on the 11th of April back to England.

   Captain Illtyd Henry Stockwood born on 29th July 1892, and formerly of the Tank Corps, joined the squadron on the 29th of September and had recently returned to duty following a spell in hospital with influenza. On the 20th of January he was attached to 9th Brigade [L'Hermitage and Morlanwelz] and then to Paris for temporary duty between the 4th and 18th of March, on which date he reported to 99 Squadron at Aulnoye before returning home on the 23rd of April.

* The *birtwistlewiki* website, which I have pleasure in acknowledging, records the Belgian built *Stad Antwerpen* was converted from her peacetime role as a Channel Passenger Ferry to a Hospital Ship and as such served in this capacity from 2nd October 1915, until 12th December 1919. Returning to her formal role, she was sold for scrap in 1934. For additional information, please refer to this very informative website. Appendix E at the end of the year will show basic information regarding these vessels.

| 70 Squadron | 2Lt R Sinclair | Safe | See 21 November 1918 |
| F.1 Camel F1548 | | | |

T/o Menin for patrol duties during which a piston snapped and he was obliged to forced-land near Saint-Sylvestre Cappel [Nord] where he ran into some old trench workings which did his aircraft no good at all. Robert Sinclair hailed from Leith in Scotland and was born on the 14th of July 1898.

| 82 Squadron | Lt T G Speake | Injured | Kortrijk [St. Jan] Communal Cemetery |
| FK.8 F7517 | Mechanic A Greenwood | Injured | |

T/o Coucou to transit to the squadron's new home at Bertangles but crashed almost immediately. Aged 19, and from Edgbaston in Birmingham, Thomas Gordon Speake died the next day. Army Form B.103-II shows his funeral being carried out on, or around, the 28th of November, with the Reverend F S Oakly, attached to 62 CCS, leading the service. Thomas's headstone is inscribed with the words: *"The Fragrance Of His Memory Remains."* This tragedy was the last to effect the squadron before returning home on 15th February 1919.

| 148 Squadron | 2nd Lt J A Amor | Safe | Unemployed list 2 May 1919 |
| FE.2b D9117 | 2Lt F Shaw | Safe | |

While in the process of taxiing at Erre in readiness for an air test the centre section collapsed. Removed to 1 Advanced Salvage Centre where it was probably reduced to components. On 17th February 1919, 148 Squadron arrived at Tangmere and disbanded on the last day of June. Nothing, so far, traced regarding the service of 2nd Lieutenant Amor, but Finlay Shaw, born on 19th September 1897, was on the squadron's strength to 10th February 1919, when he was posted to 82 Wing headquarters at Serny. This, I suspect, was purely administrative for on the same day he returned to the United Kingdom.

Wednesday 20 November 1918
In compliance with the statutes of the armistice regarding the surrender of the German High Seas Fleet, U-boats began arriving off the East Anglia port of Harwich where they were placed under the control of Royal Navy Harwich Force.

After a mere two months of service 94 Squadron disbanded at Kenley; it is unlikely any aircraft were received during these few weeks. Similarly, 116 Squadron which had formed in December 1917, as a night bomber squadron disbanded at Feltham having been issued with a handful of HP O/400s in the August.

| 88 Squadron | Lt A T Daw | Injured | |
| Bristol F.2b E2610 | | | |

T/o Aulnoye to transit to Dour where the main body of the squadron assembled two days previously. Encountering adverse weather Lieutenant Daw crashed to the NW of Bavay [Nord]. Severely shocked, he was admitted to hospital and on the 28th evacuated by to the UK aboard HMHS *Western Australia* to England to continue treatment. Army Form B.103c shows he joined the RFC on 1 May 1917, and served at 1 Aeroplane Supply Depot from December 1917, until his posting to 88 Squadron on the 5th of November 1918.

| 217 Squadron | 2Lt S J Saunders | Safe | |
| DH.4 A7875 | 2Lt T C Tyers | Safe | Retired list 18 July 1923 |

T/o Varssenaere and wrecked on return while attempting to land. 2nd Lieutenant Saunders features in my second volume, pages 163 and 229. He had recently returned to duty following the better part of a fortnight in hospital having succumbed to the influenza pandemic. He was posted home on the 19th of March 1919. 2nd Lieutenant Tyers continued to serve in the postwar air force and is almost certain to have served overseas for on 29th April 1923, he was posted to the non-effective pool at Uxbridge on transfer to Home Establishment; a few months later he was placed on the Retired List on account of ill-health.

Thursday 21 November 1918
A day for ever remembered in the annals of Naval history, the dawn surrender of the German High Seas Fleet. The importance of the occasion was not lost on the publicists of the Royal Navy who arranged for the press to present and as the sun rose majestically over the mist and bleak waters of the North Sea a column of battleships, cruisers, destroyers and a plethora of smaller vessels with their skeleton crews bore down on the Firth of Forth. In addition to the reporters and their cohorts of photographers present to witness Britannia's triumph over her adversary of the past four years, so to were several artists on hand ready to capture the scene. One was the noted marine artist James Patterson who watched the unfolding drama from the deck of HMS *Revenge* and whose vivid interpretation of the event is now in the possession of the National Galleries Scotland. For the naval officers and seamen present, what thoughts must have passed through their minds as the leviathans of the German Fleet closed on their temporary anchorage led by the C-class

Light Cruiser HMS *Cardiff*. Many, like the skeleton crews sailing into captivity, would have been present at Jutland where the thunder of war had sent so many of their compatriots to their doom.

At Port Meadow 93 Squadron disbanded. Although initially formed at Croydon as an SE.5a fighter squadron on 23rd September 1917, it never became operational and disbanded at Tangmere on 17th August. A second attempt, this time with Sopwith Dolphins, was made at Port Meadow in Oxfordshire, but as indicated this, too, came to nothing. It is worth recording, however, that IWM in their register of airfields has recently reported that an Obelisk commemorating those who served at this airfield was unveiled on the 23rd of May 2018, by the Lord Lieutenant of Oxfordshire, Tim Stevensone. It is described as black in colour on a stone base on which is inscribed the names of seventeen airmen who lost their lives while stationed at the airfield.

9 Squadron	Lt A Holdsworth	Safe	Unemployed list 2 February 1919
RE.8 C2609	Lt E R Beckwith	Safe	Unemployed list 26 July 1920
	Canada		

Presentation Aircraft: Mauritius No 7
T/o Premont tasked for Corps duties and crashed near Beaumont after running into dense fog. Built in the Daimler works at Coventry, this RE was funded by the Colony of Mauritius, the seventh such presentation made by the Colony. It was taken on charge on the last day of September. Lieutenant Holdsworth arrived with the squadron as recently as 21st October and was posted home on the last day of January. Ernest Ralph Beckwith, born 3rd December 1897, remained in the postwar air force and subsequently transferred to the Administrative Branch until his placement on the Unemployed list [LG 16 July 1920, issue 31983, page 7581].

20 Squadron	2Lt J L Boyd	Safe	Unemployed list 21 May 1919
Bristol F.2b E2252	2Lt W A Rogers	Safe	

T/o Clary-Iris Farm for a practice flight but flew into a thick mist and crash-landed near Cambrai. E2252 had been on charge since the 23rd of August. 2nd Lieutenant Boyd's service has not been recorded in any detail, and I cannot find any reference to the service of his observer.

22 Squadron	Lt L N A Caple [Canada] +	Sebourg British Cemetery
Bristol F.2b C887		

T/o Aulnoye to transit to the squadron's new base at Witheries. Encountered dense fog and probably became disorientated for it is reported he nosedived into the ground near the aerodrome at Bertangles. From Vancouver, and formerly of the Canadian Medical Corps, Leonard Norman Akerman Caple was *Gazetted* to the RFC on 20th December 1917. On completion of his training he joined the squadron, then at Serny, on the 25th of June, and apart from a spell of leave taken between the 10th and 24th of October, his service was unbroken. He was buried early in December, the service being led by the Reverend J H McKen who was attached to Headquarters 20th Division. At the bequest of his parents, Leonard's headstone is inscribed: *"Good And Faithful Servant Enter Thou Into The Joy Of The Lord."* [Taken from Matthew 25, verse 21].

70 Squadron	2Lt R Sinclair	Safe	See 22 November 1918
F.1 Camel F1548			

T/o Menin and wrecked in a crash brought about by engine failure. Robert Sinclair had walked away from a serious crash on the 19th.

87 Squadron	Lt D H P Johnson	Safe	Unemployed list 22 April 1919
5F.1 Dolphin C4158			

T/o Boussières to practice patrol procedures only to come to grief on Inchy airfield, occupied at the time by 3 Squadron. On establishment since 21st October, Lieutenant Johnson was attached on the 30th of January 1919, to 5th Brigade at Namur only to be posted 24-hours later to 23 Squadron [Dolphin] at Clermont. He was posted to 'Home Establishment' on 6th March, nine days before 23 Squadron returned to Waddington and now reduced to a cadre.

91 Squadron	Captain J L Horridge	+	Tottington [St. John's] Free Church of England Chapelyard
5F.1 Dolphin			

T/o Kenley and while climbing out, and estimated by eyewitnesses to have gained height to around 200 feet, the Dolphin's engine cut. Nose high, it stalled and dived headlong onto Kenley Common. John Leslie Horridge, born 22nd June 1896, was 22 years of age. A partial record of his service suggests he embarked for France in 1916, serving at first with 7 Squadron and later with 4 Squadron before returning to England on the 17th of June 1917. TNA has a record for him under AIR 76/238/124. A bronze plaque to his memory has been fixed to the east wall of St John's church.

92 Squadron	Lt Griffiths	Injured
SE.5a F903		

T/o Bertry and while practising aerobatics over the airfield he rolled at low altitude and, inverted, struck the ground. The SE had been with the squadron for a mere eight days.

| 104 Squadron | 2Lt W McCullagh | Safe | Unemployed list 3 July 1919 |
| DH.9 D3100 | Mechanic Potter | Safe | |

T/o Azelot to transit to Blangey and thence to Maisoncelle where the main body of the squadron had been in situ for the past 24-hours. On arrival at Blangey 2nd Lieutenant McCullagh misjudged his approach, crashed and damaged the DH beyond repair. William McCullagh was born on the 3rd of August 1892. His Record of Service is devoid of information regarding postings et al.

| 104 Squadron | 2Lt L C Pitts | Safe | Unemployed list 6 March 1919 |
| DH.9 D3248 | Mechanic S H Wilcox | Safe | |

T/o Azelot with similar intent only to crash out of control. 2nd Lieutenant Pitts had joined the squadron on 25th August and on the 8th of January was laid low with influenza. Following initial treatment he returned to England on HMHS *Brighton* on the 17th.

| 104 Squadron | Lt S T Crowe | Safe | Unemployed list 26 August 1919 |
| DH.9 E659 | Mechanic T Lee | Safe | |

T/o Azelot similarly tasked and reported to have forced-landed at the Paris Depot with a failing engine; damaged beyond economical repair. Sinclair Tudor Crowe, a Londoner born on 4th of August 1898, joined the squadron on the 18th of September. On 11th January 1919, he returned to England but returned on the 10th of March and was attached to 206 Squadron [DH.9] at Bickendorf. On the 24th of April he was taken to 34 Stationary Hospital with an un-diagnosed illness and thence on the 1st of May back to England aboard HMHS *Brighton*.

| 104 Squadron | Lt A W Hardwick | Safe | Unemployed list 20 February 1919 |
| DH.9 E8974 | Mechanic White | Safe | |

T/o Azelot heading for Blengey but crashed near Doullens [Somme]; all four DHs struck off charge on 29th November. Alfred William Hardwick, born 24th July 1899, arrived in France on the 7th of September and by the 20th feeling very unwell he was taken to 8 CCS where it was confirmed he was suffering from influenza. Thus, it was October 2nd before he reported to the squadron. Then, a week after his crash, and no doubt still feeling the effects of his recent bout of 'flu, he was admitted to 12 Stationary Hospital with tonsillitis and although discharged on the 7th of December his health was still causing concern and on the 3rd of January he was re-admitted, this time to 14 General Hospital. There are no further entries on his service file.

| 215 Squadron | Lt S H Griffiths | Safe | See 6 April 1919 - 216 Squadron |
| HP O/400 D8321 | 2Lt D F Harrison | Safe | Unemployed list 14 March 1919 |

T/o Le Bourget for Alquines only to run into bad weather and with their engines failing the crew crash-landed at Attainville [Val d'Oise]. Of the Honourable Artillery Company and Royal Air Force Stanley Henry Griffiths was posted to the squadron on 11th October and falling ill on the 28th was taken to 8 Canadian Stationary Hospital suffering from influenza. The attack was relatively mild and he returned to the squadron on the 5th of November. Subsequently, he had several postings; on 25th January 1919, he went to 97 Squadron at St. Inglevert, and next to 216 Squadron on the last day of February, both squadrons operating HP O/400s. Following his second crash on 6th April, he flew Bristol F.2bs with 88 Squadron, reporting to Nivelles on 18th April. Interestingly, Army Form B.103-II shows the squadron returning to Home Establishment on 20th September, well over a month after some records indicate disbandment at Nivelles on the 10th of August.

Friday 22 November 1918
During the day King Albert and Queen Elizabeth continued their triumphal State journey across Belgium, arriving eventually in Brussels. The occasion is recorded in the diary of the 61st Field Battery, 14th Brigade of the Canadian Field Artillery, which I acknowledge, whose march towards Germany as part of the occupying forces had halted at Mons owing to problems with supplies. Thus, the delay enabled: *"26 Officers from Corps Headquarters and 10 each from the 3rd and 4th, Canadian Division to proceed by bus to BRUSSELS this date to witness the State Entry of the King and Queens of the Belgians. A number of officers also proceeded by motor car."*

There was, by contrast, no such joy in Germany where the unrest that marked the final days of the war continued unabated and in true revolutionary fashion it was the civil powers that often bore the brunt of a disgruntled population. In Berlin the police headquarters came under attack, while the knowledge that the once powerful High Seas Fleet was no longer in German ports but on the other side of the North Sea, never to return, added to the general air of despondency.

| 2 Squadron AusFC | Captain R L Manuel | Safe | |
| SE.5a F8955 | DFC* | | |

T/o Pont-a-Marq to practice patrol leadership and on return in gathering mist and darkness crashed out of control. Though salvaged it is likely the SE was struck off charge. *Flight* August 8, 1918, page 880, reports the citation to Captain Manuel's award: *'During the past month, while on an offensive patrol, his machine was badly damaged in an encounter with an enemy aeroplane which he brought down out of control. On his return home he saw another enemy machine below him. At great personal risk, owing to the state of his machine, he nevertheless attacked and brought it down. He is a most skilful pilot of great determination.'* The citation for the First Bar appears in the magazine's issue for December 12, 1918, page 1399: *'On many occasions this officer has led his patrol with exceptionable ability and courage, notably on September 16th, when, with a patrol of 11 machines, he engaged 15 hostile aircraft. By skilful manoeuvre he completely defeated the enemy in a combat that only lasted 20 minutes, at the expiration of which period only four hostile machines remained in the air, and these retired. Six of the enemy machines were seen to fall in a manner that would justify the supposition that they would crash.'*

My remarks appended to the summaries for 3 Squadron and 4 Squadron of the Australian Flying Corps apply in respect of 2 Squadron. All have an excellent selection of photographs, many of which are no longer copyright protected. With various passages as a guide, I have traced these awards to *The Edinburgh Gazette* supplement to issue 13300, of 7th August 1918, page 2816, and supplement to issue 13362, of 5 December 1918, page 4469. The former shows his Christian names as *Roby Lewis* and this has enabled me to discover additional information regarding this courageous officer. *Wikipedia* shows he was born at Bael Bael near Kerang in the Commonwealth of Victoria on 7th October 1895, enlisting on 5th April 1916, in the 43rd Battalion, Australian Imperial Force, transferring to the Australian Flying Corps a year later - almost to the day. On completing his flying training he went to France, where he was attached to 2 Squadron Australian Flying Corps on 6th February 1918, scoring his first combat success 24-hours after the formation of the Royal Air Force on April Fools' Day 1918.

Postwar, the honour of leading the ANZAC Day [25th April] flypast over London fell, appropriately, to this decorated officer. During the Second World War he served with the Royal Australian Air Force in an administrative position. Between the wars, and post-1947, he farmed, retaining his pilots' flying licence and enjoyed taking to the skies until shortly before his death at the age of 80 on 18th October 1975. The website Gannawarra Shire Council also carries a tribute and photograph of Roby Lewis Manuel.

| 9 Squadron | Captain M Forsyth | Safe |
| RE.8 C2688 | Lt D S Robertson MC | Safe |

Presentation Aircraft: Punjab No 28 Shahpur

T/o Premont to liaise with cavalry near Leignon in the municipality of Ciney [Namur]. With dusk approaching Captain Forsyth landed on an unidentified airfield only to have the misfortune to break the undercarriage. At the time his substantive rank was 2nd Lieutenant but he had been granted Acting Captain with effect from 14th November 1918, this being *Gazetted* on 22 November 1918, and repeated on page 1361 of *Flight* November 28, 1918. In its issue of July 31, 1919, page 1018, is the announcement: *"Forsyth 2nd Lieut. [A/Capt.] M, 9th Sqdn"* was one of many mentioned in despatches at the behest of Field-Marshal Sir Douglas Haig, late Commander-in-Chief, the British Armies in France, the official wording being: *"who served under his command during the period Sept. 16, 1918, to March 15, 1919, whose distinguished and gallant service and devotion to duty be considered deserving of special mention."* This appears to be his final mention in the magazine.

Referring to Army Form B.103, Matthew Forsyth came from the Brixton area of London, being born on the 8th of August 1895, and enlisting with the RFC on 27th October 1917. He was posted to 9 Squadron on the 4th of June, serving with the squadron until he was invalided home on HMHS *St. Andrew* on the 4th of March 1919, suffering from the after effects on influenza which on 26th February caused his admission to 14 General Hospital. His decorated observer was the son of the Reverend Robertson who at the time of his son's enlistment with the 14th Battalion, South Lancashire Regiment, held a living in Gloucestershire. On the 17th of June 1918, Lieutenant Robertson joined the Royal Air Force as an Observer Officer, arriving at Agenvillers 24-hours before 9 Squadron transferred to Quevenvillers on the 17th July. Apart from leave and temporary duty with 2nd Wing [7th to 26th May 1919] he was on the nominal roll until 20th July 1919, when he returned to England. Eleven days later 9 Squadron departed Ludendorf for Castle Bromwich.

| 12 Squadron | Lt C G Burnip | Safe | Unemployed list 21 January 1919 |
| RE.8 C2867 | | | |

T/o Estourmel for aerial post duties and owing to engine failure crashed while attempting to land. It appears the RE was later returned to England and lodged with 37 Training Depot Station, Yatesbury, where on the 20th of March, a Court of Inquiry was convened to investigate the loss of instruments from C2867. What conclusions were reached has not been recorded. Although I cannot be certain, I strongly suspect this officer to be formerly 473335 Private Charles Gordon Burnip of the RAMC who was granted a temporary commission in the rank of 2nd Lieutenant for duty with the RFC on the 2nd of February 1918. At the time he was serving in Egypt, his return to the UK from Alexandria aboard the *Caledonia* being dated 24th of May. His officer status is reported in *The London Gazette* 3 May 1918, supplement 30666, page 5340.

18 Squadron	2Lt E F Wilkinson	+	Fillièvres British Cemetery
DH.4 A7857	South Africa		
	Mechanic T T Whitlock	Safe	

T/o La Brayell with the intention of returning the aircraft to 2 Aeroplane Supply Depot [possibly at Berck-sur-Mer] but, it seems, a landing was made at La Bellevue, home at the time for 4 Squadron. Resuming his journey, Ernest Fletcher Wilkinson for reasons that are unclear decided to land and while banking at 400 feet lost control and dived to the ground. Miraculously, his passenger escaped relatively unscathed. Born on the 3rd of July 1899, at least two files for this officer are held at TNA Kew, AIR 76/547/201 and AIR 339/131180, while Army Form B.103 shows he was attached to 18 Squadron with effect from 28th September. His funeral was held on the 9th of December, officiating the Reverend G S Purvis who was attached to 6 Stationary Hospital. Ernest Wilkinson's father also served; the CWGC website shows the rank Major while the casualty form suggests Lieutenant-Colonel.

22 Squadron   Captain A J F Bawden   Safe
Bristol F.2b C1035 Lt D C Davies   Safe

T/o Witheries to return to Aulnoye where on arrival a landing was made on rough ground, this damaging the Bristol beyond repair. Of the 5th Battalion, Cornwall Light Infantry, Territorial Forces, Captain Bawden was seconded for Royal Air Force duties on 27 August 1918 [LG 30 December 1918, supplement 31086, page 15177]. Postwar he returned to his army duties with the 5th Battalion and, I believe, relinquished his commission [along with hundreds of other Territorial Officers] as notified in *The London Gazette* 12 December 1921, Issue 32546, page 10119. David Clifford Davies left England for France on the 24th of August and reported to Maisoncelle and 22 Squadron on the 30th. He remained on strength until 31st July 1919 [by which time the squadron was part of the Occupation Forces and based at Spich] when he was posted home, probably to await his discharge.

43 Squadron   Lt J W Milner   Injured   Unemployed list 10 September 1919
7F.1 Snipe E8037

T/o Bissehem for a line patrol which ended with the Snipe in a canal near Courtrai, the cause attributed to engine failure. Earmarked for issue on 5th September, it eventually arrived with the squadron from 2 Aeroplane Supply Depot on the 30th; it was noted the petrol tank had been fitted with U bearers. John William Milner of Birmingham, born on 21st October 1898, had seen extensive service since his enlistment on 14th March 1917. His training finished, he arrived in France on 6th October 1917, passing through 1 Aeroplane Depot before joining 66 Squadron [F.1 Camel] at Estrée Blanche on the 13th. However, a month later he returned to the UK and on his return to the Western Front on the 19th of May, it was initially intended he should be attached to 206 Squadron [DH.4] at Alquines. This, however, did not materialise and on the 21st he reported to Clairmarais to fly Camels with 4 Squadron Australian Flying Corps. Then, on 17th July he was nominally posted to 9 Brigade Rozoy and thence to 43 Squadron the next day. At the time 43 Squadron was still equipped with Camel, but in the month following John Milner's arrival began converting to Sopwith Snipe. The last entry on this Record of Service predates his accident, noting that from the last day of August to 14th September, he was away on leave.

45 Squadron   *Not reported*
F.1 Camel F3979

T/o Izel-lès-Hameau and reported as crashed, the wreckage being sent to Laburgel [sic] where it was struck off charge on 6th December. According to *The Camel File* it had been on establishment for a mere seven days.

48 Squadron   Lt W V N Grant   Safe
Bristol F.2b E2413 Sgt R L G White   Safe

T/o Nivelles for an observation patrol between the Belgian capital and Charleroi during which the Bristol ran out of petrol and crash-landed near Lauwe, now a borough of the city of Menen. Seconded from the 4th Battalion, Northumberland Regiment [LG 23 April 1918, supplement 30647, page 4954], Lieutenant Grant's service record is lacking in detail, except to confirm his previous army service. Postwar he returned to his regiment and relinquished his commission as notified *The London Gazette* 16 December 1921, supplement 32552, page 10347.

61 Squadron   F/Cdt H H B Newbury   Injured
F.1 Camel E5130

T/o Rochford but while climbing away chocked the engine. Through lack of experience, instead of landing straight ahead he made the near fatal error of trying to return to the airfield and in doing so he lost control and crashed. I am reasonably confident that he recovered from his serious injuries and in the Second World War rejoined the service and was commissioned to the Administrative and Special Duties Branch, his appointment being confirmed on 27 February 1941 [LG 21 March 1941, issue 35114, page 1685].

64 Squadron   2Lt H B Harmsworth   Safe   Unemployed list 2 August 1919
SE.5a F5468/T

T/o Aniche to fly to the squadron's new base at Saultain where on arrival he collided with his squadron colleague, summarised below. Help was quickly to his aid and he was helped from the wreckage, shaken but otherwise unhurt.

64 Squadron   Lt Crofts   Safe
SE.5a F5612/3

T/o Aniche similarly charged and wrecked in the manner outlined above. The survival of the two officers was attributed to the collision occurring at the relatively low height of twenty feet. F5612 was received by the squadron on the 3rd of November.

70 Squadron   2Lt R Sinclair   Safe   See 24 January 1919
F.1 Camel E1595

T/o Menin for a line patrol and crashed whilst landing; this was his third serious accident in less than a week. Sent with a view for repair at 8 Salvage Section, but presumably scrapped. On charge since the 5th of September, it was in action during the morning of 9th October when a patrol led by Captain Sydney Tyndall Liversedge accounted for an LVG C and a Fokker DVII. Born at Honley in Yorkshire on 15th August 1897, Sydney enlisted with the RFC on the 15th of May 1917, and was commissioned to the General List with effect from the last day of August [LG 22 September 1917, supplement 30299, page 9826]. His service in France began on 12th November 1917, but it was not until the 6th of

March that he was attached to 70 Squadron. This lengthy delay was owing in part to ill-health and his Record of Service indicates he was hospitalised from the 28th November to the 10th of January, when he was placed on the establishment of 2 Aeroplane Supply Depot. According to his profile, as recorded by *Wikipedia*, he accounted for a total of thirteen aerial victories, achieved between the 6th of April and 9th of October, some of which were shared. Strangely, for the time, he was not decorated and it seems he left the service and settled for a long career in engineering. There are no indications of Second World War service, while the precise date of his death in Huddersfield in 1979 has yet to be established.

79 Squadron	Lt C H Church	Safe	Unemployed list 22 April 1919
5F.1 Dolphin E4712			

T/o Reckem for a line patrol and while returning to base the engine failed owing to overheating. In the ensuing force-landing the Dolphin collided with a line of telegraph wires, crashing out of control. It had been on squadron charge since the 22nd of September. Posted to the squadron on the last day of October, his service was fairly limited for on the 9th of December he was taken to 55 CCS and thence to 51 General Hospital and it was not until the 4th of March 1919, that he was discharged. Six days later he returned to England.

112 Squadron	Lt W D H Baird AFC	+	Edinburgh [Morningside] Cemetery
F.1 Camel D6629			

T/o Throwley and whilst engaging in aerobatics lost control at the top of a loop, estimated by eyewitnesses to have been in the region of 3,000 feet. Out of control his aircraft fell near Detling on the NE side of Margate in Kent. William Dodds Haldane Baird's AFC was gained while ranked 2nd Lieutenant [LG 31 December 1918, supplement 31098, page 97] and was published in the New Year's Honours List of the 1st of January 1919.

151 Squadron	Lt M S Cook [Canada]	Safe	Unemployed list 13 April 1919
F.1 Camel C1629			

T/o Bancourt for practice flying and damaged beyond repair while landing. First issued to 3 Squadron on the 7th of April, C1629 was damaged in a landing accident on the 8th of May, 2nd Lieutenant M C Kinney*escaping injury. While undergoing repairs at 2 Aircraft Salvage Depot the Camel was converted to night fighter standards and issued to 151 Squadron at Vignacourt on 30th September. With the requirement for a dedicated night fighter squadron over, the squadron returned to Gullane in Scotland on 21st February 1919, and disbanded on the 10th of September. Maynard Stephen Cook, born 21st June 1895, was formerly of the RNAS and by the 16th of June 1918, was on the nominal roll of the squadron.

* Lieutenant Mark Curtis Kinney of Ohio was born on the 7th of September 1891, joining 3 Squadron on the 11th of March 1918, and was wounded twice, the last time on the 16th of August. He relinquished his commission on account of ill-health, contracted on active service, on the 5th of March 1919 [*Flight* March, 1919].

206 Squadron	Lt G A Pitt	Safe	Unemployed list 4 February 1919
DH.9 B7680	Lt H O F B Blew	Safe	

T/o Linselles for an unspecified task and written off at Elseghem [Oost-Vlaanderen] following a burst radiator. Taken on charge on 13th June, and under the command of 2nd Lieutenant M G Perry and Sergeant W C Blyth drove down a Fokker DVII near Roeselare on 29th August, both crew being wounded during the exchange of fire. Lieutenant Pitt features in my two previous books. On Saturday the 11th of May, during an attack by 206 Squadron on the railway station at Armentières his DH.9 B7587 was badly shot about and the observer, 2nd Lieutenant Charles Edward Anketell mortally wounded [see page 139 for a full description reporting the loss of B7587]. Although unscathed, Pitt's Record of Service shows he was admitted to hospital on the 20th with an undiagnosed conditions, and two days later he was receiving treatment at 24 General Hospital Etaples from where he was granted sick leave until the 12th of June. However, it was not until the 27th that he resumed his tour of operations with the squadron. Then, during escort duties on the 15th of August he crashed on return to Alquines [please refer to page 158 on my second volume for details], after which there were no further alarms other than those experienced by all aircrew in the course of executing the war. He was posted back to the United Kingdom on the 3rd of February. Lieutenant Blew's service is recorded from when he disembarked at Alexandria on the 19th of June 1919, having sailed from the French post of Marseilles on the 14th. He remained with the squadron until late October, the final entry on Army Form B.103 reading: *"Embarked at Alexandria on H.T. "Himalaya" for Marseilles en route U.K., Cairo 29.10.19"*. It is noted he was formerly of the Royal Sussex Regiment. During the Second World War he served on operations and only relinquished his commission on the 7th of May 1948 having reached the age limit for recall to active service [LG 4 May 1948, supplement 38282, page 2814].

Saturday 23 November 1918

On this day *The Scotsman* [and no doubt other leading newspapers] published extracts from David Lloyd George's famous speech in which he intoned Britain would be *"a fit country for heroes to live in"**though a century on a more jaundiced view of the Prime Minister's pronouncements is closer to reality. With his Welsh background David Lloyd George was an orator of the highest order, equally matching the patriotic utterances of another Prime Minister who stirred the nation's hearts at times of great adversity - Winston Spencer Churchill. With the influenza pandemic showing no sign of abating for many ex-servicemen they would never witness the rose-tinted fruits of victory as proclaimed by the Welsh Wizard. Just one example among many was the passing this day in a Canadian hospital at Valenciennes of

Driver Clive Burrell [an Old Oundelian] of 126 Brigade, Honourable Artillery Company who now rests in the town's St. Roch Communal Cemetery.

* A sentiment not shared at the time by Lieutenant-Colonel Rowland Feilding of the 1st/15th London Regiment, and reported in the *Aftermath Special Edition of Stand To! The Journal of the Western Front Association,* in their 2019 issue. The Colonel's remarks are printed at the top of page 6 as a lead-in to Peter Hart's most informative article *Back Home!: "The raging desire still continues to be demobilised quickly. Nevertheless, I feel pretty sure that, there will be pathetic disillusionment. In the trenches the troops have had plenty of time for thought, and there has grown up in their minds a heavenly picture of an England which does not exist, and never did exist, and never will exist as long as men are human."* A prophetic observation.

2 Squadron AusFC 2Lt J W Coy   Safe
SE.5a H7165
T/o Pont-a-Marcq briefed to practice patrol procedures. On return to the airfield he overshot and dropped into a sunken road. Three days later the badly damaged fighter was taken to 2 Advanced Salvage Dump. Although his name is not included in the squadron's nominal roll, I have traced a Private John William Coy serving with 4 Australian Flying Corps and with this as a guide I initiated a general search and was rewarded with a positive result contained within the East Melbourne Historical Society website, which I have pleasure in acknowledging. This confirms John Coy as serving with 4 Australian Flying Corps, his enlistment being shown as 9th May 1916, with a note to the effect that he had four years cadetship to his credit. Following training at Seymour as a Engineers' Reinforcement sapper, he transferred to C Flight, 4 Squadron Australian Flying Corps on 13th October, and was posted to Laverton for further instruction. This completed, he embarked with the squadron on RMS *Omrah* and commenced the long sea journey to England on the 17th of January 1917, arriving in Plymouth on the 23rd of March. Initially to Perham Down in Wiltshire, but by April 2nd, 1918, he had been attached to 71 Squadron at Castle Bromwich for pilot training. Graduating successfully, and now commissioned, 2nd Lieutenant Coy arrived in France on the 3rd of November, joining 2 Squadron Australian Flying Corps 48-hours before the armistice called a halt to hostilities. He served with the squadron for the remainder of service which terminated in Australia on 13th September 1919. His biography has an interesting final sentence: *"He wrote from Oakland, California, in December 1926 requesting his medals be sent to him, and saying that it would be some time before he returned to Australia."* Sylvia Black, to whom I'm exceedingly grateful for what must have been many hours of research states John William Coy was born in 1898 at Jolimont, Victoria, but that the date of death remains to be traced.

7 Squadron   2Lt A D M Edwards   Safe   Unemployed list 14 September 1919
RE.8 C2981   2Lt A H McIntyre   Safe
Presentation Aircraft: Punjab No. 46 Chenab
T/o Staceghem for an air test and forced-landed at Hilleghem in Ooost-Vlaanderen, no reason being given. 2nd Lieutenant Edwards embarked for France on the 4th of September and following the usual attachment to an Aeroplane Supply Depot reported to Proven on the 8th where he joined the squadron. His observer arrived on the 29th of September, subsequently returning home from Camp Candas of the 26th of January 1919. His skipper, however, remained with the squadron until he left for England, from Heumar, on the 9th of August 1919.

15 Squadron   2Lt L D Farmer [Canada] Safe   Unemployed list 12 July 1919
RE.8 H7018   2Lt L S Greenaway   Safe   Unemployed list 12 February 1919
T/o Salvigny to work with artillery, calling down ranges for the guns. The detail completed, the crew returned to base where a strong cross-wind was blowing and on touch down the RE was caught in a severe gust and crashed out of control. Leon Denis Farmer's Record of Service is Spartan apart from showing his address and that his official acceptance by the Royal Air Force was as recent as the 13th of October. I suspect, however, this might be the date of his arrival in France for Leon Farmer was a Flight Cadet commissioned on completion of his training on 16th May 1918 [LG 5 July 1918, issue 30781, page 7948]. Although his postings are absent from his Record of Service, Leonard Syrett Greenaway was born on the 28th of October 1894, and enlisted with the Royal Air Force on the historic date of April 1st 1918. His next of kin is shown as father but without an address.

20 Squadron   2Lt W Knight   Safe
Bristol F.2b E2603 2Lt D McG Lapraik   Safe   Unemployed list 18 May 1920
T/o Clary to practice patrol flying. Owing to an error of judgement 2nd Lieutenant Knight overshot and crashed into a parked DH.9 D3233 belonging to 211 Squadron. He had joined the squadron on the 25th of October and departed for home on the 18th of April 1919. On the 30th, David McGeachie Lapraik of Ayr in Scotland followed. He had served with the squadron from the last day of September. Born on the 6th of December 1899, he qualified as an Observer Officer four days prior to his arrival with the squadron [LG 4 October 1918, issue 30934, page 11719].

70 Squadron   2Lt G R Stark   Safe   Unemployed list 29 January 1919
F.1 Camel F1898
T/o Menin ordered for a line patrol; crashed while forced-landing with engine failure near Ecclo-Ghent. Gilbert Ramsay Stark, whose address is shown as 61 Vincent Crescent, Glasgow West, was born on the last day of August 1899, and arrived with the squadron on the 9th of October. Indicative of the culling of officers is the that his operational service lasted for just over three months.

101 Squadron   Captain C W D Bell   Safe   See 30 January 1919
FE.2b A5560
T/o Catillon for an air test and written off while forced-landing with engine failure, coming down near the airfield. Despatched, crated, to France in late August 1919, and eventually issued to 102 Squadron at Surcamps, it was damaged in a night accident on 24th April, after which in languished in a repair park until late September when it was sent to 2 Air Issues. I suspect the air test may well have been its first flight with the squadron; there are no further entries for this aircraft. Formerly of the Royal Hussars, Captain Bell appears to have served in France during 1917 and arrived back on the Western Front on the 28th of August 1918. Briefly attached to 1 Aeroplane Supply Depot he reported to the squadron on 9th September, and was made an Acting Captain with effect from the 1st of November. He returned to England on the 11th of February 1919. He was, I believe, a New Zealander for it was a Captain Bell who in 1921 wrote an essay on the use of aircraft in the defence of New Zealand; his observations may be accessed on the National Library of New Zealand. His name also appears on page 365 in the *War List of the University of Cambridge 1914-1918* edited by G V Carey MA*where Bell's entry indicates he was an officer in the 10th Hussars. Another publication in which he features is the *Quarterly Army List for the Quarter Ending 31 December 1919 - Volume 1* where on page 118 his rank is shown as: *[Lt. Res. Of Off.]* and records he had been mentioned in a despatch.

* G V Carey MA was a Fellow of Clare College, late Rifle Brigade and Royal Air Force. First printed in 1921, a 2002 reprint by N & M Press may still be available, ISBN 9781843424307.

103 Squadron   Sgt H Driver   Safe
DH.9 E8918   Sgt H S Garnett   Safe
T/o Ronchin and set out for 4 Aeroplane Supply Depot to collect a new aircraft. Crashed-landed on arrival and damaged beyond repair.

108 Squadron   2Lt J S G Holmes   Injured   Unemployed list 1 February 1919
DH.9 D499   2Lt J B Fletcher   Injured
T/o Gondecourt to practice formation flying and on return the undercarriage caught the top of a small building causing the DH to dive nose first into the ground. The service records for the two officers have no information regarding their movements, though that for 2nd Lieutenant Fletcher notes he had previously served with the 5th Battalion, Lancashire Regiment. D499 was a squadron veteran having been allotted on the 18th July when the squadron was working up at Kenley. Four days after its acceptance the squadron left for France where it saw considerable operational flying and on two occasions returned from raids with members of crew wounded. The first occasion was on the 27th of August while bombing targets at Oostende when shrapnel from anti-aircraft fire struck 2nd Lieutenant J W Ritchie, the observer, in the larynx. Admitted to 35 General Hospital he was evacuated to England on the 11th of September on HMHS *New-haven*. Then, on 26th October 2nd Lieutenant C R Knott, the pilot, received a gunshot wound to his left knee which was first treated at 3[Australian] CCS before he went home on the 29th aboard HMHS *St. Denis*.

By early October D499 was frequently flown by 2nd Lieutenant Knott; on the 1st, accompanied by Lieutenant G Windle, they were included in the squadron's attack on Inglemunster Station. As the bombers withdrew so a swarm of enemy fighters pounced and a fiercely fought running battle ensued during which the combined fire from the formation accounted for at least one of the enemy, while two others dropped away, possibly out of control. On the debit side, as I report on page 279 of my second volume, three of the DHs failed to return. In the middle of the month the intrepid Knott and Windle forced-landed D499 near Mardyke, fortunately without serious damage and, as recounted, they were back in action together on the 26th.

Returning to the action in which 2nd Lieutenant Ritchie was wounded, his pilot was Lieutenant J E H Dakin whose Record of Service shows he first went out to France on the 12th of May 1917, and on the 27th was attached to 1 Squadron at Bailleul. I suspect, however, that he did little flying with the squadron for on the 4th of June he was ordered to report to the Machine Gun Corps Base Depot at Etaples, and on the 13th he was struck off the strength of the RFC.

Little is then known of his service, though at some stage he must have returned home for the next entry shows re-embarkation and attachment to 108 Squadron with effect from 22nd July, this being the date that the squadron arrived at Capelle from Kenley, leading me to suspect that he had joined the squadron during its working up phase which began at Stonehenge on 11th November, and thence to Lake Down and Kenley.

208 Squadron   2Lt R A Gibbs   Safe
7F.1 Snipe E8135
T/o Maretz for a protection patrol. Landed safely but before coming to a stop ran into a deepish hole and tipped forward. This was first Snipe written off by the squadron and it had been on charge from 2 Air Issues since the 3rd of November. A former Flight Cadet, 2nd Lieutenant Gibbs reported for duty with the squadron on the 13th of August. He returned to England on 27th February 1919.

211 Squadron   DH.9 D3233   Struck by Bristol F.2b E2603 of 20 Squadron [summarised above] and damaged beyond repair. D3233 had been issued to the squadron on the 12th of August.

Sunday 24 November 1918
Although the movement between airfields in France and Belgium were common place the passage of years has meant that the precise location of these long abandoned sites are difficult to pinpoint and it is to the commendable diligence of dedicated researchers that what is known is down to their perseverance. On this dull but reasonably clear November day

the DHs of 49 Squadron at Villers-lés-Cagnicourt SE from Arras were prepared for the move to Bavai [Bavay]which the map on the squadron's association website pinpoints as practically on the Franco-Belgian border below Mons and east of Valenciennes, the airfield itself being sited NW of the village of the same name and north of the present D649. Until recently it had been used by the German air force and so one supposes it was in reasonable order. The move, sadly, was marred by a fatal crash as DH.9 D1097 took off and another DH crashed on arrival.

3 Squadron AusFC   RE.8 C2904   Wrecked at Falumont after being struck by a 9 Squadron RE.8 F6409 [summarised below]. The impact sliced C2904 in half, fortunately without injuring Captain H N Wrigley DFC who was sitting in the cockpit. There are two useful biographies for Henry Neilson Wrigley and I acknowledge the *Australian Dictionary of Biography* for the remarks that follow. Born on 21st April 1892, in Collingwood, Melbourne, Henry's flying training was carried out in 1916 at the Central Flying School [CFS], Point Cook, and he was appointed 2nd Lieutenant in the October of that year. Attached to 3 Squadron Australian Flying Corps he sailed to England where he underwent further training before going to the Western Front with his squadron to fly RE.8s on Corps reconnaissance duties. With hostilities drawing to a close, he was involved in a bombing raid on enemy positions near Ors on the 29th of October, during which he flew at extremely low altitude in the face of intense machine-gun fire and accurately dropped his bombs on two buildings sheltering the enemy, completely destroying his objective. For this he was awarded the DFC [LG 3 June 1919, supplement 31378, page 7032].

Postwar he wrote the squadron's history, published in 1935, with the title *The Battle Below*. By this time he was climbing steadily through the ranks of the RAAF of which he had been a founding member. Prior to its formation, Captain Wrigley, accompanied by Sergeant A W 'Spud' Murphy, had achieved a quite remarkable flight in a very obsolete BE.2e trainer from Melbourne to Darwin, the purpose being to survey the route for the forthcoming historic England to Australia air race. At the time much of Australia's interior was unknown and the resultant carefully drawn map and accompanying notes were deemed to be of such value that Henry was awarded an AFC [LG 12 July 1920, supplement 31974, page 7422].

Between the wars he achieved a number of firsts, one being the first RAAF officer to attend the Royal Air Force Staff College at Andover, completing the course in 1928. Promoted Group Captain in 1936, he was appointed to command RAAF Laverton where he devoted his long experience in bringing the country's air force to a more modern and effective force. Promoted to air rank, Air Vice-Marshal Henry Neilson Wrigley DFC AFC arrived in the UK in February 1943, where for the next three years he was a very popular Air Officer Commanding RAAF Overseas Headquarters and it was to his chagrin that he was retired in June 1946.

Casting his disappointment aside he continued to serve his country well and at the age of 91 he was honoured to lead the 1983 ANZAC Day march in Melbourne. It is recorded that he marched the entire distance unaided. His death at Fairfield, Melbourne, was announced at the grand age of 95, on 14th September 1987. An *"inveterate note taker"* his widow, Zenda Wrighley, bequeathed to the RAAF in excess of twenty volumes of notes, diaries, maps, photographs et al and following editing these were published in 1990 with the title *The Decisive Factor: Air Power Doctrine by Air Vice-Marshal H N Wrigley.*

Returning to the epic Melbourne to Darwin flight, although ranked Sergeant, Arthur William Murphy who knew Henry from their schooldays, had had a distinguished war service during which he trained as a pilot and was granted a temporary commission. His war was principally in Palestine where he was attached to 1 Squadron Australian Flying Corps flying operational missions in Bristol F.2bs over Jordan in 1918. Prior to his pilot training he had been mentioned in a despatch and following his support of Colonel T E Lawrence's irregular Arab army in the Hejaz near Darra, he was awarded the DFC. Subsequent to the Melbourne - Darwin mission, he was recommissioned and awarded the AFC. His military service encompassed the years 1914 to 1946, eventually attaining Air Commodore rank. He predeceased Henry Wrigley, his death at the age of 71 being reported on the 21st of April 1963. Without a shadow of doubt these two officers were stalwarts that have contributed to aviation's rich history.

9 Squadron   2Lt W Ashford   Safe   Unemployed list 21 February 1919
RE.8 D4869
T/o Premont with instructions to deliver despatches to Moreville [Manche] but while flying over wooded countryside the RE's engine cut and the flight ended in an emergency landing. 2nd Lieutenant Ashford is described on the report as a despatch rider. Unfortunately, his Record of Service is yet to be located.

9 Squadron   Lt N Morton   Safe
RE.8 F6409   Captain E W Goldsworthy Safe
T/o Premont for aerial post duties and on landing Falumont, Lieutenant Morton realised a parked aircraft lay in his path. Opening the throttle in the hope of taking off he chocked the engine and seconds later crashed headlong into the RE belonging to 3 Squadron Australian Flying Corps, both machines being irreparably damaged. I have not been able to find a record for Lieutenant Morton but that for Everard Walter Goldsworthy shows he was formerly of the City of London Yeomanry and had been attached to 9 Squadron since the 13th of October. Postwar he returned to his army duties and relinquished his commission on 30th September 1921, under A.O. 166/21 as amended by A.O. 332/21 [LG 22 November 1921, supplement 32526, page 9438]. His date of birth is shown as the 25th of January 1892.

11 Squadron   Lt H S Malik   Safe   Unemployed list 16 August 1919
Bristol F.2b E2364   Mechanic J Watt   Safe
T/o Aulnoy and crash-landed after an oil pipe fractured, coming down near Lay-Saint-Remy airfield then being used by American units. Salvaged four days later the Bristol was taken to 6 Aircraft Park and by 28th November 1918, it had

been deposited at 3 Aircraft Depot. Lieutenant Malik received some flying instruction at the British Flying School at Vendôme*[Loir-et-Cher]commencing 24th May 1917, and on completion was posted back to England on the 18th of June. He returned to France on the 4th of October 1918, and was attached to the squadron on the 26th. He was struck off the strength of the BEF on the 13th of January 1919, on proceeding to the West Indies.

* At the time the Flying School was under RNAS control; then with the merger of the two air arms on the 1st of April 1918, 205 Training Depot Station formed here from personnel and equipment of the School, and with further expansion of training establishments 212 Training Depot Station formed here on the 20th of May 1918. Both units were disbanded in 1919. An historical note has been added by CWGC which maintains Vendôme Town Cemetery, stating that flying training commenced in November 1916, as the weather in Central France was deemed to be better than that in the United Kingdom during the winter months. Seven probationary Flight Officers of the RNAS, two RFC and ten Royal Air Force trainee pilots died during their training; all now resting in the town cemetery.

| 40 Squadron | 2Lt P Dickens | Safe | Unemployed list 13 April 1919 |
| SE.5a F598 | | | |

T/o Aniche and set out on a compass course flight. It would seem the exercise commenced rather late in the day and in the gathering gloom 2nd Lieutenant Dickens lost his bearings. Forced-landing the SE ran up against the parapet of abandoned trench workings and turned over. Please refer to pages 358 and 361 of my second volume for details of his previous flying accidents.

| 49 Squadron | 2Lt G W Waddington | Injured | Cambrai East Military Cemetery |
| DH.9 D1097 | Sgt B Riley | + | Cambrai East Military Cemetery |

T/o Marquion to continue the transfer from Villers-lès-Cagnicourt to Bavai but swung badly and crashed into the airfield's shell dump, bursting into flames. At great risk to their lives those who arrived at the scene managed to pull George Walter Waddington clear but so grievous were his injuries that he died the next day while receiving treatment at 22 CCS. His headstone is simply inscribed: *"Safe In God's Keeping"*; he had served with the squadron since the 25th of September. Benjamin Riley was just 18 years of age; trapped in the wreckage when at last freed he was pronounced dead. His epitaph reads: *"Love And Remembrance From All Belvedere, Elland, Yorkshire."*

| 49 Squadron | 2Lt C F Cogswell | Safe |
| DH.9 D3052 | Lt J D Hall | Safe |

T/o Marquion to continue the transfer from Villers-lès-Cagnicourt and on reaching its destination crash-landed, an error of judgement on the part of 2nd Lieutenant Cogswell being the cause. He had been attached to the squadron since the 9th of August. His Record of Service shows a variety of postings; attachment to 2 Aeroplane Supply Depot on arrival in France followed three days later on 26th July to 9th Brigade at Rozoy, but on the 2nd of August he returned to 2 Aeroplance Supply depot for a week before reporting to Beauvois to join 49 Squadron. Then, and still at Bavai, he was posted on the 21st of March 1919, to 99 Squadron [DH.9A] at Aulnoye, subsequently accompanying the squadron to India [he was struck of the strength of the BEF with effect 1st May 1919]. It is also noted that he was born on the 22nd of November 1898, and his next of kin address is shown as 82 Algernon Road, Lewisham.

His observer, James Douglas Hall [see my second volume, page 166] had been attached since the 10th of August and remained with the squadron until returning home, via St. Omer, on the 14th of May 1919 [he had previously served a tour of duty flying in Bristol F.2bs with 48 Squadron, returning to 'Home Establishment' on 26th August 1917].

Until its demise, D3052, which had arrived from 2 Air Issues on 8th July, became the favoured DH for Captain Clifford Bowman DFC [see page 235 of my first volume which reports his forced-landing in DH.9 D7201 and the citation for his award] in which he claimed a quartet of the formidable Fokker DVII.

His observer/air gunner for three of these combats was Lieutenant Philip Terence Holligan*whose tour with squadron lasted from the 14th of December 1917, until he returned to England on the 13th of August. Deservedly honoured with the DFC [LG 2 November 1918, supplement 30989, page 12967], the citation reads: *'This officer has taken part in fifty bomb raids and photographic reconnaissance, and has rendered valuable and gallant service. During the Battle of the Marne his reports regarding enemy movements, positions of batteries and troops were exceptionally full and accurate and were of the greatest value.'* Clifford Bowman's fourth victory was assisted by 2nd Lieutenant Charles Barnard Edwards. His Record of Service shows he was born on the 7th of November 1899, and was attached from the 20th of May until temporary service with 1 Aeroplane Supply Depot on 21st November, and thence to 98 Squadron [DH.9] at Abscon on 16th December. On the 16th of January 1919, he returned to England only to be sent back to France on 14th February and attached to 2 Aeroplane Supply Depot. There are no further entries on his service record and with the commonality of his surname and initials I have not been able to identify his discharge via *The London Gazette.*

* Incorrectly identified on Army Form B.103 as Phillip Tennance Holligan. He was born on the 20th of May 1898, and enlisted with the RGC on 29th August 1917, receiving a commission in the General List [LG 25th September 1917, supplement 30304, page 9930]. He was discharged to the Unemployed list on 1st February 1919, seven days ahead of Clifford Bowman.

Note. Purely in chronological sequence of squadron identities D3052 became the 100th casualty since the dawn of 12th November. Numerous others from training establishments et al had also been wrecked but these fall outside the parameters of this work.

53 Squadron	2Lt W R Sisson	Injured	
RE.8 C2613	2Lt J J V Barlow	Injured	Unemployed list 21 February 1919

T/o Seclin for Reumont where the squadron would be in residence for four days before continuing to Laneffe. On reaching Reumont the crew overshot and clipped the top of a shrine, sending their aircraft nosediving to the ground. Admitted to hospital, 2nd Lieutenant Sisson [he had been on establishment since 19th October], was sent home for further treatment on the 1st of December. The movements of their RE have been charted thus; 4 Squadron between 15th July and 30th September, thence to 53 Squadron on an unreported date, its only entry being the date of its crash. An examination of *Flight* for 2nd Lieutenant Sissons reveals he was granted a temporary commission on the 13th of June following successful training as a Flight Cadet.

57 Squadron	2Lt F H Thirkell	Safe	Unemployed list 9 March 1919
DH.4 D9241	Mechanic T R Field	Safe	

T/o Vert Galant and set out for Bruyers where on arrival the DH swung and finished up balanced on its nose. One of 50 DH.4s built at Hendon by the Aircraft Manufacturing Company [AIRCO], D9241 had an inauspicious start to its service for on arrival at Bois de Roche from 2 Air Issues on 11th April for 205 Squadron it crash-landed, the damage requring fitting of a new undercarriage. Two more crashes followed; the first on 16th June involving Lieutenant Joseph Charles Wilson, an American from Pittsburgh, and Sergeant S M MacKay, followed on the last day of June by Joseph Wilson's second mishap, his observer on this occasion being Sergeant S F Langstone. Sent for repair the DH passed through a series of holding units before its issue on an undisclosed date to 57 Squadron. 2nd Lieutenant Thirkell joined the squadron as recently as the 30th October, and departed to England on the 6th of December.

Note. Joseph Charles Wilson, born on the 29th of June 1893, enlisted with the RFC on 27th August 1917, arriving with 205 Squadron on the 8th of April. On the 8th of June he crashed on return from bombing operations [see page 227 of my first volume], and then on the 19th of July, seriously wounded during aerial combat, he crashed while trying to land at the squadron's base at Bois de Roche [see page 67 of my second volume]. Taken to 21 CCS doctors found he had sustained gunshot wounds to his thigh and forearms, plus additional injuries as a result of the heavy crash. For several weeks he remained dangerously ill and it was not until the 2nd of September that he was sufficiently recovered to be sent home by ship. His supreme courage on that fateful day was recognised by the award of a DFC, the citation appearing in *The Edinburgh Gazette* 23 September 1918, issue 13325, page 3538: *'While on a photographic reconnaissance the rudder controls of this officer's machine were shot away. Shortly afterwards he was attacked by three enemy scouts; he handled his damaged machine so skilfully that his observer* [2nd Lieutenant J B Leach] *was enabled to shoot down one out of control, and force the remaining two to retire. He then flew back to the aerodrome, where, owing to his rudder being out of action, he crashed, fracturing both legs and an arm. In all, he has carried out 66 bombing raids, invariably showing fine courage and initiative.'* The figure of 66 bombing raids quoted in the citation indicates crews serving with the day bomber squadrons were flying on an average of twenty-two sorties a month. The strain must have immense for it was almost inevitable that the enemy would react strongly and although some fighter escort protection might be available to engage their scouts, for the better part survival of the bomber crews relied heavily on maintaining close formation and the combined fire power from the observer/air gunners.

205 Squadron	Lt R K Rose	Safe	Unemployed list 17 June 1919
DH.9A F1007			

T/o Menin for an air test and reported to have been damaged beyond repair following a misjudged landing at Halluin. Robert Kingsley Rose, born on the 2nd of March 1899, and enlisting with the RFC on 21st March 1917, first saw active service with 24 Squadron [SE.5a] from 26th June to 7th October when he joined 205 Squadron. He returned home three days after his twentieth birthday.

208 Squadron	2Lt G L Smith	Safe	
7F.1 Snipe E8183			

T/o Maretz for flying practice. Landed heavily, ballooned and on touching down for a second time tipped onto its nose. It had been on establishment for just nine days. Lieutenant R D Gifford having brought E8183 to Maretz from 2 Air Issues. Robert D'Arcy Gifford joined 208 Squadron at Serny, then equipped with F.1 Camels, on 22nd May, and remained on strength until he was posted to St. Valery for a course on the 12th of February 1919, returning to the squadron, now operating from Stree in Belgium, on the 17th of March. On 16th May he was detached for temporary duty with 1 Enemy Aircraft Reception Park, rejoining '206, now part of the Occupation Force and based at Heumar, on the 10th of June. Soon after his return he was taken ill and went into hospital on the 28th; recovered, he was discharged to duty on the 3rd of July. 2nd Lieutenant Smith's time with the squadron was quite mundane; arriving on 13th September he was posted back to England in March 1919.

Monday 25 November 1918
A remarkable day on the Western Front in that aircraft accidents appear to have been restricted to the 213 Squadron machine, summarised on the next page.

At home David Lloyd George opened his election campaign in Wolverhampton, repeating his mantra of making the country fit for heroes.

In France, Marshal Foch flatly refused to consider a list of protests lodged by Germany over the terms of the armistice.

213 Squadron   2Lt J P S Burton   Safe
F.1 Camel F3967
T/o Bergues and damaged beyond repair [though it was not stuck off charge until 22nd February 1919] after forced-landing in gathering darkness and mist, coming down in a ploughed field near Uxem [Nord], a little over eight km E of Dunkirk. It had been with the squadron since the 14th of October. Nothing, as yet, has come to light regarding 2nd Lieutenant Burton's service.

Tuesday 26 November 1918
The last German troops march out of Belgium and the first French troops cross into Germany; the years of occupation had begun. A most informative article, illustrated, in respect of the occupation, titled *Walls of Paper vs. Walls of Steel - France, the Failings of the 1919 Peace and the Route to the Maginot Line* written by Martin S Alexander is published in *Aftermath Special Edition' of 'Stand To!' The Journal of the Western Front Association* [October 2019].

At home a provincial newspaper *The Western Times* reported on a case brought before the Launceston Borough Police Court of a crime committed at Launceston Market when a certain Mrs Hannah Shute of Trewithick sold seven pounds of butter to a Mrs Miller of the Arundel Arms at Lifton at one penny above the set retail price of two shillings and twopence. Despite a stout defence by the unfortunate Mrs Shute's stepson, Alfred Shute, he was no match for Superintendent Webber prosecuting for a breach of the Food Control Orders and a fine of £3, including cost, was imposed.

Although today this might have been the subject to wry amusement, in the immediate aftermath of the *Great War* food shortages in the United Kingdom [and across Europe] were acute it was considered she should have sold the butter to seven families and not to one person. Although purely coincidental, Herbert Hoover, who had been appointed by President Woodrow Wilson to head the Food Administration Department arrived in England from America on this day to discuss the food shortage situation.

One cannot but help reflect upon the conditions in which the country lived in that decade after the war to today where millions of tons of food go to waste each year. A sobering thought.

5 Squadron   Lt D G Mackenzie   Safe
RE.8 C2868   2Lt F M R Jones   Safe   See 22 December 1918
T/o Pecq to transit to Cognelée in advance of the main body of the squadron which was scheduled to move here on the 27th. Weather conditions were poor and the crew forced-landed at OEudeghem [Hainaut] on the NW side of Ath. Presumed struck off charge. Lieutenant Mackenzie served on the squadron for the better part of a year, arriving on the 6th of October and leaving with the squadron for Bicester on the 8th of September. Notes in regard to 2nd Lieutenant Jones are reported in the 22nd December summary.

5 Squadron   2Lt F B Peacock   Safe   See 11 February 1919
RE.8 F6044   Mechanic Clark   Safe
T/o Pecq similarly charged and in the prevailing mist and gloom came down near Namur. Rebuilt from parts salvaged from damaged airframes F6044 had been on establishment since the 30th of September. 2nd Lieutenant Peacock's service is recorded in the summary for 11th February.

12 Squadron   2Lt W E Gandell   Safe   See 27 November 1918
RE.8 C2554 Britania
T/o Estourmel for aerial post duties only to encounter extremely thick mist and while banking to try and establish his position the nose dropped followed by a wing brushing the ground causing the RE to crash at Map Reference Sheet 57 bK26. An appreciation of his service [or lack of it regarding his time in the Royal Air Force] appears on the 27th.

12 Squadron   2Lt J K Kempson   Safe   Unemployed list 2 April 1919
RE.8 C2786   Corporal Dalley*   Safe
T/o Estourmel intending to transit to Les Flache airfield but mist obliged the crew to forced-land near Genly [Hainaut] in the area of Mons. Presumed damaged beyond repair. It would seem that 2nd Lieutenant Kempson was accepted as a probationary observer in November 1917, attached from the 11th [Service] Battalion, Essex Regiment, which at the time came under the aegis of the 6th Division. On the 1st of December he was posted back to the United Kingdom and it was not until the last day of August 1918, that he arrived in France [I can only assume that in the intervening period he had re-mustered as a pilot] and following attachment to 2 Aeroplane Supply Depot he joined the squadron on the 5th of September. On the 26th of March 1919, he was ordered to report to Hangelar for temporary duty with 5 Squadron only to be posted home three days later to join the growing ranks of the unemployed.

* In respect of Corporal Dalley, whose initials are are omitted from the accident report, I suspect him to be 3884 Corporal R H Dalley who enlisted with the RFC on the 1st of March 1915, and trained as an air mechanic. On the 1st of November 1917, he was promoted Corporal and his pay increased to five shillings [presumably per week]. I am indebted to RAFM Hendon for their digitising of the Muster Rolls from where my remarks are gleaned.

| 13 Squadron | Lt A E Roberts | Injured |
| RE.8 C2723 | Lt A P Thomas | Injured |

Presentation Aircraft: Zanzibar No 2

T/o Carnières for formation practice. At the end of the exercise, and while descending through cloud, collided with the side of a house and caught fire. By the best of fortune help was immediately to hand and the crew were pulled clear with only minor injuries to show for their frightening experience. Their RE had arrived from 2 Air Issues on the 29th of August and until the accident here summarised appears to have had trouble free service. Unfortunately, Records of Service for the two officers appear not to have survived.

| 42 Squadron | 2Lt W O Goldthorpe | Safe |
| RE.8 C2419 | Lt Garner | Safe |

T/o Ascq for Marquain but believed damaged beyond repair following an emergency landing near Genly [Hainaut]. It would seem 2nd Lieutenant Goldthorpe [he was born on the 26th of June 1898] had been attached from 9 Squadron; he returned home on the 16th of April 1919. Unfortunately, apart from confirmation of his commission [LG 21 June 1918, issue 30759, page 7325] nothing else appears to have been recorded, either in the *Gazette* or in the aviation magazines such as *Flight.* Similarly, in the absence of initials, Lieutenant Garner's service remains a mystery.

| 42 Squadron | Lt Owen | Safe |
| RE.8 C3467 | Lt Wicks | Safe |

T/o Ascq similarly tasked and reported down at Harminges [sic]. Recovered to 1 Advanced Salvage Dump on 3rd December where, I suspect, it was struck off charge. Tested at 1 Air Issues on the 1st of October, it was issued to the squadron on 8th November. Without initials, and with relatively common surnames, the service of the two officers remains untraced.

| 65 Squadron | 2Lt J D H Lewis | Safe | See 2 January 1919 |
| F.1 Camel F6355 | USA | | |

T/o Bisseghem for a practice flight and on landing swung out of control and finished up against the side of a hangar; wrecked. Please refer to my summary for the 2nd of January for information pertaining to 2nd Lieutenant Lewis.

| 87 Squadron | Lt W C Walker | Injured |
| 5F.1 Dolphin F7039 | | |

T/o Boussières to join with fellow pilots and engage in formation flying. Stalled at 50 feet and nosedived to the ground. It is not clear whether the accident occurred at the beginning or at the end of the exercise. His service record is devoid of information regarding postings et al.

88 Squadron   Bristol F.2b F4474   While picketed at Aulnoye was struck by an unidentified RE.8 belonging to 42 Squadron which on landing struck the Bristol causing substantial damage. Presumed struck off charge.

This had been a pretty miserable day all round, particularly for the RE.8 equipped squadrons with seven to the extent that they probably never flew again. Weather conditions over the Continent in the winter of 1918-1919 were far from conducive to safe air operations and as a consequence nature's unpredictable elements would be a major factor in many of the accidents. And, again, I stress the rudimentary state of the airfields along with the unreliability of aero engines made flying a fairly hazardous occupation.

    Cine footage taken at the time, even allowing for the poor quality of film, shows just how poor the surfaces of the aerodromes of France and Belgium had become. Without runways the ability to take off into wind was always present and with rain and frost this had led to a myriad of criss-crossing tracks into which wheels were prone to fall thereby over stressing undercarriages or wrenching off tail skids.

Wednesday 27 November 1918
Off the East Anglia port of Harwich a fleet of 27 German submarines arrived during the day and surrendered, while across the Channel and in the Pas-de-Calais the King, accompanied by Sir Douglas Haig, drove through Montreuil to great acclaim from the population ahead of his visit to Paris.

    On the Home Front election fever gripped the nation as politicians from all parties set out their policies which they hoped would win them victory in December, the 18th being the day that those eligible to vote would go to the polling stations.

| 3 Squadron | 2Lt J E Mutty | Safe | Unemployed list 29 September 1919 |
| F.1 Camel H806 | | | |

T/o Inchy for a practice flight on return from which 2nd Lieutenant Mutty misjudged his approach. Realising his error, he decided to go round again but he opened the throttle far too quickly and by doing so choked his engine. Moments late he found himself in a field adjoining the airfield and before coming to a stop the Camel dropped into a trench and turned over; damaged beyond repair. His arrival in France was quite recent, reporting to the squadron on 21st October. Following a three day attachment to the Aerial Ranges, he reported to 5th Brigade on 30th January 1919, and thence to England on the 14th of March.

4 Squadron AusFC Lt Trim   Safe
7F.1 Snipe E8121

T/o Grand Ennetières and overturned on landing having touched down on rough ground. Taken to 1 Advanced Salvage Dump for inspection the damage was deemed uneconomical to repair and the airframe was struck off charge on the 15th of December.

12 Squadron   2Lt W E Gandell   Safe   Unemployed list 10 April 1919
RE.8 C2697
Presentation Aircraft: Gold Coast No 12

T/o Estourmel with the intention of staging to Les Flache airfield but crashed heavily while forced-landing near Vannerial [sic]. This was his second serious accident in the space of 24-hours. His Record of Service has no details whatsoever regarding postings. However, I have a suspicion that he may have been formerly of the London Regiment and had been honoured with the Military Medal [LG 21 December 1916, supplement 29873, page 12443].

15 Squadron   2Lt K G Welch   Safe   Unemployed list 25 March 1919
RE.8 D6840   2Lt R Rigby   Safe

T/o Selvigny to work with artillery on a practice puff shoot. On return struck a ridge and turned over. Kenneth Gibbs Welch was formerly of the Royal Field Artillery; his date of birth is given as the 2nd of September 1896. Apart from that, information pertaining to his service has not been appended. Reginald Rigby, born 29th December 1899, was a former Flight Cadet whose commission had been approved as recently as 9th October [*Flight* 31 October, 1918, page 1236]; similar to his pilot, Reginald Rigby's service record is devoid of posting detail.

19 Squadron   2Lt N A Weir [Canada]   +   Auberchicourt British Cemetery
5F.1 Dolphin D3585

T/o Abscon authorised for flying practice. Lost control and spun into a field close to the airfield where it broke into two pieces. From Elbow in Saskatchewan, Noble Alexander Weir was born of the 4th of January 1898, and he enlisted in the RFC on the 11th of September 1917. His early service, having qualified as a fighter pilot, was dogged by ill-health.

Having arrived in France on 19th June he was struck down ten days later with influenza and this was serious enough for him to be returned to England on the 13th of July and it was not until early October that he recrossed the Channel to join 19 Squadron at Savy on the 4th of October. He was buried at Birchecourt [sic] [possible spelling error for 'Auberchicourt'] in early December, the service being conducted by the Reverend P W Wilson whose parent unit was 20 CCS. Noble's epitaph reads: *"Gone But Not Forgotten."*

46 Squadron   Lt J W Abray   Safe   Unemployed list 6 March 1920
F.1 Camel D1823/F6051

T/o Baizieux to practice flying in formation but before becoming airborne ran onto soft ground and turned over. As D1823 it crashed at Liettres on 21st June, 2nd Lieutenant Charles Stanley Lomas Coulson of 80 Squadron walking away unharmed. Rebuilt and with its new airframe serial it was accepted by the squadron on 5th October. Although identified through *The London Gazette* Lieutenant Abray's service record appears not to have survived.

Returning to 2nd Lieutenant Coulsen, he was commissioned to the General List of the RFC on 7th June 1917, having graduated as a Flight Cadet [LG 6 July 1917, supplement 30170, page 6786]. His service record shows his birth as 28th January 1898 and enlistment 5th May 1917, and with his training completed, Charles headed to France and joined 80 Squadron at Champien on the 11th of March.

Before the month was out he had written off, or damaged, four of the squadron's Camels. A sharp introduction to what life for newly arrived fighter pilots was like in the embers of winter as the German spring offensive was at its height. The first, C1581 was within 24-hours of his arrival when during a practice flight he made a hash of his landing. Next, during the afternoon of the 21st he forced-landed in B2456, coming down between St. Quentin and Roupy. At the time fierce fighting was taking place in the area and with enemy infantry advancing towards the British outposts he high tailed it in the direction of our trenches.

This eventful start to operational flying continued when on the 26th he forced-landed C1693 with a failing engine but with enemy forces pressing towards the squadron's base at Remaisnil the Camel was put to the torch. Still in situ, the next day he choked the engine of C1635 and ended up, inverted, within the landing area.

April was uneventful but on the 10th of May, and following a late evening aerial fight in which he drove down a Fokker DrI near Morcourt, he was obliged to make a precautionary landing in a ploughed field, B7322 being recovered and repaired [issued to 151 Squadron it was written off on 28th June 1918, see page 281 of my first volume for details]. His last serious accident occurred, as noted, on 21st June.

An entry of Army Form B.103c states he was wounded on the 9th of August and was taken to 61 CCS where he was treated for gunshot wounds to his legs and right foot and which following a medical board resulted in his evacuation to England aboard the *Peter de Conicke* on the 9th of October.

Subsequently, Charles Coulson was awarded the DFC the citation appearing in the Edinburgh edition of 4 November 1918, issue 13346, page 4053: *'During the late operations this officer has set a brilliant example of courage and skill, notably on one occasion when, observing a party of the enemy in a trench firing at some of our infantry, he repeatedly dived on the trench, firing at the occupants and distracting their attention from our troops. Eventually je was wounded twice in the leg* [this dates the sortie to 9th August]*, but succeeded in reaching his aerodrome.'*

In 2017, his medals from the *Great War* came up for sale by Spink auctioneers [Auction: 17003 - Orders, Decorations and Medals Lot: 714] with the description: *"A fine Great War DFC, group of three awarded to Lieutenant C S L*

Coulson late Royal Flying Corps, a pilot who 'at all times set a brilliant example of courage and determination. Following a hair-raising introduction to aerial combat in March 1918, when he was forced land his badly damaged Camel of No 80 Squadron between advancing enemy troops and our lines, he went on to claim a Fokker triplane of Richthofen's Flying Circus' and wreak havoc on enemy ground forces in the battles of St. Quentin and the Marne." Reference is made to the leg wounds reported in the DFC citation which Spinks dates as *August 1918.* The sale took place over two days in early December 2017, the results being withheld.

79 Squadron   Lt M Munden   Safe   Unemployed list 13 June 1919
5F.1 Dolphin H7245
T/o Reckem to join the squadron now at Nivelles but a tyre burst as he took off and on reaching his destination the Dolphin landed heavily; believed damaged beyond repair. Lieutenant Munden had served with the squadron since the 25th of June. On the 7th of March, he was informed his tour of duty was at an end and six days later he reported to Blandford Camp in Dorset to await his discharge. This leads me to believe he may well have been a Canadian, though the next of kin section on Army Form B.103c is blank and, therefore, I cannot be certain.

115 Squadron   Lt S C Stevens   Safe
HP O/400 C9754 2Lt J Newhill   Safe
T/o Inglevert and wrecked here in a landing mishap. There is some confusion regarding the date: AIR 1/1739 quotes identical information for both the 22nd and 27th of November, followed by an entry on the 28th indicating Army Form W3347 had been submitted. Meanwhile, AIR 1/865 records the crash as occurring on the 27th.
    Lieutenant Stevens is thought to have joined the squadron towards the end of August remaining on establishment until shortly before its departure to Ford on the 4th of March 1919. 2nd Lieutenant Newhill's name appears on the nominal roll for the squadron at the same time as Lieutenant Stevens; however, on the 27th of January 1919, he reported to 214 Squadron at Chemy, remaining with '214' until his return to England on the 25th of April. He had been confirmed in his rank on 14th May 1918 [LG 14 June 1918, issue 30747, page 7069].

205 Squadron   2Lt P J Baker   Safe
DH.9A E8413
T/o Moislains and set out for the squadron's new home at Mauberge where on landing the DH was damaged beyond repair. Originally earmarked for 110 Squadron, it was reallotted to 205 Squadron on 9th October. On the 4th of November it was slightly damaged during operations to Charleroi, the crew being recorded as Lieutenant R J V Pulvertoft and 2nd Lieutenant W M Newton. Of the three officers named here, only the record for William Malcolm Newton has been traced. Of Kentish stock, William was born on the 8th of August 1898, and enlisted on 21st May 1918. As an Observer Officer he joined the squadron on the 3rd of October. On 17th March 1919, he was attached to 18 Squadron at Bickendorf but returned to England on the day that 18 Squadron transferred to Merheim.

Thursday 28 November 1918
Although sent into exile in Holland in the final tumultuous days of the war, the Kaiser's formal proclamation of abdication did not appear until this day and it was the 30th before the text was published in the Berlin papers.

8 Squadron   Lt Filmer*   Safe
Bristol F.2b D219 Lt Oates   Safe
T/o from an unidentified reception park, presumably bound for Bellevue but as darkness fell the crew elected to make a precautionary landing, coming down at Boveffeles [sic] - possibly a mis-spelling for Bouvigny-Boyeffles in the Pas-de-Calais. It appears that the Bristol was so badly damaged that it never took to the skies again.

* Records of Service have survived for two officers with the surname Filmer; one, Lieutenant John Russell Filmer served with the 12th Balloon Section, while Harold Ernest Filmer's Army Form B.103-I [Part 1] shows no detail whatsoever regarding units et al. Concerning Lieutenant Oates, at least five officers have this surname and it is almost a certainty that the Bristol's observer was 2nd Lieutenant Harold Oates who was attached to 8 Squadron on 22nd November. His date of birth is given as the 13th of June 1895, and his enlistment in the RFC as 1st August 1917. On arrival in France he was initially attached to 2 Aeroplane Supply Depot on 16th June, and thence to Trecon on the 22nd to join 52 Squadron [RE.8] which was engaged in a myriad of tasks including tactical reconnaissance. Then, six days after reporting he was detached for temporary duty in Paris and on his return on the 29th he was ordered to St. Omer for operations with 4 Squadron [RE.8]. On the 2nd of August he was posted home, but returned to France on the 3rd of November and the customary attachment to an Aeroplane Supply Depot ahead of joining 8 Squadron. He was still on establishment in January 1919.

28 Squadron   2Lt E F Mattock   Safe   See 17 January 1919
F.1 Camel C137
T/o Sarcedo and on return landed heavily and turned over. Information regarding his service is reported in his summary for the 17th January.

29 Squadron   Captain C G Rose   Injured
SE.5a F5543
T/o Marcke to transit to Nivelles and rejoin the squadron but while climbing away the engine lost power and he crash-landed. Apparently, the SE had been left out in the open for the past two days and, I daresay, the prevailing fog and mist might well have been a contributing factor in accident. However, as with so many incidents of this type, differing reports exist and one such source states Captain Rose ran out of petrol and forced-landed near Lobbes in the Belgian province of Hainaut. His surname and initials crop up on a number of occasions in *Flight* but so far I have not been able to find his Record of Service.

70 Squadron   Lt R H Davidson   Safe
F.1 Camel D6696
T/o Namur and crashed owing to engine failure over Vaux-Andigny [Aisne], 28 km NE from Saint-Quentin. Initially with 73 Squadron until it nosed over whilst landing at Ruisseauville on 2nd July, it arrived on the squadron on the 5th of September and when written off had at least four combat successes to its credit, all achieved by Lieutenant O A P Heron. As yet I have not located any service records for Lieutenant Davidson, but in respect of Oscar Aloysius Patrick Heron born on the 17th of September 1896, there are a number of revealing entries on Army Form B.103c. The Form shows he enlisted with the RFC three days after his 21st birthday and was posted to 70 Squadron on the 16th of May. On 11th June he was erroneously posted missing, this being amended to wounded with a note appended to say he had been admitted to 47 CCS with a dislocated jaw.

Five days hence and he reported back to the squadron at Fouquerolles and was soon back in the thick of aerial fighting. In late October he was awarded the DFC and promoted Acting Captain, the final entry being for well deserved leave from the 1st to the 15th of November during which the armistice was signed. For additional information regarding this officer, please refer to his summary as reported on the 21st of April 1919, which includes the citation for his award.

The incident at Ruisseauville on 2nd July featured Lieutenant William Samuel Stephenson, a Canadian from Winnipeg, Manitoba who was shot down on the 28th of July and taken prisoner [see page 90 of my second volume for details]. At the time of writing the second volume, I was only aware of his initials and, therefore, had not traced the citations for his decorations. I was able to note the date of his repatriation which I can now add *"arrived at Dover"*. And, importantly, the citations: *'For conspicuous gallantry and devotion to duty. When flying low and observing an open staff car on the road, he attacked it with such success that later it was seen lying in the ditch upside down. During the same flight he caused a stampede amongst some enemy transport horses on a road. Previous to this he had destroyed a hostile scout and a two-seater plane. His work has been of the highest order, and he has shown the greatest courage and energy in engaging every kind of target.'* [LG 22 June 1918, supplement 30761, page 7423]. His MC was followed by the DFC on 21 September 1918, supplement 30913, page 11255: *'This officer has shown conspicuous gallantry and skill in attacking enemy troops and transports from low altitudes, causing heavy casualties. His reports, also, have contained valuable and accurate information. He has further proved himself a keen antagonist in the air, accounted for six enemy aeroplanes.'* His service record shows he was born on 11th January 1896, and enlisting on 16th August 1917.

Friday 29 November 1918
As reported by the *Birmingham Mail*, Austen Chamberlain while addressing a large audience at Camden Street Council School outlined his thoughts on how Germany should pay compensation to *"the nations which she has outraged"*. A member of Lloyd George's War Cabinet his name is mentioned on a number of occasions in the two-volume series *War Memoirs of David Lloyd George*. Coming from a well established political family, its Austen's half-brother Neville who is better known for his time as Prime Minister in the appeasement years and for his part in the Munich Agreement.

4 Squadron AusFC Lt Cullam   Safe
7F.1 Snipe E8063
T/o Grand Ennetières and damaged beyond repair when a heavy landing caused structural damage to the airframe. Received from 1 Aeroplane Supply Depot on the 3rd of October, its final entry is for the day following the accident which merely notes it was on the squadron's establishment. I suspect, however, it was decided the damage to the longerons was sufficient for the Snipe to be struck off charge.

10 Squadron   Lt C C Summers   Safe
FK.8 F631
T/o Menin for a transit flight, possibly to Reckem where the squadron was scheduled to move on 1st December. Became lost and forced-landed at Map Reference Sheet 51 cP31d. Born on the 13th of September 1898, and enlisting on the 23 of July 1917, Charles Cyril Summers was a General List officer who was confirmed in his appointment of the 15th of February [LG 19 March 1918, supplement 30589, page 3572]. His entries on Army Form B.103c show he was posted to 82 Squadron [FK.8] on the day the squadron moved into Bertangles from Allonville on 27th March 1918. On the 21st of May he was admitted to 49 CCS suffering from Myalgia [muscular pain], returning to his squadron, now at Aggenvilliers on 3rd June. However, 48-hours later he was detached to 2 Aeroplane Supply Depot from where on the 6th he returned to hospital, this time with an arthritic right shoulder and it was the 26th before he was declared fit to resume flying duties. Then, on the last day of July he departed 2 Aeroplane Supply Depot for 1 Aeroplane Supply Depot and thence of the 9th of August to 2 Squadron [FK.8] at Mazingarbe. His date of joining 10 Squadron is, as yet, not known. However, at all three squadrons his work would have encompassed the myriad tasks associated with reconnaissance flying.

23 Squadron   2Lt J E Mavity   Safe   Unemployed list 12 March 1919
5F.1 Dolphin D3588

T/o Bertry East for a practice flight but was obliged to forced-land with carburettor trouble. Before coming to a stop the Dolphin struck a ridge and as a consequence the airframe was damaged beyond economical repair. Apart from this incident it seems 2nd Lieutenant Mavity's service was uneventful. He joined the squadron on the 2nd of September and returned home on the 1st of March 1919.

43 Squadron   Lt G R Howsam MC   Safe   See 1 January 1919
7F.1 Snipe E8012 [Canada]

T/o Cognelée for a special mission and on return overshot the landing area and ended up entangled in strands of barbed wire erected around a hangar. Although the Record of Service for George Robert Howsam is incomplete, there is sufficient material to build a reasonable picture of his time in the air force. Born on the 21st of January 1895, he enlisted as a single man on the 1st of March 1917 and was appointed to the General List as a temporary 2nd Lieutenant on the 19th of August [LG 28 September 1917, supplement 30311, page 10003]. Arriving in France, and like so many of his contemporaries, he was attached to an Aeroplane Supply Depot before reporting to Poperinghe to join 70 Squadron, a scout unit equipped with F.1 Camel, on the 13th of November. Between the 17th and 24th of the month he underwent gunnery practice at the Aerial Ranges before commencing his operational flying. Then, from the 2nd to the 19th of February he went on leave to Marseilles and though it has to be guess work on my part I suspect it might have been here that he met and fell in love with the lady that would become his wife for the section on Army Form B.103c for next of kin the name of his father, residing at Port Perry in Ontario is scored through and replaced by *Mrs H Howson [Wife] 124 Winchester Street, Toronto, Canada.*

By February he was recommended for an MC, which was duly *Gazetted* on 16 August 1918, supplement 30845, page 9565: *'For conspicuous gallantry and devotion to duty in aerial combats. He has destroyed five enemy machines and driven down others out of control, showing splendid courage and initiative on all occasions.'* At this time I suspect he was in England for on the 24th of March he had been wounded in his right shoulder and on the 1st of April, the day the Royal Air Force came into existence, he was evacuated by HS *Stad Antwerpen*. His entry on *Wikipedia* indicated he returned to the Western Front in October for Flight Commander duties with 43 Squadron. Postwar, he played a major part in the establishment of the Royal Canadian Air Force [RCAF], serving until 1945 when he retired as an Air Vice-Marshal. One final honour was bestowed upon him: *Legion of Merit - Decree of Commander* [LG 16 April 1946, supplement 37534, page 1903]. His death at the age of 83 was announced on the 16th of April 1988, at which time he was residing in Vancouver, British Columbia.

Note. In what was a relatively short tour of operations with 70 Squadron, owing to being wounded, *The Camel File* identifies the following aircraft associated with his flying. In serial order: B2311, B2530, B2534, B5598 and C8204.

53 Squadron   2Lt E H Bird   Safe   Unemployed list 1 June 1919
RE.8 C2501

T/o Reumont intending to ferry the RE to Laneffe but made what is described as a poorly executed landing at Valenciennes which damaged it beyond repair. Ernest Heneage Bird was born on the 15th of March 1899, and was posted to the squadron on the 18th of September. However, 48-hours later he was ordered to join 7 Squadron [RE.8] at Proven, returning to 53 Squadron on the 13th of October. In the New Year, and on the 1st of March he reported to Gerpinnes for attachment to 6 Squadron but with 6 Squadron heading for India, Ernest was posted to 12 Squadron at Duren on the 28th of April. A squadron move to Heumar took place on 5th May and it was from here that he returned to England on the 25th to await discharge.

84 Squadron   Lt C E Kelly   Safe   Unemployed list 2 July 1919
SE.5a E1278

T/o Betry for practice flying and on return finished up in a hedge after overshooting the landing area. E1278 had been received from 2 Air Issues on 27th October. I have not been able to trace a Record of Service for Lieutenant Kelly.

87 Squadron   2Lt A S Maltby   Injured Unemployed list 29 September 1919
5F.1 Dolphin C4159

T/o Boussières to practice patrol procedures during which the Dolphin came down near Bouin [sic]. 2nd Lieutenant Maltby's service is rather unusual. He arrived in France on the 7th of July, disembarking from a night crossing, and as was the norm he was attached to an Aeroplane Supply Depot, in his case No 2 at Hesdin. Then, instead of proceeding to an operational squadron he was posted to the Depot on the 12th and for the next two months underwent attachments to various aircraft depots on temporary duty, the last entry on Army Form B.103 being dated 17th September when he was ordered to *"3 AD on temp. duty."* Turning to the *Gazette,* he was confirmed in his rank and appointment on the 25th of May [LG 2 July 1918, issue 30776, page 7771], this information being recorded on his Record of Service.

211 Squadron   2Lt E J Stevenson   Safe
DH.9 E8962   Sgt J Smith   Safe

T/o Clary but as the tail came up 2nd Lieutenant Stevenson realised he was heading for some very uneven ground. In attempting to avoid the rutted surface he used his rudder in the hope of running onto better ground but in doing so he lost control and crashed. This particular DH had arrived with the squadron from 1 Air Issues on 8th October and during the late morning of 4th November it shared with 2nd Lieutenants C H Dickens and A M Adams [B7626] in destroying a hostile aircraft, Lieutenant E G Gaff and 2nd Lieutenant W J Large flying E8962. The combined fire from the two DHs caused their opponent to break up in the air. Traces on the officers associated with E8962 show 2nd Lieutenant Stevenson joining the squadron on the 11th of August and returning home on the 3rd of March 1919. Edward George Gaff, born 9th December 1897, joined 10th October and thence to home on the 13th of January. I have not been able to find a record for 2nd Lieutenant Large.

Saturday 30 November 1918
In anticipation of the war ending, the Birmingham Business School was established under the aegis of the Ministry of Labour Appointments Department and by the end of November the *Birmingham Daily Post* published a report on the success of what was probably a pilot scheme. Over 200 officers had attended courses with a success rate of around ninety percent finding appointments, albeit some of a temporary nature. With Birmingham being judged a success, a similar school was established in London.

Rationing was still very much in force as emphasised by the front page of the *Denbighshire Free Press* which urged its readers to register without delay with R Owen & Son which had taken delivery of a stock of jam. Other adverts prominent on the page were for Three Shell a non-alcoholic beer obtainable from Andrews & Co, Denbigh, and which could be purchased during prohibited hours; an Influenza Mixture from the pharmacy of Benson-Evans & Co, plus a notice for the immediate delivery of Fordson farm tractors from W Edwards of Denbigh.

4 Squadron AusFC	Lt Collins	Safe
7F.1 Snipe E8096		

T/o Grand Ennetières and return levelled out while still ten feet above the ground, stalled and on hitting the ground turned over. It had been on establishment since the 7th of October.

5 Squadron	Captain A D K Perkins	Safe	
RE.8 F5902	2Lt E C Eastwood	Safe	Unemployed list 25 March 1919

T/o Cognelée for a travelling flight but made a precautionary landing at Fosse. Resuming the flight, on becoming airborne the undercarriage came into contact with the top of a hedge which resulted in the RE coming to grief; wrecked. Captain Perkins had been seconded from the Royal Irish Fusiliers, effective from the last day of January 1917 [LG 21st February 1917, supplement 31711, page 1848]. His first operational tour commenced on 15th February, when he joined 13 Squadron at Savy. At the time the squadron was flying obsolete BEs but in April these were exchanged for RE.8s. Apart from two spells of leave, his tour appears to have been reasonably uneventful though reconnaissance tasks during the *Great War* were rarely free from the likelihood of being attacked by enemy scouts, or having to contend with anti-aircraft fire each time the battle-lines were crossed. Thus, on 14th December he returned to England. His time in the UK was probably spent on instructional duties though information as to where he was employed has not been entered on Record of Service. Thus, three days after the armistice came into effect he reported to 5 Squadron, but his second tour was brief and he was posted home on the 31st of January 1919, two years to the date since his secondment. Later in the year he returned to the Fusiliers [LG 31 December 19129, supplement 31711, page 16114] and he remained in the army until he exceeded the age for recall to active service, his date of retirement being recorded as 26th April 1947 [LG 29 April 1947, supplement 37941, page 1894]. Details regarding his observer is confined to his rank, name and initials.

16 Squadron	2Lt H Laycock	Safe	Unemployed list 15 April 1919
RE.8 E231	2Lt S H Hughes	Safe	Unemployed list 24 February 1919

T/o Auchy authorised for a cross-country flight which ended with a crash landing at Desvres, home for 1 Aeroplane Supply Depot. E231 had been on establishment since the 27th of August. Harry Laycock, born on 23rd January 1896, first saw active service with the East Lancashire Regiment. His time with 16 Squadron is recorded as from 6th June to 22nd December when he was posted home in time for Christmas. Stanley Harold Hughes joined the squadron on 30th August and departed on the 7th of January 1919.

53 Squadron	2Lt V Foster	Safe
RE.8 C2743		

T/o Reumont with the intention of flying to Laneffe but almost immediately he lost control and crash-landed. Formerly of the South Lancashire Regiment he was appointed as a temporary 2nd Lieutenant on the 31st of August [*Flight* October 3, 1918, page 1124]. Vandel Foster was born on the 7th of March 1894, and according to the entries on Army Form B.103 he arrived in France on 14th September, reporting to the squadron on the 27th. In the New Year, and with the squadron preparing to depart for England, he was posted on 3rd March to 9 Squadron at Ludendorf. Between the 13th of June and 18th July he was attached to 8 Squadron at Sart, returning briefly to 9 Squadron before joining 2 Aeroplane Supply Depot for six weeks. His tour of duty at an end, he returned home on the 19th of September.

112 Squadron	Lt S Davison DCM	+	Manchester [Gorton] Cemetery
F.1 Camel F2090			

T/o Throwley and while stunting sideslipped out of a loop and spun into the ground; his aircraft was a Comic two-seat conversion. Unfortunately, I have not been able to trace any details pertaining to Samuel Davidson's award, or any information regarding his flying service.

211 Squadron	Lt D F Taber	Safe	Unemployed list 6 March 1919
DH.9 D7369/V	USA		
	2Lt J H McLellan	Safe	Unemployed list 22 August 1919
	Canada		

T/o Clary for local flying but became lost and crashed while attempting to land at Boussières aerodrome, home at the time for 210 Squadron. Lieutenant Taber was confirmed in the rank of temporary 2nd Lieutenant on New Year's Day 1918 [LG 22 March 1918, supplement 30594, page 3710]. His Record of Service seems not to have survived. His observer, James Howard McLellan, born on the 28th of July 1899, gave his next of kin address as his Mother, residing at 1990, 7th Avenue, West Vancouver, British Columbia. He arrived on the squadron on the last day of September and was returned to the United Kingdom on the 22nd of March 1919. He had been graded as an Observer Officer with effect from 13th September [*Flight* October 10, 1918, page 1152].

Note. Between the 12th and the end of November, 142 aircraft from the operational squadrons had either been totally destroyed or damaged to the extent that it is likely they were struck off charge.

DECEMBER
1918

Sunday 1 December 1918

During the day the Allied units arrived in the German Rhineland, thereby heralding an occupation that would last for well over a decade.

The Great Unification of Romania in which Transylvania, Bessarabia and Bukovina became known as Romania.

5 Squadron	Lt F E Wyett	Safe	Unemployed list 15 April 1919
RE.8 C2925	Mechanic Wilson	Safe	

T/o Zeba Durma [sic] on a travelling flight and crashed on landing, presumably at Cognelée the squadron's base. It had been on charge since the 29th of October. Frederick Eden Wyett was attached to the squadron on the 3rd of June, at which time it was operating out of Le Hameau on tactical reconnaissance sorties and working with the artillery. Frederick was posted to England on 14th April and was placed on the unemployed list within 24-hours of his arrival.

40 Squadron	2Lt D L Field	Safe
SE.5a F5590		

T/o Aniche for a defensive patrol and on return landed with a force sufficient to sent his SE ballooning into the air. It was then caught by a strong gust of wind which sent it crashing into the ground, smashing the undercarriage and doing the fuselage structure no little good at all. Fitted with a Hispano-Suiza engine F5590 arrived from 1 Air Issues on the 14th of October and with Lieutenant G S Smith at the controls sent down an enemy two-seater near Valenciennes on 1st November, the final aerial combat success for the squadron in the *Great War*. Mention of this appears on page 79 of David Gunby's squadron history. I have not, however, been able to trace a Record of Service for 2nd Lieutenant Field and his name is absent from the history referred too.

204 Squadron	Lt W O G Fenton	Safe
F.1 Camel D9622		

T/o Heule for a cross-country flight but soon after flying into fog he became disorientated and forced-landed in the same area as that for his colleague, summarised below. William Oliver Geddes Fenton was very severely shaken for on landing his aircraft broke into two pieces.

At the onset of the Second World War he returned to the air force, obtaining a commission in the Administrative and Special Duties Branch, effective 1st September 1939 [LG 20 October 1939, issue 34713, page 7045]. William served until relinquishing his commission under the provisions of the Navy, Army and Air Force Reserves Act 1954, by which time he had attained Squadron Leader rank [LG 22 June 1954, supplement 40210, page 3678]. A record for this officer, covering the period 1918 - 1928 is held at TNA Kew under AIR 79/776/85745.

204 Squadron	Lt C A Morris	Safe	See 14 December 1918
F.1 Camel F3960			

T/o Heule similarly authorised and owing to fog came down in a filed near Varssenaere to the east of Oostende and on the Menin to Wervicq road. In the final moments of flight the Camel collided with a telegraph pole. The Records of Service for both officers are devoid of information regarding postings, but that for Lieutenant Morris indicates former service with the King's Liverpool Regiment.

206 Squadron	Sgt J W Duffield Harding	Injured
DH.9 D1167	Sgt G Woodgate	Injured

T/o Nivelles and came to grief in a heavy crash at Sirault [Hainaut], some 16 km NNW from Mons. Apart from mention of the crash *The DH.4/DH.9 File* has no other detail pertaining to movements of this DH.

215 Squadron   2Lt J A Phillips   Safe   Demobilised 10 March 1919
HP O/400 D8305 2Lt A V W Church   Injured   Unemployed list 4 February 1919
T/o Xaffévillers to join up with the squadron at Alquines but *en route* the weather closed in and with mist obscuring the earth below it is little wonder that the crew failed to see some farm buildings as they attempted to make a forced-landing near Foult-Saint-Léger [sic] near Doullens [Somme]. 2nd Lieutenant Church, who had been with the squadron since the 18th of September, was taken to 18 CCS and thence to England aboard the HS *Ville de Liège*. 2nd Lieutenant Phillips was posted to 97 Squadron on the 25th of January 1919.

Monday 2 December 1918
Readers of the *Birmingham Mail* learned that a service of thanksgiving and remembrance of the women war workers of the city had been held the previous day with no fewer than fifteen detachments representing workers from industry, the armed services, railway staff and many other services that employed women in roles vital to the conduct of the *Great War.*

   Across the Atlantic, President Woodrow Wilson gave a rousing address to Congress during which he praised the achievements of American forces in the recent conflict.

4 Squadron   2Lt C Kipling   Injured   Unemployed list 26 March 1919
RE.8 C2902   2Lt R P H West   Injured   Unemployed list 29 March 1919
T/o Ascq and on arrival at Linslles crashed. Charles Kipling was thrown forward with some force and he was admitted to 14 General Hospital for treatment to his facial injuries; of the 14th he was sent home on HMHS *Cambria.* He was older than most pilots having been born on the 15th July 1888, and prior to coming to the air force he had served with one of the Middlesex Regiments. Married, his next of kin is shown as *Mrs D G E Kipling, 37 Ivy Crescent, Chiswick Park W.* He had arrived with the squadron as recently as the 20th of October. His observer, who had been accepted for such duties on 17th June whilst attached to the 1st Battalion, Gloucestershire Regiment [his parent Battalion was the 3rd], returned to England for instruction on the 20th, returning to France in mid-October. Following the crash he, too, received facial abrasions for which he was treated in 10 CCS before being evacuated along with his skipper.

7 Squadron   2Lt J Browning   Safe
RE.8 C2716   2Lt G V Young   Safe
Presentation Aircraft: Johore No 1
T/o Cognelée tasked for a line patrol and crashed on return. C2716 had been with the squadron since 29th September. 2nd Lieutenant Browning joined the squadron a little less than three weeks earlier and served throughout most of the squadron's time in the Rhineland, returning home on the 9th of August from Heumar. His observer arrived on the 5th of August and left for England on the 8th of January 1919.

55 Squadron   Captain R W Rose   Safe
DH.4 A7427/J   2Lt G E Little   Safe
T/o Le Planay for a travelling flight, possibly to Saint-André-aux-Bois where the squadron was scheduled to move on the 7th. *En route* the engine began to falter and Captain Rose decided to return to Le Planay where his misfortune was to crash as he landed. The DH was a squadron veteran, arriving on the 1st of June 1917, after which it had a chequered life. On 16th August, Captain F McD C Turner and his observer 2nd Lieutenant R de R Brett crashed on landing from a reconnaissance to Inglemunster-Ghent. Taken to 2 Advanced Salvage Dump for reconstruction it returned to the squadron on the 31st of March. Then, on 20th July during a hotly contested operation it was involved in the driving down of an unidentified aircraft near Baccarat [sic]. During the fight the DH's observer, 2nd Lieutenant James Ferguson Pollock was killed. His birth date is shown as 16th August 1899, and 22nd August 1917 as the date he joined the RFC. His operational tour lasted for less than a month; he was buried in Charmes Military Cemetery, Essegny by the Reverend J B Berry attached to 8th Brigade officiating. His pilot, Lieutenant Arthur Stuart Keep*forced-landing at Rambervillers [Vosges] having sustained wounds. Repairs were put in hand and A7427 was ready for action by the 12th September and before the armistice came into effect it destroyed three more hostile aircraft; during the late morning of the 15th a Fokker DVII west of Strasbourg; in the afternoon of 6th November while raiding Saarbrücken a Fokker DVII totally destroyed [it broke up in the air] and a second last seen going down, seemingly out of control. All three successes being claimed by Captain J B Fox and Lieutenant J Parke DFC].

   With such a history it is worth looking into the records of the officers connected to this DH. Reginald Walter Rose, born on 28th of November 1896, was one of over a hundred temporary 2nd Lieutenants *Gazetted* to the Machine Gun Corps on the 5th of August 1916 [LG 1 September 1916, issue 29730, pages 8598 and 8599]. Having experienced life with the 2nd Machine Company, 1st Division, he transferred to the RFC on the 19th of March 1917, returning to the UK the same day but was back in France by the last day of May, qualified as an Observer Officer. I believe, however, that in the July he re-mustered to pilot as an entry on his Record of Service shows his transfer to the General List on the 8th and return to England five days later. His service between returning home and his accident, outlined above, has not been recorded. George Edward Little, born on the last day of July 1899, joined the RFC on the 6th of November 1917, and arrived with the squadron on the 6th of June. On the 24th of January 1919, he was went to 1 Aerial Range; four days later he was attached to the 2nd Brigade and thence on the 29th to 48 Squadron [Bristol F.2b] at Bickendorf and where on the 9th of May he was cross-posted to 18 Squadron [DH.9A].

   Captain Francis McDougall Charlewood Turner was born on 17th March 1897, and enlisted in the RFC on 3rd January 1916. He enjoyed a long association with 55 Squadron commencing in early 1917, in which year he was *Gazetted* with the MC which was published in the Edinburgh edition, without a citation, on 27 September 1917, issue

13146, page 2060. He remained in the postwar air force but owing to ill-health, contracted on active service, he relinquished his commission on the 12th of March 1920 [LG 19 March 1920, issue 31830, page 3436] by which time he had been awarded the DFC [untraced]. In the Second World War he was commissioned to the Administrative and Special Duties Branch on 30th October 1940 [LG 19 November 1940, supplement 34996, page 6640] and served until resigning his commission on 4th November 1944, retaining his rank of Squadron Leader [LG 21 November 1944, supplement 36802, page 5333]. His observer's service was equally long, commencing circa March 1917, and he, too, was *Gazetted* with the MC [as yet untraced].

John Bertram Fox was born of the 24th of July 1893, and I suspect part of his formative years were spent in Ceylon [Sri Lanka] for on joining the RFC on 18th January 1917, he gave his next of kin address as *John Fox [Father], Colombo, Ceylon.* However, this was later amended to *39 Bedford Avenue, Barnet.* His first operation tour with the squadron was from 29th July 1917 to 1st May 1918, during he was awarded the MC: *'For conspicuous gallantry and devotion to duty. During a period two months he led his formation on six long-distance bombing raids into enemy territory. On the last occasion, though engaged by three separate hostile formations, he dropped his bombs with excellent effect over his objective and brought the whole of his formation back to the aerodrome intact. His formation accounted for three enemy aeroplanes destroyed and four driven down out of control. He has carried out upwards of 40 successful operations, his skill and leadership being of the highest order.'* [LG 13 May 1918, supplement 30681, page 5699]. His second tour started on 11th September and it appears he was on the squadron's nominal role until at least 14th January 1919, on which date he was due to return from leave.

Joshua Parke was three years his senior, entering the world on 22nd August 1890, and similar to Lieutenant Keep [see the asterisked note below] he answered Lord Kitchener's call and was enrolled in the 18th Battalion [Durham Pals], Durham Light Infantry in 1914 [a photograph of the 18th practicing bayonet drills can be seen on the website Durham at War]. His tour commenced on the 14th of August 1917, and I suspect he flew most of his sorties with Captain Fox. Joshua's DFC citation reads: *'This officer has taken part in 40 long-distance day bomb raids and photographic reconnaissances. His work as an observer has been consistently good, and he displays great gallantry and determination, notably in a bombing raid when he was observer to the leader of our second formation.'* [LG 20 September 1918, supplement 30913, page 11253].

* Arthur Stuart Keep, born 15th July 1891, enlisting 21st August 1916, gained the MC [LG 16 September 1918, supplement 30901, page 10974]: *'For conspicuous gallantry and devotion to duty on long-distance bombing raids. He showed great skill and determination while raiding enemy towns. One day, with his oil feed pipe broken, he reached his objective, and disposed of an enemy machine on the way back. His work was splendid.'* Postwar he continued to serve until his health failed and he relinquished his commission on Christmas Eve 1924, retaining his rank of Flying Officer [LG 23 December 1924, issue 33004, page 9338]. His Record of Service indicates he was formerly of the 14th [1st Birmingham] Battalion, Royal Warwicks, which was raised as a Pals Battalion in Birmingham soon after the outbreak of the *Great War.* Following training the Battalion embarked for France on 21st November 1915.

81 Squadron   Lt W J Sampson   +   Oxford [Botley] Cemetery
5F.1 Dolphin *not known*

T/o Upper Heyford and having flown on a southerly course William Sampson, now in the vicinity of Oxford, encountered fog. Electing to make a precautionary landing he had the misfortune to fly into a tree and crash out of control. Born in Watford, Hertfordshire, his widow's address is recorded as *465, 48th Avenue East, Vancouver.* His headstone is simply inscribed: *"Peace Be Thine."* Although identified as 81 Squadron, at the time of the crash its official title was 1 Squadron Canadian Air Force, a classic example where change of title had yet to filter through the myriad strands of administration. The origins of 81 Squadron are traced to Gosport and the 7th of January 1917, when it formed as a training unit - this being a common procedure at the time - with the intent of becoming operational and deployment either to a theatre of war or assignment to home defence duties. However, it was August before the first Camels appeared, by which time the squadron had long since moved north to Lincolnshire and Scampton. Little is known of this period and before completing the work-up to operational readiness the squadron disbanded on the 4th of July 1918.

Then, on 25th November it was resurrected at Upper Heyford as 1 Squadron Canadian Air Force. Over the next thirteen months, during which it moved to the coastal airfield at Shoreham, it received 5F.1 Dolphins but earmarked to convert to SE.5a in the spring of 1919. Throughout this period funding for the squadron was provided by the British government but this was withdrawn in the summer of '19 and with the Canadian government deciding it was not in need of a peacetime air forces the two squadrons that had formed were run down and disbanded. For 1 Squadron CAF this came on 28th January 1920, while 2 Squadron CAF which had formed at Upper Heyford on 28th November 1918, as a day-bomber squadron and issued with DH.9A the end came on 5th February 1920.

Serial identification of the aircraft issued to 81 Squadron aka 1 Squadron CAF is, perhaps, best explained as follows. On the 21st of November 1918, 93 Squadron at Port Meadow which had received a number of 5F.1 Dolphins disbanded and records show the following being released to 81 Squadron aka 1 Squadron CAF at Upper Heyford, formation being four days hence: F7085, F7086, F7090, F7091 and F7092. On Christmas Eve F7076, F7078 and F7079 arrived followed on the 27th by F7081, F7082 and F7089. Mentioned in *The Squadrons of the Royal Air Force & Commonwealth* is the issue of a F.1 Camel B7301,*but this is not supported by the history of this aircraft as recorded in *The Camel File.* However, *The SE.5a File* identifies the following delivered to Shoreham during May and June: E5747, E5748, F9025 and F9029.

* Destroyed in a fatal crash on 8th June 1918, when 2nd Lieutenant F B Love of 39 Training Squadron, South Carlton, failed to recover from a spin; he is buried in Essex at Nevendon [St. Peter] Churchyard.

Tuesday 3 December 1918
In the Balkans the emergence of the newly formed Kingdom of Yugoslavia raised alarm that Romania might resort to force against the new State, thus France deployed 15,000 troops under the command of Generals Paul Prosper Henrys and Henri Mathias Berthelot to form a buffer zone between the two countries.

15 Squadron	Lt A B Llew-Williams	Injured
RE.8 D4950	South Africa	
	2Lt H T Ecob	Injured

T/o Selvigny and set forth the squadron's new base at Vigncourt but on flying into fog the crew lost their bearings and crash-landed at Flécy [Oise], 28 km NNE of Beauvais, their aircraft tumbling into a deep ditch. Archibald Boniface Llew-Williams, late of the South African Infantry, was taken to a hospital in Beauvais suffering from multiple contusions and on the 14th he was evacuated to England by way of HMHS *St. Andrew* to continue his recovery. He had been with the squadron since the 7th of October. Hugh Thomas Ecob, born on 13th March 1895, arrived at Selvigny on 21st October and he, too, was first treated at Beauvais before accompanying his skipper home on the 14th. Postwar he transferred from the Flying Branch to the Administrative Branch with effect from 8th May 1919 [LG 10 June 1919, issue 31396, page 7433].

20 Squadron	2Lt S E Booth	+	Charleroi Communal Cemetery
Bristol F.2b F6181	Corporal E Moors	+	Charleroi Communal Cemetery

T/o Clary and in the company of other crews headed for Ossogne where the squadron would be based until the following May when it commence making preparations for service in India. Sadly, for Sydney Edwin Booth and Richard Moors such possible deployment to the Jewel in the Crown would never be realised for as they prepared to land the Bristol stalled and spun into the ground. Their headstones are inscribed respectively: *"In Loving Memory. Transported Home To Glory Land Alive For Evermore"* and *"For Ever In Our Thoughts."*

23 Squadron	2Lt W W McGill	Safe	Unemployed list 18 July 1919
5F.1 Dolphin C3785			

T/o Bertry East and on arrival at the squadron's new abode at Clermont shed part of the undercarriage on touch down. Commissioned to the General List he was confirmed in his appointment on 20th May [LG 21 June 1918, issue 30759, page 7326]. He had been attached to the squadron on the 3rd of September, and had recently returned to duty from fourteen days leave. He returned to England on the 1st of March 1919.

155 Squadron	2Lt T Richardson	+	York Cemetery, Yorkshire
DH.9A F2740	Sgt C H C Noyes	+	Folkstone [Cheriton Road] Cemetery

T/o Chingford only for the engine to fail. It seems likely that 19-year old Tom Richardson attempted to make an emergency landing on the West Essex golf course which was near the airfield and about two miles S of Waltham Abbey. Tragically, on his approach he stalled and crashed at High Beech, the impact being particularly severe. Charles Henry Crispin Noyes was 21.

Wednesday 4 December 1918
On this day a serving American president did what none of his predecessors had ever done, or possibly even contemplated; he left his country for foreign climes. Although the United States had been late coming to the war, President Woodrow Wilson was determined to ensure that his voice would be heard on terms equal to those of the leaders of France and the United Kingdom at the Paris Peace Conference [also referred to as the Versailles Peace Conference]. So, with his entourage in tow he embarked on the aptly names SS *George Washington* to face the winter waters of the North Atlantic. There was a certain irony to the occasion in that the *George Washington* had been built and named as such in Germany specifically for the Bremen-Southampton-Cherbourg-New York crossing under the flag of North German Lloyd. At the time she was the third largest ocean going passenger liner with accommodation for close on 2,900 passengers, 520 being able to enjoy the sumptuous first-class accommodation. Interned in the United States in August 1914 and in 1917 upon America's entry into the war she became the USS *George Washington* playing a major role in the transportation of troops to Europe, this being repeated during the Second World War. During her long service she was converted from coal-burning to oil-fired propulsion and was eventually sold for scrap in February 1951.

28 Squadron	Lt R B Beevor	Safe	Unemployed list 3 March 1919
F.1 Camel E7248			

T/o Sarcedo for a practice flight which end with the Camel on the ground N of Val d'Assa. Ralph Branthway Beevor, born on the 25th of April 1895, probably enlisted on 27th December 1916, but it was not until 5th August 1918, that he was attached to 28 Squadron. Postwar he was detached to Rome for temporary duty on 26th January, and whilst in the Eternal City he was taken to hospital on 16th February suffering from tonsillitis. He was discharged a week later and returned to the United Kingdom for his final days of service.

Thursday 5 December 1918

The legacy of war was brought cruelly home with the sinking by a sea-mine in the Gulf of Finland of the C-class light cruiser HMS *Casandra*. The threat from Bolshevik forces opposing the newly formed Baltic States had seen the despatch of the 6th Light Cruiser Squadron, under the command of Rear-Admiral Alexander-Sinclair, now in passage to Estonia's capital city, Tallinn, now threatened by the Bolsheviks following their assault in late November on the border town of Narya. Although the *Cassandra**foundered quickly, loss of life was mercifully low with ten sailors reported killed when the mine exploded, and one dying as the destroyers HMS *Westminster* and *Vendetta* came alongside to take off survivors. Ten of the dead are commemorated on the Plymouth Naval Memorial, while 22 year old Richard Harold Partridge, a stoker, is named on the Chatham Naval Memorial.

* Laid down at Barrow in Furness in 1916, for construction at the Vickers Yards, HMS *Cassandra* was launched on the 25th of November of that year and commissioned the following June.

1 Squadron CAF *Not known*
5.F1 Dolphin J6
T/o Upper Heyford and reported as crashed; no further details, except that it was intended for delivery to Port Meadow and 93 Squadron, but this was cancelled. Probably the first write off of an aircraft bearing a J serial.

150 Squadron   Lt W Ridley DFC   Safe   Commission relinquished 25 March 1919
SE.5a D3495
T/o Mikra Bay and on return crashed while landing, a strong and gusting wind being a factor. Although I have yet to find the service records for Lieutenant Ridley, much has come to light regarding Captain Gerald Gordon Bell who claimed for enemy aircraft whilst flying D3495 which had been shipped to the 16th Wing in Salonika, arriving on the 17th of July and issued to the squadron on the 3rd of August. Within two days of its acceptance, Gerald Bell had claimed his first victim and this was followed by successes on the 15th and 21st, and a fourth on 18th September. He also had a fond attachment to SE.5a B692, which the squadron received on 27th April, claiming three victories - all shared. This particular SE survived the war and was last reported being sent to X Aircraft Depot on 24th May 1919.

Throughout his substantive rank was Lieutenant and records show he had been attached from the Eastern Ontario Regiment and was *Gazetted* with the DFC on 2 November 1918, supplement 30989, page 12962: *'This officer has had numerous engagements with hostile aircraft, invariably displaying marked gallantry and leadership of a high order, notably on the 1st of June, when he, accompanied by another pilot, attacked a formation of twelve enemy scouts; he shot down one in flames and drove down others out of control, only breaking off the engagement when all his ammunition had been expended.'* Subsequently, he was honoured by the President of the French Republic with the *Legion d'Honour [Croix de Chevalier]* [LG 10 October 1919, supplement 31592, page 12527].

Additional information pertaining to Captain Bell may be found on the website *Soldiers of the 38th,* which I gratefully acknowledge. Born in Ottawa on the 11th of June 1890, he joined the 38th Battalion on the 8th of February 1915. Prior to the '38th' arriving in France [13th August 1916] it served time in Bermuda. Desiring the adventures offered by becoming an airman, Gerald was seconded to the RFC on the 9th of January 1917, and he remained as one until the 6th of May 1919.

Meanwhile, *Wikipedia* shows that following his secondment he initially trained as an observer and on returning to France he joined 22 Squadron [FE.2b]. Re-mustering to pilot it was back to England and Reading in Berkshire for training at 1 School of Military Aeronautics and by October 1917, he was posted to 83 Squadron at Waddington [FK.8] which was working up to operational readiness for Corps reconnaissance duties on the Western Front. For reasons unknown, his time with '83' lasted a mere seven days before he embarked for the Middle East. Initially, he was attached to 47 Squadron before joining 150 Squadron and demonstrating his fighting skills as a scout pilot.

What little is known for Lieutenant Ridley, he came to the air force by way of the Canadian Engineers and on the 19th July he shared with Gerald Bell in the destruction of an Albatros DV west of Livanova aerodrome, a combat that also involved Captain G M Brawley and Lieutenant Arthur Jarvis.

Friday 6 December 1919

As has been reported in earlier observations, the bulk of the German High Seas Fleet were now under Royal Navy control, and on this day two more warships, the Battleship *König* and the light cruiser *Dresden,* joined those already at anchor in Scapa Flow.

In Germany, Commonwealth troops marched into the Rhineland city of Köln where they would remain until January 1926.

Without becoming operational 119 Squadron disbanded at Wyton. Formed at Andover of New Year's Day it was intended the squadron would become a day bomber squadron. Its existence was slightly Nomadic in that it moved to Duxford on the 1st of March and then to Thetford on 19th August before arriving at Wyton on 26th September. During this time various types of aircraft were issued, including DH.9s. More by coincidence than design, it was issued with biplanes in the Second World War when on reformation on 19th July 1944, at Manston from a flight of 415 Squadron RCAF, it received Albacores which in January 1945, were exchanged for Swordfish! Prior to the 19th of July, the Squadron had operated in Coastal Command from 13th March 1941, to 17th April 1943, equipped with various flying-boats including Catalinas and Sunderlands.

18 Squadron   2Lt E Carter   Safe
DH.9A F1058   Lt *Sparcrop*   Safe

T/o Mauberge and on return the crew failed to notice they were heading for a ditch, into which fell and was damaged beyond repair. The surname *Sparcrop* is not recognised on the websites for *The London Gazette* or *Flight Global.*

43 Squadron   Lt E C Robinson   Safe
7F.1 Snipe E7993

T/o Cognelée only for the engine to cut resulting in the Snipe colliding with a telegraph pole. Reported at 10 Aeroplane Acceptance Park, Brooklands, on 7th August, where in a starting accident Mechanic C Thompson received non-fatal injuries to chest after being struck by the propeller. Cleared through 2 Aeroplane Supply Depot, the Snipe reached the squadron on the 30th of August.

211 Squadron   2Lt H C Thomas   Safe
DH.9 C2210   Mechanic E W Morgan   Safe

T/o for a travelling flight, possibly from Clary, to rejoin the squadron at Thuilles where the main body arrived three days previously. On landing the DH hit a sharp ridge causing total collapse of the undercarriage; damaged beyond repair. Harold Claude Thomas was born on the 26th of June 1899, and enlisted in the RFC on the 1st of August 1917. Arriving in France on 19th June, he was temporarily attached to 2 Aeroplane Supply Depot before making his acquaintance with the squadron at Petite Synthe on the 27th. Briefly reported missing the day before the armistice came into effect, Harold bade farewell to his friends - now at Thuilles - on the 23rd of February and reported to Alquines where he joined 98 Squadron. By this time '98' was preparing to return to England and three weeks before they made the transfer to Shotwick on 28th March, 2nd Lieutenant Thomas was posted back to England.

Saturday 7 December 1919
Another day of serious unrest in the Balkans, while to protect the independence of the recently formed Baltic States from the Bolsheviks, the Baltische Landswehr [Baltic Territorial Army] formed under the command of Major Emil von Scheibler who on 6th February 1919, handed over command to Major Alfred Fletcher who in turn was relieved in July of that year by Lieutenant-Colonel Harold Alexander [subsequently Field Marshal the Earl Alexander of Tunis and post Second World War, Governor-General of Canada]. This little recorded history of German forces, at the insistence of the Inter-Allied Commission of Control, mounting operations in the Baltic regions makes for fascinating reading.

   The occupation of German airfields in the Rhineland commenced with 4 Squadron Australian Flying Corps bringing their Sopwith Snipes from Grand Ennetières to Euskirchen and at Elsenborn temporary occupation by 5 Squadron and their RE.8s.

40 Squadron   2Lt E G Carter   Injured
SE.5a E1318

T/o Aniche with ordered to ferry the aircraft to a reception park but came to grief *en route*. Prior to its demise E1318, which was delivered to the squadron on 2nd July, saw a great deal of operational flying, much of which is recorded in David Gunby's history of the squadron. Two of the officers who made their mark in E1318 were Captain George Edward Henry McElroy*and American born Lieutenant Reed G Landis who between them accounted for at least eight hostile aircraft [George McElroy bagged a DFW in the evening of the day that the SE arrived at Bryas]. Both officers were decorated for their outstanding prowess as scout pilots.

* The outstanding contribution to the air war by George McElroy who was killed in action on Wednesday, 31st July 1918, is reported on page 98 of my second volume.

56 Squadron   Lt G M McWilliams   Safe   Unemployed list 29 September 1919
SE.5a B7901

T/o Bethencourt to deliver a consignment of post to 82 Squadron at Bertangles and while flying at very low altitude in adverse weather flew into the ground at Map Reference Sheet 57 CN31 and turned over. Recovered on the 13th, the SE was taken to 2 Advanced Salvage Dump where, I presume, it was struck off charge.

75 Squadron   Captain F Barclay   +   Weston-super-Mare Cemetery
Avro 504K D9348 Lt C J McGrane   Injured Unemployed list 3 June 1919

T/o Elmswell but lost power while banking and dived to the ground. At the age of 41, Captain Barclay was well over the average age for pilots. The identity of his squadron is not recorded on the CWGC website. Some reports show the accident as occurring at the squadron's detached base at Harling Road. Late of the 10th Battalion, Royal Dublin Fusiliers, Lieutenant McGrane was accepted for observer training on the 8th of February 1917, and returned to England on the 16th. On 19th March, he was back in France and attached to 22 Squadron [FE.2b] at Chipilly. From the 8th to the 14th of August he was detached for temporary duty with 101 Squadron [FE.2b], then at Izel-lès-Hameau, and soon after return to his parent squadron he was posted home. Spending Christmas and the New Year at home, he rejoined his squadron, now flying Bristol F.2bs from Auchel, on 26th January.

| 139 Squadron | Lt J A Carr | Safe |
| Bristol F.2b E2188/V Mechanic Brown | | Safe |

T/o Grossa for an air test; on return the engine failed and the Bristol crashed while attempting to land. It has been with the squadron since September 1st. On which date it was collected from 7 Aircraft Park at Caldiero. Army Form B.103-1 Part I has been raised in respect of Lieutenant Carr, but is devoid of information regarding postings et al.

205 Squadron	2Lt F O McDonald	Safe	Unemployed list 28 September 1919
DH.9A F1013	Canada		
	Captain W Grossart DFC	Safe	Unemployed list 12 April 1919

T/o Maubeuge and crashed on, or near the airfield at Bertangles, fog being a contributory factor. Frank Oscar McDonald was born, probably in British Columbia, on 20th February 1897, and joined the RFC a little over a year previous on 19th November. He arrived with the squadron on 20th June and according to his service records was hospitalised twice, the first in 50 CCS and the second time in 55 CCS. On the 21st of February 1919, he was cross-posted to 25 Squadron and [I suspect] he served with '25' throughout their time as part of the Occupation Forces, returning to South Carlton in Lincolnshire on 6th September. William Grossart also joined the RFC at around the same time as Frank McDonald, joining the squadron as a pilot on 6th April. The citation for his DFC appeared in the Edinburgh edition of the *Gazette* on 23 September 1918, issue 13325, page 3533: *'During the last two and a half months this officer has carried out twenty-seven successful bombing raids and twenty-five special photographic reconnaissances, his service on the latter duty being exceptionally valuable. This officer possesses a fine spirit of determination; neither strong opposition nor adverse weather conditions deters him from achieving his objective.'* Born on 26th May 1896, in Crawfordjohn, Lanarkshire, he is credited with driving down of five*enemy aircraft, some of these victories shared with other pilots. His brother's address appears in the section for next of kin details; *J L Grossart, Milton, Beattock, Dumbartonshire.*

* According to the most informative Aerodrome website, this quintet of success was achieved between the 3rd of May and the 11th of August, and all his victims were Pfalz DIIIs. On four occasions, all in May, William was flying DH.4 A7811 while for his fifth he was airborne in DH.4 D8421.

Sunday 8 December 1918

Continued fighting in Russia between the Bolsheviks and what is termed as the White Russians. A description of this period and the support given to the White Russians by the Royal Air Force is described in the second chapter of Chaz Bowyer's book *RAF Operations 1918-1938.*

| 32 Squadron | 2Lt J C Carson | Safe | Unemployed list 11 February 1919 |
| SE.5a C9574 | | | |

T/o Izel-lès-Hameau and written off here in a landing accident. Apart from the casualty return and a note indicating the SE was recovered to 1 Advanced Salvage Dump, nothing else is known of its service history. And of John Combs Carson little is known, either; his service sheet indicates he was born on 18th April 1892, and that he enlisted on the 11th of March 1918. His next of kin is given as his father, residing at Holyrood, Helensburgh, Scotland.

| 57 Squadron | Captain A Newman MC | Safe | |
| DH.4 F2648 | Lt A M Barron MC | Safe | Unemployed list 17 January 1919 |

T/o Bruyers and crashed N of Namur while attempting to forced-land. The DH, ex-2 Air Issues, had been with the squadron for a week. Arthur Newman who was born on the 4th of April 1884, was a prewar territorial serving with the 4th Battalion, Essex Regiment, gaining his MC prior to transferring to the RFC, notification appearing in the London edition of 3 June 1916, supplement 29608, page 5576, but with no citation appended. His date of transfer is reported as 28th December 1916, and he joined the squadron on the historic 1st of April 1918. He is named in my first volume on page 155, when with Lieutenant E G Pernet he was obliged to forced-land DH.4 A7723 on the 17th of May. The next day, again with Lieutenant Pernet, he forced-landed DH.4 E4625 as they returned from a bombing mission. Initially, the damage to E4625 was thought to be irreparable but further examination resulted in the DH being rebuilt and reissued as F6120. Stored with 2 Air Issues, it later went to 25 Squadron at Ruisseauville on 25th of September, remaining with the squadron until 19th May 1919, by which time '25' was based at Bickendorf.

Resuming my observations concerning Arthur Newman, he was awarded a DFC on 25th January 1919 [details yet to be traced], returning to England on the 8th of March. In the Second World War he was commissioned on 2nd July 1941, to the Administrative and Special Duties Branch [LG 22 August 1941, issue 35254, page 4876], and held the rank of Squadron Leader when relinquishing his commission under the provisions of the Navy, Army and Air Force Reserves Act 1954 [LG 15 October 1954, supplement 40299, page 5830].

Although no Record of Service appears to have survived for Lieutenant Barron, I am reasonably confident he was late of the Gordon Highlanders and was promoted as such on 1st July 1917 [LG 27 November 1917, supplement 30401, page 12347]. His name appears in *Wikipedia,* associated with the late William Edward Green DFC of 57 Squadron with whom he flew as an observer on 29th August and 19th September, and playing a part in shooting down a brace of Fokker DVIIs, the first of Ytres in the Pas-de-Calais and the second soon after over Havrincourt, also in the Pas-de-Calais. Bill Green, as he was popularly known, subsequently became a Lieutenant-Colonel commanding the 5th Battalion, Northamptonshire Regiment and was killed in action on 23rd May 1940, as the BEF withdrew into the Dunkirk perimeter. He is buried in White House Cemetery, St. Jean-les-Ypres.

57 Squadron   2Lt A V Dearden   Safe   Unemployed list 5 April 1919
DH.4 F6104

T/o Bruyeres and on return, and landing at 1350, had the misfortune to collide with DH.4 A7774 [see 10 February 1919], and veering away caught fire. Arnold Vivian Dearden, born on the 6th of December 1899, no doubt exited his cockpit with alacrity. He joined the squadron on 29th September, and shortly before being returned to England spent a few weeks attached to 4 Aircraft Park at Charleroi.

59 Squadron   2Lt R K Moore   Safe   Unemployed list 30 April 1919
RE.8 C2955

T/o Ossogne only for the engine to fail. Turning towards a nearby field in which to forced-land, 2nd Lieutenant Moore went into a sideslip and crashed. His service records lack and detail regarding postings.

84 Squadron   Lt J M Bacon   Safe   Unemployed list 25 February 1919
SE.5a E6024

T/o Thuilles and on return, and while about to touch down, the engine cut and moments later the SE crashed into a ditch having overshot the landing area. With the squadron since 17th September, and much favoured by Captain Carl Frederick Falkenberg DFC, E6024 accounted for five hostile aircraft and a kite balloon. Seconded for duty with the RFC on 21st October 1917 [LG 14 January 1918, supplement 30475, page 818], Carl Falkenberg of the Quebec Regiment, was an outstanding fighter pilot. The citation for his DFC was reported in *Flight* November 7, 1918: '*A bold and skilful airman, who has destroyed four enemy machines and driven down four out of control. In addition, he has performed many gallant deeds in attacking troops, transports, etc., on the ground.*' *Flight* in its December 12, 1918, issue carries the citation for the First Bar: '*A gallant and skilful fighter who, since he was awarded the Distinguished Flying Cross, has destroyed four enemy machines and one balloon, and has driven down two more machines out of control, making in all 14 enemy aircraft and one balloon to his credit. He has further rendered gallant service in attacking ground targets and reconnoitring enemy lines.*'

According to his entry in *Wikipedia* [which I acknowledge], he was credited with seventeen victories. Born in Botwood, Newfoundland on 4th February 1897, he died aged 83 on 7th October 1980, in Edmonton, Alberta. His secondment for flying duties ceased on 10th May 1919, on which date he was attached to the CAF for Flight Commander duties [LG 28 May 1919, supplement 31363, page 6616]. On the 1st of August of that year he was one of hundreds of officers selected for a permanent commission but, it seems, he declined, notification of this being *Gazetted* on 16 September 1919, issue 31554, page 11589.

Lieutenant Bacon's records appear not to have survived the passage of time.

214 Squadron   Lt G S Lewtas   Safe   Unemployed list 19 April 1919
HP O/400 C9644 Lt F C Sumner   Safe   See 9 July 1919

T/o Gamphin and in the region of Wenduvre [sic] the petrol feed pipe to the starboard engine fractured and with fuel spilling onto hot metal a fire broke out. By good fortune the HP was near the coast and the crew managed to execute a forced-landing on a beach where the bomber was swamped by the incoming tide. Up until now C9644 had had a trouble free existence since being accepted by the squadron on 16th May. As far as I can tell, George Selby Lewtas, born on the 3rd of October 1898, was the only officer with the surnane 'Lewtas' to serve with the Royal Air Force in the *Great War*. Army Form B.103c shows his enlistment with the RNAS and on arriving in France during April 1918 [and now an officer in the fledgling Royal Air Force], he joined 207 Squadron at Coudekerque on the 15th. The date of his posting to 214 Squadron is unreadable, but it was prior to 19th July when he was granted leave for fourteen day. Entered on the Form in red ink, and dated 10th January 1919, is Mentioned in Despatches, while the final entry shows posted to Home Establishment from Merheim two days before being transferred to the unemployed list.

Lieutenant Sumner's Record of Service has no information whatsoever apart from his rank, surname and initials.

Monday 9 December 1918

96 Squadron which had had two attempts at becoming an operational squadron disbanded at Wyton where it formed for a second time on 28th September. Had the armistice not intervened, then it is almost certain 96 Squadron, working up as a ground attack squadron equipped with Sopwith TF.2 Salamander, would have deployed to the Western Front.

Red Army forces advance towards Minsk and at nightfall advance elements were within striking distance of their objective.

3 Squadron   2Lt D D Ashley   Injured   Unemployed list 1 February 1919
F.1 Camel D1796/F6227/H

T/o Inchy and while flying at extremely low altitude, and into a setting sun, he failed to see a line of telegraph wires bordering the highway between Warloy-Baillon and Varennes [Somme]. The resultant collision sent his aircraft crashing out of control. Presumably, his injuries were not of a serious nature, though 2nd Lieutenant Ashley's service records have not been located. The Camel, previously with 70 Squadron and with 2nd Lieutenant Lorne Lamond Saunders at the controls, crash-landed in a cornfield near Ramaisnil airfield on 30th June. Lorne Saunders was born on 27th February 1899, and he enlisted on 15th September 1917. He arrived with 70 Squadron 24-hours before his accident and possibly as a consequence he was sent to O Battery A.A. on temporary duty for two days. Like so many young pilots attached to Camel equipped squadrons, he found the type difficult to master and within days of returning to duty he was injured in a crash on 7th July [see page 32 of my second volume] and was out of action until the 15th. Then on the 1st of August he was attached to 1 Aeroplane Supply Depot, possibly to gain experience and regain his confidence.

Five days later he was ordered to join 46 Squadron at Serny and gradually he settled into the demands of operational flying until his death on the 4th of October [see page 288 in the second volume], at which time the squadron was based at Cappy.

| 83 Squadron | 2Lt Adams | Safe |
| FE.2b E7043 | 2Lt H Clarke | Safe |

Presentation Aircraft: Johannesburg No 2

T/o Estré-en-Chaussée to transfer to a new airfield but crashed before reaching its destination. I have not been able to fully identify 2nd Lieutenant Adams but his observer, I am confident, was Herbert Clarke who joined the squadron on the 4th of September. He was posted on the last day of February 1919; his date of birth is shown as 9th May 1899.

| 149 Squadron | Captain E S Russell | Safe |
| FE.2b D9743 | | |

T/o Fort de Cognelée intending to make a round trip to Valenciennes but before becoming fully airborne ran onto soft ground and crashed through a hedge. Issued to the squadron from Norwich on 26th April, it crossed the Channel to Alquines on 16th June, subsequently moving with the squadron to Clairmarais and Le Quesnoy. Born on the 4th of April 1888, Ernest Shaftesbury Russell of the Special Reserve joined the RFC on 18th March 1916. On the 15th of October 1916, he was posted to 34 Squadron [BE.2e] at Allonville, but on New Year's Day 1917 he was admitted to hospital [Syno L Knee Slt] and on the 8th sent home aboard HMHS St. George. He returned to France on the 2nd of June 1918; on 7th August he was laid low with gastro enteritis but recovered quickly and resumed his tour of duty with 149 Squadron. The section for his next of kin indicates he was married, his wife residing at 10 Woodlands Road, Little-hampton, a popular seaside resort in West Sussex.

| 203 Squadron | 2Lt R H Thompson | + | Loos British Cemetery |
| F.1 Camel F3098 | | | |

T/o Auberchicourt for a practice flight and totally wrecked in a crash near Auby [Nord] and on the border with the Pas-de-Calais, some 14 km ESE of Lens. From the Earls Court area of London, his headstone is inscribed: "2nd Son Of The Late R H Thompson & Kate Thompson R I P." F308 was received on 22nd September and scored at least one aerial victory when during the mid-afternoon of 29th October, Sergeant W G Jones drove down a Fokker DVII near Bruary.

| 216 Squadron | Lt Mott | Safe |
| HP O/400 | Lt I B Boyce | Safe |

T/o Quillen for an air test and crashed in the wake of a sideslip near the airfield. As yet the service records for Lieutenant Mott are untraced, but from notes on Army Form B.103c show his observer was attached from the 2nd/3rd Battalion, London Regiment and arrived with the squadron as recently as the 1st of October. Entries for 1919, indicate four long spells of leave between 3rd January and 14th May, after which he appears to have returned to England.

Turning to The London Gazette supplement 32517 for 14 November 1921, page 9023, shows Lt I B Boyce of the 3rd Battalion, London Regiment, relinquishing his commission on 30th September 1921, under A.O. 166/21 as amended by A.O. 332/21, retaining his rank.

| 218 Squadron | 2Lt M J Carroll | Safe | Unemployed list 24 April 1919 |
| DH.9 D7373 | 2Lt T James | Safe | |

T/o Vert Galant and wrecked after stalling while landing. 2nd Lieutenant Carroll, commissioned to the General List, was confirmed in his appointment on 25th April 1918 [LG 16 July 1918, issue 30798, page 8339].

Tuesday 10 December 1918
Minsk falls to the Red Army.

| 46 Squadron | 2Lt R C Mills | Safe | See 7 January 1919 |
| F.1 Camel B7897 | | | |

T/o Baizieux and completely destroyed in a forced-landing, occasioned by engine failure, near Acheux-en-Amiénois [Somme], 10 km NW of Albert. 2nd Lieutenant Mills began his tour of operational flying on 8th September, when he was attached to 208 Squadron [Camel], then operating out from Tramecourt. On 4th November he was temporarily attached to 2 Aeroplane Supply Depot before on Armistice Day he joined 46 Squadron at Busigny. He returned home on 9th January 1919. During the next conflict, I believe he received a commission in the Administrative and Special Duties, effective on 5th December 1941 [LG 27 January 1942, issue 35435, page 453] serving until his release under the provisions of the Navy, Army and Air Force Reserves Act, 1954.

Wednesday 11 December 1918
The Birmingham Mail carried a report on the city's contribution in sending aid to prisoners of war. In total an impressive total of 130,152 parcels were despatched. The same article noted that 453 former prisoners had registered their names for the allocation of Council Houses, but it was thought many others had failed to do so, and were now being urged to register as a matter of urgency.

3 Squadron AusFC Lt Heather   Safe
RE.8 H7047
T/o 6 Air Issues and on arrival at Charleroi some of the ballast fell onto the control column and jammed the flying controls. A heavy crash-landing ensued and, presumably, the RE was damaged beyond repair.

| 42 Squadron | Lt S S Owen | + | Valenciennes [St. Roth] Communal Cemetery |
| RE.8 B5041 | 2Lt W D Wicks | + | Valenciennes [St. Roth] Communal Cemetery |

T/o Aulnoye and crashed almost immediately, bursting into flames. Sidney Smith Owen had emigrated to Canada and with the war in progress he enlisted in the Depot Battalion [British Columbia], Canadian Infantry. This is entered on his service records, but, unfortunately, the date of his transfer to flying duties and subsequent postings are omitted. His epitaph reads: *"The Strife Is O'ver."* Similarly, although Army Form B.103-I has been raised for 2nd Lieutenant Wicks, it has no details of his service.

Thursday 12 December 1918
A noteworthy day in aviation's rich history in that in the skies above Fort Tilden located on the coast in New York's borough of Queens, a US Navy blimp [C.1] successfully released a Curtis JN-4 into flight. Established in 1917, as part of the harbor defences of southern New York, Fort Tilden remained a military facility until the late '70s.

   Also on this day as reported in *Flight* December 19, 1919, *Major-General W G H Salmond DSO accompanied by Captain Ross Smith AFC, has arrived at Karachi in a Handley Page aeroplane to confer with the Government of India regarding the organisation and establishment of the aerial route and service to India.*

   At the time Major General Salmond was General Officer Commanding the Royal Air Force in the Middle East and had commenced his journey from Cairo. It was further noted that the Handley Page in which the flight was undertaken had in the final weeks of the war taken part in operations against Turkish forces in Palestine.

Friday 13 December 1918
Defying superstition, a Handley Page V/1500 named HMA *Carthusian* took off at 0930 from Martlesham Heath near Ipswich on the first stage of an epic flight to India. The senior pilot was Major Archibald Stuart Charles MacLaren MC AFC and alongside him was Captain Robert Halley AFC. Crewing the bomber was Sergeant Thomas Brown, navigator, and fitters Flight Sergeant Smith and Sergeant Crockett while the passenger in there care was Brigadier-General Norman MacEwen recently appointed General Officer Commanding Royal Air Force, India. Although a qualified pilot, most of his *Great War* service was spent attending to the unglamorous, but important, duties of a Staff Officer. Retiring from the air force in July 1935, he was recalled to duty in March 1939 and for slightly less than a year [September 1939 to the 1st of June 1940], he was Air Officer Commanding No 22 Group. Hanging up his uniform for a second time, Air-Vice Marshal Sir Norman MacEwen Kt CB CMG DSO died on the 29th of January 1953.

   A report on what would be for the time a huge undertaking, plus a brief article on Major-General Salmond's arrival in India 24-hours earlier, appeared in *Flight's* issue of 19th December.

   A photograph [G S Leslie collection] printed in a Martlesham Heath newsletter of June 2014, which I dutifully acknowledge, shows HP O/400 B9464 ex-Cricklewood at Martlesham Heath in August 1918. It is possible this aircraft may have been flown by Major MacLaren on one of his two proving flights to Egypt, prior to undertaking his India flight.

   In the demilitarised zone of Germany, 70 Squadron and their F.1 Camels arrived at Bickendorf.

| 117 Squadron | Captain C C Brill | Injured | Unemployed list 5 March 1919 |
| DH.9 D1190 | Mechanic T W Moore | Injured | |

T/o Wyton and crashed following a collision with telegraph wires. A service record has been raised for Captain Claud Cecil Brill, but the entries cease as at 25th May 1917, when he was posted home. Up to this date, and beginning on 29th June 1916, he had been engaged on bombing and reconnaissance operations with 8 Squadron. In the Second World War he was commissioned to the Administrative and Special Duties Branch on 7th September 1939 [LG 27 October 1939, supplement 34718, page 7186]; as with hundreds of his compatriots he was obliged to relinquish his commission under the provisions of the Navy, Army and Air Force Reserves Act 1954 [LG 25 May 1954, supplement 40180, page 3065], retaining his rank of Squadron Leader.

Saturday 14 December 1918
The first national general election held in the United Kingdom, which at the time included the whole of Ireland, resulted in a landslide victory for the coalition government of David Lloyd George and Bonar Law. However, their triumph was overshadowed when the Irish votes were counted with the moderate Irish Parliamentary Party being heavily defeated by Sinn Féin. The consequences of this would in time lead to what is referred to as 'the troubles' and the terrible bitterness between Protestants and Roman Catholics in Northern Ireland that today, even with the 'peace accord' of the Good Friday Agreement*and power sharing at Stormont, simmers beneath the surface of everyday life.

   4 Squadron Australian Flying Corps [7F.1 Snipe] arrived at Bickendorf from Euskirchen where they had been temporarily lodged since the 7th.

* Also known as the Belfast Agreement, it was signed bilaterally on the 12th of April 1998.

8 Squadron 2Lt S N Jacobson Safe See 15 December 1918
Bristol F.2b E1906 Lt Wood Safe

T/o Bellevue to reconnoitre tank movements. During the sortie the petrol feed to the engine failed and the Bristol forced-landed near Plateau [sic] where it fell into a shell hole; wrecked. 2nd Lieutenant Jacobson reported for duty on the 26th of September and returned to England on the 14th of January 1919.

11 Squadron 2Lt J F Rowbotham Safe Unemployed list 15 May 1919
Bristol F.2b E2365 Mechanic A W Wallace Safe

T/o Aulnoy with the intention of flying to Bonneville but crash-landed near Charleroi. Before coming to a stop, the Bristol collided with a plough and turned over. John Frederick Rowbotham was born on the 17th of February 1900. He graduated from Flight Cadet to temporary 2nd Lieutenant on 7th October 1918 [LG 15 October 1918, issue 30953, page 12128]. Subsequently, he enlisted in the Royal Tank Corp on 14th May 1929, thereby forfeiting retention of his commissioned rank [LG 25 June 1929, issue 33509, page 4195]. During the Second World War he was recommissioned with effect from 18th April 1942 [LG 25 September 1942, supplement 35716, page 4163]. To the best of my knowledge he survived his second wartime experience.

11 Squadron Sgt R McGlasson Safe
Bristol F.2b E2537

T/o Aulnoye with similar intent to 2nd Lieutenant Rowbotham but was forced down at Morialmé on what is now the N975 running NW from Florennes. Before the Bristol could be recovered [it had broken an axle while landing] strong winds blew the fighter onto its back, effectively damaging it beyond repair.

11 Squadron 2Lt E W C Sharpe Safe Unemployed list 14 August 1919
Bristol F.2b F6217 Canada
    Captain A Morrison Safe

T/o Aulnoye to transit to Bonneville where on arrival it overshot the landing area; wrecked. From Toronto, 2nd Lieutenant Sharpe was born on the 1st of March 1891, and probably joined the RFC in November 1917. He arrived at Le Quesnoy on the 1st of August and was attached to the squadron. On the 29th he was wounded in combat but was back on operations by the time of the armistice. From the 15th to the 20th of January, he was at 2 Aeroplane Supply Depot before returning to the squadron and thence to England on the 4th of April. Captain Morrison, born 18th March 1894, was a squadron veteran having reported to Izel-lès-Hameau on the 4th of January 1917, at which time it was equipped with FE.2b. In the May he assumed the duties of Flight Commander, but this was short lived and he returned home on the 28th. On 6th July 1918, he returned to France and was reunited with the squadron, now flying Bristols, at Remaisnil.

49 Squadron Lt B A Whitmore Safe
DH.9A F967 Canada
    Mechanic J Dorrance Safe

T/o Bavau and wrecked here in a landing accident. Lieutenant Whitmore, formerly of the 5th Battalion, Canadian Infantry, was granted the commissioned rank of 2nd Lieutenant in the Royal Air Force on 8th May 1918 [LG 11 October 1918, issue 30947, page 11976]. He was attached to 49 Squadron between 8th October and 10th January 1919, on which date he returned to England, his secondment ceasing on this date [LG 1 February 1919, supplement 31159, page 1754]. Despite an unusual surname I have not been able to trace any details regarding Mechanic Dorrance.

62 Squadron Lt Edwards Safe
Bristol F.2b E2409 Corporal Brownridge Safe

T/o Aulnoye intending to transit to the squadron's new base at Bouge where on arrival it was damaged beyond repair whilst landing. The poor state of the landing area was a major factor in its demise.

65 Squadron Lt W R Allison Injured Unemployed list 29 September 1919
7F.1 Snipe E8007

T/o Bisseghem for a practice flight which ended in a crash at Map Reference Sheet 27 P25a. According to AIR 1/951 'E8007' was delivered to the squadron on the 29th of August; it was struck off charge eight days after the crash.

66 Squadron 2Lt P H Jenner + Montecchio Precalcino Communal Cemetery extension
F.1 Camel E7213

T/o Grossa and while over the aerodrome went into a spin from which it failed to recover. E7213 was flown in to St. Petro In Gu on 4th November by Lieutenant N S Taylor. 2nd Lieutenant Jenner's service record has no information regarding his next of kin, or postings; in their understandable grief his parents requested their son's headstone be inscribed with the words: *"May He Rest In Peace In The Lord. Father And Mother."*

204 Squadron 2Lt C A Morris Injured
F.1 Camel B7875/F6265

T/o Heule for gunnery practice. Lost power, stalled and crashed near Berck-sur-Mer in the Pas-de-Calais. This was his second crash, the first being on 1st December. As B7875 and in the hands of 65 Squadron, it was badly shot about on 8th August, resulting in Lieutenant Ferris Blundell Miseroy sustaining wounds which were treated in 55 CCS. Four days later he was sent back to England by HMHS *St. David*. Subsequently, he relinquished his commission on account of ill-health on 14th May 1919 [LG 23 May 1919, issue 31352, page 6369]. His service records show he was born on the 1st of July 1899, and had joined 65 Squadron on 16th July 1918.

| 211 Squadron | Lt M F Mousley | Safe | Unemployed list 8 April 1919 |
| DH.9 E8954 | 2Lt W Norrie | Safe | |

T/o Thuiles where, on landing. It overshot and dropped into a sunken road. The crew had been practising flying in formation. Received from 1 Air Issues on 3rd October, 2nd Lieutenant Charles Crawford Broucker and Sergeant P C Siverton drove down an unidentified enemy aircraft on the 1st of November. Charles Broucker, born on the 28th of May 1898, joined the squadron on 30th September, and three days after his aerial success he was reported missing [see page 386 of my second volume for details]. I have not been able to find the service records for his observer.

Regarding Lieutenant Mousley, he joined the squadron on 18th October and departed on the 23rd of February 1919, on posting to 98 Squadron. He was posted home on 7th April 1919. As with Sergeant Siverton, 2nd Lieutenant Norrie's service is, as yet, untraced.

Sunday 15 December 1918
Occupation of former German air force airfields in the demilitarised Rhineland continued with the arrival at Bickendorf of 7 Squadron and their RE.8 reconnaissance aircraft.

| 8 Squadron | 2Lt S N Jacobson | Safe | Unemployed list 16 January 1919 |
| Bristol F.2b D2134 | 2Lt C W Prynne MM | Safe | Unemployed list 28 September 1919 |

T/o Bellevue and flew over to Bousignies [Nord] to recover mail from the Bristol summarised below, but on arrival ran into a ditch and was damaged beyond repair. This was 2nd Lieutenant Jacobson's second mishap in 24-hours. Postwar, he became a territorial and served with the 8th Battalion, Lancashire Fusiliers [LG 22 August 1922, issue 32740, page 6161]. 2nd Lieutenant Prynne was commissioned as an Observer Officer as recently as the 1st of November. I am reasonably certain he was formerly of the Canadian Engineers, his award being *Gazetted* on 12 June 1918, supplement 30743, page 7017].

| 8 Squadron | Lt S B Trites | Safe | Unemployed list 10 August 1919 |
| Bristol F.2b E9573 | 2Lt R P Hicklin | Safe | |

T/o Bellevue with orders to deliver post, the destination not being identified, but during the flight the engine began to overheat and Lieutenant Stanley Bliss Trites decided to make a precautionary landing at Bousignies. Unfortunately, the ground was in a very poor state and before coming to a stop the Bristol was badly damaged. Its active service with the squadron had lasted for just one week. Born on the 11th of November 1888, Stanley Trites joined the squadron on 23rd August, and was posted to 9 Squadron at Ludendorf on 28th January 1919; he returned to England on the 9th of April. 2nd Lieutenant Hicklin preceded his skipper's arrival at Bellevue by 24-hours and he remained with the squadron until its return to Duxford in late July 1919. He had been commissioned as an Observer Officer on 27th July 1918 [*Flight* August 8, 1918, page 891].

| 22 Squadron | 2Lt J Sewell | Safe | |
| Bristol F.2b E2263 | | | |

T/o Witheries for a transit flight, possibly to Nivelles where the squadron was scheduled to move on the 20th. On arrival the aircraft's pressure system failed and John Sewell was unable to control his landing; presumed damaged beyond repair. Born on 10th June 1896, his address is given as Shand Cottage in the Devonshire resort of Exmouth.

| 42 Squadron | Lt J G J McDermont | Safe | |
| RE.8 D6740 | 2Lt J E Elliott | Safe | |

T/o Aulnoy for Saultain where the main body of the squadron had arrived on the 11th. On arrival Lieutenant McDermont misjudged his approach and crashed. His observer's tour of operational flying began at St. Omer on 26th July, when he was attached to 4 Squadron [RE.8]. However, he had barely unpacked when he was taken to 51 General Hospital on the 31st with an undiagnosed illness which was serious enough to keep him grounded until the 27th of September. Thus, on his discharge he was ordered to join 42 Squadron, then at Rély. It would appear, however, that his general health was not good for on 25th January 1919, he was taken to 33 CCS and thence on 7th February to 51 General Hospital having suffered a relapse. There are no further entries on his service record.

Monday 16 December 1918
Continued fighting on several fronts between the Bolsheviks and the White Russians, the latter being supported by elements of the Royal Air Force.

| 44 Squadron | Lt T R R Burns | + | Hornchurch [St. Andrew] Churchyard |
| F.1 Camel 6326 | | | |

T/o Hainault Farm and crashed in unknown circumstances. The serial quoted 6326 without a prefix equates only to B6326 or F6326 which by coincidence were at various times on establishment with 54 Squadron, the former being lost of 21st June 1918 [see page 260 of my first volume]. According to *The Camel File* 54 Squadron gave up F6326 to 151 Squadron on 23rd January 1919, '151' at the time acting as a demobilisation squadron. Thomas Roland Roth Burns is reported on page 54 of Errol Martyn's first volume devoted to New Zealand's air services dead, Errol noting that

Thomas had served with the New Zealand Army Service Corps, New Zealand Expeditionary Force. His epitaph as St. Andrew's reads: *"Deeply Mourned Sadly Missed."*

99 Squadron   Lt G Jones   Safe
DH.9A F1000   2Lt M J Poulton [Canada] Safe   Unemployed list 13 April 1919
Presentation Aircraft: Hyderabad No 7
T/o Aulnoye with a consignment of mail destined for Spy where the DH crashed while trying to land. There is some confusion as to the date of the accident. *The DH.4/DH.9 File* shows the 20th; AIR 1/865 indicates the 16th while AIR 1/1485 gives the date as the 15th. Prior to its arrival with 99 Squadron, F1000 had seen operational service with 110 Squadron, sustaining serious damage during a raid to Frankfurt on 25th September during which Lieutenant Herbert James Cockman DFC was wounded but leaving his observer, 2nd Lieutenant Cornelius Henry Bowman Stevenson un-scathed. Repairs were carried out at 3 Advanced Salvage Dump.

It is worth noting that Herbert Cockman's award was a direct result of the Frankfurt raid: *'On 25th September, when on a long-distance bombing raid, this officer performed very gallant service. Heavily attacked on the return journey, he was severely wounded, his left arm being shattered and his right leg hit. Owing to his wounds and loss of blood he was unable to control his machine, but by instructing his observer he was able to keep his formation until he crossed the lines. Owing to his condition he had the greatest difficulty in landing, and it was only due to his determined courage that he succeeded in doing so.'* [LG 3 December 1918, supplement 31046, page 14319].

His service records show he joined 110 Squadron on the last day of August and he was first treated in 8[Canadian] Stationary Hospital before being returned to England on 19th October by way of HMHS *Carisbrook Castle.* On the 31st of May 1919, he joined the growing lists of unemployed officers.

Cornelius Stevenson is believed to have arrived at Kenley 24-hours before his skipper; he remained with the squadron until it disbanded at Marquise on 27th August, returning home two days later.

Lieutenant Jones's service remains untraced, but a reasonable amount of detail is recorded on Army Form B.103 in respect of Melvin Joseph Poulton who although shown above as an observer was, in fact, a pilot. He was born in Canada, probably Toronto, on the 13th of July 1895, and joined the RFlC in the summer of 1917 and was posted to 99 Squadron on the 6th of August 1918. On 25th September, with Sergeant F L Lee DFM in the observer's cockpit, he was in the formation of DHs bombing Frankfurt. Sustaining damage from anti-aircraft fire he crash-landed on return to Azelot, his service record indicating he had been wounded but I suspect it more likely he was injured in the crash for he was taken to 8[Canadian] Stationary Hospital with a badly sprained right ankle which kept him grounded until the 14th of October. The remainder of his entries are in respect of leave until 26th February 1919, when he left the squadron in readiness to return to Canada.

17 December 1918
Unrest was not confined to Europe. In Australia the Administrator of the Northern Territories, Scottish born John Anderson Gilruth, committed in the eyes of the locals a cardinal sin; he imposed a tax on alcohol. This brought the wrath of the workers crashing around his shoulders with hundreds arriving at Government House in Darwin calling for his dismissal. Such was the anger and the escalating unrest that the government in Canberra became sufficiently alarmed to order an Australian Naval vessel to sail to Darwin to help stem the violence. Although order was restored the writing was on the wall and in February 1919, the unpopular John Gilruth departed the city. He was, however, a very learned fellow who in 1892, had been admitted to membership of the Royal College of Veterinary Surgeons, London. Subsequently, he was to appointed to positions of importance in the veterinary field in New Zealand and Australia. His death in South Yarra, Melbourne was reported on 4th March 1937.

3 Squadron   Lt W H Maxted   +   Etaples Military Cemetery
F.1 Camel H809
T.o Inchy and flew over to the ranges at Berck-sur-Mer [Pas-de-Calais] just below Le Touquet. Here, while diving on a target, 19-year old William Henry Maxwell from Hemel Hempstead in Hertfordshire, overstressed the airframe and plunged into the ground with wings of his aircraft enfolded around him. He had returned from an attachment to the ranges a mere 24-hours earlier. He was laid to rest with full military honours, the funeral service being conducted by the Reverend E H Pedley. His headstone carries the words: *"God Gave And He Hath Taken Him From Us Yet Only For A Time,"* indicating a strong conviction that in time his parents would be reunited with William in the Eternal Kingdom. He was born on 2nd July 1899, and features in a squadron summary reported on page 306 of my second volume. The Aerodrome website credits him with five aerial victories, though *The Camel File* indicates three aircraft and a kite balloon, shared with Captain G R Riley MC on the 1st of September.

In closing, a Court of Enquiry into William's death was held at 1 Aerial Ranges on Christmas Eve but the board was unable to form a definitive cause of the tragedy.

10 Squadron   Lt C Cox   Safe
FK.8 H4451   Lt Atkin   Safe
T/o Staceghem to carry out a tour of the area and while doing so the engine failed. Forced-landed near the crossroads at La Clytte [West-Vlaanderen], some eight km West of Ypres; presumed damaged beyond repair. Although retaining the name La Clytte as the identification of the nearby CWGC military cemetery, the village is now known as De Kliite. Designed by Sir Edwin Lutyens the cemetery contains the graves of 1,082 casualties from the *Great War,* of which 844 have been identified. Charles Cox, born 1st of February 1899, was attached to 2 Aeroplane Supply Depot between the

4th and 16th of June on which date he joined 10 Squadron at Droglandt. He returned to England on the 24th of January 1919. I have not been able to positively identify Lieutenant Atkin [possibly Atkins].

| 57 Squadron | Lt J Erskine | Injured |
| DH.4 B7939 | Lt W Steele | Safe |

T/o Spy with the intention of delivering mail but was caught out by a sudden and violent gust of wind which threw the DH onto its back. The observer escaped with no more than a bad fright, but James Erskine [born 7th December 1895] went into hospital with lacerations to his scalp and, subsequently, was evacuated to England on Boxing Day on HMHS *St. Denis*. B7939 was one of a number of DH.4 airframes rebuilt at Farnborough by 1[Southern] Aircraft Repair Depot, arriving in France in the final weeks of the war. On 12th October it was involved in a forced-landing - the crew not being named - at Fourneil near Paris. Recovered to 3 Aircraft Depot and thence to the squadron on an undisclosed date.

| 61 Squadron | Lt J Dunbar | Injured |
| f.1 Camel C8392 | | |

T/o Rochford for a training flight but crashed heavily after flying into mist and becoming disorientated. His injuries are described as serious.

| 92 Squadron | SE.5a E5666 | Wrecked at Thuilles when a hangar collapsed brought about by gale force |

winds that sprang up during the night. E5666 was delivered to the squadron from 2 Air Issues on 28th September and during an early morning patrol on 4th October, it shared in driving down a Hannover C between Malincourt and Bertry. The two pilots involved were Captain J M Robb flying E5666 and Captain W S Philcox in E4099.

James Milne Robb late of the Northumberland Fusiliers*and, subsequently, Air Chief Marshal Sir James Robb GCB KBE DSO DFC AFC Three times mentioned in despatches. Born on the 26th of January 1895, James Robb first saw action with 32 Squadron [DH.2] and was wounded in combat on the 11th of March 1917. With gunshot wounds to his right thigh he was taken to 8 General Hospital before being evacuated to England by HMHS *Gloucester Castle* .

He made a complete recovery and returned to the Western Front on the 29th of June 1918, as a Flight Commander with 92 Squadron and by the armistice had scored seven confirmed combat victories, including one with 32 Squadron.

Appointed to a permanent commission on the 1st of August 1919, he served with no less than four fighter squadrons in the 1920s, before being appointed Chief Flying Instructor at the CFS Wittering [later, in the mid-'30s he would become the Commandant of the CFS]. His Second World War service found him holding a range of key appointments from Air Officer Commanding No 2 Group in Bomber Command to Deputy Chief of Staff [Air] at SHAEF. Then, with the war in Europe over he became Air Officer Commanding-in-Chief, Fighter Command during which his personal Spitfire LF.16 SL721 JM-R and its allover blue colour scheme became a familiar sight at Fighter Command stations throughout the United Kingdom. His final appointment, February to November 1951, was the prestigious position of Inspector General of the Royal Air Force. His death was announced on the 18th of December 1968.

Captain Philcox was on the nominal role of the squadron by July 1918, and was badly wounded on the 4th of November [see page 384 of my second volume] and was taken to a Canadian Field Hospital with shrapnel embedded in his left ankle. He was evacuated on the 9th by HMHS *Princess Elizabeth*.

* Private James Milne Robb was *Gazetted* Second Lieutenant to the 4th Battalion, The Northumberland Fusiliers, effective from 10th November 1914 [LG 9 November 1914, supplement 28968, page 9121]. The citation for his DFC was published in issue 31170 of 8 February 1919, page 2045: *'This officer has destroyed seven enemy aircraft, and under his brilliant leadership his patrols have accounted for numerous others. On 13th October he attacked and silenced three hostile howitzers which were in action.'* Notification of his DSO, awarded for *"distinguished service in connection with the operations in Kurdistan [Choarte region] during the period 6th June to 10th July, 1925"* appeared in issue 33166, of 28 May 1926, page 3458. At the time he was ranked Squadron Leader.

His Spitfire during his tenure as Air Officer Commanding-in-Chief Fighter Command now operates in Belgium, officially as OO-XVI, but, camouflaged, still carrying the serial SL721 and the code combination GE-S. There are a number of websites which record the aircraft's history.

| 104 Squadron | 2Lt W McCullagh | Safe | Unemployed list 3 July 1919 |
| DH.9 D526 | Sgt W H Ball | Safe | |

T/o Maisoncelle tasked for photography and on return, and with the engine overheating, attempted to land in a cross-wind. This, unfortunately was the undoing for William McCullagh and the DH crashed out of control, the wreckage being struck off charge on the 27th. William was born on the 3rd of August 1897, and came from the popular Dorset seaside town of Weymouth.

Wednesday 18 December 1918
Fighting continued both in Georgia and far to the north in Estonia where Valga fell to the Bolsheviks, aided by soldiers of the Latvian Riflemen.

Inclement weather, meanwhile, continued to take its toll and from Inglevert in the Pas-de-Calais, a return from the resident 97 Squadron reported HP O/400 D5442 as being totally unfit for further use and with a mere 26.20 flying hours recorded it was struck off charge. Its service history was not exactly covered in glory in that many deficiencies were found on its arrival on 10th October, and it was not until 3rd November that it was declared ready for employment on operational duties.

Thursday 19 December 1918

The Georgian war with Armenia continued to escalate along the border between the two countries.

19 Squadron	2Lt J Ditchfield	Injured	Unemployed list 26 March 1919

5F.1 Dolphin D3755

T/o Abscone to reconnoitre the area between Valenciennes and Tournai during which the engine failed and a forced-landing was executed near Herin [sic]; presumed struck off charge. Although a Record of Service has been raised, it is devoid of any information regarding his postings et al.

29 Squadron	2Lt R Williams	Injured

SE.5a H712

T/o Nivelles to transit with the squadron to Bickendorf but stalled while climbing away and crashed. Apart from the casualty report there is no information as to when it arrived with the squadron. It was, however, one of sixty airframes ordered on 20th June from The Air Navigation Company's facility at Addlestone in Surrey. On completion of each aircraft they were taken to 10 Aeroplane Acceptance Park at Brooklands to await issue.

Roderick Williams had had an eventful last few months. Embarking on the 9th of October for an overnight crossing he was attached to 2 Aeroplane Supply Depot where he fell ill with influenza and was admitted to 2 Stationary Hospital. Discharged on the last day of the month he was attached to 1 Aeroplane Supply Depot on the 1st, before reporting to Marcke on the 12th November for attachment to 29 Squadron. Admitted to 20 CCS, he was sent back to England on Boxing Day by HMHS *St. Denis.*

64 Squadron	2Lt A B H Youell	Safe	Unemployed list 17 September 1919

SE.5a E1277/4

T/o Froidmont with other aircraft but was caught in the slipstream of the leading aircraft. At this point Alan Hamilton Bruce Youell lost control and crashed. He had joined the squadron on the 5th of September, and two days before the armistice came into effect, and flying E1277, he shot down a Fokker DVII over Givry. On the 10th of January 1919, he was sent on a course of instruction at Valery, and on the 4th of March he was attached to 1 Aerial Ranges before returning home on the 15th.

206 Squadron	2Lt N E Latham	Safe
DH.9 B7596	Corporal Lloyd	Safe

T/o Nivelles for a transit flight - possibly to Bickendorf where the squadron was earmarked to move on the 20th. During the flight the crew were overtaken by engine failure and in the forced-landing at Lissendorf [Rheinland-Pfalz] to the SW of the Kyll river and the small town of Birgel, the DH was damaged beyond repair. B7596 was one of a batch of one hundred airframes built by the Westland Aircraft Works at Yeovil in Somerset and on completion went to 10 Aeroplane Acceptance Park at Brooklands, and thence to an Air Park at Dover where it was held up from crossing to France by bad weather. However, by 26th February in was in the hands of 6 Squadron RNAS, which in time became 206 Squadron. Flown by Lieutenant L R Warren it accounted for seven hostile aircraft, either destroyed or driven down out of control. For his first success he was aided by Private J T O'Brien after which the observer's position was occupied by Lieutenant L A Christian. At the end of September it was badly damaged, but repairs were put in hand and by December it had returned to the squadron.

Concerning those named with a connection to B7596, a Form has been raised for 2nd Lieutenant Latham but apart from his name and rank is completely blank. However, a trawl of the *Gazette* reveals an entry in supplement 35698, page 3955, issued on 11 September 1942, where under the heading for the Royal Berkshire Regiment: *"War Subs. N E Latham [137229] is Cashiered by sentence of a Gen. Court-Martial. 29th June 1942."* On the same page, and beneath various headings, the names of three more officers whose careers had ended in ignominy. It has, of course, to be regarded as conjecture on my part that 2nd Lieutenant Latham who forced-landed in December 1918, and Lieutenant Latham who departed the Royal Berkshire Regiment in disgrace in 1942, are one and the same person.

Lieutenant Warren's service ended with posting to Home Establishment on 20th October. The line above this entry indicates he had been awarded a DFC, though tracing the citation without knowing his Christian names has proven unsuccessful. Similarly, Lieutenant Christian was awarded a DFC, but as his Christian names are absent from Army Form B.103c, I have not been able to find the citation, but, it would not surprise me, if the details appeared in the same issue of the *Gazette.*

RAFM Hendon has digitised records for many of the non-commissioned officers who served with the Royal Air Force but, it seems, that for Private J T O'Brien has not survived.

209 Squadron	2Lt J Bradbury	Injured

F.1 Camel F3935

T/o Froidmont and wrecked here following a collision with telegraph wires. Issued on 26th September, the loss of F3935 was first since the armistice.

Friday 20 December 1918

Following a visit in the spring to the United States where he had conferred with President Woodrow Wilson, Thomáš Garrigue Masaryk returned in triumph to the newly formed nation of Czechoslovakia, honoured to have been invited to be its first President. He would become one of the first influential political leaders to recognise the true intentions of Adolf Hitler and raise a warning voice of concern.

55 Squadron	2Lt G D Beaudry	Safe	See 7 January 1919
DH.4 A7749	Canada		
	2Lt W Ward	Safe	

T/o Saint André-aux-Boise for local flying practice but Gustave Dominique Beaudry eased the control column too far forward and as a result the propeller came into contact with the ground and was shattered. One of a large batch of 689 aircraft built by The Aircraft Manufacturing Company at Hendon, A7749 had until this incident an uneventful service life. A brief note regarding to 2nd Lieutenant Beaudry is reported in the summary for 7th January.

| 74 Squadron | Lt W C Goudie | Safe | Unemployed list 24 April 1919 |
| SE.5a F5552 | | | |

Presentation Aircraft: Australia No35 Queensland No 4 The Saltbrush

T/o Halluin and damaged beyond repair here following a misjudged landing. During its war service, and flown by Lieutenant Goudie, it shared in the destruction of two Fokker DVIIs on 30th October, the other pilot being Lieutenant W T Carew flying F892 which survived the war and was subsequently flown back to England.

   Lieutenant Goudie was on the nominal role of the squadron by the end of January 1918, and served until the 2nd of February 1919, when he was posted to 92 Squadron [SE.5a] at Thuilles. He had two spells in hospital; the first on 2nd July when he was admitted to 20 General Hospital with scabies; this kept him out of action for six days, while his second spell of ill-health, tonsillitis, was treated at 18 CCS between the 6th and 11th of September.

   William Thomas Carew joined the squadron on the 10th of October, and was posted to 92 Squadron on the 2nd of February only to be sent 24-hours later to a holding unit in readiness for repatriation.

| 99 Squadron | Lt L B Duggan | Safe | See 20 January 1919 |
| DH.9A E8561 | 2Lt W J Tremellen | Safe | See 15 February 1919 |

T/o Aulnoye tasked for a mail delivery run but forced-landed at Douvrie [sic] and damaged beyond repair. Some sources show this accident as occurring three days earlier. Formerly of the 1st Battalion, Herefordshire Regiment, Lewin Browning Duggan joined the squadron on the 30th of August, following secondment to the Royal Air Force on the 30th July [LG 20 January 1919, supplement 31134, page 1055]. Subsequently, he relinquished his army commission when he was appointed to a permanent commission on the 1st of August 1919 [LG 8 June 1920, issue 31934, page 6422]. By this time he was in India with his squadron, after which little is known of his air force career.

   2nd Lieutenant Tremellen graduated from Flight Cadet to Observer Officer as recently as 4th September [*Flight* September 12, 1918. He arrived with the squadron on the 17th of September, and would survive two more serious accidents before invalided home on the 15th of March.

| 206 Squadron | DH.9 H4256 | Damaged at Nivelles when a hangar collapsed during the night. Sent to 7 Salvage |

Section for repair, there are no further entries for H4256 which, I suspect, was scrapped.

Saturday 21 December 1918
One of the most costly days for accidents involving squadrons operating on the Western Front and in the Rhineland. It was only by good fortune that fatalities were restricted to the death of Thomas Francie McGuire of 208 Squadron.

   A snippet in *The Times* reported the Antarctic explorer Sir Ernest Shackleton was received in the afternoon at No 10 Downing Street where he spent thirty minutes in conversation with the Prime Minister, David Lloyd George, the latter then departing to spend the weekend in the country.

| 4 Squadron AusFC | Lt H W Ross | Safe | |
| 7F.1 Snipe E8199 | | | |

T/o Bickendorf for an air test but having climbed to around a hundred feet the engine cut and moments later Lieutenant Ross was walking back to the aerodrome from an adjacent field. Delivered to the squadron on 1st November, it is possible E8199 participated in operations prior to the 11th. Lieutenant Ross is mentioned on page 354 of *The Australian Flying Corps in the Western and Eastern Theatres of War 1914-1918* extensively researched and written by F M Cutlack [Andrews UK Limited, 2012].

| 12 Squadron | 2Lt J C Fraser | Safe | |
| RE.8 H7266 | Mechanic Ellwood | Safe | |

T/o Bickendorf with orders to fly to the aerodrome at Duren but *en route* the all too familiar gremlins struck and with its engine failing it crash-landed on the airfield at Clavier. 2nd Lieutenant Fraser joined the squadron at Soncamp on 4th September and served until 10th July 1919, when he was posted back to England.

| 25 Squadron | Lt C Addenbrooke | Safe | See 21 January 1919 |
| DH.4 F1551/F6096 | 2Lt H J Rayment | Safe | |

T/o Maubeuge for a practice flight only to sideslip and crash. As F1551 it was one of two replacement DH.4s and was received at 2 Aeroplane Acceptance Park, Hendon, on 22nd May, reaching 205 Squadron by 3rd June. On the 19th, it took part in a raid on the railway station at Chaulnes, crewed by Lieutenant Elie Oscar Danger and 2nd Lieutenant Alan Dudley Hollingsworth and on return crash-landed. Rebuilt as F6096 it arrived with 25 Squadron at some time in July.

   Although I have had no success in tracing any information regarding Lieutenant Addenbrooke's service, that for the other officers has been more rewarding. Henry John Rayment, born 20th September 1895, was accepted for training as an Observer Officer whilst serving with the 1st/7th Battalion, King's Liverpool Regiment and returned to England on the 25th of May, and was commissioned circa 16th September. On the 5th of October he joined 25 Squadron. Eight days after the accident, he was admitted to 5 CCS suffering from tonsillitis, returning to duty on the 4th of January. Between the 9th and 23rd of January, he was on leave and on the 17th of July, he left the squadron, now at Merheim, and returned home.

Elie Oscar Danger, born 1st July 1897, was a General List officer who joined the RFC on 21st July 1917, and arrived with 205 Squadron on the 4th of June. His first serious crash occurred during operations on 23rd August when he crash-landed A7518 near Villers-Bretonneux [see my second volume, page 175]. This was followed a month later when he returned to Proyart East with D8429 so badly shot about that it was not worth repairing [see page 228]. Wounded in the lumber region he was evacuated to England on the 27th of September. On both occasions his observer was Alan Hollingsworth. His service records show he was born on 29th November 1899, and enlisting with the RFC on the 7th of February. Qualified as an observer he reported to the squadron on the 29th of May, and served with '205' until returning home on 5th March 1919. It is noted that he went down with influenza on 7th January and spent five days in hospital.

| 41 Squadron | Lt E G Corey | Safe | Unemployed list 7 March 1919 |
| SE.5a H687 | Canada | | |

T/o Halluin for a practice flight and damaged beyond repair during landing. It has been on establishment since 29th October and as far as I can establish this was the squadron's only serious accident between the armistice and return to Tangmere as a cadre on 7th February 1919. Edward Gordon Corey was born on the 19th of March 1891, and joined the RFC circa August 1917. He served with the squadron from 28th September to the last day of January, on which date he went on leave for fourteen days and thence to the unemployed list. He, too, spent a week in hospital with influenza, his treatment being administered at 62 CCS.

| 54 Squadron | 2Lt G C Robins | Safe | Unemployed list 21 June 1919 |
| F.1 Camel F2171 | | | |

T/o Merchin for a special duties flight to Nivelles but became lost and crash-landed near Saint-Genois in the Belgian province of de Flandre Occidentale; wrecked. Similar to the above summary, this appears to have been the squadron's only serious accident between 12th November and return to Yatesbury on 17th February 1919, having transferred its aircraft to 151 Squadron. For a scout squadron equipped with Camels, this was a fine achievement.

| 64 Squadron | Lt R B Francis | Safe | Commission relinquished 17 February 1919 |
| SE.5a F906/5 | Canada | | |

T/o Froidmont authorised for a practice flight but lost his bearings in poor weather and forced-landed on a railway track near Douai and turned over. Reginald Basil Francis was late of the Canadian Machine Gun Company and he ceased to be employed on 17th February 1919 [LG 6 May 1919, issue 31327, page 5655].

At some point in his service he married a Bristol girl, her address being recorded as Newstead, Radnor Road, Henleaze, Bristol. Reginald joined the squadron on the 18th of September and was repatriated to Canada on the 17th of February 1919. Normally, I would have expected a search for Lieutenant Reginald Basil Francis to get a response from one of several websites that commemorate Canadian servicemen, but on this occasion I have not been successful.

| 107 Squadron | 2Lt C W Daggett | Injured | Unemployed list 30 April 1919 |
| DH.9 D1111 | Sgt R Reed | Injured | |

T/o from a filed near Ransart*[Hainaut] where it had forced-landed, but failed to become airborne before falling into a sunken road. Neither airman was too seriously injured. Apart from his rank, surname and initials there is nothing on 2nd Lieutenant Daggett's service record to show anything of interest. The DH arrived from 5 Air Issues on 10th October.

* Today, the community of Ransart lies just off the eastern side of Brussels South Charleroi Airport.

| 115 Squadron | Lt Bell | Injured | |
| HP O/400 D4577 | Lt Dane | Injured | |

T/o from an unidentified airfield [possibly Roville-sur-Chênes] and crashed at Meru [sic], presumably while recovering to Saint Inglevert. I have not been able to find anything that identifies the two officers.

| 139 Squadron | Lt T B Service | Safe | See 11 January 1919 |
| Bristol F.2b D7963 | Lt J G Acheson | Safe | See 11 January 1919 |

T/o Grossa for an exercise in aerial photography; crashed on return to base. Again, I have been unsuccessful in discovering service details pertaining to the two officers, apart from in the case of Lieutenant Service where his Army Form 103-I shows his rank, surname and initials.

| 204 Squadron | Lt A B Ollerenshaw | Injured | Unemployed list 31 January 1919 |
| F.1 Camel D1853/F6036 | | | |

T/o Heule for practice handling and while carrying out a forced-landing following engine failure collided with a tree near Desselghem on the road between Courtrai and Ghent. This aircraft's previous service had been with 208 Squadron, ending on 7th July when Lieutenant Hayter Kembell Scrivener, born on the last day of March 1898, forced-landed; 24-hours later and Hayter Scrivener was a prisoner of war [see my second volume, page 34].

Alfred Bernard Ollerenshaw, born 20th March 1899, enlisted in the RFC on 1st August 1917, embarking for France on the 19th of May. Two days later he reported to 208 Squadron at Serny; during August he was granted home leave returning on the 29th. Then, on the last day of October he joined 204 Squadron and remained on strength until returning home in January 1919. However, shortly before his departure he spent a couple of days in hospital with dermatitis.

208 Squadron   Lt T F McGuire   +   Charleroi Communal Cemetery
7F.1 Snipe E8269
T/o Stree for practice flying but got into a spin that he was unable to control and crashed into a field near the aerodrome at Thuilles. On impact the Snipe exploded in flames. Thomas Francis McGuire was the squadron's first fatality since converting to Sopwith Snipes. He had joined at Foucaucourt on 28th September and on 2nd November went to 50 CCS for six days where he was treated for scabies. His funeral service was conducted by the Reverend J F Fleming attached to 55 CCS.

Sunday 22 December 1918
The potential for film entertainment featuring the war just ended was tested when Universal Pictures released *The Heart of Humanity* with the Austrian-American actor Erich von Stroheim playing the part of a villainous German officer. Leading roles were played by William Stowell and Dorothy Phillips who happened to be married to the film's director, Allen Holuber.

5 Squadron   Lt F E Wyett   Safe   Unemployed list 15 April 1919
RE.8 C2919   2Lt F M R Jones   Injured
T/o Hangelar with the intention of transiting to Elsenborn where the squadron first arrived as part of the Occupation Force on the 7th, but on becoming airborne the RE stalled and crashed into a ditch. Frederick Eden Wyett served on the squadron from 3rd June to 14th April 1919. 2nd Lieutenant Jones, whom it will be recalled had walked away from an accident on 26th November, sustained injuries to his side and knees; he was treated at a Canadian hospital from where he was discharged on the 30th. His Record of Service shows he joined the squadron at Izel-lès-Hameau on the 2nd of October and was still on establishment in February 1919. He was formerly of the 7th Battalion, Duke of Cornwall's Light Infantry. Frederick Eden Wyett, who was unhurt, had served with the squadron since the 3rd of June; he returned to England on the 14th of April 1919.

6 Squadron   2Lt Bush*   Safe
RE.8 D4805   2Lt H Mottershaw   Safe   Unemployed list 4 August 1920
T/o Gerpinnes for a mail delivery flight but when the engine failed the crew crashed in a failed attempt to forced-land at Ronquières [Hainaut] on the west bank of the Brussels to Charleroi canal. The loss of the RE was the squadron's first accident in peace time.

* I am reasonably confident that 2nd Lieutenant Bush is J D Bush who was posted to the squadron on the 10th of October. His service records show two spells of leave taken in January and April 1919, the last being embarkation leave for he was struck off strength of the BEF on 30th April with the squadron's deployment for Mesopotamia. However, within weeks of settling in at Baghdad West he was taken to 51 General Hospital suffering from a variety of complaints and such was their serious nature that he was invalided home by HMHS *Brighton* on 24th July.

12 Squadron   2Lt M N Pegg   Safe
RE.8 F5895   Mechanic Norman   Safe
T/o Clavier but while gathering speed ran onto soft ground and dropped onto a road which did the RE no good at all. 2nd Lieutenant Pegg joined the squadron on 23rd September and was posted back to the UK on 6th March 1919.

12 Squadron   2Lt P F Bovingdon   Safe   Unemployed list 21 October 1919
RE.8 H7044   Sgt Turner   Safe
T/o Bickendorf and set out for Clavier but landed at Duren where it overshot the landing area and finished up against a tree. 2nd Lieutenant Bovingdon reported for duty on 23rd August, at which time the squadron was based at Soncamp. He served until 16th October 1919, on which date he was posted home.

57 Squadron   Lt R R Gilpin   +   Louvres Communal Cemetery
DH.4 F2636   New Zealand
            Major-General C D Rhodes   Injured
T/o 1205 Spa detached base and with his high-ranking American passenger set off for Paris. All went well until nearing the French capital visibility suddenly deteriorated and it was not long before the DH was enveloped in fog. Sensibly, Lieutenant Gilpin signalled he was going to make a precautionary landing but in the mist he failed to notice he was on a direct path towards a hedge and before he could take evasive action a collision occurred. The impact catapulted the passenger from his cockpit and apart from some rather painful facial injuries he was not too seriously hurt. However, his recent departure from command of the 157th Field Artillery Brigade to take command of the 42nd 'Rainbow' Division was at an end. Major-General Charles Dudley Rhodes, born on 10th February 1865, retired from the army in 1929, and died at the age of 82 on 24th January 1948. He is buried in Arlington National Cemetery.

    This accident is reported by Errol Martyn on page 54 of the first of his three excellent volumes dedicated to the supreme sacrifice of so many of New Zealand's airmen. Robert Rooke Gilpin is the sole RAF pilot from the *Great War* buried in the communal cemetery at Louvre, his grave being located on the left-hand side of the main path and towards its end. His epitaph reads: *"He Is Not Dead He Has Awakened From The Dream Of Life."*

64 Squadron	Lt Crofts	Safe
SE.5a F5624/1		

T/o Froidmont for a practice flights and crashed in the same area as his Canadian colleague, Lieutenant Francis, who came to grief 24-hours earlier. The demise of F5624 was a collision with telegraph wires.

Monday 23 December 1918

A reasonably quiet day though simmering unrest in Rijeka Crnojevića and Nikšić required the presence of Serbian Militia troops.

55 Squadron	2Lt C V Ronchi	Safe	Unemployed list 19 May 1919
DH.4 D8369	2Lt S Burbidge	Safe	Unemployed list 13 April 1919

T/o Saint André-aux-Bois on the 17th and landed with its cargo of packages at Valenciennes. Here the DH was left out in the open until the 23rd when the crew took off to return to base. However, inclement weather was encountered and as a wise precaution the crew landed at Abeele*where the DH was pushed into a hangar which so like so many of these early shelters was far from weather-proof. Over the Christmas the area was subjected to heavy rain and when the crew next attempted to continue their journey the condition of their aircraft was such that it was no longer fit to fly. Its service was over.

* Practically on the border with France, Abeele [Abele in Belgium] is the site of Abeele Aerodrome Military Cemetery but though named as such it has no air force graves.

55 Squadron	2Lt H C Pendle	Safe	See 1 March 1919 - 57 Squadron
DH.4 D9265	Lt J A Shepherd MC	Safe	Commission relinquished 30 September 1921

T/o Sanit André-aux-Bois for formation flying practice but with bad weather approaching the crew decided to land in a field near Flers [Orne] to the NW of the Parc Naturel Régional Normandie-Maine where the incessant rain reduced the DH to such a state it was no longer able to fly. Herbert Charles Pendle was born on the 11th of February 1900, the date of birth for his observer has not been recorded but it is known that he was late of the 2nd/5th Battalion, The Loyal North Lancashire Regiment and in whose commission it was relinquished on 30th September [LG 20 December 1921, supplement 32555, page 10442]. He had been accepted for observer training earlier in the year and had joined the squadron as recently as 7th November. He appears to have left the squadron on the 29th, fulfilling temporary duties at a number of establishments, including the aerial ranges, until returning home on the 2nd of February 1919. His award of the MC was gained prior to his transfer to the Royal Air Force.

97 Squadron	Lt R A Gunther	Safe	Unemployed list 5 March 1919
HP O/400 D9700	Canada		
	Lt D Neil	Safe	
	Mechanic H Horridge	Safe	
	Mechanic Wishart	Safe	

T/o Xaffevilliers to transit to Saint Inglevert but was wrecked whilst forced-landing at Breteuil [Eure] owing to engine failure. Roy Alfred Gunther of London, Ontario, served with the squadron from 25th August to 24 January 1919, when he was posted to 216 Squadron at Marquise. During his time on 97 Squadron he was laid low with scabies and spent time in 8 CCS and 42 Stationary Hospital. He was posted home from '216' on the 4th of March 1919. Lieutenant Neil's tour of duty lasted from 7th September to 3rd September 1919, when he returned to the UK. However, I am not certain if he accompanied the squadron to India as his service record makes no mention of his departure from France.

Tuesday, Christmas Eve 1918

Prisoner of war repatriations that began in late November were still continuing, many requiring further intensive care following incarceration. Coupled with the influenza pandemic many were unable to fight off the twin-effects of poor health brought about by the often appalling conditions in which they were kept as prisoners and the ravages of 'flu.

At home the thoughts of parents, wives and friends of those still serving overseas must have been very much in their minds as the first Christmas of relative peace approached, thus when news reached the next of kin of Lieutenant Masters, 2nd Lieutenant Dallas and O'Grady, and Mechanic Morton that they had perished in a crash Christmas time in the future would be a particularly poignant time as hearts ached with remembrance of their loved ones passing.

3 Squadron	Lt M C Kinney	Injured Commission relinquished 5 March 1919
F.1 Camel F2153/7 USA		

T/o Inchy and written off in a crash near Bellevue aerodrome, engine failure being the all too familiar cause. Mark Curtis Kinney was destined to have a quite adventurous tour of operations. On 25th March, with the German spring offensive gaining momentum, 3 Squadron evacuated Vert Galant at dusk for Valhereux and Mark Kinney flying C6727 crash-landed, in the dark, near the Allied lines. Unhurt, he was soon reunited with his fellow pilots while his Camel, which was little damaged, was recovered and later issued to the 17th US Aero Squadron.

Now safely ensconced at Valhereux, he had his second crash. On 8th May, flying in misty conditions he forced-landed C1629 which was salvaged and following lengthy repairs issued to 151 Squadron [please refer to summaries for 22nd November 1918, for details of its demise and an asterisked note for Mark Kinney]. The next day it was his misfortune to write off B5445, details of this can be read in my first volume on page 129.

Then, on the 10th of August came the highlight of his tour when in the morning he achieved two combat successes. Both were Fokker DVIIs, the first of which was driven down out of control at around 0930, followed just over an hour later by a second which landed intact near Arvillers [Somme]. Described on *Wikipedia* as *"a swirling confused dog-fight"* the pilot was Leutnant Paul Billik*commanding Jasta 52. A week later, Mark Kinney himself came close to being shot down. Patrolling in D6579 at 10,000 feet he was south of the Somme river when from below an unidentified hostile machine struck; by good fortune, and despite being wounded, he made good his escape and returned to base and landed safely. His wounds were treated at 38 CSS.

In respect of F2153, during its few weeks of war flying it was much favoured by Captain George Raby Riley. Born in Battersea on 23rd February 1899, George arrived with the squadron on his 19th birthday and within days of his arrival began to stamp his mark as a scout pilot when flying C1609 he drove down an Albatros DV out of control and had it not been the case that he was wounded on 20th April, by which time he had secured three more victories, there is little doubt his final total of thirteen would have been much higher. The wounds to his shoulder kept him out of action until June and it would be the 8th of August before he bagged his fifth victim, a Rumpler.

Meanwhile, he had been recommended for an MC and, subsequently a DFC, the citations for these honours appearing in *The London Gazette* of 16 September 1918, and 7 February 1919, respectively. That for his MC [supplement 30901, page 11006] reads: *'For conspicuous gallantry and devotion to duty. He obtained four direct hits on a long line of enemy transport, and afterwards caused havoc among them with his machine-gun. Several times he attacked troops and transports from low altitudes; also he brought down one enemy machine and drove down another out of control.'*

The citation for his DFC [page 2045 of supplement 31170]: *'An officer who shows the greatest dash and gallantry in leading low-bombing and offensive patrols. On 27th September ['F2153'] he obtained two direct hits with bombs on an enemy on the ground, which set it on fire. Later he attacked another balloon in the air, shooting it down in flames.'*

Neither citation focuses primarily on his aerial successes which came to eight, the rest being kite balloons which were notoriously difficult to engage successfully as invariably they were well defended by seasoned machine-gun crews. The Aerodrome website, which I am pleased to acknowledge, records George Riley as being awarded his Royal Aero Club Aviators' Certificate [5205] on 7th September 1917. In the general reduction of officers in the postwar period he was placed on the unemployed list on 11th April 1919. His death is recorded as occurring in 1983, the precise date yet to be traced.

As a general observation, both Mark Kinney and George Raby flew with 3 Squadron at the same time - Mark being posted in to Warloy Baillon on 11th March. Both would have flown numerous offensive patrols but whereas George would end the war recognised as an ace, Mark's service was less spectacular with just two confirmed victories. In no way, however, does this detract from his part in the overall success of the squadron in hunting for and engaging the enemy in the air and on the ground.

| 5 Squadron | 2Lt J L Wright | Safe |
| RE.8 C2708 | 2Lt E P Collingburn | Injured |

T/o Hangelar for a photographic reconnaissance but engine failure intervened and the RE descended onto the landing area, but in a place where the surface was extremely uneven. Presumed damaged beyond repair. I have not been able to find 2nd Lieutenant Wright's service records, but Army Form B.103 raised for his observer shows he joined the squadron on the 8th of August, and following the accident was treated by 2[Canadian] CCS for lacerations and concussion. He returned to duty on New Year's Eve and remained with the squadron until its return to Bicester on the 8th of September 1919.

| 42 Squadron | 2Lt W Y Gothorp | Safe | Unemployed list 28 February 1919 |
| RE.8 C2969 | 2Lt D T Turpin | Safe | Unemployed list 18 November 1919 |

T/o Saultain for an air test but on becoming airborne 2nd Lieutenant Gothorp realised he was heading towards a line of trees and a church. Banking steeply, he lost control and crashed. The service records for both officers are devoid of any useful detail, though that for the observer identifies his Christian names as Douglas Frederick.

| 45 Squadron | Lt E H Masters | + | Duisans British Cemetery, Etrun* |
| F.1 Camel C54 | *Croix de Guerre avec Palme* [France] | | |

T/o Izel-lès-Hameau for formation flying practice and completely destroyed following a midair collision within sight of the airfield. Ernest Harold Masters, nineteen years of age and originally from Oldbury in Worcestershire, though his entry on the CWGC website shows Coventry, was taken to 7 CCS where he was pronounced dead. He had served with the squadron since the 10th of March; his headstone is simply worded: *"Peace Perfect Peace."* During his nine months of operations he accounted for eight enemy aircraft, seven claimed while the squadron was based in Italy, and one following its return to the Western Front.

* Located in the Pas-de-Calais and NW of Arras the cemetery, which in its present state was designed by Sir Reginald Blomfield, witnessed its first burials in March 1917. Today, there are 3,284 identified graves, including eight-eight German servicemen. What is worth mentioning, this significant cemetery, bordered by a neat tightly clipped hedge, is sited in open fields approached along a gravel track with grass in its middle and which leads on to Haute-Avesnes. Imagine, if you will, walking along such a track in the UK when in the midst of nowhere you find a cemetery with upwards of hundreds of graves, each with a headstone and in serried rows and all commemorated the fallen from a war of long ago. And Etrun is not unique; follow the line of the trenches that ran from the Channel coast way down to what was the French sector of the Somme and you will discover a myriad of such graveyards [and in part of Belgium, too] all maintained by CWGC and their dedicated teams of gardeners and volunteers in pristine order.

45 Squadron   Lt E L Milborrow   Injured   Commission relinquished 10 October 1919
F.1 Camel E1500   South Africa

T/o Izel-lès-Hameau similarly tasked and wrecked in the manner described above. Edgar Leake Milborrow of the Natal and born on the 12th of December 1895, was very seriously injured and was admitted to 7 CCS with a fractured skull. He had joined the RFC on 19th October 1917, and began his tour of operations with the squadron on the 12th of June. Subsequently, he left the service, as indicated above, and was permitted to retain his rank.

55 Squadron   2Lt G P Dymond   Injured   Commission relinquished 27 June 1919
DH.4A A7828

T/o Saint André-aux-Bois with mail destined for Valenciennes where on landing he collided with a post, the DH being so badly damaged that it was scrapped. 2nd Lieutenant Dymond arrived on the squadron on 21st August and returned to the UK on 30th October for temporary duty which lasted until returning to France and rejoining the squadron on 4th December. In the accident at Valenciennes he received serious head injuries and following initial treatment in 33 CCS was admitted to 14 General Hospital, and thence to England by the HS *Jan Breydel*. On relinquishment of his commission he was allowed to retain his rank.

79 Squadron   Lt F Woolley   Safe   Unemployed list 21 October 1919
5F.1 Dolphin C8121

T/o from an undisclosed location but possibly Nivelles with the intention of rejoining the squadron at Bickendorf. However, before reaching his destination the Dolphin's engine failed and Frank Woolley found himself crawling out from beneath his aircraft near Hermalle*where it ran into mud so glutinous that it flipped C8121 onto its back.

   Born on the 8th of May 1899, his military career began as a soldier in the 7th Training Reserve Battalion at Rugeley in Staffordshire; this phase lasted from June to mid-August 1917, when as a Flight Cadet he reported to Denham for training at 5 School of Aeronautics and thence to a commission as a 2nd Lieutenant in early November 1917. The next step took him to the CFS Upavon on Salisbury Plain. Here, it seems, he impressed his tutors for he was retained as an instructor before going to Turnberry in Scotland and a course at the School of Air Gunnery.

   His training finished, he crossed the Channel on 6th July, and for a few days he was attached to 1 Aeroplane Supply Depot. On the 14th, he arrived at Ste Marie Cappel for the dual duties of pilot and squadron adjutant. A year and a day later he was posted to Bickendorf and 43 Squadron [Snipe], but this attachment lasted for less than a fortnight after which he had a series of postings before returning to the UK on 25th August 1919.

   Frank's time out of uniform lasted for eight months before being granted a short service commission on 15th June 1920, this becoming permanent seven years later. By this time he had become a qualified flying instructor, but on becoming a permanent officer the direction of his career turned towards intelligence duties and a five year posting to the Air Staff in Iraq Command, broken for five months when he returned to London and the School of Oriental Studies for an intensive course in Arabic. In September 1932, he returned to flying duties, first with 24 Squadron for refresher flying and then to 100 Squadron [Horlsey] at Donibristle as a Flight Commander. In the spring of 1936, following a spell with the Coastal Defence Development Unit, he returned to the Middle East where he resumed intelligence work.

   Although only holding Squadron Leader rank, from October 1936, he filled the post of Senior Air Staff Officer at Headquarters Far East Air Force.

   Shortly before Japan's infamous attack on Pearl Harbor which made the Second World War a global conflict, he was promoted Group Captain and took over command of 223 Group in Singapore and though it seems a certainty that he would have witnessed the chaos of those final days before the surrender by Lieutenant-General Arthur Percival to the Imperial Japanese forces on 15th February 1942, little has been recorded of his movements except a note to the effect that he was on extended leave in the UK for part of 1942, before heading once more to the Middle East and Staff Duties.

   Postwar, he was Station Commander at Lyneham before rounding off many years of distinguished service as the Assistant Director at the Joint Intelligence Bureau and retiring as an Air Commodore on the 6th of August 1954.

   His death was announced on the 23rd of June 1982, but as is recorded on the Air of Authority website [which I acknowledge] he came close to an early end when in a boisterous mess party at Henlow in 1923, a young Flying Officer Frank Woolley fractured his skull, an injury which kept him in hospital for the best part of twelve months.

80 Squadron   2Lt W A Hammerton   Safe   Unemployed list 22 October 1919
F.1 Camel H6851/C

T/o Stree for a practice flight and on return landed where the ground sloped away with an uneven surface. As a consequence the Camel turned over; presumed damaged beyond repair. William Allan Hammerton joined the squadron as recently as 4th October, and subsequently went out to Egypt. Officially he was struck off the strength of the BEF on the 27th of May 1919.

   When war was declared on that historic Sunday, 3rd September 1939, William was granted a commission in the General Duties Branch, though it was not until 28th January 1941, that the administrators caught up with his return to active service, hence official notification only appearing in issue 35057, page 564 of the *Gazette*. His service lasted until Boxing Day 1958, by which time he had transferred to the Secretarial Branch [LG 20 January 1959, supplement 41510, page 488] and was ranked Group Captain.

   Turning to *Flight,* the magazine's issue of August 30, 1923, records his commission to the Reserve of Air Force Officers, effective from the 21st August, and the following year [February 28th] noting his election to The Royal Aero

Club of the United Kingdom. Then follows a gap of nine years before on page 757 of *Flight* July 27, 1933, in an article about the Royal Air Force Reserve Flying Club meeting at Hatfield his name is mentioned.

The final prewar mention of William Hammerton was reported on June 2, 1938, on the occasion of the Club's fifth annual dinner when Flying Officer Hammerton, as chairman, was able to welcome and express his appreciation to Sir Kingsley Wood, recently appointed Secretary of State for Air, for accepting at very short notice the Club's invitation.

Postwar, he was very much involved with aircrew selection as outlined in *Flight* September 23, 1948, while the magazine's issue of 1st March, 1957, page 292, reports Group Captain Hammerton as being at the Air Ministry in the Department of the Air Member for Personnel.

101 Squadron	Lt E Evans	Safe
FE.2b D9964	2Lt G Williams	Safe

T/o Morville for a mail delivery flight but forced-landed after encountering fog, alighting at Avesnes. With an improvement in the weather, the crew took off to continue their journey but the undercarriage caught the top of a hedge sending the FE crashing out of control. Welshman, Lieutenant Evans was born on the 8th of June 1899, and enlisted in the RFC on 29th August 1917. Arriving with 2 Aeroplane Supply Depot on 20th June, he was posted to the squadron on the 2nd of July. A rather mystifying entry is made on 25th October to the effect that while on leave in the UK, he was struck off the strength of the BEF. However, it is a certainty that he returned to France to continue his tour of duty with 101 Squadron. His observer, George Williams, was born on 26th January 1899, and enlisted on 14th February 1918. He arrived at Famechon on 26th June and attached to the squadron. I suspect that he fell ill in the New Year for he was returned to England from 8 General Hospital by way of HMHS *Grantully Castle* [see Appendix E].

215 Squadron	2Lt W R Dallas	+	Longuenese [St. Omer] Souvenir Cemetery
HP O/400 D4580	2Lt J H O'Grady	+	Longuenese [St. Omer] Souvenir Cemetery
	Canada		
	Mechanic J W Morton	+	Longuenese [St. Omer] Souvenir Cemetery

T/o Alquines for a practice flight and on return crashed out of control as the bomber turned onto final approach. William Reid Dallas had first seen active service with a mechanised transport unit of the RASC; he had joined the squadron on the 17th of September. His Canadian observer came from Ottawa, his epitaph being the Latin inscription: *"Requiescat in Pace."* It is almost a certainty that the crew were buried with full military honours in a joint service, conducted on the 27th by the Reverend A C Lawson.

Wednesday, Christmas Day 1918

The first Christmas since 1913, with Europe relatively speaking at peace, though Red Army factions were active on a number of fronts. In Georgia and the Balkans tensions remained high with a number of localised wars bringing misery to many.

And it should not be forgotten that the vexed problems in getting Allied prisoners of war, many of them suffering from illness or wounds, home from camps across Germany was far from settled.

On the airfields some form of traditional celebrations were held, though flying duties continued.

5 Squadron	Lt Stevenson	Safe
RE.8 C2989		

Presentation Aircraft: Rhodesia No 2

T/o 1 Aeroplane Acceptance Park on a delivery flight to Hangelar but became lost and in the forced-landing near Hohenberg*the RE ran onto rough ground and was damaged beyond repair.

* There are fourteen locations in Germany with this name and although many can be discounted, it would be misleading of me to say which Hohenberg matches the summary description.

53 Squadron	2Lt A Knox	Safe
RE.8 C2870	Canada	

T/o Ohey and set out for the squadron's base at Laneffe but forced-landed at Lamontzée [Liège] where the RE fell onto a sunken road. Before it could be recovered strong winds blew C2870 onto its back and the damage was such that it was declared beyond economical repair. Arthur Knox, born 1st July 1896, received his commission on 29th October 1917, and arrived at Abeele on 5th October for duties with the squadron. On 6th February 1919, he was admitted to 55 CCS and thence to 14 General Hospital where he stayed for 24-hours before being taken to 51 General Hospital and it was not until the 9th of March that he was declared fit.

Attached to 1 Aerial Ranges, he then came under the authority of 2nd Wing and was posted to 12 Squadron at Duren on 28th March. However, on 27th April he received orders to leave Germany and proceed to Mesopotamia and catch up with 6 Squadron which had left Sart on the 14th. Officially, he was struck off BEF establishment on the 30th April.

This is where his service record ends, though it is possible his name appears in 6 Squadron's Operations Record Book.

Thursday, Boxing Day 1918

Naval operations off Estonia resulted in the Royal Navy capturing two Russian destroyers, the *Aytroil* and the *Spartak* which were preparing to shell the port of Talliin. Both vessels later became the nucleus of the Estonia Navy and were renamed *Lennuk* and *Vambola* respectively. Meanwhile, negotiations were taking place for the return of the Russian sailors and on 27th May 1919, seventeen British prisoners of war were handed over in exchange for the captain of the *Spartak.*

7 Squadron   RE.8 H7263   While picketed in the open at Spich was blown over in gale-force winds and broken in half,

85 Squadron   Lt S A Gomez   Injured
SE.5a F923
T/o Asc intending to fly to Bruges but became hopelessly lost in the prevailing fog and approaching dark. Forced-landed in an area described as devastated by war, running into the stump of what once had been a substantial tree. The impact was severe and Lieutenant Gomez was found wandering in a very dazed state and suffering from mild concussion. He had been seconded on 16 November 1917, from the Dorset Regiment [LG 4 December 1917, supplement 30414, page 12753]. Postwar he returned to his regiment, the 3rd Battalion, and relinquished his commission with effect from 1st April 1920 [LG 24 September 1920, supplement 32065, page 9525]. It is noted that the 3rd Battalion had demobilised late in 1919, while garrisoned in Londonderry.

85 Squadron   Lt S C Elliot   Safe   Unemployed list 28 September 1919
SE.5a H702
T/o Ascq with similar intentions and lost in the manner reported above. H702 was issued to the squadron on or by the 14th November, and with F923 were the first serious accidents reported from 85 Squadron since the armistice.

98 Squadron   Lt J H W Haswell   Safe
DH.9 D582   Mechanic A S Jay   Safe
T/o Abscon with the intent of delivering the DH to Marquain but owing to inclement weather a landing was made at Hasnon where the bomber ran into a ditch; presumed damaged beyond repair. Born on 5th October 1898, Lieutenant Haswell's parents lived at 1 Holt Terrace, Birkenhead. On his arrival in France he joined 211 Squadron at Petite Synthe on 18th August, his tour of operations being interrupted on 25th September when he was struck down with scabies and taken to hospital. On being discharged on 5th October, he was attached to 1 Aeroplane Supply Depot from where he was posted to 98 Squadron on November 1st. Entries on Army Form B.103 cease on New Year's Day when he succumbed again to scabies and was sent to 51 CCS for treatment.

I suspect that at some point in his life he was ordained for an entry in *The London Gazette* 2 March 1948, supplement 38223, page 1548, shows J H W Haswell held a Permanent Commission as a Chaplin with seniority from 27th February 1936, his service now being extended by four years in the rank of Squadron Leader. He retired from the air force on 27th February 1956 [LG 6 March 1956, supplement 40725, page 1370].

Friday 27 December 1918
In Greater Poland tension between the Polish and German communities were exacerbated by a speech delivered in Poznań by the pianist and politician Ignacy Jan Paderewski who was spokesman for Polish Independence and who by the time of the signing of the Peace Treaty in June 1919, was Poland's Prime Minister. As with Thomáš Masaryk [see my lead-in for Friday, 20th December], Ignacy Paderewski had conferred with Woodrow Wilson, gaining his support for an independent Polish nation.

53 Squadron   RE.8 E1112   Destroyed on the ground at Laneffe after being blown over by strong winds.

Saturday 28 December 1918
The gales that had become an all too familiar feature of the Continent's weather continued to effect air operations.

73 Squadron   2Lt R H Gowan   Safe   Unemployed list 14 August 1919
F.1 Camel D8200
T/o Baizieux and headed for Bellevue where on landing in exceptionally strong surface winds it was blown over as it taxied towards the hangars. Taken on charge by 4 Squadron Australian Flying Corps on 29th July, it was exchanged for a Snipe on 4th October. Passed to 73 Squadron it narrowly escaped being wrecked when on 9th November, and landing at Malencourt, it fell into a shell hole. The pilot on that occasion was Captain Emile John Lussier who had been recently been *Gazetted* with the DFC [Edinburgh edition, 4 November 1918, issue 13346, page 4059]: *'During recent operations this officer has driven down out of control or destroyed seven enemy machines, and, with the aid of two other pilots, has accounted for a further two. Three of these he destroyed in one day. In these combats he has proved himself an officer of very high courage, eager to attack without regard to the enemy's superiority in numbers.'*

Born in Chicago, Illinois, on the 10th of October 1895, the young teenager Emile moved with his parents northwards to Canada where his father, Joseph Lussier, secured a job constructing railroad stations in Western Canada, Emile joining his father in this profession until enlisting with the RFC in late 1917.

Postwar, he returned to the United States and set up home in Westminster in the State of Maryland where he became a farmer. Come the Second World War he left his farm and joined the RCAF and rising to Squadron Leader rank played a significant role in radio training. By this time his marriage had produced four daughters, one, Betty Ann Lussier* becoming a pilot and crossing to the UK where she joined the Air Transport Auxiliary.

The war over, Squadron Leader Emile John Lussier returned to his farm in Westminster from where his death was reported on 11th December 1974.

Returning to 2nd Lieutenant Gowan, he joined the squadron on 28th September and remained on strength until returning to the UK on the 9th of February 1919.

* Internet searches for Betty Ann Lussier will result in several websites devoted to her life, the most informative being the Central Intelligence Agency site which describes her as *"a fiercely independent, hardworking, adventurous woman with a craving for excitement."* Her death at the age of 86, was reported as recently as 2017.

73 Squadron   2Lt F M Stieber   Safe   Unemployed list 14 August 1919
F.1 Camel F1532/1
T/o Baizieux similarly tasked and on landing at Bellevue suffered the same fate as that for D8200. Arriving with the squadron on 11th August, F1532 was initially coded J. Similar to the Camels lost by 85 Squadron on Boxing Day, this duo from 73 Squadron were the first to be written off since the armistice. 2nd Lieutenant Stieber had joined '73' on 26th July and was posted to 3 Squadron at Inchy on the last day of January 1919, but I doubt if he had time to unpack before being ordered to a repatriation camp the next day.

Sunday 29 December 1918
The *Sunday Express* is published for the first time. The banner across the first page reads: *Landslide for the Coalition - Asquithian Liberals Disappear.* Most of the front page is devoted to election results, but world affairs are also reported. It cost three halfpence.

40 Squadron   2Lt G S Smith   Safe
SE.5a E4066
Presentation Aircraft: Britons in Malaya No 2
T/o Aniche and on arrival at Orcq made a poor landing and nosed over; presumed damaged beyond repair. Gerald Stewart Smith joined the squadron at Bryas on 24th August and apart from temporary detachments remained on establishment until 8th March 1919, when he reported to Bickendorf to fly SE.5as with 29 Squadron. On the 27th of June he was admitted to hospital with an undisclosed illness and invalided to England on the 2nd of July.

Monday 30 December 1918
The fighting between Georgian and Armenia forces continued but behind the scenes peace negotiations were making good progress

24 Squadron   2Lt A L Bloom   Injured   Unemployed list 22 February 1919
SE.5a E5790
T/o Bisseghem for a practice flight but before becoming fully airborne he hit the top a ditch, damaging the under-carriage. However, 2nd Lieutenant Bloom managed to retain control and continued his flight. On return the damaged unit gave way and he was quite badly injured. Taken to 62 CCS with cuts to his face he was sent by HS *Jan Breydel* to England on the 7th Of January. He had been with the squadron since the 9th of August, and earlier in the month had spent a few days of detached duty at Nivelles. The loss of E5790 was the squadron's first serious accident since the war ending.

44 Squadron   Lt W A H Ellercamp   +   Hornchurch [St. Andrew] Churchyard
F.1 Camel D6637
T/o Hainault Farm and while making a climbing turn flew into the 78 Squadron aircraft summarised below. Little is known of Lieutenant Ellercamp. I can find no records for his service and his entry on the CWGC website is devoid of Christian names and next of kin; however, the IWM website identified him as Wilfred Alan Herbert Ellercamp.

64 Squadron   2Lt H G Yerg   Injured   Unemployed list 12 July 1919
SE.5a E4003/F
T/o Froidmont authorised for practice flying but climbed far too steeply, stalled and crashed. It would seem from entries on Army Form B.103 that 2nd Lieutenant Yerg arrived in France on the overnight ferry 14th-15th September and was attached to 2 Aeroplane Supply Depot. Here, he was taken ill and admitted to 51 General Hospital where he remained until the 9th of December and it was not until the 29th that he joined 64 Squadron. His crash, therefore, was perhaps hardly surprising for he was seriously out of flying practice. Now seriously injured he was first treated for abdominal injuries in 57 CCS before being transferred to 20 General Hospital from where he was sent back to the UK on the 4th of January aboard HMHS Brighton.

Note. As an indication of how rapidly the RAF was reducing the number of officers, on 12th July 1919, the day on which 2nd Lieutenant Yerg's services were no longer required, ninety-seven in total were discharged [LG 29 July 1919, issue 31478, pages 9589 to 9592].

78 Squadron   Lt C D Hurndall   +   Southend-on-Sea [Sutton Road] Cemtery
F.1 Camel D9459
T/o Sutton's Farm and destroyed in the Hainault Farm circuit after coming into collision with the 44 Squadron Camel featured above.

Tuesday, New Year's Eve 1918

After a fortnight of fighting in the disputed border region between Armenia and Georgia a British-brokered peace deal was agreed between the two sides and a ceasefire was announced.

In the Baltic State of Estonia the fight for independence showed no sign of abating, while to the south beyond Latvia, Lithuania was occupied by Bolshevik forces.

The winter weather continued to be a factor with rain sodden landing grounds producing a crop of accidents as undercarriages sank into softened ground, while aircraft that were picketed outside were prone to structural damage as was illustrated by a report from 59 Squadron at Gerpinnes that three of their RE.8s were now so waterlogged that glue joints of C2312 and H7054 were giving way and the mainplanes of C3407 were so warped it was no longer safe to fly.

| 18 Squadron | 2Lt D L H Moore | Safe | See below |
| DH.9 E8970 | 2Lt H S Cranfield | Safe | See below |

T/o Maubeuge but came to a violent stop after a wing skid dug into the rain-soaked surface, swinging the DH onto its nose and minus the undercarriage. David Lucius Henry Moore was born on the 7th of April 1894, joining the squadron on 11th October. On 28th January 1919, he fell ill with influenza and was admitted to 20 CCS and thence to 14 General Hospital before arriving back in England on 4th February aboard the HS *Jan Breydell.*

Herbert Stanley Cranfield, born just after the turn of the century on 7th January, qualified as an Observer Officer on 26th August [*Flight* September 5, 1918, page 1007] and joined the squadron on 5th September. He, too, went down with influenza and was treated in 47 CCS between the 21st and 31st of January. He was posted home on 2nd September 1919, the day on which the squadron returned to Weston-on-the-Green.

| 18 Squadron | 2Lt D L H Moore | Safe | unemployed list 8 April 1919 |
| DH.9A E9730 | 2Lt H S Cranfield | Safe | |

T/o Maugeuge for an engine test and came to grief in the manner described above.

20 Squadron	2Lt S L Walters	Safe	Unemployed list 25 July 1919
Bristol F.2b E2644	South Africa		
	Lt E W Kirkpatrick	Safe	

T/o Ossogne for a practice flight and believed damaged beyond repair after becoming embedded on soft ground. From Durban, Stanley Leslie Walters arrived in the world on the 7th of April 1894. On completion of his training he was posted to 22 Squadron [Bristol F.2b] at Maisoncelle but a fortnight after his arrival he was taken to 51 General Hospital suffering, it was thought, from the most painful condition of Epididymis. On his release, he was attached to 1 Aeroplane Supply Depot and thence on 9th September to 20 Squadron. A record for his observer has yet to be found.

| 59 Squadron | 2Lt H S R Burt | Safe | |
| RE.8 C2875 | Lt O'Halleron | Safe | |

T/o Gerpinnes to take Lieutenant O'Halleron to Spa but on encountering mist a precautionary landing was made. With conditions improving and attempt was made to complete the journey, but on becoming airborne its progress was rapidly arrested with the undercarriage entangled in wire fencing. 2nd Lieutenant Burt had been with the squadron since 23rd of August, departing on 29th July 1919, to Buchheim to join 7 Squadron [RE.8]. On the 5th of September he returned home from Heumar.

| 98 Squadron | Lt R L Lawson | Safe | |
| DH.9 E9014 | Lt R U Hoddinott | Safe | Commission relinquished 1 April 1920 |

T/o Marquain and on arrival at Abscon overshot and in trying to avoid running into a hangar swung and lost the DH's undercarriage. I have not located Lieutenant Lawson's service record, but that for Robert Uriah Hoddinott shows he had at least two years of distinguished service as an officer in the Royal Field Artillery before becoming an Observer Officer with effect from 22nd December 1917. Two Record of Service cards have been raised, one providing an extensive outline of his army service, but the second is devoid of any details pertaining to his air force movements.

| 104 Squadron | Lt E C Stringer | Safe | |
| DH.9 D2862 | 2Lt J N Ogilvy | Safe | |

T/o Maisoncelle for 2 Aeroplane Supply Depot to collect a new aircraft but on reaching Fienvillers a fish-bolt sheared and a serious crash followed, wrecking D2862. Edward Carpenter Stringer was formerly of the London Regiment, Territorial Forces and had been seconded to the RFC on the last day of August 1916 [LG 25 September 1916, supplement 29762, page 9322]. Posted, probably as an observer on 24th September, to 27 Squadron [Martinsyde] he returned to England on 31st March, returning to France as a pilot on 9th August and was attached to 1 Aircraft Depot and thence to 22 Squadron for three days of temporary duty before arriving at Ste Marie Cappel on 16th August as a scot pilot with 45 Squadron. On 11th September, he returned to 1 Aircraft Depot and this is where the surviving service record for Lieutenant Stringer, born in London on 29th January 1898, ends.

I am reasonably confident that he had been awarded the MM [LG 8 August 1916, supplement 29701, page 7890] and that in the Second World War he was commissioned as a Lieutenant to the General List on 2nd August 1940 [LG 3rd September 1940, supplement 34936, page 5528] and served until disability meant he had to relinquish his commission on 1st May 1945, by which time he was attached to the Army Catering Corps [LG 1 May 1945, supplement 37056, page 2286]. I have not been able to discover any details in respect of 2nd Lieutenant Ogilvy.

Appendix 1A - Squadron Losses Table 12th November 1918 - 31st December 1918

In a departure from the lay out of appendices as shown in the first two volumes, the following statistics show:-

1. Accidents in which it believed the aircraft was either a total wreck, or deemed to be beyond economical repair.
2. Fatalities, either at the time of the crash, or subsequently reported to have died from injuries.
3. Miscellaneous; ground accidents being the common cause.
4. Totals of the three columns.
5. Unless annotated to the contrary, the area of operations post-armistice was either Belgium, France or Germany. 'Home defence', self explanatory, though as recorded by John Rawlings are included in *Fighter Squadrons of the RAF and their Aircraft.* As is evident in the table, the balance of roles was fairly even and though disbandment affected the majority of squadrons, here recorded, with the gradual expansion of the Royal Air Force in the 1930s to meet the growing threat from Nazi Germany a sizeable proportion resurrected the duties of their predecessors.

ROYAL AIR FORCE

Squadron	1	2	3	4	Description
3 Squadron	4	1		5	Fighter squadron equipped with F.1 Camel
4 Squadron	1			1	Reconnaissance squadron equipped with RE.8
5 Squadron	7			7	Reconnaissance squadron equipped with RE.8
6 Squadron	1			1	Reconnaissance squadron equipped with RE.8
7 Squadron	2		1	3	Reconnaissance squadron equipped with RE.8
8 Squadron	4			4	Reconnaissance squadron equipped with FK.8
9 Squadron	5			5	Reconnaissance squadron equipped with RE.8
10 Squadron	3	2		5	Reconnaissance squadron equipped with FK.8
11 Squadron	4			4	Fighter squadron equipped with two-seat Bristol F.2b
12 Squadron	7			7	Reconnaissance squadron equipped with RE.8
13 Squadron	1			1	Reconnaissance squadron equipped with RE.8
15 Squadron	5	1		6	Reconnaissance squadron equipped with RE.8
16 Squadron	1			1	Reconnaissance squadron equipped with RE.8
18 Squadron	4	1		5	Bomber squadron equipped with DH.4/DH.9A
19 Squadron	3	1		4	Fighter squadron equipped with 5F.1 Dolphin
20 Squadron	4	2		6	Fighter squadron equipped with Bristol F.2b
22 Squadron	3	1		4	Fighter squadron equipped with Bristol F.2b
23 Squadron	4	1		5	Fighter squadron equipped with 5F.1 Dolphin
24 Squadron	1			1	Fighter and ground attack squadron equipped with SE.5a
25 Squadron	1			1	Day bomber squadron equipped with DH.4
27 Squadron	2			2	Day bomber squadron equipped with DH.4/DH.9
28 Squadron	2			2	Fighter squadron equipped with F.1 Camel and operating in Italy
29 Squadron	2			2	Fighter squadron equipped with SE.5a
32 Squadron	1			1	Fighter squadron equipped with SE.5a
35 Squadron	1			1	Reconnaissance squadron equipped with FK.8/Bristol F.2b
40 Squadron	4			4	Fighter squadron equipped with SE.5a
41 Squadron	1			1	Fighter squadron equipped with SE.5a
42 Squadron	5	2		7	Reconnaissance squadron equipped with RE.8
43 Squadron	3			3	Fighter squadron equipped with 7F.1 Snipe
44 Squadron	2	2		4	Home defence squadron equipped with F.1 Camel/7F.1 Snipe
45 Squadron	3	1		4	Fighter squadron equipped with F.1 Camel/7F.1 Snipe
46 Squadron	4			4	Fighter squadron equipped with F.1 Camel
48 Squadron	2			2	Fighter squadron equipped with Bristol F.2b
49 Squadron	4	2		6	Day bomber squadron equipped with DH.9
50 Squadron	1	1		2	Home defence squadron equipped with F.1 Camel/SE.5a
53 Squadron	3		1	4	Reconnaissance squadron equipped with RE.8
54 Squadron	1			1	Fighter squadron equipped with F.1 Camel
55 Squadron	6			6	Bomber squadron equipped with DH.4
56 Squadron	2			2	Fighter squadron equipped with SE.5a
57 Squadron	6	1		7	Bomber Squadron equipped with DH.4
59 Squadron	2			2	Reconnaissance squadron equipped with RE.8/Bristol F.2b
61 Squadron	3			3	Home defence squadron equipped with F.1 Camel
62 Squadron	1			1	Fighter squadron equipped with Bristol F.2b
64 Squadron	7			7	Fighter squadron equipped with SE.5a
65 Squadron	2			2	Fighter squadron equipped with F.1 Camel
66 Squadron	1	1		2	Fighter squadron equipped with F.1 Camel
70 Squadron	5			5	Fighter squadron equipped with F.1 Came/7F.1 Snipe
72 Squadron			1	1	Fighter squadron equipped with Bristol M.1c/SE.5a
73 Squadron	2			2	Fighter squadron equipped with F.1 Camel
74 Squadron	2			2	Fighter squadron equipped with SE.5a
75 Squadron	1	1		2	Home defence squadron equipped with Avro 504K
78 Squadron	1	1		2	Home defence squadron equipped with Avro 504K/F.1 Camel
79 Squadron	6			6	Fighter squadron equipped with 5F.1 Dolphin
80 Squadron	2			2	Fighter squadron equipped with F.1 Camel/7F.1 Snipe
82 Squadron	2	2		4	Reconnaissance squadron equipped with FK.8
83 Squadron	2			2	Bomber squadron equipped with FE.2b/FE.2d
84 Squadron	2			2	Fighter squadron equipped with SE.5a

Squadron				Total	
85 Squadron	2			2	Fighter squadron equipped with SE.5a
87 Squadron	3			3	Fighter squadron equipped with 5F.1 Dolphin
88 Squadron	1		1	2	Fighter squadron equipped with Bristol F.2b
91 Squadron	1	1		2	Home defence squadron equipped with 5F.1 Dolphin
92 Squadron	2		1	3	Fighter squadron equipped with SE.5a
97 Squadron	1			1	Bomber squadron equipped with HP O/400
98 Squadron	4			4	Bomber squadron equipped with DH.9
99 Squadron	2			2	Bomber squadron equipped with DH.9/DH.9A
101 Squadron	2			2	Bomber squadron equipped with FE.2b/FE.2d
102 Squadron	1			1	Bomber squadron equipped with FE.2b/FE.2d
103 Squadron	1			1	Bomber squadron equipped with DH.9
104 Squadron	6			6	Bomber squadron equipped with DH.9
105 Squadron	2	3		5	Army support squadron equipped with RE.8/Bristol F.2b
107 Squadron	1			1	Bomber squadron equipped with DH.9
108 Squadron	2			2	Bomber squadron equipped with DH.9
110 Squadron	2			2	Bomber squadron equipped with DH.9A
112 Squadron	2	2		4	Home defence squadron equipped with F.1 Camel
115 Squadron	2			2	Bomber squadron equipped with HP O/400
117 Squadron	1			1	Bomber squadron equipped with DH.9
138 Squadron	1	1		2	Home defence squadron equipped with Bristol F.2b
139 Squadron	3			3	Fighter squadron equipped with Bristol F.2b
148 Squadron	1			1	Bomber squadron equipped with FE.b/FE.2d
149 Squadron	1			1	Bomber squadron equipped with FE.2b/FE.2d
150 Squadron	1			1	Fighter squadron equipped with Bristol M.1c/SE.5a
151 Squadron	2	1		3	Fighter squadron equipped with F.1 Camel
155 Squadron	1	2		3	Bomber squadron equipped with DH.9A
203 Squadron	3	2		5	Fighter squadron equipped with F.1 Camel
204 Squadron	4			4	Fighter squadron equipped with F.1 Camel
205 Squadron	3			3	Bomber squadron equipped with DH.4/DH.9
206 Squadron	4		1	5	Bomber squadron equipped with DH.9/DH.9A
207 Squadron	1			1	Bomber squadron equipped with HP O/400
208 Squadron	6	1		7	Fighter squadron equipped with F.1 Camel/7F.1 Snipe
209 Squadron	1			1	Fighter squadron equipped with F.1 Camel
210 Squadron	1	1		2	Fighter squadron equipped with F.1 Camel
211 Squadron	4		1	5	Bomber squadron equipped with DH.9
213 Squadron	1			1	Fighter squadron equipped with F.1 Camel
214 Squadron	1			1	Bomber squadron equipped with HP O/400
215 Squadron	3	3		6	Bomber squadron equipped with HP O/400
216 Squadron	1			1	Bomber squadron equipped with HP O/400
217 Squadron	1			1	Bomber squadron equipped with DH.4
218 Squadron	1			1	Bomber squadron equipped with DH.9
Total	244	41	7	292	

AUSTRALIAN FLYING CORPS

Squadron				Total	
2 Squadron	2			2	Fighter squadron equipped with F.1 Camel
3 Squadron	3		1	4	Reconnaissance squadron equipped with RE.8
4 Squadron	6	1		7	Fighter squadron equipped with 7F.1 Snipe
Total	11	1	1	13	

CANADIAN AIR FORCE

Squadron				Total	
1 Squadron	2	1		3	Fighter squadron equipped with 5F.1 Dolphin
Combined total	257	43	8	308	

Appendix 1B - Losses by Aircraft Type 12th November 1918- 31st December 1918

The statistics for this appendix follow the same lines as those shown in Appendix A.

Aircraft Manufacturing Company Limited: DH.4

18 Squadron	1	1		2
25 Squadron	1			1
27 Squadron	1			1
55 Squadron	6			4
57 Squadron	6	1		7
217 Squadron	1			1
Totals	16	2		18

The prototype DH.4, designed by Geoffrey de Havilland, flew for the first time at Hendon towards the middle of August 1916. A total of 1,461 airframes were built and its role as a day bomber was acknowledged to be one of the finest.

Aircraft Manufacturing Company Limited: DH.9

18 Squadron	2	1		3
27 Squadron	1			1
49 Squadron	3	2		5
98 Squadron	3			3
103 Squadron	1			1
104 Squadron	6			6
107 Squadron	1			1
108 Squadron	3			3
117 Squadron	1			1
206 Squadron	4		1	5
211 Squadron	4		1	5
218 Squadron	1			1
Totals	30	3	2	35

Envisaged as an improved DH.4, in reality the DH.9 failed to rise to expectation and its operational performance was well below that of the DH.4. Such were its short-comings, particularly in respect of the Puma engine with which it was powered, that Major-General Trenchard [having been so advised by Geoffrey de Havilland], attempted to prevent the DH.9 entering service. However, owing to production and contractual arrangements signed off, he was bluntly informed by Sir William Weir, Controller of Supplies in the Ministry of Munitions that it was a case of *fait accompli* or nothing at all. Consequently, the type saw wide-spread service on the Western Front and in other theatres of war, as well as use in coastal defence patrols and at flying training establishments. Postwar, large numbers of surplus DH.9s were sold to foreign air forces.

Aircraft Manufacturing Company Limited: DH.9A

18 Squadron	2			2
49 Squadron	1			1
99 Squadron	3			3
110 Squadron	2			2
155 Squadron	1	2		3
205 Squadron	3			3
Totals	12	2		14

With an American built 400-hp Liberty engine the DH.9A was a marked improvement over the DH.9, and though its operational service was limited [110 Squadron commenced equipping with less than three months of hostilities remaining], it was to become the Royal Air Force's day bomber aircraft until the early 1930s seeing extensive service in the Middle East and over the North West Frontier of India.

The proven success of the DH day bomber squadrons operating on the Western Front was an influencing factor in the reasoning of the air chiefs during the late 1930s, hence the intention to use Bomber Command as a day bombing force. The DH.9A was able to operate at 17,000 feet and providing the crews maintained tight formation, the excellent visibility afforded to the air gunners reduced the effectiveness of the German scout pilots. Perusing the individual aircraft histories reported in *The DH.4/DH.9 File* there are numerous examples of claims submitted, either for the destruction, or the driving down out of control of German fighters. One such example features DH.9 D5845, a presentation aircraft, which arrived with 108 Squadron at Capelle on 29 September 1918. Two days later it was part of a formation attack on Ingelmunster station [crewed by 2nd Lieutenant A G Kershaw and 2nd Lieutenant W L Walker]; at 1725 the formation was attacked by a force of at least 33 enemy scouts which the report shows *'1 BU and 2 OOC shared C2205, D499, D5835, D7342, E605, E5435, E8871 & F5847 then crashed.'* Repaired, and transferred with the squadron to Bisseghem, it was in action on the 9th of November, again with 2nd Lieutenant Kershaw at the controls but with Lieutenant H S Gargett in the observer/air gunner's seat *'on Denderleeuwe raid EA OOC E of Sotteghem, shared C2216, D613, D7357, E8980 & E9028 0905.'* On return Lieutenant Gargett received attention to his wounds. Then, 24-hours before the signing of the armistice, and flown by Lieutenants W Marsden with observer W McGowen, the pilot was wounded during a reconnaissance sortie. On 23rd January, D5845 was transferred to 98 Squadron and thence on the 13th of February, it was despatched to 8 Aircraft Acceptance Park at Lympne.

Armstrong Whitworth: FK.8

10 Squadron	3	2		5
35 Squadron	1			1
82 Squadron	2	2		4
Totals	6	4		10

A general reconnaissance aircraft which although of sturdy construction and, reputedly, easier to fly that its counterpart, the RE.8, was considered rather pedestrian in performance. Despite these shortcomings, 1,650 were built and saw service on all fronts, home defence, and in home training establishments.

Between the formation of the Royal Air Force on the 1st of April 1918, and the armistice, at least 222 FK.8s were lost on operations, plus another 35 in accidents. Details of the breakdown of these casualties are recorded in the appendices of volumes one and two of this series. One of the most notable of the FK.8 losses occurred on Saturday, the 10th of August 1918, and is reported on page 135 of the second volume. The crew were Captain Freddie West and his observer, Lieutenant J A G Haslam. Both were attached to 8 Squadron, then based at Vignacourt, and flying in FK.8 C8602. Their mission was to try and make contact with tanks heading in the direction of Roye, southeast of Amiens. What happened in the sortie resulted in Freddie West being awarded the nation's highest honour for gallantry in the face of the enemy, namely the Victoria Cross. It would be remiss of me not to mention that Freddie and his regular observer, James Haslam, had both being *Gazetted* with Military Crosses, indicative of their devotion to duty during their many hazardous operations undertaken in the pursuit of war operations. Prior to Freddie's epic sortie, and pre-formation of the Royal Air Force, Canada born 2nd Lieutenant Alan Arnett McLeod of 2 Squadron won the Victoria Cross during a protracted operation on 27th March 1918. The details of this are recorded by Chaz Bowyer in *For Valour - The Air VCs*, while his gallant observer, Lieutenant A W Hammond, received a First Bar to his Military Cross. Reading the account, Lieutenant Hammond's actions appear worthy of similar recognition afforded to his young pilot, for Arthur William Hammond was so gravely wounded that the injuries to one of his legs were so severe that surgeons were unable to save the limb and amputation became necessary [by awful coincidence Freddie West was destined to suffer amputation of one his legs]. Their FK.8 B5773 crash-landed, burning, in No Mans Land by which time Arthur Hammond was unconscious. Although seriously wounded and suffering from burns, Alan McLeod braved the flames and hoisting his observer onto to his shoulder, set off on the perilous journey towards some trenches which at the time were manned by South African Scottish. Before reaching the dubious safety of the lines, he was wounded again but such was the intensity of the German artillery fire evacuation was impossible. For five hours the two airmen endured the rain of shells plunging into the torn earth until, at last, they were taken to the reserve trenches and a field dressing station and thence, eventually, to Etaples. By this time it appeared that neither officer would survive and 24-hours later Alan McLeod was ensconced in the Prince of Wales' Hospital, London where he was joined by his father who had been summoned to his bedside from Canada. Subsequently, he recovered and with the aid of two sticks was able to be received by the King at Buckingham Palace and invested with the Victoria Cross. Still extremely weak he returned to his home in Stonewall, Manitoba to convalesce but, tragically, fell victim to the influenza pandemic and died on the 6th of November 1918. He was nineteen years of age.

Avro Aircraft Company: Avro 504K

75 Squadron	1	1		2

A number of Avro 504Ks were attached to the Home Defence squadrons where they performed useful, if unproductive, night patrols.

The longevity of the Avro 504 was quite staggering; taking to the air for the first time on the 18th of September 1913, and going on to serve with every major training and a high proportion of operational units, the type remained in service until being officially retired in 1934, but for a very short period in the Second World War a small number of '504s that had been sold for private use were impressed for glider towing. It is believed G-ADEV aka BK892 was the last Avro 504N to be retired when on the 9th of June 1942, it was down graded for instructional duties and issued as 3118M to 1264 Squadron Air Training Corps at Ashville College, Windermere. Including licence built airframes, 11,303 were built.

Bristol Aeroplane Company: Bristol F.2b

8 Squadron	4			4
11 Squadron	4			4
20 Squadron	4	2		6
22 Squadron	3	1		4
48 Squadron	2			2
62 Squadron	1			1
88 Squadron	1		1	2
138 Squadron	1	1		2
139 Squadron	3			3
Totals	23	4	1	28

One of the most effective fighter aircraft of the *Great War* and continued in Royal Air Force service until the 1930s, during which time it was employed as the standard army co-operation aircraft, particularly in the Middle East and in India. The last squadron to give up its 'Brisfits' was 20 Squadron at Peshawar where the last examples were disposed of in March 1932, giving way to the Westland Wapiti.

Handley Page Limited: HP O/400

97 Squadron	2		2
115 Squadron	2		2
207 Squadron	1		1
214 Squadron	1		1
215 Squadron	3	3	6
216 Squadron	1		1
Totals	10	3	13

Employed as a night bomber the Handley Page O/400 was retired from service in 1919, when it was replaced by the Vickers Vimy.

Royal Aircraft Factory: BE.12

207 Squadron	1	1

Royal Aircraft Factory: FE.2b

83 Squadron	2	2
101 Squadron	2	2
102 Squadron	1	1
148 Squadron	1	1
149 Squadron	1	1
Totals	7	7

Initially used for fighter duties, by 1916 the type was outclassed but a new role was found as night bomber. When the Royal Air Force was formed, seven squadrons were operational and four had been formed in the United Kingdom for night flying training. Its genesis dates from 1911, and when phased out of service close on 2,000 had been built. 149 Squadron appears to have had a few examples on its charge until as late as August 1919.

Royal Aircraft Factory: RE.8

4 Squadron	1			1
5 Squadron	7			7
6 Squadron	1			1
7 Squadron	2		1	3
9 Squadron	5			5
12 Squadron	7			7
13 Squadron	1			1
15 Squadron	5	1		6
16 Squadron	1			1
42 Squadron	5	2		7
53 Squadron	3		1	4
59 Squadron	2			2
105 Squadron	2	3		5
Totals	42	6	2	50

Accepted as the standard reconnaissance machine from mid-1917 onwards, the RE.8 was not universally popular and its reputation as being a difficult aircraft to fly was never entirely dispelled. Nevertheless, in excess of 4,000 were built and by the time of the armistice it was employed in every theatre of war. Regarded soon after as obsolete the type was quickly withdrawn from service and unlike many wartime designs the RE.8 was never taken up by civilian operators or by private flyers.

AUSTRALIAN FLYING CORPS

3 Squadron	3		1	4

Combined totals	45	6	3	54

Royal Aircraft Factory: SE.5a

24 Squadron	1	1
29 Squadron	2	2
32 Squadron	1	1
40 Squadron	4	4
41 Squadron	1	1
56 Squadron	2	2

This was a fine record in that not a single death was reported between the armistice and the end of the year from squadrons equipped with the SE.5a. Generally regarded as a superior fighter to its counterpart, Sopwith's F.1 Camel, problems associated with its Hispano-Suiza engine meant that it was not until well into 1918, was the type available in large numbers. Postwar the SE.5a squadrons were quickly run-down, the last of its type being stood down

64 Squadron	7		7
74 Squadron	2		2
84 Squadron	2		2
85 Squadron	2		2
92 Squadron	2	1	3
Totals	26	1	27

AUSTRALIAN FLYING CORPS

2 Squadron	2		2
Combined totals	28	1	29

by 56 Squadron in January 1920. In total a shade over 5,200 were produced.

Sopwith Aviation Company: F.1 Camel

3 Squadron	4	1	5
28 Squadron	2		2
44 Squadron	2	2	4
45 Squadron	3	1	4
46 Squadron	4		4
50 Squadron	1	1	2
54 Squadron	1		1
61 Squadron	3		3
65 Squadron	2		2
66 Squadron	1	1	2
70 Squadron	5		5
73 Squadron	2		2
78 Squadron	1	1	2
80 Squadron	2		2
112 Squadron	2	2	4
151 Squadron	2	1	3
203 Squadron	3	2	5
204 Squadron	4		4
208 Squadron	3		3
209 Squadron	1		1
210 Squadron	1	1	2
213 Squadron	1		1
Totals	50	13	63

Acknowledged as one of the finest fighter aircraft of the *Great War*, the Camel required a highly skilled pilot at the controls to realise its full potential. With so much of its weight packed into the first seven feet of the fuselage, plus the gyro-scopic effect of the rotary engine, it was little wonder that embryo pilots found Tommy Sopwith's design*beyond their capabilities. In level flight the Camel became tail-heavy, thus necessitating the need for forward pressure on the control column to maintain level flight. With such demanding characteristics flying accidents were frequent, particularly at the Training Depot Stations, where many a pupil crashed while attempting his first solo on type, often with fatal consequences or serious injury. Although the majority of Camel production [5,490 built] went to Royal Air Force units, a development known as the 2F.1 Ship's Camel was used for carrier operations, or for launching from platforms build atop the gun turrets of capital ships.

* The lead designer throughout the development of the Camel was Sopwith's chief engineer, Herbert Smith.

Sopwith Aviation Company: 5F.1 Dolphin

19 Squadron	3	1	4
23 Squadron	4	1	5
79 Squadron	6		6
87 Squadron	3		3
91 Squadron	1	1	2
Totals	17	3	20

Early in 1917, Herbert Smith turned his attention to designing the 5F.1 Dolphin which following successful testing entered operational service early in 1918.

CANADIAN AIR FORCE

1 Squadron	2	1	3
Combined total	19	4	23

1

Sopwith Aviation Company: 7F.1 Snipe

43 Squadron	3		3
208 Squadron	3	1	4
Totals	6	1	7

Herbert Smith's successor to the F.1 Camel. Remained in frontline service after the war.

AUSTRALIAN FLYING CORPS

4 Squadron	6	1	7
Combined totals	12	2	14

Appendix 1C - Squadron Locations as at 31st December 1918

The rundown of the squadrons, although contemplated now that the war had ended, had yet to gain momentum, but numerical strength at the turn of the year would soon become a distant memory and would not be repeated for several decades yet to come. As with my previous volumes, I have prepared this appendix from information reported in Air-Britain's *The Squadrons of the Royal Air Force & Commonwealth 1918-1988* compiled by James J Halley. One minor departure, instead of showing the theatre in which they were based, I have shown the country and additional comment. The majority of squadrons, on their return to the United Kingdom, were reduced to a cadre while awaiting disbandment. Those squadrons assigned to bases in Germany were supporting the Allied Occupation Force in the Rhineland. On paper, 14 Squadron, without aircraft, was *en route* from Greece, arriving in England on New Year's day. It is also worth noting that some of the United Kingdom Royal Air Force stations mentioned in the fifth column were still in existence when the Second World War broke out on Sunday, 3rd September 1939, since when such familiar names can be counted on the fingers of one hand. Among the most famous survivors, Waddington is still a very active station.

1 Squadron	Izel-lès-Hameau	France	SE.5a	To London Colney 1 March 1919.
2 Squadron	Genech	France	FK.8	To Bicester 12 February 1919.
3 Squadron	Inchy	France	F.1 Camel	To Wye 15 February 1919.
4 Squadron	Ascq	France	RE.8	To Linselles, 3 February 1919.
5 Squadron	Hangelar	Germany	RE.8/Bristol F.2b	To Bicester 8 September 1919.
6 Squadron	Gerpinnes	Belgium	RE.8/Bristol F.2b	To Sart, 19 March 1919.
7 Squadron	Spich	Germany	RE.8	To Buchheim 11 May 1919.
8 Squadron	Bellevue	France	Bristol F.2b	To Sart 11 May 1919.
9 Squadron	Cognelée	Belgium	RE.8/Bristol F.2b	To Ludendorf 3 January 1919.
10 Squadron	Reckem	France	RE.8	To Ford 17 February 1919.
11 Squadron	Nivelles	Belgium	Bristol F.2b	To Spich 20 May 1919.
12 Squadron	Duren	Germany	RE.8/Bristol F.2b	To Heumar 5 May 1919.
13 Squadron	Vert Galant	France	RE.8	To St Omer 19 January 1919.
15 Squadron	Vignacourt	France	RE.8	To Fowlmere 15 February 1919.
16 Squadron	Auchy	France	RE.8	To Fowlmere 12 February 1919.
17 Squadron	Amber-Koj	Greece	DH.9/F.1 Camel	To San Stephano 28 January 1919.
18 Squadron	Maubeuge	France	DH.9A	To Bickendorf 24 January 1919.
19 Squadron	Abscon	France	5F.1 Dolphin	To Genech 9 February 1919.
20 Squadron	Ossogne	France	Bristol F.2b	To India 30 May 1919.
21 Squadron	Coucou	Belgium	RE.8	To Fowlmere 18 February 1919.
22 Squadron	Nivelles	Belgium	Bristol F.2b	To Spich 21 May 1919.
23 Squadron	Clermont	France	F.5F Dolphin	To Waddington 15 March 1919.
24 Squadron	Bisseghem	Belgium	SE.5a	To London Colney 12 February 1919.
25 Squadron	Maubeuge	France	DH.4/DH.9A	To Bickendorf 26 May 1919.
27 Squadron	Bavay	France	DH.9	To Shotwick 18 March 1919.
28 Squadron	Sarcedo	Italy	F.1 Camel	To Yatesbury 10 March 1919.
29 Squadron	Bickendorf	Germany	SE.5a	To Spittlegate 10 August 1919.
30 Squadron	Kifri	Mesopotamia	Martinsyde G.100	To Baghdad 2 April 1919.
31 Squadron	Risalpur	India	BE.2e/Bristol F.2b	
32 Squadron	Izel-lèz-Hameau	France	SE.5a	To Serny 18 January 1919.
33 Squadron	Kirton Lindsey	England	Avro 504K	To Harpswell 2 June 1919.
34 Squadron	Villaverla	Italy	RE.8	To Caldiero 28 February 1919.
35 Squadron	La Bellevue	France	FK.8/Bristol F.2b	To Ste Marie Cappel 19 January 1919.
36 Squadron	Usworth	England	Bristol F.2b	
37 Squadron	Stow Maries	England	F.1 Came/7F.1 Snipe	To Biggin Hill 17 March 1919.
38 Squadron	Serny	France	FE.2b	To Hawkinge 14 February 1919.
40 Squadron	Orcq	Belgium	SE.5a	To Tangmere 13 February 1919.
41 Squadron	Halluin	France	SE.5a	To Tangmere 7 February 1919.
42 Squadron	Abscon	France	RE.8	To Netheravon 17 February 1919.
43 Squadron	Bickendorf	Germany	7F.1 Snipe	To Eil 12 August 1919.
44 Squadron	Hainault Farm	England	F.1 Camel/7F.1 Snipe	To North Weald 1 July 1919.
45 Squadron	Izel-lès-Hameau	France	F.1 Camel/7F.1 Snipe	To Rendcombe 17 February 1919.
46 Squadron	Baizieux	France	F.1 Camel	To Rendcombe 8 February 1919.
47 Squadron	Janes	Greece	FK.8/DH.9	To Amberkoj 16 February 1919.
48 Squadron	Bickendorf	Germany	Bristol F.2b	To India 26 May 1919.
49 Squadron	Bavai	France	DH.9	To Bickendorf 29 May 1919.
50 Squadron	Bekesbourne	England	SE.5a	
51 Squadron	Marham	England	F.1 Camel	To Suttons Farm 14 May 1919.
52 Squadron	Aulnoye	France	RE.8	To Netheravon 17 February 1919.
53 Squadron	Laneffe	France	RE.8	To Old Sarum 17 March 1919.
54 Squadron	Merchin	France	F.1 Camel	To Yatesbury 17 February 1919.
55 Squadron	St. André-aux-Bois	France	DH.4	To Renfrew 30 January 1919.
56 Squadron	Bethencourt	France	SE.5a	To Narbrough 15 February 1919.
57 Squadron	Spy	Belgium	DH.4	To Morville 7 January 1919.
58 Squadron	Proven	France	HP O/400	To Heliopolis 2 May 1919.
59 Squadron	Gerpinnes	Belgium	Bristol F.2b	To Bickendorf 14 March 1919.
60 Squadron	Inchy	France	SE.5a	To Narborough 28 February 1919.
61 Squadron	Rochford	England	F.1 Camel	
62 Squadron	Nivelles	Belgium	Bristol F.2b	To Spich 2 May 1919.
63 Squadron	Samarra	Mesopotamia	BE.2e/DH.4	To Baghdad 17 February 1919.

70

64 Squadron	Froidmont	France	SE.5a	To Narborough 14 February 1919.
65 Squadron	Bisseghem	Belgium	F.1 Camel	To Yatesbury 12 February 1919.
66 Squadron	San Pietro	Italy	F.1 Camel	To Yatesbury 10 March 1919.
70 Squadron	Bickendorf	Germany	F.1 Camel/7F.1 Snipe	To Spittlegate 3 September 1919.
72 Squadron	Baghdad	Mesopotamia	Bristol M.1c/SE.5a	Left for England 13 February 1919.
73 Squadron	Baizieux	France	F.1 Camel	To Yatesbury 8 February 1919.
74 Squadron	Halluin	France	SE.5a	To Lopcombe Corner 10 February 1919.
75 Squadron	North Weald	England	Avro 504K	
76 Squadron	Ripon	England	Avro 504K	To Helperby 18 March 1919.
77 Squadron	Penston	England	Avro 504K	
78 Squadron	Sutton's Farm	England	F.1 Camel/7F.1 Snipe	
79 Squadron	Bickendorf	Germany	5F.1 Dolphin	
80 Squadron	Stree	Belgium	F.1 Camel/7F.1 Snipe	To Clermont in March 1919.
82 Squadron	Bertangles	France	FK.8	To Shoreham 15 February 1919.
83 Squadron	Serny	France	FE.2d	To Hawkinge 14 February 1919.
84 Squadron	Thuilles	Belgium	SE.5a	To Bickendorf 13 May 1919.
85 Squadron	Ascq	France	SE.5a	To Lopcombe Corner 16 February 1919.
87 Squadron	Boussieres	France	5F.1 Dolphin	To Ternhill 9 February 1919.
88 Squadron	Nivelles	Belgium	Bristol F.2b	
90 Squadron	Buckminster	England	Avro 504K	
91 Squadron	Kenley	England	5F.1 Dolphin	To Lopcombe Corner 7 March 1919.
92 Squadron	Thuilles	Belgium	SE.5a	To Eil 14 June 1919.
94 Squadron	Izel-lès-Hameau	France	SE.5a	To Tadcaster 3 February 1919.
97 Squadron	St. Inglevert	France	HP O/400	To Ford 4 March 1919.
98 Squadron	Marquain	France	DH.9	To Alquines 19 January 1919.
99 Squadron	Aulnoye	France	DH.9A	Left for India in May 1919.
100 Squadron	Ligescourt	France	HP O/400	To St. Imglevert 16 June 1919.
101 Squadron	Morville	France	FE.2d	To Filton 16 March 1919.
102 Squadron	Serny	France	FE.2d	To Lympne 26 March 1919.
103 Squadron	Ronchin	France	DH.9	To Mainsoncelle 25 January 1919.
104 Squadron	Maisoncelle	France	DH.9	To Turnhouse 1 February 1919.
105 Squadron	Omagh	Ireland	Bristol F.2b	To Oranmore 28 January 1919.
106 Squadron	Fermoy	Ireland	RE.8	
107 Squadron	Nivelles	Belgium	DH.9	To Maubeuge 8 January 1919.
108 Squadron	Gondecourt	France	DH.9	To Lympne 16 February 1919.
110 Squadron	Mainsoncelle	France	DH.9/DH.9A	To Tardinghem 1 February 1919.
111 Squadron	Kantara	Egypt	SE.5a	To Ramleh 6 February 1919.
112 Squadron	Throwley	England	F.1 Camel	
113 Squadron	Kantara	Egypt	BE.2e/RE.8	To Ismailia 16 February 1919.
114 Squadron	Lahore	India	BE.2e	To Quetta 26 March 1919.
115 Squadron	St. Inglevert	France	HP O/400	To Ford 4 March 1919.
117 Squadron	Wyton	England	DH.9	To Tallaght 29 March 1919.
120 Squadron	Wyton	England	DH.9	To Hawkinge 20 February 1919.
123 Squadron	Upper Heyford	England	DH.9A	To Shoreham 31 March 1919.
138 Squadron	Chingford	England	Bristol F.2b	
139 Squadron	Grossa	Italy	Bristol F.2b	To Blandford 25 February 1919.
141 Squadron	Biggin Hill	England	Bristol F.2b	To Tallaght 1 March 1919.
142 Squadron	Kantara	Egypt	BE.2e/RE.8/FK.8	To Suez 17 February 1919.
143 Squadron	Detling	England	F.1 Camel	
144 Squadron	Ford	England	*Without aircraft*	
145 Squadron	Kantara	Egypt	SE.5a	To Suez 16 February 1919.
148 Squadron	Serny	France	FE.2d	To Tangmere 17 February 1919.
149 Squadron	Bickendorf	Germany	FE.2d	To Tallaght 26 March 1919.
150 Squadron	Mikra Bay	Greece	Bristol M.1c	To San Stephano 11 June 1919.
151 Squadron	Lièttres	France	F.1 Camel	To Gullane 21 February 1919.
152 Squadron	Lièttres	France	F.1 Camel	To Gullane 21 February 1919.
153 Squadron	Hainault Farm	England	*Without aircraft*	
157 Squadron	Upper Heyford	England	Salamander	
166 Squadron	Bircham Newton	England	HP V/1500	
167 Squadron	Bircham Newton	England	HP V/1500	
185 Squadron	East Fortune	Scotland	Cuckoo	
186 Squadron	HMS *Argus*		Avro 504K *various*	
187 Squadron	East Retford	England	Avro 504K *various*	
188 Squadron	Throwley	England	Avro 504K *various*	
189 Squadron	Sutton's Farm	England	Avro 504K *various*	
190 Squadron	Upwood	England	Avro 504K *various*	
191 Squadron	Upwood	England	FE.2b/BE.2c	
192 Squadron	Newmarket	England	FE.2b/FE.2d	
199 Squadron	Harpswell	England	FE.2b	
201 Squadron	Bethencourt	France	F.1 Camel/7F.1 Snipe	To Lake Down 15 February 1919.
202 Squadron	Varssenaere	Belgium	DH.4	To Driffield 24 March 1919.
203 Squadron	Orcq	Belgium	F.1 Camel	To Boisdinghem 18 January 1919.
204 Squadron	Heule	France	F.1 Camel	To Waddington 7 February 1919.
205 Squadron	Maubeuge	France	DH.4/DH.9	To La Luveterie 9 January 1919.
206 Squadron	Bickendorf	Germany	DH.9/DH.9A	To Maubeuge 27 May 1919.
207 Squadron	Carvin	France	HP O/400	To Merheim 1 January 1919.
208 Squadron	Stree	Belgium	7F.1 Snipe	To Heumar 23 May 1919.
209 Squadron	Froidmont	France	F.1 Camel	To Scopwick 13 February 1919.
210 Squadron	Boussieres	France	F.1 Camel	To Scopwick 17 February 1919.
211 Squadron	Thuilles	Belgium	DH.9	To Wyton 15 March 1919.
212 Squadron	Great Yarmouth	England	DH.4/DH.9	To Swingate Down 7 March 1919.

213 Squadron	Stalhille	Belgium	F.1 Camel	To Scopwick 19 March 1919.
214 Squadron	Chemy	France	HP O/400	Left for Egypt 3 July 1919.
215 Squadron	Alquines	France	HP O/400	To Ford 2 February 1919.
216 Squadron	Marquise	France	HP O/400	To Qantara 3/19 July 1919.
217 Squadron	Varssenaere	Belgium	DH.4	To Driffield 28 March 1919.
218 Squadron	Vert Galant	France	DH.9	To Hucknall 7 February 1919.
219 Squadron	Westgate and Manston	England	*Various*	
220 Squadron	Imbros	Aegean	DH.4/DH.9	To Mudros during February 1919.
221 Squadron	*En route* to Russia		DH.9/DH.9A	To Petrovsk 15 January 1919.
222 Squadron	Mudros	Aegean	*Various*	
223 Squadron	Mudros	Aegean	*Various*	
224 Squadron	Pizonne	Italy	DH.4/DH.9	
228 Squadron	Great Yarmouth	England	F.2A	To Killingholme 5 June 1919.
229 Squadron	Great Yarmouth	England	*Various*	To Killingholme 3 March 1919.
230 Squadron	Felixstowe	England	*Various*	
231 Squadron	Felixstowe	England	F.2A/F.3/F.5	
232 Squadron	Felixstowe	England	F.2A/F.3	
233 Squadron	Dover	England	*Various*	
234 Squadron	Tresco	England	*Various*	
235 Squadron	Newlyn	England	Short 184	
236 Squadron	Mullion	England	DH.6/DH.9	
237 Squadron	Cattewater	England	Short 184	
238 Squadron	Cattewater	England	*Various*	
239 Squadron	Torquay	England	Short 184	
240 Squadron	Calshot	England	*Various*	
241 Squadron	Portland and Chickerell	England	*Various*	
242 Squadron	Newhaven	England	Short 184/DH.6	
243 Squadron	Cherbourg	France	Short 184/Wight	
244 Squadron	Bangor	Wales	DH.6	
245 Squadron	Fishguard	Wales	Short 184/Baby	
246 Squadron	Seaton Carew	England	Short 184	
247 Squadron	Felixstowe	England	F.2A/F.3	
248 Squadron	Hornsea Mere	England	Short 184	
249 Squadron	Dundee	Scotland	*Various*	To Killingholme 3 May 1919.
250 Squadron	Padstow	England	DH.6/DH.9	
251 Squadron	Hornsea	England	DH.6/DH.9	To Killingholme 31 January 1919.
252 Squadron	Tynemouth	England	DH.6	To Killingholme 31 January 1919.
253 Squadron	Bembridge	England	*Various*	
254 Squadron	Prawle Point	England	DH.6/DH.9	
255 Squadron	Pembroke	Wales	DH.6	
256 Squadron	Sea Houses	England	DH.6	To Killingholme 31 January 1919.
257 Squadron	Dundee	Scotland	F.2A/Campania	
258 Squadron	Luce Bay	Scotland	DH.6	
259 Squadron	Felixstowe	England	F.2A/F.3	
260 Squadron	Westward Ho	England	DH.6/DH.9	
261 Squadron	Felixstowe	England	F.2A/F.3	
263 Squadron	Taranto	Italy	*Various*	
264 Squadron	Calafrana	Malta	Short 184	
265 Squadron	Gibraltar		Short 184/F.3	
266 Squadron	Mudros	Aegean	*Various*	To Petrovsk 10 March 1919.
267 Squadron	Calafrana	Malta	*Various*	
268 Squadron	Calafrana	Malta	Short 184/Short 320	
269 Squadron	Alexandria	Egypt	*Various*	
270 Squadron	Alexandria	Egypt	*Various*	
271 Squadron	Otranto	Italy	Short 184/F.3	
272 Squadron	Machnhanish	Scotland	DH.6	
273 Squadron	Great Yarmouth	England	*Various*	
274 Squadron	Seaton Carew	England	HP V/1500	To Bircham Newton 15 June 1919.

Appendix 1D - A Comparison Between the F.1 Camel and the SE.5a

The Camel and the SE.5a were two outstanding scout aircraft of the *Great War*, both types being produced in large numbers. Including all variants, approximately 5,490 of the former rolled off the productions lines and were in service from May 1917 [the first examples reaching the Royal Naval Air Service squadron ahead of their Royal Flying Corps counterparts which began to equip in June 1917], until January 1920, when it was withdrawn from Royal Air Force service. The Royal Aircraft Factory designed SE.5a [the first 77 airframes were designated SE.5, with the remainder of production totalling over 5,000 airframes having a more powerful engine and designated SE.5a] entered service a few months earlier than the Camel and for the novice scout pilot was a far easier aircraft to handle than the inherently unstable Sopwith design. Regarding the date of issue, for some serials this was the first time its identity had appeared on a squadron return. For as complete a picture as possible, I have included dates and incidents prior to the 1st of April 1918. An asterisk against a serial shows it was issued to the squadron on two or more occasions, or it received a new airframe serial either during its time with the squadron, or as a result of being rebuilt at a repair facility. Likewise, an asterisk placed ahead of the serial identifies a rebuilt aircraft. Against a name it indicates the pilot was involved in more than one incident, and against a date draws attention to an aircraft that failed to return with the entire entry in italics for further emphasis. A double asterisk against a date shows the pilot was killed, or died from his wounds. Note. I have omitted the handful of examples of paper issues between 80 Squadron and 73 Squadron which occurred at the end of March and beginning of April 1918.

No 80 Squadron came into existence at Montrose on 1 August 1917, earmarked for scout duties on the Western Front and to be equipped with Sopwith F.1 Camels. On 1 November, the squadron moved south to Beverley and thence to France and St.Omer on 20 February 1918. Post-armistice, the squadron commenced converting to the Sopwith 7F.1 Snipe in readiness for deployment to the Middle East, but a handful of F.1 Camels were still on establishment at the turn of the year with some examples still remaining in February 1919.

Serial	Date of issue and disposal	Remarks	Aircraft/kite balloons destroyed
B6264	01.11.17 - 06.11.17	Crashed and struck off charge the same day.	
B6265	01.11.17 - ?	Disposed to 73 Training Squadron Turnhouse.	
B9165	14.12.17 - 24.12.17	Crashed [2Lt H N S Anderson killed].	
B9173	14.12.17 - 01.07.18	Disposed to 2 Aeroplane Supply Depot.	
B9175	14.12.17 - ?	Disposed to 44 Squadron.	
B9171*	20.12.17 - 25.01.18	Disposed to 4 Aeroplane Acceptance Park Lincoln	
B9209	27.12.17 - 17.03.18**	*Failed to return [Captain St. Clair C Tayler MC killed].*	4
B9179	20.12.17 - 26.03.18**	*Failed to return [Captain D D G Hall MC died from wounds].*	
C6709	20.12.17 - 28.02.18	Crashed; repaired and reissued [2Lt J L Holt].*	
B9170	12.17 - 12.17	Crashed; no further details.	
B9223	04.01.18 - 25.03.18**	*Failed to return [2Lt R S F D Radcliff killed].*	
B9239	13.01.18 - 24.03.18	Crashed in forced-landing [2Lt W A Pell].*	
B9185	03.02.18 - 19.02.18**	*Failed to return [2Lt S R Pinder].*	
B9323	03.02.18 - 27.06.18	Crashed on landing [2Lt V S Bennett].*	
B9171*	09.02.18 - 19.02.18*	*Failed to return [2Lt E Westmoreland reported as a prisoner of war].*	
B9205	09.02.18 - 21.03.18	Crashed [2Lt R M Lees killed]	
B9219	09.02.18 - 16.07.18	Crashed [Captain R A Preeston].*	
B9229	09.02.18 - 17.03.18**	*Failed to return [2Lt J L Holt killed].*	
B9235	09.02.18 - 10.07.18	Crashed on landing; repaired and reissued as F6314 [2Lt J A C Randall].*	
B9243	09.02.18 - 10.05.18	Damaged on operations; repaired and reissued as F6064 [Lt T S Nash].	
B9247	09.02.18 - 01.04.18	Crashed on take off [2Lt O C Bridgeman].	1
B9255	09.02.18 - 27.03.18	Crashed and burnt out.	
B9237	09.02.18 - 31.05.18	Crashed in forced-landing; repaired and reissued as F6148 [Lt L C Welford].*	
B9293	09.02.18 - 16.04.18	Crashed [Captain H A Whistler].	
B9325	09.02.18 - 15.03.18	Crashed on take off [2Lt D Gardiner].*	1
C1557	20.02.18 - 21.02.18**	*Failed to return [2Lt R C Brown killed].*	
B9181	23.02.18 - 24.03.18	Crashed on landing [2Lt W A Pell].*	
C6719	26.02.18 - 10.03.18*	*Failed to return [2Lt C H Flere reported as a prisoner of war].*	
C1581	28.02.18 - 12.03.18	Crashed; repaired and reissued [2Lt C S L Coulson].*	
C1665	04.03.18 - 12.03.18	Crashed on landing [2Lt G Miller].	
C1651	11.03.18 - 17.03.18	Crashed [2Lt H R Jones killed].	
B2456	13.03.18 - 21.03.18*	*Failed to return [2Lt C S L Coulson safe].*	
B2479	14.03.18 - 06.04.18*	*Failed to return [2Lt E L Smithers reported as a prisoner of war}.*	
B5420	16.03.18 - 21.03.18	Flying accident; repaired and reissued [2Lt D Gardiner].*	
B898	17.03.18 - 22.03.18	Flying accident; repaired and reissued [2Lt D Gardiner].*	
C1673	18.03.18 - 27.03.18	Damaged during operations; repaired and reissued.	
C6724	18.03.18 - 25.03.18*	*Failed to return [2Lt G Miller missing - possibly died from wounds].*	
B4617	22.03.18 - 21.04.18*	*Failed to return [2Lt A L Code wounded but safe].*	
B5154	22.03.18 - 12.04.18**	*Failed to return [2Lt G L Murray killed].*	
C1693	22.03.18 - 26.03.18	Crashed and later burnt during retreat [2Lt C S L Coulson].*	
D6419	22.03.18 - 10.05.18**	*Failed to return [2Lt G A Whateley killed].*	
C1635	24.03.18 - 27.03.18	Crashed in forced-landing [2Lt C S L Coulson].*	
B2311	27.03.18 - 30.03.18	Flying accident; repaired and reissued [2Lt J R Orr].*	
C1699	27.03.18 - 12.04.18*	*Failed to return [2Lt W A Pell reported as a prisoner of war].*	1
D6457	27.03.18 - 10.05.18*	*Failed to return [2Lt A V Jones reported as a prisoner of war].*	
C1681	31.03.18 - 01.04.18**	*Failed to return [2Lt J J Meredith killed].*	
B2524	01.04.18 - 16.06.18*	*Failed to return [2Lt G H Glasspoole reported as a prisoner of war].*	
B5587	01.04.18 - 29.04.18	Crashed on landing; repaired and reissued [2Lt M V Barker]. [See 05.07.18].	
B7322	01.04.18 - 10.05.18	Crashed on landing; repaired and reissued [Lt C S L Coulson].*	1
C1683	01.04.18 - 12.04.18*	*Failed to return [2Lt A L Code injured].*	

C1687	01.04.18 - 26.07.18	Crashed on landing [Lt E O'C Parsons].	
C6723	01.04.18 - 23.04.18	Crashed; repaired and reissued.	
D6507	01.04.18 - 26.07.18	Crashed in forced-landing [2Lt V G Brindley].*	1
D6481	02.04.18 - 09.07.18	Crashed on landing; repaired and reissued as F6199 [Captain O C Bridgeman].	5
D6495	13.04.18 - 25.04.18	Crashed on landing; repaired and reissued [2Lt A W Chadwick].	
D6499	13.04.18 - 20.05.18	Crashed on landing [Lr J R Paisley injured].	
B5447	17.04.18 - 17.04.18	Crashed during delivery; salvaged, repaired and reissued [2Lt C G S Shields].*	
D6591/V	22.04.18 - 10.05.18*	*Failed to return [2Lt H V Barker safe].*	
D6619	02.05.18 - 10.05.18**	*Failed to return [Lt C G S Shields killed].*	
B2429	27.04.18 - 19.05.18*	*Failed to return [2Lt J Patenaude reported as a prisoner of war].*	
B7346	08.05.18 - 24.07.18	Disposed to 5 Air Issues and thence to England.	5
B5639	11.05.18 - 16.05.18	Crashed on landing; repaired and reissued as F6147 [Lt A J Patenaude].*	
B9191	11.05.18 - 22.05.18	Crashed on landing; repaired and reissued as F6182 [Lt C S Dunn].	
C1647	11.05.18 - 11.08.18	Crashed on landing [2Lt R E Thompson].*	1
D6581	11.05.18 - 25.07.18	Crashed on take off [2Lt H E Hudson].	
D6611	11.05.18 - 14.06.18	Crashed on take off [Lr W R Archibald]	
D6633/N	11.05.18 - 29.06.18	Crashed on landing [2Lt L L McFaul injured].*	
B7294	13.05.18 - 07.06.18**	*Failed to return [Lt L C Welford died from injuries].*	
B6235	15.05.18 - 31.05.18	Crashed; repaired and reissued as F6105 [2Lt H W Russell].*	
D1849/M	20.05.18 - 08.07.18	Crashed on take off [Lt J A McGill].*	2
D6597	21.05.18 - 14.06.18*	*Failed to return [2Lt P R Beare wounded].*	
B7292/B	25.05.18 - 15.09.18	Disposed to a repair facility; no further information.	3
C8232	25.05.18 - 01.06.18	Crashed on landing [2Lt E G Hayes].*	
D1831	25.05.18 - 09.07.18	Crashed on landing; repaired and reissued as F6211 [Lt L K Baker].	1
D1839	25.05.18 - 25.06.18	Crashed on take off; repaired and reissued as F5986 [Lt E N Ruffle].*	
D6463	25.05.18 - 10.07.18**	*failed to return [Lt L L McFaul killed].*	
D1777	31.05.18 - 26.06.18**	*Failed to return {2Lt B Critchley died from wounds].*	
D6414	01.06.18 - 04.06.18	Crashed [Lt L C Welford].*	
D6420	01.06.18 - 14.06.18**	*Failed to return [2Lt A R Melbourne killed].*	
C8254	02.06.18 - 17.07.18*	*Failed to return [2Lt E G Hayes safe].*	1
C8203	09.06.18 - 15.07.18	Crashed on landing [Lt W A Hallgren].*	1
D1797	09.06.18 - 16.06.18	Crashed on landing [2Lt W G Hales].	
B2396	15.06.18 - 08.08.18**	*Failed to return [2Lt H E Hudson killed].*	
C1623	15.06.18 - 02.09.18	Crashed in forced-landing; repaired and reissued as F6297 [2Lt R A H Shelford].	1
D9429	17.06.18 - 09.08.18**	Failed *to return [Lt J R Orr killed].*	
D9431	17.06.18 - 16.08.18	Crashed on landing; repaired and reissued as F6269 [2Lt R E Thompson].*	
D9433	24.06.18 - 04.09.18	Crashed on landing [2Lt R E Thompson].*	
B6335	27.06.18 - 11.07.18	Crashed on landing [2Lt E N Ruffle].*	
B9133	27.06.18 - 25.08.18	Wrecked on the ground.	
B5599	29.06.18 - 03.07.18	Crashed on landing; repaired and reissued as H7280 [2Lt W A Hallgren].*	
C8205	29.06.18 - 15.07.18	Crashed in forced-landing [Lt E N Ruffle].*	1
D6530	30.06.18 - 04.07.18	Crashed on landing; repaired and reissued as F6312 [2Lt H N Price].	
D6453	05.07.18 - 08.08.18*	*Failed to return [2Lt G Wignall safe].*	
B7434	09.07.18 - 14.09.18	Hit by anti-aircraft fire and crashed [Major F J Tanner injured].*	1
B5587	05.07.18 - 08.08.18**	*Failed to return [Lt T S Nash died from wounds].*	
B5241	10.07.18 - 17.07.18	Crashed in forced-landing [Lt V S Bennett].*	
B7199	10.07.18 - 13.08.18	Crashed on landing; repaired and reissued as F6261 [Lt A W Chadwick].	
D6657	11.07.18 - 08.08.18	Crashed; repaired and reissued as F6241 [Lt J R Rogers].	
D9501	11.07.18 - 04.09.18*	*Failed to return [2Lt E O Champagne safe].*	
F2154	11.07.18 - 25.08.18	Crashed on landing; repaired and reissued as H6854 [Major F J Tanner].*	
*F5922	11.07.18 - 20.07.18	Crashed in forced-landing [Lt H J Welch].*	
D6663	17.07.18 - 31.07.18	Crashed in forced-landing [Lt H W Russell].*	
F6148	17.07.18 - 25.07.18	Damaged on operations [2Lt W A Hallgren wounded].*	
*F6151	17.07.18 - 30.08.18	Crashed in forced landing [2Lt V G Brindley killed].*	
*F5921	19.07.18 - 02.10.18*	*Failed to return [2Lt J E Jennings reported as a prisoner of war].*	
*F5927	20.07.18 - 31.08.18	Crashed in forced-landing [[Lt G B Wootten].*	1
D9449	21.07.18 - 12.10.18	Damaged on operations [2Lt H P Sharkey safe].*	
D9485	24.07.18 - 30.10.18*	*Failed to return [Lt R C Fyson safe].*	8
D9483	26.07.18 - 06.09.18**	*Failed to return [Lt J A McGill killed].*	
*F5930	26.07.18 - 12.10.18	Crashed on landing [2Lt J H Waddington].*	
C8335	28.07.18 - 10.08.18	Crashed on landing; repaired and reissued as F6287 [Lt J A C Randall].*	
D9467	28.07.18 - 10.10.18	Crashed on landing [2Lt J Lightoller].	
F2085	07.18 - 02.08.18	Disposed to 51 Wing.	
*F5949	01.08.18 - 16.11.18	Still on establishment.	
F2133	04.08.18 - 05.09.18*	*Failed to return [2Lt A R Thatcher reported as a prisoner of war].*	
E5177	08.08.18 - 27.08.18	Damaged on operations; repaired and reissued as H6855 [2Lt H W Phear wounded].	
*F5924	08.08.18 - 07.09.18	Crashed in forced-landing [2Lt H Walker].*	
*F5954	08.08.18 - 04.10.18**	*Failed to return [2Lt T Whitman killed].*	
*F5956	08.08.18 - 15.08.18	Crashed on take off [2Lt G Smith killed].*	
*F5964	08.08.18 - 12.08.18	Crashed on landing [2Lt G Smith].*	
F6182	08.08.18 - 13.08.18	Crashed on landing; repaired and reissued [2Lt J A C Randall].*	
*F5931	13.08.18 - 23.09.18	Crashed on landing; repaired and reissued as H6875 [2Lt H N Jubb].*	
*F6184	13.08.18 - 15.09.18	Crashed in forced-landing; repaired and reissued as H6840 [2Lt A E Watson].	
F1969	16.08.18 - 22.08.18**	*Failed to return [2Lt A L Tupman killed].*	
F1967	17.08.18 - 04.09.18	Crashed in forced-landing [Lt G A Hodgetts].*	
F2170	23.08.18 - 02.09.18	Crashed in forced-landing; repaired and reissued [Captain R A Preeston].*	
F1968	26.08.18 - 01.19	Still on establishment.	1
F1975	26.08.18 - 26.09.18**	*Failed to return [2Lt H Walker killed].*	
*F5989	26.08.18 - 14.09.18	Crashed in forced-landing; repaired and reissued as H6863 [2Lt T Whitman].*	
F2156	30.08.18 - 25.09.18	Crashed on landing [2Lt F Chalcroft].	
F2143	31.08.18 - 05.09.18	Damaged on operations; disposed to 2 Aircraft Salvaged Depot [2Lt G B Wootten].*	

F6306	31.08.18 - 17.09.18	Crashed on landing [Lt J R Andrews].	
C3378	05.09.18 - 10.10.18	Crashed in forced-landing [2Lt J H Waddington].*	
F2174	05.09.18 - 23.09.18**	*Failed to return [2Lt F A Fairburn killed].*	
F2177	05.09.18 - 06.10.18*	*Failed to return [2Lt O V Judkins reported as a prisoner of war].*	
*F6026	05.09.18 - 01.10.18*	*Failed to return [2Lt R E Thompson reported as a prisoner of war].*	
F6309	06.09.18 - 16.09.18	Crashed in forced-landing [2Lt H N Jubb}.*	
F6307	07.09.18 - 26.09.18	Still on establishment; no further trace.	
F2139	13.09.18 - 04.11.18	Damaged on operations; repaired and reissued as H6897 [2Lt G A Hodgetts].*	
C3377	15.09.18 - 26.09.18	Wrecked on the ground.	
F1965	15.09.18 - 30.10.18	Crashed on landing [Lt H W Russell DFC].*	
*F6056	15.09.18 - 15.11.18	Still on establishment.	
*F6188	15.09.18 - 22.09.18**	*Failed to return [Captain H J Welch killed].*	1
F1990	18.09.18 - 04.10.18**	*Failed to return [Lt J Winthrop-Andrews killed].*	
*F6224	18.09.18 - 05.10.18*	*Failed to return [2Lt E E Middleton safe].*	
H831	19.09.18 - 30.10.18*	*Failed to return [2Lt G B Wootten wounded].*	
F2001	25.09.18 - 28.01.19	Still on establishment.	
*F6244/Y	28.09.18 - 22.01.19	Still on establishment.	
H750	28.09.18 - 22.10.18	Midair collision with F6412 [2Lt G P McCaig safe].	
H770	28.09.18 - 28.09.19	Disposed to 2 Aeroplane Supply Depot.	
*H7274	09.18 - 29.09.18**	*Failed to return [2Lt R Bramwell killed].*	
H765	01.10.18 - 04.10.18	Wrecked on the ground.	
H773	01.10.18 - 12.02.19	Crashed on landing [2Lt H R Messinger injured].*	1
C8378	02.10.18 - 17.11.18	Disposed to 2 Air Issues.	
C8380	03.10.18 - 04.10.18	Crashed on landing [2Lt H C R Grant].	
C8382	05.10.18 - 09.11.18	Disposed to 2 Air Issues.	
*F6251	05.10.18 - 08.10.18	Damaged on operations; repaired and reissued [2Lt H R Messinger].*	1
H752	05.10.18 - 28.02.19	Disposed to 2 Aeroplane Supply Depot.	
C8363	08.10.18 - 28.01.19	Disposed; squadron now equipped with 7F.1 Snipe.	
C8364	08.10.18 - 28.02.19	Disposed; squadron now equipped with 7F.1 Snipe.	
C8376	08.10.18 - 22.01.19	Disposed; squadron now equipped with 7F.1 Snipe.	
C8385	10.10.18 - 30.10.18*	*Failed to return [2Lt W C Kinnesten safe].*	
*F6241	13.10.18 - 25.10.18	Crashed in forced landing [2Lt H P Sharkey].*	
F6412	13.10.18 - 22.10.18	Midair collision with H750 [2Lt J H Waddington killed].*	
C8387	17.10.18 - 22.10.18*	*Failed to return [2Lt T M MacIntyre safe].*	
F6261	24.10.18 - 08.11.18*	*Failed to return [Lt H W Russell DFC reported as a prisoner of war].*	
H800	24.10.18 - 28.01.19	Still on establishment.	
*F6292	30.10.18 - 04.11.18	Damaged on operations [2Lt G A Muschamp safe].	
*F6110	02.11.18 - 04.11.18*	*Failed to return [Lt R C Fyson wounded].*	
*H6848	02.11.18 - 28.01.19	Still on establishment.	
*H7091	02.11.18 - 28.01.19	Still on establishment.	
F6287	07.11.18 - 15.11.18*	Crashed on landing [2Lt H P Sharkey}.*	
*H6851/C	07.11.18 - 24.12.18	Crashed on landing [2Lt W A Hammerton].*	
*H6852	09.11.18 - 28.01.19	Still on establishment.	
*H6856	15.11.18 - 28.01.19	Still on establishment.	
*H7086	15.11.18 - 28.01.19	Still on establishment.	

Total number of aircraft issued, either from new, rebuilt with a new serial and reissued and rebuilt airframes: 276

No 64 Squadron commenced re-equipping with SE.5a early in 1918, and retained the type throughout the remainder of the *Great War.* Typical of a scout squadron, the table serves as an illustration of how the type fared in the vagaries of flying on the Western Front.

Serial	Dates of issue and disposal	Remarks	Aircraft/kite balloons destroyed
B4852	12.01.18 - 24.02.18	Disposed to 2 Air Issues for re-allotment.	
C9499	12.01.18 - 12.01.18	Crashed in forced-landing during delivery from 1 Air Issues [Lt Blythe].*	
B673	20.01.18 - 19.03.18	Damaged by gunfire [2Lt J F T Barrett].*Disposed to a Repair Park.	
B674/W	20.01.18 - 03.06.18	Unserviceable; disposed to 1 Air Issues and thence to United Kingdom.	1
B8276	20.01.18 - 23.03.18	Crashed [2Lt E E Ashton].	
B8296	20.01.18 - 11.03.18	Damaged in combat [2Lt J W Bell wounded]. Disposed to a Repair Park.*	
C6356	20.01.18 - 26.03.18	Crashed on landing [Lt R C Hardie].	
B76	22.01.18 - 06.05.18	Major B E Smythies aircraft; disposed to 41 Squadron.	2
B4866/1	23.01.18 - 01.05.18	Unserviceable; disposed to a repair facility and thence to England.	
B7770/V	23.01.18 - 23.04.18	Disposed to 41 Squadron.	
C1755	23.01.18 - 08.03.18	Undercarriage collapsed after landing [Captain E R Tempest].*	1
C9499	23.01.18 - 23.01.18	Crashed into a shell hole during delivery from 1 Air Issues [Lt Blythe].*	
C9603/3	23.01.18 - 06.05.18	Disposed to 41 Squadron.	3
C9604	23.01.18 - 08.05.18	Wrecked on the ground [Lt A C Hendry].	
C9605	23.01.18 - 13.03.18	Crashed [2Lt V W Thompson].*	
B684/V	28.01.18 - 17.03.18	Damaged by anti-aircraft fire [2Lt P S Burge].*Disposed to a Repair Park.	
B697	28.01.18 - 03.05.18	Crashed on landing [Lt W P Southwell].	
B8263	28.01.18 - 02.05.18	Crashed on landing [Lt J J Carroll].*	1
B8264/X	28.01.18 - 08.03.18*	*Failed to return [2Lt H R Topliss wounded and made a prisoner of war].*	
C9493/B	28.01.18 - 18.04.18	Unserviceable; disposed to a repair facility and thence to England.	1
C9602	28.01.18 - 25.03.18	Crashed on landing [2Lt E E Ashton].	1
B147/U/X	24.02.18 - 21.04.18	Unserviceable; struck off charge 25.04.18.	
C6398/X	09.03.18 - 25.03.18	Crashed on landing [2Lt B A Walkerdine].*	
C5392	13.03.18 - 02.05.18	Unserviceable; struck off charge 08.05.18.	2
C5390	14.03.18 - 17.03.18	Crashed on take off [2Lt V W Thompson].*	
C5393	15.03.18 - 11.05.18	Disposed to 41 Squadron.	
B143	09.03.18 - 13.03.18	Crashed and turned over [Captain E R Tempest].*	
D3430	15.03.18 - 20.03.18	Crashed in forced-landing [2Lt C B Stringer injured].	
B124	18.03.18 - 29.04.18	Crashed on landing [Lt D Lloyd-Evans].*	3

B125/Y	18.03.18 - 25.04.18	Crashed on take off [2Lt M L Howard].*	2
B58	24.03.18 - 13.06.18	Undercarriage collapsed after landing [Captain P S Burge].*	5
B74	22.03.18 - 30.08.18	Forced-landed in tranches and wrecked [Lt D Lloyd-Evans].*	6
C1100	26.03.18 - 02.05.18	Wrecked [2Lt J F T Barrett].*	
D289	26.03.18 - 06.07.18	Crashed in forced-landing [Lt J F T Barrett].*	6
B7796	27.03.18 - 15.04.18	Disposed to 1 Aeroplane Supply Depot.	
B2	17.04.18 - 03.05.18	Forced-landed in trenches and wrecked [2Lt W C Daniel].*	1
C9517	20.04.18 - 04.07.18	Crashed in forced-landing [Lt A S Rawlinson].	3
B132/V	23.04.18 - 22.05.18*	*Failed to return [Lt G A Rainier reported as a prisoner of war].*	1
C6447/1	25.04.18 - 14.07.18*	*Failed to return [2Lt B N Garrett reported as a prisoner of war].*	1
C6448	25.04.18 - 31.05.18	Crashed in forced-landing [Lt J J Carroll].*	3
B8492/3	03.05.18 - 08.05.18	Forced-landed in trenches [2Lt B A Walkerdine].*	
C1860	03.05.18 - 02.09.18	Crashed on landing [2Lt W A F Cowgill].*	6
B8498	03.05.18 - 07.09.18	Crashed [Lt A W Elliott injured].	
C6461	03.05.18 - 08.05.18	Crashed in forced-landing [Lt W H Farrow].	
D336/5	03.05.18 - 18.05.18	Damaged in combat [2Lt W C Daniel].*	
C6418/2	04.05.18 - 30.06.18	Crashed in forced-landing [Lt M L Howard]. *	1
C6470/4	04.05.18 - 18.05.18	Damaged in combat [2Lt W P Southall].*	2
B8488	06.05.18 - 09.08.18	Crashed [Sgt A S Cowlishaw].	2
B7786	09.05.18 - 18.07.18	Crashed in forced-landing [2Lt G W Schermerhorn].*	5
C1857/3	09.05.18 - 15.07.18	Crashed in forced-landing [2Lt B A Walkerdine].*	
C1859	09.05.28 - 16.05.18	Forced-landed with structural damage [Lt S B Reece].*	
C6402	09.05.18 - 17.06.18	Crashed on landing [2Lt G W Schermehorn].*	
B8516	11.05.18 - 18.05.18	Crashed in forced-landing [Lt J J Carroll].*	
B7737	18.05.18 - 21.05.18*	*Failed to return [Lt S B Reece*reported as a prisoner of war].*	
B7765/5	19.05.18 - 27.06.18	Crashed on landing [Lt J A Van Tilburg].*	
C6455	19.05.18 - 28.05.18**	*Failed to return [2Lt W P Southall killed].*	
C6471	19.05.18 - 22.05.18	Crashed in forced-landing [Lt G Wood].	
C1880	22.05.18 - 08.07.18	Crashed on landing [Lt A M Stahl]*	2
D6861	25.05.18 - 16.08.18	Unserviceable; struck off charge 22.08.18.	5
D6865	25.05.18 - 13.07.18	Crashed during operations {Lt G W Wood].	
C6475	28.05.18 - 25.07.18**	*Failed to return [Lt M L Howard died from wounds].*	3
C6476	01.06.18 - 02.06.18	Crashed on landing [Lt W J Cockburn injured].	
C1817	04.06.18 - 17.08.18	Forced landed in trenches [Lt J K Chatham].	
C6487	04.06.18 - 08.07.18	Crashed on landing [2Lt G W Schermehorn].*	
D6900	14.06.18 - 24.07.18**	*Failed to return [Captain P S Burge MC killed].*	3
E1292	18.06.18 - 08.07.18	Crashed on landing [Captain W H Farrow].	
D6901	28.06.18 - 30.06.18	Crashed in forced-landing [Lt J A Van Tilburg].*	
C1122	01.07.18 - 11.08.18	Crashed on landing [Lt L E Bickel].	1
C1929	01.07.18 - 25.07.18*	*Failed to return [2Lt W R Henderson reported as a prisoner of war].*	2
E1354	05.07.18 - 25.08.18	Crashed on landing [Lt J K Chatham].	
C8734	06.07.18 - 25.07.18	Damaged in combat [Lt A S Barrett].	
D6907	09.07.18 - 10.08.18	Crashed on landing [Lt A M Stahl].*	
E5941/U	09.07.18 - 02.11.18	Damaged on operations [Lt J W Bell].*	1
C8733	10.07.18 - 17.07.18	Crashed in forced-landing [2Lt G W Schermerhorn].*	
E3921	16.07.18 - 19.07.18*	*Failed to return [Lt J A Van Tilburg reported as a prisoner of war]. *	
D6929	28.07.18 - 04.09.18	Crashed in forced-landing [Captain A F Buck].	1
E1391	14.07.18 - 04.09.18	Crashed on landing [Lt T Ross].	1
E1392	15.07.18 - 04.09.18	Crashed in forced-landing [Lt S H Arding].	1
E3918	19.07.18 - 25.08.18	Crashed on landing [Lt A T Sheldrake].*	1
E3920	20.07.18 - 03.08.18	Crashed in forced-landing [2Lt G W Schermehorn].*	
D6930	28.07.18 - 18.09.18	Crashed on landing [Lt Watson].	
D6931	28.07.18 - 12.08.18	Wrecked on the ground.	
D6945	28.07.18 - 20.09.18	Crashed in forced-landing during operations [2Lt H F V Battle wounded].	
D6952	28.07.18 - 30.09.18	Unserviceable. Disposed to a repair facility and thence to England.	6
E5977/5	28.07.18 - 31.08.18**	*Failed to return [Captain T St P Bunbury killed].*	
E5988/N	06.08.18 - 31.12.18	Unserviceable; returned to England.	2
D6978	10.08.18 - 26.08.18	Forced-landed during operations [Lt J B Edwards}.	1
C9244	11.08.18 - 29.09.18	Crashed on landing [2Lt G W Graham]*	
D6988	11.08.18 - 04.09.18	Midair collision [Lt T G Sifton injured].	
C9061/4	14.08.18 - 29.08.18**	*Failed to return [2Lt E A Parnell killed].*	
E4002/Z	21.08.18 - 04.09.18*	*Failed to return [Lt H T McKinnie wounded].*	
C6456/C	24.08.18 - 30.08.18*	*Failed to return [2Lt R B Luard reported as a prisoner of war].*	
B7900/B	26.08.18 - 28.09.18**	*Failed to return [2Lt A T Sheldrake killed].*	
C1874	27.08.18 - 02.10.18	Forced-landed in shell holes [2Lt J B Forrester].	1
E1273/V	27.08.18 - 04.09.18**	*Failed to return [Lt A M Stahl killed]. *	
E1271/4	30.08.18 - 19.12.18	Crashed on take off [Lt A Youell].	
E1270	31.08.18 - 02.09.18	Crashed in forced-landing [Captain D Lloyd-Evans].*	
E4100	01.09.18 - 04.10.18	Damaged on operations [Captain D Lloyd-Evans].*	
E5979/5	01.09.18 - 04.09.18*	*Failed to return [Lt V Harley reported as a prisoner of war].*	
C1909/D	03.09.18 - 05.09.18*	*Failed to return [2Lt W A F Cowgill*reported as a prisoner of war].*	
C1135/Z	05.09.18 - 30.10.18*	*Failed to return [2Lt T A Priestley wounded].*	
C9191	05.09.18 - 05.10.18	Crashed on take off [Lt J A Massey injured].	
D6030/Y	05.09.18 - 17.09.18*	*Failed to return [Lt W W Chreiman reported as a prisoner of war].*	
E4003/F	05.09.18 - 30.12.18	Crashed on take off [Lt H G Yerg injured].	
E4083	05.09.18 - 23.09.18	Crashed in forced-landing [Lt H C Hayes].	
F6427*	05.09.18 - 23.09.18	Renumbered H7254.	
F6431*	05.09.18 - 23.09.18	Renumbered H7259.	
F6432*	05.09.18 - 23.09.18	Renumbered H7260.	
F5452/3/A	05.09.18 - 01.11.18	Crashed on take off [Lt F Fawcett injured].	
E6011	10.09.18 - 07.10.18	Crashed on landing [Lt C A Sperry].	

F5510	18.09.18 - 08.10.18	Crashed in forced-landing [Lt A S G Rodway].
C9242	20.09.18 - 04.11.18	Crashed in forced-landing [Lt R B Francis].
H7259*	05.09.18 - 27.09.18	Crashed on landing [Lt T Bullough].*
H7254*	23.09.18 - 24.10.18	Hit by anti-aircraft fire; crashed in forced-landing [Lt Channing].
H7260*	23.09.18 - 17.10.18	Forced-landed; no further details.
F5460/S	25.09.18 - 20.01.19	Disposed to 32 Squadron.
F5468/T	25.09.18 - 22.11.18	Midair collision [Lt H B Harmsworth].*
E5661	28.09.18 - 01.10.18	Crashed [Lt T Bullough].*
F857/B	29.09.18 - 14.01.19	Disposed to England.
F5451	30.09.18 - 01.10.18	Crashed in forced-landing [2Lt G W Graham].*
E5759/W	03.10.18 - 20.01.19	Disposed to 32 Squadron.
F864/5	03.10.18 - 02.11.18**	*Failed to return [2Lt J Bullough killed].*
F869/6	03.10.18 - 28.10.18	Damaged on operations [Captain C W Cudemore].
F870/2	03.10.18 - 20.01.19	Disposed to 32 Squadron.
F5612/3	03.10.18 - 22.11.18	Midair collision [Lt Crofts].*
E5664/E	05.10.18 - 16.11.18	Crashed [Captain D Lloyd-Evans].*
F582/D	07.10.18 - 17.12.18	Crashed into a shell hole [Lt C D Notley].
F887/C	09.10.18 - 27.10.18	Crashed in forced-landing [Lt A S G Rodway].
F890/V	11.10.18 - 20.01.19	Disposed to 32 Squadron.
C1150/3	27.10.18 - 01.11.18**	*Failed to return [2Lt G W Graham died from wounds].*
F5500/6	30.10.18 - 24.01.19	Disposed to 32 Squadron.
E5746/A	02.11.18 - 24.01.19	Disposed to 32 Squadron.
E5809/U	02.11.18 - 20.01.19	Disposed to 32 Squadron.
H688/C	03.11.18 - 20.01.19	Disposed to 32 Squadron.
H696/Z	03.11.18 - 20.01.19	Disposed to 32 Squadron.
F5624/1	07.11.18 - 21.12.18	Crashed [Lt Crofts].*
F906/5	08.11.18 - 21.12.18	Crashed in forced landing [Lt R B Francis].
D389/E	19.11.18 - 20.01.19	Disposed to 32 Squadron.
F5668	27.11.18 - 14.01.19	Disposed to England.
F8954	27.11.18 - 21.01.19	Disposed to 32 Squadron.
D7009	26.12.18 - 20.01.19	Disposed to 32 Squadron.
B108	30.12.18 - 20.01.19	Crashed on delivery [Lt H B Harmsworth]. Disposed to 32 Squadron.*
E5904	30.12.18 - 20.01.19	Disposed to 32 Squadron.
F8969	30.12.18 - 30.01.19	Disposed to 32 Squadron.

It seems that at least 141 Sopwith SE.5a aircraft were issued to the squadron and it is interesting to note that of this considerable total, only twenty-one failed to return from operations from which nine pilots were killed, ten taken prisoner and two safe, but suffering from wounds. This is at odds with the popular belief that survival rates for pilots fighting on the Western Front could be measured in a few weeks.

Appendix 1E - Hospital Ships

The information imparted in this appendix has been drawn from the website BirtwistleWiki which I gratefully acknowledge. Thus, any errors in interpretation are mine for which I apologise. I also draw attention to the asterisked note following a summary for 82 Squadron on 14th November 1918, and in particular mention of John H Plumridge's book *Hospital Ships & Ambulance Trains* which I have no doubt whatsoever will expand ten-fold on the information disclosed in this appendix.

HMHS *Brighton*   Two funnelled and with a displacement of just 1,384 tons and a speed of 21 knots, as SS *Brighton* she was operated by London, Brighton and South Coast Railway on the Newhaven to Dieppe route. On the advent of war in August 1914, *Brighton* was requisitioned by the Admiralty and until her conversion to a Hospital Ship she was operated as as a troopship. Among the illustrious passengers that graced her saloon over the next five years was King George V on his visit to troops of the British Expeditionary Force in November 1914, while postwar during the course of the peace negotiations at Versailles such luminaries as the prime minister Lloyd George and the American President Woodrow Wilson were among those who crossed and recrossed the Channel during the duration of the talks. In 1930, and now back in the ownership of South Coast Railway, SS *Brighton* was sold to Mr W E Guinness, distinguished soldier and a director fo the Guinness brewing firm, who had her converted as his private yacht and named *Roussalka*.

HMHS *Cambria*   Following requisitioning by the Admiralty, *Cambria's* initial service was as an Armed Boarding Steamer, but in in the summer of 1915, she was converted for Hospital Ship duties, At various time she reverted to troop carrying, but it believed she was still fitted as a Hospital Ship when the armistice was signed. Pre-hostilities, SS *Cambria,* owned by London and North Western Railways, was a familiar sight on the Holyhead to Dublin ferry route. Returned to ferry work in January 1919, in 1921 she was renamed *Arvonia* and after a somewhat chequered last few years she was broken up for scrap in the summer of 1925. Similar to HMHS *Brighton, Cambria* was twin funnelled; displacement is shown as 1,862 tons and, I suspect, her top speed would have been in the region of 21 knots.

HMHS *Carisbrook Castle*   Built for the Union Castle Line, RMS *Carisbrook Castle* operated the Southampton to Cape Town route with accommodation for two hundred and fifty first class passengers and one hundred and forty who could not afford the luxury of what in the halcyon days of late Victorian and early Edwardian sea travel must have been something to behold. Her displacement was 7,626 tons and she cut through the seas at a modest 16 knots. Postwar, her return to service was relatively brief and she was laid up at Netley in 1922, with the entry into service of her replacement, RMS *Windsor Castle.*

HMHS *Grantully Castle*   With a displacement of 7,606 ton and a sedate speed of 13 knots, *Grantully Castle* performed the duties of a Hospital Ship from June 1915 until March 1919, after which she returned to her owners, the Union-Castle Mail Steamship Company of London. Scrapped 1939.

HMHS *Newhaven*   Despite her very British name, *Newhaven* was French constructed and at the outbreak of the *Great War* operated for the French Navy as an auxiliary cruiser. However, by the summer of 1916, she had been British flagged, serving until March 1919, as a Hospital Ship. Still in service [and now returned to French ownership] and with the fall of France in 1940, the German Navy took her over for operations as a troop ship in the Baltic. With the surrender in 1945, she was reclaimed by the French with a view to refitting her as a passenger carrying vessel, but the costs proved prohibitive and *Newhaven* was sold for scrap in 1949.

HMHS *Princess Elizabeth*   Still under investigation.

HMHS *St Andrew*   From the 19th of August 1914, to the 29th of May 1919, this vessel fulfilled the role of a Hospital Ship. Built by John Brown & Co. of Scotland in 1908, *St Andrew* had a displacement of 2,495 tons and if required could attain a speed of 21 knots. Owned by Great Western Railways, *St Andrew* in her peacetime environment was used as a passenger ferry plying the Irish Sea between the Welsh port of Fishguard and Rosslaire in Leinster. On the outbreak of the *Great War,* she was one of the first ships to be commandeered for war service as a Hospital Ship and when fitted out could accommodate a staff of four medical officers, four nurses and twenty-six assistants. Postwar, she returned to service with Great Western Railways and in the year [1932] before she was withdrawn, sold and broken down for scrap, the name *Fishguard* replaced *St David.*

HMHS *St David*   Served throughout the *Great War* as a Hospital Ship. Prewar and postwar, operated by Great Western Railways on the same route as that described for HMHS *St Andrew.* Briefly named *Rosslaire* before being broken down for scrap in 1933.

HMHS *St George*   It was not until 1917, when *St George* was requisitioned from the Canadian Pacific [who had purchased the vessel from Great Western Railways in 1913] and converted as a Hospital Ship. Postwar, *St George* came into the ownership of Great Eastern Railways and until scrapping in 1929, operated the Harwich to the Hook of Holland sea crossing.

HMHS *Western Australia*   Built in Trieste for the Russian Government, her original name was *Mongolia* but changed, appropriately, to *Western Australia* when purchased from its then Danish owners by the Western Australia Government. However, it was found unsuited for what the Australians had in mind, so with the name *Western Australia* still emblazoned she was despatched to the UK for sale; however, before any commercial transactions could take place, war was declared and at this point the Admiralty stepped in and as history now shows, she was converted for Hospital Ship duties. During her time performing this vital role, she survived one attack by a U-boat whose torpedo missed its intended target. Postwar, she was sold to an unnamed foreign owner.

HM *Jan Breydel*   Remains to be investigated.

HM *Stad Antwerpen*   Remains to be investigated.

Appendix 1F - Additions and Amendments to Volumes 1 and 2

Additions are marked with an asterisk.

Volume 1

Page 10   8 Squadron   C3684   Lt E J Brabrook   Army Form B.103c shows Edward John Brabrook as being born on the 1st of October 1893 and enlisted with the Royal Flying Corps on the 15th of September 1917. He joined 4 Squadron on the 5th of December and was posted to 8 Squadron on the 25th of March. He was admitted to 13 Australian Field Hospital with severe gunshot wounds to his right arm.

Page 71   4 Squadron   C4557   Lt D Elliott   Army Form B.103c shows Duncan Elliott was formerly of the 1st Battalion, Border Regiment, and was accepted as a potential Observer Officer circa 24th November 1917, and was returned to England for training. On the 15th of March 1918, he joined 4 Squadron at Chocques. His date of birth is recorded as the 19th of February 1894.

Page 165   62 Squadron   C4630   2Lt H A Clarke   Army Form B.103c 26.07.18: *"Officially reported as prisoner of war. 30.12.18 Repatriated & arrived at Hull. Op 11196 Daag 2 Cas c970/11 9.01.19."* He had been with the squadron since the 26th of April.

Page 238   74 Squadron   C6497   Lt G F Thompson   Army Form B.103c 08.10.18: *"Officially accepted Prisoner of War. List R M 531 & Cas C/909/6."* He had joined the squadron on the 17th of May 1918.

Page 263   149 Squadron   D9777   Lt J W Thompson   Army Form B.103c 25.07.18: *"Believed Unwounded Prisoner of War.'* 13.09.18; *'Officially reported as Prisoner of War. W O List No PM 512 DAAG 2 Cas C8911/3 S/19.9.18. Extract 3rd Edn d/25.9.18."*

Volume 2

Page 29   104 Squadron   D2868   Lt A Moore   Army Form B.103c 08.10.18: *"Officially accepted Prisoner of War List R M 523 & Cas 909/8 a/d".* Andrew Moore's date of birth is shown as Christmas Day 1890 and his enlistment with the RFC 23rd June 1917. He was a Canadian.

Page 34   208 Squadron   D1955   Lt H K Scrivener   Army Form B.103c 8.10.18: *"Officially accepted Prisoner of War List P.M. 583 & Cas, 909/8 a/d 16/10.18."*

Page 54   54 Squadron   D9437   Lt R B Thompson   Army Form B.103c shows he was a General List officer who was attached to the squadron on the 7th of April 1918.

Page 70   99 Squadron   D1679   Lt F E Thompson   Army Form B.103c shows his Christian names as 'Frederick George' and his date of birth as 8th February 1894. He enlisted on 24th August 1915, and joined the squadron on the 20th of April 1918. Between the 2nd and the 6th of July he was treated in 8 Casualty Clearing Station for influenza. His release from a prisoner of war camp came on 6th December, whereupon he was taken to 42 Stationary Hospital with an undiagnosed condition; he was sent home on the 27th by Ambulance Transport *Aberdonian*.

Page 119   35 Squadron   D5120   2Lt H Elliott   Army Form B.103c 16.09.18 *"Presumed Prisoner of War."* Missing on the opening day of the *'Battle of Amiens'* [8th August 1918], 2nd Lieutenant Elliott was attached to the squadron as recently as 28th July.

Page 126   209 Squadron   D9619   Lt L Thompson   Army Form B.103c 10.08.18: *"Buried at Military Cemetery Asylum, Amiens by Rev. J Parker att. 48 CCS. G.1047/6 undated."* Leonard Thompson born of the 5th of November 1898, and enlisting 14th August 1917, joined the squadron on the 19th of June. His father at 52 Whitworth Road, Rochdale, was named as his next of kin.

Page 135   6 Squadron   B5893   Lt A R Thompson   Army Form B.103c shows he joined the squadron on the 27th of May 1918.

Page 152   104 Squadron   D3088   2Lt E C Clarke   Army Form B.103c 29.05.19: *"Death accepted by the Air Council as having occurred on or after 13.08.18. Lapse of time. Memo P.2.Cas."* Edwin Cedric Clarke was born on 23rd June 1896, and enlisted on 20th January 1918. He was initially attached to 99 Squadron at Azelot on the 30th of June and was cross-posted to 104 Squadron on the 8th of July.

Page 156   99 Squadron*   D1019   2Lt D F Brooks   T/o Azelot for a practice flight and wrecked whilst landing. The appropriate
                                       2Lt R Buckby   appendices require amending. His serve record is reported in my summary for the 8th of February 1919. 2nd Lieutenant Ralph Buckby, born 16th May 1895, joined 99 Squadron on the 6th of August 1918, and was killed on operations on 26th September, the details of his loss being recorded in my second volume on page 253.

Page 167   5 Squadron   C2596   Lt G W H Parlee   Army Form B.103c Born 13th July 1897, George William Hugh Parlee had served with the squadron since 27th May; I have not been able to find any additional information regarding his pilot, Lieutenant Fothergill.

Page 167   30 Squadron*   B6611   Capt. L St A M Page T/o Baqubah to practice firing the RE.8s machine-gun but while flying at a height
                                       Lt L Kirwan   of 600 feet stalled and spun to the ground. Lance St. Allard March Page was the senior Flight Commander and was in charge of C Flight. He had been with the squadron since 1916. He was formerly of the 10th [Royal East Kent and West Kent Yeomanry] Battalion and later The Buffs [East Kent Regiment]. Twice mentioned in despatches his epitaph reads: *"God Gave His Soul Brave Wings."* His observer, who had arrived as recently as the 1st, was late of the 1st Battalion, South Lancashire Regiment. No less than four Army Form B.103s have been raised for this officer, charting his service from 5th October 1915, when he arrived in Gallipoli. Both are buried in Baghdad [North Gate] Cemetery.

Page 188   55 Squadron   D8396   2Lt R A I Hickes   55 Squadron Association website. In the Association's superb collection of photographs is one showing the twisted remains of 'D8396' lying in front of the church of Latour-en-Woeuvre where the crew now rest. The caption states that the DH was shot down by Johannes Voigt-Christiansen and who is included in the photograph standing beside a fellow officer and with a host of soldiers in the background.

Page 197   40 Squadron   D8445   Lt H W Clarke   Army Form B.103c 13.10.18: *"Killed in action or died of wounds shortly after. Daag 2 Burial Report S6153."* Hubert Wilton Clarke was born on the 30th of June 1899, and enlisted on the 4th of July 1917. He joined the squadron on the 13th of May and was admitted to 12 Stationary Hospital on 6th July, with bullet wounds to his thigh. He was discharged to 1 Aeroplane Supply Depot on the 1st of August, rejoining his squadron on the 9th.

Page 201   25 Squadron   D9235   2Lt E F Boyce   Army Form B.103c. Edward Francis Boyce was born on the 19th of November 1897, and enlisted in the RFC on 23rd October 1917. On 27th May he was posted to 11 Squadron [Bristol F.2b] at Remaisnil and was admitted with a sprained right ankle to 21 CCS on 16th June and was discharged to duty on the 26th. On the 5th of July he was attached to 25 Squadron.

Page 219   Sunday 15 September 1918 3 Squadron Lt S A Kemp Safe See Appendix G - Roll of Honour 1919
F.1 Camel D9425/H T/o Valhereux and written off in a forced-landing, brought about by engine failure, at Bucquoy. Salvaged, the airframe was struck off charge five days later. Taken on charge 20th June 1918, Lieutenant W H Boyce shot down a 2-seater machine in the early morning of 10th August, his victory shared with Lieutenant J R Montgomery flying F5958.

Page 221   84 Squadron   F6420   2Lt C R Thompson   Army Form B.103c records his date of birth as 4th December 1894, and his enlistment as 11th April 1917. He was well into his tour of operations having reported to the squadron on the 26th of May. Cecil Robert Thompson was evacuated by Ambulance Transport *St. Andrew* on the 18th of September.

Page 245   30 Squadron*   B3445   *Not reported*   RE.8 reported wrecked in a crash-landing at Surmil landing ground.

Page 249   99 Squadron   C2197   2Lt M J Poulton   Insert [Canada] after his surname.

Page 252   99 Squadron   B9347   Captain P E Welchman Army Form B.103c *"Died of wounds [Returned PoW] 28.11.18 W3743 42 Sty. Buried at Charmes Military Cemetery. Row D. Grave A. By Revd A G W Bullock attd. 42 Stat. Hosp.G.1665/11 undated. Burial report 67403."*

Page 258   20 Squadron   E2568   2Lt C E Clarke   Army Form B.103 10.06.19: *"Death accepted by the Air Council as having occurred on or after 27.09.18. Lapse of time. Memo P.2.Cas."* 2nd Lieutenant Clarke joined the squadron ten days before his death.

Page 270   22 Squadron   E2517   Lt C W M Thompson Army Form B.103c 29.09.18: *"Believed Prisoner of War. 2u.12.18 Released Prisoner of War Admitted [Old GSW Knee R]. 30.12.18 T. England Per A T 'Cambria."* Born on 11th April 1899, Chester William McKinley Thompson enlisted on the 13th of June 1917, and was posted to the squadron on the 16th of April.

Page 276   46 Squadron*   F5950   2Lt H P Clarke   T/o Cappy for an offensive patrol only to lose control, spin and crash near the airfield and was admitted to 27 Casualty Clearing Station where he was pronounced dead. He was posted in six days previously.

Page 278   80 Squadron   F6026   2Lt R E Thompson   Army Form B.103c shows Robert Ellerton Thompson was born on the 21st of November 1899. He had served with the squadron the 10th of August 1918.

Page 294   206 Squadron   D560   2Lt J H Perring   Army Form B.103 indicates he was repatriated to Leith, and placed on the unemployed list on 12 April 1919. Interestingly, however, it seems a track was kept on officers who served in the *Great War* for many decades and in respect of John Hubert Perring, late of the Welsh Regiment and who joined the squadron on the 3rd of September 1918, there is handwritten entry *Died 26.7.66 [per M N I]*.

Page 310   107 Squadron   F5846   Lt W M Thompson   Army Form B.103c 22.05.19: *"Death accepted by the Air Council as having occurred on or after 9.10.18 on evidence being gathered by lapse of time."* He had joined the squadron on the 23rd of August 1918.

Page 367   88 Squadron   E2451   2Lt C M W Elliot   Army Form B.103c identifies his surname as 'Elliott' and with Christian names Charles Morris William. He was born on the 1st of June 1898, and joined the Royal Air Force on 21st June 1918. He arrived in France on 26th September and was hospitalised the next day with scabies. Discharged on 3rd October, he joined 88 Squadron four days later. Admitted to 1[Australian] Casualty Clearing Station he was returned to England on 2nd November by HMHS *Princess Elizabeth*.

Page 377   208 Squadron   E7179   Lt W V Skall   New insertion after 70 Squadron: T/o Maretz for an unreported task and on return crashed whilst landing. Removed to 2 Air Issues and probably scrapped. Amend appendices A and B as appropriate.

Appendix 1G - The Roll of Honour 12th November to 31st December 1918

At the going down of the sun and in the morning
We will remember them

[Laurence Binyon]

In a departure from previous volumes, the names will be reported in alphabetical order rather than by chronological date. Within 24-hours of the armistice being signed, at least twenty-two Royal Air Force personnel died. Two of the ten squadron deaths on the 12th, were from air accidents, while the remainder died either from wounds or from natural causes. An asterisk against a surname indicates killed that day, or died soon after, in a flying accident. Of the five entries recorded on the 7th of December, four are in respect of 7 Squadron airmen, three of whom are buried in Belgium at Herzele Churchyard. Also buried here, and who died on the 7th, are Private W Foster of the 13th Balloon Company and Corporal V Hugo of 1 Aircraft Depot along with three soldiers, namely Sappers L Boff and H Hawes of the 184th Tunnelling Company, Royal Engineers and Private James Turnbull of the Royal Army Service Corps. This leads me to suspect that all fell victim to an accident of serious proportion; all are located near the North wall of the Chancel. The village of Herzele [Oost-Vlaanderen] lies to the southwest Aalst. The fourth 7 Squadron airman who perished was Private James Rourke who has no known grave and is commemorated on the Arras Flying Services Memorial. It is sad fact that deaths from squadrons featured every day until the 12th of December. Furthermore, deaths in many cases can be attributed to the influenza pandemic that sweeping across the world.

ROYAL AIR FORCE

Captain	ARMSTRONG*	D'urban Victor	13 November 1918	151 Squadron
	DFC South Africa			
Corporal	ARMSTRONG	William James	12 November 1918	48 Squadron
2Lt	AYLES	Walter Matthew William	20 December 1918	21 Squadron

Although no Army Form B.103 appears to have survived regarding 2nd Lieutenant Ayles, who is buried in Tourcoing [Pont-Neuville] Communal Cemetery, a section of the IWMs website [Lives of the First World War] shows he was born on 26th October 1899, while his entry on the CWGC website notes that he came from Southfield, London, and that prior to enlisting he had been a Civil Servant working in the Admiralty.

Corporal	BAILEY	William	22 November 1918	90 Squadron
Lt	BAIRD*AFC	William Douglas Haldane	22 November 1918	112 Squadron
Mechanic	BARRETT	John	19 December 1918	205 Squadron
Mechanic	BELFITT	William Arthur	16 December 1918	149 Squadron
Mechanic	BLAIN	David	3 December 1918	148 Squadron
2Lt	BOOTH*	Lawrence Howard	13 November 1918	105 Squadron
	Canada			
2Lt	BOOTH*	Sydney Edwin	3 December 1918	20 Squadron
Lt	BOURNS	Arthur Eldridge	14 November 1918	57 Squadron

See my summary for 4th November, page 382, for details of his loss. According to Army Form B.103-11, Arthur Bourns was attached to 57 Squadron on 25th September, and was wounded on 27th October. An undated entry indicates he was *"buried at Ghissignies"* [this is at odds with his entry on the CWGC website] with the Reverend D'Arcy Ward, attached 112 Brigade, conducting the service.

Mechanic	BOYLE	Joseph Aloysius	23 November 1918	9 Squadron
Corporal	BRADBURY	Stanley	17 November 1918	6 Squadron
Corporal	BRADSHAW*	Thomas George	13 November 1918	105 Squadron
Private	BROWN	John	7 December 1918	7 Squadron
Corporal	BRUNSDEN	Cecil Stuart	18 November 1918	11 Squadron
Mechanic	BULL	Percival Henry	30 November 1918	9 Squadron
Mechanic	BURKITT	Frank Henry	18 November 1918	52 Squadron
Lt	CAPLE*	Leonard Norman Akerman	21 November 1918	22 Squadron
	Canada			
Mechanic	CLEVERLY	William John	26 November 1918	43 Squadron
Mechanic	COOK	Frank Lockwood	12 November 1918	102 Squadron
Lt	CRAWFORD	James Currie	12 November 1918	56 Squadron
	Canada			

James Currie Crawford proceeded overseas in 1916 with the 74th Battalion, Canadian Infantry. His death on the 12th was from injuries [described on Army Form B.103-11as *"[burns multiple]"* received when his aircraft crashed on 9th of November; see page 394 in my second volume for details.

Captain	CRUMMEY	Francis Cyprian	20 November 1918	27 Squadron
	Canada			

Born on the 2nd of July 1899, Francis Crummey [on Army Form B.103c his Christian names are recorded as *"Frank Charles"*] joined the Royal Flying Corps on 16 June 1917, arriving with 27 Squadron on the 7th of June 1918, and was appointed to the rank of Captain [Flying] with effect from the 15th of October. Stricken down with influenza on the 30th, he died from Bronchial Pneumonia. His funeral at St. Sever Cemetery extension, Rouen on, or around, the 30th of November, was conducted by the Reverend T Healy of No 11 Stationary Hospital.

Sgt	CUMMINS	Alfred George	21 November 1918	98 Squadron
2Lt	DALLAS*	William Reid	24 December 1918	215 Squadron
	Mechanical Transport, RASC			
Corporal	DAVIDSON	Falconer	26 November 1918	43 Squadron
Lt	DAVISON*DCM	Samuel	30 November 1918	112 Squadron
Mechanic	DE FRANCESCO	Michele	15 November 1918	191 Squadron
	Italy	Formerly of Fratta Maggiore, Napoli. Aged 30, and married, his widow is shown as living in Genoa.		
Private	DICKENSON	Robert	28 December 1918	149 Squadron
Sgt	DOLPHIN	Oliver	15 November 1918	205 Squadron
2Lt	DOUGLAS	Roland Keith	26 November 1918	19 Squadron

Canada   Born on the 7th of June 1898, Roland Douglas enlisted with the Royal Flying Corps on the 1st of September 1917, and following his qualification as a scout pilot embarked for France three days before his 20th birthday. Arriving at Clairmarais South on the 6th, He joined 1 Squadron, but a week later he was posted to 19 Squadron at Savy and it was while serving with '19' that he failed to return from an offensive patrol on the 11th of August [see my second volume page 141 for details]. The following statements have been entered on Army Form B.103c: " *Believed prisoner of war* ' followed by *'29.5.19 Death accepted by the Air Council as having occurred on or after 11.8.18, and to believe that date of death was 26.11.18. Lapse of time.. Memo P.2 Cas.* "

Mechanic	EGGETT	Victor James	22 November 1918	192 Squadron
Lt	ELLERCAMP*	Wilfred Alan Herbert	30 December 1918	44 Squadron
2Lt	FAWCETT	Fred	12 November 1918	64 Squadron

Died from injuries, as recorded on Army Form B.103-11. Part II [Service and Casualty Form Part II]. See my summary for 1st November 1918, page 373, for details of his crash during which he suffered from severe burns to his hands and face.

2Lt	FOLKARD*	William Lucas	15 November 1918	138 Squadron

Squadron identity omitted; reported from other sources to have commenced his military service as a private soldier in the Royal Engineers.

Private	FOSKETT	William George	5 December 1918	149 Squadron
Mechanic	GIBB	Thomas Ritchie	30 November 1918	34 Squadron
Mechanic	GIBSON	Albert Claude	15 November 1918	27 Squadron
2Lt	GILPIN	Robert Rooke	22 December 1918	57 Squadron
	New Zealand			
Mechanic	HALL	Donald Charles	14 November 1918	27 Squadron
Lt	HANNA	William Neil	20 November 1918	34 Squadron
	Canada	40th Battery, 25th Brigade, Royal Field Artillery		

Army Form B.103c carries the sad statement that William Hanna died from self inflicted wounds. He was laid to rest in Montecchio Precalcino Communal Cemetery extension on the 22nd of November, the funeral being conducted by the Reverend C J Rae, attached to 24 CCS. According to the Casualty Form he had been posted to 34 Squadron on the 16th of October, and three days later was admitted to hospital suffering from influenza. He was discharged to his squadron on the 12th of November. Prior to being accepted as an observer, he had served with the 40th Battery, 25th Brigade, Royal Field Artillery.

Mechanic	HARRIS	Thomas White Ford	19 November 1918	44 Squadron
Private	HARRISON	William Frederick	12 November 1918	199 Squadron
Corporal	HENDERSON	William	15 November 1918	36 Squadron
Mechanic	HICKS	Henry	24 November 1918	153 Squadron
Private	HILLIER	Bert Sidney	20 November 1918	46 Squadron
Mechanic	HOLMES	Frank Eyre	14 November 1918	36 Squadron
Private	HOOPER	Alfred James	5 December 1918	35 Squadron
Captain	HORRIDGE*	John Leslie	21 November 1918	91 Squadron
Mechanic	JACKSON	Edgar Harold	24 November 1918	34 Squadron
Mechanic	JAKES	Leonard Frederick	13 December 1918	12 Squadron
	Royal Garrison Artillery			
Mechanic	JELLEY	Herbert Harold	24 November 1918	24 Squadron
2Lt	JENNER	Percy Herbert	14 December 1918	66 Squadron
Mechanic	JOHNSON	William George	15 November 1918	27 Squadron
Mechanic	KAPLANSKY	Wolfe	20 November 1918	90 Squadron
	Lithuania			

Joined the Royal Flying Corps on the 21st of August 1916. He succumbed to influenza while being treated in 4th Northern General Hospital, Lincoln.

Corporal	KING	Thomas Allister	10 December 1918	1 Squadron
Private	LAMB	Matthew	18 November 1918	5 Squadron
Corporal	LEDGER mid	William Henry	27 November 1918	17 Squadron
Mechanic	LEES	Edward	22 November 1918	3 Squadron
Mechanic	LEGGETT	Charles Wales	23 November 1918	150 Squadron
Mechanic	MADDOCK	Thomas	24 November 1918	43 Squadron
2Lt	MANDERS*	Arthur	16 November 1918	15 Squadron
Private	MARSH	Edwin William	14 November 1918	25 Squadron

At the time of his death 25 Squadron was based in France at La Brayelle, but Private Marsh is buried in Italy at Staglieno Cemetery, Genoa.

Mechanic	MARTIN	R Washington	18 November 1918	58 Squadron
Lt	MASTERS*	Ernest Harold	24 December 1918	45 Squadron
	Croix de Guerre [France]			
Lt	MAWER	John Bailey	28 November 1918	57 Squadron

Army Form B.103c shows John Bailey Mawer joining the RFC on 14th of October 1917, and *Gazetted* 2nd Lieutenant 1st December 1917. Army Form B.103c in respect of 'J B Mawer' leads me to suggest the two documents concern the same person, the latter showing: *"55293 L/Cpl J B Mawer, Lincs Yeo, to be Temp 2/Lieut Gen List for duty with RFC at 1.12.17."* He was the posted 57 Training Squadron at Abu Sueir [subsequently re-designated No 17 Training Depot Station here on 21st July 1918] where on the 10th of January 1918, he was admitted to 26 Stationary Hospital with concussion of the brain and placed on the dangerously ill list. However, with 48-hours his condition had improved and by the 19th he was out of danger and was discharged to No 1 Convalescence Home. By the end of March he was declared fit for duty. The final entry confirms my suspicion that 'John Bailey Mawer' and 'J B Mawer' are one and the same person: *"1.4.18 Lon. Gazette L/Cpl J B Mawer from the Yeo T.F. to be Temp. 2/Lieut Gen List RFC 1.12.17."* John Mawer is the sole service burial in Goltho [St. George] Churchyard, Lincolnshire.

Lt	MAXTED*	William Henry	17 December 1918	3 Squadron
Sgt	McDONALD	Alexander	25 November 1918	66 Squadron
2Lt	McGUIRE	Thomas Francis	21 December 1918	208 Squadron
Lt	MEES	Ian Rudolph	14 November 1918	48 Squadron

Casualty Form - Officers in respect of Lieutenant Mees shows he was posted to 48 Squadron on the 22nd of September 1917. Various administrative entries follow, until the 12th of March 1918, when he was posted to Home Establishment. His date of birth is shown as 14th July 1898, and that he banked with Cox & Company.

Mechanic	MOORE	Edward Charles	29 November 1918	214 Squadron
2Lt	MORRIS	Corbet Wiley	30 November 1918	120 Squadron
	Nova Scotia			
Mechanic	MORRIS	Joseph	9 December 1918	57 Squadron
Corporal	MOORS	Richard	3 December 1918	20 Squadron
Mechanic	MORTON*	James Walter	24 December 1918	215 Squadron
Private	MORTON	William	28 November 1918	14 Squadron
Mechanic	NEALE	Walter Charles	15 November 1918	6 Squadron
Sgt	NICHOLLS*	James Albert	12 November 1918	203 Squadron
Sgt	NOYES*	Charles Henry Crispin	3 December 1918	155 Squadron
Mechanic	ODLING	Arthur	6 December 1918	222 Squadron

Lt	O'GRADY*	James Henry	24 December 1918	215 Squadron
	Canada			
Mechanic	PAGE	Alfred George Elsha	20 November 1918	13 Squadron
2Lt	PALMER	John William	25 December 1918	2 Squadron

Second Lieutenant Palmer's first posting following his arrival in France on 29th September, was to 7 Squadron at Proven, reporting here on the 30th, but was immediately admitted to hospital suffering from bronchitis which kept him out of action until 6th October, and on his discharge he ordered to Mazingarbe for attachment to 2 Squadron. On the 26th, the squadron moved to Genech where he was killed in a fatal accident on Christmas Day. He was buried in the local Communal Cemetery, his funeral being conducted by the Reverend H C Perry who was attached to 1st Wing at Valenciennes. A Court of Enquiry was held into the circumstances leading up to his death and the conclusion reached was; *"that this Officer's death was caused by his own negligence in handling explosives."* A record for this officer is held at TNA Kew under AIR 76/386/177.

Lt	PARKS	Herbert Clifford	19 December 1918	29 Squadron

Lieutenant Parks left England for 29 Squadron on the 4th of September, arriving at La Lovie the same day. On the 14th he was treated for a gunshot wound to his left leg, this keeping him grounded until the 3rd of November, on which date he rejoined the squadron, now at Marcke. From the 27th through to 11th December, he was on leave and then, on the 16th, he was accidentally shot in the abdomen and rushed to 55 Casualty Clearing Station where he died. Details of his burial in Charleroi Communal Cemetery have not been entered on Army Form B.103.

Sgt	PARRY	John	4 December 1918	214 Squadron
Mechanic	PEARCE	Emrys	22 November 1918	4 Squadron
Sgt	PEEL	Frank Robinson	18 November 1918	5 Squadron
Mechanic	PENKETH	George Ernest	7 December 1918	214 Squadron
Major	PLENTY	Edward Pellew	22 November 1918	96 Squadron
Mechanic	PLOWMAN	Rowland Harry	8 December 1918	192 Squadron
2Lt	POOLE	Roland Barrett	18 December 1918	221 Squadron
Mechanic	PRESTON	Edmund George	7 December 1918	7 Squadron
Corporal	PRIEST	Ronald	28 November 1918	98 Squadron
Mechanic	PRIME	Leonard Sidney	29 November 1918	5 Squadron
Mechanic	PRINCE	John Arthur	12 November 1918	243 Squadron
Lt	PROCTOR*	Leslie Horner	17 November 1918	10 Squadron
	Army Service Corps and 2/Royal Irish Rifles			
Lt	PUGH	John Edwin	13 November 1918	210 Squadron
Private	RENN	Frederick Henry	23 November 1918	34 Squadron
2Lt	RICHARDSON*	Tom	3 December 1918	155 Squadron
Mechanic	RICHMOND	Alfred Howard Daniel	7 December 1918	7 Squadron
2Lt	RILEY*	Benjamin	24 November 1918	49 Squadron
Mechanic	ROSS	Robert Philip	19 November 1918	6 Squadron
Private	ROURKE	James	7 December 1918	7 Squadron
Mechanic	ROUTLEDGE	Albert Edward	18 November 1918	11 Squadron
Mechanic	RUSSELL	Thomas Stark	16 December 1918	104 Squadron

Formerly of the Highland Light Infantry, Mechanic Thomas Stark Russell died in France at 12 Stationary Hospital where he was being treated for influenza and broncho pneumonia. Paul McMillan also adds, TNA Kew has a record for Mechanic Start under WO 372/17/128849 38094 29066.

Corporal	RYLAND	Arthur Cleve	27 November 1918	110 Squadron
2Lt	SALTON*	William Kenneth	17 November 1918	10 Squadron
Lt	SAMPSON*	Wilfred John	2 December 1918	81 Squadro
Mechanic	SEARSON	Bertie	29 November 1918	96 Squadron
Sgt	SILLS	Thomas	4 December 1918	48 Squadron
Mechanic	SIMMONITE	Frank	15 December 1918	145 Squadron
Private	SKEELS	William Robert	3 December 1918	214 Squadron
Mechanic	SKINNER	William	12 November 1918	14 Squadron
2Lt	SLOSS	James Duncan	23 November 1918	108 Squadron
	New Zealand			

New Zealand See page 395 of my second volume for details of the operation during which he was severely wounded. His funeral, undated, but prior to the 10th of December, was overseen by the Reverend A M Maclean from Boulogne.

2Lt	SPEAKE*	Thomas Gordon	20 November 1918	82 Squadron
Private	STANMORE	William Henry	22 December 1918	232 Squadron
Mechanic	STEELE	Morton	12 November 1918	32 Squadron
Mechanic	STEPHENS	George Frances	17 November 1918	26 Squadron

At the time of Mechanic Stephens death, 26 Squadron's 'number plate' was laid up, the squadron having disbanded on 8th July 1918, at Blandford Camp on its return from South Africa.

Mechanic	STOCKMAN	Frederick	1 December 1918	199 Squadron
2Lt	STRONG	Robert Abraham	1 December 1918	273 Squadron
Mechanic	SUMMERS	John William	13 November 1918	35 Squadron
Mechanic	SUTCLIFFE	Frank	27 December 1918	203 Squadron
Lt	SYMONDSON*	Vernon Francis	13 November 1918	21 Squadron
Corporal	THOMAS	Horace Lee	15 November 1918	104 Squadron
2Lt	THOMPSON*	Robert Henry	9 December 1918	203 Squadron
Mechanic	TURNER	William Henry	3 December 1918	9 Squadron
Mechanic	VALLANCEY	Robert Victor	18 November 1918	9 Squadron
2Lt	WADDINGTON	George Walter	24 November 1918	49 Squadron
Mechanic	WALKER	Frederick Arthur	19 December 1918	144 Squadron
LAC	WALSH	John	29 November 1918	112 Squadron

The revised rank structure for non-commissioned officers came into effect from January 1919, with Aircraftman replacing Air Mechanic, Private and Clerk, though throughout 1919, these redundant ranks continued to be reported from record offices.Thus 'LAC' translates as Leading Aircraftman and this pre-dated use appears to be the first recorded on the CWGC website. From Merthyr Tydfil, John Walsh is buried in Aberfan Cemetery.

Mechanic	WARWICK	Henry Thomas	3 December 1918	222 Squadron
2Lt	WEIR*	Noble Alexander	27 November 1918	19 Squadron
	Canada			
Captain	WELCHMAN MC DFC	Patrick Eliot	29 November 1918	99 Squadron

Formerly of the 2nd Battalion, King's Own Scottish Borders, Patrick Eliot Welchman was born on the 17th of March 1895, and joined the Royal Flying Corps in May 1916. He was posted to 99 Squadron on the 14th of September 1918, and was taken prisoner of war on the 29th of September [full details of his capture and the citation for his DFC are reported in my second volume, page 252]. His wounds, sadly, were to prove fatal and he died soon after being returned to Allied care. His funeral at Charmes Military Cemetery took place on, or around, the 10th of December, officiated by the Reverend A G W Bullock attached to the 42nd Stationary Hospital.

AC1	WHITE	Harry Leslie	23 December 1918	232 Squadron

2Lt	WHITTALL*	Garth	12 November 1918	23 Squadron

2Lt	WICKS*	William Dixon	11 December 1918	42 Squadron
Lt	WILKINSON	Charles	21 November 1918	42 Squadron

The cause of his death has not been recorded on Army Form B.103c, but the few entries that have been made indicate he was formerly of the Royal Field Artillery before joining the Royal Air Force on 8 June 1918, as a trained observer. He arrived with 42 Squadron at Rely on 28th June and was posted to Home Establishment on the 5th of November. Charles Wilkinson is buried in Essex at East Hannington [All Saints] Churchyard.

2Lt	WILKINSON* South Africa	Ernest Fletcher	22 November 1918	18 Squadron
Mechanic	WILLS	Arthur Herbert	19 November 1918	102 Squadron
Mechanic	WILSON	George Leslie	17 December 1918	10 Squadron
2Lt	WILSON*	James Murdoch	13 November 1918	105 Squadron
Private	WILSON	Richard Thomas	24 December 1918	191 Squadron
2Lt	WREATHALL*	Robert Scott	15 November 1918	82 Squadron
Private	WRIGHT	Albion Albert	3 December 1918	57 Squadron
2Lt	WRIGHT	Sydney Hopewell	17 December 1918	33 Squadron
Mechanic	WRIGHT	Walter John	26 December 1918	47 Squadron
Mechanic	WYLIE	James	26 November 1918	43 Squadron

AUSTRALIAN FLYING CORPS

Lt	SWANN*MM	Lyell Keith	14 November 1918	3 SquadronAusFC

CANADIAN INFANTRY

Lt	OWEN*	Sidney Smith	11 December 1918	42 Squadron

From Bootle, Liverpool, Sidney Owen had emigrated to Canada where he responded to the call to arms and enlisted with the Infantry and was attached to the Depot Battalion, British Columbia.

There was a huge variation in the ages of airmen serving at the time, a vivid example being recorded on the 10th of December when Boy Albert Victor Patterson died at 18 years of age and Private W J Hinwood, who was 60, and who had served with the Hazare Expedition of 1888. Boy Patterson is buried in Dundee [Balgay] Cemetery, while Private Hinwood rests in Exeter Higher Cemetery.

Addendum to the Roll of Honour 1st July to 11th November 1918.

Second Lieutenant Cyril George Russell mortally wounded on 30th August flying as observer to Second Lieutenant W A Warwick in 99 Squadron DH.9 D3215, was buried the next day in a Military Cemetery on the south side of the Damas-aux-Bois road, three km from Charmes, the funeral service being conducted by the Reverend H J Blake, attached 8th Canadian Stationary Hospital.

Part 2 - Squadron Losses 1st January 1919 - 31 December 1919

The first full year of "peace", a year in which decisions taken at the Versailles Peace Conference by the Allied powers would impact upon Germany for the next two decades and in no small part sowed the seeds that by the middle '30s blossomed into the rise of Nazism and, ultimately, to the Second World War.

Presently, with the dawning of 1919, a state of armistice continued and though extensions would come into effect it would be late June before agreements were signed and a further six months before the terms came into effect.

This was for the future and for the Royal Air Force the next twelve months would result in swinging cuts in man-power and a savage reduction in front-line squadrons, most of those that survived the axe being deployed to the Middle East and India.

Although I refer to "peace' in my opening remarks, in many regions of world factional fighting was claiming hundreds of lives, particularly in the power struggle between the Bolsheviks and their White Russian opponents, and if this was not enough the influenza pandemic had yet to run its course.

On the home front "peace" was not bringing prosperity. Factories that had been geared for war work now faced reduced orders and for thousands of ex-servicemen hoping to resume their prewar employment the future was bleak.

JANUARY
1919

Wednesday New Year's Day 1919
A terrible maritime tragedy occurred during the hours of darkness when HMY *Iolaire* struck the Beasts of Holm rocks in the entrance to Stornoway harbour and in storm lashed seas sank with the loss of 201 passengers, the majority being Royal Navy Reservists returning home to the Isle of Lewis. The effect on the tight-knit communities of Lewis has never been fully assuaged and to this day descendants of those who perish remember the immense sorrow that came upon the island when the full impact of the tragedy became clear.

During the day returns from squadrons continued to report aircraft no longer fit for service. From 5 Squadron at Hangelar three of their RE.8s B7893, C2731 and C2974 were waterlogged and from Gerpinnes where 59 Squadron was based three of their RE.8s were in a similar state C2710, C2865 and F6050.

At Tangmere in Sussex personnel of 14 Squadron arrived from Greece.

1 Squadron	Lt F P Magoun	Safe	Unemployed list 13 June 1919
SE.5a B8501	USA		

T/o Izel-lès-Hameau for flying practice. Overtaken by engine failure and in the ensuing forced-landing near Courcelles-le-Compte in the Pas-de-Calais, fell into an old shell hole. On squadron charge since 26th August, B8501 was struck off charge on the 2nd. An incomplete Army Form B.103 has been found for Francis Peabody Magoun but what details remain make for interesting reading. Born on the 6th of January 1895, in Cambridge, Massachusetts, Francis enlisted with the RFC on 11th April 1917. Commencing 11th July, he was attached to the British Flying School, presumably in France, for the entry on 8th August records his return to Home Establishment.

On 10th November he returned to France, joining 1 Squadron at Bailleul on the 14th, at which time the squadron was equipped with Nieuport 27s. Between 2nd and 9th December he attended a course at the aerial ranges and shortly after his return made his acquaintance with the SE.5a.

From 8th to 22nd February he was on leave and then on the 10th of April, he was shot through his right shoulder and admitted to hospital. This was the final entry on the Form.

Turning to *The SE.5a File* I have been able to piece together a reasonable picture of his operational flying. In chrono-logical sequence his first success came on 10th March while flying C5306/R he deflated a kite balloon on the Roulers to Menin road, followed five days later in A8904 he shared in the destruction of an LVG C to the south of Ledeghem. On the 26th he made a heavy landing A8904, which was struck off charged on the 29th.

His most successful day appears to have been on the 28th; first, with the help of Captain G B Moore*[C1083] he sent down an LVG C over the Pas-de-Calais between Gavrelle and Oppy, followed by a solo claim for an Albatross DD on the north side of Oppy, both victories coming during the same patrol in C5306. When wounded he was flying C9621 which although damaged was repaired and remained in squadron service.

I am not able to say for how long he was out of action, but he was certainly back in the fray by the autumn for on 28th October, and piloting E5778, he drove down a Fokker DVII north of Hirson.

* Killed in action on the 7th of April 1918, the circumstances of his death are summarised in my first volume on page 34. Concerning Gavrelle, there is an excellent website which describes the assault by the 63rd [Royal Naval] Division on the village in April 1917, and the heroic capture of the Gavrelle Windmill.

72 Squadron   Lt T L Williams   +   Baghdad [North Gate] War Cemetery
Spad VII A8824

T/o Baghdad and while in flight suffered complete structural failure. From Pontardulais, Swansea, 21 year old Trevor Lewis Williams is commemorated by a simple epitaph: *"Asleep In Jesus."* He was commissioned to the General List RFC on the 5th of July 1917 [LG 24 July 1917, supplement 30203, page 7608].

A photograph of Lieutenant Williams, submitted by Dimitrios Corcodilos on 21st August 2019, appears on the Find a Grave website. Also, a photograph of his grave taken at around the time of his funeral showing a propeller as the marker, this being added by Mary Petroff as recently as 9th May 2019.

110 Squadron   Lt G T Griffith   Safe
DH.9A F1065   2Lt R W Jones   Safe

T/o Maisoncelle to practice map reading and came to grief in a landing accident. One of a batch of 150 airframes built by the Westland Aircraft Works at Yeovil in Somerset, F1065 arrived with the squadron at Bettencourt on the 22nd of October 1918. Gerallt Tegwyn Griffin of 52 Marians Terrace, Aberystwyth was born 4th February 1896, and was commissioned to the General List RFC on 21st June 1917 [LG 6 July 1917, supplement 30170, page 6787] at which time he had been serving as an NCO since the 15th of February. On 29th September, he embarked for France and was attached four days later to 45 Squadron [Camel] at Ste Marie Capel. For reasons not stated he returned to England on 11th October, and it was not until a year later [the 8th to be precise] that he returned to France and joined 110 Squadron at Bettencourt.

Shortly before the squadron disbanded at Marquise on 27th August, Gerallt was posted to a Reinforcement Park at Arques where he remained for 24-hours before returning to the UK.

Postwar he served for three years, 20th April 1923 to 4th June 1926, in the Reserve of Air Force Officers, holding the rank of Flying Officer, the relevant entries being *Gazetted* on 20 April 1923 and 4 June 1926, issues 32816 page 2892 and 33169 page 3657 respectively.

Then, like so many of his generation, when war came for the second time he immediately offered his services and was granted a commission in the Administrative and Special Duties Branch [LG 14 June 1940, issue 34892, page 4184]. In the majority of cases where officers who had served in the *Great War* and returned to duty in the second, served until the mid-'50s when under the Provisions of the Navy, Army and Air Force Reserves Act 1954, they were obliged to relinquish their commissions. Tragically, in the case of Flying Officer Gerallt Tegywn Griffin he lost his life on the 17th of December 1944, while *en route* for active service on the Continent. He is buried in Schoonselhof Cemetery at Antwerpen where his headstone bears the lengthy inscription: *"The Busy World Is Hushed, The Fever Of Life Is Over, Lord, Abide With Me."* It is noted he held a Bachelor of Science degree [Birmingham] and was a Fellow of the Geographical Society. There are fourteen burials in Schoonslehof Cemetery where the date of death is recorded as the 17th of December 1944.

203 Squadron   Lt D B Barbour   Injured   Unemployed list 16 May 1919
F.1 Camel D9597

T/o Orcq and crashed at Tournai. With the squadron since the 30th of May 1918, it accounted for at least three hostile aircraft, the first being an LVG C which Lieutenant Arthur Edgar Rudge sent crashing into a canal near Merville early in the morning of 20th July. Two days later, and in the capable hands of Lieutenant Richard Stone, a Fokker DVII was driven down in mid-morning near Carvin followed during the evening of 11th August by another Fokker DVII east of Bray by Lieutenant William Sidebotham.

Apart from his single entry in *The Camel File,* nothing is known for Lieutenant Barbour but records have survived regarding the other officers mentioned. Arthur Rudge, from Effingham in Surrey, was born on the 8th of August 1898, joining the RFC on 7th July 1917. On 25th November he arrived at Bailleul where he was attached to 65 Squadron [Camel] which had arrived on the Western Front from Wyton on 27th October, initially using La Lovie but moving to Bailleul on 4th November. His time with the squadron was brief, but not uneventful for on 6th December he misjudged his landing, undershot and crashed B2440. The damage was not too serious, but four days after his accident he was sent back to the UK, probably for additional training.

His second spell of operational service was with 66 Squadron [Camel] on the Italian Front, Arthur reaching Grossa on 23rd January, only to be sent home on 12th April having been involved in three more crashes. The first, on 8th February damaged B3840/F while landing, while on 16th March he probably wrote off B5594 while taking off from San Pietro [the squadron having arrived here from Treviso four days earlier]. Then on 3rd April he lost control of B6413/J while landing and finished up hitting a hangar door.

Despite these false starts, Arthur's tour continued for on 26th June he reported to 203 Squadron at Filescamp and, as reported, accounted for an LVG C reconnaissance aircraft on 20th July. Sadly, two days after this success and within minutes of driving down a Fokker DVII he was shot down and killed, details of this being reported in my second volume on page 77. A tragic end to a determined young scout pilot whose life was snuffed out over the skies of France at the tender age of nineteen.

Richard Stone who drove down a Fokker DVII on the 22nd while flying D9597 also lost his life. He had been posted to 203 Squadron on the 17th of April 1918, transferring to 201 Squadron at Poulainville on the 9th of August. At the time practically every squadron on the Western Front was heavily involved in the *Battle of Arras* that had kicked off the previous day. Richard must have arrived in the morning of the 9th for by the afternoon he was in the air for the final time in his all too brief life. The circumstances of his death appear on page 133 of my second volume, to which I can add by way of the entry on his Army Form B.103c: *"Buried near Vauvillers Rd W 13C 70.7030 by o/c 3rd Field Coy A E D.8296 undated."* The date in the left hand margin for this entry is shown as 23/8/18. His operational flying, traced through entries in *The Camel File* provide an excellent backdrop to the life of scout pilots fighting in the last months of the war. On 17th May, he was airborne in D3362 and while in the region of Estaires-Merville the patrol, led by Captain Leonard Henry Rochford [B7197], pounced on a Pfalz DIII. It was a fierce encounter during which 2nd Lieutenant Edwin Ravenhill Prideaux, a South African, was shot down and killed [see my first volume, page 158]. Also lending a hand was 2nd Lieutenant Charles Frederick Brown flying C61, and Charle Brown would also be involved in Richard's second claim, a DFW C over Estaires on 16th June. Again, it would take the combined efforts of five of the patrol to destroy their opponent; one, unnamed, was flying B7185 while others were the patrol leader Captain E T Haine [D3417] and Lieutenant Yvone Eustace Sutton Kirkpatrick in D3414.

Richard was born on 12th March 1899, his next of kin being recorded as his father, John M Stone at 3 Stone Buildings Lincolns Inn, London WC2. He had enlisted in the RFC on the 2nd of August 1917.

And so to William Sidebottom, born on the 11th of October 1893, who enlisted with the RFC in September 1916. Prior to his arrival on the squadron he had been hospitalised on 24th April 1918, suffering from frostbitten fingers. This must have been a severe case for he was not discharged until 7th May, after which he was attached to 2 Aeroplane Supply Depot before arriving at Filescamp on the 18th.

Note. Two officers with the name William Sidebottom served with the RFC and Royal Air Force, their service being almost in parallel and both were accomplished fighter pilots, each gaining a DFC. William Sidebottom who flew with 203 Squadron claimed at least seven hostile aircraft and a kite ballon, all falling to the guns of C197 between the 24th of September and 2nd October. His DFC is noted for later in the month, but see my next paragraph. Army Form B.103c shows his next of kin address as 11 Stockport Road, Hyde, Cheshire, while the other William Sidebottom gained his victories with 73 Squadron and was awarded his DFC in February 1919. His date of birth is shown as 3rd October 1898, enlisted 1st August 1917, and a next of kin address in Derbyshire, the precise details being unreadable.

A trawl of *Gazette* entries for William Sidebottom results in 672 hits, though not all show the name in full. However, one positively identifies the William who flew with 203 Squadron. Issue 31170 of 7 February 1919, page 2046: *'This officer has carried out numerous offensive and low bombing patrols with courage, skill and judgement. He has also proved himself a bold and resolute fighter in aerial combats, having nine enemy machines to his credit.'*

206 Squadron	Lt C L Cumming	Safe	See 31 January 1919
DH.9 H4249	2Lt H O Brown	Safe	

T/o Bickendorf for mail delivery duties and forced-landed, owing to a burst radiator, at Andrimont [Liège] on the eastern side of Verviers. Charles Linnaeus Cumming was posted in to 206 Squadron on 8th August 1918. Although a Record Service Form has been raised for his observer, it has no details regarding his movements.

Thursday 2 January 1919
Further reduction in Germany's military forces was announced this day with the disbandment of the 18th Imperial German Army. Formed towards the end of 1917 and beginning of 1918, principally from divisions and formations from the Eastern Front where the fighting had dwindled, the 18th Army, commanded by *General der Infanterie* Oskar von Hutier would be a welcome addition to the German Spring Offensive planned for March 1918.

43 Squadron	Lt G R Howsam MC	Safe
7F.1 Snipe E8206		

T/o Bickendorf authorised for a practice flight. By the time George Robert Howsam returned to the airfield the strength of the wind had increased and in the gusty conditions he was unable to control his landing, the Snipe dropping a wing and cartwheeling onto its back. For an appreciation of Lieutenant Howsam's service, please refer to my summary of the 29th November 1918.

48 Squadron	Sgt N Hunt	Safe
Bristol F.2b E2511	Sgt C F Perkin	Safe

T/o Bickendorf and wrecked in circumstances similar to those outlined above. E2511 had been received from 2 Aeroplane Supply Depot on 27th August 1918. The service numbers for the crew, 100083 and 240349 identify them as joining the service more or less at the same time, Sergeant Perkins being a 1917 RNAS entrant automatically transferred on 1st April 1918, while Sergeant Hunt was a direct RFC entrant as a Flight Cadet circa October/November 1917.

65 Squadron	2Lt J D H Lewis	Safe
F.1 Camel E7217	USA	

T/o Bisseghem authorised for a practice flight and on landing in a strong crosswind he lost control and finished up nose down, the propeller shattered. This was his second accident, the previous being on the 26th of November, a month or so after he arrived with the squadron. John Digby High Lewis was born on the 31st of October 1890, and prior to his arrival on the Western Front he had married *Annie Laurie Lewis, Box 19, Poughkeepsie, New York* [Poughkeepsie being a city in Dutchess Country, New York State]. Although it has to be conjecture on my part, it seems likely that the authorities decided he should be removed from being a fighter pilot and on the 4th of February he was ordered to Reckem to join 10 Squadron which until recently had been a Corps reconnaissance unit. However, on his arrival he found the squadron in the throws of returning to Ford in Sussex so, on the 8th, he was sent to Gondecourt for attachment to 108 Squadron only to discover '108' was preparing to cross the Channel to Lympne in Kent. The final entry on his service record reads: *"To Mancherton Barracks for demob 26.4.19."*

201 Squadron   2Lt V S G Hawkins   Safe   Unemployed list 3 July 1919
F.1 Camel C195
T/o Bethencourt and on return executed a heavy landing, ballooned and overturned. It had served with the squadron since the 12th of August 1918. A record of Service card exists for 2nd Lieutenant Hawkins; unfortunately, it has no information regarding his movements.

209 Squadron   2Lt G T Parker   Safe
F.1 Camel F3942
T/o Froidmont and came to grief in circumstances similar to those reported above. In each case the surface wind is described as strong and blustery. F3942 had been on establishment since 9th October 1918. 2nd Lieutenant Parker's service records appear not to have survived the passage of time.

Friday 3 January 1919
Laid to rest in All Saints Church cemetery extension at Harrow-Weald in Middlesex was one of the air VCs from the recent conflict. Captain William Leefe Robinson VC had gained his honour, and with it the adoration of the nation when on the night of 2nd-3rd September 1916, he succeeded, following a torturous flight in and out of cloud, in shooting down a Zeppelin which fell, burning, near the village of Cuffley in Hertfordshire. His victory, however, brought with it a period of being grounded as he was considered far too valuable an asset to be risked on further hazardous operations.

By nature a modest young man, William was embarrassed by the publicity being placed upon him and after pleading with the authorities he returned to active duty as a Flight Commander attached to 48 Squadron which was the first squadron to receive the Bristol F.2b.

Participating in the squadron's first operational sorties with their new aircraft, William Robinson and his observer, 2nd Lieutenant E D Warburton, were shot down in A3337 and captured.

In the remaining months of the war, during which William made several unsuccessful escape attempts, he was very harshly treated and on arriving home on 14th December 1918, was a desperately weak and sick man. Lodging in the home of his friend Captain Noel Clifton and for much of the time confined to his bed, he fell victim to influenza and died from heart failure on New Year's Eve.

The nation had not forgotten William Leefe Robinson VC, thousands lined the streets as the funeral cortege slowly made its way to the cemetery. Leading, appropriately, was the Central Band of the Royal Air Force while overhead an aircraft dropped a wreath which was later placed on the grave.

For a biography of this courageous airmen I recommend Chaz Bowyer's *For Valour - The Air VCs*.

2 Squadron   2Lt H G Marsay   Safe   Unemployed list 21 March 1919
FK.8 D5173   Lt Stewart   Safe
T/o Genech where it crashed on completion of a navigation flight. D5173 had been with the squadron since the last day of September 1918. To the best of my knowledge this was the only serious accident suffered by the squadron since the armistice. 2nd Lieutenant Marsay was born on 10th September 1898 and enlisted in the RFC on February 1st, 1918. He started his operational tour on 26th June with 13 Squadron [RE.8] at Izel-lès-Hameau but on the 1st of July went to Mazingarbe and attachment to 2 Squadron. From the 30th January to 13th February he was on leave, and on his return discovered that the squadron had departed on the 12th to Bicester.

16 Squadron   2Lt J A L Harris   Safe   Unemployed list 26 January 1919
RE.8 C2937   2Lt W Lowe   Safe
T/o Auchy for a navigation exercise, on the face of it a simple task of flying to Cambrai and return. All seems to have gone well until the crew returned to Auchy at which point a misjudged approach resulted in a heavy landing and damage that was beyond economical repair. Both officers joined the squadron in August 1918 at Camblain l'Abbé, 2nd Lieutenant Harris on the 5th and his observer on the 19th. It is likely both returned to the UK on 25th January.

40 Squadron   2Lt A B Dunn   Safe   Unemployed list 29 September 1919
SE.5a C9258   USA
T/o Orcq where in was damaged beyond repair in a crash-landing. Arriving from 1 Air Issues on 16th August, Canadian born Captain George Clapham Dixon, late of the 16th Battalion, Highland Light Infantry, drove down a Fokker DVII SW of Cambrai on the 21st, while the next day Lieutenant Louis Bennett, an American from Weston in West Virginia, bagged a couple of kite balloons east of La Bassée followed on the 23rd by driving down an LVG C reconnaissance aircraft near Ouiéry-la-Motte in the Pas-de-Calais. Sadly, within 24-hours of this victory he was dead, the circumstances leading to his death being recorded in my second volume on page 176. Louis had been with the squadron since the 23rd of July.

George Dixon hailed from Vancouver and was accepted for training as an observer, returning home on 31st March 1917. On return to France he joined 43 Squadron [Sopwith 1½ Strutter] at Treizennes on the 17th of May, but went back to the UK on 20th September having re-mustered for pilot training. In these five months and flying with 2nd Lieutenant Charles Henry Harriman*he claimed an Albatros DIII north of Lens on 16th June and on 13th August near Pont-à-Vendin in the Pas-de-Calais an Albatros DV.

Now qualified as a fighter pilot he arrived back on the Western Front on 22nd May 1918, posted to 85 Squadron at St. Omer. Within two months of his return to operations he was promoted Acting Captain and had accounted, according to the Aerodrome website, a couple of Pfalz DIIIs, the first on the 13th July west of Armentières, followed by a second over Estaries on the 14th, both victories while flying SE.5a D6923. However, *The SE.5a File* has only a record for the combat on the 13th. Arriving from 1 Air Issues three days earlier, D6923 was written off on the 17th of August [see my second volume and page 165 for details].

Meanwhile, Captain Dixon had taken over Flight Commander duties with 40 Squadron, reporting to Bryas on 24th July, and with '40' and between 21st August when he drove a Fokker DVII down out of control SW of Cambrai and 2nd September, another Fokker DVII west of Escourt St. Quentin he added five more enemy scouts and a kite balloon to his score, the last four being achieved while flying SE.5a E3979.

Born in Vancouver on 3rd November 1895, he died there on the 1st of February 1975. TNA Kew has a non-digitised record for Lieutenant George Clapham Dixon of the Highland Light Infantry under WO 339/62259.

Arnold Browning Dunn joined the squadron on 17th October, just in time to take part in the last few weeks of air operations. From 14th to 23 December, he was attached for temporary duty at the aerial ranges and on the 26th of February he was posted back the UK. For his next of kin he indicated his sister at 2544-C-Street, San Diego, California.

* Born on 17th November 1893, Charles Harriman was shot down and killed shortly after 43 Squadron converted to Camels, the date of his death being 29th October 1917. He was patrolling in B2357 when he was attacked by an unidentified hostile aircraft and crashed into Oppy Wood. According to entries in his service record he was buried at Lapugnoy [now Lapugnoy Military Cemetery] by the Reverend B W Reymer attached to the 1st Briagde, RFC. His headstone is inscribed: *"Tenderly Loved And Deeply Mourned By Father And Mother."* Oppy Wood is the subject of a 1918 work by the artist John Nash and held by the IWM.

56 Squadron	Lt E W Graham	+	Caudry British Cemetery
SE.5a E5900	Canada		

T/o Bethencourt for firing practice and it was while recovering from a dive, described by the accident report as gentle, the starboard wing collapsed sending the SE plunging into the ground whereupon it burst into an all consuming fire. It is thought Lieutenant Edward William Graham, formerly of the Canadian Service Corps, was thrown clear for the entries pertaining to his death state he was taken to 3 CCS having sustained multiple injuries. Edward had been with the squadron since 5th October 1918. His funeral service was conducted by the Reverend E S Ellis attached to 13th Corps.

210 Squadron	2Lt B J Dearlove	Injured
F.1 Camel B7159/F6246		

T/o Boussières and came to grief at Bavay aerodrome. At first it was considered for another rebuild but on the 24th it was reduced to produce. Formerly with 201 Squadron, on 10th June 1918, Lieutenant John Hugh Paton crash-landed and in the process turned over near Doullens. He had been with the squadron since 24th April 1918, and postwar was posted on 26th June 1919, to 208 Squadron [7F.1 Snipe] at Heumar.

2nd Lieutenant Dearlove's overseas service was dogged by illness. Having embarked for France on 11th September and arriving at 1 Aeroplane Supply Depot, he was taken ill on the 15th and it was not until the 16th of November 1918 that he was discharged from hospital, and it would be a further month before he joined 210 Squadron. His injuries must have been minor for there are no entries indicating admittance to hospital.

Subsequently, following leave in January he joined 43 Squadron [7F.1 Snipe] at Bickendorf, remaining with '43' until returning to the UK on 25th August.

Saturday 4 January 1919
In the Ukraine the conflict between the Bolsheviks and the White Russians, an army group being formed to bolster the fortunes of the latter.

9 Squadron	Lt C Dotzert	Safe	Unemployed list 20 May 1919
RE.8 F1667	Canada		
	Mechanic Phillips	Safe	

T/o Cognelée to rejoin the squadron now at Ludendorf. It was, perhaps, not the best of flying weather and not for the first time an aircraft was wrecked before it became airborne owing to the gusting conditions of the surface wind. Clayton Dotzert, an ex-Flight Cadet, had been granted a temporary commission on 3rd June 1918 [LG 12 July 1918, issue 30793, page 8205], joining the squadron at Amiens on the 19th of August. A most informative website, sponsored by Waterloo Public Library [which I am most pleased to acknowledge] reveals that Clayton was of German extraction with his Canadian roots in Waterloo, Ontario, and on his release from the Royal Air Force and return to Canada became a maker of high quality leather gloves, first with his brother-in-law but later setting up on his own as the Dotzert Glove Company.

It appears, however, that making gloves was not his only passion for, as his biography records, he became a highly respected postmaster, serving the community for twenty-five years.

In 1934, he helped to establish the Waterloo Siskins Junior B hockey team while throughout his life he never lost a very special interest in air force development. He was a member of Wing 404 RCAF commanding for a time K-W 80th Air Cadet Squadron.

Born on the 13th of October 1896, his long and very rewarding life ended on the 6th of December 1988. Clayton Dotzert, airman, glove maker, postmaster and respected member of Waterloo's community is buried in the town's Parkview Cemetery.

| 94 Squadron | Lt E C Mogridge | Safe | Unemployed list 2 March 1919 |
| SE.5a H680/D | | | |

T/o Izel-lès-Hameau for a practice flight and reported as being damaged beyond repair while landing. H680 was one of the squadron's initial issues during the working up period at Upper Heyford. Late of the Machine Gun Corps, Lieutenant Mogridge joined the RFC on 18th December 1917 [LG 18 March 1918, supplement 30582, page 3399]. With the squadron preparing to return to England, he was cross-posted on the 18th to 1 Squadron and thence to the UK on the last day of February.

| 104 Squadron | Lt F Wallis | Safe | |
| DH.9 C6153 | 2Lt C B Parker | Safe | |

T/o Maisoncelle and reported as being wrecked in a forced-landing at Sommelsdijk on Overflakkee, some 12 km SSE of Goeree, Holland, after becoming lost and running out of petrol. Records of Service for both officers are Spartan in content; Frank Wallis was born on 11th March 1899, while Cecil Billsdon Parker came into the world on the last day of March 1900, and joined the Royal Air Force on the 29th of April 1918.

104 Squadron	2Lt R F Lynch	Safe	
DH.9 D481	USA		
	Mechanic Linion	Safe	

T/o Maisoncelle to test the engine and was damaged beyond repair in a poorly executed landing. On charge by the 6th of June 1918, it had survived a crash-landing at Essey-lès-Nancy on 9th November, the identity of its crew not being recorded. Richard Faulkner Lynch, born 24th January 1899, joined the RFC on 13th September 1917, embarking for France on 17th of August last. On the 21st he was attached to the squadron, then at Azelot.

When the squadron departed for Turnhouse on the 1st of February, Richard Lynch was posted to 1 Aeroplane Supply Depot, remaining on establishment until the 10th of June when he was ordered to Köln for temporary duty. Eleven days later he returned to England. Despite an unusual surname, I have not been able to discover any information regarding Mechanic Linion.

| 104 Squadron | Lt P C Saxby | Safe | Commission relinquished 31 January 1919 |
| DH.9 D5773 | Lt E D Aldridge | Safe | Unemployed list 10 October 1919 |

T/o Mainsoncelle for formation flying and it while in formation at 3,000 feet that the engine spluttered and died. With no option but to forced-land the crew headed for what appeared to be a reasonably large field which turned out to have been recently ploughed. Consequently, on touching down on the soft earth the wheels dug in and catapulted the DH onto its back. Having extracted themselves from their cockpits, the crew discovered they were near Trequess [sic].

Lieutenant Percy Charles Saxby, born 3rd November 1897, arrived with the RFC on 31st January 1918, following service with the 5th Battalion, Royal West Kent Regiment [LG 24 May 1918, issue 30702, page 6111] and with his training finished he joined the squadron at Azelot on the 2nd of July.

Flying for him was not always straight forward and between 4th and 15th September he was treated in 8 General Hospital for chronic air sickness. This was followed by a period of convalescence during which he was struck down with Stomatitis, a painful condition that effected his mouth, and was admitted to a New Zealand administered Stationary Hospital. Consequently, it was not until the 6th of November that he returned to the squadron.

On 24th January he was posted home and relinquished his air force commission soon after. So far I have not been able to trace any information for his observer, apart from the *Gazette* entry reporting his placement on the unemployed list.

D5773 was one of three hundred airframes built by the furniture makers, Waring & Gillow and arrived in France by way of Hendon on 29th August 1918. Its service with the squadron got off to an inauspicious start in that on delivery from 3 Aeroplane Supply Depot it crashed on landing. Repaired, it was accepted on 31st October and during the early afternoon of 6th November while raiding Buhl aerodrome 2nd Lieutenant Jack Wrighton and Sergeant W H Bell sent a Fokker DVII down with flames streaming back from its engine.

Born on 23rd June 1898, Jack Wrighton joined the squadron on 18th August 1918. Laid low with tonsillitis between the 1st and 4th of November [he was treated in 8 CCS], he returned to the UK soon after on the 5th of December.

| 110 Squadron | Lt R P Brailli | Safe | Unemployed list 22 April 1919 |
| DH.9A F1032 | 2Lt C H B Stevenson | Safe | Unemployed list 26 August 1919 |

T/o Mainsoncelle and wrecked after landing on rough ground at Béthune. My summary for a 99 Squadron mishap on 16th December 1918, mentions 2nd Lieutenant Cornelius Henry Bowman Stevenson who arrived with 110 Squadron as recently as 27th November and remained on establishment until returning home and placement on the unemployed list. Lieutenant Rudolph Paul Brailli had reported as recently as 11th December after treatment in 42 Stationary Hospital where he was taken on 1st November suffering from influenza.

Sunday 5 January 1919
Casualty returns, filed by 3 Squadron Australian Flying Corps at Charleroi, report the following RE.8s as unfit for further service owing to the ravages of winter weather: B4088, C2728 and C2748.

Monday 6 January 1919
In Poland a Supreme Peoples' Council of Greater Poland came into existence and immediately Polish troops advanced on the German-held airport near Lawica, quickly over running and securing their objective.

An inspection of 53 Squadron's RE.8s at Laneffe revealed a sorry state of affairs and by the time the inspection was completed no less than eight badly waterlogged aircraft were deemed unfit for further use: C2545, C2602, C2901, D4871, D6703, F5897, F6018 and H7033. Relatively new H7033 had flown for a total of 25.15 hours while D4871 had, at least, logged a useful 161.05 hours.

From Gerpinnes 59 Squadron sent in a return for RE.8 D6823 as being waterlogged.

29 Squadron   2Lt H H Swanton   Safe   Unemployed list 11 May 1919
SE.5a H675/A
T/o Bickendorf for camera gun practice but with the wind gusting in all directions it was not too surprising that 2nd Lieutenant Swanton lost control and crashed without becoming airborne.

45 Squadron   2Lt A V Green   Injured   Unemployed list 12 July 1919
F.1 Camel D9392/B Canada
T/o Izel-lès-Hameau and written off in a landing accident at Maisoncelle. During its time in Italy it was flown by a number of pilots and accounted for at least three hostile aircraft. Born on the 8th of April 1891, Albon Victor Green joined the RFC on 10th October 1917, reporting to the squadron at Grossa on the 6th of August. Now seriously injured he was taken to 12 Stationary Hospital and it was not until the 11th of March was he fit enough to be discharged. During his period of incapacity he received treatment in 3 General Hospital and 51 General Hospital. By the time of his release 45 Squadron had returned to the UK, so Albon was ordered to report to the Pool of Pilots station at Lilques [sic] and I suspect he remained here until his discharge. A married officer, his wife's address is shown as 774, 13th Avenue West, Vancouver, British Columbia.

45 Squadron   Lt J H Dewhirst   Safe   Unemployed list 4 February 1919
F.1 Camel E7204
T/o Izel-lès-Hameau and wrecked after landing on a rain-soaked airfield at Bethencourt. Lieutenant James Henry Dewhirst came from Bingley in Yorkshire, where he was born on 26th September 1892. He enlisted with the RFC on 25th April 1917, and saw extensive operational service with the squadron which began in Italy at Astrana on 10th February. By the summer he was attached to C Flight, commanded by Captain Cedric Ernest Howell*and though I have no evidence that Captain Howell flew E7204 his prowess as a fighter pilot is, nonetheless, worth setting down.

Meanwhile, James Dewhirst whose name crops up several times in the squadron's published history, was posted home of 25th January.

* Born in Adelaide, South Australia, on 17th June 1896, there are several websites recording the life of this outstanding fighter pilot who sailed out of Melbourne on the 14th of March 1916, as a private soldier attached to the 14th Infantry Battalion of the Australian Imperial Forces. Reaching the Western Front, Cedric Howell, now a sniper with the 46th Battalion, transferred to the RFC on the 16th of November at a time when the fighting on the Somme was beginning to peter out.

With his training over, he was posted to 45 Squadron on 27th October 1917, at which time The Flying Camels were in France at Ste Marie Cappel. However, operations on the Italian Front beckoned and by Christmas '45' were settling in, moving in quick succession from Padova to San Pelagio and on Boxing Day to Istrana from where the business of engaging the enemy began in earnest.

Referring to the Aerodrome website, between 14th January, when he opened his account by shooting down an Albatros DIII in the Cimetta-Cadogne region, and 15th July when he destroyed a Phönix DI [an Austro-Hungarian fighter built by the Phönix Flugzeug-Werke] near Mount Forcellona, Captain Howell had scored nineteen victories, all but the first two during morning patrols.

His most productive day was May 13th, when in the space of just twenty-five minutes he drove down a quartet of Albatros DIIIs, two over Coldarco, a third near Costa and the last in the region of Brenta-Rocca. According to *The Camel File* Cedric was associated with five aircraft, his favourite being D9394 in which he gained ten of his victories though in those hectic minutes of combat on the 13th he was flying B5238 in which he had the misfortune to bend in a crash-landing on the 14th [it was repaired and returned to the squadron].

It is no surprise, therefore, that his outstanding record was rewarded with an MC and a DFC, the citations being published in *Gazette* supplements 30901, page 10968 and 30913, page 11252 of 13th and 20th September 1918, respectively: *'For conspicuous gallantry and devotion to duty. He bombed an electrical power-house with great skill, obtaining three direct hits from 100 feet. With two other machines he carried out a most dashing attack on twelve enemy aeroplanes. Although badly hampered by frequent jams in both of his machine guns, he destroyed three and drove down one out of control [this refers to the combat on 13th May]. He is a most successful and gallant patrol leader, and has destroyed six enemy aeroplanes and shot down one out of control.'*

This was followed by: *'On a recent occasion this officer, leading his patrol of three machines, attacked nine enemy aeroplanes, destroying six and driving down one out of control; he himself accounted for two of these. On a former occasion he destroyed three enemy aeroplanes in one fight [again, this is in reference to the patrol on May 13th]. He is a fine fighting officer, skilful and determined.'*

One further honour awaited him, namely the DSO which was conferred upon him by the King at an investiture held at Buckingham Palace on 13th December 1918. Sadly, a year on and he was dead. It seems that following his release from the air force he accepted an invitation to take part in an attempt to fly from the United Kingdom to Australia within thirty days, the prize for achieving this as offered by the Australian Government being a handsome £10,000. With the backing of the Martinsyde aircraft manufacturer, Captain Howell would pilot an aircraft of their design and with a Rolls-Royce engine the prospects of success appeared favourable.

Thus, on 4th December, accompanied by a fellow Australian, Lieutenant George Henry Fraser as his navigator and flight engineer, Cedric was airborne from Hounslow Heath Aerodrome and heading across the Channel to France. The weather, however, closed in and an unscheduled landing was made at Dijon.

With conditions improving the pair pressed on and by the 10th, and now at Taranto, they were hopeful of crossing the Mediterranean and into Africa but once again the weather forced a change of plan and course was set for Crete. What happened next is a matter of some conjecture but apparently in mid-evening the Martinsyde was over St. George's Bay making for Corfu but before reaching land the aircraft alighted in the sea. It is said by people living close by that cries for help were heard but the rough seas prevented any boats being launched and both airmen drowned.

Captain Howell's body was eventually washed ashore and returned to Australia for burial on 22nd April 1920, in Heidelberg's Warringal Cemetery. An account of this sombre occasion can be read on *Wikipedia,* while additional reading is available on the Australian Dictionary of Biography website where the notes were penned by T H Cooke.

On 10th November 2019, the Australian newspaper *The Courier* carried a lengthy article about the race in which the Martinsyde is identified as being registered G-EAMR and has a photograph of a smiling Cedric Howell in uniform and alongside a fellow pilot which, I suspect, was taken in Italy.

To close, Cedric was married and on his service record his wife is shown as his next of kin and during the war she was resident at 24 Breden Gardens, Cambourne Avenue, West Ealing.

| 73 Squadron | Lt D G Reid | Safe | Unemployed list 13 April 1919 |
| F.1 Camel D6462 | USAS | | |

T/o Baizieux and while attempting to land at Bovelles flew into a telegraph pole and crashed. At the time he had run low on petrol. The history of D6462 can be traced back to the 30th of March 1918, and prior to being sent for a major overhaul on 9th July, it had two hostile aircraft to its credit, both at the hands of Lieutenant Gerald Pilditch MC.

Born in South Africa on 27th October 1892, he enlisted in the RFC on the 2nd of October 1917, and by early '18 and following a brief spell in hospital returned to duty with 73 Squadron. The closeness of dates between joining the air force and his posting as a scout pilot to an operation squadron leads me to suggest he may have trained as a pilot before arriving in the UK.

Including D6462, Gerald flew at least half-a-dozen Camels in which *The Camel File* mentions him by name. Two, C1590 and C1619 came to grief on the same day, 26th March. The former was recovered from near Cachy in the Somme, WSW of Villers-Bretonneux and following inspection was repaired. The second incident occurred near the village of Franvillers, roughly midway between Amiens and Albert and was abandoned to its fate.

Gerald opening his scoring on 11th March during an early afternoon patrol and when at the controls of B7298. Hunting southeast of Cambrai the patrol came across a gaggle of enemy scouts, one of which, a Fokker DrI was picked out and driven down. Then, early in the morning of the 24th, and over the Somme, he accounted for a two seater near Vraignes [there are two locations where Vraignes is the first part of the name; Vraignes -lès-Horney and Vraignes-en-Vermandois.

His association with D6462 and combat success came during an evening patrol on 11th April when over Villers-Bretonneux his sharp eyes fastened on a Albatros which was soon despatched; then shortly before sunset on 21st May, he drove down a Fokker DrI southwest of Armentières.

Finally, while on strafing operations in the far south of the Somme on 11th June he came to the rescue of a squadron colleague Lieutenant J H Ackerman of the USAS who was scrapping hard with a scout. Seeing that the American was getting the worst of it, Gerald, flying D6572, piled in and sent the Fokker DVII down to crash near Rollot. Meanwhile, Lieutenant Ackerman crash-landed, his Camel being totally wrecked; see my first volume and page 236 for details.

Unsurprisingly, these clashes with the enemy in the air and, as the citation shows, on the ground were rewarded with an MC, *Gazetted* 22 June 1918, supplement 30761, page 7420: *'For conspicuous gallantry and devotion to duty. He engaged the enemy massed ready for an attack from a height of 300 feet, using up all his ammunition and scattering the enemy in all directions, inflicting very heavy casualties. Previously to this he had dived and fired on a hostile battery until he had silenced it, and had also destroyed an enemy triplane and a two-seater machine. His work has been of the highest order, and he has shown the greatest courage and energy in attacking ground targets.'*

On 18th July he was taken to 14 General Hospital, and two days later he was evacuated to England on the HS *Jan Breydel.*

Arriving in France on 24th July 1918, Lieutenant Reid in the space of 48-hours passed through 2 Aeroplane Supply Depot, 9 Aircraft Park and thence to 73 Squadron at Le Touquin. He had one confirmed victory on 19th September, but an early claim made on 25th August was disallowed. On each occasion he had fought with the formidable Fokker DVII.

| 85 Squadron | Lt C C Wood | Safe |
| SE.5a F5613 | South Africa | |

T/o Ascq for air test only for the engine to cut. Crashed-landed and overturned. Charles Campbell Wood was born on 8th December 1891, probably in Johannesburg and joined the RFC on 11th April 1917. His commission to the General List was promulgated 18 September 1917 in supplement 30292, page 9711. His first operational posting dates from 14th February 1918, when he was attached to 2 Squadron [FK.8] at Floringhem and lasted until June 21st, when he returned to the UK on temporary duty. By the 5th of July he was back in France and on the 14th proceeded to Paris on a seven day assignment. It is not clear if he returned to 2 Squadron, for the next entry on Army Form B.103, shows his return to England, again on temporary duty, for three days between the 21st and 24th of September. Post armistice was spent on leave and then an attachment to 1 Aeroplane Supply Depot before reporting to Ascq and 85 Squadron on 11th December. At this point entries on his service record cease.

99 Squadron	2Lt W T Jones	Safe	
DH.9A E9743	Canada		
	Sgt A J Renfree	Safe	

T/o Aulnoye for mail delivery duties and on return crashed while trying to land. Born on 16th July 1898, William Thomas Jones likely hailed from Toronto where his next of kin address is shown as 228 Pape Avenue. His first posting was to 104 Squadron at Azelot on 19th July 1918, but on 1st August he was cross-posted to 99 Squadron. I have not been able to discover any information regarding his observer. Their DH was one of a batch of 150 airframes built at the Mann, Eggerton facility in Norwich and was tested in late October 1918 at 3 Aeroplane Acceptance Park, Norwich.

| 103 Squadron | Captain R Jackson | Safe | |
| DH.9 E660 | Lt E A Slater | Safe | Unemployed list 26 August 1919 |

T/o Ronchin for formation flying practice and on return landed heavily, breaking the fuselage into two sections. Unlike the DH summarised above, E660 saw several weeks of operational service. Arriving with the squadron from 1 Air Issues on 25th September 1918, it was selected for a late afternoon reconnaissance on 25th October, the crew being Sergeants H Driver and H Huckle. Ever alert to danger, it was around 1630 that a brace of Fokker DVII were seen preparing to attack, but skilful flying by Sergeant Driver enabled his observer to drive one of their assailants down out of control, while his companion broke of his attack and was soon out of sight, leaving the crew to complete their task.

I have not been able to find Captain Jackson's service record, but that for Edward Albert Slater shows he was Devonshire born on the 3rd of March 1900. He joined the squadron on 24th September and on 23rd October, teamed with 2nd Lieutenant Leslie Weston Marchant in C2204 took part in an afternoon raid on Hirson Railway Station. Invariably, these operations were hotly contested and with the formation east of Tournai they were engaged by a swarm of Fokker DVIIs, but as the enemy fighters came within range so they were met by a storm of well directed defensive fire, two of the attackers going down out of control from the aim of Edward Slater. In his post raid report, he said that one of his bursts hit the scout with such force that it *"fell like a stone."*

Post armistice he remained in France until long after '103' had returned to England on 26th March, eventually Edward returned to the UK on 20th August.

| 204 Squadron | Lt R E Baty MC | Safe | Unemployed list 5 February 1919 |
| F.1 Camel F8501 | | | |

T/o Heule and on return flew into a raised bank; wrecked. A late production aircraft F8501 was at 1 Air Issues by the 13th of October 1918, and reached the squadron on the 26th. In the final days of aerial combat, and flown by Lieutenant Edward Stanton, it destroyed a Fokker DVII near Melle [Oost-Vlaanderen] in the early morning of 4th November.

Edward had recently joined the squadron from 203 Squadron with whom he had served since 27th September 1918. His service record shows he was born on 10th February 1898, and enlisted in the RFC on 14th August 1917, and on 17th April he reported to Bruay and joined 4 Squadron Australian Flying Corps; three days later and he was in 23 CCS suffering from injuries to his head and arms having stalled and crashed on a practice flight [see page 82 of my first volume for details]. Discharged on the 25th, he was sent back to England on the 27th, no doubt to undergo further training and it was not until 21st September that he returned to the France.

Reginald Elphinstone Baty, late of the Northumberland Fusiliers, was appointed to the Royal Air Force on 2nd May 1918 [LG 31 May 1918, issue 30714, page 6385] and, I suspect, like many of his fellow officers he opted for service in the skies over the Western Front rather than continue his fight with the enemy on the ground for as the citation that follows his reasoning becomes clear: *'For conspicuous gallantry and devotion to duty in leading a raiding party. Although severely wounded, he continued to lead his men, and entered the enemy trench. He has previous done fine work.'* [LG 26 April 1917, supplement 32446, page 7047].

At the time his rank was Temporary Second Lieutenant. Although placed on the unemployed list, I suspect he retained a link with his old regiment until relinquishing his commission 5th July 1922 [LG 5 September 1921, supplement 32446, page 7047].

With the situation in Europe once again giving cause for alarm he returned to uniform and was commissioned as a Flying Officer to No 936[County of Northumberland] Squadron, Auxiliary Air Force,*but subsequently he was transferred to the Administrative and Special Duties Branch with which he served until relinquishing his commission on 6th February 1945, retaining his Squadron Leader rank [LG 20 February 1945, supplement 36945, page 990]. A document in his name held at TNA Kew under AIR 76/28/45 shows his date of birth as 1st August 1895.

* Coming within the barrage balloon section of the Auxiliary Air Force, the squadron existed from 20th February 1939 to 4 June 1943, when it amalgamated with 937[County of Northumberland] Squadron. Bearing both number plates disbandment took place on 1st December 1944.

Tuesday 7 January 1919
Easily the worst day of the year so far with thirteen aircraft reported as being written off owing to crashes caused through weather and a run of engine failures.

In Poland the German Air Force arrived over Lawica airport which Polish troops had captured 24-hours earlier and bombed the area; this may well have been the first operational sorties flown by their air force since the armistice.

4 Squadron AusFC   Lt N C Johnson   Safe
7F.1 Snipe E8088

T/o Bickendorf for formation flying which went well until Lieutenant Johnson came into land. Probably through the inclement weather the Snipe came down hard on one wheel, bounced and before control could be regained hit the ground and turned over. Issued on 30th September 1918, from 1 Aeroplane Supply Depot its service up until the crash-landing had been free of incident.

24 Squadron   2Lt G Abrahams   Safe   Unemployed list 29 September 1919
SE.5a F5508

T/o Bisseghem for a practice sortie but having climbed to around fifty feet the engine cut and upon turning to avoid some buildings the wind took charge and blew the SE onto its back, much, I daresay, to the concern of 2nd Lieutenant Abrahams whose Record of Service has yet to be found.

   Arriving with the squadron on 18th September 1918, it was taken over by Captain Walter Hunt Longton who accounted for a kite balloon south of Busigny [Nord] on 8th October and before the month was out he had destroyed a quartet of Fokker DVIIs, thus bringing his total of aerial combat successes to eleven and the award of a DFC and First Bar. The citations for these honours were published in the *Gazettes* of 2nd November 1918, supplement 30989, page 12969 and 8th February 1919, supplement 31170, page 2033.

   'On the 22nd August this officer led his formation of six machines to attack an equal number of the enemy scouts. All the latter were account for, four being crashed and the remaining two driven down out of control. A brilliant perform-ance, reflecting the greatest credit on this officer as leader, and all who took part in the engagement. During the last seven weeks Lieutenant Longton has destroyed seven enemy machines.'

   This assertion of seven enemy machines is at odds with research carried out and published on the Aerodrome website. Up to the 22nd August, and commencing on 7th July, Walter had sent down five, thus making his victory on the 22nd his sixth, secured in D6963, the action taking place over Haut Allines.

   'Between 29th September and 9th October, this officer carried out twelve tactical reconnaissances, bringing back most valuable information; he also displayed great gallantry in attacking enemy troops on the ground. On 9th October when on a low patrol, he observed a machine-gun nest which appeared to be the sole obstacle to our calvary advance. Having informed the cavalry and field artillery of the situation, he co-operated with the former in their attack, and, after the enemy had been driven out, pursued them with machine-gun fire as they retreated.'

   This First Bar citation is a reflection on much of the work being carried out by the scout squadrons since the opening of the 100 days campaign. The static days of trench warfare over, both armies were now out in the open with the British and Commonwealth forces, and their French and American counterparts relentlessly harassing the enemy as they gave ground that had been in their possession since the opening months of the war.

   Born on 10th September 1892, Walter Longton joined the RFC on 29th April 1916, following service as a Territorial with the 1st Worcestershire Yeomanry, and was *Gazetted* as a Temporary Second Lieutenant [LG 10 May 1916, supp-lement 29575, page 4649]. He first saw action with 85 Squadron, gaining an AFC [LG 3 June 1918, supplement 30772, page 6520]. At the time he had been laid low with Rubella and was to remain incapacitated until 4th June. His posting as Acting Captain for Flight Commander duties with 24 Squadron was promulgated on 27th September.

   Postwar, and following a brief spell back in civilian life, Walter, now with a Second Bar added to his DFC [LG 30 May 1919, supplement 31378, page 7030] but without the citation added, was granted a permanent commission with seniority from 1st August 1919. Within a much reduced in size air force promotion was slow but by the summer of 1927, he had attained the rank of Squadron Leader. This was a time when air races were all the vogue and wealthy private owners often recruited service pilots to fly their aircraft in events held up and down the country. It was also an age when what today we refer to as Health and Safety assessments for such events were unheard of and already the meeting, the third Whitsun Races held near Bournemouth with Ensbury Park Racecourse as their venue, had got off to a terrible start with the fatal crash of a DH.37A G-EBDO. It was a practice flight ahead of the main programme and with Major Harold Hemming at the controls and accompanied by 24-year old Claude St. John Plevins as a passenger the crash occurred within moments of becoming airborne when the DH stalled in a tight turn. Claude Plevins was killed and Major Hemming was helped from the wreckage seriously injured.

   This accident occurred on the 4th, and two days later with the races now in full swing came the next tragedy when piloting a Blackburn Bluebird G-EBKD Walter came into a midair collision with a Westland Widgeon G-EBPW flown by Flight Lieutenant Lawrence Pratt Oppenshaw, the two aircraft plunging into the ground at West Parley on the northern outskirts of Bournemouth.

   Contemporary newspapers local to the Bournemouth area reported these crashes in detail along with reaction from those living in the vicinity to aircraft flying perilously low to the ground, so low that a local farmer was enraged to the point of loosing off both barrels from his shot gun as one passed over his land on the 25th - this was Bluebird G-EBKD and the pilot Squadron Leader Walter Hunt Longton.

40 Squadron   2Lt L A Brais   Injured   Unemployed list 20 May 1919
SE.5a F5582   Canada

T/o Orcq having been briefed for practice flying but with seconds of becoming airborne 2nd Lieutenant Louis Alexis Brais collided with a tree and crashed out of control. Louis's Record of Service is confined to recording his date of birth as 11th October 1894, his next of kin details, name and rank.

   The incident here reported is mentioned on page 80 of David Gunby's excellent history of 40 Squadron, the author stating that the crash was owing to engine failure.

42 Squadron	Lt F W Mesinger	Safe	Unemployed list 12 July 1919
RE.8 C2689	2Lt G E Muir	Safe	Unemployed list 15 December 1919

T/o Marquise and on arrival at Abscon the wind strength was such that on touch down the RE was blown onto its back. Born on the 20th of August 1893, Frederick William Mesinger joined the squadron the 1st of June 1918, and his Record of Service is completely at odds with his placement on the unemployed list for the final entry on his 'Casualty Form - Officers' aka Record of Service shows *"26.5.20 To Home Est."*

George Esson Muir, born on 23rd November 1892, first saw operational service with 9 Squadron, commencing on 19th August. However, on 12th October he was admitted to 14 General Hospital with an undisclosed condition and on discharge on the 27th was temporarily attached to 1 Aeroplane Supply Depot. Then, between the last day of October and 24th November, he was hospitalised again, this time suffering from a very painful abscess in his right ear.

Returned as fit to 1 Aeroplane Supply Depot, he was attached to 42 Squadron on the 12th of December. Shortly after the accident he proceeded on leave, this being the final entry on his Record of Service.

43 Squadron	Lt G M Smith	Safe
7F.1 Snipe E8041	Canada	

T/o Bickendorf and crashed near Köln while practising his flying. Of Victoria in British Columbia, Gerald Mackie Smith entered the world on the 5th of November 1893, and joined the RFC on 18th April 1917. He was commissioned to the General List on 13th August [LG 30 October 1917, supplement 30357, page 11130], embarking for France on the 2nd of February. However, unlike the majority of newly trained fighter pilot, Gerald spent the next eight months moving twixt a number of non-operational units, plus leave, and it was not until 25th September that he reported for duty with 43 Squadron, then based at Fienvillers.

His travels not yet an end, he was sent on temporary duty on 10th October to 83 Wing at Bainville-sur-Madon, the date of his return to 43 Squadron going unreported and the last entry on his Record of Service is for leave between the 17th and 31st of January 1919.

46 Squadron	Lt R C Mills	Safe
F.1 Camel D1958		

T/o Baizieux and believed damaged beyond repair following a landing mishap during which the Camel turned over. For an appreciation of Lieutenant Mills's service, please refer to my summary of 10th December 1918. This accident was the fifth to effect the squadron since the armistice and, I suspect, for Lieutenant Mills his final flight with the squadron.

55 Squadron	Lt G D Beaudry	Safe	Unemployed list 28 September 1919
DH.4 A7936	Canada		
	2Lt W H S Kingsland	Safe	

T/o Saint André-aux-Bois to practice map reading and both officers were most fortunate to escape serious injury when the DH nosedived into woods close to the airfield. For Gustave Dominique Beaudry, this was his second serious accident, the first being on 20th December 1918. His service records merely indicate his home as being in Montreal and his date of birth as 9th of May 1898. That for his observer is much more detailed: William Henry Kingsland, born 20th January 1900, hailed from Stenage in Hertfordshire and was posted to 55 Squadron at Azelot on 26th September 1918. Shortly before the squadron returned to Renfrew on January 20th, he was ordered to report to the Reinforcement Pool from where he was attached to 20 Squadron on the 19th of February. Following home leave in March, he accompanied the squadron to India. At this point entries on Army Form B.103 cease and attempts at tracing his service via the *Gazette* and *Wikipedia* have failed to bear fruit. The loss of A7936 was the last from the squadron before disposing of their aircraft to storage on the 17th.

62 Squadron	Captain F G C Weare MC	Safe	See 18 March 1919
Bristol F.2b E2595	2Lt S B Perry	Safe	

T/o Nivelles for an air test and wrecked in a crash occasioned by engine failure, the Bristol stalling into trees near the airfield. Of The Buffs [East Kent Regiment] and as 2nd Lieutenant, Frank Gerald Craven Weare was seconded to the RFC on 11th July 1917 [LG 2 August 1917, supplement 30214, page 7892]. Postwar he was one of a select group of officers appointed to a permanent commission, thereby becoming the bedrock of the Royal Air Force [LG 1 August 1919, issue 31486, page 9868]. The citation for his MC, *Gazetted* 22 June 1918, supplement 30761, page 7425 reads: *'For conspicuous gallantry and devotion to duty. In the course of eight days' operations he destroyed two enemy machines, drove down one out of control and enabled his observer to destroy two others. During an earlier engagement he carried out two valuable reconnaissances at a low altitude. He showed a splendid fighting spirit and displayed great skill and judgement in leading his formation'.* Having attained Flight Lieutenant rank, he resigned his permanent commission of 30th January 1924, and was permitted to retain his rank [LG 29 January 1924, issue 32902, page 875].

Come the Second World War and he was appointed as a 2nd Lieutenant in the Special List of officers for service with the Army Cadet Corps, this being effective from 25th November 1942 [LG 24 August 1943, supplement 36142, page 3782]. His biography, as reported on *Wikipedia,* and which I acknowledge, shows his birth as 15th June 1896, and on completing his education at Charterhouse School he entered Sandhurst as a Gentleman Cadet. A table showing his fifteen aerial combat victories, all attained while attached to 22 Squadron and flying Bristol F.2bs is recorded. His death is reported to have occurred in London on 6th July 1971. The excellent Aerodrome website also produces his table of victories, noting that his observer for all bar the first two was Lieutenant George Hayward, while 2nd Lieutenant S J Hunter was present for the combats fought on 13th and 16th March 1918. Information regarding 2nd Lieutenant Perry is lacking, merely a record showing his rank, name and initials.

65 Squadron   Captain A Storey DFC   Safe

F.1 Camel F1925

T/o Bisseghem for local flying practice and on landing in a gusting wind a wingtip brushed the ground and catapulted the Camel onto its nose. Alan Storey, born on the 20th of September 1896, enlisted with the RFC on the 1st of March 1917, eventually joining 208 Squadron at Tramecourt of 22nd September and thence on the 23rd to Foucacourt and it was from here on the 26th that he was wounded and taken to hospital with gunshot wounds to his legs.

The Camel File shows he was flying in D8168 and following a scrap with an unidentified hostile aircraft he forced-landed near Villachottes [sic] from where the Camel was recovered by 7 Advanced Salvage Section and though badly damaged it was repaired and reissued to the squadron by the 3rd of October.

Meanwhile, Captain Storey was undergoing treatment in 41 Stationary Hospital before being evacuated on 8th October on HMHS *Western Australia.* Fully recovered, he returned to the squadron on the 14th of November, but was posted out a week later to 65 Squadron. According to his Record of Service he had been *Gazetted* with a DFC, but I have yet to find the citation for this award. Searches of the paper merely highlight administrative entries in respect of pay and allowances, and his attachment to 65 Squadron is the final entry on his service sheet.

However, an internet search brings up his name in the book *Images of War - Royal Flying Corps - Rare Photographs from Wartime Archives* by Alistair Smith [Pen & Sword Aviation, 2012]. Thus, on page 89 is a photograph of a wrecked Avro 504K which was privately owned by Captain Alan Storey in which he took off from Weymouth with a female passenger on Saturday, 16th August 1919 [this is at odds with the book's title] intending to fly eastwards along the coast to Bournemouth. What should have been a very pleasant experience for the young lady ended rather abruptly when the Avro's engine backfired so violently that part of the propeller was blown away and it was only Captain Storey's skill in handling a crippled aircraft that he alighted in the water just off the pavilion.

Two more images of the wrecked Avro are published on the website devoted to Dorset Aircraft Crashes, admirably compiled by Dave Fagen to whom I am indebted.

Delving further into the history of D8168, prior to Alan Storey forced-landing, Captain James Butler White, born in Canada on the 9th of July 1893 and enlisting in the RNAS on 7th February 1917, drove down an enemy reconnaissance aircraft east of Oppy during a first light patrol on 14th August 1918. So skilled were the crew of the two-seater that it needed three of Captain White's patrol to come to aid. Then, during the evening of 6th September James sent a Fokker DVII down burning furiously to crash onto the east bank of a canal on the Arras to Cambrai road.

Although, as noted, I have not found the citation for Alan Storey's DFC, I have located that for Captain White. It was *Gazetted* on 3 December 1918, supplement 31046, page 14327: *'A fine fighting pilot who has accounted for eight enemy aeroplanes. He has led numerous offensive and low bombing raids, and by his able and daring leadership has achieved great success with a minimum of casualties to his patrol.'*

Turning to the Aerodrome website, James White actually accounted for eleven enemy aircraft, two prior to the formation of the Royal Air Force when 208 Squadron was 8 Squadron RNAS. He opened his scoring on the 24th of January 1918, and rounded off on the 3rd of October. His death on the 2nd of January 1972, was announced from Toronto.

85 Squadron   2Lt E H Henson   Safe   Unemployed list 19 April 1919

SE.5a E5763

T/o Ascq and on return, and with the engine misfiring, it was caught in a violent gust of wind which blew the SE onto its back. It had been on establishment since the 13th of November 1918. Army Form B.103 indicates 2nd Lieutenant Henson joined the squadron on 4th September last, and had only returned to duty 24-hours earlier from temporary duty in Brussels. On the 13th he was posted back to England to await demobilisation.

205 Squadron   Lt K K Gould   Safe

DH.9A E8437

T/o Maubeuge with orders to ferry the DH to La Louveterie but the engine seized and a crash-landing resulted near the aerodrome. It is is not clear, however, whether this occurred on departure or on arriving at its destination. Built at Hendon by AIRCO E8437 was issued from 2 Air Issues on 25th September 1918, and until the accident appears to have had a trouble free existence. From a perusal of *The DH.4/DH.9 File* it seems this was the only DH associated with Lieutenant Gould whose Army Form B.103 appears not to have survived the passage of time.

205 Squadron   Lt W H Clarke   Safe

DH.9A F1025   2Lt N R McKinlay   Safe   Unemployed list 21 May 1919

T/o Maubeuge similarly tasked and wrecked in a landing accident near Germund [sic]. Both flights were ahead of the planned move of the squadron, scheduled for the 12th. William Henry Clarke was born on the 11th of September 1892, his next of kin address being 2 Wedderburn Road, Harrogate, Yorkshire. He enlisted with the RFC on 26th April 1917, and in time was commissioned to the General List.

He reported to the squadron at Bois de Roche on 20th May 1918, and, apart from three spells of leave, served without a break until 17th March when he was posted home.

His observer's details indicate home was at 39 Radnor Drive, Liscard on the Cheshire Wirral and that he entered the world on the 19th of January 1899. He arrived with the squadron on 5th September 1918, after joining the RFC eleven months previously on 21st October. According to his service records the accident is recorded as occurring five days earlier and that on the 12th he was taken into 50 CCS suffering from concussion and shock. Transferred soon after to 14 General Hospital he was evacuated to the UK aboard the HS *Jan Breydel* on the 22nd January.

During his operational flying, Lieutenant Clarke had one close call, this was during operations on 21st September when he returned in F1015 with his observer, 2nd Lieutenant Walter Tunstall in much distress having been shot through the upper part of one of his legs. Initially to 5 CCS before transfer to 8 General Hospital his Record of Service has been annotated 'GSW Blighty' and so on the 26th he was put on HMHS *Gloucester Castle**to continue his recovery in more tranquil surroundings. Walter, born on 9th December 1898, and enlisting 3rd December 1917, had been with the squadron for just seven days.

* HMHS *Gloucester Castle* survived an attack off the Isle of Wight on the 31st of March 1917, when she was struck by a torpedo from *UB-32* [Kapitänleutnant Max Viebeg]. Three members of crew died during their transfer to a rescue vessel; although seriously damaged *Gloucester Castle* was salvaged and repaired. During the Second World War, and now in use as a passenger/cargo liner, she was sunk on the 15th of July 1942 with heavy loss of life off Angola by the German auxiliary cruiser *Michel*. The survivors, which included women and children were taken aboard the *Michel* and landed at the Japanese port of Yokohama where they were interned in less than favourable conditions for the rest of the war

209 Squadron   2Lt L H Parsons   Safe   Unemployed list 12 July 1919
F.1 Camel E1536   Canada
T/o Froidmont to practice flying in formation, and in the prevailing weather conditions this must have been a most demanding task. On return the surface winds were blowing hard and though an experienced pilot Lloyd Holman Parsons crashed while attempting to land. Lloyd features in my second volume on page 95, but without being acknowledged as a Canadian. Born on the 1st of February 1893, he joined the RFC as a Flight Cadet on 1st September 1917, and was commissioned on 13th December 1917 [LG 20 December 1917, supplement 30438, page 13326]. He arrived in France on the 5th of June and was attached to 43 Squadron [Camel] at Fouquerolles on the 13th. During an offensive patrol on the 30th of July he was seriously wounded in his right side and chest and following lengthy treatment in 8 General Hospital was returned to England on 29th August. By mid-November he was declared fit to resume flying duties and on the 21st he arrived back in France and was initially attached to 6 Issues Section. On the 30th he was posted to 1 Aeroplane Supply Depot after which there are no further entries on his Record of Service.

Wednesday 8 January 1919
The litany of reports advising terminal damage to aircraft after becoming waterlogged continued. At Laneffe, an inspection of RE.8s held by 53 Squadron resulted in five being declared unfit for further use; from 6 Squadron at Gerpinnes a better situation with only one of their REs being struck off.

62 Squadron   2Lt R C McHenry   Safe
Bristol F.2b C959
T/o Nivelles for an air test which passed off successfully. However, after landing and while taxying across the airfield the Bristol dropped into a deepish depression in the ground and was damaged beyond repair. A Record of Service form has been raised for 2nd Lieutenant McHenry but it is devoid of detail in respect of postings, next of kin et al.

107 Squadron   2Lt J McB Sillars   Safe   Unemployed list 16 September 1919
DH.9 D5697   AC1 A Adams   Safe
T/o Nivelles intending to transit to the squadron's new home at Maubeuge but on leaving the ground climbed too steeply, stalled and crashed. Born on 7th November 1897, and enlisting in the RFC on 19th June 1917, John McB Sillars probably joined 107 Squadron soon after arriving in France on 6th June 1918 [he is summarised, but without his the initial 'McB' on page 71 of my second volume when on 20th July he crashed whilst landing].
    On March 6th, and having enjoyed three weeks leave, he was ordered to go to Bavai and join 49 Squadron remaining with '49' until three days before disbandment on 18th July. At this point John Sillars was posted to 18 Squadron at Merheim for duties in the Rhineland. This was his final posting and he returned to England 1st of September, followed 24-hours later by the main body of 18 Squadron which arrived at Weston-on-the-Green.

216 Squadron   Lt Logan   Injured
HP O/400 D5410 2Lt E Conning   Injured
T/o Marquise carrying a large consignment of mail and on reaching Cognelée airfield some seven km NNW from Namur crashed with a force sufficient to wreck the HP. Lieutenant Logan's service records elude me, but those for 2nd Lieutenant Conning show he was attached to the squadron on 22nd September 1918. Taken to 48 CCS with contusions of the knee he was sent back to England on the 27th aboard HS *Jan Brydel*.

Thursday 9 January 1919
During the day, and in conjunction with recent events at Lawica in Greater Poland, the Polish Air Force despatched six bombers [type not identified] to raid Frankfurt *Flugplatz* where a number of German military units were ensconced. This was the first time that the Poles had mounted air operations against a foreign power.
    Into the large expanse of water in the Orkney Islands known as Scape Flow sailed the last German battleship to join the surrendered High Sea Fleet. With a great roar as her anchor chains dropped into the chill depths of the anchorage the seventy-fourth ship of all types was now present to await its fate - the *Baden's* operational days were over.

100 Squadron	2Lt J H Gardner	+	Cologne Southern Cemetery
Gotha	2Lt J Wood	+	Cologne Southern Cemetery

T/o Bickendorf presumably to test the flying characteristics of this German bomber and subsequently reported as crashed near Sedan. The circumstances of this accident raises several points. At the time 100 Squadron was not part of the Occupation Force policing the Rhineland; therefore, I assume, the crew had been detached from Ligescourt in France to conduct the test.

A second mystery centres on their burial. If the location *"near Sedan"* is correct, why then were they not laid to rest in France and even the positions of their their graves in the Southern Cemetery seems rather odd. John Harrison Gardner, he was twenty years of age, rests in plot XV row B grave 56, while his nineteen year old co-pilot, James Wood, is in plot XVI row 3 grave 1A. Perhaps as explanation is the entry on 2nd Lieutenant Gardner's Record of Service which reads *"Undated DAAG 2 Buried @ Montjow [Germany] by Rev W H Brown att 6th Infantry Bde G1730/26 Burial Report 79356 undated."*

I have searched the place-name index in my*Grosser Auto Atlas Deutschland Europa* but I cannot find any location that remotely resembles Montjow or possibly Moritjow.

Prior to joining the squadron on the 5th of December 1918, John Gardner had been attached since 16th of October to 115 Squadron, while James Wood, born 1st December 1899, and enlisting 4th October 1917, had been with 100 Squadron since 15th September 1918.

It would appear both officers were the first postwar Royal Air Force burials in Germany, though historical records presented by CWGC show over a thousand Allied prisoners of war from the *Great War,* along with dozens of German servicemen, were laid to rest in this cemetery. In total 2,591 identified Allied personnel from both wars are buried in the city's southern cemetery.

Friday 10 January 1919

During the day the Prime Minister, David Lloyd George, appointed Winston Spencer Churchill to the twin-posts of Secretary of State for War and Secretary of State for Air. As far as Lloyd George was concerned, he had little interest in the future of a fledgling Royal Air Force and would not have shed a tear if the air force was disbanded. For a fascinating insight as to how the service survived amid, at times, a highly charged atmosphere as General Sir Hugh Trenchard and Winston Churchill clashed over all manner of subjects from deployment to resources, I recommend Richard Overy's *The Birth of the RAF 1918* published by Allen Lane, 2018.

With planning for the forthcoming Peace Conference in Paris and the requirement for fast despatch of ministers and papers, an order for a number of DH.4s to be converted for this purpose was promulgated.

3 Squadron	2Lt A J O'Neill	Safe
F.1 Camel D8121/F6138	Canada	

T/o Inchy for a practice flight and crash on landing. As D8121 it was badly damaged in a ground collision with a Bristol F.2b on 18th June 1918, its 73 Squadron pilot, Lieutenant Daniel Bryan Sinclair injuring his hand. Canadian born on the 5th of December 1896, Daniel joined the squadron on 2nd June 1918, but almost immediately was hospitalised, first with an injured thumb [this as a result of the accident] and then with influenza and so it was not until the 27th of July that his operational tour started in earnest.

Arol John O'Neill joined 3 Squadron on the 6th of September and returned to England on the 9th of February. Single, and from Georgetown in Ontario, he was born on 21 September 1899, and enlisted in the RFC on 8th December 1917.

Saturday 11 January 1919

139 Squadron	Lt T B Service	Safe
Bristol F.2b D7954	Lt J G Acheson	Safe

T/o Grossa and reported to have forced-landed, out of petrol, at Borgo. The crew, apparently, had been flying in cloud when their fuel ran out. For both officers this was their second mishap, the first being on 21st December 1918. On charge since 28th December, what remained of D7954 was taken on the 23rd to 7 Air Park where, presumably, it was struck off charge.

Sunday 12th January 1919

20 Squadron	Lt J D Boyd	Safe
Bristol F.2b E2407	Canada	
	Lt S P B de Moyse- Bucknall	Safe

T/o Ossogne for a practice flight but when the land over which they were flying became shrouded in mist the crew decided it would be prudent to forced-land. This they did, coming down in a field near the Arsenal at Ghent but as the Bristol trundled over the grass its progress was arrested when the tail skid became caught in an unseen obstruction and the airframe was damaged beyond repair. James Dunbar Boyd, born 28th September 1889, enlisted on 28th August 1917, and by 11th November, a year to the date before the armistice, he joined the squadron at Ste Marie Cappel.

Formerly of the 1st/5th London Regiment, Silvio Paul Bernini de Moyse-Bucknall was accepted for observer training in the spring of 1918, and returned to England on the 24th of May. He arrived with the squadron on the 27th of September and in April 1919, was struck off the strength of the BEF on being posted to India with his squadron. A record for this officer, who was born on the 21st of May 1896, is held at TNA Kew under AIR 76/131/13.

97 Squadron	Lt C F Hunt		Safe	See below
HP O/400 C9760	2Lt R McKinnon		Safe	See below

T/o Saint Inglevert heading for Rely and during the transit the leading edge of the top planes buckled. It is not clear from the accident report if the crew reached their destination but, it seems, the bomber was left out in the open and eventually became waterlogged. A second report indicates it was taken to 4 Advanced Salvage Dump. It had been with the squadron since 3rd November 1918.

97 Squadron	Lt C F Hunt		Safe	See 23 April 1919
HP O/400 D4575	2Lt R McKinnon		Safe	

T/o Saint Inglevert heading for Rely but upon realising the top planes were starting to distort the crew forced-landed at Ennettieres [sic] where its fate mirrors that of the HP reported above. D4575 was assigned to the squadron as early as 26th June 1918, at which date it was undergoing inspection at Castle Bromwich. On the 6th of July it was flown to Netheravon and moved with the squadron to Xaffévillers on the 9th of August. Cyril Frank Hunt joined the squadron on 28th November 1918, and preceded the squadron's transfer to Ford on the 4th of March by 24-hours. As yet, I have not located a Record of Service for 2nd Lieutenant McKinnon.

97 Squadron	2Lt F C Salmon		Safe	See below
HP O/400 D8320	2Lt Russell		Safe	See below

T/o Saint Inglevert and reported as being destroyed in a violent storm at Nivelles.

97 Squadron	2Lt F C Salmon		Safe	See 1 May 1919
HP O/400 D9704	2Lt Russell		Safe	

T/o Saint Inglevert for Rely where during landing the wind blew the HP sideways [whether this was to port or starboard, is not made clear]. Presumed damaged beyond repair. Frederick Charles Salmon joined the squadron on September 21st last.

Note. I believe it possible that the casualties from 97 Squadron shown for the 12th may have been an amalgamated from reports submitted over several days.

Monday 13 January 1919

19 Squadron	Lt J C Morris		+	Denain Communal Cemetery
5F.1 Dolphin F7056	Mechanic H T Ford	Injured		

T/o Abscon for a practice flight but lost control and crashed either into or against the side of hangar in which Mechanic Ford was working on an RE.8. From the Blackheath district of London, John Morris briefly served with the 3rd Battalion, Duke of Wellington's [West Riding Regiment]. His headstone has been inscribed *"God Bless Thee Whereso'er In His Great Universe Thou Art Today."* As to the extent of Mechanic Ford's injuries, I am not able to report.

Since 12th November, this was the squadron's fourth serious accident and the second where death occurred.

36 Squadron	Lt F Yorke		+	Sunderland [Bishop Wearmouth] Cemetery
Sopwith Pup B1763				

T/o Usworth and collided in the air with the aeroplane reported below, both machines falling to crash near Ashington in Northumberland. Formerly of the Cheshire Regiment, Frederick Yorke was the son of the Reverend H Lefroy Yorke and Margaret Yorke, *nee* Warrington. Prior to his service with 36 Squadron, Frederick had trained as an observer and on 24th May 1917, reported to Hesdigneul where he was attached to 2 Squadron. On the 11th of September 1917, during the course of a photographic reconnaissance his FK.8, serial and pilot not known, was shot about and he sustained a gunshot wound to his left foot. After being treated locally, he was sent back to the UK on the 17th aboard the HS *Ville de Liège*. There are no further entries on his service record.

36 Squadron	Lt H Croudace		+	Putney Vale Cemetery and Crematorium
Sopwith Pup B1805				

T/o Usworth and destroyed in the circumstances reported above. Harold Croudace's entry in the cemetery register is devoid of information regarding next of kin.

Note. An internet search in the hope of discovering additional information has been most rewarding and it gives me great pleasure to acknowledge the North East War Memorials Project, which carries a detailed report of the tragedy under the heading Parish Notes - Ashington and in particular the article published in the *Morpeth Herald* in their issue of 17th January: *'Lieut. Frederick Yorke, of Hylton, and Lieut. Harold Croudace, of Sunderland, were killed at Ashington on Monday. The airmen were flying in one-seater machines, and collided in a mist. Both airmen died almost immediately on reaching earth.*

An inquest was held on Wednesday at Ashington by Mr C Percy MP on the bodies of Lieut. Frederick Yorke [24] and Lieut. Harold Croudace [24] of the Royal Air Force, who had been killed by a collision in mid-air. Both officers belonged to Usworth, and were attached to the Hylton Aerodrome. Lieut. Sydney Denham Chard, in command of the Ashington Aerodrome, stated that the deceased officers went to Ashington on duty on Monday. Both were flying Sopwith scouting biplanes. They arrived at 12.30 and left half an hour later. Witness watched them for about eight minutes. They were flying in an ordinary manner, and about 50 yards apart, which witness considered was rather close. The weather was misty, and the machines entered the mist at about 1,500 feet high. Looking into the mist with the sun at their backs, they would be able to see a long way, but with the sun shining through the mist into their faces it would be almost impossible to see at all. Undoubtedly, said the witness, the condition of things prevented them seeing one another. Both were very experienced flyers.

Two other witnesses, ex-Gunner Langdown and Christopher Wilson, a farm labourer, gave evidence to the effect that they saw the machines rise from the aerodrome and make south. One aeroplane was slightly higher than the other.

Suddenly the engine of the highest machine stopped, and it dropped down on the other machine. The machines separated and spiralled to the ground in a field on Coneygarth Farm. The officers were alive when found, but unconscious, and they died almost immediately afterwards.

Lieut. Chard was recalled and questioned with regard to the statement that one of the engines had stopped. He said he saw both engines run before the ascent was made, and they were all right then.

A verdict was recorded to the effect that the officers were accidentally killed through their aeroplanes colliding in mid-air.'

Tuesday 14 January 19
The 2nd Army, commanded by *General der Infanterie* Adolph von Carlowitz, of the German Imperial Army was disbanded. Adolph von Carlowitz had taken command during the last major offensive of the war when the fighting was no longer confined to the trenches.

108 Squadron	Lt W H L Oxland	Safe	Unemployed list 21 May 1920
DH.9 E9034	Mechanic Waite	Safe	

T/o Gondecourt and set off for Tardinghem but while over the Pas-de-Calais the engine failed and while attempting to land at Baraques airfield the DH sideslipped and crashed. Postwar William Henry Lionel Oxland was granted a short service commission in the rank of Flying Officer, effective from 5 December 1919 [LG 5 December 1919, issue 31674, page 15062]. However, regarding his transfer to the unemployed list, as shown above, and where his rank is given as Lieutenant it may be that he decided to leave the service. On the same page indicating his unemployed status [page 6485 of issue 31939, dated 11 June 1920] is an interesting Notice to Airmen No 66 which repeats French Notice to Airmen No 7, advising that a Customs Aerodrome had opened at St. Inglevert on May 20th, and that Marquise-Calais was now closed. Thus, all aircraft landing, or departing France now had the choice of two aerodromes, namely Le Bourget or St. Inglevert.

218 Squadron	2Lt R A Whitehead	Safe
DH.9 E8957	Mechanic Barnes	Safe

T/o Vert Galant and on return from the aerial range at Tardinghen crashed whilst landing. Although the records for 2nd Lieutenant Whitehead are lacking in detail regarding his units, his next of kin is shown as *"Major D C Whitehead [F], Colombo Cottage, Queens' Walk, Ealing, London W."*

Wednesday 15 January 1919
The HP V/1500 which departed Martlesham Heath on Friday the 13th of December last [see my lead-in for the day], arrived in Karachi.

In the Strait of Messina a terrible tragedy occurred when a French passenger ship *Chaouia* struck a sea-mine and went down with the loss of 476 souls.

191 Squadron	2Lt G G Duncan	Safe
FE.2b A5778	F/Cdt J Stubbing	Safe

T/o Upwood and crashed owing to engine failure.

Thursday 16 January 1919
85 Squadron	Major J O Leach	Safe
SE.5a F895		

T/o Ascq for a practice flight and on return struck a ridge, bounced and on its second arrival hit the ground tail first which did the SE no good whatsoever. Attached to the RFC from the Middlesex Regiment, Major Leach's Record of Service shows he was wounded on the 7th of May 1917, and was evacuated to England aboard the HS *St. Denis*.

The next entry shows he was appointed as Temporary Captain and to assume the duties of a Flight Commander with effect from the 4th of June 1917, after which there is a gap until the 7th of January 1919, when he left 56 Squadron to take command of 85 Squadron, vice Major Cyril Marconi Crowe.

A partial record for Cyril Crowe is quite revealing. Born 6th of January 1894, he joined the RFC on 2nd of October 1914. The first entry of importance records his admittance to 8 General Hospital with a fractured right radius on 13th January 1916, and thence to the UK aboard HMHS *St. Andrew*.

It was not until 18th April 1917, that he returned to operations, 56 Squadron being noted against the date, and soon after gained an MC. On the 13th of July, he was taken to 10 Stationary Hospital having sustained minor gunshot wounds, but although described as minor, he was sent home via HS *St. Denis* on the 22nd, this being the final entry. However, annotated on the top right corner of his Army Form B.103, *'DFC'* has been entered in addition to the MC.

Referring to the *Gazette* and the issue for 18 July 1917, supplement 30188, page 7225, the citation for his MC reads:
'For conspicuous gallantry and skill as a leader of offensive patrols, many times attacking hostile formations single-handed, and descending to low altitudes under heavy anti-aircraft fire. He has been responsible for the destruction of several enemy machines.'

That for his DFC was published on 21 September 1918, supplement 30913, page 11250: *'This officer has been engaged in active operations over the lines for over twelve months, and has accounted for ten enemy aeroplanes. He is a most successful leader, distinguished for skill and bravery. On a recent occasion he, accompanied by two other machines, attacked an enemy formation consisting of four biplanes and one triplane. Having destroyed a biplane he engaged the triplane at close range and destroyed that also.'*

Turning to the Aerodrome website, here researchers [to whom I am most appreciative] have discovered much additional background to this officer's life. It would seem that in 1918, he was promoted Major but following a party in Dieppe on 29th July, Cyril Crowe with two passengers in his car smashed into a tree. By a miracle he was only slightly hurt but his two companions, Captain Owen Scholte and a Major Cyril Edgar Foggin of 40 Squadron were fatally injured and died within hours of the crash. Their graves are in the Somme at St. Riquier British Cemetery, a relatively small cemetery some nine km northeast of Abbeville. A Court Martial followed and he was reduced in rank to Captain for a month and posted out to 85 Squadron.

His impressive victory tally, achieved in SE.5as, opened in the morning of 24th April 1917 and closed during the evening of 16th September 1918, when he achieved his single victory with '85', despatching a Fokker DVII in the vicinity of Sauchy-Couchy.

During the Second World War he was commissioned to the Royal Air Force [Volunteer Reserve], eventually attaining the rank of Wing Commander before reverting to Flight Lieutenant in the Reserve of Air Force Officers. On the 27th of May 1954, he relinquished his commission. Cyril Marconi Crowe died in Swindon on the last day of May 1974.

110 Squadron	2Lt W A Peters	Safe	Unemployed list 7 April 1919
DH.9 E703	2Lt L R Robins	Safe	Unemployed list 7 March 1919

T/o Mainsoncelle intending to fly as far as Namur and return. On return 2nd Lieutenant Peters misjudged his approach and crashed. His service record is restricted to his rank, name and initials, as is that raised for 2nd Lieutenant Robins.

Friday 17 January 1919
During the day 55 Squadron at Saint André-aux-Bois ferried the last of their DH.4s to 2 Aircraft Supply Depot having been stood down from operating mail delivery services. Since the turn of the year they had lost a single aircraft in a non fatal accident on the 7th.

Jagdstaffel 50 of the *Luftstreikräfte* disbanded.

16 Squadron	Lt J Douglas	Injured	
RE.8 E226	Lt G T Learmond	Safe	Commission relinquished 5 March 1919

T/o Auchy for a navigation exercise and it was while west of Charleroi, and on the return leg, that the crew flew into a snowstorm and crashed-landed. John Douglas, born on the 4th of August 1896, joined the squadron on the 19th of May 1918, and apart from leave and a course of instruction in December appears to have had a trouble free tour of duty. His injuries must have been of a minor nature as the accident has not been recorded on his Record of Service; he was posted out to a Reinforcement Park on the 21st and back to the UK soon after.

Formerly of the 2nd/1st Northumberland Hussars, George Thomas Learmond, born 3rd August 1887, reported for duty with the RFC as a Recording Officer on probation on New Year's Eve 1917, and on the 2nd of January proceeded to La Bellevue where until the 5th of February he was attached to 11 Squadron.

His next attachment, from the 5th, was to 16 Squadron. It appears he was not of robust health for an entry in early June reads *"Fit for Light Duty only"* as advised by the Medical Officer at 24 General Hospital, Etaples, and this is followed with entries for leave in July, August and September before he went to HQ 1st Wing at Bruay on the 1st of October. Here the entries cease, but I assume his parent unit throughout was 16 Squadron.

28 Squadron	2Lt E F Mattock	Injured Unemployed list 14 September 1919
F.1 Camel B7383		

T/o Sarcedo and on landing turned over, this being Edwin Frank Mattock's second such incident, the first being on 28th November 1918 on which occasion he escaped injury. This time he was not so fortunate and was admitted to hospital with an injured shoulder. On the 8th of February he was sent to convalesce at an Officers Hospital at Portifino from where, it appears, he was sent back the UK on the 25th of March. It is noted he was born on the 15th of December 1899, and enlisted on the first of October 1917. His address is shown as Swan House, North Heigham, Norwich.

49 Squadron	Lt L W Boland	Safe	Unemployed list 24 April 1919
DH.9 D3165	Canada		
	2Lt J S Tinn	Safe	

T/o Bavai for a practice flight and owing to a lack of good judgement crashed on landing. Formerly of the Canadian army, Lloyd Winton Boland was born on the 12th of October 1895. This was his second serious accident, the first have occurred on the 12th November 1918. John Stuart Tinn's birth date is recorded as 29th August 1897, and he likely hailed from Grantham in Lincolnshire.

57 Squadron	2Lt W F Smith	Safe
DH.4 D8412/F6511/H7118		

T/o Morville carrying mail to Köln where it crashed while landing at Crab Aerodrome. As D8412 the DH saw operational service with 205 Squadron and was badly shot about by a Pfalz DIII over Chaulnes [Somme] on the 10th of

August 1918. Its crew were Lieutenant John Gordon Kerr, who was unhurt, and Herbert William Hopton who was mortally wounded and died two days later.

Herbert's Record of Service reports his birth 29th March 1899, and joining the RFC on 4th February 1918. He arrived with 205 Squadron on 29th May, and when wounded was admitted to 41 Stationary Hospital with wounds to his lower body. He was buried in Pont-Remy British Cemetery, his funeral service being overseen by the hospital's padre the Reverend F L Ree.

John Kerr, whose home address is shown as 21 Park Road, West Kirby, Cheshire, was born on the 9th of September 1898, enlisting on 2nd April 1917. He served with the squadron from 4th June to 4th January 1919, on which date he was taken to 14 General Hospital with an undisclosed illness. On the 10th he was shipped back to England aboard the HS *St Denis.*

| 84 Squadron | Lt A E Hill | Safe |
| SE.5a D387 | | |

T/o Thuilles but stalled from a climbing turn, crashed and caught fire. Lieutenant Hill served with the squadron from 8th August 1918, until the 2nd of April when he reported to one of the reception camps to await his discharge; the final entry on his Record of Service was entered on the 18th when he was posted home.

| 103 Squadron | Lt W N Wilson | Safe | See 8 June 1919 -110 Squadron |
| DH.9 D496 | 2Lt G Butters | Safe | See 8 March 1919 |

T/o Ronchin for an exercise in photography; crashed, owing to a misfiring engine, on return. The DH was reduced to produce on the 25th. William Nichol Wilson, born 19th August 1899, and enlisting with the RFC on 11th September 1917, reported to the squadron on the 11th of July and was still on establishment during January 1919.

Geoffrey Butters, whose address is shown as 5 Wilson Street, Derby, was born on the 5th of September 1899, and joined the RFC five days after his 18th birthday. His operational tour began on the 13th of July, during which he played a full part in the squadron's bombing operations. On the 9th of August, his aircraft D489 was hit by anti-aircraft fire over Erquinghem [Nord] and on landing at Serny the undercarriage collapsed. Six days later, this time in E631,*and raiding Péronne the formation became split up as a thick mist shrouded the ground. Uncertain of their position, the crew landed at Ligescourt where they stayed the night being entertained by 207 Squadron.

On both these operations, Geoffrey is shown as the pilot; for the raid on the 9th, William Wilson is recorded as the observer while on the 15th, 2nd Lieutenant Michael Solomon Lewin was fulfilling this role. However, as shown here, and on the 8th March, Geoffrey appears to have been the observer. One further note of interest, the heading of his Army Form B.103 has been annotated late USAS, but I suspect this was a clerical error, for it was crossed through.

* See my Second Volume and page 347 for the subsequent fate of this bomber.

| 204 Squadron | Lt T Whittaker | Safe |
| F.1 Camel F3100 | | |

T/o Heule for an undisclosed task and on return, and preparing to land, the engine cut causing the fighter to overshoot the landing area. Damaged beyond repair. Taken over by the squadron on 30th October, in the dying days of the *Great War*, its guns achieved one combat success when during an early morning patrol on 4th November, Thomas Whittaker drove down a Fokker DVII over Melle in Oost-Vlaanderen.

Born on the 15th of August 1899, and with his address shown as 30 Kirkstone Road, Hillsborough, Sheffield, Thomas joined the RFC in the last month of its existence, reporting on the 7th of March. Qualified as a pilot he arrived at Beugnatre on 20th October and was attached to 201 Squadron but ten days later, during which time '201' commenced converting from Camel to Snipe, he was ordered to Heule and 204 Squadron.

On the 6th of February his Record of Service indicates posting to 108 Squadron [DH.9] at Gondecourt; however, '108' were in the midst of getting ready to leave on the 16th for Lympne in Kent, their aircraft being disposed to storage units. So, with their personnel joyfully heading for home, Thomas was packed off on the 18th to the aerial ranges and on the 10th of March was instructed to go to Clermont and acquaint himself with Major C M Leaman and his officers of 80 Squadron [Snipe].

Settled in, he was granted leave from the 15th to 29th April, but a recall was sent and he returned on the 21st and soon after departed with the squadron for duties in the Middle East.

| 208 Squadron | 2Lt G V Snell | Safe | Unemployed list 23 May 1919 |
| 7F.1 Snipe E8042 | | |

T/o Stree for a practice flight and was wrecked in a manner similar to that recorded above in that on regaining the airfield the engine cut without warning and the Snipe finished up beyond the landing area. 2nd Lieutenant Snell served with the squadron from 8th September 1918, until 21st March.

Saturday 18 January 1919

| 205 Squadron | Lt H F Taylor | Safe |
| DH.9A F1019/C | | |

T/o La Louveterie for postal duties and crashed near Valenciennes. Harold Fenton Taylor, born 20th July 1899, was on the squadron's strength from the 20th of July 1918, until the 9th of March when he went to the Rhineland to serve with 18 Squadron [DH.9A] at Bickendorf. However, about six weeks later on 19th April, he returned to England.

205 Squadron   Lt A S M Meyrick-Jones   Injured Commission resigned 12 October 1921
DH.9A F2751
T/o 6 Air Issues and set off for La Louveterie but *en route* he forced-landed at Condre-Vaux airfield and while doing so the undercarriage caught the top of a bank. The impact sent the DH careering out of control and on coming to a stop a fire broke out. The Record of Service for Lieutenant Meyrick-Jones is devoid of any useful information regarding his service. However, by referencing *The London Gazette this* shows he was formerly of the Royal Artillery and was seconded for duty with the RFC on 8th March 1918 [LG 22 April 1918, supplement 30642, page 4802].

   Postwar he returned to the Royal Garrison Artillery until resigning his commission, as indicated above [LG 11 October 1921, supplement 32484, page 8036].

236 Squadron   2Lt R J Cotterell   +   Whiteparish [All Saints] Churchyard
DH.9 C1304
T/o Mullion [Cury Air Station] and almost immediately spun back to the ground with the engine misfiring. Robert James Cotterell was an Oxford graduate from Magdalen College; his epitaph reads: *"In Ever Loving Memory In The Midst Of Life We Are In Death."*

   Little is known about the Cornish RNAS station sited on the Lizard Peninsular, but a map of the area shows Cury as being a couple of miles NNE from Mullion. Neither Cury or Mullion are mentioned in Chris Ashworth's contribution to the *Action Station* series of books on military airfields covering the UK and published by Patrick Stephens, Cambridge.

Sunday 19 January 1919
The turmoil of war in Russia remained ongoing, while in Germany the 17th Army of the Imperial German Army was disbanded. The standing down of the 17th took place against a background of elections in the Weimar Republic where the Social Democratic Party secured most of the votes. Meanwhile, the internal defence of Germany was recognised by the establishment at Zossen of the Reichswehr under Paul von Hindenburg,*late commander of the Imperial German Army. The agreed establishment of troops was put at 100,000 thousand, while that for the Reichsmarine was a force of 15,000 sailors headed by *Vizeadmiral* Adolf von Trotha. Although the Allies were determined that the German navy would no longer be a dominant threat, nevertheless it was foreseen that a strong Baltic Fleet would be a useful counter to Soviet expansion in the area.

* Paul von Hindenburg and Erich Friedrich Wilhelm Ludendorff were the *bête noire* of the Allied general in the *Great War.* An ardent nationalist, Ludendorff persistently argued that German had been betrayed in 1918, by the combined forces of communist inspired politicians and, ominously, the Jews.

35 Squadron   2Lt A L Corson MM   Safe
FK.8 F644   Canada
                    Mechanic Dyson   Safe
T/o La Bellevue with the intention of flying to the squadron's new base at Ste. Marie Cappel but as was so often the case within minutes of departing engine failure took over and descending on to rough ground the FK was damaged beyond repair. Arthur Leopold Corson won his MM while ranked Sergeant [LG 14 January 1918, supplement 30476, page 833]. His Royal Air Force service started with 2 Squadron [FK.8] at Mazingarbe on 23rd September 1918, while his attachment to 35 Squadron came post-armistice on the 3rd of December.

   With the squadron disposing of its equipment in early March in readiness to return to Netheravon, Arthur Corson was posted on the 8th to Blandford Camp in Dorset to await repatriation to his home at Welland in Ontario. It is noted it was born on the 27th of March 1897.

Monday 20 January 1919
Estonian forces were gaining the upper hand in the country's war of independence, forcing the Bolsheviks to retreat beyond the Narva river.

   From Thuilles, 92 Squadron signalled that four of their SE.5as were no longer flyable owing to weather related issues.

5 Squadron   2Lt A Douglas   Safe
RE.8 C2914   LAC W Loudon   Safe
T/o Hangelar for an air test and wrecked in a misjudged landing. 2nd Lieutenant Douglas arrived with the squadron on the 27th of September 1918, and remained on establishment until his posting to a demobilisation camp on 7th May.

18 Squadron   2Lt G P H Carter   Safe   Retirement 29 August 1950
DH.9A E8424   Major Ewen   Safe
T/o Maubeuge to ferry the DH to Marquise but when engine failure obliged the crew to forced-land at Estrée, a heavy arrival caused the bomber to bounce and turn over. Gerald Paul Halliday Carter was born on the 18th of February 1900, and joined the RNAS as a potential pilot on the 3rd of March 1918, but less than a month later he would continue his flying training in the newly formed Royal Air Force. Reporting to the squadron on the 4th of September, he later went to 206 Squadron [DH.9] on 21st August and thence to 47 Squadron on the re-numbering of '206', now at Helwan in the Middle East, on the 1st of February 1920.

   By now he had been granted a permanent commission and as such his career followed the usual path of spells spent on the ground interlinked with active flying. In Gerald's case, he specialised in wireless communications and between the wars he served at stations both at home and abroad, an example being between April 1930 and October 1932 during which time he was a Flight Lieutenant attached to Air Staff [Signals] at Headquarters RAF Middle East.

Prior to this he had attended the long course at the Electrical and Wireless School at Flowerdown near Winchester, spent two years at Cambridge University, served for a year as Signals Officer on 25 Squadron at Hawkinge in Kent, no doubt acquainting himself with the squadron's Gloster Grebe fighters.

From January 1935 to the following January he was at Andover attending Staff College, after which came a lengthy tour as an instructor with the Electrical and Wireless School, now located at Cranwell.

The Second World War found him employed in a variety of posts, including six months [May to November 1944] as Station Commander at Kirmington in Bomber Command, and home to the Lancasters of 166 Squadron.

Between the winter of 1946 and the spring of 1949, he enjoyed the delights of Seletar in the Far East, before rounding off his service as Senior Air Staff Officer at 47 Group, headquarters at Abingdon. Retiring as an Air Commodore, Gerald Carter died on the 17th of September 1989.

With no initials as a guide the service of Major Ewen remains untraced.

40 Squadron   Captain S J Stewart   Safe
SE.5a F5532
T/o Orcq and subsequently forced-landed with his engine failing at Allennes-les-Marais [Nord]. All might have been well but while still running at speed the tail skid became caught in wire and the SE turned over. Taken to 1 Advanced Salvage Dump, I am the opinion its flying days were over. Sidney Joseph Stewart was born on the 10th of May 1895, joining the RFC on the 5th of August 1916. His first operational tour was with 27 Squadron [DH.4], reporting to Fienvillers on 26th April 1917. On the 1st of May, he sustained gunshot wounds to his left arm and wrist, these injuries being treated in 3 Canadian Stationary Hospital, and it was not until the 3rd of June that he was passed fit to resume flying duties. His tour finished at Serny on 24th October, the following eleven months spent in England during which time he switched to flying scouts. Thus, on 27th September 1918, he returned to France and joined 40 Squadron at Bryas.

85 Squadron   Captain L D Baker   Safe
SE.5a E5987
T/o Ascq and flew to Berck-sur-Mer where Captain Baker misjudged his approach and crashed. He is reported to have been quite seriously injured but I have yet to find any information regarding his service. On 23rd October 1918, E5987 was flown on an offensive patrol led by Captain C B R MacDonald during which he destroyed a kite balloon near Le Quesnoy. Charles Beverley Robinson MacDonald enlisted with the RFC on 20th August 1917, and served for the best part of a year from early May 1918, until he returned to the UK, ahead of the squadron, on the 13th of February. Between the 25th and 31st of July, he was treated for slight wounds to his left arm.

99 Squadron   Lt L B Duggan   Injured See 14 February 1919
DH.9A E8563   2Lt E E Bricknell   Injured Unemployed list 11 February 1920
T/o Aulnoye and totally wrecked after crashing headlong into a tree. An appreciation of Lewin Browning Duggan's service is summarised on 20th December 1918. Evans Edward Bricknell was born on 20th February 1899; his next of kin is shown as his mother, residing at 24 Kensington Crescent, Swansea, South Wales.

110 Squadron   Lt S B Bradley   Safe   Unemployed list 3 May 1919
DH.9A F1060   Sgt H B Banks   Safe
T/o Maisoncelle carrying a consignment of mail to Morville where the DH was wrecked after overshooting the landing ground. Lieutenant Bradley joined the squadron in early September 1918, and departed on 29th April, when he was posted to 91 Wing to await demobilisation. For his next of kin he chose his brother, the Reverend W E Bradley of Crosthwaite*Vicarage, Keswick, Cumberland.

* Undoubtedly Great Crosthwaite on the west side of Keswick between Bassenthwaite Lake and Derwent Water; Crosthwaite is inland on the eastern side of Windermere.

205 Squadron   Lt R E Morton   Safe   Unemployed list 10 May 1919
DH.9A F990
T/o La Louveterie for aerial postal duties and damaged beyond repair in a forced-landing near Dinant [Namur] on the banks of the Meuse. All might have faired well but before coming to a stop the DH crashed against some pretty stiff fencing. Robert Edwin Morton was on establishment from 24th September 1918, until the squadron returned to Hucknall in Nottinghamshire on 18th March; in fact, at the time of its departure Robert was on leave, returning on the 20th. Subsequently, he was attached to 1 Aeroplane Supply Depot and eventually left for England on 25th April.

208 Squadron   Captain W E G Mann   Safe   Unemployed list 29 August 1919
7F.1 Snipe E8066   DFC
T/o Stree for practice and local flying. On return made a fast landing and collided with the Snipe featured below. Born on 20th April 1899, William Edward George Mann joined the RNAS on 30th May 1917, and undoubtedly served prior to April 1st, 1918, with 8 Squadron RNAS, subsequently 208 Squadron gaining his thirteen combat victories starting on the 8th of May, when he claimed an Albatros DV near Provin and finally a Fokker DVII to the SE of Saint Quentin on the 26th of September, four days after he had been recommended for the DFC. This was duly *Gazetted* on 3rd Dec-

ember 1918, supplement 31046, page 14323: *'This officer has led many patrols in action, and invariably displays marked fearlessness and ability, setting a fine example to other Pilots. He has accounted for nine enemy aeroplanes, and in these combats his success has been largely due to his skill in manoeuvre and bold daring in closing to short range with the enemy.'* In mid-March he began to feel unwell and was soon admitted to 20 General Hospital at Etaples where he remained until the 26th of June. On the 27th, he reported to the aerial ranges at Berck-sur-Mer and from here he returned to England, 24-hours before being placed on the unemployed list.

His time as a civilian must have been relatively brief for by the 2nd of January 1920, he was again in air force blue and undergoing a refresher flying course after which his his initial career centred on flying instruction. In September 1924, he re-acquainted himself with squadron activities when he was posted to Hawkinge for Flight Commander duties with 25 Squadron. At the time the squadron was in the process of converting from *Great War* issue Snipes to Gloster Grebes. Early in 1926, he attended the Electrical and Wireless School at Flowerdown and from then on his principal contri-bution to the air force was in the developing world of wireless communications, a role touched upon in my summary on the 20th January for Air Commodore Gerald Carter.

During the Second World War, spent for the better part in the Middle East, he was a driving force behind the development of mobile signals and radar units, vital for the close air support being provided for the armies as they wore the enemy down in this theatre and across the rest of Europe.

Rising to Air Commodore rank, William Mann completed his long and dedicated service at Iver in Buckinghamshire where he served as Senior Air Staff Officer at Headquarters No 26[Signals] Group. Retiring on 18th of April 1945, he maintained his expertise in communications with various bodies, subsequently returning to the Middle East as the Decca Navigator Company's representative. Sadly, his health gave way and he died at the relatively early age of 67 on the 4th of May 1966. In addition to his DFC, William was appointed CBE, CB and twice mentioned in despatches.

208 Squadron   Major H G Smart   Safe   Retirement 1 September 1945
7F.1 Snipe E8162
While stationary of the airfield hit by the Snipe summarised above. Harry George Smart was born in Newmarket, Suffolk, on the 28th of June 1891, and when he embarked for France on 25th May 1916, it was on posting to 60 Squadron [Morane], temporarily based at St. Omer whilst awaiting deployment for operations. I strongly suspect that Harry had initially reported to the squadron while it was working up at Gosport, for it was here that it had formed on the last day of April 1916. His Record of Service shows he was sent on a machine-gun course between the 8th and 15th September, by which time the squadron had disposed of their Moranes in favour of Nieuports.

Between the 17th and 20th of December, he went to Paris on temporary duty, and shortly after returned to England. By now he had been promoted Lieutenant and it would appear he spent the next two years in the UK before returning to Belgium to command 208 Squadron, the effective dates of his command being between early January and 28th August 1919, his departure from the Rhineland coinciding with the squadron's pending move to Netheravon in September and disbandment in November.

Major Smart was now a permanent officer and though entries on his service record end with his return to the UK, the Air of Authority website, which I am always pleased to acknowledge, show his steady rise to air rank and at his retirement on the 1st of September 1945, he was ranked Air-Vice Marshal and had been honoured with a CBE, DFC, AFC and a mention in a despatch.

The early years of his permanent service were spent in Iraq where he served with 6 Squadron [Bristol F.2b],*while between November 1927 and February 1930, he was attached to the RAAF. This was followed by a switch to bombers and command of 99 Squadron which was based at Upper Heyford in Oxfordshire and equipped with a mixture of Hyderabad and Hinaidi biplanes, modernisation of the air force to meet any future conflict continuing to move at snail-like pace.

Various appointments followed, these being as diverse as taking charge of the engineering requirements for the Inland Area, Commandant of the Central Flying School, first at Wittering and later at Upavon, Commandant of Martlesham Heath where the important task of testing aircraft prior to their entry into front-line service, or rejection as the case might be, was being conducted by the Aeroplane and Armaments Experimental Establishment.

With war now looming he was appointed Senior Air Staff Officer at Headquarters No 12[Fighter] Group at Uxbridge but shortly after war was declared in September 1939, he was sent out to Iraq as Air Officer Commanding British Forces. It was during his time in Iraq at his headquarters at Habbaniya that with the encouragement of Germany rebel forces rose up in the spring of 1941. On the 5th of May he was seriously injured and evacuated to India.

What appears to be his final appointment was in Coastal Command when in November 1941, he became Air Officer Commanding No 17[OperationalTraining] Group at Lee-on-Solent.

Most unusually his Army Form B.103 has been stamped, in red, *"DECEASED 28th June 1963."*

* It was while attached to 6 Squadron that he was awarded the DFC, this being *Gazetted* on 28 October 1921, issue 32501, page 8496: *'For energy, gallantry and leadership.This officer has shown a very fine example to his fellow officers, especially during low bombing raids, when he has frequently descended among heavy rifle fire to very low altitude to ensure accurate bombing of small targets. He has taken part in 25 bombing raids and two night raids.'*

213 Squadron   Major A G Taylor AFC   Safe
F.1 Camel F3944
T/o Stalhille for a practice flight and on returned went onto its nose after the undercarriage sank into soft ground. Sent for repair, the Camel was struck off charge on 2nd February. Army Form B.103-I has been raised for Major Taylor, but no information regarding his service has been appended.

Tuesday 21 January 1919

During the day the 8th Army, commanded by *General der Infanterie* Hugo von Kathen, of the Imperial German Army was disbanded.

Another day of accidents on the Western Front, eleven aircraft in total written off for a myriad of reasons, while two more SE.5as from 92 Squadron at Thuilles were declared unfit to fly owing to exposure to the weather.

10 Squadron	2Lt D R Morford	Safe	Unemployed list 28 October 1919
FK.8 F7489			

T/o Reckem on a travelling flight but after becoming uncertain of his position Douglas Rippon Morford forced-landed at Map Reference Sheet 27 O34c1010. Presumed damaged beyond repair. As with a considerable percentage of Army Form B.103-I, although a card exists, it is devoid of detail regarding postings et al.

10 Squadron	Lt P Coyle mid	Safe
FK.8 H4426		

T/o Reckem similarly charged and probably in the company of Douglas Morford, and crashed, owing to engine failure, at Map Reference Sheet 27 K31b97. The two accidents here recorded were the last to be reported from 10 Squadron prior to leaving for Ford in Sussex on 17th February. Peter Coyle's service record is interesting in that although he arrived in France as early as 17th February 1918, where-upon he was attached to 4 Aeroplane Supply Depot, his posting to 10 Squadron is not mentioned. Between 21st May and 4th June, he was on leave, prior to which he had been sent to 1 Aircraft Depot. The next entry is dated 14th June 1919 [by which time, as indicated above, 10 Squadron had long since left the Continent] when he was attached to Rhine HQ. This is followed by a spate of entries, mainly to non-operational units and leave, before a final note on 4th May 1920, posting him back to England.

25 Squadron	Lt C Addenbrooke	Safe
DH.4 F7598	Sgt J Bourne	Safe

T/o Maubeuge for a practice flight but stalled and finished up in a collision with telegraph wires. A month previous to the date, Lieutenant Addenbrooke had written off a DH.4 in similar circumstances. Although badly damaged F7598 remained on establishment until 19th May, this being noted on page 212 of Francis K Mason's *Hawks Rising - The Story of 25 Squadron Royal Air Force*.

43 Squadron	Lt E G L Weaver	Safe
7F.1 Snipe		

T/o Bickendorf for a practice flight and wrecked on return when a wheel sheered from the axle and moments later the Snipe was slithering to a stop, inverted. Born, probably in Stoke on Trent, on the 4th of February 1899, Lieutenant Weaver enlisted with the RFC on 29th August 1917. He was posted to 43 Squadron [Camel] at Lièttres on 29th June, returning home on the 14th of March.

57 Squadron	Lt F O Thornton	Safe	See 26 January 1919
DH.4 F2662	2Lt J F Blick	Safe	

T/o Morville for a travelling flight and having become lost the crew made a precautionary landing at Remicourt where a helpful staff explained in which direction they should travel. Unfortunately, within seconds of resuming their journey the DH crashed out of control as a consequence of its undercarriage catching in the top of a bank, or mound.

Frederick Oswell Thornton was born on 24th April 1897, joined the RFC on 11th June 1917, and reported to Le Quesnoy on 25th June. He was destined to be involved in two more crashes, the second being fatal.

John Francis Blick, born on the last day of October 1896, was formerly of the 1st Battalion, Hampshire Regiment and on qualifying as an observer first saw service with 20 Squadron [Bristol F.2b], joining three days after the armistice came into effect. He had been with 57 Squadron for just eleven days. By the end of April he had rejoined 20 Squadron and left for India at the end of May.

I am reasonably confident that in the Second World War he received a commission in the Administrative and Special Duties Branch, effective from 23rd September 1939 [LG 3 October 1939, issue 34700, page 6662], and continuing to serve until relinquishing his commission under the provisions of the Navy, Army and Air Force Reserves Act 1954. He left the service as a Squadron Leader.

57 Squadron	2Lt W E Hall	Safe
DH.4 D8377/H7147	Lt W Steele	Safe

T/o Morville carrying sacks of mail to Spa. On arrival it was damaged while landing and with crew leaving the DH to seek assistance [this suggests, possibly, their arrival had gone unnoticed] a group of civilians gathered and looted the contents and made off, not only with the mail but parts of the aircraft as well which on inspection deemed it would not be economical to repair. A most strange affair.

As D8377 it had served with the squadron until 4th September 1918, when Major Cuthbert Ambrose Anthony Hiatt, accompanied by Mechanic W J Brinsden, landed heavily at Le Quesnoy and damaged the undercarriage. Only a partial record exists for Major Hiatt; this shows he was born on the 20th of March 1890, and transferred from the Norfolk Regiment to the RFC on the 17th of February 1915. On the 28th of September of that year he joined 4 Squadron at Baizieux for reconnaissance duties and was made a Flight Commander on March 29th, returning home on the 17th of July 1916, at a time when the *Battle of the Somme* was beginning to achieve limited successes, albeit with heavy casualties for every yard of ground gained and held. During his time on the Western Front he had one spell of sickness when he was grounded for six days with sciatica between the 10th and 15th of February.

Mechanic Brinsden, service number 210857, enlisted in the RFC on the 30th of April 1917. His service record indicates he was being paid three shillings a day.

2nd Lieutenant Hall joined the squadron as recently as the 3rd January, though he had been in France since September last and for the most part on the strength of 3 Aircraft Depot. He remained on the Continent after the squadron returned to the UK, the final entry on service sheet indicated a posting to a reception camp at Duren on 16th September.

I have not been able to locate any identifiable records for Lieutenant Steele.

Note. By entering his full name into the *Gazettes* on-line website, three notices show in respect of Major Hiatt. On page 35 of the Edinburgh edition of 1st January 1917, issue 13033, page 35, is notification of the honour made to him of the MC [no citation], while the London editions for 19th September 1939, issue 34687, page 6355, and 14th March 1941, issue 35106, page 1530, show his return to a form of active duty. That for September, under the heading General Duties record his rank as Honorary Flight Lieutenant with effect from 10th July 1939, while the March issue quotes his service number 76977 and under the heading Administrative and Special Duties Branch confirms his appointment as a Pilot Officer on probation. Tracing his service through the same medium and by using his service number for the search, this produces four more reports, that for supplement 40226, page 4028, of 6th July 1954, indicating he had to relinquish his commission under the provisions of the Navy, Army and Air Force Reserves Act 1954, and with permission to retain the rank of Squadron Leader.

A Google search has proved most rewarding for his name appears in one of the hundreds of records on the Aviation Safety Network [which I hereby acknowledge], this particular report ASN *Wikibase* Occurrence 220621 outlining the fate of a BE.2d of 66 Squadron which was destroyed in a fatal crash at Filton on the 21st of December 1916, while being flown by 2nd Lieutenant George Douglas Pechell who, it appears, lost control while climbing out of the airfield and from a height of sixty feet sideslipped and crashed.

Quoting from various sources, 220621 reads as follows: *"The second fatal incident occurred on 21 December 1916, and involved 2nd Lieutenant George Douglas Pechell [ex-Indian Army Reserve of Officers], who had been training with No 66 Squadron since 9 November. The 25 year old pilot was killed during the afternoon while flying B.E.2d 6735, which had been manufactured by the Vulcan Motor & Engineering Co. It appears that the aircraft went out of control at an altitude of 60 feet, side-slipped, and then crashed on Filton aerodrome.*

2nd Lieutenant Pechell was the younger son of Lieutenant-Colonel Sir A. Alexander Brooke-Pechell, 7th Baronet, of Larrau, Licq, Basses Pyrenees, France, and the Royal Hospital, Chelsea. He had been gazetted to the Indian Army Reserve of Officers in November 1914, and in the following January was attached to the 108th Infantry Regiment, and later the R.F.C.

The inquest on his death was held on 22 December, at which Captain Gilbert Dobbyn, a doctor with the Royal Army Medical Corps, stated that he saw the deceased fall with his machine about five o'clock. Death was instantaneous.

Captain Cuthbert Ambrose Anthony Hiatt, [ex-2nd Battalion, Norfolk Regiment], a Flight Commander with No 66 Squadron, said he saw the deceased in the air at 3.45 p.m. He was rising, when the machine turned to the right. The turn became steeper and steeper, and after one complete turn it fell through the roof of a store building, from a height of about 100 feet. He attributed the accident to the machine getting out of control through lack of experience of the aviator, who was under instruction. Captain Hiatt said he examined the machine and found all the controls in working order."

The inquest next heard from Lieutenant Alfred Reginald Boeree who had served previously with the 4th Battalion, Suffolk Regiment, but was now a Flight Commander serving with 66 Squadron. His statement was confined to reporting four test flights, undertaken by himself, prior to the George Pechell's fateful flight. On each of the four flights the aircraft responded as he expected with everything working perfectly. Lieutenant Boeree added that the deceased had flown the FE previously and appeared not to have displayed any serious flying faults.

A verdict of accidental death was recorded; 2nd Lieutenant Pechell being laid to rest in Bristol's Canford Cemetery.

65 Squadron   2Lt P T Grant   +   Kortrijk [St. Jan] Communal Cemetery
F.1 Camel E1591/D Canada

T/o Bisseghem for gunnery practice, the target being laid out on the airfield. Paul Thomas Grant climbed to the height that he had been briefed but, tragically, eyewitnesses considered he then dived at far too steep an angle before suddenly swerving away in a desperate attempt to recover. Out of control his aircraft hurtled into the ground.

2nd Lieutenant Grant, born on the 12th of July 1896, joined the RFC circa 8th October 1917, and had reported to the squadron at Petite Synthe on 28th September, so he was not inexperienced in the flying characteristics of the Camel.

His injuries as described on the Service and Casualty Form Part II as being egg shell fractures to the head and multiple fractures; there are no indications that he suffered burns. He was buried with full military honours in a service officiated by the Reverend F S Oakley, attached to 62 CCS.

92 Squadron   Lt B Mignault   Safe
SE.5a F8956

T/o Thuilles for a practice flight and on return overshot the landing area and crashed. Lieutenant Mignault joined the squadron on 26th September 1918, and was wounded in acton on the 27th of October [see page 354 of my second volume for details]. It appears his injuries were not of a serious nature and over the Christmas he enjoyed ten days leave in France. On the 6th of March he reported to Blandford Camp in Dorset and, I much suspect, soon after he sailed for

Canada, though there are no indications on his Record of Service that he was a Canadian. As in so many cases, his full service records has not been preserved.

| 103 Squadron | Lt J G H Crispin | Safe | Unemployed list 4 May 1919 |
| DH.9 D7249 | Lt C G Bannerman | Safe | |

T/o Ronchin to practice air-to-air firing but owing to incorrect gear settings the propeller fractured causing the engine to overspeed; damaged beyond repair.

Accepted on the 19th of June 1918, D7249 had at least four enemy machines to its credit, the first, a Fokker DVII, being claimed by Lieutenant Crispin and 2nd Lieutenant Bannerman during the morning of 24th September. Three days later, again during a morning patrol, Captain Donald McKenzie Darroch accompanied by 2nd Lieutenant Eric Appleyard Wadsworth, settled the fate of another Fokker DVII.

A relatively quiet few weeks followed before on October 30th, Lieutenant G B Hett observer accounted for a brace of these very potent scouts; sadly, these victories were offset by return fire which mortally wounded 2nd Lieutenant John James Nicholls. News of his death at 39 Stationary Hospital would be conveyed to his father residing at 8 Yardside Road, Barrow-in-Furness, Lancashire, by which time his son had been laid to rest at Lille, his funeral being overseen by the Reverend C H D Hodges attached, I believe, to 39 Signal Regiment.

I believe John Nicholls joined the Royal Air Force on or around the 2nd of May 1918, reporting for observer duties on the 19th of September.

A Record of Service form has survived for Lieutenant Crispin but, unfortunately it, like a number of contemporary records of the time has nothing of interest appended. However, the air history website, to which I am indebted, identifies him as Joel Gordon Hirst Crispin and armed with this information I have been able to trace his elevation from Flight Cadet to 2nd Lieutenant on probation from 11th October 1917 [LG 17 October 1917, supplement 30337, page 10656]. For his observer, I have yet to trace any details.

Donald McKenzie Darroch was born on the 5th of October 1893, enlisting circa December 1917, and reported for his operational tour with the squadron around the middle of May 1918, this being terminated on the 23rd of October when he was badly wounded whilst leading his flight on bombing operations [see my second volume and page 341 for details] sustaining a colles' fracture to his left wrist, a fractured radius and injuries to his ribs; four days later he was sent home aboard the HS *Jan Breydel*. His observer was Lieutenant Frank Masterman Loly born 2nd November 1894, and late of the 3rd Battalion, East Surrey Regiment. Frank Loly came to the RFC on 13th January 1918, and began his tour of duty with 18 Squadron on 20th March and thence to 103 Squadron on 12th June. His wounds must have been minor and there is no mention of treatment at a CCS. He was posted home on the 5th of September.

Eric Appleyard Wadsworth, who was with Captain Darroch on 27th September, had been commissioned to one of the East Yorkshire battalions, transferring to the RFC on the 1st of December 1917. His operational tour lasted from the 8th of May to the 16th of October. His birth date is shown as the 3rd of April 1894.

Finally, Lieutenant Geoffrey Bruce Hett who returned to base with his observer dying is recorded as having served with three DH equipped squadrons; 103 Squadron from 14th June 1918 to 18th February 1919; then to 206 Squadron until the 8th of May on which date he reported to 18 Squadron before heading for England on the 6th of June.

On the 11th of February 1919, the Edinburgh edition of the *Gazette* issue 13400, page 799, published the citation for his DFC: *'This officer has taken part in fifty bombing raids, proving himself a capable and resolute officer. On 30th October, during a return journey, his formation was attacked by thirty scouts. Lt. Hett, flying in the rear, bore the brunt of this heavy attack. With skill and cool judgement he so manoeuvred his machine that his observer was enabled to destroy two of the hostile aircraft before he was seriously wounded. Facing the enemy scouts, Lt. Hett maintained a successful combat until they were driven off by the arrival of some of our scouts.'*

| 204 Squadron | 2Lt W R Stewart | Safe |
| F.1 Camel F4990 | | |

T/o Heule authorised for practice flying. On completing the detail, Second Lieutenant Stewart overshot his landing and crashed after striking part of a raised road. A Record of Service form has been raised, but apart from his name, initials and rank it has no other information.

| 216 Squadron | Lt Moore | Safe |
| HP O/400 B8806 | Lt Taylor | Safe |

T/o Marquise carrying mail and wrecked while landing at Duren.

Wednesday 22 January 1919

| 3 Squadron AusFC | Lt W R G Frayne | Safe |
| RE.8 B7917 | Lt C T Brown | Safe |

T/o Charleroi for a practice flight. Overshot on return and in attempting to avoid a sunken road the RE turned sharply and overturned.

| 74 Squadron | Lt F Thornton | Safe |
| SE.5a H713 | | |

While taxying at Halluin the undercarriage dropped into some deep ruts and the impact overstressed the airframe. Its engine and flying instruments were salvaged with what remained set alight. Frank Thornton was posted to 74 Squadron on the 3rd of October 1918, and remained so attached until the 30th of January when he was posted to a holding camp to await his return to the UK.

208 Squadron   Lt W V Skall   Safe
7F.1 Snipe E8051
T/o Stree for a practice flight but crashed out of control before becoming airborne. A rather badly creased Record of Service form show Lieutenant Skall arriving with the squadron on the 26th of July 1918, at which time it was flying Sopwith Camels. It is believed he wrote off E7179 in a landing accident on the 3rd of November. Omitted from my second volume, I have added the incident to the Additions and Amendments appendix. He returned to England on the 25th of February.

Thursday 23 January 1919
Territorial issues continued to dominate, this time a border dispute between Poland Czechoslovakia which lead to Czech forces occupying Bohumin and Karyiná.

65 Squadron   Lt F A Green   Injured
F.1 Camel B5585   USA
T/o Bisseghem for a disposal flight to Lièttres where it was to be placed in the care of 151 Squadron whose role was now a demobilisation unit. However, *en route* the engine began misfiring and seeing he was close to Reckem airfield Lieutenant Floyd Ambrose Green elected to land; however, dame fortune was against him and he crashed with a force sufficient to wreck his aircraft.

   His Record of Service is quite illuminating. Nominating his mother as his next of kin at P.O.Box 1201, Detroit, Michigan, his date of birth appears to have been the 15th of January 1891, though the hand-writing is none too clear. He probably joined the RFC on 28th June 1917, his bank details, effective from this date, being London City and Midland at 27 Haymarket, London. Floyd Green arrived in France on the 2nd of October and while attached to 1 Aeroplane Supply Depot was admitted to 14 General Hospital suffering from an undiagnosed illness and it was not until the 9th of December that he was declared fit for duty.

   Initially, he returned to 1 Aeroplane Supply Depot before being posted to 12 Brigade on the 12th, and thence on Christmas Day to 65 Squadron. Between the 10th and 19th of January, he took leave in France, and shortly after the accident, here reported, Floyd was ordered to report to Reckem where, briefly, he was taken on the nominal roll of the resident 10 Squadron [Bristol F.2b.

   However, with the squadron preparing to return to England, he was posted out on the 8th to 108 Squadron [DH.9] at Gondecourt only to find himself in similar circumstances in that '108' was in the throws of crossing the Channel to await disbandment. Thus, on the 4th of March he was ordered to a dispersal camp at Setques in the Pas-de-Calais SW of St. Omer. There is little doubt he was demobilised soon after.

203 Squadron   *Not reported*
F.1 Camel C191
T/o Bethencourt [201 Squadron] assigned for 203 Squadron at Boisdinghem but forced-landed near Saint Quentin. Salvaged, it eventually arrived at Boisdinghem where it was broken down for spares and produce.

Friday 24 January 1919
A costly day in terms of fatalities with three singe-seater pilots killed.

1 Squadron   Lt H G Freeman   Safe   Unemployed list 2 March 1919
SE.5a F5661/B
T/o Izel-lès-Hameau for an air test and crashed, owing to a failing engine, at Avesnes-le-Comte in the Pas-de-Calais. Accepted on 27th October 1918, it was struck off charge 24-hours following the crash. This was the squadron's second major accident since the turn of the year. I have yet to locate any information regarding Lieutenant Freeman's postings.

22 Squadron   Lt D G Davis   Safe
Bristol F.2b E2617 Captain F J Phillips   Safe
T/o Nivelles to take Captain Phillips to rejoin 48 Squadron at Bickendorf but became lost in mist and in making a forced-landing the Bristol ran into a tree; wrecked. Lieutenant Davis's Army Form B.103 has, apart from his name and initials, a single entry *"7/9/18 Posted to No 22 Squad."* I believe he had reported on 30th August.

   Francis John Phillips, born 13th April 1895, and enlisting 28th July 1917, was still on establishment in early 1919 [he was on leave between between the 20th of February and the 1st of March]. His service record indicates he had one spell back in the UK following sickness; on the 29th of May 1918, he went home aboard HMHS *Grantully Castle,* returning to 48 Squadron on 27th June, only to fall ill with influenza two days later. Treated at 55 CCS he was deemed fit to resume operations on the 4th of July. He assumed Flight Commander duties on the 4th of October.

   On the 1st of May, he was still carrying out such duties and for this purpose, although his substantive rank was Lieutenant, his pay and allowances matched those of Captain [LG 19 August, issue 31510, page 10478].

70 Squadron   Lt A Webster   +   Cologne Southern Cemetery
F.1 Camel E7241/2
T/o Bickendorf for formation flying practice and collided with the Camel reported below. Born on the 5th of February 1893, and from Montrose in Scotland, Alexander Webster enlisted in the RFC on the 5th of May 1917, and had flown with the squadron since May 18th last, so on this evidence he was a very experienced scout pilot. His funeral, and that

of 2nd Lieutenant Sinclair, a fellow Scotsman, were conducted with full military honours by the squadron's Chaplin, the Reverend C D R B Bankes. Alexander's grave is inscribed with the words: *"Beloved Son Of Gordon Webster Brechin In Sweet Remembrance."*

70 Squadron   2Lt R Sinclair   +   Cologne Southern Cemetery
F.1 Camel F4001
T/o Bickendorf similarly tasked and lost in the manner described above. Although a Record Service form has been raised for 2nd Lieutenant Sinclair it has no details pertaining to his service with the squadron. His epitaph reads: *"Dearly Beloved Only Son Of Mr And Mrs R Sinclair Fillyside, Leith."*

112 Squadron   2Lt J T Mitchell   +   Throwley [St. Michael] Churchyard
F.1 Camel F2091   Canada
T/o Throwley and lost control at the top a loop and spun into a wood near Favershan, Kent. His entry in the cemetery register shows only his initials, but he is reported as the son of Mrs Eliza Mitchell of Wingham in Ontario.

Saturday 25 January 1919
A draft proposal agreed between the British Under Secretary of State for Foreign Affairs, Robert Cecil and Jan Smuts, the South Africa Prime Minister, for the establishment of a League of Nations, received approval at the Paris Peace Conference. A most laudable aim but which in reality, as history now shows, proved totally ineffective when war threatened for a second time in Europe .

20 Squadron   2Lt W Knight   Safe
Bristol F.2b F4275
T/o Ossogne and thought to have been damaged beyond repair at Thuilles when the tail skid snapped on landing. 2nd Lieutenant Knight's service with the squadron commenced on 25th October 1918 and ended when he was posted back to England on 18th April, six weeks before 20 Squadron left for India.

66 Squadron   Lt S J Osborne   Safe   Unemployed list 26 February 1919
F.1 Camel E7246
T/o San Pietro and believed damaged beyond repair when a wheel came away from the axle on landing. Possibly born in Wiveliscombe near Taunton in Somerset on 15th February 1899, 2nd Lieutenant Osborne enlisted in the RFC on or around 15th August 1917. His training finished, he unpacked his bags at San Pietro on 25th July 1918. From the 11th to the 27th of September, he was treated in 24 CCS for jaundice, and then between the 1st of November and the 14th, he received attention in an unidentified hospital for a gunshot wound to his right thigh. He left Italy ahead of the squadron's return to England and was placed, as indicated, on the unemployed list.

84 Squadron   2Lt R Johnston   Safe
SE.5a E5767
T/o Thuilles authorised for practice flying. On return overshot the landing area and crashed. I believe this to be Robert Johnston who was born on the 2nd of August 1897, and whose address is shown as 15 Spring Street, Stockton-on-Tees.

208 Squadron   Lt L F A Green   Safe   Unemployed list 5 November 1919
7F.1 Snipe E8184
T/o Stree for a practice flight and believed to have been damaged beyond repair in the all too familiar circumstances of a forced-landing brought about by engine failure. Lionel Frederick Augustus Green who was born on 28th August 1899, joined the RNAS the day before his eighteenth birthday. He arrived in France in time to serve with 8 Squadron RNAS before the amalgamation of the two air arms resulted in the squadron becoming 208 Squadron of the Royal Air Force.
   On the 4th of February 1919, he was treated at 55 CCS for diphtheria and on the 20th sent home by way of the HS *Jan Breydel*. On the 17th of June 1940, he was granted a commission in the Administrative and Special Duties Branch [LG 13th September 1940, issue 34945, page 5493] and rose to the rank of Wing Commander before the provisions of the Navy, Army and Air Force Reserves Act 1954, obliged him to relinquish his commission.

Sunday 26 January 1919
57 Squadron   Lt F O Thornton   Safe   See 6 March 1919
DH.4 B3957
T/o Morville carrying mail to Spa but soon after setting course a fire broke out in the carburettor and Frederick forced-landed at Ivoz-Ramet where an inspection revealed such extensive fire damage that the Dh was written off charge. This was his second narrow shave, the first occurring at Remicourt on the 21st.
   Prior to issue to 57 Squadron, B3957 had seen operational service with 55 Squadron and it was certainly not without incident. Raiding Mannheim in the early afternoon of 18th March 1918, 2nd Lieutenants Cecil Alchin Bridgland and Earle Richard Stewart, a Canadian from Vancouver, drove down an Albatros in the target area. Two months later, Captain F Williams returned to Tantonville with his observer, 2nd Lieutenant John Stewart Bradley, wounded [the portion of his Army Form B.103 covering this period has not survived].
   Early morning operations on 30th July resulted in an Albatros being driven down over Offenburg, the victorious crew being Captain Williams and 2nd Lieutenant Stewart. Then, on 12th August, tragedy struck when the DH was badly shot about; Cecil Bridgland escaped unharmed but Earle Stewart was mortally wounded. Born 14th September 1898, and

enlisting in the RFC on the 22nd of August 1917, Earle had served with the squadron since the 12th of March, and was nearing the end of his tour of operations. He was buried in a military cemetery on the south side of Damas-aux-Bois [now Charmes Military Cemetery, Essegney] some two to three km east of Charmes, the service being conducted by the Reverend H J Blake attached to 8 Canadian Stationary Hospital. On 21st September 1918, he was *Gazetted* with the DFC, supplement 30913, page 11255: *'For gallantry and skill as an observer on long-distance bombing raids. During a raid a few months back he was in the deputy-leaders machine [which usually has to bear the brunt of an attack], and in the course of repelling vigorous enemy attacks he had a breakage in his gun, with the result he could only fire single shots. In these circumstances he would have been justified in causing his pilot to close up under the remainder of the formation, but with great coolness and sound judgement he maintained his place, and thus avoided the risk of impairing the squadron's defensive efficiency. By his action he rendered the valuable assistance to his formation in holding off the enemy, and by the time the enemy had been dispersed he had fired 200 rounds by single shots with excellent effect. Lieut. Stewart has rendered further distinguished service during the past month, displaying very great ability and absolute fearlessness.'*

And what of the others mentioned in regard to 55 Squadron? For Captain Williams I have drawn a blank, but in respect of Cecil Bridgland whose address is shown as The Cedars, Gravesend, Kent, it is shown he was born on the 10th of April 1896, and making his acquaintance with the RFC on 4th May 1917. He joined the squadron on 13th February 1918, and completed his tour of duty on 4th September, on which date he was posted back to England. Subsequently, he was awarded the DFC [no citation attached, unfortunately], *Gazetted* 3 June 1919, supplement 31378, page 7031. It is noted he had seen army service with the 3rd Battalion, East Surrey Regiment being *Gazetted* 2nd Lieutenant on 1st October 1913, late Cadet Lance-Corporal, King's School [Rochester] Contingent Officers Training Corps [LG 28 October 1918, issue 28768, page 7523].

As noted the portion of John Bradley's form recording his wounds is missing but it is known that he was of the 11th Machine Gun Squadron, returning home to commence his observer training on the 21st of September 1917. Three months later he was back on the Western Front and reported to the squadron at Tantonville on 29th December. From Co. Derry, he was born on the 9th of December 1892.

Repaired, the DH arrived with 57 Squadron from 2 Air Issues on 8th December.

203 Squadron   F.1 Camel D1929/F6037   Burnt out at Boisdinghem. Previously with 4 Squadron Australian Flying Corps as D1929 it accounted for an impressive total of eleven aircraft and two kite balloons, all at the hands of Arthur Henry Cobby who rose to Captain rank in the *Great War* and subsequently became a permanent officer in the RAAF, attaining the rank of Air Commodore.

As recorded on the Aerodrome website, which I acknowledge, his fighting qualities were second to none. Between the 21st of March 1918 and the 4th of September he destroyed, or was assisted, twenty-four aircraft and five kite balloons. In this relatively short span of just over six months he gained a DFC and Two Bars and the DSO. The citations for these honours read as follows:

'Has proved himself a very gallant and successful fighter and patrol leader, setting a fine example to the squadron. Within the last few months he has destroyed a number of enemy balloons and aeroplanes.' [LG 3 August 1918, page 9199 of supplement 30827].

'An officer whose success as a leader is due not only to high courage and brilliant flying, but also to the clear judgement and presence of mind he invariably displays. His example is of great value to other pilots in his squadron. During recent operations he shot down five machines in eleven days, accounting for two in one day.' [LG 21 September 1918, supplement 30913, page 11248].

'One evening this officer, in company with another machine, attacked five Pfalz Scouts, destroying two; one fell in flames, and one broke up in the air. The officer who accompanied him brought down a third machine out of control. While engaged in this combat they were attacked from above by five triplanes. Displaying cool judgement and brilliant flying, Captain Cobby evaded this attack and returned to our lines in safety, both machines being undamaged. A determined and most skilful leader, who has destroyed twenty-one hostile machines or balloons, accounting for three machines and two balloons in four days.' [LG 21 September 1918, supplement 30913, page 11248].

'On the 16th August, this officer led an organised raid on an enemy aerodrome. At 200 feet altitude he obtained direct hits with his bombs and set on fire two hangars; he then opened fire on a machine which was standing out on the aerodrome. The machine caught fire. Afterwards he attacked with machine-gun fire parties of troops and mechanics, inflicting a number of casualties. On the following day he led another important raid on an aerodrome, setting fire to two hangars and effectively bombing gun detachments, anti-aircraft batteries, etc. The success of these two raids was largely due to the determined and skilful leadership of this officer.' [LG 2 November 1918, supplement 30989, page 12959]. This citation for the DSO reflects in part the intensity of air operations during the *Battle of Amiens*.

In the Second World War he was awarded the George Medal for his part in rescuing fellow survivors from the crash of a Catalina flying-boat at Townsville on the 7th of September 1943. The pinnacle of his service came when he was appointed to Australia's First Tactical Air Force operating in the area of the South West Pacific and it must have been to his sorrow that owing to differences of opinion between him and some of his squadron leaders that he was relieved of his command in April 1945. Retiring from the service on the 19th of August 1946, he maintained his life-long interest in aviation by joining the Department of Civil Aviation.

Born in Prahran in the State of Victoria on 26th August 1894, his sudden, and unexpected death, came on Armistice Day 1955, following his collapse in his Melbourne office. Rushed into hospital Arthur Henry Cobby DSO DFC** GM died that same evening of hypertensive cerebrovascular disease.

Monday 27 January 1919

20 Squadron   Bristol F.2b C808   While being taxied towards the hangars at Ossogne by Chief Mechanic A P Welton the tail skid fractured and the rest of the unit collapsed. A similar accident of Thuilles on the 25th resulted in one of the squadron's Bristols being written off in similar circumstances.

58 Squadron   2Lt G E Newton   Safe
HP O/400 D9706 2Lt F H Langmaid   Safe   Unemployed list 18 April 1919
T/o Proven with the Brigade's sports' officer as passenger and set a course for Marquise where, I suspect, the crew would clear customs, and then continue to the UK. With weather forecasting still in its infancy it is unlikely anyone was aware that dense fog lay along their route and when it was met a precautionary landing seemed advisable. Unfortunately in the poor visibility a line of trees went unseen and it was into these obstructions that the bomber flew, the location reported as five km east of Desvres in the Pas-de-Calais.

Born in Devon - his next of kin address is shown as Sea View House, Seaton - on the 1st of May 1898, George Ewart Newton joined the RFC on 24th February 1918, and commenced his service with the squadron on 27th September. He eventually started out for Egypt on the 27th of May.

On 18th October 1920, he was granted a short service commission [LG 29 October 1920, issue 32105, page 10456] and served until 18th October 1928, on which date he was transferred from Class A to Class C. No doubt aware of the worsening situation in Europe, George returned to the service, this time in the Administrative and Special Duties Branch, his commission being effective from 20th June 1938 [LG 12 November 1939, issue 34752, page 8256].

With the drastic reduction in officer strength in the mid-'50s, and now ranked Wing Commander, he relinquished his commission under the provisions of the Navy, Army and Air Force Reserves Act 1954.

Frederick Harold Langmaid left the quiet surroundings of 56 Alwyne Road, Wimbledon for the RFC on the 10th of February 1917 [his birth date is recorded as 26th July 1895] and with his observer training over, he joined the squadron at Fauquembergues on 30th August but had barely time to take in the camp before he moved over to Alquines on the 31st. From the 16th to the 22nd of September, he was treated for an unidentified condition in a hospital attached to the New Zealand Expeditionary Force.

With the squadron making ready to move to Egypt, Frederick was posted to 214 Squadron at Chemy on the 12th of April, but after a mere five days in getting to know his new colleagues he returned to England and joined the mounting numbers of officers whose service was no longer required.

Tuesday 28 January 1919

The scaling down of the Imperial German Army continued with the announcement that the 4th Army had disbanded. I believe its commander at the time was *General der Infanterie* Friedrich Bertram Sixt von Armin.

75 Squadron   2Lt A H Thomas   Safe
F.1 Camel F2175
Presentation Aircraft: Nabha No 6
T/o North Weald and reported as wrecked in unrecorded circumstances. It had been presented by His Highness the Maharajah of Nabha.

75 Squadron   F/Cdt J R Lloyd   Safe
F.1 Camel F6336
T/o North Weald and reported as *"wrecked."* I would not be surprised if there is a connection between its demise and the loss of the Camel summarised above.

84 Squadron   Captain F H Taylor MC   Safe   Unemployed list 16 September 1919
SE.5a F5663   Canada
T/o Thuilles to maintain his flying skills and believed to have been damaged beyond repair and a heavy landing on ground frozen hard by recent frosts.

The service records that have survived in the form of Army Form B.103 show Frank Harold Taylor as born on the 11th of August 1896 and that he transferred to the RFC on the 14th of July 1917, having until then served with the 3rd Battalion, Canadian Infantry [Lieutenant-Colonel Joseph B Rogers CMG DSO MC] and, I suspect, he had taken part in the *Battle of Arras** which was fought between the 9th of April and 16th May 1917. Like every major offensive on the Western Front it was a brutal affair; the Canadians and British under the command of General Henry Sinclair Horne's First Army succeeding in taking the key sector of Vimy Ridge.

Frank's initial flying training probably started on June 12th in France at Vendôme before returning to the UK on 14th July, his transfer from the army now approved.

On the 22nd of September he was back on the Western Front, reporting to 41 Squadron at Lielvilliers where he flew DH.5s before converting to SE.5as in November; it was in a DH.5 that he claimed his first combat success when on the last day of November on a patrol over Bourlon Wood he shared with three others pilots the driving down on a hostile machine. This was followed twixt 25th January and 24th March with successful claims for six aeroplanes and a kite balloon.

For these actions he was *Gazetted* with the MC [LG 22 June 1918, supplement 30761, page 7429]: *'For conspicuous gallantry and devotion to duty. On one occasion, whilst on offensive patrol, he shot down a hostile scout in flames and a second out of control* [23rd March while flying SE.5a C1752 in the vicinity of Bourlon Wood, both victims being Albatros DVs]. *On the following day he shot down an enemy triplane* [over Vaulx], *which finally crashed to earth.*

During the recent operations he has carried out many successful attacks on enemy infantry from low altitudes, and has taken part in over 80 offensive patrols. His gallantry and good service merit the highest praise.'

Shortly before the armistice he was appointed as a Flight Commander to 84 Squadron [C Flight] and flying SE.5a F855 he chalked up two more victories, the first in the gloom of late afternoon, 3rd November, when he drove down a Fokker DVII out of control over Forêt de Mormal and then on the morning of the 10th he destroyed a Fokker DVII SE of Faynolle. In between his service with the two fighter squadrons, he was able to return for a welcome spell of leave in Canada. His death, reported on the 7th of June 1985, occurred in Mattituck in Suffolk County, New York.

* Sir Douglas Haig favoured operations further north in the Ypres sector coupled with the aim of a break-out from the Ypres Salient and an advance towards the Belgian ports, thereby denying the enemy of facilities for their submarine operations. This did not sit well with the Prime Minister, David Lloyd George, who vetoed its implementation. There are numerous books and websites that deal in great depth to this battle and its outcome.

Wednesday 29 January 1919
At the Paris Peace Conference, Poland, through their diplomat Roman Dmowski formerly met with the Supreme War Council to press the case for his country to be recognised as the rightful owner of certain German territories, including Greater Poland where tension remained high following recent fighting.

28 Squadron   2Lt A E Hitchcock   +   Montecchio Precalcino Communal Cemetery extension
F.1 Camel E7171
T/o Sarcedo and came down at Ville Franca. Salvage teams removed the the Clerget 9Bf engine and all armaments which were deposited at 7 Aeroplane Park. A Record of Service card has been raised for Albert Edward Hitchcock on which his date of birth is shown as 11th November 1899, and enlistment to the RFC on 28th November 1917. He listed his mother as next of kin, her address being 12 Melfort Road, Thornton Heath, Surry. Unfortunately, information regarding postings and the like have not been entered. His poetic epitaph reads: *"You Bravely Answered Duty's Call, You Gave Your Life for One And All."*

35 Squadron   Lt R Lazarri   Safe
FK.8 F7406
T/o Ste Marie Cappel intending to cross the Channel but before reaching the coast he forced-landed in a ploughed field near Lieppe [sic]. Lieutenant Lazarri first served with 8 Squadron [RE.8] reporting to Estrée-en-Chaussèe on 26th September 1918. By 11th October, he was undergoing treatment in 39 General Hospital and it was not until 9th December that he was discharged to a reception centre at Rouen.

On the 13th he came under the aegis of 10th Brigade, but was re-admitted to hospital on the 15th for two days. Eventually, on the 8th of January he was declared fit enough to resume flying duties and was posted to 35 Squadron. His general health, however, was not good and by 4th February he was back in hospital, this time with 3 Canadian Stationary Hospital and thence to England on the 17th by way of HMHS *Brighton.*

98 Squadron   Lt J M Brown   Safe
DH.9 E8931
T/o Alquines for an air test following its temporary loan to 40 Squadron but owing to the extreme cold the oil was so sluggish it failed to circulate properly and with its engine spluttering the DH forced-landed. It is likely that additional damage occurred thus making likely that following recovery to 1 Advanced Salvage Dump it was scrapped.

Lieutenant Brown first saw operational service with 103 Squadron, joining the squadron at Old Sarum three days before its departure to Serny. On the 9th of August he was ordered to Clairmarais where he was attached to 98 Squadron. His service record ceases on 21st December, at which time he was still on the squadron's nominal roll.

Thursday 30 January 1919
55 Squadron [DH.4] arrived at Renfrew in Scotland and was reduced to a cadre. During the day the Imperial German Army disbanded its 3rd, 5th and 7th armies.

101 Squadron   Captain C W D Bell   Safe
FE.2b F5859   Lt W J P Dicks   Safe   Unemployed list 10 February 1919
T/o Morville for a cross-country but when the crew were obliged to forced-land between the war torn countryside between Laon and Soissons their FE dropped into an old shell hole and was damaged beyond repair.

An overview of Captain Bell's service is recorded in my summary for 23rd November 1918. That for Lieutenant Dicks is confined to his rank, name and initials.

Friday 31 January 1919
The month ended with a combined force of Estonian and Finnish troops defeating a mixed Russian and Latvian force. On a more positive note, the fighting between Poland Czechoslovakia that had embroiled the two countries since the 23rd ended.

29 Squadron   2Lt S E Allenby   Safe   See 11 May 1919
SE.5a E5658
T/o Bickendorf for an air test and on return misjudged his approach, stalled and crashed.

206 Squadron	Lt C L Cumming	+	Cologne Southern Cemetery
DH.9 E8877	2Lt A J Waters	+	Cologne Southern Cemetery

T/o Bickendorf carrying mail only to catch fire in the air and crash out of control at Buschbell [Nordrhein-Westfalen], SSW from the centre of Köln and on the south side of the railway leading to the border town of Aachen. It will be re-called that Charles Cumming had crashed on New Year's Day while carrying out a similar mission. Both officers were were buried side-by-side with full military honours, the service being conducted by 70 Squadron's Padre, the Reverend C R D Banks. Andrew John Walters had previously flown with 21 Squadron [RE.8] and had joined '206' as recently as 18th January. His headstone is inscribed with the well known phrase: *"Till The Day Breaks And The Shadows Flee Away."* He was nineteen years old.

FEBRUARY
1919

Until now squadron strength on the Continent and in the Middle East had altered little since the armistice but through-out February a seed change witnessed the rundown of squadrons that by the end of the year would leave the Royal Air Force a mere shadow of its former glory. This savage reduction is illustrated by a list of squadrons in Appendix C that survived the axe. It is worth comparing the table with Appendix C for 1918.

Saturday 1 February 1919
Celebrations in Estonia with the news that Bolshevik forces had been expelled from Valga and Vōru thus bringing to an end Estonia's War of Independence.
    104 Squadron returned to Turnhouse from Maisoncelle.

43 Squadron	Lt W E Thomas	Injured
7F.1 Snipe E8186		

T/o Bickendorf for a practice flight. Forced-landed with a failing engine near the village of Weiler*where the under-carriage became stuck in ruts deep enough to pitch the Snipe onto its nose. William Elias Thomas, born 19th November 1899, had served on the squadron since the 12th of August 1918. His injuries must have been minor as there are no in-dications that he went to hospital. He remained on establishment until 20th August; five days later 43 Squadron returned to England to await disbandment.

* There are no less that thirteen locations in Germany named Weiler and twenty-six others where Weiler is associated with a larger town.

61 Squadron	2Lt F Lloyd	+	Walsall [Bloxwich] Cemetery
F.1 Camel H799			

T/o Rochford and while flying at extremely low altitude a wingtip struck an overhead tramway standard and within seconds H799' was on the ground, a mass of flames. It is noted from CWGC records the cemetery contains thirty-eight service burials, nineteen from the *Great War* and an equal number from the Second World War.

Sunday 2 February 1919
215 Squadron arrived at Ford from Alquines. Formed out of 15 Squadron RNAS on the 1st of April 1918, '215' had operated in the night bombing role, first with Handley Page O/100s and later with the improved O/400s. Since August 1918, it had come under the aegis of 83 Wing, VIII Brigade of the Independent Force of the Royal Air Force.

43 Squadron	Lt G P Geiger	Safe	Unemployed list 20 May 1919
7F.1 Snipe E8033	Canada		

T/o Bickendorf for a practice sortie and crashed out of control when on landing the pulsator glass shattered sending a spray of hot oil onto George Feltmeth Geiger's goggles. Born on the 5th of December 1894, he had flown with the squadron since the 9th of August 1918. For an explanation of the pulsator glass and its purpose, Barry Schiff [whom I gratefully acknowledge] provides on his website a fascinating insight regarding the skill required to fly and get the best out of these aeroplanes of the day. In a lengthy discourse he comments on why Sopwith deliberately made the Camel an unstable aircraft in order to maximise its performance. In retrospect I suspect many a young pilot, freshly qualified, wished that the Camel's flying characteristics were a little more docile.

Monday 3 February 1919
94 Squadron [SE.5a] departed Izel-lès-Hameau for the delights of Tadcaster. Throughout its time on the Western Front, first at Senlis on the last day of October 1918, and to the chagrin of its pilots, it was never called upon to participate in the final operations of the war.

221 Squadron	Captain J W B Grigson	Safe
DH.9 D2803/I	DSC	
	Lt O R Gayford DSC	Safe

T/o Petrovsk and reported as crashed but without details regarding the location. A photograph of D2803 from the extensive J M Bruce/G S Leslie collection] is printed on page 171 of *The DH.4/DH.9 File.* This shows it struck the ground on its starboard side causing extensive damage to the lower and upper wings, while the rear fuselage appears fractured just ahead of the tail assembly where the starboard elevator has the letter C painted on the upper surface. The wreck has attracted a gathering of personnel - possibly including the crew - while in the background are a large number of tall poles.

John William Boldero Grigson, born 26th January 1893, commenced his military service as a sailor in the Royal Navy Volunteer Reserve [RNVR] and by mid-April 1915, he was serving aboard HMS *India,* an Armed Merchant Cruiser, which on the 8th of August 1915, was sunk by U-22 off Helligyaer, Norway. At the time of the sinking *India* was engaged in intercepting neutral flagged shipping suspected of carrying iron ore from Sweden to Germany. Although reported to have been interned in neutral Norway, John Grigson was back in England by August 1916, where he obtained a commission in the RNAS.

By July 1918, he was a Flight Commander with 221 Squadron and in August 1919, he was one of many officers appointed to a permanent commission. His Record of Service shows he was in South Russia by 21st August and on the strength of 47 Squadron and when '47' became A Squadron of the Royal Air Force Mission supporting White Russian forces, John Grigson was included in its strength.

Eventually, he arrived in Constantinople on March 31st, 1920, where he was struck off strength of Allied forces in the area. At this point it is appropriate to record the citation for his DSC [LG 21 September 1918, supplement 30913, page 11256] awarded jointly with Lieutenant Oswald Robert Gayford: *'[Sea Patrol]. These two officers have flown together for a period of twelve months, during which they participated in a number of bombing raids, carried out a large number of valuable reconnaissance patrols and escort flights in all weathers, by day and night, during the performance of which duties they have brought down hostile aircraft on several occasions. No task is too difficult for these two officers.'*

Recorded on his service records below the Constantinople entry appears the following: *"Distinguished Service Order 18.3.20', 'St Vladimir 4th Class with Sword & bow No 2834 17.3.20'* and *'St Vladimir 3rd Class with Sword & now No 2874 23.3.20."*

For the time being Captain Grigson remained in Turkey and although I cannot be certain I believe it likely he joined 55 Squadron*at Maltepe on appointment as a Flight Commander. This was followed by a return to the UK, probably in 1921, for Flight Commander duties with 205 Squadron at Leuchars, the only squadron in the Royal Air Force to equip with Parnall Panther two-seater Fleet spotter biplanes. His association with naval-style flying lasted until May 1924, when he attended Staff College and for the next few years he was confined to ground based work, including a course at the School of Oriental Studies from April to October 1925. This stood him in good stead for returned to Iraq where for the next four years he was attached to Headquarters Iraq Command assuming duties concerned with intelligence. Then, and no doubt to his delight, he was appointed on 21st March 1929, to command 55 Squadron at Hinaidi.

As an illustration of the paucity of Royal Air Force equipment in the interwar years, the squadron was still operating DH.9As with which John Grigson had been familiar with over a decade earlier.

This was his last active flying post. In January 1930, and now back in England, he attended the Imperial Defence College after which he performed Staff Duties at home and in India while in the Second World War he was in the Middle East and Balkans before, very sadly, dying on the 3rd of July 1943, during his appointment as Acting Air Officer Commanding, Rhodesian Air Training Group.

Air Commodore John William Boldero Grigson DSO, DSC, DFC**, twice mentioned in despatches was buried in Harare [Pioneer] Cemetery, his headstone inscribed with the words: *"And All The Trumpets Sounded For Him On The Other Side."*

Regarding his observer of long standing, Oswald Robert Gayford, I have turned to his records as shown on The Air of Authority website, which I have delight in acknowledging.

Oswald was born on the 18th of May 1893, making him four months younger than his skipper, and like John Grigson his service began in the navy enlisting as a humble sailor in the RN Division on the 4th of September 1914. For at least two years he served as a signaller until mid-October 1916, when he began commenced training as an observer.

By 1917, he was attached to C Squadron of No 2 Wing RNAS on HMS *Ark Royal.* In the wake of the accident, and by September 1919, he was a Staff Officer on Z Force in British Somaliland where he received the news that he had been appointed to a permanent commission.

Over the next two decades his career was filled with numerous postings, during which he re-mustered to pilot and was trained by 29 Squadron before serving as a Flight Commander between November 1924 and February 1927, first at Hinaidi with 1 Squadron [Snipe] and then 47 Squadron, which had a mixture of DH.9A and Fairey FIIIF, at Helwan.

However, perhaps one of his most interesting posts was at Upper Heyford in Oxfordshire where he commanded the Long Range Development Unit. For an insight into its history, I recommend accessing the History Net website where Derek O'Connor has written a most informative article.

During the early days of the Second World War he commanded two key airfields in No 2 Group, Wattisham and Wyton before being serving for six months in 1941 at Litchfield in the dual posts of station commander and officer in charge of 27 OTU. Then, in quick succession, he commanded 152 Wing at Predannack in Cornwall before heading to the Middle East to take over 231 Wing which he oversaw until 1943, at which time he became Air Officer Commanding 205 Group. I suspect his general health now began to show signs of failing for in the same year he returned home to assume control of 33 Base at Waterbeach. Less than a year later he retired from the Royal Air Force [LG 24 November 1944, supplement 36814, page 5443]. Sadly, his well deserved retirement from serving his country lasted for only a year and on the 10th of August 1945, he died. Air Commodore Oswald Robert Gayford CBE DSC DFC*AFC mentioned in a despatch is buried in Suffolk at Naughton [St. Mary] Churchyard; he is the sole service burial here and many years later when his widow passed away, his headstone was inscribed with the words: *"Also His Wife Irene Helen 26 December 1977 Age 80."*

* Following disbandment at Shotwick on the 22nd of January 1920, 55 Squadron was reborn out of 142 Squadron at Suez on the 1st of February 1920, equipping with DH.9A. On the 12th of July the squadron moved into Maltepe as part of Q Force before settling on 30th September 1920, in Iraq which would be its spiritual home for close on two decades.

Tuesday 4 February 1919
144 Squadron which had been at Ford since leaving Mikra Bay in December last, disbanded. Just qualifying as an RFC squadron having formed at Port Said on 20th March 1918, it flew corps reconnaissance support sorties in the Palestine and Egyptian theatres and prior to operations in the Dardanelles supported Field Marshal Edmund Allenby's successful pursuit of two Turkish armies falling back from through Palestine and the Jordan Valley into Syria.

Also disbanding this day was 14 Squadron which arrived at Tangmere from Salonika on New Year's Day. Similar to 144 Squadron, '14' had operated in support of the army. However, whereas 14 Squadron would reform in 1920 and remain active in the Middle East during the interwar years, 144 Squadron's number-plate would lie dormant until the expansionist period of the late 1930s.

As far as I can determine there were no squadron air accidents on this day, though from Thuilles came reports that DH.9s B7679 and B9348 belonging to 211 Squadron were no longer fit for service in the field. The former was written off with 230 flying hours recorded, the latter with a total of 235 hours.

Wednesday 5 February 1919

53 Squadron	2Lt J H Weatherill	Safe	Unemployed list 10 October 1919
RE.8 C2908	2Lt T R Young	Safe	

T/o Laneffe for a reconnaissance sorties but failed to clear a line of trees and crash-landed; presumed wrecked. For the time being 2nd Lieutenant Weatherill's service is confined to the remarks above; that for Thomas Reginald Young is more rewarding. Born on the 19th of February 1900, Thomas nominated his father, Henry Young, as his next of kin showing his address as 128 Weston Park, Crouch End, N.8. His granting of Temporary 2nd Lieutenant from Flight Cadet on successful completion of his observer training was *Gazetted* on 6th September 1918, issue 30887, page 10554, his seniority dated 31st August 1918.

He was posted to 53 Squadron at Abeele on 19th September, and following the armistice took leave from the 8th to the 22nd of December. A month after the accident, he was posted to 7 Squadron [RE.8] at Spich in the Rhineland, and apart from four days of temporary duty with an unidentified artillery unit at the end of May, remained on the squadron's establishment until returning home from Heumar on the 9th of August.

During the Second World War he received a commission as a Pilot Officer in the Training Branch, effective 28th March 1941 [LG 11 July 1941, issue 35217, page 4006], and served as such until resigning his commission, still ranked Pilot Officer on the 18th of June 1947 [LG 8 July 1947, supplement 38009, page 3127].

205 Squadron	Lt S J Furze	Safe
DH.9A E8438		

T/o La Louveterie probably with the intention of delivering the aircraft to a storage unit but owing to engine failure forced-landed near Tournai. Although salvaged, I doubt if it ever took to the skies again. It had been with the squadron since October 13th last.

Stanley Jack Furze, born 3rd September 1897, joined the RFC on 19th August 1917, and on arriving in France was attached to 1 Aeroplane Supply Depot from 26th May until 4th June, when he reported to 205 Squadron at Bois de Roche. Between the 19th and 21st of June he was on temporary duty at 30th Division; on return he continued to serve until the squadron returned to Hucknall on 18th March.

Apart from his mishap in E8438 he was involved in a crash 24-hours before the cease fire came into effect on 11th November [see page 400 of my second volume].

216 Squadron	2Lt J H V Wood	Safe	Unemployed list 14 May 1919
HP O/400 D8345	Lt I B Boyce	Safe	

T/o 1225 Liège carrying mail to La Lacque southeast of St. Omer. Ran into bad weather and by around 1330 the crew were being forced lower and lower in close to blinding snow. Eventually, the bomber was down to two hundred and flying over a landscape pitted with shell holes and it was when almost within sight of their destination that they crash-landed and turned over.

Neither officer was seriously hurt. A photograph of the wrecked aircraft, along with the flying log book of James Wood, is preserved in the BDAC library at Old Sarum.

Lieutenant Boyce was formerly of the 2nd/3rd Battalion, London Regiment, joining the squadron on the 1st of October 1918. Following the crash he appears to have spent most of his time on leave, the final entry on his Record of Service being *"S O S of B E F whilst on leave in England 14.5.19-21.5.19."*

Thursday 6 February 1919
Flight in their issue for 6th February, under the heading Items, carried three requests from parents seeking information regarding their loved ones whom they had been officially notified as *"missing."* Two feature in my first volume on pages 89 and 162 respectively. The mother of Lieutenant Cecil John Mason of 54 Squadron who was shot down on the 21st of April 1918, wishes for persons who may have witnessed her son's final flight to write to her at Wimbledon Common [Cecil's Army Form B.103c shows his mother living at 54 High Street, Wimbledon], while Mrs Havilland-Roe residing at 6 Annesley Grove, Addison Street, Nottingham, was anxious for news of her son, Lieutenant H A

Havilland-Roe who failed to return from a raid on Zeebrugge on the night of 18th-19th May 1918, while serving with 214 Squadron.

From my second volume, page 400, the fatal wounding on 10th November 1918, of John Edwin Pugh, 210 Squadron, information was being sought by John V Pugh of Allesley, Coventry.

29 Squadron	Lt E G Davies DFC*	+	Cologne Southern Cemetery
SE.5a H7162/E	*Croix de Guerre* Belgium		

T/o Bickendorf for an air test and it was while performing a high-speed roll as he crossed the aerodrome that the wings folded and the SE hit the ground and burst into flames. According to Army Form B.103, Edgar George Davies reported to the squadron on the 1st of September 1918, and as is evident from his biography on The Aerodrome website he set about pursuing the enemy at every opportunity. Between the 16th September and 10th November he accounted for nine aircraft and a kite balloon. His first victim, a Fokker DVII was sent down east of Lille and his last, another Fokker DVII, was destroyed in the Moorleghen region.

The citation for his DFC was published in the Edinburgh edition of the *Gazette* issue 13400, page 795, of 11th February 1919: *'Bold in attack and skilful in manoeuvre, this officer never hesitates to attack the enemy when opportunity occurs, without regard to disparity in numbers. On 7th October, with three other machines, he attacked seven Fokkers, four of these were destroyed, 2nd Lt. Davies accounting for one. Since 16th September, he has to his credit four enemy machines and one kite balloon.'*

A biography of this dashing young 20 year old pilot appears in Norman Franks *Fallen Eagles* along with a photograph of the SE in which he met his maker standing on a snow covered airfield - probably Bickendorf. The First Bar, without a citation, and the Belgian honour, were published on 5th June and 22 July 1919 respectively, issues 13458, page 2047 and 13476, page 2457.

He was buried on the 8th with full military honours, the Reverend C D R B Bankes of 70 Squadron leading the service.

100 Squadron	Lt L S Hewett	+	Cologne Southern Cemetery
Gotha 99 No 527	2Lt B Carlton-Smith	+	Cologne Southern Cemetery

T/o Ligescourt presumably to test the flying characteristics and performance of this enemy bomber. Leonard Stanley Hewett was born on the 20th of July 1897, enlisting in the RFC on 14th August 1917. He joined the squadron on the 7th of May 1918, and was wounded in action on the 11th of July. Unfortunately, his Record of Service form has been cut off at this point, thus his return to duty and other information is missing. However, the record for Beavan Carlton-Smith is complete; born 27th October 1899, he arrived on the squadron on the 27th of September 1918.

It is a certainty that both were buried in joint funerals, these being conducted on the 8th by the Reverend T G Sharpe attached to 44 CCS. The headstones carry the inscriptions: *"Greater Love Hath No Man'* and *'in Proud & Loving Memory "Brampton Shropshire".'* respectively.

103 Squadron	Sgt C R Haigh	Safe	See 26 February 1919
DH.9 C2204			

T/o Maisoncelle and probably scrapped after a forced-landing brought about by engine trouble, the DH descending into a ploughed field.

208 Squadron	Captain D M Faure	Safe	Unemployed list 6 September 1919
7F.1 Snipe E8177			

T/o Stree for a practice flight which ended with the Snipe losing its undercarriage on landing. It was brought to the squadron on 19th November 1918, by Captain John Sutherland McDonald.

Formerly of the Royal Army Service Corps [Captain Faure's commission as a temporary Second Lieutenant effective 25th February 1915] was *Gazetted* on 19th March 1915, issue 29106, page 2740]. Less than a year later he transferred to the RFC and was attached to 2 Squadron [BE.2] at Hesdigneul on the 24th of January. It would seem his observer training was carried out in house for the next entry on his Record of Service reads *"Graded Qualified Observer 14/3/16."*

Preferring, it appears, to be a pilot, he returned to England on the 14th of July, and on his return to the Western Front was posted to 32 Squadron[DH.2] at Lealvilliers on 8th December 1916. His service with '32' was short-lived for on the 5th of January*he was wounded and following treatment in 3 CCS went back to England aboard HMHS *Brighton.*

At this point he service history ceases, thus the date of his attachment to 208 Squadron is, for the present, not known. However, his date of birth is shown as 8th October 1895, and he requested his uncle, C A Freeman, to be his next of kin.

Picking up on the service of Captain McDonald, he was born on the 8th of April 1895, and joined the RNAS on the 25th of October 1917. With the merging of the two air arms in April 1918, he automatically became a Royal Air Force officer, 8 Squadron RNAS becoming 208 Squadron, with which he served until returning to the UK on 30th January.

Prior to joining the RNAS, John McDonald has been commissioned from his Officer Cadet Unit to Second Lieutenant on 30th May 1917, to the Scottish Rifles [LG 12 June 1917, supplement 30127, page 5825].

* Through the magnificent generosity of Andrew Pentland who has permitted me to use his records collected during numerous visits to TNA Kew, I have been able to ascertain that Lieutenant Faure was flying DH.2 7890 and during a line patrol he was obliged to forced-land, running into a tree near Auchonvillers in the Somme and just to the SW of Beaumont-Hamel.

Friday 7 February 1919

During the day three squadrons left France for bases in the UK and to await disbandment. 41 Squadron, having disposed of their SE.5as to storage, arrived at Tangmere from Halluin; 204 Squadron arrived at Waddington from Heule ['204' was the only squadron to operate from this airfield]. Like 41 Squadron their aircraft [Camels] had been ferried to holding units, while at Hucknall a welcome was extended to Major C H Hayward and 218 Squadron, their DH.9s, too, being left in dispersal units.

| 205 Squadron | Captain P J Barnett | Safe |
| DH.9A E9721 | | |

T/o La Louveterie and written off here in a landing accident. I have not been able to trace his Record of Service.

| 205 Squadron | Captain A R McAfee | Safe | Unemployed list 4 April 1919 |
| DH.9A F1074 | | | |

T/o La Louveterie and crashed almost immediately. It is believed Alan Rodman McAfee had been tasked for mail delivery/collection duties. Born on the 8th of July 1898, Alan McAfee first saw active service with the RNAS [1st April 1917, precisely one year before the merger], attached to 9 Squadron RNAS [Camel], subsequently 209 Squadron, and thence to 205 Squadron on the 8th of May 1918. On the 3rd of April he returned to England and 24-hours later joined the ranks of the unemployed.

With 9 Squadron RNAS he was involved in two accidents, the second resulting in the loss of Camel B3857 in which he ditched with a failing engine near No 3 Buoy [wherever that may be]. His DH flying brought him one combat victory when in the late afternoon of 11th of October, accompanied in F1043 by Sergeant W Jones, an all over green coloured Fokker DVII went down in flames near Grougis [Aisne] a hamlet to the SSE of Bohain-en-Vermandois.

Saturday 8 February 1919

From Baizieux on the Somme, WSW of Albert, their Camels now in storage, 46 Squadron arrived at Rendcombe in Gloucestershire while 73 Squadron went to Yatesbury in Wiltshire.

| 12 Squadron | Lt W Massey | Safe |
| RE.8 D4913 | LAC Harris | Safe |

T/o Duren for a practice flight and when flying some five km distant from the airfield a spin developed and the RE finished up on a road leading to Köln. William Massey arrived in France in the final weeks of the war and while attached to 2 Aeroplane Supply Depot, awaiting posting, was admitted to 51 General Hospital.

Discharged to duty on 21st December, he came under the authority of 9th Brigade and on 18th January he reported to 15 Squadron [RE.8] at Vignacourt. Hardly had he settled in, he was ordered on the 26th to go to Genech for duties with 2 Squadron [FK.8]. Within days of his arrival, William must have thought he was the proverbial pass the parcel for on the 31st he came under the umbrella of 2nd Brigade and on 3rd February he was posted to 12 Squadron.

As if this was not enough, by close of play on the 8th he was handed a posting order to report to 103 Squadron [DH.9] at Mainsoncelle, but this was almost certainly cancelled for under 12 Squadron authority he went off on leave on the 10th, returning on the 24th.

This was not the end of his travels for in quick succession on 15th and 18th March two more squadrons are recorded on Army Form B.103-II - 99 Squadron [DH.9A at Aulnoye] and 110 Squadron [DH.9A at Tardinghem]. At this point the form was filled with entries, so what happened to Lieutenant Massey after the 18th, I am not able to say.

His date of birth is shown as 22nd December 1896, and his enlistment as 27th May 1918. But there is an interesting twist to this summary, for a second Army Form B.103 has been raised in respect of William Massey and this form pre-dates the information reported above, though it confirms his temporary commission as a 2nd Lieutenant on the 27th of May, his previous service being a gunner serving in the Middle East. Although I cannot be certain, I consider it likely that he received his basic flying instruction in Egypt for it was not until the 4th of July that he boarded the SS *Kaiser-i-Hind* at Alexandria bound for the UK.

Had William Massey being given a second Christian name it is probable that I would have been able to discover his discharge through *The London Gazette* but on entering W Massey this produces 6,184 notices and William Massey marginally less at 6,080. A search, I fear, too far.

| 18 Squadron | Lt D F Brooks | Safe |
| DH.9A E8577/D | LAC F Beaumont | Safe |

T/o 6 Air Issues and set out for Bickendorf where on arrival the DH struck the lip of a sunken road and crash-landed, heavily, onto ground frozen solid by frost. Damaged beyond repair. Douglas Frederick Brooks, born 16th January 1898, flew with 99 Squadron [DH.9] between 6th August and 15th December 1918, and features in my second volume on page 179 and 180 when he wrote off C6092 in a forced-landing. He also wrecked D1019 on 14th August, omitted from the second volume, but included in this book in the Additions and Amendments appendix.

On 15th December he was posted to 18 Squadron and remained on establishment until returning to England on the 9th of April.

| 18 Squadron | Lt W B Henderson | Safe |
| DH.9A E9735/H | Corporal C Bradley | Safe |

T/o 6 Air Issues and on landing at Bickendorf ran into a deep depression and was damaged beyond repair. Lieutenant Henderson joined the squadron on 18th August 1918, and was on the nominal roll until 12th March, when he was posted to Letques [sic]. Here he contracted scabies and on 26th March he was hospitalised to England aboard HMHS *St. Andrew*. There are no further entries for this officer.

18 Squadron	Lt L A C Hudson	Safe
DH.9A E9742	Canada	
	Corporal A Henson	Safe

T/o 6 Air Issues and on arrival at Bickendorf overshot and swerving to avoid a collision with a line of hangars over-stressed the undercarriage, which collapsed. Lionel Augustus Croucher Hudson served with the squadron from 29th July 1918 to the 1st of August 1919, when he returned to the UK from Merheim.

| 70 Squadron | 2Lt J W Abray | Safe | Unemployed list 6 March 1920 |
| F.1 Camel F3999 | | | |

T/o Bickendorf authorised for flying practice, a detail that ended in the all too familiar engine failure followed by a crash-landing. Recovered the same day from near Esch [sic], it was conveyed by road to 8 Salvage Section with a view to repair, but there are no further entries, so it is likely it was broken down for scrap. Presently, his service records have eluded all searches.

Sunday 9 February 1919
Leaving their Sopwith Dolphins in storage, 87 Squadron left Boussieres for Ternhill in Shropshire.

| 25 Squadron | DH.9A F1045 | Wrecked while parked at Maubeuge when an unidentified French aeroplane landed |

and collided with the DH.

| 43 Squadron | 2Lt J S Swales | Safe |
| 7F.1 Snipe E8013 | | |

T/o Bickendorf for a practice flight and on return, and while taxying towards the hangars, ran into the 206 Squadron DH summarised on the next page. Most likely born in Keighley, Yorkshire, on 27th December 1895, 2nd Lieutenant Swales reported to 43 Squadron at Lièttres on 29th June 1918, and apart from leave and attachments for temporary duties, remained with the squadron until returning home on on the 14th of March.

206 Squadron	Captain T Roberts DFC	Safe
DH.9 D5782	*Croix de Guerre*	
	Sgt Pugh	Safe

T/o Bickendorf for an air test and on return the crew failed to realise they were on a collision course with the Snipe featured in the last summary. Sent to 9 Salvage Section, I suspect D5782 was reduced to produce.

Captain Thomas Roberts was on establishment from the 5th of April 1918, until he was posted to 18 Squadron on 11th July 1919. He features in reports for two of the squadron's aircraft; flying D1663 on the 3rd of May 1918, with Sergeant James Chapman DFM*they made it home to Alquines with their aircraft seriously damaged by anti-aircraft fire. Taken to a repair park it was rebuilt as F5843.

On 23rd June, accompanied this time by 2nd R W Brigstock, he forced-landed with engine failure, the resultant damage being beyond economical repair. This crash is summarised on page 263 of my first volume. Four days later, 2nd Lieutenant Brigstock was admitted to hospital suffering from concussion, but whether this was a consequence of the accident is not clear. On July 5th, he was discharged and sent on three weeks sick leave. On his return, he was attached to 1 Aeroplane Supply Deport at which point indication of continued service ends.

With the commonality of his Christian name and surname, I have yet to trace his honours.

* *Gazetted* 21st September 1918, supplement 30913, page 11257: *'During a recent raid four of our machines were attacked by twelve enemy aeroplanes. The pilot of this observer's machine was badly wounded, and lost consciousness. The machine fell out of control, but Pte Chapman took control from his seat and flew the machine back to our aerodrome, and landed without breaking a wire, exhibiting skill and presence of mind worthy of the highest praise.'*

On 30th May 1919, he received a First Bar, supplement 31378 of 3rd of June 1919, page 7035. No citation appended. Of interest is the observation that the recipient's city/town is attached, and in the case of Sergeant Chapman this is shown as Newcastle-upon-Tyne.

His name appears once more, this time in supplement 31457, page 8988, of 15 July 1919, when the King of the Belgians conferred on him [and many others] the *Croix de Guerre*.

Monday 10 February 1919
74 Squadron arrived at Lopcombe Corner from Halluin and is believed to have brought their SE.5as with them. This airfield is located NE of Salisbury on the Wiltshire-Hampshire border. The airfield was first known as Hollom Down and unofficially as Jack's Bush while lies a little further along the A343 heading in the direction of Andover. The station opened in September 1917, its principle role, as overseen by 3 Training Depot Station was bringing pilots up to proficiency on the Sopwith Camel, a task that for many proved beyond their capabilities and crashes, often fatal, were common place. Lopcombe Corner closed in November 1919.

23 Squadron   2Lt C F Yokum   +   Charleroi Communal Cemetery
5F.1 Dolphin F7048   Canada
T/o Clermont for a practice sortie and on return, and while turning off the downwind leg, stalled and spun to the ground where on impact his aircraft burst into flames. From Pasqua in Saskatchewan, Chester Frank Yokum was just 19; his epitaph simply reads: *"For His Country."*
   His squadron details are incorrectly reported in the cemetery register as '59 Squadron'.

57 Squadron   2Lt F K Damant   Safe
DH.4 A7774   2Lt W A Ford   Safe
T/o Morville with a consignment of mail and set forth for Verviers. The delivery completed, the crew prepared to return to base but within seconds of becoming airborne the engine cut and having extracted themselves from amongst the branches of a tree into which they fell, walked back to the airfield.
   On 8th December 1918, A7774 had been slightly damaged when it was hit by DH.4 F6104 piloted by 2nd Lieutenant A V Dearden, his aircraft being damaged beyond repair.

Tuesday 11 February 1919
5 Squadron   2Lt F B Peacock   Safe   Unemployed list 21 March 1919
RE.8 H7025   2Lt M de Verteuil   Safe   Unemployed list 11 June 1919
                Trinidad
T/o Hangelar to fly a compass course and on return to base crashed and damaged beyond repair. 2nd Lieutenant Peacock had forced-landed near Namur on the 26th of November 1918. He joined the squadron five months previously on 26th September, and apart from three days between the 16th and 19th of November when he was treated for an undisclosed condition in 4 Canadian Hospital, his service was relatively uneventful; he returned to England on the 3rd of March.
   Marc de Verteuil, whose address is reported as 165 Charlotte Street, Port of Spain, Trinidad, was born on the 10th of March 1894, enlisting with the RFC on 30th January 1918. His first operational posting was to 10 Squadron on the 2nd of September, transferring to 5 Squadron on 26th January. He is believed to have returned to the United Kingdom on or around the 6th of May.

43 Squadron   Lt E B Brodie   +   Cologne Southern Cemetery
7F.1 Snipe E8169
T/o Bickendorf and totally destroyed following a midair collision with a Camel belonging to 70 Squadron. Eric Brownlee Brodie was born on the 23rd of September 1898, enlisting with the RFC on 24th July 1917. By the 6th of December he was a qualified scout pilot, reporting to Warloy Baillon to fly Camels with 3 Squadron.
   His operational tour, however, never got underway and parts of his service records make for disturbing reading. It would appear that on the 28th of December, possibly while handling a firearm, an explosion occurred which resulted in injuries to his arms and face. Taken to 56 CCS he was soon transferred to 3 General Hospital where he remained until the 23rd of March 1918.
   An official enquiry into the circumstances concluded that his injuries were *"Negligently Self Inflicted"* and acting on these finding the General Officer Commanding 3rd Army [General Sir Julian Byng] ordered his records be endorsed *"Censured"*.
   On his release he was attached to 2 Aeroplane Supply Depot to await posting, but 48 hours after his discharge he was taken to 24 General Hospital with a gunshot wound to his left hand.
   These entries filled one side of Army Form B.103c and, unfortunately, the reverse of the form has not been copied. His services were retained and eventually he reached 43 Squadron and, as reported, lost his life in a midair collision.
   The address of his next of kin is recorded as Aigburth Hall, Aigburth, Liverpool, and this matches the entry in the cemetery register, thus confirming Eric Brownlee Brodie late of 3 Squadron and Eric Brownlee Brodie of 43 Squadron are one and the same person.

57 Squadron   2Lt J H Lorimer   Safe
DH.4 A7926   2Lt G B Allen   Safe   Unemployed list 20 October 1919
T/o Morville for an engine test. On return 2nd Lieutenant Lorimer misjudged his approach and crashed-landed; as yet, his record of service is unknown. What is known is that on 7th January, after collecting A7926 from 2 Air Issues, he forced-landed near Tubize [Walloon Brabant], Belgium, completing his transit to Morville two days later.
   Similarly, 2nd Lieutenant Allen's service is an unknown factor.

70 Squadron   2Lt H C Hammond   +   Cologne Southern Cemetery
F.1 Camel E7228
T/o Bickendorf and destroyed following a midair collision with the 43 Squadron Snipe reported above. Harry Charles Hammond, born 30th May 1899, joined the squadron on the last day of September 1918, and had one confirmed combat victory to his name when during an offensive patrol in the late morning of 28th October, and flying in E7161 he despatched a Fokker DVII over the Bois de Breuze in Belgium.
   His funeral, and that for Eric Brodie, was held on the 13th, the squadron's padre, the Reverend C D R B Bankes officiating. This was his third military funeral since 24th January. Harry Hammond's headstone carries the words: *"Lord All Pitying Jesus Grant Him Thine Eternal Rest."*
   For the fate of E7161 on 8th November, please refer to my second volume and page 390.

110 Squadron   Lt T G Griffiths   Safe
DH.9A E9711/A 2Lt W W Pritchard   Safe   Unemployed list 8 March 1919
T/o Tardinghem carrying mail. Crashed at Valenciennes. I have had no success in tracing the service of Lieutenant Griffiths, but that for his observer shows he joined the squadron on the 8th of September 1918, was hospitalised, first at 8 Canadian Stationary Hospital and then in 39 General Hospital between 26th September and 9th December. He returned home five days before his discharge from the air force.

208 Squadron   Lt E Jackson   Safe   See 12 April 1919
7F.1 Snipe E8108
T/o Stree for a practice sortie. On return and landing a swing developed and before Edwin Jackson could bring his fighter under control it crashed, and was damaged beyond repair. Collected from 2 Air Issues by Captain J B White on the last day of October 1918, its service had been free from incident until now. Edwin's service history is reported in my summary for his accident on the 12th of April.

   Captain James Butler White, born 9th of July 1893, was a Canadian from Toronto, commencing his service with the RNAS on 7th February 1917. It is safe to assume he flew with 8 Squadron RNAS before the April 1st merger, after which he served with '208' until returning to the UK on the 3rd of April.

   On the 3rd of December 1918, he was *Gazetted* with the DFC, supplement 31046, page 14327: *'A fine fighting pilot who has accounted for eight enemy aeroplanes. He had led numerous offensive and low bombing raids, and by his able and daring leadership has achieved great success with a minimum of casualties to his patrol.'*

   The Aerodrome website records his total tally as twelve, made up by the destruction of nine scouts and three reconnaissance machines. His first two victories were with 8 Squadron RNAS, destroying an Albatros D.V on 24th January followed on 3rd February by a second Albatros driven down out of control. On both occasions he was at the controls of Camel B6321. His final victim, claimed during a late afternoon patrol on the 3rd of October, was a Fokker DVII which went down near Premont to the guns of Camel E7165.

   Reverting to his substantive rank of Lieutenant he was placed on the unemployed list on 7th July 1919. As a civilian he turned to stockbroking and in 1924 founded J B White & Company in his home city of Toronto. Post-Second World War he was appointed President of the Toronto Stock Exchange. James White DFC died on the 2nd of January 1972.

Wednesday 12 February 1919
With their FK.8s left in France, 2 Squadron returned to Bicester; 16 Squadron less their RE.8s arrived at Fowlmere from Auchy; 24 Squadron, having given up their SE.5as and reduced to a cadre, arrived at London Colney; at Yatesbury 65 Squadron flew in with their Camels.

80 Squadron   2Lt H R Messinger   Injured
F.1 Camel H773   USA
T/o Stree and while banking stalled and crashed. Issued to the squadron on 1st October it was soon in action and on the 3rd, Captain Maurice Michael Freehill landed from a patrol to report an indecisive engagement with a Fokker DVII NE of Brancourt [possibly Brancourt-le-Grand [Aisne]]. When last sighted the Fokker was in a vertical bank and appearing to be out of control. Harry Read Messinger joined 80 Squadron on 12th September, his service record showing his address as Everett, Massachusetts. His injuries were first treated in 14 General Hospital, followed by further care in the UK to where he was taken on the 20th.

   Maurice Michael Freehill had joined the RFC [8th March 1917] within a couple of months of celebrating his 17th birthday [he was born on 21st January 1918] and five days after his 18th, he joined 46 Squadron at Filescamp. On 8th February he attended a course at the aerial ranges followed on the 7th of March by a six day detachment to 59 Squadron [RE.8] at Lealvilliers. His natural leadership ability led to promotion to Acting Captain on 30th September and a posting to 80 Squadron for Flight Commander duties. Thus, it is no little surprise that an award of the DFC was imminent, the citation appearing in the *Gazette* on 8 February 1919, issue 31170, page 2039: *'A brilliant leader who has destroyed five enemy aircraft and has displayed conspicuous bravery in attacking enemy troops on the ground. On 4th November, observing that a machine-gun post was holding up the advance of our infantry, he attacked it from a very low altitude, inflicting heavy casualties on the crew and putting them to flight. Later on he carried out a reconnaissance of the Army front at a height of 50 feet in the face of intense machine-gun fire, bringing back most valuable information.'*

84 Squadron   Lt R Johnson   Safe
SE.5a F5657
T/o Thuilles and wrecked here when landing from a practice sortie. While running across the landing area the main wheels dropped into some deep ruts causing them to be ripped off.

208 Squadron   Lt G Swannell   Safe
7F.1 Snipe E8140
T/o Stree for practice flying and believed damaged beyond repair when on return the engine seized just as Lieutenant Swannell was about to touch down. An incomplete service form shows he joined the squadron on the 6th of June 1918. Like so many young fighter pilots, he found the Camel [which the squadron was equipped with at the time] rather a handful and taking off from Serny for a training exercise on 16th June he lost control and crashed. Fortunately, although the damage was extensive a rebuild programme was initiated and C8266 eventually became F5957. Stored for a while at 2 Air Issues it was issued to 43 Squadron on 24th August and when '43' began to equip with Snipes it returned to 208

Squadron on the 18th of September, before being given up to 2 Air Issues on 30th October, after which reports of its movements cease.

216 Squadron Lt P S Primrose	Safe
HP O/400 C9685 Lt Clarke	Injured
General Hogg	Injured
Lt Weston	Safe
Mechanic Batman	Safe

T/o Marquise with passengers and packets of mail destined for the Allied occupation forces in the Rhineland. Crashed, and wrecked, near Geven-Pulheim [Nordrhein-Westfalen], roughly midway between Grevenbroich and the centre of Köln. Lieutenant Primrose first arrived in France on 26th August 1918, but went back to the UK on October 31st.

Returning to France on 28th November, he was posted to 115 Squadron at Saint Inglevert but on December 5th, he went to Quinlen where he was attached to 216 Squadron. Entries of his service record cease on 26th February when he was taken into hospital, possibly ass a result of the accident summarised here.

Although lacking initials, I am confident that his high ranking passenger was Brigadier-General Rudolph Edward Trower Hogg CMG CIE whose service began with a gentleman cadetship at the Royal Military Academy, Woolwich. Graduating in 1896, he was commissioned to the Royal Artillery.

Transferring to the RFC he commanded 23 Squadron FE.2b] from January to April 1916, and by the end of the *Great War* he had risen to Brigadier-General rank and holding the position of Acting Brigade Commander. It would not surprise me to discover his injuries were serious enough to cause his retirement soon after, for I would have fully expected him to have been offered a permanent commission. There are no indications that he returned to any form of service in the Second World War. His death was announced on the 29th of June 1955.

Thursday 13 February 1919
4 Squadron returned to Northolt from Linselles and although reduced to a cadre may well have brought some of their RE.8s with them as records show the type was not finally disposed of to September. A move to Uxbridge is also mentioned, while be the end of April 1920, the squadron was occupying South Farnborough and receiving Bristol F.2b two-seater fighters.

Sopwith Snipe E8088 of 4 Squadron Australian Flying Corps came to grief after a hard landing at Bickendorf on 7th January 1919. Fortunately Lt. N. C. Johnson was unharmed. The accident was due, at least in part, to poor weather (Crown Copyright.)

Also on this day 40 Squadron [SE.5a] left Orcq for Tangmere, while Mesopotamia personnel of 72 Squadron bade farewell to Baghdad and set out on the long journey home, their aircraft safely in the hands of storage depots. From Froidmont 209 Squadron, having despatched the last of their Camels to store in January, arrived at Scopwick.

4 Squadron AusFC Lt Bishop   Safe
7F.1 Snipe E8058
T/o Bickendorf for a training flight but swung badly and crashed out of control.

99 Squadron   Lt E H Buxton   Safe   Unemployed list 30 April 1919
DH.9A F983
Presentation Aircraft: Hyderbad No 1
T/o Aulnoye where, upon landing from a practice sortie, it crashed out of control. Army Form B.103-1 raised for Eric Harold Buxton is lacking in detail regarding his postings but it does show his next of kin address at Much Hadham which in the *Great War* was likely to have been a quintessential Hertfordshire village to the SSW of Bishop's Stortford.

205 Squadron   Lt Y H Sox   Safe
DH.9A F1618
T/o 6 Air Issues intending to deliver the DH to La Louveterie but crash-landed while trying to land at Verviers. Although an unusual surname, I have not found any reference to an officer bearing this name. Was he, perhaps, a French or Belgian pilot attached to 6 Air Issues - I float this possibility on the evidence of his first initial.

   As far as I am to ascertain, this was the last DH to be struck from charge ahead of the squadron returning to Hucknall on the 18th of March.

Friday 14 February 1919
Three more squadrons returned this day to the UK from duties in France. Personnel from 38 Squadron and 83 Squadron until recently operating their FE.2s out of Serny accompanied each other to Hawkinge, while 64 Squadron may well have brought their SE.5as from Froidmont to Narborough.

   Turmoil in Europe continued with fighting breaking out between Polish forces and the Bolsheviks in what is recorded as the *Battle of Bereza Kartuska*. In Georgia, meanwhile, elections were held during which for the fist time women were able to take part.

48 Squadron   Lt G Thornton-Norris   Safe
Bristol F.2b F5995 Captain Campbell   Safe
T/o Bickendorf with the intention to fly to Nivelles in Belgium but *en route* the crew encountered fog and persistent rain and this, eventually, led to a forced-landing at Albaneyck [sic] which resulted in the Bristol being damaged beyond repair. Lieutenant Thornton-Norris joined 48 Squadron at Boisdinghem on the 28th of August 1918. In January he underwent a course of instruction with the 2nd Guards Brigade, while from late March to mid-May he received treatment in several hospitals, subsequently being discharged from 56 General Hospital and posted to 88 Squadron [Bristol F.2b] at Nivelles on 19th May. The reverse of service records has not been copied.

80 Squadron   2Lt A E Watson   Safe
7F.1 Snipe E8190
T/o Stree and came to grief near the aerodrome at Thuilles. Alexander Erskine Watson entered the world on the 27th of August 1899, and following his cadetship in the RFC was appointed as a temporary 2nd Lieutenant on 14th October 1917 [LG 19 November 1917, supplement 30388, page 11933].

   For his next of kin he chose his mother who resided at 133 Union Grove, Aberdeen. Joining 80 Squadron [Camel] at Assévillers on the 9th of September; six days later he forced-landed F6184 with engine trouble near Bapaume. He controlled his arrival fairly well, and although damaged his aircraft was recovered and rebuilt as H6840.

   The final entry on his service record coincides with the departure from Clermont of 80 Squadron to the Middle East on the the 26th of May 1919.

99 Squadron   Lt L B Duggan   Safe   Retirement 29 September 1946
DH.9A F1018   Captain T E H Birley   Safe
T/o Aulnoye with a consignment of mail for Köln. With its destination in sight the DH's engine cut and the ensuing crash-landing damaged it beyond repair. This was Lewin Bronwing Duggan's third serious accident since joining the squadron on the 30th of August 1918, the previous being on 20th December, and 20th January. On the 1st of May he was struck off the strength of the BEF with the departure to India of the squadron.

   Lieutenant Duggan was one of many officers appointed on the 1st of August 1919, to permanent commissions and I believe his service was unbroken until his retirement, as noted above.

   I am reasonably confident that Captain T E H Birley relates to Thomas Eaton Hornby Birley who by the outbreak of the Second World War had been granted a commission in the Administrative and Special Duties Branch and having completed a probationary period as a Pilot Officer was confirmed in his appointment and promoted Flying Officer on 14th August 1939 [LG 31 October 1939, issue 34721, page 7276]. His service continued until 18th May 1954, at which point he relinquished his commission under the provisions of the Navy, Army and Air Force Reserves Act of 1954. He was permitted to retain the rank of Group Captain.

111 Squadron	Captain E G Bannister	+	Ramleh War Cemetery
Bristol F.2b *Not reported*	Captain F Jefcoate	+	Ramleh War Cemetery
	MBE mid South Africa		

T/o Ramleh and stalled, with great force, into the ground near Aboukir. Edward Gentleman Bannister's honour appeared in the New Year's Honours List of 1919 [LG 1 January 1919, supplement 31098, page 97]. His passenger, 37 year old Frank Jefcoate, had been commissioned to the Suffolk Regiments, though his entry in the cemetery register records 111 Squadron. His mention in a despatch was *Gazetted* on 3 June 1919, supplement 31378, page 7029, while the Edinburgh edition published on 16th July 1920, issue 13615, page 1668, amends the date of his appointment to the MBE from 3rd June 1919, to 1st January 1919.

Saturday 15 February 1919

The running down of active squadrons continued with 3 Squadron leaving their Camel scouts behind arrived at Wye in Kent from Inchy; 15 Squadron departed Vignacourt, I believe with their RE.8s, to settle for the remainder of the year at Fowlmere; likewise, 56 Squadron brought their SE.5as from Bethencourt to Narborough; 82 Squadron, less their FK.8s, arrived at Shoreham from Bertangles and 201 Squadron, their Camels deposited to store, reported to Lake Down from Bethencourt. The activities of these squadrons from now on, I suspect, were very much relaxed.

2 Squadron AusFC	Lt J W Coy	Safe
SE.5a E5765		

T/o Hellemmes for mail duties and crashed into a ploughed field near Aire [sic] the all too common result of engine failure. This was the squadron's last flying accident ahead of disbandment. Formed at Kanatara, Egypt as 68[Australian] Squadron on 20th September 1916, it was retitled 2 Squadron Australian Flying Corps on 4th January 1918, by which time it had been active in France as a scout unit since September 1917.

Initially equipped with DH.5, on becoming part of the Australian Flying Corps it re-equipped with SE.5a and was to the fore in all the major engagements on the Western Front.

Its War Diary AWM 4: 8/6/1-8/6/28 notes that following the armistice part of its duties was to evaluate captured enemy aircraft, of which there were plenty.

Returning to Australia aboard RMS *Kaiser-i-Hind* it disbanded with the disembarkation of the last members of the squadron left the ship in Sydney harbour.

3 Squadron AusFC	Lt J B Tait	Safe
RE.8 H7023	Lt H Howard	Safe

T/o Charleroi for an exercise in photography, a task that ended in a forced-landing at Map Reference Sheet 62 BG4 central following engine failure overhead Bellincourt. This was the squadron's last reported accident before packing their stores and heading for Hurdcott Camp near the cathedral city of Salisbury.

With no gainful employment in the offing, squadron personnel entrained to Southampton on the 6th of May and in good cheer boarded RMS *Kaiser-i-Hind* for home, reaching Port Adelaide on the 6th of June.

Note. A precise explanation regarding the formation and re-titling of these two squadrons is difficult to report with accuracy. Reading James J Halley's *The Squadrons of the Royal Air Force & Commonwealth 1918-1988,* this shows formation of 68 Squadron at Harlaxton in Lincolnshire on the 30th of January 1917, for fighter duties but it seems the first of the DH.5s did not arrive until it crossed the Channel to Baizieux on the 21st of September; I can only assume, therefore that the squadron received various types in which to work up to operational efficiency.

Meanwhile, 69 Squadron had formed at South Carlton, Lincolnshire, on the 28th of December 1916, and received a variety of types before leaving for Savy with RE.8s for Corps reconnaissance work.

Rather than add to a confusing situation, I will leave it to my readers, if they so wish, to investigate the histories of these two squadrons which appear to have been recognised on formation in Australia as 2 Squadron and 3 Squadron respectively.

In regard to Hurdcott Camp, this lies to the west of Salisbury and was sited between the villages of Barford St. Martin and Fovant, the latter now famous for the military unit badges carved into the chalk downs bordering the main road leading to Shaftesbury. The camp was officially taken over by Australian Imperial Forces on the 12th of March 1917. A photograph, supported by much fascinating information, can be viewed on the website map-of-Australia.

12 Squadron	Captain C J S Dearlove	Safe
RE.8 E1211	Lt Armitage	Safe

T/o Bickendorf for an air test but before becoming fully airborne a wheel sheared from the axle and though the RE staggered into the air it was, unsurprisingly, damaged beyond repair on its return.

Cuthbert Joseph Stanley Dearlove's association with the squadron goes back to the 24th of February 1917, his first tour with the squadron finishing on the 15th of June when he returned to the UK. However, by late September of that year he was back in France, rejoining the squadron on the 5th of October. The reverse of his service record has not been copied, but in the upper portion, where it is noted he was born on the 9th of February 1898, his promotion to Captain was effective from the 4th of May 1918. His enlisted with the RFC on 21st August 1916, and his next of kin address as 32 Oakfield Street, Cardiff. I have not been able to positively identify Lieutenant Armitage.

59 Squadron   Lt F A Markham   Safe
Bristol F.2b C9877   Mechanic G G Stewart   Safe

T/o possibly from Gerpines for a delivery flight and on landing the undercarriage collapsed and the Bristol turned over. The location is not reported; therefore, its departure may have been from one of the air issues depots still functioning.

     Lieutenant Markham*joined 8 Squadron [FK.8] at Bellevue on 2nd September 1918, and was posted in to 59 Squadron on 28th January. Attached to the Army of Occupation in the Rhineland, it was one of only a handful of squadrons to be disbanded in situ, in '59's' case at Duren on the 4th of August 1919. By this time the majority of its personnel had been returned to England, Lieutenant Markham departing for home on the 29th of July.

* He was formerly of the Royal Lancashire Regiment, Special Reserve of Officers, and promoted Lieutenant on the 1st of July 1917 [LG 4 March 1918, supplement 30553, page 2704]. On the 16th of September 1919, he relinquished his commission in the Royal Air Force on return to army duties with the Royal Lancashire Regiment. Under the new system of air force ranks he is reported as Pilot Officer [Honorary Flying Officer] [LG 27 January 1920, issue 31755, page 1100]. Then, with effect from the 1st of April 1920, he relinquished his commission with the regiment, retaining the rank of Lieutenant [LG 21 July 1920, supplement 31988, page 7740].

99 Squadron   Lt T C S Tuffield   Safe   See 4 March 1919
DH.9A F978   2Lt W J Tremellen   Safe   See 4 March 1919

T/o Aulnoye tasked to deliver mail to Morville where the crew crashed while attempting to land. Some sources report the crash as occurring 24-hours previously. Thomas Cecil Silwood Tuffield, born 17th February 1893, had been accepted for training as an Observer Officer in the spring of 1917, and returned to England for training on the 29th of May. Prior to this he had served as a Corporal in a Signal Squadron attached to the 1st Indian Cavalry Division and thence had been commissioned to the 16th Battalion, Welsh Regiment [LG 2 February 1917, issue 29928, page 1171]. On the 4th of July he reported to Bellevue where he was attached to 48 Squadron [Bristol F.2b], completing his first tour of operational flying by 25th November, on which date he returned home and re-mustered for pilot training. Successful, he returned to France on 29th December 1918, and joined 99 Squadron.

     For his observer, this was his second accident, the previous being on the 20th of December 1918.

Sunday 16 February 1919
In Greater Poland where fighting had been taking place, news that prolongation between Germany and the Allies of the armistice helped in ending major conflict, though as with all cease fires localised breaches continued. Sadly, racial tension between opposing ethnic groups resulted in well over four hundred Albanians being massacred by Yugoslavian soldiers, adding to the atrocities in Ukraine where 24-hours earlier paramilitary groups entered villages and murdered around 1,500 people of Jewish ancestry.

     95 Squadron returned from Ascq to Lopcombe Corner and 108 Squadron departed Gondecourt for Lympne.

62 Squadron   Lt E R Danks   Injured
Bristol F.2b E2416

T/o Nivelles for a cross-country exercise during which Lieutenant Danks became hopelessly lost in mist and on forced-landing discovered he had crossed the border into Holland and had alighted near the village of Yerseke [Zeeland] on the southern shore of the Oosterscheldt estury. His injuries were not, it is thought, of a serious nature.

     Army Form B.103-I in respect of this office contains only his rank, surname and initials.

Monday 17 February 1919
The exodus of squadrons from the Continent continued apace with no less than seven returning across the Channel. In numerical sequence 10 Squadron arrived at Ford, 19 Squadron at Ternhill, 42 Squadron into Netheravon on Salisbury Plain where they were joined by 52 Squadron which to the best of my knowledge had operated since the armistice without any serious flying accidents, a remarkable achievement. 54 Squadron went to Yatesbury, 148 Squadron to Tangmere and 210 Squadron to Scopwick.

Tuesday 18 February 1919
At Fowlmere in Essex a welcome was extended to 21 Squadron which since January 1916, had performed a variety of duties before settling for Corps reconnaissance and artillery spotting from February 1917. It is worth mentioning that since the armistice the squadron had had a trouble free existence. As with so many famous squadrons of this era, having arrived home it existed merely as paper formations and it was not until 3rd December 1935, that its number plate would be resurrected. Equipped with Hawker Hinds at Bircham Newton it was assigned the role of a light-bomber squadron.

70 Squadron   2Lt S Green   +   Cologne Southern Cemetery
F.1 Camel F2010/S

T/o Bickendorf and found on the east bank of the Rhine southeast of the city centre in the Köln-Deutz area, totally smashed. 2nd Lieutenant Green's first posting had been to 204 Squadron [Camel] at Teteghem on 18th October 1918, followed on 12th December by an attachment to 5th Army School for a course, the nature of which not being reported. On 28th December he returned to '204', now at Heule, and on the 7th of January he was posted to 70 Squadron.

     His funeral, with full military honours, was conducted by the Reverend C D R B Bankes, attached to 70 Squadron.

| 101 Squadron | 2Lt K L Graham | Injured | Unemployed list 13 April 1919 |
| FE.2b D9967 | 2Lt J H Pringle | Injured | Unemployed list 12 July 1919 |

T/o Morville for local flying practice and wrecked after control was lost in a turn, the FE sideslipping to the ground. Record of Service cards have been raised for both officers, but only that for 2nd Lieutenant Pringle has any reports regarding the crash. This states he was admitted to 20 CCS with injuries to his scalp and following initial treatment was evacuated to England on the 22nd aboard the HS *Jan Breydel*. I much suspect a similar report exists somewhere for his pilot.

| 206 Squadron | Lt C Workman | Injured | Unemployed list 16 April 1919 |
| DH.9 E9001 | Mechanic E Rogan | Injured | |

T/o Bickendorf tasked for a mail-run but became lost in fog and crash-landed at an undisclosed location in Holland. Born on 20th September 1898, Colin Workman joined the RFC on the 14th of August 1917, and on completion of his training arrived in France and reported on 21st August to 104 Squadron at Azelot. His time with '104' was minimal; from 30th October to 29th December he was in the UK on temporary duty and on return was detached to Tardingham, this detachment lasting from the 14th to the 24th of January, and on completion of which he was posted to 206 Squadron. Hospitalised, I suspect Lieutenant Workman had made his final flight in the air force.

Wednesday 19 February 1919

48 Squadron	Captain L A Payne MC mid +		Cologne Southern Cemetery
Bristol F.2b F4475	South Africa		
	2Lt R L Ford	Safe	

T/o 1045 Bickendorf for local flying and roughly forty-five minutes later came down in the Rhine opposite Köln-Merheim, the Merheim district of the city being inland from the river and on its east side.

With the fast-flowing current taking command, Lawrence Allan Payne took off his trench coast and indicated to his observer that they should swim to the nearest bank. On entering the water, Lawrence Payne, a strong swimmer, was soon making good progress until suddenly he was no longer in sight. By this time 2nd Lieutenant Ford had become so exhausted that he decided to turn onto his back and allow the current to take him, hopefully to a bank where he could get out of the water.

Fortunately, the drama of the crash had been witnessed by a couple of German boatmen who reached the young observer and pulled him to safety. The entry on his Record of Service reads: *"Injured [acc.]. Shock & exhaustion from immersion in water [not severe]. Machine was flying low over river when it struck a bump & touched the water."* This was his second narrow shave since joining the squadron on the 8th of September last, for on the 14th of that month during an operational patrol he received a gunshot wound to his thigh for which he was treated in a New Zealand Stationary Hospital. Discharged on 4th October, he was sent to 1 Aeroplane Supply Depot from where he was re-posted to 48 Squadron the 10th.

Only a partial record has survived for Captain Payne, but this is illuminating; he was born on the 14th of July 1894, probably in Barberton in the Transvaal and on arriving in England he joined the RFC on 17th February 1917. His association with 48 Squadron goes back to the 12th of September 1917, and appears unbroken apart from leave and a return to the UK for a course of instruction from 8th to 19th February.

In April he was recommended for the MC and this was duly approved, and *Gazetted* on 26 July 1918, supplement 30813, page 8832: *'For conspicuous gallantry and devotion to duty. Volunteering to proceed on a special reconnaissance under adverse weather conditions, he penetrated for a distance of nine miles behind the enemy's lines, flying at an altitude of 200 feet, despite the most intense machine-gun and rifle fire. H returned later, his machine riddled with bullets, with the required information. Previous to this, he had bombed and engaged with machine-gun fire bodies of hostile infantry with the most effective results. He has destroyed one hostile plane and driven down two others out of control. He has at all times displayed great fearlessness and dash.'*

Meanwhile, on June 3rd he became ill and was taken to 24 General Hospital from where he was despatched to England on the 5th aboard HMHS *Princess Elizabeth*.

It is at this point that a record of his movements cease, but it may be safely assumed that on regaining his health he returned to the Western Front and resumed his duties with the squadron.

Following the crash an intensive search for his body was initiated but it was some while before notification was received from Belgian authorities that his remains had been recovered, and identified, from the Rhine north of Düsseldorf. His headstone is inscribed: *"He Gave Up His Life For The Good Of Humanity."* His biography is published between pages 12 and 15 of Norman Franks' *Fallen Eagles*.

Friday 21 February 1919

Two squadrons returned to Drem in East Lothian, the station also being referred to Gullane or Fenton Barnes, a point possibly of little interest to the personnel of 151 Squadron and 152 Squadron whose wartime operations had been concerned with night fighting. Both had ended up at Liettres in the Pas-de-Calais.

With the winter weather continuing to exact its toll on aircraft, 6 Squadron signalled from Gerpines that five of their RE.8s were no longer in an airworthy state; C2929 was reported to have a twisted fuselage and wood parts thoroughly sodden, D4803 was in a similar state, E1148 also, its fuselage warped, H7027 reduced to a rain soaked hulk and H7057 having broken elevators, a damaged rudder and longerons and wing struts swollen out of true after been picketed in the open for the past two months.

Radio communications in the United States witnessed an historic day when from station 1XE at Medford in Massa-chusetts established contact with the SS *George Washington* homebound with the country's President, Woodrow Wilson, fresh from attending the ongoing peace talks in Paris.

Saturday 22 February 1919
Three home-based squadrons disbanded; 235 Squadron [Short 184] at Newlyn, 254 Squadron [DH.6/DH.9] at Prawle Point and 260 Squadron at Westward Ho, also DH.6/DH.9 equipped.

The day also witnessed the demise of seven aircraft in accidents, five of the casualties being from 70 Squadron. Out in the cold waters of the North Sea the surrendered U-boat U-21 under tow foundered.

57 Squadron	Lt A D Stubbs	Safe	Unemployed list 8 October 1919
DH.4 F2635	2Lt L E Morris	Safe	

T/o Morville and believed damaged beyond repair when landing at Spa, its consignment of mail being recovered from the hedge in which the DH finished up.

70 Squadron	Lt F R L Lazier	Safe	Unemployed list 28 September 1919
F.1 Camel D1953			

T/o Bickendorf to deliver his aircraft to Boisdinghem but with insufficient petrol to complete the journey he forced-landed at Gembloux [Namur], some 20 km or so NE of Charleroi. Recovered to 7 Salvage Section, I suspect it was struck off charge. An Army Form B.103 has been raised for Lieutenant Lazier but it has no information whatsoever in regard to postings et al.

During its war service, 2nd Lieutenant Francis Edward Wilford drove down a Fokker DVII over Bois de Breuze, a forest in the Belgian province of Hainault, in the late morning of 28th October 1918. Born on the last day of August 1897, Francis joined the RFC two days before his twentieth birthday. He was attached to the squadron from the 2nd of June 1918 until returning to England on 14th April, 48-hours before he was placed on the unemployed list.

70 Squadron	Lt W J Nicholl	Safe
F.1 Camel F1930		

T/o Bickendorf with similar orders and believed wrecked while forced-landing in the same area as the Camel reported above.

70 Squadron	2Lt C R Peters	Safe
F.1 Camel F1933		

T/o Bickendorf similarly instructed and crashed-landed with a faulty ignition switch near Ans aerodrome. Again, a not unfamiliar occurrence where a Record of Service form has been opened, but without any supporting details.

70 Squadron	Lt G P Alexander	Safe
F.1 Camel F1935		

T/o Bickendorf likewise ordered and after running out of petrol crashed-landed at Lonsee [sic] near Nivelles in the Belgian province of Brabant.

70 Squadron	2Lt S B Atkinson	Safe	Unemployed list 21 June 1919
F.1 Camel H7003			

T/o Bickendorf and subsequently came down in the same vicinity as Lieutenants Lazier and Nicholl. An unconfirmed report suggests H7003 was later taken in hand by the French.

It is thought all five aircraft were being transferred to 203 Squadron, which seems rather odd as '203' would return to the UK before the end of March.

78 Squadron	Lt J B Perring	Injured	Unemployed list 28 December 1919
F.1 Camel C8355			

T/o Sutton's Farm and wrecked after colliding with a wireless aerial, causing the pilot serious injuries.

Sunday 23 February 1919

23 Squadron	2Lt J L Bowie	Safe	Unemployed list 16 August 1919
5F.1 Dolphin E4737			

T/o Clermont intending to ferry the Dolphin to 6 Air Issues but, subsequently, forced-landed at Dottignies [Hainaut], roughly midway between Courtrai to the north and Tournai to the south. At the time the squadron was preparing to dispose of its aircraft before returning to England.

Monday 24 February 1919
A casualty return from 12 Squadron at Bickendorf reported RE.8 E228 was no longer safe to fly; the airframe, already waterlogged, had received further damage after been run into [culprit not identified]. Total flying hours 151.45.

Tuesday 25 February 1919

Personnel from 139 Squadron arrived at Blandford in Dorset from duties in Italy, the squadron having formed at Villaverla on the 3rd of July 1918. Equipped with Bristol F.2b throughout and Sopwith Camels up to October, '139' flew fighter patrols and reconnaissance sorties over the Plave front.

75 Squadron	Lt E G Forder	+	Winterborne Stickland [St. Mary] Churchyard

F.1 Camel H3997

T/o North Weald and crashed on, or close to, Elmswell airfield, eyewitnesses stating the aircraft hit the ground in an inverted spin. Ernest George Forder's entry on the CWGC website is devoid of Christian names, unit and next of kin, but a general search on the web results in his full name recorded on the Canadian Virtual War memorial, while the IWM website has chapter and verse with a digitised copy of F.S.Form 559 Casualty Card with details of the crash and stamped KIILED in red.

This shows, he was born on the 26th of July 1893, in Winterborne Stickland, a Dorset village some three miles SW of Blandford Forum, and had emigrated to Canada where he enlisted as a private soldier on the 18th of September 1914, and by the 13th of February 1915, he was serving with the 5th Battalion, Canadian Expeditionary Force. He transferred to the RFC in May 1917.

Turning to *The London Gazette,* supplement 30170, page 6787, shows he was commissioned on 21st June 1917. It is rare to find an Army Form B.103 for officers killed in the United Kingdom but in the case of Ernest Forder a Record of Service does exist and this confirms his place of birth and date, and indicates he went to the RFC in the March and not May as recorded by IWM.

On the 12th of March 1918, he reported to Grossa in Italy and joined 28 Squadron but on the 11th of May he failed to return from an offensive patrol [for details, please refer to my first volume page 138, though the summary has nowhere near the amount of information now reported above].

An entry on the form dated 16th July reads; *"Officially reported as having been interned at Satzerbad'* This is followed by two more entries; *'Released Prisoner of War & attd. To 28 Sqdn 14.11.18. Repat. PoW to UK 28.11.18."*

Additional to the Camel in which he was shot down, Ernest forced-landed B4615 with engine failure on the 21st of March, the location being reported as near San Giórgio, while on the 25th of April he stood B7351 on its nose. Repaired, B7351 was written off with fatal consequences on the 15th of June, for a report as to what happened, please refer to page 245 of my first volume.

Note. I was able to visit St. Mary's on 19th October 2019, where a most helpful lady explained that although he has no headstone of the pattern used by CWGC, the Commission has it hand to place a notice on the church boundary wall notifying that the churchyard contains service graves. In addition to Lieutenant Forder's stone, Private Harry George Whittingham, originally of the 4th Battalion, Dorsetshire Regiment, but at the time of his death on 28th February 1919, was attached to the 494th Agricultural Company of the Labour Corps. Both graves are in the middle of the NW area of the churchyard.

80 Squadron	Captain M M Freehill	Safe

7F.1 Snipe E8092   DFC

T/o Stree for local flying but crashed into a ploughed field near the airfield after a cylinder burst. On hitting the rough surface the Snipe turned onto its back. The citation to his DFC is recorded in my summary for the loss of F.1 Camel H773 on February 12th, flown at the time by 2nd Lieutenant Messinger. Postwar, Captain Freehill was appointed to a permanent commission [LG 1 August 1919, issue 31486, page 9870] after which his career followed the path of a permanent officers with spells of duty at home and abroad. He attended two specialist courses, the first in the early '20s when he underwent a course of instruction at the Electrical and Wireless School, Flowerdown and then in the mid '30s, following a tour with 41 Squadron flying Bulldog IIAs, he was posted to Farnborough and the School of Photography. On 1st April 1937, he was promoted Squadron Leader and later in the month he reported to Boscombe Down for flying duties with 58 Squadron. At the time the squadron was equipped with obsolete Vickers Virginia bombers, their most modern equipment being a flight of Avro Ansons which were used to train the squadron's observers. However, in the autumn the first of the Whitley twin-engined bombers arrived, the early Mk.Is soon being replaced the Mk.IIs which the squadron took to Linton-on-Ouse in April 1938.

And it was here that Squadron Leader Maurice Michael Freehill fell ill and was admitted to York Military Hospital from where his early death was reported on the 3rd of February 1939. I have little doubt that had he lived he would have risen to air rank.

88 Squadron	Captain K R Simpson	Safe

Bristol F.2b F4309

T/o Nivelles and after landing at Marquise for fuel the Bristol was blown onto its nose while taxying towards the fuel point. Kenneth Roy Simpson, born on the 13th of July 1895, reported to the squadron, then at Capelle, on the 16th of June 1918, and according to his service records, assumed command of the squadron on the 8th of April. This, I suspect, was at the time when Major E N Montagu-Stuart-Wortley was departing and Major C C Darley was about to take his place.

In his analysis of the squadron, John Rawlings reports that 88 Squadron was one of the most aggressive Bristol F.2b squadrons operating on the Western Front. In seven months of operations, '88' claimed 164 hostile aircraft destroyed.

99 Squadron	2Lt D C Bain	Safe	See 23 April 1919
DH.9A E720	2Lt F S Smith	Safe	

T/o Aulnoye tasked for mail delivery. Crashed whilst landing on Gerpinnes airfield. Although I have not been able to find the records for 2nd Lieutenant Bain, those for 2nd Lieutenant Smith show he was posted to the squadron as recently as 17th January, and departed for home on the 9th of April.

Previously he had served with 52 Squadron [RE.8] from 28th July 1918 to the 14th of December. It is believed he was on a course of instruction during the intervening period.

Wednesday 26 February 1919

6 Squadron	Lt H G Lomberg	Safe	Unemployed list 13 November 1919
RE.8 C3016	South Africa		

T/o Gerpinnes with the intention of ferrying the RE to St. Omer for disposal. For reasons not stated Harry Graham Lomberg landed at Laneffe from where a casualty report indicated his aircraft was wrecked.

Born on the 29th of September 1897, probably at Germiston in the Transvaal Lieutenant Lomberg joined 15 Squadron at Vert Galant on 30th August 1918, and at the time of the accident was on the nominal roll of 53 Squadron which was based at Laneffe. I suspect, therefore, that Harry Lomberg had decided to pay his squadron a visit before continuing to St. Omer.

The movements for C3016 show it arrived at Port Rouen aboard the SS *Teviot**on 26th October last and was issued to 6 Squadron from 1 Aeroplane Supply Depot, the date of acceptance going unrecorded. Shortly after the accident Lieutenant Lomberg was returned to the UK on the 6th of March.

In general the 26th was a bad day for the squadron with casualty returns for three more of their aircraft being unfit for further service; C2727, E1157 and H7038 all reported as waterlogged.

* A file for this vessel is held at TNA Kew under MT 23/425/9. A note attached reports the ship was damaged in 1915, when tugs pushed her against the quayside at Le Havre.

18 Squadron	Lt J K S Smith	Safe	
DH.9 E707	2Lt R H Walker	Safe	

T/o Bickendorf for an air test but at the point of becoming airborne the undercarriage caught the wreckage of a German aircraft that was awaiting clearance. The impact threw the DH out of control and the ensuing crash ended its days.

James King Steel Smith of Mosagul Castlehead, Paisley, Scotland, was born on the 27th of March 1899, enlisting in the RFC on 27th April 1917. He joined the squadron on the 18th of May, following treatment for scabies. He returned to England on the 8th of May.

Belfast born [2nd July 1899] Ralph Hamilton Walker was an 18 Squadron officer from 28th August 1918, to 21st July 1919, his service being broken between 19th January and 10th February when he was back in the UK on a course of instruction.

44 Squadron	2Lt A D Simmons	+	Knottingley Cemetery
F.1 Camel F1993			

T/o Hainault Farm and while flying in formation lost control and spun to the ground near Chadwell Heath, roughly three miles WNW from Romford in Essex. Arthur Donald Simmons' entry in the cemetery register indicates he had been attached from 189 Squadron at Sutton's Farm.

103 Squadron	Sgt C R Haigh	Safe	
DH.9 D7371			

T/o Maisoncelle and crashed in the course of a travelling flight to Linselles aerodrome. It will be recalled that Sergeant Haigh had crash-landed earlier in the month on the 6th.

Thursday 27 February 1919

222 Squadron disbanded at Mudros; it had formed at Thasos from A and Z squadrons of the former 2nd Wing of the RNAS, which upon for merger of the two air arms on April 1st, became 62 Wing. Equipped with DH.4 and DH.9, the squadron's remit was to maintain raiding Turkish targets in the Macedonia and Thrace areas. In addition to the DHs, Sopwith Camels were issued to provide fighter escort. The squadron moved from Thasos to Mudros on 22nd May and thence, briefly, to San Stephano on 15th November before returning to Mudros on the 23rd of that month.

As with the majority of squadrons that disbanded in 1919, 222 Squadron would lie dormant until after the outbreak of the Second World War.

An interesting item published in *Flight* on this day reports that Cambridge University received a most generous offer of £20,000 of 5 percent War Stock from Mr Emile Mond of Hyde Park Square *"for the endowment if a Professorship of Aeronautical Engineering as a memorial to his son, Lieut. Francis Mond, who was killed in action whilst flying on the Western Front on May 15, last. The Chair*is to be designated the Francis Mond Professorship of Aeronautical Engineering."* This generous offer was greeted with gratitude and the Air Ministry, too, signalled its approval.

Turning to my first volume, page 145 summaries the death of Captain F L Mond and his Canadian born observer, Lieutenant E M Martyn of 57 Squadron who were shot down during a photographic reconnaissance mission. Francis Leopold, born 20th July 1895, had been educated at Peterhouse, Cambridge. His Record of Service shows he joined the squadron on the 3rd of April 1918, and that he had previously been an officer with the Royal Field Artillery.

From the same issue of *Flight*, obituaries for three officers who had succumbed to the influenza pandemic were published; Captains Herbert Andrew Patey DFC, Robert Bruce Stanley and Lieutenant Joseph Waterhouse.

Herbert, whose birth is shown on his service records as 29th September 1898, died on the 18th February, was formerly of 210 Squadron and in his all too short life had experienced the horrors of Gallipoli where he served with *Howe* Battalion of the Royal Naval Division. He now rests in peace in Hampstead Cemetery. His award of the DFC was published in *The London Gazette* 21 September 1918, supplement 30913, page 11253: *'Whilst leading his flight on an offensive patrol eight enemy machines were encountered. Captain Patey was cut off from his patrol by two of the enemy who got on his tail, and continued in that position until within 2,000 feet of the ground, at which point his machine was hit in the petrol tank. Notwithstanding his serious handicap, he turned four times on his pursuers, destroying one and driving the remainder away. On previous occasions this officer has destroyed two enemy machines and brought down two more out of control, and, in company with other pilots, he has assisted in destroying or bringing down out of control five additional enemy aircraft.'*

Consulting *The Camel File* shows he flew with the squadron when it was known as 10 Squadron RNAS and his name appears in conjunction with the following Camels B5749, B6391, B7195, B7249, B7280, D3391, D3410 and D9622.

* The first incumbent of the Chair was Bennett Melvill Jones [1919-1952], with the present incumbent William Nicholas Dawe appointed in 1996.

Friday 28 February 1919
60 Squadron, their SE.5as transferred to storage, arrived at Narborough from Inchy. To the best of my knowledge '60' had carried out its post-armistice tasks without losing a single aircraft, a quite remarkable achievement should my assumption prove correct.

An unusual occurrence is reported this day regarding the death of 2nd Lieutenant Lloyd Dietz St A Lyon MM who was born in Jamaica on the 1st of May 1898, and who, with his mother left the island as passengers on the SS *Obidense* docking in New York, the year being given as 1913, at which time Lloyd was age fifteen.

On the 22nd of September 1914, he convinced the authorities that he was eighteen, and was accepted in the Canadian Army, eventually arriving in France on the last day of July 1915, by which time he was serving with the 3rd Battalion. His transfer to the RFC seems to have been on, or around, 24th January 1918, though I can find no Record of Service for an officer bearing his surname. Nevertheless, his entry on the Hollybrook Memorial [Southampton] register states he was attached to 54 Squadron. By the end of February, the squadron had been reduced to a cadre and was stationed in Wiltshire at Yatesbury.

In my search for this officer I was rewarded by the website cairogang, which I have pleasure in acknowledging, and from where I gleaned the above details [the website is headed by a photostat of his Medal Card]. However, it is the two extracts from Irish newspapers, namely the *Sunday Independent* and the March 3rd issue of *The Irish Times* that provide a fascinating account into his death. That reported in the former will suffice: *"Canadian Drowned Dublin Bay - Comrades' Attempt at Rescue. Dublin Bay was the scene of a lamentable fatality on Friday evening, when Light-Lieut. J Lyon, MM, Canadian RAF was drowned owing to engine trouble in his machine, which fell into the water, near the Kish Lighthouse, between Kingstown and Howth.*

About 4.15 five aeroplanes were observed crossing the Channel from the direction of Holyhead, and when approaching land one of them was sen to 'waver', being apparently unable to maintain itself in the air, and subsequently it dropped into the sea. The flight commander and the deputy commander followed the descending aeroplane as closely as they could go with safety to the water, and sent out signals of distress calling for help. The flight commander flew for the nearest point of land to procure assistance to effect rescue; he was unable to land in the vicinity of the Howth Lighthouse, but eventually succeeded in getting to the ground in Major Robinson's field.

All this time the deputy commander continued to fly over the spot, where the aeroplane entered the water, while the flight commander also returned to the place where the lieutenant was in difficulties. About 5.30 a patrol boat put out from Kingstown, but was unable to discover any trace of Lieutenant Lyon.

It is stated that the machine struck the water with considerable force, and was practically broken to pieces. Lieut. Lyon's comrades displayed great activity in endeavouring to obtain help, and at considerable risk to themselves. In rather a strong wind kept hovering over the spot where the young aviator lost his life. The machines were coming from Chester, and had for their objective Bathdonnell[sic] as a landing place.*

Search parties yesterday failed to find the machine, a single-seater, or its unfortunate occupant. Mr Herbert Muxwell who witnessed the coming of the three machines across the water, said to a Sunday Independent representative said that "It was really very hard luck on the plucky man in the machine after coming so far he should be knocked over just in sight of land. The wind was very squally and heavy all the afternoon though, otherwise the day was more like one in summer."

Another resident of Howth recalls a similar incident some years ago on the Dublin coast when, fortunately, the airman escaped. The aviator on that occasion was the well-known actor, Sir Robt. [unreadable]. He flew across the Channel from England, and fell into the sea at a point between Howth and Skerries."

Lloyd Dietz Lyon's mother, Mrs Emma Lyon was residing at 98 Northcliffe Block, Toronto.

* The location reported in *The Irish Times* correctly refers to the landing place as Baldonnel and that the field where the flight commander landed was near Baily where he telephone Kingstown for assistance.

Note. Aware than on occasions 54 Squadron can be confused with 54 Training [ex-Reserve] Squadron, I have checked information regarding this unit and find that it was re-designated 50 Training Depot Station on the 15th of July 1918.

70 Squadron   2Lt H E Minton   Safe   Unemployed list 6 March 1920
7F.1 Snipe E8212   Canada
T/o Bickendorf with orders to ferry the Snipe to 6 Air Issues for storage as the squadron was being reduced to a cadre
but crashed whilst attempting a forced-landing at Somain. It seems, however, that the squadron remained in the Rhineland until the September when personnel returned to Spittlegate.

   Harold Edward Minton joined the squadron on the last day of October 1918. Prior to that, he was operational on
Camels with 43 Squadron until a sprained knee put him in hospital for the latter part of September and the first week in
October. His service began with the RFC when he was commissioned to the General List on 20th December 1917 [LG
1st January 1918, supplement 30452, page 96].

211 Squadron   Lt A Adams   Injured
DH.9 D551/X
T/o Thuilles to dispose of the DH to 98 Squadron at Alquines, '98' assuming the role for the next few weeks at a
demobilisation unit. Within sight of his destination, Lieutenant Adams, whom I believe was a 98 Squadron pilot,
encountered bad weather and crashed-landed about a kilometre west of the airfield.

MARCH
1919

Throughout the month the process of reducing the number of active squadrons in all theatres continued and with it a
massive scaling back of manpower. The land *"fit for heroes"* was coming under immense strain with thousands of ex-
servicemen and women now looking for gainful employment. But, it would be the opposite for many as factories that
had been geared for war production were facing up to cancelled orders and with it the shedding of labour. For months,
even years in some cases, the reality of a country at peace would not be a bed of roses.

   What made life for many who had endured months of living in near unimaginable conditions on the battlefields of the
Continent so hard to bear was the indifference shown to them by former employers and those employees who had
stayed in protected jobs.

Saturday 1 March 1919
1 Squadron, less their SE.5as and now reduced to a cadre, arrived at London Colney from Izel-lès-Hameau. On the
Continent the duties of 80 Wing based at Wattignies on the SSW side of Lille ceased and with it disbandment.

   Also this day, the resurgence of German civilian aviation with Deutsche Luft-Reederei starting scheduled flights to
Hamburg.

18 Squadron   Lt R W O Thurburn   Safe   See 22 March 1919
DH.9A F1080/R   Sgt T Carr   Safe
T/o Bickendorf for an air test and on return undershot its approach and came down in a ploughed field where it turned
over. Lieutenant Thurburn had joined the squadron at Maisoncelle on 8th August 1918.

32 Squadron   SE.5a D7002   While in the process of taxying from its hangar to commence a flight to the UK the
tail skid snagged in the rails of a light railway. Taken to 1 Advanced Salvage Dump it was struck off charge on the 8th.
The identity of the pilot is unknown.

57 Squadron   2Lt H C Pendle   Safe   Unemployed list 24 September 1919
DH.4 A7970
T/o Morville with a consignment of mail to Spa but after losing his way Herbert Charles Pendle forced-landed in
Holland. No location has been recorded and it is assumed the DH was taken over by the Dutch authorities. It will be
recalled that Herbert Pendle was formerly of 55 Squadron and had been involved in an accident on 23rd December last.

80 Squadron   2Lt L C Mullins   Safe   See 6 March 1919
7F.1 Snipe E8069
T/o Stree for a practice flight and wrecked when the engine cut and a crashed-landing into a ditch near Donstiennes
[Hainaut] ensued. 2nd Lieutenant Mullins Army Form B.103-I has not postings information whatsoever.

107 Squadron   2Lt C F Robinson   Safe   Unemployed list 1 November 1919
DH.9 C1179
T/o Maubeuge with orders to take the DH to 98 Squadron for disposal; however, before becoming airborne he ran into
the DH summarised below which was also awaiting ferrying to Alquines.

   2nd Lieutenant Robinson arrived with the squadron from 2 Aeroplane Supply Depot on the 23rd of October 1918, and
48-hours after his accident he was posted to 49 Squadron at Bavai, moving with the squadron to Bickendorf towards the
end May. From here, and two days before '49' disbanded, he joined 25 Squadron at Merheim.

   It most likely he left the Rhineland with the squadron in early September, and was placed on the unemployed list as
indicated.

107 Squadron   DH.9 F6073   Struck by 2nd Lieutenant Robinson's aircraft. Sitting in the cockpit was 2nd Lieutenant W F Long who although shaken was otherwise unharmed. Posted to 108 Squadron on the 9th of August 1918,

131

this was cancelled and on the same day he went to 107 Squadron. According to his Record of Service, he was attached to 98 Squadron on the day of the mishap. The final entry on Army Form B.103 for this officer shows he returned to the UK on the 13th and joined the numbers of the unemployed on the 28th of March 1919.

F6073 was one of many rebuilt DHs. Its original identity was C1178 which with 49 Squadron saw four days of active service before it was seriously damaged on the 25th of May 1918. Crewed by Sergeants S J Oliver and W Lee it came to grief while landing at Conteville in gusting winds which caught the DH as it touched down and threw it violently to port to finish with its nose buried in the grass.

| 110 Squadron | 2Lt W L Carroll | Safe | |
| DH.9A H3411 | 2Lt A R Wylde | Safe | Unemployed list 27 August 1919 |

T/o Tardinghem tasked for a mail delivery flight but thought to have been damaged beyond repair after forced-landing in fog near Saint Pol [probably Saint-Pol-sur-Ternoise in the Pas-de-Calais]. Little, apart from this entry, is known of 2nd Lieutenant Carroll's service.

His observer had seen service with the 7th Loyal North Lancashire Regiment, subsequently joining the squadron on the 27th of September 1918. From the 13th to the 22nd of October he was treated for influenza, eventually returning home on the 16th of April.

| 208 Squadron | Lt Hope | Safe |
| 7F.1 Snipe E8313 | | |

T/o Stree for practice flying. On landing, and before coming to a stop, the undercarriage sank into the mud which caused the Snipe to turn onto its back. I have not been able to positively identify Lieutenant Hope.

Monday 3 March 1919
35 Squadron arrived at Netheravon from Ste Marie Cappel. Equipped with FK.8, which they operated throughout their time on the Western Front, and adding Bristol F.2bs in the final weeks, 35 Squadron had been operational since January 1917, initially to support the Cavalry Corps, but from March 1918 as a general reconnaissance formation.

Continuing the advance of aviation this day witnessed the first delivery of international mail in the United States when William E Boeing, founder of the aircraft company that continues to this day to bear his name, flying a Boeing CL-4S arrived at Seattle in Washington State with post from Vancouver.

| 12 Squadron | Lt Welch | Safe |
| RE.8 F1677 | Lt D V Hoskins | Safe |

T/o Duren for an air test and crashed-landed here on return. I have yet to trace the Record of Service for the pilot, but that for his observer shows he served with the squadron from 22nd August 1918, until the 6th of March when he was posted to a holding camp before returning to Blandford Camp in Dorset to await discharge. This leads me to suspect he was a Canadian, despite the lack of an address on the form.

| 57 Squadron | Lt W J Barber | Safe | Unemployed list 17 July 1919 |
| DH.9A E8525 | | | |

T/o Morville and probably wrecked here whilst landing. The loss of E8525 was probably the first of its type from the squadron.

| 70 Squadron | Lt V S Parker | Safe | Unemployed list 27 June 1919 |
| 7F.1 Snipe E8205 | | | |

T/o Bickendorf and on return from a practice flight Vivian Steel Parker made a hash of his approach and crashed. What survives from his service records show that he was born on the 4th of December 1898, and enlisted with the RFC on 15th February 1917, and before the year was out joined 43 Squadron at Auchel on 28th October. Vivian was on the squadron's nominal roll until 26th January 1918, on which date he returned to England.

Consulting *The Camel File* it is shown he forced-landed near La Gorgue in B6365 on the 8th of December. He was unhurt and the Camel was recovered and was soon back in service.

Although his return to the UK is the last entry on Army Form B.103, by the summer of 1918, he was serving as an instructor with 40 Training [ex-Reserve] Squadron at Croydon. Here, during a sortie in E1531 on 19th August, the lower front spar on the starboard wing collapsed. Skilfully maintaining control of his crippled aircraft, Lieutenant Parker forced-landed in a field near the airfield which had been cropped with potatoes. Moments after his arrival E1531 turned over and was damaged beyond repair.

| 88 Squadron | 2Lt W R Kellough | + | Charleroi Communal Cemetery |
| Bristol F.2b E2458 | Canada | | |

T/o Nivelles having been briefed for a practice flight, possibly his first in a Bristol. Tragically, William Roy Kellough climbed far too steeply and while turning stalled and spun to the ground. Although a Record of Service form has been raised, it has no details regarding his postings or his sad demise. His headstone bears a rhyming inscription: *"God Will Bind The Broken Chain Closer When We Meet Again."*

Tuesday 4 March 1919
During the day Tangmere welcomed 32 Squadron from Serny; at Ford just along the coast to the east, 97 Squadron arrived from Saint Inglevert to commence re-equipping with DH.10 in readiness for service in India. Also arriving at

Ford from Saint Inglevert, 115 Squadron but unlike '97' its 'number plate' would soon be placed in abeyance until major rearmament of the Royal Air Force in the 1930s.

84 Squadron	*Not reported*	Safe
SE.5a F5669		

T/o from an Air Issues unit and on arrival at Bickendorf landed on very soft ground and lost its undercarriage. The name of the ferry pilot has been lost in the annals of time.

99 Squadron	Lt T C S Tuffield	Injured	Unemployed list 1 October 1919
DH.9A F1031	2Lt W J Tremellen	Injured	

T/o Aulnoye with a consignment of post but as the DH gathered speed so it was caught by a violent gust of wind which threw it out of control with such force that both crew were quite badly injured. For notes regarding Lieutenant Tuffield, please refer to my summary for 15th February. I suspect he was admitted to 57 CCS, for this is where his observer was taken for initial treatment for a compound fracture to his right femur and concussion. He was then transferred to 20 General Hospital and back to England on the 15th by way of HS *Jan Breydell*.

Wednesday 5 March 1919

3 Squadron AusFC   RE.8 E224   Burnt out at Jemappes in the Belgian province of Hainaut, Jamappes now part of the conglomerate of Mons. By one of those odd quirks of coincidence, Jampappes was an airfield in Algeria, occupied during the Second World War by 43 Squadron [Spitfire] from 13th March to 19th April 1943, and by the Beaufighters of 153 Squadron at various times between 15th February and 20th June 1943.

110 Squadron	Lt A R MacDonald	Safe
DH.9A E8482	Lt H C Hincliffe	Safe

T/o Tardinghem for mail delivery duties, this time to England, but on crossing the Channel and over the Kent country-side the crew flew into a bank of fog and crashed attempting to forced-land near Sittingbourne on the Gillingham to Faversham road.

An incomplete Record of Service for Lieutenant MacDonald indicates he served with the squadron from 30th August 1918, until the squadron disbanded at Marquise on 27th August 1919. His next of kin address, typed, shows he lived at 180 Soho Hill, Handsworth, Birmingham. Lieutenant Hincliffe's form is devoid of details.

Thursday 6 March 1919

5 Squadron	Lt R V N Makepeace	Safe
RE.8 C2932	2Lt W H Whale	Safe

T/o Hangelar for an air test but before becoming airborne crashed into the RE summarised below. Lieutenant Make-peace had served previously with 11 Squadron [Bristol F.2b] for eleven days between the 20th and 30th January 1918, on which day he went back the UK. He returned to France in the autumn and joined 5 Squadron on 3rd October.

Sent to a holding unit on the 6th of March, he was posted to Blandford Camp two days later. As with Lieutenant Hoskins of 12 Squadron, summarised on the 3rd of March, I suspect 2nd Lieutenant Makepeace was a Canadian.

2nd Lieutenant Whale joined the squadron on the 26th of September 1918; on the 12th of March he was admitted to 14 General Hospital from where five days later he was evacuated to the UK by way of HMHS *St. Andrew*.

5 Squadron	RE.I H7055	Wrecked in the manner described above.

30 Squadron	Captain A P Adams DFC mid +	Tehran War Cemetery
Martinsyde G-100 7461		

T/o Kifri for bombing operations during which the aircraft was hit by ground fire and crashed on scrub-land near Khun Bushire in Southern Persia. Allen Percy Adams' biography, along with a photograph of his crashed aircraft, is reported between pages 15 and 17 of Norman Franks excellent tribute to decorated airmen who fell post-11th November 1918.

The cemetery register shows 21 year old Captain Adams as being attached to 47 Squadron which at the time was many miles away at Amber-Koi in Greece. Furthermore, the biographical details indicates he was one of 30 Squadron's longest serving officers and at the time of his death he was commanding C Flight.

An explanation as to how this error came about may be found on page 71 of John Hamlin's detailed history titled *Flat Out - The story of 30 Squadron Royal Air Force* where he writes; *"Capt. Adams had been an observer with 47 Squadron in Salonika and had served with 30 Squadron since August 1917."*

He also reports that Lieutenant Bull and his observer who had been participating in the same operation and who had witnessed the crash landed alongside the wrecked Martinsyde but before they could recover Allen's body they were driven off by sustained and accurate rifle fire. Then, on the 12th of March, Captain Adams was recovered and brought to Chaghdaz where it was found he had died from a bullet wound to the head. He was buried with full military honours on the 13th, *"a firing party of 100 Sepoys from the Punjabi Regt. providing a last salute."*

57 Squadron	Lt F O Thornton DFC	+	Theux Communal Cemetery
DH.4 A7940	Lt P S Burnay	+	Theux Communal Cemetery

T/o Spa loaded with mail and set off the squadron's base at Morville but *en route* visibility deteriorated. Descending, no doubt to try and establish their position, the crew failed to see they were on a direct collision course with a belt of trees into which they flew near La Reid.

This was Frank Thornton's third crash, the two previous being on 21st and 26th January. Percy Samuel Burnay first saw service with 3 Squadron [Camel] at Valhereaux on 18th May 1918 [this leads me to suspect he was a pilot] and joined the squadron as recently as 11th February.

Both were buried with full military honours with the Reverend L L Chaplin officiating. Frederick's epitaph reads: *"He Died That We Might Live New Chester Sale, Cheshire"* while Percy is remembered with the words: *"In Loving Memory Of My Son Rest In Peace."*

The village of Theux [Liège] lies to the SW of Verviers and until April 1919, was the site of 61 CCS. A relatively small cemetery, it contains thirty-one service graves, all post-armistice, six with dates in November and December and the rest in 1919. The two officers, here named, are the sole Royal Air Force personnel buried here.

80 Squadron	2Lt L C Mullins	Safe	
7F.1 Snipe E8318			

T/o 6 Air Issues for Clermont but near Maubeuge the engine cut through lack of petrol, an inexcusable oversight on the personnel at 6 Air Issues. Gliding down, 2nd Lieutenant Mullins for the second time in six days found himself climbing out a ditch.

99 Squadron	Lt H A L Pattison	Safe	Retired list 1 December 1937
DH.9A F1062	2Lt W E Lowrie	Safe	Unemployed list 3 December 1919

T/o Aulnoye with mail destined for Spa where on arrival the crew crashed-landed. Harold Arthur Langston Pattison was formerly of the Bedfordshire Regiment, commissioned as a temporary 2nd Lieutenant, on probation, on 7th July 1916 [LG 26 July 1916, supplement 29682, page 7416].

Postwar, on the 1st of August 1919, he was appointed to a permanent commission, *Gazetted* this date in issue 31486, page 9870. His service as a permanent officer is, to say the least, Spartan but the website devoted to the Gander Airport Historical Society suggests that a very lengthy summary written by Frank Tibbo may well be referring to Squadron Leader Pattison, though unfortunately the author only refers to him by his initials. In this piece it is reported that he *"joined the Royal Air Force and flew in France on the India Frontier and in Palestine."*

A trawl of *Flight* results in several entries, the earliest being April 15, 1920, where under the banner Air Routes in India it reports Flying Officer H A L Pattison proving the route between Calcutta and Delhi. His retirement in December 1937, was at his own request.

William Edward Lowrie, born 9th June 1894, joined the RFC on 2nd September 1915. However, his first posting detail does not appear until Boxing Day 1917, when he was attached to 20 Squadron [Bristol F.2b] at Ste Marie Cappel. On the 1st of July he was posted to L Flight [no location indicated], remaining with this formation until 24th January when he reported to 99 Squadron. Although there are no indications of illness, the final entry, dated 26th of May, is for evacuation to the UK on HMHS *Brighton.*

202 Squadron	2Lt E Tompkins	Safe	
DH.4 N5988			

T/o Varsseneare intending to deliver the DH to 233 Squadron at Dover but was late in departing and on crossing the Channel found himself flying in the dark, and with little hope of finding the destination airfield, forced-landed on the golf links at West Cliffe near St. Margaret's Bay, a few miles NE from Dover.

Delivered in July 1917, to 5 Squadron RNAS, the DH passed into the hands of 2 Squadron RNAS and on 24th March 1918, made an unscheduled landing on sands near Niewpoort. Salvaged, and little damaged, it remained with the squadron [now 202 Squadron] and throughout carried the individual letter K.

202 Squadron	2Lt L S Clarke	Safe	
DH.9A D8400			

T/o Varsseneare similarly ordered but by the time the Southern Coast was crossed the light was fading and in attempting to make a precautionary landing in a field belonging to Wanstone Court Farm near Swingate Downs airfield 2nd Lieutenant Clarke came to grief.

At the time 202 Squadron was in the process of disposing of their aircraft ahead of returning to England.

Saturday 8 March 1919

103 Squadron	2Lt M S Lewin	Safe	Commission relinquished 20 July 1954
DH.9 E8884	South Africa		
	2Lt G Butters	Safe	Unemployed list 25 September 1919

T/o Maisoncelle for postal duties and damaged beyond repair following a landing on unsuitable ground at Morville. Michael Solomon Lieutenant, mentioned in respect of my summary for 17th January in which Geoffrey Butters features, was born in the Cape in 1898, and reported for operational service with the squadron on the 20th of July 1918. He was posted back to England on 14th January, but returned to the squadron, at Maisoncelle, on the 6th of February.

On the 10th of March, he joined 110 Squadron at Tardinghem from where on June 19th, he was posted to 91 Wing at Marquise and thence back to the UK on the 24th.

During the Second World War he obtained a commission in the Training Branch, effective from the 1st of March 1941 [LG 20 June 1941, issue 35196, page 3529], but, I suspect, between the wars he had qualified as a dentist for on the 6th of August 1942, he relinquished his commission in favour of a commission on transfer to the Dental Branch [LG 29th September 1942, supplement 35721, page 4220]. His service then continued until being obliged to step down under the provisions of the Navy, Army and Air Force Reserves Act 1954, retaining his rank of Flight Lieutenant.

Sunday 9 March 1919

18 Squadron	Lt B Champion	Safe	See 28 March 1919
DH.9A E717	2Lt E Lay	Safe	

T/o Bickendorf for a mail delivery flight which ended rather abruptly when the radiator sprang a leak and the engine seized. The crew tried to land near Charleroi but crashed in the attempt. Lieutenant Champion served with the squadron from the 3rd of August 1918, until he was sent back to the UK on the 16th of May, by which time '18' had moved to Merheim.

His observer preceded him, arriving on the 29th of July 1918, and was very briefly attached to 8 Squadron from the 16th to the 20th of April when he, too, returned to England.

18 Squadron	Captain R T Minors	Safe	See 27 March 1919
DH.9A E8426	2Lt W Ballentine	Safe	

T/o Bickendorf to visit 20 Squadron at Ossogne where on landing the DH struck a sharp ridge and was damaged beyond repair. For an appreciation of Ronald Towers Minors service, please refer to my summary of the 27th. I have yet to find 2nd Lieutenant Ballentine's service records.

110 Squadron	2Lt R R Spencer	Safe	Unemployed list 12 May 1919
DH.9A F1054			

T/o Tardinghem with mail intended for the authorities in Köln but crashed while forced-landing near Moresnet, a village at the junction with Belgium, Germany and the Netherlands. Its history is outlined on the website Neutral Moresnet'

Monday 10 March 1919

Two more squadrons arrived in the UK during the day from foreign climes; personnel from 28 Squadron and 66 Squadron reported to Yatesbury having sailed earlier from Sarcedo in Italy.

12 Squadron	Lt Barnum	Safe
RE.8 F5909	Captain Peacock	Safe

T/o Duren across the prevailing wind intending to deliver the RE to 1 Aeroplane Storage Depot but the wind took charge and soon the crew were walking back from a recently ploughed field, their aircraft minus its undercarriage and damaged beyond repair.

208 Squadron	Lt Carey	Safe
7F.1 Snipe E8134		

T/o Stree for local flying and reported to have crashed whilst approaching at an unsafe slow speed.

Note. Most unusually I have not been able to positively identify the three officers whose initials are absent from the casualty returns.

Wednesday 12 March 1919

48 Squadron	2Lt C A Allen	+	Cologne Southern Cemetery
Bristol F.2b F5817	South Africa		
	2Lt W Kennedy	+	Cologne Southern Cemetery

T/o Bickendorf entrusted as the leading crew in formation flying practice and it was while flying at several thousand feet over Lohmar [sic] that something of a very serious nature overtook the Bristol which eyewitnesses say dived at a near vertical angle into the ground.

Charles Arthur Allen, 24 years of age, hailed from Derwent Siding, Middelburg in the Transvaal, while 19 year old William Kennedy, born in Lancashire but at the time of his death his parents had moved to Glasgow, rest side-by-side in plot 1, row F, graves 3 and 4 respectively.

Thursday 13 March 1919

57 Squadron	2Lt A S Smith	Safe	See 20 March 1919
DH.9 E8603	Lt R M Dixon	Safe	See 20 March 1919

T/o Morville and thought to have been written off during a forced-landing near Clavier - probably in the province of Liège and, I suspect, while carrying a consignment of mail. A Record of Service form has been raised for 2nd Lieutenant Smith but it shows merely his rank, name and initials, plus his next of kin address in Sheffield.

That for Ralph Melville Dixon is much more forthcoming. He was senior in years to most of his contemporaries in that he was born on the 19th of October 1884. His Record of Service is incomplete, but he was wounded on operations on either the 9th or 10th of June 1917, with a gunshot wound to his right thigh. At the time he was flying in DH.4 A7469 of 55 Squadron piloted by Lieutenant P J Barnett, and engaged in a photo reconnaissance sortie when they were attacked by an enemy scout whose fire holed the DH's petrol tank and in the ensuing forced-landing it crashed out of control and was wrecked.

First treated in 1 Canadian CCS, he was transferred to 14 General Hospital and on the 1st of July sent back to the UK aboard HMHS *St. Patrick.*

The next, and final, entry of any significance is his posting to 57 Squadron on the 9th of March 1919.

Thursday 13 March 1919

57 Squadron	2Lt A S Smith	Safe	See 20 March 1919
DH.9 E8603	Lt R M Dixon	Safe	See 20 March 1919

T/o Morville and thought to have been written off while forced-landing near Clavier - probably in the province of Liège and, I suspect, whilst carrying a consignment of mail.

Friday 14 March 1919

78 Squadron	2Lt W A Raw	Injured	Hornchurch [St. Andrew] Churchyard
Avro 504 E9715	South Africa		
	Lt W C Mortimer-Phelan	Injured	Unemployed list 8 August 1919

T/o Hornchurch for local flying only to stall and dive headlong into the ground. From the Transvaal, 19 year old Wilfred Addison Raw succumbed to his injuries on the 16th. Lieutenant Mortimer-Phelan, as reported by Trevor Henshaw on page 36 of *The Sky Their Battlefield,* had been shot down and taken prisoner on 1 April 1916, when his 11 Squadron Vickers FB.5 5079 was driven down over Boyelles in the Pas-de-Calais. However, as *Flight* in their issue of May 23, 1918, reported, Mortimer-Phelan was among a large group of Allied officers recently released to Holland for internment. The serial, as reported, is incorrect as it belongs to a batch of DH.9As E9657-E9756.

80 Squadron	2Lt E F Adams	Safe
7F.1 Snipe E8011		

T/o Brellendorf and on arrival at Thuilles misjudged his approach and crash-landed.

80 Squadron	Sgt B T Lindsey	Safe
7F.1 Snipe E8099		

T/o Brellendorf similarly charged and, unfortunately, wrecked the Snipe in the manner reported above. Sergeant Lindsey's service number 110448 indicates enlistment as a cadet between November 1917 and January 1918.

99 Squadron	2Lt J H W Wilcox	Safe	Unemployed list 18 April 1919
DH.9A E711	2Lt P E Bullock	Safe	

T/o Aulnoye for a travelling flight during which the engine cut and in the forced-landing that followed the DH was brought to a halt when it ran into some trees. I am reasonably confident that 2nd Lieutenant Wilcox returned for service during the Second World War for on 11 January 1940, a John Harold Walton Wilcox was granted a commission in the Administrative and Special Duties Branch [LG 2 February 1940, issue 34784, page 658], though I can find no further entries for this officer following promotion to Flight Lieutenant, as promulgated in *The London Gazette* 3 July 1942, issue 35618, page 2929.

Saturday 15 March 1919

Widespread rioting accompanied by the burning of buildings and entire villages reported from Egypt; this news, no doubt, would have caused concern within the Foreign Office.

   23 Squadron arrived at Waddington from Clermont;

17 Squadron	Captain G C Gardiner	Safe
F.1 Camel D6553		

T/o San Stephano for an air test but in a wind blowing close to a gale. Unsurprisingly, the Camel failed to become airborne and was completely wrecked after crashing out of control.

48 Squadron	Major F W Stent	Injured
Bristol F.2b E2281	2Lt Lang	Injured

T/o Bickendorf for an air test and local flying, taking with him 2nd Lieutenant Lang of the 18th Royal Hussars. Ditched in the Rhine close to the city's Schiffbrücke Bridge. Major Stent had assumed command of the squadron from Major Keith Park*MC at around the time of the armistice and held the chair up to the time of his accident. On the 1st of August 1919, he was one of many officers selected for a permanent commission. The Bristol, reported here, had been with the squadron since 22 September 1918.

* Subsequently, New Zealand born Air Chief Marshal Sir Keith Park was Air Officer Commanding 11[Fighter] Group throughout the *Battle of Britain* going on to serve with distinction in the Middle East theatre , including 18 months as Air Officer Commanding AHQ Malta. Additional information concerning Keith Park can be read in my second volume, page 393.

202 Squadron	Lt P R Spivey	Safe
DH.4 N5969		

T/o Varssenaere with the intention of delivering the DH to 98 Squadron at Alquines for its disposal, but *en route* the engine failed and a crash-landing was made at Setques Pool Pilot's Range where the undercarriage dropped into a deep hole. Six days after this incident, 202 Squadron returned to the United Kingdom, settling at Shotwick to await disbandment.

208 Squadron   Lt G Smith   Safe
7F.1 Snipe E8167
T/o Stree and on arrival at Donstiennes overshot the landing area and while attempting to make a steep climb over a line of telegraph wires, stalled and crashed.

Sunday 16 March 1919
Continued fighting between White Russian forces and Bolshevik formations resulted in the former expelling the 5th Red Army from Ufa [now the capital of the Russian Republic of Bashkortostan].
    101 Squadron arrived at Filton from Morville;

98 Squadron   Captain R V James DFC   Injured
DH.4 D8390
T/o Alquines and flew over to Varssenaere to visit 217 Squadron. Shortly after leaving Varssenare to return to base, the engine of his DH failed and in forced-landing WSW of Bruges in an area heavily wooded his aircraft crashed into trees.

Monday 17 March 1919
At Bolshie Ozerki, a village near the port of Onega, a small Allied garrison was overwhelmed by a Brigade of Red Army troops and over fifty French soldiers were captured; meanwhile, the scaling down of the British Army witnessed the disbandment of three Brigades and four Infantry Divisions.
    53 Squadron arrived at Old Sarum from Laneffe; 107 Squadron arrived at Hounslow from Maubeuge.

62 Squadron   2Lt E G Schafter   Injured
Bristol F.2b H7065
T/o Nivelles for a cross-country exercise which ended with 2nd Lieutenant Schafter*straying across the border into Holland where he crash-landed at Foedekenskerke in the province of Zeeland, and roughly 22 km ESE from Middelburg.

* An unusual surname which has defied searches via *The London Gazette* and *Flight.*

99 Squadron   2Lt R R Martin   Safe
DH.9A E8562   Major Cameron   Safe
T/o Aulnoye carrying mail and reported to have crashed at Louverie [sic].

Tuesday 18 March 1919
Although 3 Squadron Australian Flying Corps ceased flying at the end of February, it appears disposal of its aircraft had yet to be completed for on this day three RE.8s C5105, F6016 and H7265 were the subject of casualty returns [AIR 1/866]. The report indicates all were being ferried from Tarcienne to St Omer for issue to 25 Squadron, but owing to inclement weather all three forced-landed at Maubeurge. The names of the pilots are reported as Lieutenants Robinson, Grigson and Heathcote respectively. There is a degree of confusion in that when 3 Squadron Australian Flying Corps ceased operations it was based at Charleroi, and why the REs had to be delivered to St. Omer seems pointless as 25 Squadron was operating from Maubeuge where the forced-landings took place. 27 Squadron arrived at Shotwick from Bavay, though it would be over a year before official notice of disbandment would be promulgated. 205 Squadron arrived at Hucknall from La Louveterie but would remain in existence until 22 January 1920.

62 Squadron   Captain F G C Weare MC Safe   See 7 April 1919
Bristol F.2b F4299 2Lt E G Holloway   Safe   See 7 April 1919
T/o Nivelles for an air test and thought to have been written in a crash on the aerodrome. A biography of Captain Weare is recorded in my summary for the 7th of January. 2nd Lieutenant Holloway was posted in on 9th October 1918, and three days before the squadron disbanded at Spich on the last day of July, he was cross-posted to 11 Squadron. On the 3rd of September, 11 Squadron returned to Scopwick by which time 2Lt Holloway had been in the UK for 24-hours.

Wednesday 19 March 1919
6 Squadron   Lt D McD Northcombe   Injured
Bristol F.2b F5997 Canada
T/o Sart for a practice flight but collided with an RE.8 that was on the point of landing. This was the squadron's first mishap at Sart having arrived here earlier in the day from Gerpinnes. Of the Western Ontario Regiment, Lieutenant Northcombe had been seconded for duty with the Royal Flying Corps on 16 November 1917 [LG 14 August 1918, supplement 30842, page 9530] and ceased his attachment on 13 August 1919 [LG 27 August 1919, supplement 31524, page 10841].

20 Squadron   Captain Addis   Safe
Fokker DVII
T/o from unidentified airfield and overturned on landing, probably at Ossogne, after experiencing uneven throttle control.

| 70 Squadron | 2Lt J W Abray | Safe | Unemployed list 6 March 1920 |

7F.1 Snipe E8057

T/o Bickendorf for local flying and wrecked following a misjudged landing.

| 84 Squadron | 2Lt R A Whyte | Safe |

SE.5a E5920

T/o Thuilles authorised for local flying but failed to become airborne owing to the wheels sinking into mud which resulted in the SE turning over.

| 99 Squadron | 2Lt J G Kershaw | Safe | Unemployed list 16 April 1919 |

DH.9A F977

T/o Aulnoye and crashed at Morville where Lieutenant Kershaw had intended making a safe delivery of mail.

Thursday 20 March 1919

A most informative report was published in *Flight* March 20, 1919, on the subject of the mail/passenger system currently employed between Hendon and Paris, where the Peace Conference was in progress. Because of the infancy in weather forecasting, the telephone became a vital tool in deciding whether flying was possible, or not. Each morning reports on the weather are exchanged between the two countries, after which a call is made to the British Peace Commission to advise on the feasibility of sending mail or passengers across the Channel by air, or whether recourse to the morning boat train is the safer option. The report goes on to quote some of the recent notable achievements; *"on March 16, Mr Bonar Law was in conference with the Prime Minister in Paris at 10.30 a.m. An hour later he left Paris on a DH.4* [No 2 Communications Flight detachment]*, landed at Hendon at 1.55 p.m. and at 2.15 p.m. was in his study in Downing Street.'* The report continues; *'Gen. Seeley on Saturday flew from Folkestone to Paris in the fast time of 1h.14min, for the 172 miles."* Regarding Mr Bonar Law's journey by car from Hendon to Downing Street in less than twenty minutes, I doubt if that could be bettered today.

| 57 Squadron | 2Lt A S Smith | + | Houyet Churchyard |
| DH.4 F2653 | Lt R M Dixon | Safe |

T/o Bickendorf to return to Morville with packages of mail but *en route* flew into a snowstorm and in attempting to make a precautionary landing the DH stalled and crashed near Anhée [Namur] on the west bank of the Meusse and roughly 15 km S of Namur. The village of Houyet, as reported by Commonwealth War Graves Commission, contains twenty-three service burials from the *Great War* and two from the Second World War, both being soldiers of the Royal Engineers who died on Boxing Day 1944. Of the *Great War* deaths all bar one [Private Frank Brown of the King's Own Yorkshire Light Infantry] died post-armistice and by pure coincidence the two Royal Air Force graves contain the remains of airmen from 57 Squadron. For 20 year old Algernon Sydney Smith the circumstances of his death are explained in this summary, but how Aircraftman Ewart Oswald Challenor, also 20 years of age, met his end on the last day of February is not known [his name does not appear in the DH.4 index of *The DH.4/DH.9 File*]. Their respective epitaphs are: *"Peace Perfect Peace'* and *'Rest In Peace."* Regarding Ralph Merville Dixon, who appears to have escaped unscathed, his name appears in *The London Gazette* 3 June 1919, supplement 31378, page 7033, publishing the names of those awarded the DFC, but without citations appended. He was formerly of the 9th Berkshires.

Friday 21 March 1919

| 12 Squadron | Lt Blackford | Safe |

Bristol Fighter D7952

T/o Duren and heavily damaged while landing from a practice flight. Although primarily a reconnaissance squadron equipped with RE.8s, Bristol F.2bs were introduced in March 1918 and remained in use until July 1922, by which time the RE.8s had long since being disposed of. The movement card for D7952 indicates it was ferried to France by an unnamed pilot from 8 Squadron and deposited by 28 January 1919, with 2 Aeroplane Supply Depot. Its only mention as a 12 Squadron aircraft is recorded for the day of its accident.

| 84 Squadron | Lt H L Hall | Safe |

SE.5a E5813

T/o Thuilles and damaged beyond repair following the undercarriage collapsing on landing from a practice flight.

| 84 Squadron | 2Lt C V Forsyth | Safe |

SE.5a H710/P

T/o Thuilles for local flying practice. Landed on soft ground and moments later 2nd Lieutenant Forsyth was extracting himself from the cockpit of his overturned fighter

Saturday 22 March 1919

| 18 Squadron | Lt R W O Thurburn | Safe | Commission relinquished 1 April 1920 |

DH.9A F2734/W

T/o Bickendorf for postal duties and it was on return, and in limited visibility, that Lieutenant Thurburn misjudged his approach and came down in a ploughed field and turned over. It will be recalled that he had suffered a similar accident on the 1st and this second incident might well have been in the same field. The casualty report, forwarded on the 23rd, states that he ran into the farmer's plough, which proved the DH's undoing. It is noted from his service records that he was late of the 3rd Scottish Rifles. The *Gazette* 29 October 1917, supplement 30356, page 11116, under the heading Special Reserve of Officers, records his promotion to Lieutenant on 1st July 1917, and that he remained seconded. On relinquishing his commission he was permitted to retain his rank [LG 24 June 1920, supplement 31952, page 6870].

70 Squadron   2Lt F W Perrin   Safe
7F.1 Snipe E7358
T/o Bickendorf for local flying practice and crashed on return, the familiar story of misjudgement while landing.

Monday 24 March 1919
202 Squadron arrived at Driffield from Varssenaere, its aircraft having been left behind in France. Disbanding this day was the Army's 66th Infantry Division.

5 Squadron   Lt R Blake   Safe
Bristol F.2b F6042 2Lt R Franklin   Safe
T/o Hangelar on what is described as a travelling flight and on arrival at an airfield near Koblenz was obliged to go round again after being baulked by another aircraft approaching to land from the opposite direction. While doing so the Bristol's engine cut and the crew crash-landed on rough ground. Similar to my remarks for 12 Squadron, and the crash of one of their Bristols on the 21st, 5 Squadron was a Corps reconnaissance squadron but began to receive some Bristol F.2bs, though unlike the former that had experience of the type for a year, 5 Squadron's involvement was recent and in the case of F6042 it had been received within the last few days.

Tuesday 25 March 1919
6 Squadron   Captain H J Hunter   Safe
RE.8 F6277   Lt McEwan   Safe
T/o Sart for an air test and probably damaged beyond repair in the aftermath of a landing accident.

43 Squadron   Lt C E James   Injured
7F.1 Snipe F2361
T/o Bickendorf authorised for a practice sortie and while flying west of the centre of Köln, and at a very low altitude, clipped high-tension wires between Königsdorf and Lovenich.

Wednesday 26 March 1919
102 Squadron arrived at Lympne from Serny; 103 Squadron returned to Shotwick from Mainsoncelle.

110 Squadron   Lt R Burgess   Safe
DH.9A F987   Lt W D C Hutton   Injured   Cologne Southern Cemetery
T/o Tardinghem loaded with mail destined for Köln but ran into a near blinding snowstorm and crashed while attempting a forced-landing near Vaals a small town in the Dutch province of Limburg, and on the border with Germany five km W of Aachen. It is a heavily wooded area in the Ardennes-Eifelrange.
   William Douglas Campbell Hutton, 19 years of age, died from his injuries on the 27th. Born in Madras, his headstone is inscribed thus: *"Dearly Loved Son Of William And Anne Hutton Madras And Edinburgh."* His father, William, had been Chief Engineer of the Public Works Department Madras.

Thursday 27 March 1919
13 Squadron arrived at Sedgeford from St. Omer;

9 Squadron   Lt G Miller   Safe
RE.8 E1207   *Not named*   Safe
T/o Ludendorf for local flying and with an officer from the Camerons occupying the rear cockpit, but at the point of becoming airborne a gust of wind caught the aircraft side-on and moments later the sortie ended with the RE upside down on the airfield. Two rather shaken officers emerged from the wreck, probably in need of a stiff brandy.

18 Squadron   Captain R T Minors   Injured   Belgrade Cemetery, Belgium
DH.9A E9715
T/o Bickendorf with a consignment of post; encountered a violent snowstorm and crashed out of control near the sanatorium at Profondeville which straddles the Meuse south of Namur. Formerly of the Worcestershire Regiment Ronald Towers Minors died the same day from his injuries; a single word epitaph: *"Wolverhampton"* commemorates his passing. He had crashed earlier in the month on the 9th. According to *The London Gazette* 17 August 1915, supplement 29268, page 8270, he was commissioned from the rank of Private on 20 August 1915, having initially served with the 28th[County of London] Battalion, The London Regiment [Artists' Rifles]. His secondment from the Worcestershires to the Royal Flying Corps, effective from 8 June 1917, was promulgated in *The London Gazette* 30 June 1917, supplement 30158, page 6508.

114 Squadron	*Not reported*		Injured	
BE.2e	Mechanic A Adams	+	Quetta Government Cemetery

T/o Jacobabad but struck a mound and rolled over, bursting into flames. Mechanic Adams is also commemorated on the Delhi Memorial [India Gate].

Friday 28 March 1919

8 Squadron	Lt G A Gowler	Safe	Unemployed 26 September 1919
Bristol F.2b D7855	Lt Fitzgerald	Safe	

T/o Bellevue for an engine test; crashed on landing. Lieutenant Gowler was formerly of the Royal Berkshire Regiment. This was the squadron's first reported serious accident of the year.

18 Squadron	Lt B Champion	Safe
DH.9A E8479		

T/o from 3 ELG Namur for postal duties but while gathering speed the port wheel sank into soft ground causing the undercarriage to collapse. Lieutenant Champion had crash-landed during similar duties on the 9th.

Saturday 29 March 191

12 Squadron	2Lt P F Bovingdon	Safe	Unemployed list 21 October 1919
Bristol F.2b D2167	Lt C G Turpin	Safe	Unemployed list 30 November 1919

T/o Duren for an air test in weather that was most inclement; on return to the airfield the Bristol crash-landed.

62 Squadron	Lt H V Edwards	Safe
Bristol F.2b E2559	Lt Davidson	Safe

T/o Nivelles for an air test which ended in a forced-landing at Marcq [probably Marcq-en-Baroeul [Nord] in the NNE suburbs of Lille].

110 Squadron	Lt M J Lewin	Safe
DH.9A E704		

T/o Tardinghem with instructions to deliver mail to Köln, but was forced down at Olne [Liège], roughly 10 km of so W of Verviers owing to a snowstorm.

216 Squadron	2Lt F H Sullivan USA	+	Terlincthun British Cemetery, Wimille
HP O/400 B8807	2Lt A Westall	Injured	Terlincthun British Cemetery, Wimille
	AC1 G W Tucknott	Injured	

T/o Marquise with mail destined for Valenciennes*but failed to clear a line of trees near Ferques in the Pas-de-Calais some five km ENE from the airfield. Frank Harrington Sullivan's epitaph reads: *"With Faith In God He Gave His Life For Liberty And Humanity."* His second pilot, 18 year old Arthur Westall, is remembered by the inscription: *"We Must Not Murmur Or Complain Trusting In Heaven To Meet Again."*

* 2nd Lieutenant Sullivan's entry in the cemetery register indicates the HP was bound for Köln with post for the Army of Occupation. The entry continues: *"Previous to enlistment was a student at Stevens Technical Institute, Hoboken, N.J., preparing for profession of mechanical engineer."*

Monday 31 March 1919

57 Squadron	2Lt D P Fulton	Injured	Unemployed list 26 April 1919
DH.9A F5730			

T/o Morville with the intention of delivering mail to Köln but soon after departing the DH's engine cut and 2nd Lieutenant Fulton was unable to prevent his machine from diving to the ground. Considering his transfer in less than a month following the crash, it is unlikely his injuries were of a serious nature. Furthermore, I strongly suspect him to be Douglas Patison Fulton commissioned with many others to the Administrative and Special Duties Branch on 26 September 1939 [LG 3 October 1939, issue 34700, page 6662]. As with large numbers officers whose former service had been in the *Great War*, their service stretched well beyond the ceasing of hostilities in 1945, and it was not until the huge culls of the '50s that they relinquished their commissions under the provisions of the Navy, Army and Air Force Reserves Act, 1954. In the case of Douglas Fulton, his commission was relinquished with effect from 22 June 1954, at which time he held the rank of Flight Lieutenant.

92 Squadron	Lt T S Horry DFC	Safe
SE.5a C8898		

T/o Thuilles for a cross-country flight but encountered driving snow and in attempting to forced-land crashed into a ploughed field near Mettet [Namur], 20 km SE of Charleroi. Thomas Stanley Horry was awarded the DFC as promulgated in *The London Gazette* 8 February 1919, supplement to issue 31170, page 2041: *'An officer of exceptional courage and daring. On 5th November, in face of driving rain and low clouds, he led his patrol far into enemy territory in order to engage enemy troops and transport that were retiring. Reaching his objective, he attacked the enemy with vigour, causing heavy casualties. He has in all destroyed three enemy aircraft and driven down out of control, and has, in addition, taken a leading part in the destruction of six others.'* Although not named in the initial promulgation of officers appointed to permanent commissions on 1 August 1919, an Air Ministry release of 28 October 1919, published the names of a further list of officers, including Thomas Horry, appointed to permanent commissions with seniority back-dated to 1 August 1919. On 4 June 1928, Flight Lieutenant Thomas Horry was awarded the AFC [LG 4 June 1928, supplement 33390, page 3862]. His service then continued until retirement, at his own request, on 16 November 1944, retaining the rank of Group Captain [LG 19 December 1944, second supplement 36844, page 5795]. Turning to *Flight,* he is mentioned in their issue of November 29, 1923, as transferring to Home Establishment on 13 October 1923, thus indicating he had recently served at an overseas location. On 12 February 1924, he was posted to Biggin Hill where he was attached to the Night Flying Flight, followed by a return overseas, this time to Iraq and 5 Armoured Car Company on 12 February 1926. As was common in many of these postings for a permanent officer, his ground tour was relatively brief and on 22 October of that same year, he resumed flying duties with 70 Squadron [Vickers Vernon/Victoria] at Hinaidi and it was during his time with 70 Squadron that he was awarded the AFC, as notified early in this summary. Still ranked Flight Lieutenant, he returned to England and on 3 September 1929, went to Martlesham Heath for duties with 22 Squadron which at the time was an integral part of the Aeroplane and Armament Experimental Establishment [15 Squadron was also so employed at this time]. By 4 October 1932, he was back at Hinaidi, this time attached to 55 Squadron [Wapiti IIA], but in less than a year he was home, this time to Duxford and Station Headquarters with effect from 4 July 1933. On 1 April 1937, promotion at last and as Squadron Leader he headed on the 24th to Dishforth and Flight Commander duties with 10 Squadron [Whitley I], where the squadron was visited by the magazine's Staff Reporter, Major F A de V Robertson who produced for *Flight's* November 18th, 1937, issue an excellent report on the squadron's role as a night-bomber unit, including several photographs of the Whitleys and the squadron's officers which show Wing Commander Graham flanked by his Flight Commanders, Squadron Leaders Horry and E B Steadman. In 1938, Squadron Leader Horry went out to Singapore where on 1 August, he became the first commander of 4 Anti-Aircraft Co-operation Unit at Seletar which was equipped with a variety of types including Vickers Vildebeest, an example being K2818 which is known to have been on its establishment in. 1938. He was promoted Wing Commander on 1 March 1940 [LG 12 March 1940, issue 34810, page 1472]. Although his date of death is unknown, his *Wikipedia* entry shows he was born in Boston, Lincolnshire on 21 May 1898.

| 110 Squadron | Lt H G Bennett | Safe |
| DH.9A E719 | | |

T/o Tardinghem carrying mail destined for Köln and wrecked in a crash-landing near Nivelles. Although not stated, I suspect weather was a factor.

| 208 Squadron | Lt Davidson | Safe |
| 7F.1 Snipe F2344 | | |

T/o Heumar reportedly to inspect a new location and damaged beyond repair in a crash near the German border town of Aachen.

APRIL
1919

At last, the weather began to show signs of improvement though spring did not witness the end of snow. Squadrons continued to submit accident returns on a regular basis but it was not until the 23rd that the first fatalities for the month were reported. As entries continue to show, squadrons employed on the Western Front came to the end of their duties. On return to the United Kingdom the majority were reduced to cadres while awaiting disbandment.

Tuesday 1 April 1919
The 1st anniversary of the formation of the Royal Air Force. Appropriate for the occasion, the military charity RAF Benevolent Fund was established by Chief of the Air Staff, Sir Hugh Trenchard.

Fierce fighting between Bolsheviks and Allied troops around Bolshie Ozerki continued; although heavily out-numbered well directed artillery and machine-gun fire held the Red forces at bay.

Wednesday 2 April 1919

| 88 Squadron | 2Lt T Blythe | Safe |
| Bristol F.2b E2474 | 2Lt H Bradbury | Safe |

T/o Nivelles for firing practice, an exercise which ended with a forced-landing near the aerodrome after the crew managed to shoot away the propeller!

Thursday 3 April 1919
The aviation magazine *Flight* in their issue for this day, on page 447, carried a poignant item originating from Mr Arthur Smith of Morningside, Aldershot, seeking information regarding his son, Captain Sydney Philip Smith, a Flight Commander with 46 Squadron, who *"was last seen on April 18th over Lamotte, flying a Camel O 6491. Will repatriated officers and men who can give information concerning this officer please write."* As can be read in my first volume, page 33, Captain Smith failed to return on the 6th of April 1918, and is commemorated on the Arras Flying Service Memorial.

| 6 Squadron | Lt A Turner | Safe |
| RE.8 C3008 | AC2 H J Bilbe | Safe |

T/o Sart for an air test and crashed on return.

20 Squadron   2Lt Knight   Safe
Bristol F.2b F4439   AC2 Creed   Injured
T/o Ossogne authorised for local flying practice but the Bristol's engine failed and a crash-landing resulted in a field close to the airfield.

57 Squadron   Lt E G Gaff   Safe
DH.9A E8572   Lt A S White   Safe
T/o Morville and reported to have crash-landed near Sorennes [sic]. Formerly of the Royal West Kent Regiment, Lieutenant Gaff relinquished his commission in the army having been appointed on 1 August 1919, to a permanent commission in the Royal Air Force [LG 26 March 1920, supplement 31838, page 3740]. However, on 7 January 1922, and now ranked Flying Officer, he resigned his permanent commission and was permitted to retain the rank of Lieutenant [*Flight* January 19, 1922].

Friday 4 April 1919
22 Squadron   Lt Lavery   Injured
Bristol F.2b E2269
T/o Nivelles for local flying but swung and went onto its nose before becoming airborne.

57 Squadron   2Lt H A Griffiths   Safe
DH.4 C4521   2Lt E C W Bray   Injured Unemployed list 18 November 1919
T/o Morville and landed at Bickendorf to pick up mail and it was while taking off that the DH came into collision with an RE.8 that was landing. It is almost a certainty that the RE was the 59 Squadron aircraft summarised below.

59 Squadron   Lt Johnson   Safe
RE.8 C2869   Lt Richardson   Safe
T/o Bickendorf for a practice sortie and wrecked in the manner described above.

70 Squadron   2Lt C L Hurst   Safe
7F.1 Snipe E8157
T/o Bickendorf for local flying practice and owing to a misjudged landing the Snipe was damaged beyond repair.

Saturday 5 April 1919
12 Squadron   Lt Frost   Safe
Bristol F.2b C9947 Lt Jenkins   Safe
T/o Duren for formation flying practice. On return landed on soft ground and, presumed, damaged beyond repair. The movement record for this aircraft is quite Spartan but it appears to have arrived in France during February 1919. Its date of issue to 12 Squadron is not recorded, the sole entry being the landing mishap, here reported.

18 Squadron   Lt E Peskett   Safe
DH.9A F1036   AC1 G Tunks   Safe
T/o Bickendorf for an air test and wrecked on return when an uneven landing was made, the DH touching down on its starboard wheel.

18 Squadron   Lt H R Leach   Safe   Unemployed list 21 April 1919
DH.9A F1046
T/o Bickendorf tasked for mail delivery duties but became lost and on landing at Flamesheim*where Lieutenant Leach intended to ascertain his position, he ran into a concealed dyke; damaged beyond repair.

* Possibly Euskirchen-Flamersheim [Nordrhein-Westfalen] and on the NW side of the Flamersheme Wald.

22 Squadron   Captain J M Heap   Safe   Commission relinquished 27 October 1919
Bristol F.2b D7908 2Lt H K Pople MC   Safe   Unemployed list 19 May 1919
T/o Nivelles for an air test but while running at speed Captain Heap eased the control column too far forward and by doing so the propeller struck the ground and swung the Bristol round with such force that it was damaged beyond repair. Both officers were badly shaken. Joseph Milne Heap's commission was relinquished owing to ill-health contracted while on active service; he was permitted to retain his rank. His observer had been seconded from the 4th Battalion, Somerset Light Infantry for duty with the Royal Air Force with effect from 7 November 1918 [LG 20 January 1919, supplement 31134, page 1052]. He returned to his battalion but relinquished his commission on 30 September 1921, under the terms of A.O. 166/21 as amended by A.O. 332/21 and granted the rank of Captain [LG 13 December 1921, supplement 32548, page 10207].

43 Squadron   Lt W H Statham   Safe   Unemployed list 21 April 1919
7F.1 Snipe E8321
T/o Bickendorf for a practice sortie and on return Lieutenant Statham, formerly of the Leicestershire Regiment, made a sharp turn to avoid running into the wreckage of a DH that had not been cleared from the landing area. In doing so, a wingtip brushed the ground sending the Snipe crashing out of control.

57 Squadron   Captain A MacGregor DFC Safe   Unemployed list 23 May 1919
DH.9A F1048   Captain J F D Tanqueray   Safe
T/o Morville for an air test and on return landed on uneven ground, bounced and turned over. Born at Glen Gyle, Scotland, on 25th October 1897, Andrew MacGregor's service began in April 1917, with the Argyll and Sutherland Highlanders but before the year was out he had transferred to the General List of the RFC, joining 57 Squadron at the same time [this suggests that his pilot training was carried out whilst with the Argylls], and on 1st May 1918, he was appointed a Flight Commander with the squadron. In the summer of 1919, he returned to the service and was one of many officers appointed to a permanent commission on the 1st of August. From then on his career followed the path of a permanent officer with postings as a pilot to a number of squadrons, along with the mandatory ground duties both at home and abroad. During the Second World War, and now of air rank, he was posted as Senior Air Staff Officer at 4 Group, Bomber Command, an appointment that he held between November 1940 and November 1942. This was followed by two years in the Mediterranean theatre, while his final post was as Air Officer Administration at Fighter Command. Retiring on 9th September 1949, Air-Vice Marshal Andrew MacGregor died at Glen Gyle on 24 October 1983. Returning to his *Great War* service with 57 Squadron, his DFC's citation, as reported in *The Edinburgh Gazette* April 11th, 1919, issue 13431, page 1442, reads: '*This officer has accounted for five enemy aircraft and has proved himself an exceptionally capable leader of patrols, notably on 14th August, when his formation of five machines was attacked by eight enemy aircraft. By his skilful leadership five of the latter were brought down without his own formation sustaining a single casualty.*'

70 Squadron   Sgt Lindsay   Safe
7F.1 Snipe E8263
T/o Bickendorf and wrecked here as a consequence of a misjudged landing.

207 Squadron   Lt R Pughe   Safe
HP O/400 C9676/J 2Lt S Pike   Safe   Commission relinquished 6 January 1920
T/o Guines tasked for a passenger flight to Hawkinge in Kent, but before becoming airborne the HP collided with a goalpost and was damaged beyond repair. 2nd Lieutenant Pike's health failed, hence the relinquishment of his commission. He was permitted to retain his rank.

Sunday 6 April 1919
18 Squadron   2Lt L R Haskell   Safe   Unemployed list 10 December 1919
DH.9A F1047
T/o Bickendorf for mail delivery duties and written off while landing at Maisoncelle.

88 Squadron   2Lt N L Head   Safe   Unemployed list 10 December 1919
Bristol F.2b D7942
T/o Nivelles for a cross-country sortie during which engine failure obliged 2nd Lieutenant Head to forced-land near Antwerpen.

216 Squadron   Lt S H Griffiths   Safe
HP O/400 D8319 Lt A C Taylor   Safe
              Mechanic Shephard   Safe
T/o Bickendorf carrying parcels of mail and damaged beyond repair after crashing into a hedge bordering the airfield at Ans. On 21st November 1918, Lieutenant Griffiths, then serving with 215 Squadron, crash-landed at Attainville in Val d'Oise.

Monday 7 April 1919
6 Squadron   Lt J G Bush   Safe
RE.8 C2964   2Lt F C Mildenhall   Safe   Unemployed list 7 June 1919
T/o Sart for an exercise in reconnaissance which went well until the crew returned to base and an unfortunate collision with trees during landing. Little is recorded in respect of C2964 apart from an entry on 22nd October 1918, when it was in storage at 2 Aeroplane Supply Depot. As far as I am able to report with any certainty, I believe this was the squadron's last accident before packing up and commence moving to Mesopotamia on the 14th. Since the armistice 6 Squadron had written off five RE.8s and a Bristol F.2b, the latter type now being surplus to requirement. Overseeing the move was Major George Clark Pirie MC who had commanded the squadron since July 1918, and who would be awarded a permanent commission on 1 August 1919, and eventually rise to air rank and retire as Air Chief Marshal Sir George Pirie KCB KBE MC DFC and a mention in a despatch. Born on 28 July 1896, his *Great War* service began as an officer in the 3rd Battalion, The Cameronians [Scottish Rifles] but by early March 1916, he was undergoing observer training, on completion of which he was attached to 2 Squadron, though within months he was back in training, this time as a potential pilot and on 6th November 1916, he reported to 34 Squadron, a Corps reconnaissance squadron operating their BEs from Allonville though soon to transfer to Italy where Gordon Pirie was appointed a Flight Commander. As has been reported on several occasions, his service as a permanent officer was a mixture of tours at home and abroad which for Gordon Pirie took him to the Middle East, India and in the summer of 1945, out to South East Asia. His final appointment ahead of retirement on 15 October 1951, was as Head of Royal Air Force Staff, British Joint Service Mission, Washington [he would have been very familiar with Washington for between October 1937 and August 1941,

he had been Britain's Air Attache in the United States]. Although I have yet to trace the citation for his MC, *The London Gazette* 28 October 1921, issue 32501, page 8496, carries the citation for his DFC: *'For great gallantry and good work, especially during operations in the relief of Diwaniyah and during our retirement to Hillah. This officer showed remarkable ability in quick initiative when leading his flight during operations. '*. Born on 28 July 1896, his death was announced on 21 January 1980.

| 49 Squadron | 2Lt W H Isted | Safe | Unemployed list 20 September 1919 |
| DH.9A H3467 | 2Lt D M Fraser | Safe | |

T/o Nivelles to return to the squadron's base at Bavai where owing to an error of judgement the DH crashed while landing. Tested at Yeovil [Westland Aircraft Works] on 20th February 1919, it was flown the next day to 5 Aeroplane Acceptance Park at Bristol, and was in squadron hands at sometime in March. I am reasonably confident that the pilot was William Henry Isted who was granted a commission in the Administrative and Special Duties Branch on 7th January 1942 [LG 24 February 1942, issue 35467, page 912], and who served until relinquishing his commission on 12th November 1946, retaining the rank of Flight Lieutenant [LG 18 February 1947, supplement 37883, page 802].

| 62 Squadron | Captain F G C Weare MC | Safe | |
| Bristol F.2b F4333 | Lt E G Holloway | Safe | |

T/o Nivelles for a cross-country and was totally wrecked following a crash in the Rhineland at Stolberg on the western side of Aix-le-Chapelle, more commonly referred to as Aachen. Biographies for the two officers are recorded on 7th January and 18th March respectively.

| 99 Squadron | 2Lt H W Atherton | Safe | Unemployed list 27 June 1919 |
| DH.9A E718 | Lt J S Fletcher-Watson | Safe | |

T/o Aulnoye for mail delivery duties; landed on rough ground at Clermont and damaged beyond repair. Army Form B.103 seems not to have survived for 2nd Lieutenant Atherton, but that for his observer shows that while serving with the Royal Garrison Artillery and attached to the 180th Siege Battery, his application for transfer to the Royal Air Force and train as an observer was accepted and he returned to England on the 19th of June 1918.

Returning to the Western Front on 29th October, he was attached to 52 Squadron [RE.8] at Avesnes-le-Sec and it was not until the 17th of January that he was posted in to 99 Squadron. On the 1st of May he was struck off the strength of the BEF with the departure of the squadron to India.

| 208 Squadron | 2Lt E K Dashwood | Safe | Unemployed list 4 November 1919 |
| 7F.1 Snipe E8129 | | | |

T/o Stree for a cross-country only to come to grief at Donstiennes where on landing it ran onto sloping ground, ballooned into the air and out of control hit the ground for a second time and turned over. 2nd Lieutenant Dashwood's movements since arriving at 2 Aeroplane Supply Depot on 6th October 1918, were fairly frequent. On the 11th he joined 85 Squadron [SE.5a] at Estrée-en-Chaussée and post-armistice he was temporarily attached to what appears to be *"5th Army RAF School on ....."*, rejoining 85 Squadron at Ascq on 6th January.

On the 8th of February, he came under the authority of 91 Wing at St. Omer and thence 24-hours later to 32 Squadron [SE.5a] at Serny. With the squadron leaving France for Tangmere on the 4th of March, 2nd Lieutenant Dashwood was attached to 2 Aircraft Depot from where on the 26th he was posted to 208 Squadron.

Eventually ending up with '208' in the Rhineland, he left Heumar on the 4th of August for the UK, his active service at an end.

Tuesday 8 April 1919

| 11 Squadron | 2Lt A K Doull | Safe | Unemployed list 1 August 1919 |
| Bristol F.2b C955 | Sgt L K Ward | Safe | |

T/o Nivelles for a formation flying exercise and crashed-landed near the Belgian capital. Unfortunately, apart from his rank, surname and initials, Army Form B.103 Part 1 has no information pertaining to his service.

| 11 Squadron | Lt C Simar | Safe | |
| Bristol F.2b E2554 | 2Lt Jackson | Safe | |

T/o Nivelles for local flying practice and crashed, owing to an error of judgement, during landing. Taken on charge from 2 Aeroplane Supply Depot on 17th September 1918, E2554 appears to have had a trouble free life until the incident here recorded. Regarding the crew, no supporting information has yet come to light.

57 Squadron	2Lt F de M Hyde	Safe	Unemployed list 18 January 1920
DH.9A F1100	New Zealand		
	Captain Todd	Safe	

T/o Sart with his passenger, Captain Todd, and set a course for Morville where on landing Frederick de Mulford Hyde failed to impress his senior officer by executing a landing with a force sufficient to throw the DH onto its back; fortunately, neither airman suffered serious injury.

Born on the 29th of December 1898, possibly in Hamilton in New Zealand's North Island, Frederick enlisted with the RFC on 13th October 1917, and joined the squadron on the last day of August 1918. Apart from the embarrassment of the incident, here outlined, his operational tour was uneventful and he left France for England a week or so after the squadron returned to South Carlton in readiness to disband.

However, although I have been able to find just this single reference to his time with 57 Squadron, *Flight* in its issue for 9th October, 1919, which replicates many of the entries published in *The London Gazette* of 30th September 1919, mentions him as being a recipient of the AFC which His Majesty had been pleased to approve for Lieutenant Hyde's distinguished services rendered during the war.

62 Squadron   2Lt N P B Giddens   Safe   Unemployed list 1 March 1920
Bristol F.2b E2408 2Lt F D R McLaren   Safe
T/o Nivelles for an air test and reported as *"smashed."* Between 14th October 1918, when he joined 20 Squadron [Bristol F.2b] at Moislains, 2nd Lieutenant Giddens and his departure to India on the 30th of April [he had been re-posted to 20 Squadron on the day of the crash], he had spent time in 14 General Hospital, followed on 27th March with a posting to 52 Squadron which was likely to have been an administrative error as 52 Squadron had by this time being reduced to a cadre and was back in the UK. Thus, on the 30th March, the posting order was amended to 62 Squadron which, as indicated, lasted until the day of the crash.

   2nd Lieutenant Fred Downie Rattray McLaren, Scotland born on 14th January 1900, rejoined the service in the Second World War and received a commission in the Training Branch on 30th April 1941 [LG 18 July 1941, issue 35222, page 4138] and served until relinquishing his commission on 10th October 1947, still ranked Pilot Officer [LG 4 November 1947, supplement 38115, page 5200].

84 Squadron   Lt H Egan   Safe
SE.5a E6008
T/o Thuilles for an air test. On return landed heavily and collapsed the undercarriage. E6008 arrived from 2 Aeroplane Supply Depot on 10th September 1918. Of Lieutenant Egan's service, I can find information whatsoever.

Wednesday 9 April 1919
48 Squadron   2Lt L C Taylor   Safe
Bristol F.2b E2430
T/o Sart amd on return to Bickendorf, 2nd Lieutenant Taylor [he had been with the squadron since the 14th of October 1918, so was now reasonably experienced] was confronted with a gale-force wind which made the landing extremely difficult to control and as a consequence he crashed-landed and damaged the Bristol beyond repair. On 7th May, he was posted to a holding camp to await demobilisation.

Thursday 10 April 1919
Although no reports of squadron casualties, it is noted that the Russian Spring Offensive was continuing with the fortunes of both opposing forces swaying back and forth.

Friday 11 April 1919
8 Squadron   Lt W J Tarring   Safe   Commission resigned 28 May 1946
Bristol F.2b C9873 2Lt H E Sheffield   Safe
T/o Bellevue with mail destined for St. Omer where it crashed during landing. Lieutenant Tarring's Record of Service contains merely his name, initials and rank; however, on the 26th of April 1941, a William John Tarring was granted a commission in the Training Branch [LG 4 July 1941, issue 35208, page 3841] and served until handing in his resignation, still in the rank of Pilot Officer.

   I fear it is a similar story regarding 2nd Lieutenant Sheffield. Army Form B.103-1 has been raised but merely notes his name, initials and rank.

20 Squadron   Lt Talbot   Safe
Bristol F.2b E2419 Lt Ford   Safe
T/o Ossogne for a practice flight and wrecked after landing and running onto uneven ground. In the absence of initials it has been impossible to identify either officer. The Bristol was issued from 2 Aeroplane Supply Depot on 26th September 1918, and until its demise had operated without incident.

216 Squadron   2Lt P McNaught   Safe
HP O/400 D4621 2Lt D E Haighton   Safe   Unemployed list 18 June 1919
T/o Marquise with a consignment of mail and totally wrecked in a crash-landing at Roubrouck [Liège]. Although little is known of 2nd Lieutenant McNaught's early service, a second service record has been raised which shows that he rejoined the squadron at Ismailia on 4th November 1919, having disembarked from the HMT *Caledonian.* He was now ranked Pilot Officer. However, his time in the Middle East lasted for just on three months and on the 20th of February he embarked on the HMT *Kural* at Alexandria and sailed for England.

   A single Record of Service exists for Donald Edward Haighton but it merely shows he was born on 9th of February 1900, and that his parents resided in Crewe Road, Nantwich, Cheshire.

Saturday 12 April 1919
208 Squadron   Lt E Jackson   Injured
7F.1 Snipe E8143
T/o Stree for the purpose of inspecting what the accident report describes as a *"new location"* but, it seems, Edwin Jackson encountered lowering visibility accompanied by heavy raid and as a result he failed to see he was on a collision

course with a line of trees into whose tops he flew. He was down, injured though to what extent is not recorded, some fifteen km SE of Verviers [Liège] which, if the distance given is correct would place the crash in the vicinity of wooded countryside around Belle Croix. This was his second accident, the first being on the 11th of February.

Born of 15th June 1893, it appears at the time of his enlistment with the RFC on 28th August 1917, he had married, his wife living at 36 Theobold Road, Leyton, London E.10. His operational flying got off to a slow start for although he joined 80 Squadron [Camel] at La Bellevue on June 1st, 1918, within a week he had been admitted to 8 General Hospital and thence to 51 General Hospital with an illness that kept him grounded until his discharge to 1 Aeroplane Supply Depot on 30th August.

From here he was ordered to join 208 Squadron [Camel] at Tramecourt on 4th September. His service records indicate two periods of leave, one prior to Christmas and the second from the 18th to the end of March. The last entry shows the date of his accident and although it is conjecture on my part I suspect he was returned to England soon after.

Sunday 13 April 1919
This must be regarded as one of the most inglorious days as far as the British Army in British India is concerned for at Amritsar in the Punjab, British and Gurkha soldiers under the command of Acting Brigadier-General Reginald Edward Harry Dyer [his substantive rank was Colonel] were ordered to open fire on a crowd, estimated from anywhere between 10,000 and 20,000 that had gathered for an illegal public meeting at Jallianwala Bagh; a total of at least three hundred and seventy-nine Sikhs were killed and many more lay injured in the panic that following the first shots.

Subsequently removed from his post, Colonel Dyer was allowed to leave the army without any formal reprimand for his actions. Settling in England, he died following a series of strokes at his cottage at Long Ashton in Somerset on the 24th of July 1927, aged sixty-two.

17 Squadron	Major S G Hodges MC AFC	Safe	Commission resigned 16 March 1920
DH.9 C6312	South Africa		
	2Lt H A Fourte	Safe	Unemployed list 22 November 1919

T/o San Stephano for a demonstration flight which, unfortunately, ended with the DH damaged beyond repair. An entry in *The London Gazette* 9th November 1917, supplement 30373, page 11572, under the heading *"Sqdn. Comdr."* shows *"2nd Lt [temp Capt] S G Hodges MC Wilts R. From a Flight Comdr. and to be temp Maj whilst so empld 19 Oct 1917,"* while the paper's issue for 30 September 1921, supplement 32474, page 7745, carries the following: *"Wilts R, Lt S G Hodges MC AFC resigns his commn. on appt. to a permanent commn. in the R A F 1st Aug. 1919."* It seems, however, his service as a permanent officer was short-lived for *Flight* in its issue for April 29, 1920, shows he resigned his commission, while ranked Squadron Leader on 16 March 1920. His death, in most unusual circumstances, was reported in *Flight* January 25, 1934,*under the heading : *"An Imperial Airways Loss."* At the time Major Swithin Gane Hodges was the airline's Station Superintendent at Broken Hill, South Africa, where he recently suffered an embolism in one of his knees and was told by his doctor that the affected leg would have to be amputated, the procedure to be carried out in Johannesburg. Thus, it came to pass he was on a flight to the city when he collapsed and died between Pietersburg and Germiston. The report notes that in addition to his honours shown above, he had been awarded a *Croix de Guerre,* the Greek Medal of Military Merit and had been mentioned in a despatch. His military service had been extensive with operational duties in Egypt, Macedonia, Russia, Bulgaria, Turkey, Palestine and France. The report ends: *"His loss will be keenly felt by all air travellers in South Africa."* Turning to my copies [facsimile] of the Wiltshire Regiments war diaries, the index for the 1st Battalion is devoid of any entry for S G Hodges, while, unfortunately, the diary for the 2nd Battalion is restricted to date entries only and has no index.

* I am indebted to researcher Di Ablewhite for kindly drawing my attention to the *Flight* issue of January 1934, and in addition to forwarding a copy of AIR 76/232/97 which is held at The National Archives showing hand-written notes pertaining to his military service. Unfortunately, although it is noted that he had been awarded the MC and AFC, and that his former service had been with the Wiltshire Regiment, there is nothing to guide a researcher to the citations for his decorations. The file confirms his South African heritage and that he was born on 21 April 1892; also notes as to the units on which he served and remarks confirming his appointment to a permanent commission and the resignation of his commission in the Wiltshire Regiment, though, frustratingly, to which battalion is not recorded.

Monday 14 April 1919
At Sart in Belgium, 6 Squadron began moving with their RE.8s to Mesopotamia, their Bristol F.2bs being left behind, though it would be three months before the move to Mesopotamia would be completed. Interestingly, however, there is a casualty return for this day from the squadron indicating Bristol F.2b F4472 forced-landed at St. Andre while *'on special duty'*, the crew being identified as Lieutenant J Owen and Major Ford.

7 Squadron	2Lt Edwards	Safe
Bristol F.2b E2440	2Lt Boyd	Safe

T/o Spich to practice flying in cloud. On return, and in strong winds, the Bristol turned over.

Tuesday 15 April 1919
Tensions in British India were still running high following the shooting by British and Gurkha troops at Amritsar and such was his concern that Brigadier-General N D K MacEwen, commanding Royal Air Force formations in British India, sanctioned the use of aircraft to assist the police in quelling unrest in Gujiranwala where the population was much

angered on learning of the killing of Sikhs. Aircraft were armed with bombs and in addition machine-gun fire from Lewis guns were employed, leaving a dozen civilians dead and nearly thirty wounded.

Note. What took place on that fateful Sunday in April 1919, was witnessed by an ardent nationalist, namely Udham Singh. Determined to take revenge for the massacre of his fellow countrymen he decided that the main culprit was the Lieutenant Governor of the Punjab, Michael O'Dwyer and it was on Wednesday. 13th March 1940, at London's Caxton Hall that Udham Singh fired a number of rounds at what *The Times* describes as *"a group of eminent men;"* O'Dwyer fell, mortally wounded, and three others were wounded, including the Secretary of State for India, Lord Zetland.
   Udham Singh was hanged in Pentonville Prison on the last day of July 1940.

99 Squadron	Captain W D Thom	Safe	
DH.9A E8509			

T/o Aulnoye carrying mail and crash-landed on Sart airfield.

Friday 18 April 1919

110 Squadron	Lt G A Walker	Safe	
DH.9A H3437	Lt H S Cook	Safe	

Took off Tardinghem with mail and wrecked in a crash-landing at Weiden*near Aachen.

* It is almost a certainty that the crew were making for Bickendorf and though I cannot find Weiden near Aachen there is such a location on the Western outskirts of Köln.

Saturday 19 April 1919

9 Squadron	Captain J McBain	Injured	
Bristol F.2b C9242	Lt J A Williams	Safe	

T/o Ludendorf for formation flying and reconnaissance during which the Bristol's engine failed, resulting in a heavy crash-landing on the airfield. The wreckage was deposited with 8 Salvage Section.

Sunday 20 April 1919

92 Squadron	Lt Flynn	Safe	
SE.5a B8331			

T/o Thuilles for a cross-country flight. On return the strength of the wind had increased and on landing the undercarriage collapsed followed by a strong gust blowing the SE onto its back.

Monday 21 April 1919

12 Squadron	Lt J B Purefoy mid	Safe	Unemployed list 3 November 1919
Bristol F.2b E2233	Lt Taylor	Safe	

T/o Duren for an air test and on return, and just about to land, the engine cut swinging the Bristol out of control, its left mainplanes striking some trees. Lieutenant Purefoy was one of hundreds of officers and airmen whose names were brought to the notice of the Secretary of State for Air by Field-Marshal Sir Douglas Haig as having served under his Command between 16 September 1918, and 15 March 1919: *"whose distinguished and gallant services and devotion to duty he considered deserving of special mention."* *Flight* July 31, 1919, pages 1018, 1019 and 1020, under the heading *"Mentioned in Despatches."*

49 Squadron	Lt J N Bitton	Safe	Unemployed list 9 September 1919
DH.9 E623	Lt H Taylor MC	Safe	

T/o Bavai for flying practice and crashed on landing. On establishment since the last day of July 1918, this DH had seen action aplenty with claims for four enemy scouts in hard-fought combats. The first claim, lodged on 24 August by Lieutenant M D Allen and 2nd Lieutenant W A Owens, was for a Pfalz which sported a red tail and yellow wings sent down in the late afternoon West of Forêt de Mormal. In total it was estimated the squadron had to fight off upwards of forty scouts as they headed back to Beauvois; the following evening, Allen, this time with Lieutenant F Maudesley as his observer fought with scouts over Moeuvres [Nord] which left his observer wounded. Promoted Captain, Allen, now reunited with 2nd Lieutenant Owens, accounted for a trio of Fokker DVIIs between 9 October and 4 November, their final victim going down near Blangy burning furiously.

66 Squadron	Captain H K Goode DSO DFC Injured Resigned commission 15 December 1941		
Avro 504K D7789	Sgt T W Cockerill	+	New Malton Cemetery

T/o Yatesbury for local flying during which the Avro went into a spin and crashed. Reduced to a cadre, this was the squadron's first serious accident since arriving at Yatesbury from San Pietro in Italy on the 10th of March. Thomas Wray Cockerill's service number 25416 suggests he enlisted circa 1917. Harry King Goode, whom I summarise in my second volume on page 92, escaped with a broken wrist. Additional to the information reported in that summary, the citations for his awards are as follows: *'A brilliant fighting pilot who sets a fine example of courage and determination to the officers of his squadron. He has destroyed six enemy aeroplanes and two kite balloons'* [LG 3 December 1918, supplement 31046, page 14321] and: *'During the recent operations this officer has displayed magnificent courage and determination in attacking enemy aerodromes, kite balloons and retreating columns inflicting very heavy loss. On 29th October he led two other machines in a bombing raid against an enemy aerodrome; he completely destroyed with a* *bomb one hostile machine on the ground, and, attacking the hangars and workshops with machine-gun fire, he caused many casualties amongst the mechanics. Later on in the same day he returned alone to attack the same aerodrome, and found the enemy about to evacuate it. Flying at a very low altitude - at times his wheels almost touched the ground - he destroyed one machine with a bomb and set fire to another with machine-gun fire. The enemy personnel were driven back into the village by the vigour of his attack. Captain Goode's utter disregard of personal danger inspired all who served with him.'* [LG 7 February 1919, issue 31770, pages 2031 and 2032]. Both honours were gained when his substantive rank was 2nd Lieutenant but holding the acting rank of Captain. Subsequently, he was granted, along with many others, a permanent commission on 1 August 1919, and from then on until he resigned his commission on 15th December 1941, his career followed the channels of all permanent officers with spells at home and abroad. His overseas postings included India and various stations in the Middle East, including Heliopolis and Helwan where he was attached to 47 Squadron [DH.9A]. One of the highlights of his pre-Second World War service came in April 1939, when he flew General Viscount Gort VC, then Chief of the Imperial General Staff*on an inspection tour of the Maginot Line, a defensive barrier which in the advent of the German *Blitzkrieg* of May 1940, proved totally ineffective against the armoured offensive of the Wehrmacht. On 1 March 1941, he was promoted Group Captain, taking command of 60 Operational Training Unit at Leconfield, later moving to East Fortune in Scotland, from where he left the service to take up a position with the Accident Investigation Board, and it was while so in post that he was killed on 21st August 1942, when a 120 Squadron Liberator III LV340 /X in which he was a passenger crashed while in transit from the squadron's base at Ballykelly to Nutts Corner. Weather conditions at the time were poor with a persistent mist which hampered visibility and this may well have been a contributory cause when the bomber flew into Limnalary Mountain, Gortnacory, in County Antrim. Group Captain Harry King Goode DSO DFC AFC is buried in Tamlaght Finlagen Church of Ireland Churchyard, his epitaph reads: *"God Is Light, And In Him Is No Darkness At All."* He was 47 years of age.

Note. There are 17 burials in Tamlagaht Finlagen churchyard and apart from Private Jean McCarron, a local girl who died postwar while serving with the Auxiliary Territorial Service, all are airmen and include two who died with Group Captain Goode. They are identified as Sergeant Arnolous Bothma Meyer [no next of kin details, but his service No 776185 indicates enlistment in the Middle East circa July 1940], second pilot to the aircraft's captain, Pilot Officer Michael Franci Dear who was cremated in Liverpool's Anfield Crematorium, and New Zealand born, Sergeant Thomas William Taylor RNZAF, whom Errol Martyn, in his first volume dedicated to New Zealand's airmen who died, identifies as having flown sixteen operational sorties.

* Born 10 July 1886, Field Marshal Viscount Gort was appointed by the Prime Minister, Neville Chamberlain, in September 1939, as Commander-in-Chief of the British Expeditionary Force in France, a post that he held until 1st June 1940, having overseen the evacuation of his forces from Dunkirk. On his return to England, Winston Churchill, who had replaced Neville Chamberlain as Prime Minister, consider Gort to be unsuited for any further field command. His final post was as High Commissioner for Palestine and Transjordan by which time his health was failing and he died in Guy's Hospital on 31 March 1946, at the relatively early age of 59, from cancer of the liver. He rests in the Sidney family vault at St. John The Baptist Church at Penshurst, Kent.

70 Squadron   Captain O A P Heron   Safe   Unemployed list 10 August 1919
7F.1 Snipe E8198 DFC *Croix de Guerre* Belgium
T/o Bickendorf for a cross-country exercise in the course of which one of the undercarriage wheels fell off. Crash-landed on return. Considerable information in respect of Oscar Aloysius Patrick Heron is imparted in my summary for a squadron Camel D6696 on Thursday 28th November 1918. Born in Ireland on 17th September 1896, his military service prior to becoming a pilot was with the Connaught Rangers but it was his air force service that his fighting spirit came to the fore. Between the evening of 30th June and the late morning of 28th October, thirteen enemy aircraft of various types fell to his aim, though some were shared with fellow pilots. The citation for his DFC [LG 8 February 1919, issue 31170, page 2041] reads: *'An officer conspicuous for his skill and daring in aerial combats. On 28th September* [Camel F.1 D6696] *he attacked, single-handed, three Fokkers, one of these he shot down. On another occasion he, in company with five other machines, engaged six Fokkers, all six being destroyed, 2nd Lt Heron accounting for two.'* His *Croix de Guerre* was *Gazetted* in the Edinburgh edition, 22 July 1919, issue 13476, page 2457. Within a couple of months of being placed on the unemployed list, he was offered a short service commission, which he accepted and though of relatively of short duration he enjoyed a spell of duty in India where he was attached to 3 Squadron at Ambala flying Sopwith Snipes. On his return, and reversion to the Reserve of Air Force Officers, Oscar went back to Ireland and joined the National Army Service which in 1924 was retitled the Air Corps. For much of his time he was based at Baldonnel Airfield and employed as a flying instructor, during which he which he relinquished his Royal Air Force commission [LG 9 November 1926, supplement 33219, page 7258].

Seven years later, and in the August of 1933, the Air Corps held its first Pageant at Phoenix Park, Dublin, where on the 2nd during practice his great friend, Lieutenant J P Twohig, was killed following a midair collision, his funeral being held on the 5th, Oscar being one of the pall bearers. That same afternoon he was airborne in a Vickers Vespa V6, accompanied by Private Robert Tobin who was to act as his air gunner in the mock-fight with a trio of Avro Cadets. To the applause of the crowd, which included Oscar's wife, all appeared to be going well and as a final flourish to end the display the Vespa flew at speed over the park at around 500 feet; then, without hint of warning it suddenly went into a spinning nosedive and crashed into the ground, inverted. Many rushed to the scene [thankfully there was no fire] but for this popular and very experienced pilot his life was over and a few days later he was laid to rest by his fellow officers in

Glasnevin Cemetery. Robert Tobin was alive, but critically injured and despite the best efforts of the doctors and nurses he died the following day.

A brief biography of this gallant Irishman who served with such distinction in the *Great War* is published along with an accompanying photograph between pages 216 and 218 of Norman Franks' *Fallen Eagles*.

Tuesday 22 April 1919

11 Squadron	Lt J P Cox	Safe	
Bristol F.2b E2565	Lt P C Bayley	Safe	Unemployed list 6 December 1919

T/o Nivelles for what is described on the accident report as a *"travelling flight"* but before reaching flying speed a wheel dropped into a hole; probably damaged beyond repair as a result. Apart from his rank, surname and initials, Lieutenant Cox's Record of Service is a blank, while that his observer appears to have been lost in the mists of time.

Wednesday 23 April 1919

6 Squadron	Captain H J Hunter	Safe
Bristol F.2b F4470		

T/o Sart with the intention of ferrying the Bristol to 6 Air Issues but turned back with a failing engine and crashed while attempting to land.

84 Squadron	Sgt R E Surman	Safe
SE.5a H692		

T/o Thuilles for local flying but owing to an error of judgement crashed before becoming airborne.

97 Squadron	Lt C F Hunt	+	Richmond Cemetery, Surrey
DH.10 E5444			

T/o Ford for practice flying during which 20 year old Cyril Frank Hunt lost control and spun into the ground. His epitaph reads: *"Killed While Flying At Ford Yet He Died For England's Sake."* This was the squadron's first fatal accident since arriving at Ford from Saint Inglevert on 4 March, and converting from HP O/400 to DH.10. Although of de Havilland lineage, E5444 was from an order of 100 airframes built by Avro, not all, according to Bruce Robertson's compilation of *British Military Aircraft Serials 1878 - 1987,* delivered to service. Cyril Frank Hunt was commissioned to the General List of the Royal Flying Corps on 20 April 1917 [LG 6 June 1917, supplement 30117, page 5604].

99 Squadron	2Lt D C Bain	Safe	Unemployed list 2 May 1919
DH.9A E706	AC1 A Mace	+	Cabaret-Rouge British Cemetery, Souchez
	LAC F J Clark	Injured	
	AC1 C R Peploe	+	Cabaret-Rouge British Cemetery, Souchez
	Mechanic C G Lincox	Injured	
	Mechanic J McCallum	Injured	
	Mechanic J O'Donnell	Injured	

T/o Aulnoye and headed for 6 Air Issues where on arrival 2nd Lieutenant Bain realised he was in danger of over-shooting the landing area. Deciding to go round again he opened the throttle, but choked the engine and to his horror he hit the side of hangar where a group of airmen were working. He had been involved in an accident on the 25th of February.

The aftermath of this awful tragedy left two airmen killed and four injured. Aircraftman Mace had enlisted in the RFC in 1913. His squadron details, and those for Aircraftman Peploe, show he belonged to 6 Squadron.

Thursday 24 April 1919

In their issue of this day *Flight* magazine names three recently repatriated officers; Captain C T Porter and Lieutenants D H Macintyre and K G W Withers. I have not located a Record of Service for Captain Porter, but Army Form B.103 for Lieutenant Macintyre of 11 Squadron shows he was reported missing on 9th July 1916, when he failed to return to Bertangles. Referring to Trevor Henshaw's magnificent *The Sky Their Battlefield,* I discover on page 43 that he was piloting a FE.2b 6952 and was shot down by a Fokker scout to crash near Beaulincourt. The combat left him and his observer, 2nd Lieutenant H Floyd, wounded, the latter dying from his injuries on the 11th. I have had no fortune in tracing details for Lieutenant Withers via Army Form B.103.

However, Captain C T Porter is almost certain to be Captain G T Porter recorded on page 27 of the above named title and who was made a prisoner of war on 27th December 1915, when his 2 Squadron Bristol Scout C4673 went down west of Lille with engine failure. To prevent it from falling into enemy hands, Captain Porter managed to set the Scout on fire.

Using the same source, Lieutenant Withers is shown in the index as being made a prisoner of war on the 17th of October 1918, but I can find no supporting detail in either *The Sky Their Battlefield* or in my second volume.

22 Squadron	Lt Col Strange	Safe
Bristol F.2b E2615		

T/o Nivelles and headed for Bickendorf only to encounter adverse weather and crashed-landed at Cognelée airfield. Eleven Record of Service forms have survived for officers with the surname Strange, one of which is for Lieutenant-Colonel Louis Arbon Strange, formerly of the Dorset Regiment.

Reverting to *The London Gazette* issue 28762, page 6984, of the 7th of October 1913, beneath the heading Royal Flying Corps - Military Wing shows *"Louis Arbon Strange to be Second Lieutenant [on probation]. Dated 8th October, 1913."*

Returning to his Army Form B.103, which has not been fully digitised, shows:-

Embarked 16.8.14

	Arrived in England on leave till	*12.12.14*	*AWO 173*
	By air	*16.12.14*	*AWO 132*
	Rejoined from leave	*19.12.14*	*B.213 RO 164*
17.2.15	*"Mentioned in Despatches"*		*Ldn Gaz*
27.3.15	*Granted the "Military Cross"*		*Lists 20*
	Granted leave from	*2.4.15*	*B.213 RO 337*
	Rejoined from leave	*7.4.15*	*B.213 RO 350*
	To RFC in England	*31.7.15*	*B.213*
	Re-embarked		
21.9.15 16 Sqn	*To RFC in England*	*19.9.15*	*B.213*

This being the final entry on the surviving form. However, the *Gazette* enables me to map out some of his operational service which shows he was very much a hands-on officer. The citation for his MC is presently untraced but that for his DFC was published in the paper's edition of 2 November 1918, supplement 30989, page 12974: *'To this officer must be given the main credit of the complete success attained in two recent bombing raids on important enemy aerodromes. In organising these raids his careful attention to detail and well-thought-out plans were most creditable. During the operations themselves his gallantry in attack and fine leadership inspired all those taking part.'*

This was followed on 7th February 1919, issue 31170, pages 2032 and 2033, for the citation for his richly deserved award of the DSO: *'For his exceptional services in organising his wing and brilliant leadership on low bombing raids this officer was awarded the Distinguished Flying Cross not long ago. Since then, and by his fine example and inspiring personal influence, he has raised his wing to still higher efficiency and morale, the enthusiasm displayed by the various squadrons for low-flying raids has been most marked. On 30th October he accompanied one of these raids against an aerodrome; watching the work of his machines, he waited until they had finished and then dropped his bombs from one hundred feet altitude on hangars that were undamaged; he then attacked troops and transport in the vicinity of the aero-drome. While thus engaged he saw eight Fokkers flying above him; at once he climbed and attacked them single-handed; having driven one down out of control he was fiercely engaged by the other seven, but he maintained the combat until rescued by a patrol of our scouts.'*

Turning to Alex Henshaw's *The Sky Their Battlefield,* Alex, in his introduction to the 30th October 1918, page 241, reports the 30th as *'the heaviest day of fighting of the war'* and in his lengthy analysis comes to the part involving the squadrons of the X Brigade, operating with the Fifth Army, north of the First Army. A morning reconnaissance had detected a great deal of enemy activity at Rebaix aerodrome and the outcome was a decision taken to commit every squadron in the 80th Wing to bombing this key target. Thus, in the early afternoon a total of sixty-two aircraft took off led by Louis Strange in his personal Camel D1943. It was the single largest attack of the day and resulted in consider-able damage to the aerodrome and at least nine enemy fighters driven down. Returning to their airfields, the force overflew columns of retreating troops and transports which were heavily engaged by Lewis fire, thus adding to the general carnage.

Come the Second World War and this indomitable officer returned to the air force and was granted a commission in the Equipment Branch, effective 18th April 1940 [LG 7 May 1940, issue 34844, page 2726] and within weeks of his return he added a First Bar to the DFC won two decades earlier: *'Pilot Officer Strange was detailed to proceed from Hendon to Merville to act as ground control officer during the arrival and departure of various aircraft carrying food supplies. He displayed great skill and determination whilst under heavy bombing attacks and machine-gun fire at Merville, where he was responsible for the repair and successful despatch of two aircraft to England. In the last remaining aircraft, which was repaired under his supervision, he returned to Hendon, in spite of being repeatedly attacked by Messerschmitts until well out to sea. He had no guns in action and had never flown this type of aircraft previously, but his brilliant piloting enabled him to return with this much needed aircraft.'*

One other honour came his way when postwar he was conferred by the President of the United States [Harry S Truman] the Bronze Star Medal [LG 15 March 1946, supplement 37501, page 1380]. By this time he had been made a Member of the Order of the British Empire in the New Year's Honour's list of 1945.

Born in the Dorset village of Tarrant Keynsham on 27th July 1891, to farming stock, he retained a pilot's licence and for several years owned and flew a Taylorcraft Auster Plus D G-AHCR. Sadly, in his declining years his health failed and his death in Poole was announced on the 15th November 1966, at the age of 75.

Part of him possibly lives on through his ownership of G-AHCR for this venerable aeroplane is believed to be still current having being restored by Edward H Gould of Bedchester near Shaftesbury.

99 Squadron	2Lt V C Varcoe	Safe	Unemployed list 30 April 1919
DH.9A H3410	2Lt P G Addie	Safe	Unemployed list 2 May 1919

T/o Aulnoye loaded with mail and wrecked following engine failure which occurred at 500 feet, coming down in a ploughed field near Dousois [sic]. Born, probably in Launeston, Chorleywood in Hertfordshire on the 4th of July 1899, Vivian Charles Varcoe was appointed as a 2nd Lieutenant on the 8th of November 1917 [LG 14 November 1917, supplement 30379, page 11759]. He joined the squadron at Azelot on 19th September 1918, departing to a holding camp on the 25th of April 1919, from where he crossed the Channel four days later.

With threatening for a second time he returned to the air force and was commissioned to the Administrative and Special Duties Branch on 18th September 1939 [LG 25 April 1939, issue 34619, page 2758]. His second spell in uniform far outstripped his first and when relinquishing his commission on 7th September 1954, under the provisions of the Navy, Army and Air Force Reserves Act, 1954, he was ranked 'Wing Commander'.

Peter George Addie's service was not dissimilar; his appointment from 21st October 1917, was *Gazetted* on the 1st of November 1917, supplement 30361, page 11279. Postwar his name appears under the heading Reserve of Air Force Officers, his service encompassing the years 6th April 1924 to 15th May 1926, as reported in issue 32931, page 3430 of 29th April 1924 and 4th June 1926, issue 33169, page 3657.

During the Second World War, I suspect he assisted with the Air Training Corps as he was commissioned as a Pilot Officer in the Training Branch, serving from the 1st of February 1941 to the 19th of June 1943, the relevant entries being 9th May 1941, issue 35158, page 2680 and 6th July 1943, supplement 36079, page 3044.

208 Squadron	Lt C R Davidson	Injured
7F.1 Snipe E8132		

T/o Stree and crashed at Donstiennes airfield whilst on a practice flight.

Friday 25 April 1919

88 Squadron	Lt R J Twilton	+	Marcinelle New Communal Cemetery
Bristol F.2b E2649	Sgt P Gaillard	+	
	Belgium		

T/o Nivelles for local flying practice and totally destroyed in a crash on the aerodrome. Born on the 10th of October 1895, Reginald John Twilton reported to the squadron at Serny on the 19th of October 1918. He had recently returned from a fortnight's leave; his epitaph reads: *"God Takes Our Loved Ones From Our Homes But Never From Our Hearts."*

Saturday 26 April 1919

18 Squadron	2Lt K E M Holmes	Safe
DH.9A E8578		

T/o Bickendorf for mail delivery duties and damaged beyond repair at Maisoncelle after landing on soft ground and nosing over, smashing the propeller and distorting the engine bearers.

Kenneth England Maxwell Holmes was born on 26th June 1898, and lived at Millon Road, Hornsea in East Yorkshire. He had served with the squadron since the 6th of October 1918, and returned home from Merhaim on the 7th of May 1919. Apart from this incident, his tour of air force duty appears to have been, by war standards, fairly mundane, but I daresay his time with the Royal Garrison Artillery had been far from quiet. After returning to the army he relinquished his commission, as *Gazetted* on 22nd December 1921, supplement 32557, page 10482.

Sunday 27 April 1919

18 Squadron	2Lt J A Watton	Safe	
DH.9A E8508	2Lt W G Perry	Safe	Unemployed list 9 May 1919

T/o Bickendorf with a consignment of post and while flying in the vicinity of Thuilles airfield the engine seized through lack of water. Crashed-landed near Thuilles in a field that had recently been put to the plough. I have yet to find a record of service for the pilot, but that for William Garfield Perry shows his birth as the 12th of March 1900, and his next of kin address as 34 Reservoir Road in the Edgbaston district of Birmingham. He joined the Royal Air Force soon after his 18th birthday, reporting for duty on the 22nd of April, and on completion of his training was posted to 205 Squadron [DH.9] at Proyart East on 20th September. He arrived at Bickendorf on the 17th of March and departed Merheim for the UK on the 3rd of May, soon to join the ranks of the unemployed.

142 Squadron	Lt H M Fletcher	Safe
DH.9 D573	Mechanic Johnson	Safe

T/o Port Said for an undisclosed task and reported as *"crashed."*

Monday 28 April 1919

Considering the importance of Bickendorf aerodrome near Köln, it is somewhat surprising that it has received scant mention in the aviation press. *Flight*, a leading aviation magazine of the time, mentions it but once and this was in the context of two photographs showing the King and Queen of Belgium at Bickendorf in the company of General Sir William Robertson CGB, Commander-in-Chief of the British Army on the Rhine.

The trio are standing by the rear fuselage of a DH.9 which from what is visible has an F block serial - F12... Consulting *The DH.4/DH.9 File* three DH.9s F1204, F1275 and F1293 were sold to the Belgian Government, so it is likely that the royal couple were using one of these.

The Aerodrome website, which I acknowledge, reports Bickendorf between June and August 1919 was base for the Royal Air Force Meteorological Flight, initially equipped with DH.9s which were soon replaced by Bristol F.2bs.

Other websites mention the aerodrome, several of which indicate it later became Butzweilerhof where the author of this series was stationed between 1956 and 1958.

49 Squadron	2Lt J Turner	Safe
DH.9A E8486	Lt J N Britton	Safe

T/o Bavai for local flying but within seconds of becoming airborne came down just beyond the airfield after the engine suddenly lost power. I am reasonably confident the observer is James Nimmo Britton who was granted a commission in the Administrative and Special Duties Branch on 5th July 1940 [LG 30 July 1940, issue 34910, page 4680] and relinquishing this, while holding Wing Commander rank, under the provisions of the Navy, Army and Air Force Reserves Act, 1954.

Tuesday 29 April 1919

8 Squadron   Lt Weaver   Safe

Bristol F.2b E2161

T/o Bellevue with an unnamed passenger who was to join 22 Squadron at Nivelles. On arrival here the Bristol landed safely but moments later fell onto a sunken pathway and was damaged beyond repair.

9 Squadron   Lt Bell   Injured

RE.8 D4936

T/o Ludendorf for circuits and landings but got into difficulties and from a fairly low altitude spun to the ground.

70 Squadron   2Lt C W Pattison   Safe   Unemployed list 13 November 1919

7F.1 Snipe E8325

T/o Bickendorf for local flying and damaged beyond repair following a misjudged landing. A Record of Service has been raised for this officer but apart from his rank, name and initials nothing else has been appended.

Wednesday 30 April 1919

208 Squadron   Major C E Bryant   Safe

Fokker DVII 6539

T/o Denstiennes to assess the flying characteristics of this formidable German fighter. All went well until Major Bryant came into land when he realised he was on a collision course with a line of telegraph wires; pulling up sharply he stalled and crashed. Two Record of Service forms exist for this officer, who was formerly of the 11th Hussars, though one only contains details of name and rank. The second has entries up to July 1917, and these I show as follows:-

16.12.16	*Posted to No 23 Squadron*	*2.12.16*	*B.213 23 Sqdn*
11.1.17	*To be Flight Commander*	*22.12.16*	*LG*
13.1.17	*Appointed Actg F/Comdr*	*22.12.16*	*B.213 23 Sqdn*
10.2.17	*Leave 9.2.17 to 23.2.17*		*" "*
7.4.17	*Posted to 18 Sqdn*	*5.4.17*	*" 18 Sqdn*
23.5.17	*Award Bar to DSO*		*RO 973 HQ*
9.6.17	*Leave 3.6.17 to 17.6.17*		*B.213 18 Sqdn*
15.7.17	*To Home Establishment*	*8.7.17*	
16.8.17	*Appointed Sqdn Comdr*	*9.7.17*	*LG*

Turning to the *Gazette* of 18th February 1915, supplement 29074, page 1689, this announces the award of the DSO but the citation has not been reported. However, the citation to the First Bar is reported: *'For conspicuous gallantry and devotion to duty. He has displayed the utmost gallantry and skill in leading photographic reconnaissances. In spite of overwhelming opposition by hostile aircraft, he has never failed to carry out his difficult task.'* [LG 18 July 1917, supplement 30188, page 7209].

    The next entry of importance was published on 21st September 1918, supplement 30913, page 11259, recorded his award of the *Croix de Guerre,* and this was followed on the 3rd of June 1919, supplement 31378, page 7040, by: *'The undermentioned officers and other ranks of the Royal Air Force have been mentioned in Despatches and Reports received in the Air Ministry for valuable services rendered during the war - Major Charles Edgar Bryant DSO [France].'*

    In the Second World War he received a commission in the Administrative and Special Duties Branch with seniority from 17th June 1940 [LG 9 July 1940, issue 34892, page 4184] and during his service was for the second time mentioned in a despatch [LG 14 June 1945, supplement 37119, page 2993].

    Born in Surbiton on the 6th of April 1885, he married Gillian Mary Spencer Warwick on the 4th of February 1919. Charles Bryant died in Cirencester at the comparatively early age of 64 on the 22nd of February 1950.

MAY
1919

In Germany, Soldiers of the *Freikorps* mounted a major assault on Munich, now masquerading as the capital of the Bavarian Soviet Republic. Ferocious fighting continued throughout the day with the *Freikorps* securing the city street by street. Throughout the night, and well into the Friday the battle raged until the last of the forces loyal to the Soviets were crushed. As a measure of the fierceness of the fighting, those killed exceeded six hundred, many of which were civilians, and I have little doubt the number wounded and injured exceeded the total of those who died.

    In contrast to April where squadron fatalities amounted to six, May witnessed a huge increase to twenty-two.

Thursday 1 May 1919

97 Squadron	Lt G Harwood AFC	+	Chislehurst [St. Nicholas] Churchyard
DH.10 E5446	2Lt F C Salmon	+	Beckenham Crematorium and Cemetery
	2Lt N de Gersigny	Injured	Unemployed list 4 November 1919
	France		

152

T/o Ford for local flying and practice on type in readiness for the squadron's pending move to India scheduled for July. At some point the engine failed and out of control the DH spun into the ground. Gerald Harwood was formerly of the 3rd Battalion, Suffolk Regiment, his details appearing in several editions of the *Gazette*. A report in the paper for 9th October 1914, issue 28932, page 8046, concerned cancellation of his appointment *"to a Second Lieutenancy, which appeared in the Gazette dated 25th September, 1914."* However, restoration of his commission to the 3rd Battalion, effective from 14th January 1915, appeared in issue 29044, page 612.

To date I have not found an entry for his award of the AFC, and his Record Service form appears not have survived. Frederick Charles Salmon commenced his military service with the RNAS and was granted a temporary commission with the Royal Air Force on 2nd August 1918 [LG 6 September 1918, issue 30887, page 10554]. He joined the squadron at Xaffévillers on the 21st of September 1918.

Noel de Gersigny was born on Christmas Day 1898 [and I have little doubt that the significance of this is reflected by his Christian name], and he joined the RFC on the 1st of December 1917. His service records are devoid of postings, but it identifies his father as living at the Royal Hotel, 33 Avenue Friedland, Paris [its current address being 33 Avenue de Friedland, 75008 Paris].

Friday 2 May 1919
At Proven pilots, observers, mechanics and all the paraphernalia associated with the major move of a squadron was in train as 58 Squadron prepared to start their transit to Heliopolis in Egypt.

Saturday 3 May 1919
During the day disturbing reports from British India reached England that Afghanistan fighters, in strength, had come through the Khyber Pass and overrun the border town of Bagh. This had serious implications for the British Indian Army garrison at Landi Kotal for whoever occupied Bagh had direct control over the water supply to the garrison where two companies were in billets.

34 Squadron which had seen operational service as a reconnaissance squadron in France and Italy arrived from the latter, less their RE.8s, at Old Sarum to await further instructions.

25 Squadron	2Lt A H B Stace	+	Mons [Bergen] Communal Cemetery
DH.4 *Not reported*	Major H H Robinson MC*	+	Mons [Bergen] Communal Cemetery

T/o Maubeuge and whilst in the process of climbing the engine cut and within seconds the bomber stalled and out of control fell to the ground. Arthur Howard Bartlett Stace who entered the world on the last day of February 1899, had been with the squadron since September 29th, last. From Brackley in Northamptonshire he is commemorated with the familiar inscription: *"At The Going Down Of The Sun And In The Morning We Will Remember Them."*

His passenger, Major Hugh Huntley Robinson had recently transferred from the RAMC for service with the Royal Air Force. His name first appears in the *Gazette* in its publication of 19th June 1914, issue 28841, page 4803, under the heading For Attachments to Units other than Medical Units and to be graded Lieutenant with effect from 25th April 1914. He was to prove, like so many of his colleagues, a brave and resourceful medical officer whose duties took him out onto the battlefield in the most dangerous of conditions. The citation for his MC was published on 14th November 1916, supplement 29824, page 11065: *'For conspicuous gallantry and devotion to duty. He tended the wounded with great courage and skill, quite regardless of personal danger. He has, on many previous occasions, displayed the greatest bravery.'*

A First Bar was *Gazetted* on the 3rd of June 1918, supplement 30716, page 6462, but without a citation attached. The website devoted to RAMC in the Great War [which I gratefully acknowledge] carries a short biography of Major Robinson who was attached to the 9th Wing of the Royal Air Force. His war service, in the main, was spent serving the 5th London Division Field Ambulance. It also records he was a graduate of The London Hospital which he entered in 1905, qualifying in April 1912, LRCP and MRCS. A photograph of his headstone is attached, courtesy of Barbara Janman - CWGC notes it is inscribed: *"On Active Service From Aug. 1914."*

186 Squadron	2Lt C Harrison	+	Gosport [Ann's Hill] Cemetery
Sopwith Cuckoo N6927			

T/o Gosport and crashed on the railway line near Fort Grange. There are no next of kin details appended against Cuthbert Harrison's name and neither have I been able to locate his Record of Service.

Although ordered from Pegler & Company in 1917, the firm advised that delivery of the Cuckoo could not be actioned before 1919, thus the construction of airframes N6090 to N6929 was entrusted to Blackburn Aircraft.

Tuesday 6 May 1919
With the *Great War* and the ongoing peace talks in Paris still very much the government's focus, the decision to formally declare the *Third Anglo-Afghan War* could not have been taken likely, particularly in the knowledge that previous conquests in that far-flung regions have ended in humiliation.

8 Squadron	Lt H J Weaver	+	Terlincthun British Cemetery, Wimille
Bristol F.2b D2721	AC1 E J Tricker	+	Terlincthun British Cemetery, Wimille

T/o Sart and crashed on or near the aerodrome at Marquise. Herbert John Weaver, born on the 14th of November 1898, enlisted at the age of 17, and was commissioned to the 6th Battalion, Queen's Own Regiments, West Kent Regiment. On his transfer to the RFC he trained as an observer, joining 22 Squadron [Bristol F.2b] at Estrée Blanche on the 11th of

December 1917. The reverse of his Army Form B.103 has not been digitised, so I can only surmise that on finishing his first operational tour he re-mustered and underwent training to become a pilot.

His epitaph reads: *"Ever In Our Thoughts Until We Meet Again Father, Mother, Brother."* Ernest James Tricker's commemoration is similar: *"Ever In Our Memory."* Both were just 20 years of age.

Wednesday 7 May 1919
In Paris the ire of Belgium was expressed most forcefully when the decision was made that Great Britain should be awarded all territories in East Africa that until now had been in the domain of Germany.

141 Squadron   2Lt W F K Kretmar   +   Grangegorman Military Cemetery
Bristol F.2b E2763
T/o Tallaght where, on return, the Bristol crashed whilst in the landing phase. I have yet to locate William Forrest King Kretmar's service records, and as far as I have been able to ascertain his sole entry in the *Gazette* appeared on the 14th of June 1918, issue 30747, page 7071, reporting his Lieutenancy from the 24th of April 1918.

Friday 9 May 1919
25 Squadron   2Lt J G Barclay   Injured   Mons [Bergen] Communal Cemetery
DH.4 D8415/H7121   AC2 J Borthwick   +   Mons [Bergen] Communal Cemetery
T/o Maubeuge and on return eyewitnesses report seeing the DH bank steeply at around fifty feet, stall and dive into the ground. Prior to its issue to 25 Squadron, as D8415 it was on establishment with 57 Squadron where it was coded A6 and on 22nd August 1918, damaged in a crash-landed, the crew being 2nd Lieutenant J P Ferreira and Lieutenant L B Simmonds, both escaping with little more than a severe shaking. Following repair it arrived with '25' [date not known] adorned with its new identity H7121.

John George Barclay was alive, though grievously injured, and he died the following day; he was 23 years of age. James Borthwick's headstone is inscribed with the words: *"Gone But Not Forgotten."* His life had been tragically short for he was only seventeen when it came to an horrific end.

Concerning South African born Julien Percy Ferreira, born [probably in Cape Province] on the 13th of February 1899, he joined 57 Squadron on the 21st of July 1918, and failed to return from operations on 16th September, the details of his loss, and that of Leslie Bernard Simmonds, are recorded in my second volume on page 226. Neither have a known grave and thus are commemorated on the Arras Flying Services Memorial.

Sunday 11 May 1919
29 Squadron   Lt S E Allenby   Safe
SE.5a E6033
T/o Bickendorf and damaged beyond repair in a landing accident. It will be recalled that he had written off an SE.5a in similar circumstances on the last day of January. E6033 had been with the squadron since the 10th of October 1918, and flew, with the squadron, to Bickendorf on 19th December. Late of the 8th Battalion, West Yorkshire Regiment, Lieutenant Allenby was seconded for duty with the Royal Air Force on the last day of October 1918 [though I suspect he was undergoing flying training before this date], as reported in the *Gazette* 22 January 1919, supplement 31137, page 1144, this secondment being continued from the 1st of May [LG 31 December 1919, supplement 31711, page 16120].

Wednesday 14 May 1919
206 Squadron   Lt S Gibbs   Injured   Cologne Southern Cemetery
DH.9 D7380   Sgt A B Page   +   Cologne Southern Cemetery
T/o Bickendorf and destroyed in a flying accident, the circumstances for which are unknown. Stanley Gibbs died later in the day from his injuries. To date, his service records remain untraced.

The service number for 19 year old Arthur Baden Page 176156 identifies him as an ex-flight cadet, enlisting between May and October 1918. For his parents, Arthur's death was the second tragedy to fall upon them for on the 17th of July 1918, his brother Private Hector John Page, formerly of the Glamorgan Field Company, Royal Engineers but at the time of his death serving with the 1st/5th Battalion, North Staffordshire Regiment fell. He is buried in the province of Aisne in Montcornet Military Cemetery.

Thursday 15 May 1919
A number of quite poignant notices appeared this day in *Flight*, which relate to summaries in my second volume, pages 235 and 250 respectively. The first from the parents of Lieutenant Thomas Martin Phillips of 103 Squadron who, along with his observer, perished during bombing operations and the second from the mother of Lieutenant Leonard Charles Scroggie. All were seeking information regarding their sons. Mr and Mrs Phillips of Swansea appear to have accepted that their son had been killed but were anxious to hear from any of his squadron colleagues who might have witnessed his final moments.

Mrs Scroggie of Aberdeen, however, as at May 1919, was under the impression that Leonard may have been taken prisoner for since being notified on the 4th of October that he was missing she had not received further news from the authorities. Sadly, as my book shows, Leonard had been killed and as his remains had never been positively identified his name is amongst the thousands commemorated on the Arras Flying Services Memorial.

78 Squadron   2Lt H C Smith   +   Hornchurch [St. Andrew] Churchyard
7F.1 Snipe E8139
T/o Hornchurch for local flying practice and reported to have spun out of control to crash near Dagenham, Essex. Hugh Cassillis Smith was 19 years of age and his parents requested, and were granted, the following commemoration which in part embraces the Nicene Creed: *"Called To The Fuller Life While Flying I Believe In The Communion Of Saints & The Life Everlasting."*

221 Squadron   Lt B E N Turner   +   Haidar Pasha Memorial
DH.9A *Not reported* 2Lt G E Jemmeson   +   Haidar Pasha Memorial
T/o Petrovsk and reported to have side-slipped and crashed on Chechen Island on the western shores of the Caspain Sea, presumably while trying to land on the island.

Note. Although outside the parameters of this volume, DH.9A H5894 belonging to 1[Communications] Squadron at Kenley came to grief when it crashed into the waters of Boulogne Harbour taking with it the lives of Captain Elgie Blyth Barwise Jefferson and 42 year old Mr Aaron Aaronsohn who, at the behest of Chaim Weizman, was involved with the Versailles Peace Conference. An incomplete service record exists for Captain Jefferson, late of the 1st Battalion, The King's [Liverpool] Regiment:-

5.5.16	*No 18 Sqdn*	*Attached to 18 Sqdn*	*1.5.16*	*B.213*
20.5.16	*"*	*Leave 18.5.16 to 27.5.16*		*B.213/1287*
27.5.16	*AG*	*Accepted for permanent*		*Memo No.*
		employment with RFC		*AG/A/1665/614*
22.7.16	*No 18 Sqdn*	*Graded qualified observer*	*15.7.16*	*B.213*
2.9.16	*"*	*Posted to No 16 Sqdn*	*1.9.16*	*B.213*
9.9.16	*22 CCS*	*Admitted [Debility]*	*3.9.16*	*ED 29op*
16.9.16	*"*	*Discharged to duty*	*12.9.16*	*ED 31g4*
16.9.16	*No 16 Sqdn*	*Leave 13.9.16 to 19.9.16*		*B.213*
30.9.16	*"*	*Leave extended to 3.10.16*		*B.213*

Captain Jefferson's body was recovered and his grave can now be visiting in Dunkirk Town Cemetery.

Saturday 17 May 1919
58 Squadron   2Lt F G Prince   +   Rome [Testaccio] Protestant Cemetery
HP O/400 D5439 2Lt S Spratt   +   Rome [Testaccio] Protestant Cemetery
                 Colonel T E Lawrence   Injured
                 AC2 F J Daw   Injured
                 AC2 Henely   Injured
T/o *Not reported* with their esteemed passenger Colonel T E Lawrence, known around the world today as Lawrence of Arabia, *en route* to Egypt. Approaching Roma-Centocelle aerodrome disaster overtook the bomber and it crashed with fatal consequences for the two pilots and serious injury to Lawrence and the two airmen; Colonel Lawrence being taken to hospital with a broken should blade and two fractured ribs. During his incarceration, and with news banded about that a famous person was in their care, he was visited by Italy's King Victor Emmanuel III. Before commenting further on this complex character, a word or two about the two pilots Frederick George Prince and 19 year old Sidney Spratt who hailed from Wallasey in Cheshire.
   Frederick Prince was born, probably in Dulwich, on 17th July 1891, joining the RFC circa 8th February 1918. His flying training completed he reported to the squadron, then operating out of Fauquembergues on the 11th of August 1918. Sent back to England on the 1st of April, he was recalled and rejoined '58' on the 10th, and is believed to have begun the fateful flight on the 3rd of May. His epitaph and that for Sidney read respectively *"Steadfast And Brave Unto Death He Did His Duty Thy Will Be Done'* and *'The Gardener Who Has Plucked One Of My Choicest Flowers The Master."*
   Returning to Lawrence his many exploits both in Arabia and with the Arabs in their opposition to the threat from Turkey have been so well reported that it is unnecessary for me to comment further. However, it is noted that at the Paris Peace Conference he was a member of Emir Faisal's delegation. But it is the years between his brief employment with the Foreign Office and his work with Winston Churchill at the Colonial Office that I will conclude the main part of this summary.
   Tiring of the bureaucracy that is part and parcel of all great offices of State he changed his name to John Hume Ross and enlisted as an airmen in the Royal Air Force, this being August 1922, but when his true identity became known and the furore that ensued it became untenable for him to continue and he left the air force in February 1923.
   Determined not to be thwarted he changed his name for a second time and as 'T E Shaw' he joined the Tank Corps. Sadly, Shaw and army life did not jell and, eventually, in August 1925, he succeeded with his desire to serve in the Royal Air Force.
   Thus, the years twixt the summer of '25 and March 1935, when his term of service ended, were probably the happiest that he could wish for. Retiring to Clouds Hill [now a National Trust property], a cottage near Wareham in Dorset, Lawrence never lived to see out the summer for on the 13th of May, out on one of his beloved motorcycles and indulging in his passion for speed, he failed owing to a dip in the road to see two young boys out on the bicycles. Swerving to avoid them, he mounted a bank was thrown over the handlebars. Rushed to hospital he lingered for six days before dying from his injuries; he was 46 years of age. His grave is in the churchyard of St. Nicholas at Moreton some six miles or so east of Dorchester. His awards included a Companion of the Order of the Bath, DSO and two

awards from the French, despite being viewed with suspicion in some quarters, Knight of the Legion of Honour and a *Croix de Guerre.*

Lawrence published two books, the best known being *Seven Pillars of Wisdom* which is regarded as an auto-biographical account of his part in the Arab Revolt, and *Mint* which describes his postwar life in the army and air force.

Returning to the graves in Rome's Testaccio Protestant Cemetery, there are just seven Commonwealth burials - six from the *Great War* and one from the Second World War, this being for Sub-Lieutenant Roy Charlton of HMS *Saracen*. *Saracen* was an S-class submarine sunk on the 14th of August 1943. At the time *Saracen* was patrolling off Corsica when she was detected by an Italian *Gabbiano-class* corvette *Minerva* and forced to the surface by depth charging. From the submarines complement of forty-eight, only two lost their lives, while the remainder went into captivity. I can only surmise that when in. September 1943, Italy threw in the towel and some Allied prisoners found themselves on transports heading for camps in Germany, Roy Charlton was left behind.

Finally, Roma-Centocelle was Italy's first airport and flight school, opening with a demonstration by the pioneering aviator, Wilbur Wright, who flew the Wright Flyer on the 15th of April 1909. *Flight* mentions Centocelle aerodrome on eight occasions in 1909, several of the reports featuring flights made by Wilbur Wright, several of which were in the presence of King Victor Emmanuel.

Sunday 18 May 1919

Harry Hawker and his co-pilot, Lieutenant-Commander Kenneth Mackenzie-Grieve took off from St. John's in New-foundland on the first attempt to make an air crossing of the Atlantic; success eluded them and after a little over 1,000 miles of flight they were obliged to ditch. Much confusion followed; hope were raised only to be dashed within hours. A report from the Admiralty that their Sopwith Atlantic machine had alighted in the mouth of the Shannon on Ireland's west coast and some forty miles west of Loop Head had later to be denied.

Subsequently, fears that both airmen had perished vanished with the news that the Sopwith had come down near a Danish tramp steamer, the SS *Mary*. Owing to the fact that the vessel was not equipped with wireless equipment, it was several days before the good news of their survival could be announced.

Monday 19 May 1919

7 Squadron   Captain L I Barker   +   Cologne Southern Cemetery
Fokker type
T/o Buchheim and crashed on the airfield while test-flying, thus demonstrating the perils associated with flying aircraft of an unfamiliar nature.

The Buchheim district of Köln lies on the east bank of the Rhine, more or less opposite the city centre, and to where the squadron arrived eight days earlier and from where they would depart to Heumar on the 7th of August.

Tuesday 20 May 1919

59 Squadron   Lt N McEachran   +   Cologne Southern Cemetery
RE.8 C2910   2Lt H Davis MM   +   Cologne Southern Cemetery
T/o Duren to practice firing the Lewis gun, and exercise that ended with the RE a blazing wreck after Niall McEachran failed to recover from a stall. Late of the Highland Light Infantry, and born on the 4th of April 1895, possibly at Thornton Hall, Lancashire, he first saw operational service with 7 Squadron [RE.8] at Proven East , joining precisely one year before the armistice came into effect.

He enjoyed two spells of leave; the first between the 10th and 14th of February, exploring the delights that the French capital could offer, followed almost immediately by home leave twixt 20th February and 3rd March. Soon after his return he came under the aegis of the 5th Brigade and was posted to 59 Squadron on the 25th of March 1918. He must have been close to being tour expired.

His epitaph reads: *"God's Finger Touched Him And He Slept."* Harry Davis, the observer, had served with the 3rd Battalion, Royal Warwickshire Regiment. The words of his commemoration are taken from the Song of Solomon: *"Until The Day Dawns And The Shadows Flee."*

Thursday 22 May 1919

For the second time in less than a week a senior officer would lose his life while testing the flying characteristics of an enemy fighter. This time the tragedy would unfold over English soil.

2 Squadron CAF Major A D Carter DSO*   +   Old Shoreham Cemetery
Fokker DVII 8482/18 *Croix de Guerre* [Belgium] Three times mentioned in a despatch Canada
T/o Shoreham to examine the merits of what was considered to have been one of the enemy's most formidable fighter aircraft. Climbing hard, Albert Desbrisay Carter was probably impressed by its rate of climb and then eyewitnesses on the ground watched in awe as he rolled into a dive, the speed building until he began to recover. Then, to the horror of all those watching the wings suddenly folded and moments later it was just a completely broken heap of wreckage on the airfield. Photographs of this, and one taken with Major Carter sitting in the cockpit prior to the test, appear in his biography reported between pages 31 and 34 of *Fallen Eagles.*

This biography records the occasion when he was shot down and wounded on May 19th, 1918, and made a prisoner of war after forced-landing behind enemy lines [see page 163 of my first volume for additional details]. At the time of his death he had been attached to the squadron from 1 Training Group, Royal Air Force.

Omitted from my report in the first volume was the citation for his DSO which was *Gazetted* on 18th July 1918, supplement 30801, page 8444: *'For conspicuous gallantry and devotion to duty. He destroyed two enemy aeroplanes, drove down several others out of control, and on two occasions attacked enemy troops from a low altitude. He showed great keenness and dash as a patrol leader.'*

The First Bar followed in supplement 30901, page 10861, of the paper issued on 16th September 1918: *'For conspicuous gallantry and devotion to duty as a fighting pilot. In three and a half months he destroyed thirteen enemy machines. He showed the most determination, keenness and dash, and his various successful encounters, often against odds, make up a splendid records.'*

Although I have shown 2 Squadron CAF, some documentation refer to the Fokker as belonging to 123 Squadron which, in effect, was about to become 2 Squadron CAF. This unit had first formed at Waddington on the 1st of February 1918, equipping with DH.9As, but did not become operational and eventually disbanded at Duxford on 17th August.

Then, on 3rd November it reformed as a Canadian Fighter Squadron at Upper Heyford, moving to Shoreham on the last day of March. Two dates are given for its formation as 2 Squadron CAF - *Wikipedia* shows 20th November 1918, while James J Halley's *The Squadrons of the Royal Air Force & Commonwealth 1918 - 1988* suggest it occurred eight days later.

Monday 26 May 1919

48 Squadron [Bristol F.2b] at Bickendorf was stood down from its duties as part of the Occupation Force and over the course of the next month prepared for its move to India where it would set up home at Quetta and in less than a year see its number plate transferred to 5 Squadron. In similar vein, 80 Squadron [Snipe] prepared to make their transfer from Clermont in France to the Middle East.

Thursday 29 May 1919

During the day 49 Squadron transferred from Bavai to Bickendorf as part of the Allied Occupation Force policing the Rhineland. As the two summaries that follow show, the move was not entirely successful, though no one was hurt in the two accidents.

49 Squadron	2Lt L W D Peacock	Safe	Unemployed list 20 November 1919
DH.9 E695	AC2 R J Ashton	Safe	

T/o Bavai to transit to Bickendorf but forced-landed, and believed damaged beyond repair, at Maubeuge. E695 was received from 2 Air Issues on 22nd November 1918. Posted to the squadron on the 12th of August 1918, 2nd Lieutenant Peacock features in my second volume on page 285, his observer on that occasion being Sergeant R Read.

On the 15th of July as the squadron prepared to disband, he was posted to Merheim and 25 Squadron [DH.9A] and when '25' made ready to return home in early September, 2nd Lieutenant Peacock preceded the move and crossed the Channel on the 5th, his service days nearing their end.

49 Squadron	Captain S H Gaskell	Safe
DH.9A E8481	Sgt F W Thomson	Safe

T/o Bavai with similar intent and on arrival at Bickendorf crashed-landed. Briefly on establishment with 110 Squadron, the DH was returned to 2 Air Issues from where it was ferried to the squadron on 28th November 1918. A Record of Service form has been raised for Sydney Hodson Gaskell which shows he was born in the October of 1889, and that his home address was Handley, St, Georges Road, Worthing. Unfortunately, his military service has not been appended. However, come the Second World War he was commissioned to the Administrative and Special Duties Branch on the 10th March 1940 [LG 26 March 1940, issue 34817, page 1782] and served until relinquishing his commission under the provisions of the Navy, Army and Air Force Reserves Act, 1954, at which time he was ranked Wing Commander.

Friday 30 May 1919

20 Squadron [Bristol F.2b] based at Ossogne in France [it was the only Royal Air Force squadron to occupy the airfield] began preparations to transfer to India, a move which would be completed in less than a month.

Sadly, May 1919 in respect of squadron losses ended as it had started with a crash that claimed the lives of those involved.

11 Squadron	Captain G W N R Hayes	+	Cologne Southern Cemetery
Bristol F.2b *Not reported*			

T/o Spich and recorded as being written off in a flying accident, though the location was not given. From Crosshaven in Co Cork, George William Norman Risdale Hayes was late of the 6th Battalion, Royal Munster Fusiliers. His epitaph reads: *"Blessed Are The Pure In Heart For They Shall See God."* A non digitised record for this officer is held at TNA Kew under WO 339/14718.

JUNE
1919

The huge reductions of late in both the number of operational squadrons and manpower had practically run its course; also coming to end were the protracted talks in Paris that would title *The Treaty of Versailles* and bring closure on the

Great War. Much has been written on the rights and wrongs of the agreement that leaders of the various Allied nations put their signature too, but the consensus of historians whose minds have broached the subject general conclude that the terms imposed on Germany and the subsequent lack of will by the Allies to follow these through gave rise to events that heralded the outbreak of the Second World War in September 1939.

Thursday 5 June 1919

105 Squadron	2Lt F Clarke	+	Reigate Cemetery
Bristol F.2b F4669	2Lt D W Beard	Injured	Commission relinquished 25 December 1920

T/o Oranmore and reported down at Castlebar the county town in Co Mayo having failed to recover from a spinning nosedive. This crash is thought to have been the last fatal accident involving an operational squadron in the UK in 1919. Although shown as the pilot, Fred Clarke may have been the observer. I have not been able to trace his service records but his entry on the CWGC website indicates he held the Territorial Efficiency Medal and was formerly of the Surrey Yeomanry [Queen Mary's Regiment]. He was 34 years of age and was born in Sutton Bridge, Lincolnshire, since when his parents had moved to Redhill in Surrey.

Donald Wainwright Beard was born on the 20th of May 1895, probably in Sandbach, Cheshire. His entries on an in-completed Army Form B.103 show:-

28.4.18	839 Sgt D W Beard, R A F to be	3.4.18	B.213 11 Sqdn
	2/Lieut for duty with R A F		
26.5.18	Leave 19.5.18 to 2.6.18		B.213 11 Sqdn
7.7.18	To Home Est.	2.7.18	" "

The relevant *Gazette* entry for his commission was published on 16th July 1918, issue 30798, page 8339. Owing to ill-health [probably as a result of this serious air accident] it was relinquished on Christmas Day 1920 [LG 31 December 1920, issue 32176, page 12759].

Between the wars his health recovered and on the 18th of November 1940, he was granted a commission in the General Duties Branch [hence my suggestion that Fred Clarke may have been an observer] but, subsequently, transferred to the Technical Branch [LG 31 December 1940, issue 35028, page 7299 and LG 8 August 1941, issue 35241, page 4576] being the respective entries.

Less than a year later his general well being failed and, reluctantly, on the 13th of March 1942 he was obliged to relinquish his commission for a second time [LG 24 March 1942, supplement 35498, page 1337]. However, having left the service I believe he was accepted as an Air Training Corps officer, eventually resigning on the 8th of April 1947.

Sunday 8 June 1919

57 Squadron	Lt H S Round	Safe	Unemployed list 2 September 1919
DH.9A H3470	2Lt P A Savoie	Safe	Unemployed list 13 November 1919
	Canada		

T/o Morville with a consignment of mail and on landing [the location omitted] the port wheel sheered from the axle and the imbalance turned the DH onto its back. A Record of Service form has been raised for Lieutenant Round but, I'm afraid, apart from his rank, name and initials nothing of interest has been recorded.

Fortunately, that for his observer is more forthcoming. Born in Canada on the 23rd of August 1893, Joseph Philippe Auguste Savoie came to the Royal Air Force on the 4th of April 1918, and with his observer training successfully completed he joined the squadron at Le Quesnoy on the 18th of September. Shortly before the orders to return to England on the 2nd of August, Joseph was posted to a holding camp on the 29th of July to await repatriation. I would not be too surprised if he returned to Canada by way of Blandford Camp in Dorset.

110 Squadron	Lt G G Bannerman	+	Belgrade Cemetery, Belgium
DH.9A E9898	Lt W N Wilson	+	Belgrade Cemetery, Belgium

T/o Tardinghem with mail destined for the Allied Occupation Forces in the Rhineland but before reaching Bickendorf the DH came down at Floreffe [Namur] on the River Sambre, some ten km WSW from Namur. Gilbert Gunn Bannerman's entry in the register has no information regarding his next of kin, and I have not been able to locate his Record of Service. However, as with 2nd Lieutenant Savoie of 57 Squadron, William Nichol Wilson's record has survived and this shows his birth in Consett, Co Durham, on 19th August 1899, and his enlistment with the RFC on 11th September 1917, less than a month after his 17th birthday.

On the 11th of August 1918, he reported to Serny where he was attached to 103 Squadron. On the 17th of January he crashed-landed during a photography exercise [see my summary for details]. The entries on his Army Form B.103 cease as at the 2nd of January, thus his posting to 110 Squadron, I suspect, occurred on or around 26th March when '103' returned to England.

Tuesday 10 June 1919

80 Squadron which departed Clermont as recently as the 26th of May, arrived at Aboukir.

Friday 13 June 1919

On this day a vast pruning of squadrons that until now had been tasked for the defence of the United Kingdom were stood down, many not to re-emerge until the expansionist years of the mid'30s. Thus, removed by one bureaucratic stroke of the pen 33, 50, 51, 61, 75, 76, 77, 90 and 112 Squadrons ceased to exist. The defence of the realm was near stripped bare.

Saturday-Sunday 14-15 June 1919
The challenge, initiated in 1913 by the *Daily Mail* but held in abeyance owing to the *Great War,* for the first successful crossing of the Atlantic was achieved by Captain John Alcock and his co-pilot and navigator Arthur Whitten Brown when flying a twin-engined Vickers Vimy they crossed from St. John's in Newfoundland to Clifden in Co. Galway where the Vimy finished up nose-down in an Irish bog. Both would now share the *Mail's* £10,000 prize and within days of their historic achievement be invested with knighthoods by King George V.

Sunday 15 June 1919
99 Squadron which had departed from Aulnoye in May arrived at Ambala.

57 Squadron   Lt W S Eason   Safe
DH.9A E729
T/o Morville and crashed while *en route* to Bickendorf. I am reasonable confident that the Record of Service for William Stanley Eason, whose record I show below, relates to Lieutenant Eason of 57 Squadron. Presuming my assumption to be correct, Stanley was born in Norfolk at East Tuddenham on the 24th of August 1897, and enlisted with the RFC on the 7th of July 1917;-

10.2.18	*Attached to No 2 ASD*	3.2.18	B.213 2 ASD
3.3.18	*Posted to No 29 Sqdn*	27.2.18	" "
7.4.18	*Attached to No 206 Sqdn*	3.4.18	" 29 Sqdn
20.4.18	*Posted to No 98 Sqdn*	16.4.18	" 98 Sqdn

The next line on the form has been left blank, before continuing:-

12.6.18	*Admitted [GSW slt]*	11.6.18	W3034 1 BRX
16.6.18	*Discharged to duty*	15.6.18	" "
23.6.18	*To Home Est*	20.6.18	B.213 2 ASD

Although referencing *The DH.4/DH.9 File* I can find no reference to him being wounded, I have traced two accidents involving Lieutenant Eason which resulted in his aircraft being written off and these are summarised in my first volume on pages 185 and 200. In each case, please delete the remark that he relinquished his commission.

63 Squadron   Lt C Gattens mid   +   Baghdad [North Gate] War Cemetery
RE.8 B6591   South Africa
                 Sgt H Lindley   +   Baghdad [North Gate] War Cemetery
T/o Mosul for local flying and crashed in the general vicinity of the airfield. Charles Gattens hailed from Johannesburg and was 27 years of age. Hirst Lindley's service number 20845 indicates enlistment circa 1916-1917, either as a transfer from another service, or by direct entry from civilian life. His next of kin has not been appended.

Monday 16 June 1919
Negotiations in Paris were coming to a head with the Allied delegation piling pressure on the German representatives. A draft of the peace treaty was set before them with the stark message; accept or risk a resumption of hostilities within five days. In retrospect, with the armies on all sides having been considerably reduced this threat may not only have been difficult to implement, but public opinion both at home and in Germany may not have been supportive of a renewal of fighting.

   20 Squadron and their Bristol F.2bs were now, on paper at least, domicile in India at Risalpur where their duties would involve policing the North West Frontier and working closely with the army. In light of recent events in the region, the squadron would be kept busy for the foreseeable future.

84 Squadron   2Lt H T Clark   +   Cologne Southern Cemetery
SE.5a C8709
T/o Bickendorf for local flying and crashed, the location not being reported. C8709 was one of 650 airframes built in Birmingham by the Austin Motor Company at their Longbridge factory. Apart from a note recording its demise, no other details are available regarding its previous use or arrival with the squadron.

Friday 20 June 1919
Turmoil in Germany with Chancellor Philipp Scheideman resigning as head of the Weimar Republic and dissolving the government in protest at the Allied ultimatum demanded in Paris on the 16th.

47 Squadron   Lt G E Clavey   Safe   Commission relinquished 24 October 1919
DH.9 C6236   Mechanic F J Smith   Safe
T/o Ekaterinodar and reported to have been wrecked whilst landing, or, as the squadron recorded on 11th August *"lost through enemy action on special mission with the Caucasian Army."* Lieutenant Clavey had been attached from the Royal Field Artillery and ceased to be employed with effect from 24th October 1919 [LG 28 October 1919, issue 31620, page 13140]. Again, I recommend Chaz Bowyer's *RAF Operations 1918 - 1938* for an insight into this phase of the squadron's history and in particular pages 37 to 54 of the second chapter, titled *Russian Interlude.*

Saturday 21 June 1919
At Scapa Flow an act of defiance at what was being demanded of Germany in regard to the future of her naval forces witnessed the scuttling of the entire German High Seas Fleet which had been interned at the anchorage for the past eight

months. Plans for such an eventuality had long been in place and now it was ordered by Rear-Admiral Hans Hermann Ludwig von Reuter.

There are several occasions during my searches for air accidents involving Royal Air Force squadrons that I come across material of interest, though not matching that which form the majority of entries in this volume. One such example I reported in the form of a note on May 15th, and now I impart a second example.

During the course of the day a DH.9 [airframe serial not known] belonging to 2 Squadron Slavo-British Aviation Corps is reported to have crashed near Topsa after being hit by shrapnel during bombing operations. The pilot, 21 year old Lieutenant Clarence Raymond Wentworth Knight died, possibly in Bolshevik hands, and was buried in Topsa Churchyard. His entry on the CWGC website indicates he is now commemorated by a Special Memorial B.79 in Archangel Allied Cemetery as his grave could not be found. He was the only son of Mr and Mrs W H Knight of Towns End House, Limington near Ilchester in Somerset.

It is not uncommon for the records of officers killed during operations against Red Army factions to be missing from the forms digitised recently by RAFM Hendon, but a part record for Clarence Knight has survived and it is worth recording. It shows he was born on the 8th of October 1897, and opens with a note indicating that by April 1917 he was a scout pilot flying SE.5s with 56 Squadron:-

12.5.17	To be Temp. Lieut.	1.5.17	L of Appts. HQ RFC
"	Posted to No 2 AD	9.5.17	B.213 56 Sqdn
26.5.17	Posted to No 55 Squadron	23.5.17	" 55 Sqdn
14.7.17	To Home Est.	13.7.17	" "
	Re-embarked & Disembarked	16.6.18	N. Roll No 151 Sqdn
29.6.18	Attached 101 Squadron from 151 Squad.	25.6.18	B.213 101 Squad.
6.7.18	Posted to 151 Sqdn	3.7.18	" "
4.10.18	Leave 13.9.18 to 23.9.18		Memo 151 Sqd
19.10.18	To Home Establishment	16.101.18	B.213 "

Turning to *The Camel File* I found several entries of interest concerning Clarence's time with 151 Squadron, a night fighter unit tasked to patrol and intercept enemy night raiders. Flying B5206 he carried out an anti-Gotha patrol during the night 19th-20th May [this is at odds with the information shown above which suggests he reached France in mid-June]. Patrolling on 10th-11th August in company with Lieutenant John Hamilton Summers*in B5412 together they accounted for a Gotha type which they drove down out of control.

However, it was in D6660 that Clarence enjoyed most success when in the space of 48-hours between the 23rd and 25th of August he intercepted and shot down two twin-engine Friedrichshafen GIII bombers. The first of these went down in flames at 0115 north of Doullens and Arras. When the wreckage and the bodies of the crew were examined identification revealed they were from 378/17 Boghohl VI/8, its crew being *Lieutnant* Kaiserbrecht and *Vizefeldwebel* Ludwig and Piepenkotte.

His second victim hit the ground three km or so east of Arras at 0033 on the 25th, exploding into a ball of flame on impact thus rendering identification of its unit and crew impossible.

Returning to events in North Russia, according to the website Nominal Roll Australians in North Russia, which I gratefully acknowledge, has a collection of twenty-six photographs, courtesy of Gareth Morgan, President of the Australian Society of WWI Aero Historians. The unit, which was supporting the White Russians was commanded by Major Charles Roderick Carr until disbandment of the Force in September 1919. Thus, on October 19th, 1919, he found himself on the unemployed list, but within three years was back in the air force after being granted a short service commission on 19th September 1922. In the years between leaving and rejoining he was employed briefly as Chief of Air Staff, Lithuania before returning home and joining Sir Ernest Shackleton's second Antarctic Expedition. His first attempt had ended in heroic failure, the story of the crew making a hazardous sea and overland trek in appalling conditions to South Georgia is well known and needs no further comment here, except to say that the heart trouble that would eventually kill him was brought about by the hardships endured between November 1915 and May 1916.

I believe it likely that Roderick Carr met Shackleton while in North Russia for in October 1918, Shackleton went to North Russia to advise on the training and equipping of our forces operating in Arctic conditions. Thus, on the 21st of September, the expedition aboard the *Quest* sailed from England and making its first stop at Rio de Janeiro where Sir Ernest had a suspected heart attack. Ignoring advice to rest and recuperate he insisted on continuing and on the 4th of January 1922, *Quest* reached South Georgia where within 24-hours he suffered major heart failure and died; he was 47 years of age. Perhaps fittingly, instead of being returned home as Lord Nelson was a century earlier, Sir Ernest is buried in a simple grave at Grytviken, South Georgia.

Roderick, again in the comforting surrounds of the air force enjoyed a most successful career. For most of the Second World War he was Air Officer Commanding No 4 Group, Bomber Command. On leaving the service on the 1st of February 1947, he had risen to the rank of Air Marshal and honoured with the KBE CB DFC AFC mentioned in a despatch and *Croix de Guerre* [France]. His DFC is interesting in that it was one few such awards issued in recognition of his service in Russia: *'On the 17th of June 1919, this officer flew a scout machine over the enemy aerodrome at Puchega at an average height of only 50 feet, for thirty minutes. During this time he succeeded in setting fire to a Nieuport enemy machine, to a hangar which contained three aeroplanes [all of which were destroyed], drove all the personnel off the aerodrome, and killed some of the mechanics.'* This appeared in the Edinburgh edition of 21st November 1919, issue 13528, page 3628. The citation was repeated by *Flight* on November 20th, where it is supported by information identifying Acting Wing Commander Robin Grey, Grenadier Guards, as commander of the Archangel Area, his leadership being rewarded with the DSO. He, personally, undertook several hazardous reconnaissance sorties and during one such sortie on 22nd April, he crashed. Although physically shaken he continued to head the Force until the conclusion of operations in September.

Page 1501 of *Flight* records a number of citations awarded to officers serving with "Syren" Force in North Russia.

* Lieutenant Summers remained in France after 151 Squadron returned home and was admitted to 51 General Hospital on the 21st of March, subsequently transferred to 56 General Hospital from where on the 11th of July 1919, he was sent home aboard HMHS *Brighton*. Both hospitals were based in Etaples.

Sunday 22 June 1919
High-stakes were now being played out in Paris as Germany made last minute pleas for certain amendments to the draft peace treaty; Germany's new chancellor, Gustav Bauer telegraphed acceptance, provided that articles viewed as detrimental to his country's economy and security were removed. The Allied response was swift and brutal; accept, or forces stationed in the Rhineland would within twenty-four hours cross the Rhine and advance into German.

111 Squadron	Lt J M D Mills AFC mid	+	Ramleh War Cemetery
Bristol F.2b C4728	Lt-Col A C Boddam-Whetham DSO	Injured	Ramleh War Cemetery

T/o Ramleh and totally destroyed after John McFarlane Denholm Mills lost control while banking at low altitude and attempting to land following complete loss of power at 1,000 feet. From Retirement, Montego Bay, Jamaica in the British West Indies, his epitaph simply reads: *"Faithful Unto Death."* His first entry in the *Gazette* under the heading 'The British West Indies Regiment' records his appointment as temporary 'Second Lieutenant' with effect from 30th September 1916, supplement 29867, page 12316, of the paper published on 16th December 1916. To date I have not found a Record of Service or any information pertaining to his honours.

Lieutenant-Colonel Arthur Courtney Boddam-Whetham was on the Staff of HQ Middle East, Royal Air Force, and was on his way to Damascus where he was to survey suitable landing stations to aid flights on the air route from the UK to India. Critically injured, he died before reaching hospital. His military service appears to have begun when he was commissioned to the 5th Battalion, Northumberland Fusiliers on 20th April 1901 [LG 3 May 1901, issue 27310, page 3038]. By 1909, he was on the Reserve of Officers and promoted Lieutenant [LG 2 March 1909, issue 28229, page 1661] and then, on 22nd October 1913, he was promoted Captain and attached from the General Reserve of Officers to the 4th Battalion, Princess Louise's [Argyll and Sutherland Highlanders], this being published in issue 28766, page 7340 of 21st October 1913.

However, I am of the belief that his service with the RFC began early on in the *Great War* for in its issue of 15th November 1915, supplement 29367, page 11302, under the heading Flying Officers to be Flight Commanders his name appears along with his army details. His promotion to temporary Lieutenant-Colonel was reported in the *Gazette* of 16th October 1917, supplement 30335, page 10586; I have yet to find the citation for his DSO.

His headstone bears the lengthy inscription: *"For A Tomb They Have An Altar And For Lamentation Memory."*

Note. There are five military casualties with the surname 'Boddam-Whetham' and I have little doubt that are related.

Monday 23 June 1919
His bluff called, Gustav Bauer telegraphed acceptance of the draft and a delegation would leave forthwith for Paris with instructions to sign without reservation, though five days would elapse before their signatures were penned.

79 Squadron	2Lt I Turkington	+	Cologne Southern Cemetery
5F.1 Dolphin *Not reported*			

T/o Bickendorf and crashed in unknown circumstances. Aged 18, Ivan Turkington was the son of the Reverend James and Mrs Turkington of Sheffield. Ivan's epitaph reads simply: *"In Loving Memory."*

Tuesday 24 June 1919
Personnel attached to 87 Squadron at Ternhill, 94 Squadron at Tadcaster and 98 Squadron at Shotwick, were informed that their squadrons were now disbanded. All three number plates would lie dormant for close on three decades. Two would reform in the UK but 94 Squadron was resurrected on the 26th of March 1939 at Khormaksar.

Thursday 26 June 1919
Two squadrons, namely 35 Squadron and 42 Squadron, were officially disbanded at Netheravon.

Saturday 28 June 1919
Amid the splendour of the Palace of Versailles a peace treaty that had been hammered out over months of talks in Paris between delegates of the Allied powers and German was, at last, signed. The *Great War* formally was over.

Appropriately, this momentous act came exactly five years after the assassination of Archduke Franz Ferdinand of Austria and his wife, Sophie, on his ill-advised visit to Sarajevo.

At Lopcombe Corner, 52 Squadron was stood down and would not be called upon until the expansion years of the mid '30s when it reformed at Abingdon.

Monday 30 June 1919
Three more squadrons were stood down by close of play; 82 Squadron at Tangmere, 104 Squadron at Crail and '107' at Hounslow.

Tuesday 1 July 1919

One of the oddities known only to the administrators in the Air Ministry occurred this day when at Biggin Hill the cadre of 37 Squadron became 39 Squadron. However, it remained as a cadre for nearly three years before arriving at Spittlegate from Kenley [it transferred to Kenley from Biggin Hill on April 12th, 1920] to equip with DH.9A.

Wednesday 2 July 1919

73 Squadron was stood down at Yatesbury.

Thursday 3 July 1919

Five more squadrons ceased to exist on this day, three at Lopcombe Corner where 74 Squadron, 85 Squadron and 91 Squadron had been waiting for the axe to fall, while at Lympne in Kent 102 Squadron and 108 Squadron were stood down. The Royal Air Force was shrinking by the day.

Friday 4 July 1919

And so it continued; 38 Squadron disbanded at Hawkinge and at Tangmere a similar fate befell 40 Squadron, and in the Rhineland at Duren 59 Squadron was ordered to cease its duties as a reconnaissance unit.

Tuesday 8 July 1919

49 Squadron	2Lt J Turner	Safe
DH.9 D9836		

T/o Bickendorf with instructions to deliver the bomber to 1 Air Issues but failed to complete the transit, coming down at Morschenich [Nordrhein-Westfalen], some four km NNE from Merzenich. 2nd Lieutenant Turner had a most fortunate escape for the DH caught fire and was burnt out. He had arrived with the squadron on the 6th of March 1919 and was still on establishment when the squadron disbanded later in the month.

Wednesday 9 July 1919

The perils associated with long-distance flights was tragically recognised this day with the loss of another Handley-Page as it attempted to leave what had been the Western Front for Egypt. It will be recalled that on the 17th of May a similar accident occurred near Rome involving a 58 Squadron crew and which nearly claimed the life of Lawrence of Arabia. Now it was the fate for a 214 Squadron crew whose bodies were recovered from the mountains near Trets in the Bouches-du-Rhône some considerable distance WSW from Draguigan in the Var.

214 Squadron	Lt C Hall	+	Mazargues War Cemetery, Marseilles
HP O/400 D4591	Lt F C Sumner	+	Mazargues War Cemetery, Marseilles
	Corporal E H Flintoff	Injured	Mazargues War Cemetery, Marseilles
	Corporal L H Jaffe	Injured	Mazargues War Cemetery, Marseilles

T/o Chemy with the intention of making the transit to Abu Sueir in Egypt, the first aircraft having commenced leaving France six days previously. Clifford Hall's home forms part of his epitaph: *"Loved By All Who Knew Him St. Anne's On Sea."* Clifton was aged 20, his co-pilot a year younger as was Elton Humpherus Flintoff who with Louis Hyman Jaffe died from injuries on the 10th. Francis Cyril Sumner features in a summary for 8th December 1918, when the HP in which he was flying forced-landed on a beach where before it could be salvaged it was engulfed by the incoming tide.

Friday 11 July 1919

31 Squadron	Lt F V Devonshire	+	Delhi Memorial [India Gate]
BE.2e A2931			

T/o Risalpur for operations over the North West Frontier and concentrating on the region near Fort Chuna in the vicinity of the Kyber Pass. Feray Vulliamy Devonshire had served with the 7th [Queen's Own] Hussars. Unusually, a very detailed account of his RFC and Royal Air Force service has survived, which I now copy. In particular it traces the process of his flying training, something which I have not previously encountered:-

		Embarked Bombay		per H.T.
		Disembarked Suez	18.6.17	"Chakdina"
30.6.17	No 3 School of Military Aeronautics. Attached for instruction Abbassia		23.6.17	B.213
21.7.17	21 Res. Sqdn " from S M A Abbassia		19.7.17	B.213
19.8.17	22 Res. Sqdn Transferred from 21 Res. Sqdn Aboukir		12.8.17	B.213
26.8.17	23 " " 22 "		18.8.17	B.213
23.9.17	SN Gunnery Attached from 23 Res. Sqdn Aboukir		19.9.17	B.213
7.10.17	23rd L Sqdn Trans. for duty from S A G pending posting		2.10.17	B.213
	Graded as Flying Officer subject app of War Office		6.9.17	B.213
"	Qualified to wear Wings		2.10.17	B.213
14.10.17	Posted to 23 Training Squadron on probation		6.9.17	B.213
9.11.17	3rd Echelon App passage for Mesopotamia on posting to 31 Wing ME/A/M/575/7 of 8.11.17		9.11.17	MFC/25480

This completes the entries on the first B.103. At various times two persons entered data to the form. Sheet 2 reads:-

	Group 40 Army	Father R L Devonshire Esq	
		Maadi, Cairo, Egypt	
11.10.18	Middle East	Embarked Basrah 11/11/18 per H.T. "Eastern"	
		en route to India on transfer &	GOC ME
		struck off strength from that date	Basrah 11.11.18 Idm A7473 d
			11/10/18

The form is signed [unreadable signature] in red by a Lieutenant from *British Army, Record Office 3, 3rd Echelon GHQ Mid. Ex. Force*. At this time his rank is shown as Acting Captain. TNA Kew holds a non digitised file for Feray Vulliamy Devonshire of the County of London Yeomanry under WO 339/55849. His date of birth is shown as the 17th of April 1891.

Sunday 13 July 1919
80 Squadron which settled at Aboukir from France on the 10th of June suffered its first fatal accident since arrival.

80 Squadron   Captain A J B Tonks   Injured   Alexandria [Hadra] War Memorial Cemetery
Sopwith Pup C480   DFC*

T/o Aboukir and crashed while trying to land at Cairo. Alive when released from the wreckage, Adrian James Boswell Tonks had sustained serious head injuries and he succumbed the following day. Born on the 10th of May 1898, his military service began on the 13th of August 1916, when he joined the RNAS and in the wake of protracted flying training reported to 4 Squadron RNAS on 17th August 1917, after which he was in continuous action for the next twelve months, gaining a DFC and First Bar. The citations for these honours appeared in the Edinburgh editions of the *Gazette* on 4th November 1918, issue 13446, page 4064 and 5th December 1918, issue 13363, page 4469 respectively:

'*Sea Patrol. A brave and determined airman who has destroyed four enemy aeroplanes and driven down six out of control. In a recent engagement with twelve enemy scouts he destroyed one and drove off others who were attacking some pilots in his flight. In these combats he expended all his ammunition, but seeing three enemy machines attacking one of ours, he, with great gallantry, dived amongst them with a view to distracting their attention. In this he succeeded. A courageous and meritorious action.*'

The First Bar: '*Sea Patrol. FLANDERS. Since 28th September this officer has led eleven low bombing raids, displaying conspicuous courage and skill, and inflicting serious damage on the enemy from low altitudes. During bombing raids Capt. Tonks has destroyed two enemy machines, proving himself a bold and daring fighter.*'

According to the indispensable website The Aerodrome, Adrian Tonks was born in Solihull on the 10th of May 1898 [though on Army Form B.103 the next of kin address for his father is shown as 31 Addison Mansion, Kensington], and was credited with the destruction of a dozen enemy aircraft between the 22nd of August 1917 and the 28th of September 1918. He flew a variety of Sopwith Camels, though C66 was one of his favourites in which he claimed victims six to ten inclusive [see my second volume and page 249 for the loss of this aircraft on 25th September].

The same website, which I have pleasure in acknowledging, reports Adrian as gaining his Royal Aero Club Aviator's Certificate on 28th December 1916, at RNAS Cranwell, flying a Maurice Farman biplane.

His Army Form B.103 shows he joined 92 Squadron [SE.5a] at Thuilles on 25th April 1919, and thence to 80 Squadron on the 3rd of May. He was officially struck off the strength of the BEF on the 27th May.

In conclusion, his biography is published in *Fallen Eagles*, pages 37 to 39.

Tuesday 15 July 1919
He drawdown of the Rhineland squadrons continued with 79 Squadron [Dolphin] disbanding at Bickendorf.

Wednesday 16 July 1919
216 Squadron   *Not reported*
HP O/400 D5418

T/o from an undisclosed location and crashed at Istres in Southern France whilst *en route* to Qantara. Earlier in the year this HP had forced-landed at Cognelée during a ferry flight to Bickendorf. The crew on that occasion were recorded as Lieutenant Edward Claud Middleton who had been commissioned to the 1st Battalion, East Yorkshire Regiment before joining the RFC on 27th April 1917. Born on the 15th of November 1896, an incomplete Record of Service shows the following;-

16.4.17	Accepted as Obs on probation	AG/D/2030/2/144 CR 8174 B 17.4.17
29.4.17	To Home Establishment	28.4.17 RO 952
	Re-embarked & Disembarked	15.5.17 LR 25 Sq
19.5.17	Attached to No 25 Sqdn	17.5.17 B.213 25 Sq
21.7.17	Admitted [Synovitis*R Knee]	18.7.17 ED 7831 23 CCS
28.7.17	Discharged to Unit	23.7.17 ED 8202. "
13.7.17	Appt Flying Officer [Obs] with seniority from 27 - 4 - 17	25.6.17 LG
5.8.17	Leave 4.8.17 to 18.8.17	B.213 25 Sq
13.10.17	To Home Est.	8.10.17 " "

Alan James Taylor, who may have been the second pilot, entered the world on the 10th of January 1899, and was accepted by the RFC on June 1st, 1917. His service records show:-

| 29.6.18 | Posted to No 100 Sqdn | 27.6.18 B.213 100 Sqdn |

25.10.18	Leave 10.9.18 to 24.9.18	Memo	"
13.11.18	Admitted [Scabies]	13.11.18 N3034-42 Stny	
24.12.18	Discharged to Duty	23.12.18 " 8 Gen.	
11.1.19	Posted to 100 Sqdn	4.1.19 " 100 Sqdn	
25.1.19	Posted to 97 Sqdn	23.1.19 B.213 97 Sqdn	
15.2.19	Posted to No 100 Sqdn	10.2.19 " 100 Sqdn	
27.2.19	Posted to No 214 Sqdn	23.2.19 " 214 Sqdn	
"	Leave 26.2.19 to 12.3.19	" "	

The names of two more officers are appended to the report. A form been has raised in respect of Lieutenant H G Shaw, this showing his date of birth as the 9th of February 1896, and an address in Canada but little else and the same for Lieutenant Ckifford Harold Bowen Price who was born on 4th March 1900, and who came from Radnorshire.

* Inflammation of the joint lining of the knee.

Friday 18 July 1919

6 Squadron reached Baghdad while in the Rhineland at Bickendorf 49 Squadron personnel were informed their duties were over. It would be the 10th of February 1936, before its number plate was raised to meet the concern being felt as Germany under Adolf Hitler continued to flout the dictates of the Treaty of Versailles.

47 Squadron	Lt A H Day	Safe
DH.9 D1142	Lt S T Fripp	Safe

T/o Ekaterinodar and crashed here where it was assessed to be a total wreck. Records for both officers are, as yet, not located.

Saturday 19 July 1919

At Ford in Sussex aircrew, mechanics and sundry personnel of 97 Squadron, now equipped with DH.10, started out on the long haul to India. The ground staff went to Tilbury for embarkation on the troopship *Mandala* which reached Allahabad on the 13th of August.

From Qantara in Egypt, 216 Squadron signalled it was ready to commence duties as a transport squadron.

Friday 25 July 1919

By coincidence both losses on this day feature aircraft that came down in the sea, one illustrating, again, the hazards of transiting over long distances which a century on pass without thought.

117 Squadron	*Not reported*
DH.9 D1181	*Not reported*

T/o Gormanston and reported to have alighted in the sea. The squadron, which had formed as an RFC unit at Waddington in Lincolnshire on New Year's 1918, was intended for the role of day bombing but this never materialised and following several transfers to stations in England, the squadron left for Dublin and Tallaght towards the end of March 1919. Within a month of its arrival it moved to Gormanston in Co Meath to continue its internal security duties which continued until disbandment in early October 1919.

There are a number of websites devoted to the history of the station, one of which records its occupancy by the infamous *Black and Tans* of the Royal Irish Constabulary.

216 Squadron	Lt C I Collinge	Injured	Ravenna War Cemetery
HP O/400 F304	Lt Adams	Injured	
	Sgt Ashley	Injured	
	AC1 A Balfour	Injured	

T/o Marseilles setting a course that would eventually take them to the squadron's base at Qantara but technical problems overtook them and the crew ditched in the Ligurian Sea off Monterosso at Mare in the province of La Spezia near Cape Mesco in NW Italy. A report in *Flight* 7th August, 1919, incorrectly identifies the bomber as an Italian Caproni F.304.

Formerly of the Tank Corps and from Larkfield in Kent, 21 year old Charles Ingham Collinge was freed from the cockpit by his crew who managed to get him ashore but despite their heroic efforts his injuries were mortal and he died not long after. His entry on the CWGC website notes that while on active service in France in 1917, he had been wounded. I have little doubt that after recovering Charles decided to apply for transfer to the air arm and in this he was successful, his commission being effective from 28th October 1918, as *Gazetted* on 12th November 1918, issue 31005, page 13315. A Record of Service exists for him, but with only the barest of detail appended.

Monday 28 July 1919

Personnel from 8 Squadron arrived at Duxford from Sart in Belgium. It is possible that their Bristol F.2bs accompanied them.

Wednesday 30 July 1919

A day of remarkable courage displayed by all those involved.

| 47 Squadron | Captain W Elliot DFC | Safe |
| DH.9 D2846 | Lt H S Laidlaw | Safe |

T/o Ekaterinodar in the company of Captain W F Anderson and Lieutenant J Mitchell and Captain S G Frogley and Lieutenant N Greenslade, their mission to bomb and photograph targets in the Tcherni-Yar region.

In the wake of the bombing Walter Fraser Anderson descended to around a thousand feet in order that his observer could take photographs and he was accompanied by William Elliot acting in the role of protection in the event of any interference from the air. Captain Frogley, meanwhile, remained above as top cover.

As the DHs descended so they were met by a hail of machine-gun fire and Elliot's engine was damaged to the extent that a forced-landing was his only option. Gliding down he was able to distance himself from the scene of their attack, and to his relief he could see Anderson following him down.

With both bombers on the ground, William set fire to his aircraft and then with his observer raced over to where Walter Anderson was waiting. It was then found that a bullet had penetrated the gravity tank, whereupon Mitchell got out of his cockpit and standing on the port wing plugged the hole with his thumb. Thus, with Elliot and Laidlaw in the vacant cockpit Walter Anderson opened the throttle and to everyones relief they achieved a good take off and were soon on their way home, the young Mitchell hanging on grimly and being subjected to the intense heat coming from the DH's exhaust. The entire action, and other exploits of the squadron at this time are featured in the second chapter of Chaz Bowyer's oft quoted book *RAF Operations 1918 - 1938*. It is worth, however, to record the citations for the honours subsequently awarded and background to the officers concerned in the operation. First, the citation for William Elliot's First Bar which was *Gazetted* on the second anniversary of the formation of the Royal Air Force, supplement 31847, page 4020: *'On the 30th July 1919, whilst on special duty for the Russian Volunteer Army, Flying Officer Elliot was shot down about five miles behind enemy lines, He then burnt the crashed machine, and kept off the enemy calvary by machine-gun fire until rescued by another machine which flew to his aid. This gallant and highly skilful pilot has carried out forty-five long-distance raids over the enemy lines during a period of four months, and has been continuously on active service since August 1917, during which period he has taken part in ninety-five raids, and brought down six enemy machines.'*

His distinguished military career began shortly after leaving Tonbridge School when in 1915, he joined the Army Service Corps before transferring two years later to the RFC. Postwar, he was granted a permanent commission after which he career followed the well trodden path of a permanent officer with a succession of flying appointments mixed with Staff Duties both at home and abroad. From November 1947 to April 1949, he was Air Officer-Commanding-in-Chief Fighter Command and following a brief posting as Chief Staff Officer to the Ministry of Defence took up the duties as ADC to The King and was still in this prestigious post when George VI died on February 5th, 1952; he then continued these duties to The Queen before retiring on the 18th of April 1954.

Born on the 3rd of June 1896, Air Chief Marshal Sir William Elliot GCVO KCB KBE DFC*ADC died on the 27th of June 1971. For readers who may wish to delve further into the life of Sir William are guided towards King's College, London and the Liddell Hart Centre for Military Archives.

The same *Gazette* issue announcing William Elliot's award, also carried citations in respect of four of the officers that took part in this operation. To Walter Fraser Anderson and John Mitchell a twin-citation for their DSO: *'On 30th July 1919, near Cherni Yar [Volga], these officers were pilot and observer respectively, on a DH.9 machine, which descended to an altitude of 1,000 feet to take oblique photographs to take oblique photographs of the enemy's positions. A second machine of the same flight which followed as escort was completely disabled by machine-gun fire, and forced to land five miles behind the enemy's foremost troops. Parties of hostile cavalry which attempted to capture the pilot and observer of the crashed machine were kept away by the observer's Lewis gun whilst the pilot burnt the machine.*

Flight Lieut. Anderson, notwithstanding that his petrol tank had been pierced by a machine-gun bullet, landed alongside the wrecked machine, picked up the pilot and observer, and got safely home.

The risk involved in attempting this gallant rescue was very great, as had any accident occurred in landing the fate of all four officers can only be conjectured. The difficult circumstances of the rescue will be fully appreciated when it is remembered that Observer Officer Mitchell had to mount the port plane to stop the holes in the petrol tank with his thumbs for a period of fifty minutes flying on the return journey.'

Sydney Gilbert Frogley DFC and his observer are honoured in the same issue, but not necessarily in relation to the rescue. Nevertheless, I consider it beneficial to include their citations; Sydney Frogley DFC gained a DSO and Norman Greenslade MC, late of the 4th Battalion, Devonshire Regiment, a DFC.

First the DSO: *'A fleet of about forty Bolshevik vessels, armed with all descriptions of guns, having broken through the defences of the Volunteer Army, commenced a bombardment of Tzaritzin. Flying Officer Frogley led a formation of machines on 15th October 1919, and at a height of 1,000 feet dropped his bombs with such effect that the fleet was dispersed p several vessels having been destroyed. During a period of four months this officer has rendered invaluable services in South Russia.'*

The same *Gazette* edition published his DFC: *'On the 15th July 1919, Flying Officer Frogley led a most successful raid on the Bolshevik flotilla of vessels [about 40 in number] 150 miles from his base, which resulted in the capture of the town of Kamyshin [Volga] by our Allied troops. He then led his formation at almost ground level, attacking the retreating enemy with machine-guns and causing complete disorganisation amongst them. A very risky and noteworthy performance, seeing that the distance back to base was 150 miles.'*

Norman Greenslade's citation reads: *'On 27th August 1919, at Cherni Yar, this Officer carried out a raid at very low altitude on the assembled flotilla of Bolshevik vessels, and by accurate bombing was largely instrumental in the success which followed. The anti-aircraft fire from the enemy was particularly severe during the engagement, and almost all the vessels carried such guns.'*

Thus, only Lieutenant Laidlaw missed out on an award. I have, however, found his Record of Service, or part thereof, which shows:-

11.12.19   HQ RAF   And Novoeossish from sick leave from
Constantinople 8/12 & re-taken on
strength from that date & attd. To HQ. South Russia 10.12.19 HQ/RO/107/11/12/19
15.12.19   HQ RAF   To C Flight for duty   " " 16.12.19 HQ/RO/151/16.12.19
29.3.20.   " "   To Constant, & struck off strength.   " " 28.3.20   HQ/RO/35 29.3.20

On leaving the air force, Walter Fraser Anderson became a civil pilot and by the summer of 1936, he was British Airways Chief Pilot. On the night of 15th September 1936, he took off with his crew of three from Gatwick in DH.86A G-ADYF to operate a mail flight to Hamburg. Climbing away the DH suddenly yawed through 180 degrees and dived to the ground, striking a tree just before impact, killing Captain Anderson and two of the crew. An enquiry into the crash came to the conclusion that the radio operator may have got his foot jammed between the second rudder bar control and a fire extinguisher.

Thursday 31 July 1919
At Castle Bromwich remnants of 9 Squadron reported, their duties as part of the Rhineland Occupation Force at an end, while at Spich, 62 Squadron [Bristol F.2b] received orders to stand down.

**AUGUST
1919**

The dominant theme throughout August was an acceleration in reducing the squadron strength of the Royal Air Force.

Saturday 2 August 1919
57 Squadron's duties to provide mail deliveries to the Rhineland and other area of the Continent had ceased and on thus on this day personnel from the squadron arrived at South Carlton.

Monday 4 August 1919
The rundown of Rhineland based formations continued when at Duren 59 Squadron [Bristol F.2b] were ordered to cease operations.

Thursday 7 August 1919
At Eil in Germany, 92 Squadron [SE.5a] was stood down; two decades would pass before it would re-form as a fighter squadron.

Friday 8 August 1919
On this day an Armistice was agreed between Great Britain and Afghanistan, thus ending the *Third Afghan War* {please refer to my entry for 6th May 1919]. It would not, however, prove to be end of hostilities between various tribes living on the British India side of the agreed border between the two countries.

Sunday 10 August 1919
29 Squadron, less aircraft, arrived at Spittlegate from Bickendorf; at Nivelles in Belgium the services of 88 Squadron were no longer required.

Monday 11 August 1919
47 Squadron recorded the loss of one of their DH.9s during a special operation in support of the Caucasian Army. No further details known at this time.

Tuesday 12 August 1919
84 Squadron returned as a cadre from the Rhineland and settled for the remainder of the year at Tangmere.

Wednesday 13 August 1919
97 Squadron and their DH.10s which left Ford in Sussex on 19th July, arrived at Allahabad.

Friday 15 August 1919
Although reduced to a cadre, it seems that personnel from 1 Squadron were still on the nominal roll while lodged at London Colney and on stand by for any task that might be required, and so it was that Lieutenant Gore William Hemsworth was ordered to Amiens from where he was to ferry SE.5a F9123 to Lympne.

Sadly, *en route* and over the Channel his aircraft came down in the sea and he was drowned. Eventually, the tides washed his body onto the French coast and he now rests in Terlincthun British Cemetery at Wimille where his head-stone carries the inscription: *"Safe In The Arms Of Jesus."* The section of his service records that have survived show he was born on the 25th of March 1899, and enlistment in the RFC on the 4th of April 1917.

On 25th November 1917, he reported to 60 Squadron [SE.5a] at Ste Marie Capel, serving with '60' until the 18th of February 1918, when he was attached to 20 Squadron to fly Bristol F.2bs, '20' at the time operating from the same air-field. Then, on the 25th of March he was instructed to proceed to Remaisnil and continue his operational tour flying Bristols with 62 Squadron. Within days of his arrival, '62' moved to Planques and it was here on the 15th of April that he took a tumble and fractured a clavicle. The injury was deemed serious enough for him to be evacuated to England and with his shoulder strapped he boarded the HS *Ville de Liège* on the 19th.

Post-armistice he returned to France and, I assume, was posted to 1 Squadron, though the reverse of the form that might show this has not been digitised. Gore Hemsworth came from Rathgar, then a village, but now incorporated into the southern suburbs of Dublin.

Turning to *The SE.5a File,* F9123 was recorded as being at 10 Aeroplane Acceptance Park at Brooklands by 19th December 1918, followed by a note to indicate it arrived at Amiens on the 12th of August where it was replenished with oil and petrol.

Wednesday 20 August 1919

5 Squadron	Lt R R Evans	+	Cologne Southern Cemetery
Bristol F.2b *Not reported* Lt V Limerick		+	Cologne Southern Cemetery

T/o Hangelar and reported to have crashed in the general vicinity of Köln. For both officers I have located partial Records of Service both of which show that having been returned to the UK in 1919, they subsequently found themselves back on the Continent. First, Army Form B.103 entries for Richard Ralph Evans who embarked for Italy on the 13th June 1918:-

22.6.18	Posted to "Z" Flight 34 Squadron	20.6.18	B.213 Z Flt 34 Sqd
13.7.18	Posted to No 139 Sqdn	3.7.18	B.213 34 Sqdn
3.8.18	Attached to No 34 Sqdn	1.8.18	" "
12.10.18	Leave 7.10.18 to 21.10.18		" "
23.11.18	Attached to no 7 A Park	22.11.18	" "
7.12.18	Leave 6.12.18 to 16.12.18 Italy		" 7 AP
9.12.18	To T/W in Italy	6.2.19	" "
15.2.19	Rejoined 7 AP from T/W in Italy	10.2.19	" "
8.3.19	To Home Estb	3.3.19	" "

His headstone is inscribed with the words: *'In Ever Loving Memory Father, Mother & Margie.'* Victor Limerick's epitaph reads: *'Dearly Beloved Only Son Of M. And The Late Geo. Limerick N Shields.'* Victor's Army Form B.103 indicates he was formerly of the Royal Field Artillery:-

23.4.18	Accepted as Observer on probation	AG 2154/136[O] WR No8174/757 Bd/24.4.18	
14.5.18	To Home Est.	8.5.18	
	Re-embarked	3.11.18	
9.11.18	Attd to 1 ASD	4.11.18	B.213 1ASD
12.11.18	Adm [Sprd ankle L]	11.11.18	W3034 NY 847
1.12.18	Dis. To Base Depot	30.11.18	" 38 Gen
2.12.18	Attd to 1 ASD	30.11.18	RO 397
14.12.18	To Home Establishment	9.12.18.	B.213
	Re-embarked	19.6.19	
24.6.19	Posted to 9 Sq	24.6.19.	LR A34

It is reasonably safe to assume that when 9 Squadron returned home from Ludendorf on the last day of July, Victor was posted to 5 Squadron.

Monday 25 August 1919

43 Squadron, their aircraft safely deposited to storage, arrived from Eil in the Rhineland to Spittlegate in Lincolnshire. With a Gamecock as their badge, '43' was known as *The Fighting Cocks* and prior to the armistice at least ten pilots with the accolade Ace served with the squadron. One, Henry Winslow Woollett is believed to have brought down more kite balloons that any other pilot on the Western Front, his total of eleven being included in his overall tally of thirty-five aerial victories.

Wednesday 27 August 1919

At Marquise, Major H R Nicholl who had commanded 110 Squadron since January 1918, was informed the squadron would disband this day, so ending its task of delivering consignments of mail to Bickendorf. As many summaries show, a task that produced its fair share of accidents. Major Nicholl's service records show he received a mention in a despatch in the New Year's Honours list of 1916, and in the March of that year had conferred upon him the *Legion d'Honour.* In addition to his duties as Squadron Commander, on the 22nd of December 1918, he assumed command of the 41st Wing at Bachincourt Château.

SEPTEMBER
1919

The pace of disbandment of squadrons continued unabated throughout September, of particular note was the number of squadrons leaving the Rhineland Occupation Force and either returning to the UK, or being stood down in situ.

Monday 1 September 1919

22 Squadron [Bristol F.2b] arrived at Ford from the Rhineland. Some documents indicate the squadron arrived with its aircraft, but on this point I am not certain.

Tuesday 2 September 1919

18 Squadron , their DHs delivered to store, returned to Weston-on-the-Green from Merheim. Since the armistice the squadron had been commanded by Major John Farquhar Gordon DFC, formerly of the Gordon Highlanders. Born in Aberdeenshire on the 23rd of March 1893, John Gordon transferred to the RFC on on 22nd November 1915, and by the 8th of February 1918, when as a Flight Commander he joined 25 Squadron at Boisdinghem, he had flown operationally with 6 Squadron and 5 Squadron. His DFC was *Gazetted* on 2 November 1918, supplement 30989, pages 12965 and 12966: *'An exceptionally able leader, who has carried out thirty-one bombing raids and twenty photographic reconnaissances. Many of these flights were of great distance and carried out at a very high altitude, calling for great courage and stamina. This officer possesses these qualities in a marked degree, and his example has been of the greatest service to his squadron.'* Postwar he continued in service, eventually retiring at his own request on 25th November 1936, when ranked Squadron Leader [LG 24 November 1938, issue 34343, page 7576].

Referencing *The DH.4/DH.9 File* and I find his name associated with two DH.4s; on 8th July 1918 with Corporal H Emerson as his observer, he snapped the axle of A7626/N while landing at Ruisseauville, the casualty report noting that as A7626 it had been rebuilt on two occasions and on inspection it was discovered the fuselage was strained and its woodwork saturated with oil. This notwithstanding it was sent for another rebuild, this time emerging as F6215 in which guise it was ferried to England on the 8th of January 1919.

Then on the 30th of July he forced-landed A7877 with engine trouble, this incident being summarised on page 95 of my second volume.

Wednesday 3 September 1919

11 Squadron [Bristol F.2b] which had been in the Rhineland since late May arrived at Scopwick, while at Spittlegate personnel from 70 Squadron [Snipe] reported from service at Bickendorf. Both squadrons now reduced to a cadre.

Saturday 6 September 1919

With their DHs left in storage 25 Squadron, commanded by Major G G A Williams, reported to South Carlton from Merheim. Major Williams had been commissioned to the 5th Dragoon Guards before his transfer to the RFC. During operations on the 6th of September 1916, and flying in 19 Squadron BE.12 6538 he received a gunshot wound to his ankle, this resulting in him being evacuated to England on the 13th by way of HMHS *St. David.*

Monday 8 September 1919

On this day 5 Squadron, which was one of the few RFC squadrons in existence at the outbreak of the *Great War* and which went to France and Maubeuge as early as 18th August 1914, for reconnaissance duties arrived at Bicester.

Friday 12 September 1919

100 Squadron arrived as a cadre at Baldonnel from Saint Inglevert.

Monday 22 September 1919

7 Squadron, the last of the pre-August 1914, units to form and whose Rhineland duties began in December last, arrived at Old Sarum. 72 Squadron formerly disbanded on this day.

Thursday 25 September 1919

34 Squadron which had been at Old Sarum since early May disbanded.

Saturday-Sunday 27-28 September 1919

274 Squadron   Captain C H Darley   +   Rome [Testaccio] Protestant Cemetery
Vickers V/1500   DSC* DFC Cross of Merit [Spain]
F8622   Captain C C Darley mid   Injured

T/o from a forced-landing site but on becoming airborne the bomber hit a telegraph pole, crashed and caught fire, the location being reported as Bracciano some thirty km NW of Rome. At the time, 274 Squadron was based at Bircham Newton in Norfolk.

The tragedy is reported in *Flight* October 2nd, 1919, page 1325, and quotes from the Italian newspaper *Epoca*. *"A British aeroplane en route for Rome and Cairo, when near Lake Bracciano, crashed and caught fire, Capt. C H Darley, the pilot being burned to death, and Capt. Chas Darley injured."*

A partial record of Service exists for Cecil Hill Darley who was born on the 11th of March 1889 and enlisted with the RNAS on the 1st of September 1915. This shows he was attached to 214 Squadron by the spring of 1918, and was awarded a First Bar to his DSC on the 2nd of April followed on the 13th of June by a DFC.

Turning to *The London Gazette* supplement 30227, page 8207, of the paper published on 11th August 1917, records the following: *'For conspicuous skill and gallantry on the night of 2nd July 1917. One of his engines having seized whilst he was over Bruges, he dropped his bombs on the objective and managed to fly his machine home on one engine and effected a safe landing on the aerodrome.'*

The citation for the First Bar appeared in the edition of 17th April 1918, supplement 30635, page 4647: *'For zeal and determination in carrying out numerous night bombing raids on enemy aerodromes, docks, etc. On the night of 18th-19th February 1918, he carried out two attacks on the St. Denis Westrem Aerodrome.'*

That for his DFC was reported in supplement 30827, page 9199, of 2nd August 1918: *'An officer with a fine record of gallantry to his credit. During the past two years he has been flying in active operations, twelve months of which were on night-flying bombing work, being on one occasion in the air in bad weather for 7 and a half hours. On several* occasions he has carried out two raids on the same night, and during the past month he successfully attacked a very formidable enemy position from a height of 200 feet in the face of very intense fire.'

I have little doubt that throughout his operational flying with the RNAS he was attached to 14 Squadron RNAS which on the 1st of April 1918, became 214 Squadron. Recently, Cecil had been appointed to a permanent commission and but for his tragic death would most likely have risen to high rank. His epitaph reads: *'Thanks Be To God Which Giveth Us Victory Through Jesus Christ.'*

His brother, Captain Charles Curtis Darley, displayed the utmost bravery in trying to release Cecil from the wreckage, his heroic efforts being recognised by the award of the Albert Medal, *Gazetted* 25th July 1922, issue 32732, pages 5511-5512: *'The KING has been pleased to award the Albert Medal to Squadron Leader Charles Curtis Darley of the Royal Air Force, in recognition of his gallantry in endeavouring to save life. On the night of 27th September 1919, a Vickers-Vimy Aeroplane, piloted by Captain Cecil Hill Darley, brother of Squadron Leader [then Flight Lieutenant] Darley, who was acting as Navigation Officer, made a forced-landing by Lake Bracciano, some twenty miles north of Rome, when on a flight from England to Egypt. On the following morning, in taking off, the aeroplane failed to clear a telegraph pole, and crashed, immediately bursting into flames. Squadron Leader Darley was thrown clear, but at once rushed to the blazing wreckage and displayed very conspicuous bravery and devotion in persistent, but unavailing, attempts to rescue his brother, who was pinned in the pilot's seat. His efforts to release his brother were only brought to an end by his collapse. He sustained such severe burns that he was a patient in hospital for over eighteen months.'*

No citation, however compassionately worded, can fully convey the desperation that must have been coursing through his mind as he fought tooth and nail to free his brother who, perhaps, mercifully may have been rendered unconscious by the crash.

Following his recovery, Charles, who had been appointed along with his brother to a permanent commission, continuing to serve [mainly in Staff appointments at home and abroad] until ill-health obliged him to resign his commission on 14th September 1939. At the time he was ranked Air Commodore. His death was announced on the 10th of June 1962.

Retracing the narrative to the *Great War,* Charles Darley, already an officers of some years standing having graduated from the Royal Military Academy at Woolwich and thence serving with the Royal Field Artillery in India, transferred to the RFC and served on the Western Front, initially with 3 Squadron [Morane Parasol] and then with 11 Squadron [Vickers FB.5] as Flight Commander "C" Flight. Thus, on the 26th of October 1915, and flying an offensive patrol out of Auchel in FB.5 5462 to the Cambrai area with 2nd Lieutenant R J Slade as his observer, he was shot down and made prisoner. Both officers were wounded; subsequently, they escaped from their prison camp, Charles making it to Switzerland in May 1916, and 2nd Lieutenant Slade to Holland by April 1918 - though this may have been an arranged repatriation as opposed to an actual escape. Charles's Record of Service shows he was mentioned in a despatch in the New Year's Honours list for 1916, and that on 28th May 1919, he had been posted to 88 Squadron [Bristol F.2b] at Nivelles. Identified only by his initials, 2nd Lieutenant Slade's Army Form B.103, shows he eventually reached Hull on the 18th of November 1918.

The loss of their FB.5 is recorded by Trevor Henshaw on page 23 of *The Sky Their Battlefield,* but it was the *Daily Mail* of Monday 10th April 1916, which carried a quite exciting account having received a letter from young Slade. The *Mail's* report reads: *"Graphic details of the manner in which Fokker 'star' Lieutenant Immelmann, attacks his adversaries have reached England in a letter from Lieutenant R J Slade, an observer of the Royal Flying Corps, now a prisoner of war at Fürstenberg."* Slade writes that they were over the German lines in *'a French machine'* when Immelmann attacked from the rear, his opening burst holing the petrol tank. Diving away, fortunately without catching fire, Immelmann continued to fire bursts into the machine hitting Charles Darley in his right arm and left hand and in the words of Lieutenant Slade *"the thumb of his left hand was pounded to a jelly"* which the writer states he carried out an amputation, in the air, with his penknife! Then in the best tradition, Darley brought the aircraft down to a *"stunt landing."* Slade continues by saying their assailant, realising his victim was not going to escape, drew off to one side and then observing the safe landing, himself alighted and rendered what assistance he could. The account ends, *"He [Immelmann] is a gentleman, and if we ever capture him I hope he will be treated as such."*

But, as history tells us, this was not to be for Max Immelmann and his Fokker E.III Eindecker fell in a late evening combat with an FB.5 from 25 Squadron on Sunday the 18th of June 1916, his machine breaking up in the air. The much decorated *Oberleutnant* Max Immelmann was afforded a State funeral in his home city of Dresden; he was 26 years of age and was credited with seventeen aerial victories.

OCTOBER
1919

Wednesday 1 October 1919
During the day formal disbandment of 21 Squadron took place at Fowlmere and at Shotwick 103 Squadron was stood down. The number plates for both squadrons would be abed until the 1930s.

Thursday 2 October 1919

99 Squadron	Lt J Clarke MC	+	Ambala Cantonment Cemetery
DH.9A J585	Sgt M G Spong	+	Ambala Cantonment Cemetery

T/o Amala to rejoin the squadron at Mianwale but crashed near the airfield soon after becoming airborne. This was the squadron's first fatal accident since arriving in India from Aulnoye. Joseph Clarke was formerly 2729 Corporal Clarke of the 17th Lancers and an officer with the Worcestershire Regiment. As yet I have not traced the citation for his award.

Maynard George Spong's service number 11010 indicates he came to the RFC circa October - November 1917, either as a direct entrant as a civilian or on transfer from one of the armed services.

Monday 6 October 1919
At Gormanston personnel from 117 Squadron moved to Tallaght where they merged with 141 Squadron [Bristol F.2b].

Tuesday 7 October 1919
At Ekaterinodar in South Russia, 47 Squadron which had been playing an important role in aiding White Russian forces in the long-running civil war against the Bolsheviks, adopted the title A Squadron RAF Mission. As I have remarked on several occasions, operations and general comment on the work of 47 Squadron and, subsequently, A Squadron are recorded by Chaz Bowyer in *RAF Operations 1918 - 1938.*

Wednesday 8 October 1919
106 Squadron disbanded at Fermoy.

Friday 17 October 1919
The administration involved with re-titling 47 Squadron as A Squadron RAF Mission had not quite worked its way through the system, hence the inclusion of the two summaries set out below.

47 Squadron	Lt V J Clow	Safe
DH.9 F1187	Lt W Bourne	Safe

T/o Ekaterinodar and on return, and landing, collided with the DH recorded below. Two Record of Service exist for Victor James Clow, the content of which reads as follows:-

19.3.18	5236759*Corp. V J Clow ASC to be temp.		*List of apps. No 349*
	2/Lieut. Gen. List for duty with RFC	16.2.18	*GHQ EEF*
15.3.18	Graded as Flying Officer subject W O app.	12.3.18	*7 Bde RO 74 HQME*
13.6.18	Posted to Home Establishment	13.6.18	*MFG 34117*
17.6.18	Embarked Alexandria for UK per HT 'Indarra'	17.6.18	*D 27755*

This completes the first form. * Possibly 52/6759.

14.9.19	*HQ RAF*	*Arr. S. Russia 12.9.19 taken on strength*	14.9.19	
	"	*HQ RAF & posted to S. Russia*		
15.10.19	"	*To Volnavkha on temporary duty*	14.10.19	*HQ/RO/98/16.10.19*
9.12.19	"	*To Kislovka & Z Sqdn by air*	9.12.19	*HQ/RO/115/9.12.19*
31.1.20	"	*From Z Sqdn to ..K awaiting embarkation*	29.1.20	*HQ/RO/114 9.2.20*
9.2.20	"	*To Constant. & struck off strength*	7.2.20	*HQ/RO/10 9.2.20*
15.4.20	"	*St. Stanislaus with Sword & Bow 2785**	19.1.20	*HQ/RO/37 15.4.20*

This completes the second form.* Possibly 2786.

47 Squadron	DH.9 F1196	Damaged beyond repair while parked at Ekaterinodar after being struck by the

aircraft reported above.

Saturday 18 October 1919
115 Squadron disbanded at Ford.

Tuesday 21 October 1919
At Lympne 120 Squadron was officially stood down from duty.

Friday 24 October 1919
Still the paperwork had yet to be completed in respect of the change to A Squadron RAF Mission.

47 Squadron	Captain B G H Keymer	+	Krasnodar Cemetery, Krasnodar, Russia
DH.9A F1086	DFC* *Croci di Guerre* [Italy]		
	Lt D B Thompson	+	Krasnodar Cemetery, Krasnodar, Russia

T/o Beketovkar for bombing operations but on becoming airborne a bomb fell off and exploded, the blast destroying the DH. Basil Graham Homfray Keymer arrived in South Russia on 21st August 1919, and was attached to 47 Squadron. Aged only 20, he was the son of the Reverend Basil Nathaniel Keymer of Gosbeck Rectory, Ipswich. Basil Keymer's name appears in the list of officers appointed to a permanent commission on the 1st of August 1919, and until recently had being fly DHs with 221 Squadron.

The citations for his awards read as follows: *'Sea Patrol MEDITERRANEAN - A very gallant flight leader of exceptional ability and determination. On 24th July, when on a long-distance raid, Lieut. Keymer was attacked by three hostile aeroplanes and three seaplanes. Undaunted by these heavy odds, he engaged the enemy for thirty-five minutes and eventually succeeded in driving them off.'* Issue 13363, page 4475 of the Edinburgh edition of 5th December 1918.

The First Bar appeared in the Edinburgh paper of Boxing Day 1919, issue 13543, page 4138, though without a citation appended, merely noting it was for operations in South Russia and was effective on 22nd December 1919. Sadly, Captain Keymer, whose rank is recorded as Flying Officer, would never be aware of this second honour bestowed upon him.

Douglas Blaxland Thompson, whose service records I have yet to find, was aged 27, and was formerly of the Royal Field Artillery.

Both officers are now commemorated on the Haidar Pasha Memorial in Turkey where their names are engraved on panel 8 of the screen wall.

Note. I strongly suspect that Basil Keymer had an elder brother who took Holy Orders for a Record of Service is extant for Captain Bernard William Keymer, Chaplin, who joined the RFC in February 1917. He was married, and his next of kin address is given as The Vicarage, East Leigh. He was attached to a number of squadrons:-

> *27.2.17 40 Squadron; 24.7.17 25 Squadron; 13.8.17 10 Squadron; 20.8.17 25 Squadron; 11.9.17 16 Squadron and 16.9.17 25 Squadron. Returned to 1st Brigade 28.9.17.*

Saturday 25 October 1919
Four more squadrons were officially informed that their duties ceased with effect from this day; 53 Squadron at Old Sarum, 54 Squadron and 65 Squadron at Yatesbury and 66 Squadron at Leighterton.

Monday 27 October 1919
3 Squadron disbanded at Dover.

**NOVEMBER
1919**

For the first time since the armistice, a month passed without any fatal casualties reported from squadrons that were attributed to air accidents.

Tuesday 11 November 1919
The first anniversary of the Armistice.

Friday 14 November 1919
At Stan Stephano in Turkey 17 Squadron which had operated a variety of aircraft since arriving in Egypt shortly before Christmas 1915, subsequently operating its flights at various locations including Macedonia, disbanded.

**DECEMBER
1919**

Tuesday 23 December 1919
To receive news that a son, daughter or husband had been killed whilst on military service was always a painful experience for parents and wives. Some just could not accept that it was the end for one loved so much, this being true for both wars. In the Somerset village of Isle Brewers where I grew up, my brother [at the time he was serving with the Royal Air Force as a driver and stationed in North Africa] lost his best friend, Kenneth Brice who had volunteered for aircrew and in 1943, was a flight engineer attached to 408 Squadron RCAF. He was well into his tour of operations when on the night of 3rd-4th April 1943, in the course of a raid on Essen, his Halifax II JB866 EQ-T captained by Pilot Officer Ebenezer Alfred Sirett RCAF was shot down while outbound over Holland. No one survived and all now rest in Uden War Cemetery. When Kenneth's parents were eventually informed that their son had died, Mrs Brice would never accept that Kenneth had been killed and as a consequence his brother and two sisters never knew what fate had befallen him until I went to the Public Record Office at Kew and took photocopies of all his operational flights and presented them to the family [both Mr and Mrs Brice had long since died]. Also, through the kindness of the late Haans de Hann, a truly dedicated Dutch researcher, who went to Uden and photographed Kenneth's grave, I was able to provide them with pictures of his grave.

Since then I have long since completed my work on the Bomber Command losses series where in the 1943 volume on page 92 is the summary explaining what befell Kenneth and his crew. In the Roll of Honour [Volume Nine] his name appears on page 178, left hand column, his skipper being commemorated in the RCAF section on page 281 right hand column.

48 Squadron   P/O M H Tisdall   +   Quetta Government Cemetery 2272 [Delhi Memorial, India Gate]
Bristol F.2b H1551 AC2 A J S Jordan   +   Quetta Government Cemetery 2390 [Delhi Memorial, India Gate]
T/o Quetta and crashed close to the airfield thus becoming the first fatal accident to befall the squadron since arriving at Quetta in July. There are no next of kin details appended for Michael Henry Tisdall [was the trauma like that for Mrs Brice over two decades later so overwhelming that Michael's parents were unwilling to have their details recorded].

Official notice of his short service commission, effective from 30th January 1920, in the rank of Flying Officer from Pilot Officer appeared in the *Gazette* on 30th January 1920, issue 31761, page 1264.

Aircraftman Jordan came from Willenhall in Staffordshire. His service number 248631 identifies him as having transferred from the RNAS on formation of the Royal Air Force in April 1918.

Monday 29 December 1919
The remaining personnel of 32 Squadron at Croydon were stood down. On the 1st of April 1923, at nearby Kenley, the squadron would reform.

Tuesday 30 December 1919
56 Squadron [SE.5a] arrived at Bircham Newton from Narborough.

New Year's Eve 1919
As if to emphasise that the need to retain a healthy residue of squadrons was no longer necessary, then this brought into sharp focus on this Wednesday with the disbandment of twenty-one squadrons at various locations across the UK. The cull included 7, 9, 10, 11, 13, 15, 16, 18, 19, 22, 23, 41, 43, 44, 45, 46, 57, 64, 78, 83 and 101.

31 Squadron   F/O J Pipe   Injured Karachi 1914-1918 War Memorial
Bristol F.2b E2538
T/o Risalpur and stalled into the ground while making a steeply banked climbing turn. James Pipe died the following day from his injuries. I have not been able to locate a Record of Service.

His father, Major Alfred William Pipe, late of the Royal Garrison Artillery, and retired from regular service prior to the start of the *Great War,* rejoined as a Territorial and was made a temporary Captain on the 24th of June 1915 [LG 23 June 1915, supplement 29203, page 6140].

Appendix 2A - Squadron losses table 1919

1. Accidents in which it is believed the aircraft was either a total wreck, or deemed to be beyond economical repair
2. Fatalities, either at the time of the crash, or subsequently reported to have died from injuries
3. Miscellaneous
4. Totals of the three columns
5. Squadron's role

ROYAL AIR FORCE

Squadron	1	2	3	4	5
1 Squadron	2	1		3	Fighter equipped with SE.5a
2 Squadron	1			1	Corps reconnaissance equipped with FK.8
3 Squadron	1			1	Fighter equipped with F.1 Camel
5 Squadron	5	2	1	8	Rhineland occupation equipped with RE.8 and Bristol F.2b
6 Squadron	7		6	13	Reconnaissance equipped with RE.8 and Bristol F.2b
7 Squadron	2	1		3*	Rhineland occupation equipped with Bristol F.2b
8 Squadron	4	2		6	Reconnaissance equipped with Bristol F.2b
9 Squadron	4			4	Rhineland occupation equipped with RE.8 and Bristol F.2b
10 Squadron	2			2	Reconnaissance equipped with FK.8
11 Squadron	5	3		8	Fighter equipped with Bristol F.2b
12 Squadron	8		1	9	Rhineland occupation equipped with RE.8 and Bristol F.2b
16 Squadron	2			2	Reconnaissance equipped with RE.8
17 Squadron	2			2	White Russian support equipped with DH.9 and F.1 Camel
18 Squadron	16	1		17	Rhineland occupation equipped with DH.9A
19 Squadron	1	1		2	Fighter equipped with 5F.1 Dolphin
20 Squadron	5		1	6*	Fighter equipped with Bristol F.2b
22 Squadron	3			3	Rhineland occupation equipped with Bristol F.2b
23 Squadron	2	1		3	Fighter equipped with 5F.1 Dolphin
24 Squadron	1			1	Fighter equipped with F.1 Camel
25 Squadron	3	4	1	8	Rhineland occupation equipped with DH.4 and DH.9A
28 Squadron	2	1		3	Fighter equipped with F.1 Camel
29 Squadron	4	1		5	Rhineland occupation equipped with SE.5a
30 Squadron	1	1		2	Fighter/bomber equipped with Marinsyde and SE.5a
31 Squadron	2	1		3	Army co-operation equipped with BE.2e and Bristol F.2b
32 Squadron			1	1	Fighter equipped with SE.5a
35 Squadron	2			2	General purpose equipped with FK.8 and Bristol F.2b
36 Squadron	2	2		4	Training equipped with Sopwith Pup
40 Squadron	2			2	Fighter equipped with SE.5a
42 Squadron	1			1	Reconnaissance equipped with RE.8
43 Squadron	9	1		10	Rhineland occupation equipped 7F.1 Snipe
44 Squadron	1	1		2	Fighter equipped with F.1 Camel
45 Squadron	1			1	Fighter equipped with F.1 Camel
46 Squadron	1			1	Fighter equipped with F.1 Camel
47 Squadron	5	2	1	8	White Russian support equipped with DH.9
48 Squadron	8	5		13	Rhineland occupation equipped with Bristol F.2b
49 Squadron	7			7	Rhineland occupation equipped with DH.9 and DH.9A
53 Squadron	1		13	14	Reconnaissance equipped with RE.8
55 Squadron	1			1	Bomber equipped with DH.4
56 Squadron	1	1		2	Fighter equipped with SE.5a
57 Squadron	20	3		23	Mail delivery equipped with DH.4, DH.9 and DH.9A
58 Squadron	2	2		4	Bomber equipped with HP O/400
59 Squadron	3	2		5	Rhineland occupation equipped with RE.8 and Bristol F.2b
61 Squadron	1	1		2	Fighter equipped with F.1 Camel
62 Squadron	8			8	Rhineland occupation equipped with Bristol F.2b
63 Squadron	1	2		3	Army co-operation equipped with RE.8
65 Squadron	4	1		5	Fighter equipped with F.1 Camel
66 Squadron	2	1		3	Fighter equipped with F.1 Camel
70 Squadron	19	4		23	Rhineland occupation equipped with F.1 Camel and 7F.1 Snipe
72 Squadron	1	1		2	Army co-operation equipped with various types
73 Squadron	1			1	Fighter equipped with F.1 Camel
74 Squadron	1			1	Fighter equipped with SE.5a
75 Squadron	3	1		4	Fighter equipped with F.1 Camel
78 Squadron	3	2		5	Training equipped with various types
79 Squadron	1	1		2	Fighter equipped with 5F.1 Dolphin
80 Squadron	7	1		8	Fighter equipped with various types
84 Squadron	11	1		12	Rhineland occupation equipped with SE.5a
85 Squadron	4			4	Fighter equipped with SE.5a
88 Squadron	6	3		9	Fighter equipped with Bristol F.2b
92 Squadron	3		6	9	Rhineland occupation equipped with SE.5a
94 Squadron	1			1	Fighter equipped with SE.5a
97 Squadron	6	4		10	Bomber equipped with HP O/400 and DH.10
98 Squadron	2			2	Bomber equipped with DH.9

173

99 Squadron	16	4		20	Bomber equipped with DH.9A
100 Squadron	2	4		6*	Bomber equipped with HP O/400
101 Squadron	2			2	Bomber equipped with FE.2b
103 Squadron	6			6	Bomber equipped with DH.9
104 Squadron	3			3	Bomber equipped with DH.9
105 Squadron	1	1		2	Army co-operation equipped with Bristol F.2b
107 Squadron	2		1	3	Bomber equipped with DH.9
108 Squadron	1			1	Bomber equipped with DH.9
110 Squadron	13	3		16	Mail delivery equipped with DH.9A
111 Squadron	1	2		3	Army co-operation equipped with Bristol F.2b
112 Squadron	1	1		2	Fighter equipped with F.1 Camel
114 Squadron	1	1		2	Army co-operation equipped with BE.2e
117 Squadron	1			1	Internal security equipped with DH.9
139 Squadron	1			1	Fighter equipped with Bristol F.2b
141 Squadron	1	1		2	Internal security equipped with Bristol F.2b
142 Squadron	1			1	Reconnaissance equipped with various types
186 Squadron	1	1		2	Torpedo development equipped with various types
191 Squadron	1			1	Training equipped with various types
201 Squadron	1			1	Fighter equipped with F.1 Camel
202 Squadron	3			3	Bomber equipped with DH.4
203 Squadron	3		1	4	Fighter equipped with F.1 Camel
204 Squadron	2			2	Fighter equipped with F.1 Camel
205 Squadron	8			8	Bomber equipped with DH.9A
206 Squadron	5	4		9	Rhineland occupation equipped with DH.9
207 Squadron	2			2	Rhineland occupation equipped with HP O/400
208 Squadron	16			16*	Rhineland occupation equipped with 7F.1 Snipe
209 Squadron	2			2	Fighter equipped with F.1 Camel
210 Squadron	1			1	Fighter equipped with F.1 Camel
211 Squadron	1			1	Bomber equipped with DH.9
213 Squadron	1			1	Fighter equipped with F.1 Camel
214 Squadron	1	4		5	Bomber equipped with HP O/400
216 Squadron	10	3		13	Transport equipped with HP O/400
218 Squadron	1			1	Bomber equipped with DH.9
221 Squadron	2	2		4	White Russian support equipped with DH.9 and DH.9A
236 Squadron	1	1		2	Coastal reconnaissance equipped with DH.9
274 Squadron	1	1		2	Training equipped with V/1500
Total	353	95	33	481	

AUSTRALIAN FLYING CORPS

2 Squadron	1			1	Fighter equipped with SE.5a
3 Squadron	2		4	6	Reconnaissance equipped with RE.8
4 Squadron	2			2	Fighter equipped with 7F.1 Snipe
Total	5		4	9	

CANADIAN AIR FORCE

2 Squadron	1	1		2*	Training equipped with DH.9A
Combined totals	359	96	37	492	

* Indicates included within their losses the crashes of German aircraft under test

174

Appendix 2B - Losses by Aircraft Type 1919

Data in the columns follow the same pattern as Appendix A. An explanation as to role performed by the various types is recorded in Appendix B for 12th November to 31st December 1918.

Aircraft Manufacturing Company Limited: DH.4

25 Squadron	3	4		7
55 Squadron	1			1
57 Squadron	10	3		13
98 Squadron	1			1
202 Squadron	2			2
Totals	17	7		24

Aircraft Manufacturing Company Limited: DH.9

17 Squadron	1			1
47 Squadron	5	2	1	8
49 Squadron	4			4
57 Squadron	2			2
98 Squadron	1			1
103 Squadron	6			6
104 Squadron	3			3
107 Squadron	2		1	3
108 Squadron	1			1
117 Squadron	1			1
142 Squadron	1			1
206 Squadron	5	4		9
211 Squadron	1			1
218 Squadron	1			1
221 Squadron	1			1
236 Squadron	1	1		2
Totals	36	7	2	45

Aircraft Manufacturing Company Limited: DH.9A

18 Squadron	16	1		17
25 Squadron			1	1
49 Squadron	3			3
57 Squadron	8			8
99 Squadron	16	4		20
110 Squadron	13	3		16
202 Squadron	1			1
205 Squadron	8			8
221 Squadron	1	2		3
Totals	66	10	1	77

Aircraft Manufacturing Company Limited: DH.10

97 Squadron	2	3	5

Developed as a replacement for DH.4, the DH.10 arrived too late to see active service and as a consequence only four squadrons operated the type and by 1923 it had been withdrawn from use.

Armstrong Whitworth: FK.8

2 Squadron	1	1
10 Squadron	2	2
35 Squadron	2	2
Totals	5	5

Avro Aircraft Company: Avro 504

66 Squadron	1	1	2
78 Squadron	1	1	2
Totals	2	2	4

Bristol Aeroplane Company: Bristol F.2b

5 Squadron	2	2		4
6 Squadron	2			2
7 Squadron	1			1
8 Squadron	4	2		6
9 Squadron	1			1
11 Squadron	5	3		8
12 Squadron	4			4
20 Squadron	4		1	5
22 Squadron	3			3
31 Squadron	1			1
48 Squadron	8	5		13

59 Squadron	1			1
62 Squadron	8			8
88 Squadron	6	3		9
105 Squadron	1	1		2
111 Squadron	1	2		3
139 Squadron	1			1
141 Squadron	1			1
Totals	54	18	1	73

Handley Page Limited: HP O/400

58 Squadron	2	2		4
97 Squadron	4			4
207 Squadron	2			2
214 Squadron	1	4		5
216 Squadron	10	3		13
Totals	19	9		28

Handley Page Limited: V/1500

274 Squadron	1	1		2

Martinsyde: G-106

30 Squadron	1	1		2

Royal Aircraft Factory: BE.2e

31 Squadron	1	1		2
114 Squadron	1	1		2
Totals	2	2		4

Royal Aircraft Factory: FE.2b

101 Squadron	2			2
191 Squadron	1			1
Totals	3			3

Royal Aircraft Factory:RE.8

5 Squadron	3		1	4
6 Squadron	5		6	11
9 Squadron	3			3
12 Squadron	4		1	5
16 Squadron	2			2
42 Squadron	1			1
53 Squadron	1		13	14
59 Squadron	2	2		4
63 Squadron	1	2		3
Totals	22	4	21	47

AUSTRALIAN FLYING CORPS

3 Squadron	2		4	6
Combined totals	24	4	25	53

Royal Aircraft Factory:SE.5a

1 Squadron	2	1		3
24 Squadron	1			1
29 Squadron	4	1		5
32 Squadron			1	1
40 Squadron	2			2
56 Squadron	1	1		2
74 Squadron	1			1
84 Squadron	11	1		12
85 Squadron	4			4
92 Squadron	3		6	9
94 Squadron	1			1
Totals	30	4	7	41

AUSTRALIAN FLYING CORPS

2 Squadron	1			1
Combined totals	31	4	7	42

Société Pour L'Aviation et ses Dérivés: SPAD VII

72 Squadron	1	1		2

Sopwith Aviation Company: F.1 Camel

3 Squadron	1			1
17 Squadron	1			1
28 Squadron	2	1		3
44 Squadron	1	1		2
45 Squadron	1			1
46 Squadron	1			1
61 Squadron	1	1		2
65 Squadron	4	1		5

66 Squadron	1			1	
70 Squadron	10	4		14	
73 Squadron	1			1	
75 Squadron	3	1		4	
78 Squadron	1			1	
80 Squadron	1			1	
112 Squadron	1	1		2	
201 Squadron	1			1	
203 Squadron	3		1	4	
204 Squadron	2			2	
209 Squadron	2			2	
210 Squadron	1			1	
213 Squadron	1			1	
Totals	40	10	1	51	

Sopwith Aviation Company: Cuckoo

186 Squadron	1	1		2	

Sopwith Aviation Company: 5F.1 Dolphin

19 Squadron	1	1		2	
23 Squadron	2	1		3	
79 Squadron	1	1		2	
Totals	4	3		7	

Sopwith Aviation Company:Pup

36 Squadron	2	2		4	
80 Squadron	1	1		2	

Sopwith Aviation Company: 7F.1 Snipe

43 Squadron	9	1		10	
70 Squadron	9			9	
78 Squadron	1	1		2	
80 Squadron	5			5	
208 Squadron	15			15	
Totals	39	2		41	

AUSTRALIAN FLYING CORPS

4 Squadron	2			2	

Combined totals	41	2		43	

German Aircraft

7 Squadron	1	1		2	Fokker type
20 Squadron	1			1	Fokker type
100 Squadron	2	4		6	Gotha type
Totals	4	5		9	

CANADIAN AIR FORCE

2 Squadron	1	1		2	Fokker type

Combined totals	5	6		11	

Appendix 2C - Squadron Locations as at 31st December 1919

The year 1919, had witnessed a massive change in squadron fortunes. The need to retain Royal Air Force strength, as it stood on the 1st of January, could not be sustained in a country coming to terms with a peace that had only been achieved at a terrible cost in human life and resources. The entire structure of the armed forces had to undergo a seed change and the Royal Air Force was no exception. The table that follows has been constructed from the late James J Halley's work *The Squadrons of the Royal Air Force & Commonwealth 1918-1988* and published by Air-Britain[Historians] Ltd in 1988. Squadrons that had been reduced to a cadre and without aircraft are omitted.

The table shows squadrons that were extant at the end of the year.

6 Squadron	Baghdad West	Mesopotamia	RE.8	Patrol duties
8 Squadron	Duxford	England	Bristol F.2b	Awaiting disbandment
12 Squadron	Heumar	Germany	Bristol F.2b	Rhineland Occupation
20 Squadron	Bannu	India	Bristol F.2b	Patrol duties over the North West Frontier
31 Squadron	Risalpur	India	Bristol F.2b	Patrol duties over the North West Frontier
48 Squadron	Quetta	India	Bristol F.2b	Patrol duties over the North West Frontier
56 Squadron	Bircham Newton	England	SE.5a	Fighter
58 Squadron	Heliopolis	Egypt	HP O/400 & Vimy	Transport
63 Squadron	Baghdad	Mesopotamia	RE.8	Awaiting disbandment
80 Squadron	Aboukir	Egypt	7F.1 Snipe	Awaiting disbandment
97 Squadron	Lahore	Indi	DH.10	Patrol duties over the North West Frontier
99 Squadron	Mianwali	India	DH.9A	Patrol duties over the North West Frontier
105 Squadron	Oranmore	Ireland	Bristol F.2b	Army support
111 Squadron	Ramleh	Palestine	Bristol F.2b	Army support
113 Squadron	Ismailia	Egypt	RE.8	Amy suppor.t
114 Squadron	Ambala	India	Bristol F.2b	Indian army support.
123 Squadron	Shoreham	England	DH.9A	Bomber
141 Squadron	Baldonnel	Ireland	Bristol F.2b	Army support
142 Squadron	Suez	Egypt	DH.9	Army support
186 Squadron	Gosport	England	Various	Torpedo development
206 Squadron	Helwan	Egypt	DH.9	Army support
212 Squadron	Swingate Downs	England	DH.9	Coastal duties
214 Squad4on	Abu Sueir	Egypt	HP O/400	Bomber
216 Squadron	Abu Sueir	Egypt	HP O/400 & DH.10	Transport
230 Squadron	Felixstowe	England	Various	Coastal duties
267 Squadron	Calafrana	Malta	Various	Seaplane duties
274 Squadron	Bircham Newton	England	HP V/1500	Bomber

Appendix D - Permanent Commissions

This appendix, and Appendix E , should be read in conjunction with entries in *The London Gazette* and similar websites, particularly Malcolm Barrass's expertly compiled 'Air of Authority - A History of RAF Organisation'. Other sources, such as air accident reports et al have been accessed to provide additional information and I am indebted to my co-author Paul McMillan whose 'detective' expertise has enable me to enter data against some of the names that defied my attempts to discover the date on which they left the service.

On the 1st of August 1919, the establishment of permanent commissions was signalled from the Air Ministry: *"The attention of the officers named in this Gazette is directed to the Air Ministry Weekly Order, now in course of issue, relating to the grant of permanent commissions and to the new rates and conditions of pay and other emoluments.*
The following are granted permanent commissions in the RAF in the ranks stated. Dated 1st August:-"

MAJOR-GENERALS
6

Sir H M TRENCHARD KCB DSO	MRAF	01.01.30	Retirement

Marshal of the Royal Air Force, The Viscount Trenchard of Wolfeton GCB OM GCVO DSO ten times mentioned in despatches, died on Friday, 10th February 1956. He is buried in the Royal Air Force Chapel in Westminster Abbey. Note. He resigned his commission as Air Marshal and was granted the Honorary Rank of Major-General in the Army whilst holding the appointment of as Colonel of the Royal Scottish Fusiliers [LG 25 May 1920, supplement 31916, page 5898]. However, in February 1919, he was summoned by Official Telegram to report to the War Office where Winston Churchill, Secretary of State for War and Secretary of State for Air, insisted he return to the service and on 31st March 1919, Trenchard took up the appointment of Chief of the Air Staff.

Sir G M PAINE KCB MVO	AV-M	12.05.20	Retired list

At his own request [LG 11 May 1920, issue 31894, page 5362]. Rear Admiral [Air-Vice Marshal] Sir Godfrey Paine KCB MVO died on Wednesday, 23 March 1932, and was buried at his request in the sea off Portsmouth's Nab Tower.

Sir J M SALMOND KCB CMG CVO DSO	MRAF	01.04.33	Retirement

Marshal of the Royal Air Force Sir John Salmond GCB CMG CVO DSO* seven times mentioned in despatches, died on Tuesday, 6th April 1968. His brother, Air Chief Marshal Sir Geoffrey Salmond pre-deceased him. With his death, so passed the last surviving officer of Major-General rank appointed on the 1st of August 1919.

J F A HIGGINS CB DSO AFC	AM	01.09.30	Retirement**

Air Marshal Sir John Higgins KCB KBE DSO AFC six times mentioned in despatches, died on Tuesday, 1st June 1948. It is recorded that on the outbreak of the Second World War at which time Sir John was employed by an aircraft company in India, resumed the mantle of Air Marshal on 6th October 1939, serving until August 1940, as Air Officer Commanding in Chief, Air Forces India. On retiring from the Service for the second time he returned to the United Kingdom.

E L ELLINGTON CB CMG	MRAF	04.04.40	Retirement**

Marshal of the Royal Air Force Sir Edward Ellington GCB CMG CBE three times mentioned in despatches, died on Tuesday, 13th June 1967.

Sir W G H SALMOND KCMB CB DSO	ACM	+	27.04.33	Chief of the Air Staff

Air Chief Marshal Sir Geoffrey Salmond KCB KCMG DSO seven times mentioned in despatches and elder brother of Marshal of the Royal Air Force Sir John Salmond died in King Edward VII's Hospital on Thursday, 27th April 1933. He was the only appointee from the rank of Major-General to die while on active service.

COLONELS
17

A V VYVYAN CB DSO	AV-M	01.09.25	Retirement

At his own request [LG 11 September 1925, issue 33083, page 5974]. Air Vice-Marshal Sir Vyell Vyvyan KCB DSO Twice mentioned in despatches, died on Monday, 30th September 1935.

P W GAME CB DSO	AV-M	01.01.29	Retirement

Air Vice-Marshal Sir Philip Game GCB GCVO GBE KCMG DSO Mentioned in despatches, died on Saturday, 4th February 1961.

O SWANN CB CBE	AV-M	02.11.29	Retirement

Air Vice-Marshal Sir Oliver Swann KCB CBE died on Sunday, 7th March 1948.

F R SCARLETT CB DSO	AV-M	31.12.31	Retirement

Air Vice-Marshal Francis Rowland Scarlett CB DSO Mentioned in despatches, died on Sunday, 15th April 1934.

C L LAMBE CB CMG DSO	AV-M	01.10.31	Retirement

Air Vice-Marshal Sir Charles Lambe KCB CMG DSO, died on Saturday, 25th April 1953.

J M STEEL CMG CBE	ACM	12.09.37	Retirement

Air Chief Marshal Sir John Steel GCB KBE CMG twice mentioned in despatches, died on Thursday, 2nd December 1965.

C A H LONGCROFT CMG DSO AFC	AV-M	02.11.29	Retirement

Air Vice-Marshal Sir Charles Longcroft KCB CMG DSO AFC mentioned in despatches, died on Thursday, 20th February 1958.

T I WEBB-BOWEN CB CMG	AV-M	26.09.33	Retirement

Air Vice-Marshal Sir Tom Webb-Bowen KCB CMG three times mentioned in despatches, died on Monday, 29th October 1956.

L E O CHARLTON CB CMG DSO	A/Cmdr	01.04.28	Retirement

Air Commodore Lionel Evelyn Oswald Charlton CB CMG DSO three time mentioned in despatches, died on Friday, 18th April 1958.

D le G PITCHER CMG DSO	A/Cmdr	12.04.29	Retirement

Air Commodore Duncan le Geyt Pitcher CMG CBE DSO twice mentioned in despatches, died on Friday, 1st September 1944.

R M GROVES CB DSO AFC	A/Cmdr	+	27.05.20	A.AOC RAF ME

Although recorded as '70 Squadron' on the CWGC data base, at the time of his death in an air accident [see my summary for the date in question] he was Acting Air Officer Commanding RAF Middle East Area and had been in post since 3rd April 1920. Air Commodore Robert Marsland Groves CB DSO AFC aged 40, is buried in Cairo New British Protestant Cemetery, Egypt.

E A D MASTERMAN CMG CBE AFC	A/Cmdr	01.03.29	Retirement

Air Commodore Edward Alexander Dimsdale Masterman CB CMG CBE AFC, died on Monday, 26th August 1957.

J H W BECKE CMG DSO	A/Cmdr	29.02.20	Retirement

Air Commodore John Harold Whitworth Becke CMG DSO AFC twice mentioned in despatches, died on Monday, 7th February 1949.

E L GERRARD CMG DSO	A/Cmdr	15.11.29	Retirement

Air Commodore Eugene Louis Gerrard CMG DSO, died on Thursday, 7th February 1963.

H P SMYTHE-OSBOURNE CMG	A/Cmdr	12.11.24	Retirement

Air Commodore Sir Henry Smythe-Osbourne Kt CMG CBE mentioned in despatches, died on Friday, 28th March 1969.

F C HALAHAN CMG DSO MVO	AV-M	01.01.30	Retirement

Air Vice-Marshal Frederick Crosby Halahan CMG CBE DSO MVO mentioned in despatches, died on Sunday, 17th October 1965.

01026	P R C GROVES CMG DSO	Brigadier-General	03.02.22	Retirement

Returned to service: Commissioned 21st September 1939, to the Administrative and Special Duties Branch. 10.02.54 Relinquished

Air Commodore Percy Robert Clifford Groves CB CMG DSO, died on Wednesday, 12th August 1959.

LIEUTENANT-COLONELS
79

C R SAMSON CMG DSO AFC	A/Cmdr	06.11.29	Retirement

Air Commodore Charles Rumney Samson CMG DSO*AFC twice mentioned in despatches, died on Thursday, 5th February 1931.

R H CLARK-HALL DSO	AM	11.08.34	Retirement

Air Marshal Sir Robert Clark-Hall KBE CMG DSO mentioned in despatched, died on Sunday, 8th March 1964.

T C R HIGGINS CMG	A/Cmdr	01.11.29	Retirement

Air Commodore Thomas Charles Reginald Higgins CB CMG, died on Tuesday, 22nd September 1953.

A M LONGMORE DSO	ACM	01.03.42	Retirement**

Air Chief Marshal Sir Arthur Longmore GCB DSO mentioned in despatches, died on Thursday, 10th December 1970.

I M BONHAM-CARTER OBE	A/Cmdr	01.10.31	Retirement

Air Commodore Ian Malcolm Bonham-Carter CB OBE, died on Thursday, 31st December 1953. During the *Great War* and while serving with 4 Squadron RFC, he visited his old regiment, the Northumberland Fusiliers which were in the line and while present an enemy shell exploded nearby resulting in him losing a leg. Despite this he continued to fly and towards the end of his air force career, and while Air Officer Commanding, No 23 Group, he had an Avro 504 specially adapted for his personal use.

P L W HERBERT CMG	A/Cmdr	03.12.29	Retirement

Air Commodore Herbert Philip Lee William Herbert CMG CBE, died on Thursday, 26th November 1936.

J G HEARSON CB DSO	A/Cmdr	01.09.27	Retirement

Air Commodore John Glanville Hearson CB CBE DSO mentioned in despatches, died on Thursday, 9th January 1964.

E R LUDLOW-HEWITT CMG DSO MC	ACM	19.11.45	Retirement**

Air Chief Marshal Sir Edgar Ludlow-Hewitt GCB GBE CMG DSO MC six times mentioned in despatches, died on Wednesday, 15th August 1973.

U J D BOURKE CMG	G/Capt	13.04.30	Retired list

Group Captain Ulick John Deane Burke assumed command of No. 3 Group on 30th November 1919, though by 5th November 1920, he was in the Middle East where he assumed command of Palestine Group vice Wing Commander S Grant-Dalton. The 'Air of Authority' website further indicates that on 10th April 1922, he was appointed as Station Commander to one of the Royal Air Force stations in the central area of the United Kingdom.

C L N NEWALL CMG AM	MRAF	24.10.40	Retirement**

Marshal of the Royal Air Force The Lord Newall of Clifton upon Dunsmoor Baron GCB OM GCMG CBE KStJ AM three time mentioned in despatches, died on Saturday, 30th November 1963.

A E BORTON CMG DSO AFC	AV-M	23.08.33	Retirement

Air Vice-Marshal Amyas Eden Borton CB CMG DSO AFC mentioned in despatches, died on Friday, 15th August 1969.

A FLETCHER CMG CBE MC	A/Cmdr	01.07.30	Retirement

Air Commodore Albert Fletcher CMG CBE MC, died on Sunday, 29th January 1956.

R GORDON CMG DSO	A/Cmdr	26.08.25	Retirement

Air Commodore Robert Gordon CB CMG DSO twice mentioned in despatches, died on Saturday, 25th September 1954.

C R J RANDALL CBE	G/Capt	04.10.23	Retired list

On account of ill-health [LG 2 October 1923, issue 32867, page 6586].

A G BOARD CMG DSO	A/Cmdr	10.09.31	Retirement

Air Commodore Andrew George Board CMG DSO, died on Sunday, 25th February 1973.

F V HOLT CMG DSO	AV-M	+	23.04.31	AOC Fighting Area

Killed in a midair collision while returning from Tangmere to Uxbridge when when the DH 60M Moth in which he was a passenger came into collision with a Siskin, both machines coming down at Seahurt Park, near Chichester. The pilot of the Siskin, Sergeant C G Wareham managed to land safely, but Air-Vice Marshal Felton Vesey Holt CMG DSO twice mentioned in despatches and his pilot, Flight Lieutenant H M Moody MC perished

K G BROOKE CMG	G/Capt	06.03.29	Retired list

At his own request [LG 5 March 1929, issue 33474, page 1578].

P B JOUBERT de la FERTÉ CMG DSO	ACM	06.11.43	Retirement**

Air Chief Marshal Sir Philip Joubert de la Ferte KCB CMG DSO five times mentioned in despatches, died on Thursday, 21st January 1965.

W R FREEMAN DSO MC	ACM	19.10.42	Retirement**

Air Chief Marshal Sir Wilfrid Freeman Baronet GCB DSO MC three times mentioned in despatches, died on Friday, 15th May 1953.

N D K MacEWEN DSO	AV-M	05.07.35	Retirement

Air Vice-Marshal Sir Norman MacEwen Kt CB CMG DSO, died on Thursday, 29th January 1953.

P H L PLAYFAIR MC	AM	20.07.42	Retirement**

Air Marshal Sir Patrick Playfair KBE CB CVO MC twice mentioned in despatches, died on Saturday, 23rd November 1974.

01090	R P MILLS MC	AV-M	01.01.36	Retirement

Air Vice-Marshal Reginald Percy Mills CB MC AFC, died on Thursday, 4th July 1968.

I T COURTNEY OBE	W/Cdr	01.03.46	Relinquished
G B HYNES DSO	G/Capt	12.04.31	Retired list

On account of ill-health [LG 14 April 1931, issue 33707, page 2422]. Paul McMillan adds, Group Captain Hynes died on Monday, 30th May 1938. His entry on *Wikipedia* shows he was born in Malta on 12th April 1887, gaining a commission in the Royal Artillery in 1905. One of the first army pilots, he gained his aviator's certificate No. 77 from the Royal Aero Club , and subsequently to the Royal Flying Corps in 1912.

Hon J D BOYLE DSO	A/Cmdr	09.07.32	Retirement

Air Commodore The Honourable John David Boyle CBE DSO, died on Wednesday, 25th September 1974.

01110	P K WISE CMG DSO	G/Capt	01.09.45	Retired list**
	W F MacN FOSTER DSO DFC	AV-M	06.02.37	Retirement

Appointed as W F MacNEECE but changed his surname to FOSTER by deed poll in 1927; recalled to service in September 1939, Air Vice-Marshal William Foster MacNeece Foster CB CBDE DSO DFC mentioned in despatches, died on Tuesday, 28th March 1978.

A B BURDETT DSO	G/Capt	12.06.30	Retired list

At his own request [LG 17 June 1930, issue 33616, page 3812].

W G S MITCHELL DSO MC	ACM	01.07.41	Retirement**

Air Chief Marshal Sir William Mitchell KCB CBE DSO MC AFC five times mentioned in despatches, died as a result of heart failure on Tuesday, 15th August 1944, while serving as Commandant of London Command, Air Training Corps. It is also recorded that he was the first Royal Air Force officer to hold the post of Gentleman Usher of the Black Rod. He is buried in Putney Vale Cemetery.

H le M BROCK DSO	A/Cmdr	01.08.37	Retirement

Air Commodore Henry le Marchant Brock CB DSO mentioned in despatches, died on Wednesday, 11th March 1964.

G F PRETYMAN DSO OBE	W/Cdr	30.11.29	Retired list

On account of ill-health [LG 3 December 1929, issue 33557, page 7868].

E F BRIGGS DSO	G/Capt	13.02.30	Retired list

At his own request [LG 25 February 1930, issue 33583, page 1224].

C E RISK DSO	W/Cdr	07.12.22	Retired list
C L COURTNEY CBE DSO	ACM	09.11.45	Retirement**

Air Chief Marshal Sir Christopher Courtney GBE KCB DSO mentioned in despatches, died on Friday, 22nd October 1976.

C E H RATHBORNE DSO	A/Cmdr	13.10.35	Retirement

Air Commodore Charles Edward Henry Rathbone CB DSO*, died on Tuesday, 21st December 1943.

A W BIGSWORTH CMG DSO	A/Cmdr	22.09.35	Retirement

Air Commodore Arthur Wellesley Biggsworth CMG DSO* AFC mentioned in despatches, died on Friday, 24th February 1961.

R P ROSS DSO	A/Cmdr	01.01.34	Retirement

Air Commodore Robert Peel Ross DSO AFC, died on Monday, 30th December 1963.

S A HEBDEN	G/Capt	17.05.30	Retired list
G I CARMICHAEL DSO	G/Capt	01.09.33	Retired list

At his own request [LG 5 September 1933, issue 33975, page 5802].

J A CHAMIER CMG DSO OBE	A/Cmdr	07.12.28	Retirement

At his own request [LG 11 December 1928, issue 33446, page 8173]. In 1938, he was appointed Commandant of the Air Defence Corps and in February 1941, undertook the establishment of the Air Training Corps, earning himself the title 'Father of the ATC'. Air Commodore Sir John Chamier Kt CB CMG DSO OBE twice mentioned in despatches, died on Friday, 3rd May 1974.

L W B REES VC MC AFC	G/Capt	01.08.31	Retired

At his own request [LG 4 August 1931, issue 33741, page 5113]. LG 5 August 1916, supplement 29695, page 7744: *'For conspicuous gallantry and devotion to duty. Whilst on flying duties, Major Rees sighted what he thought to be a bombing party of our own machines returning home. He went up to escort them, but on getting nearer discovered they were a party of enemy machines, about ten in all. Major Rees was immediately attacked by one of the machines, and after a short encounter it disappeared behind the enemy lines, damaged. Five others then attacked him at long range, but these he dispersed on coming to close quarters, after seriously damaging two of the machines. Seeing two others going westwards, he gave chase to them, but on coming nearer he was wounded in the thigh, causing him to lose temporary control of his machine. He soon righted it, and immediately closed with the enemy, firing at a close-contact range of only a few yards, until all his ammunition was used up. He then returned home, landing his machine safely in our lines.'* Group Captain Lionel Wilmot Brabazon Rees VC OBE MC AFC, died in Nassau in the Bahamas on Wednesday, 28th September 1955 and is buried in Nassau War Cemetery.

C R S BRADLEY OBE	G/Capt	23.04.32	Retired list

At his own request [LG 33822, Page 2891].

N J GILL CBE MC	A/Cmdr	01.01.37	Retirement

Air Commodore Napier John Gill CB CBE MC, died on Wednesday, 20th October 1948. In retirement, at his own request, he was General Manager of Boulton Paul Aircraft Limited until 1942, when he joined Marine Mountings Limited as their General Manager.

01109	H A WILLIAMSON CMG	G/Capt	30.09.28	Retired list

At his own request [LG 2 October 1928, issue 33426, page 6349]. Returned to service: Commissioned to General Duties Branch and with effect from 1st December 1940, promoted Group Captain [temporary] [LG 10 December 1940, issue 35010, page 6982]. TNA Kew records that a collection of the Group Captains memoirs and naval aviation papers are held by Cambridge University, Churchill Archives Centre.

D A OLIVER DSO	W/Cdr	22.06.33	Retired list

The award of his DSO was *Gazetted* on 22nd June 1916, supplement 29635, page 6212: *'In recognition of his services on the morning of the 25th April, 1916, when he pursued out to sea the enemy fleet which had bombarded Yarmouth, and flew along the line dropping bombs, being subjected to intense anti-aircraft fire.'* At the time he was ranked 'Lieutenant' but is recored as Squadron Commander. In the New Year's Honours List for 1919, and now ranked Lieutenant-Colonel, he was mentioned in despatches for his distinguished services in the Adriatic. He was *Gazetted* OBE in his Majesty's Birthday Honours list of 1919 [LG 3 June 1919, supplement 31378, page 7028].

F W BOWHILL DSO	ACM	01.07.42	Retirement**

Air Chief Marshal Sir Frederick Bowhill GBE KCB CMG DSO* seven times mentioned in despatches, died on Saturday, 12th March 1960.

E D M ROBERTSON DFC	A/Cmdr	01.08.35	Retirement

At his own request [LG 6 August 1935, issue 34187, page 5055]. Re-employed 2nd September 1939.

		10.10.45	Retired list**

Air Commodore Edmund Digby Maxwell Robertson CB DFC, died on Sunday, 24th July 1956.

J T CULL DSO	G/Capt	06.08.34	Retired list

At his own request [LG 7 August 1934, issue 34076, page 5057].

H M CAVE-BROWN-CAVE DSO DFC	AV-M	18.09.40	Retirement**

Air Vice-Marshal Henry Meyrick Cave-Brown-Cave CB DSO DFC, died on Thursday, 5th August 1965.

A L GODMAN CMG DSO	A/Cmdr	25.02.31	Retired list

At his own request [LG 24 February 1931, issue 33692, page 1288]. Air Commodore Arthur Lothian Goodman CMG DSO twice mentioned in despatches, died on Thursday, 26th July 1956.

A J L SCOTT MC AFC	G/Capt +	16.01.22	

New Zealand Group Captain Alan John Lance Scott CB MC AFC was born in Christchurch on the 29th of June 1883, and on graduating with a a degree in law from Oxford University took silk and as a Barrister practiced in London. As a pilot in the Royal Flying Corps he was attached to 43 Squadron and then in March 1917, was appointed to command 60 Squadron. Flying Nieuport 23 B1575/B on 10th July 1917, he was wounded in combat and the following day handed the squadron over to Major W J C K Cochran-Patrick. In 1920, he published a history of the squadron with the title *Sixty Squadron RAF : A history of the squadron from its formation*. Group Captain Scott died from double pneumonia. Copies of his book are still available, ABE Books UK from as little as £1.82 for an ex-library copy, while second-hand copies vary from £10 upwards.

A V BETTINGTON CMG	G/Capt	19.0.45	Retired list**
J H A LANDON DSO	G/Capt	05.08.35	Retired list

At his own request. Seriously ill, Group Captain Joseph Herbert Arthur Landon DSO died on Sunday, 8th December 1935.

R A COOPER DSO	Lt-Col	06.01.20	Resigned
R G CHERRY MC	Lt-Col	01.08.19	Cancelled
J C HALAHAN CBE	G/Capt	28.02.26	Retired list
A E CAIRNES DSO	Lt-Col	01.08.19	Cancelled
00051	C D BREESE AFC	AV-M +	05.03.41	AOC 18 Group

Air Vice-Marshal Charles Dempster Breeze CB AFC twice mentioned in despatches, was killed in a flying accident on Wednesday, 5th March 1941, the details being recorded in Ross McNeill's *Royal Air Force Coastal Command Losses of the Second World War - 1939-1941* which I gratefully acknowledge. The Hudson I N7315 QX-Y of 224 Squadron Leuchars, in which he was a passenger, took off from Leuchars at 0910 on a ferry flight to Sumburgh during which a fault on one of the engines occurred and in the attempted forced-landing near Wick airfield control was lost and the aircraft spun to the ground and caught fire killing the entire crew which was captained by Flight Lieutenant Ronald Nicholas Selley DFC. Air Vice-Marshal Breeze was buried at sea. On 21st April 1941 [some records show 19th April 1941] his son, Flight Lieutenant Henry Francis Dempster Breese of 210 Squadron lost his life whilst on operations. He is commemorated on the Runnymede Memorial.

R G D SMALL W/Cdr 17.12.32 Retired list

Owing to ill-health [LG 20 December 1932, issue 33894, page 8138]. He received a mentioned in despatches for his war services in France, notification appearing in the Edinburgh edition of the *Gazette* January 6th, 1919, issue 13378, page 82.

C S BURNETT DSO ACM + 09.04.45 Commandant ATC

Air Chief Marshal Sir Charles Burnett KCB CBE DSO seven times mentioned in despatches, died on Monday, 9th April 1945, while serving as the Commandant, Central Command of the Air Training Corps. He is buried in Halton [St. Michael] Churchyard.

N GOLDSMITH OBE Formerly of the Royal Hussars and Royal Field Artillery, Lieutenant N Goldsmith OBE resigned his commission on appointment to a permanent commission in the Royal Air Force [LG 7 December 1920, supplement 32158, page 12160].

J B BOWEN OBE A/Cmdr 04.10.37 Retirement

Air Commodore James Bevan Bowen CBE, died on Tuesday, 12th August 1969.

W H C MANSFIELD DSO Lt -Col 01.08.19 Cancelled
A H MEASURES OBE W/Cdr 31.03.20 Resigned
M SPICER G/Capt 30.11.32 Retired list
01043 R G BLOMFIELD DSO W/Cdr 04.05.24 Retired list

Australia Wing Commander Richard Graham Blomfield returned to service. W/Cdr + 16.03.40

His death, according to the website Home of the Firebirds - 56 Squadron History : Commanding Officers which I acknowledge, was by his own hand having been dismissed the service by sentence of General Court Martial on 5th March 1940. His offence had been to write a private letter to a friend in America using official headed note-paper outlining details of the magnetic hoop fitted to a Wellington conducting trials in detecting and destroying magnetic mines. Although written in all innocence he had breached the Official Secrets Act. Details of the court martial can be found at TNA Kew AIR 43/13 and AIR 44/10. Wing Commander Blomfield is buried in Aldershot Military Cemetery.

S GRANT-DALTON DSO W/Cdr 06.05.29 Retired list

At his own request [LG 14 May 1929, issue 33495, page 3242].

C G S GOULD W/Cdr 08.07.33 Retired list

At his own request [LG 22 August 1933, issue 33971, page 5554].

P F M FELLOWES DSO A/Cmdr 17.07.33 Retirement

Air Commodore Peregrine Forbes Morant Fellows DSO* mentioned in despatches, died on Sunday, 12th June 1955.

W H PRIMROSE DFC A/Cmdr 03.07.33 Retirement

Air Commodore William Harold Primrose CBE DFC, died on Saturday, 15th June 1957.

C F KILNER DSO* G/Capt + 20.10.25 Aide-de-Camp HM King

Group Captain Cecil Francis Kilner DSO* born at Kemsing in Kent on 8th October 1883, was appointed Aide-de-Camp to HM King George V on the 1st of January 1925, vice Air Commodore Cyril Lewis Norton Newall [LG 17 February 1925, issue 33021, page 117]. Sadly, within weeks of taking up his appointment he fell dangerously ill and died at 16 Beaumont Street, London, on Tuesday, 20th October 1925. He is buried in Kensal Green Cemetery. His awards were *Gazetted* on 16th February 1915, supplement 29076, page 1721 and 6th March 1917, issue 29772, page 2255.

H R BUSTEED OBE AFC A/Cmdr 14.11.32 Retirement

Air Commodore Henry Richard Busteed OBE AFC, died on Monday, 14th June 1965.

G V FOWLER AFC G/Capt + 02.07.42 Delhi
M G CHRISTIE CMG DSO MC G/Capt 15.01.30 Retired list

At his own request [LG 17 January 1930, issue 33571, page 348].

H BLACKBURN W/Cdr 29.08.29 Retired list
01089 J MEAD MC W/Cdr 14.03.23 Retired list

On account of ill-health contracted on active service.

R C M PINK A/Cmdr + 07.03.32 SASO HQ ADGB

Air Commodore Richard Charles Montagu Pink CBE mentioned in a despatch, died Monday, 7th March 1932. He is the only Royal Air Force officer to have a campaign named after him when he commanded No 2[Indian] Wing during operations on the North West Frontier. The success in quelling dissident tribesmen resulted in the accolade "Pink's War". Struck down with cancer within days of assuming the duties of Senior Air Staff Officer at Headquarters Air Defence Great Britain, he died a few months later in RAF Hospital Halton.

G C St P de DOMBASLE OBE W/Cdr + 07.07.29

Canada The website 'The Regimental Rogue' detailing the service of officers of The Royal Canadian Regiment lists in excess of ten entires pertaining to this officer as published in *The London Gazette*. It also notes he was appointed to command No. 1 Squadron at Bailleul on Christmas Eve 1916, vice Major C F Pretyman [see one page previous to this appendix].

R A BRADLEY CMG Lt-Col 01.08.19 Cancelled

MAJORS
177

F J ROBERTS [A] Major 01.08.19 Cancelled
01107 L A STRANGE DSO MC DFC [A] W/Cdr 24.02.21 Retired list

On account of ill-health contracted in the Service [LG 29 April 1921, issue 32307, page 3440]. Returned to service: Commissioned to the Royal Air Force Volunteer Reserve, General Duties Branch, in the rank of Pilot Officer for the duration of hostilities with effect from 18th April 1940 [LG 7th May 1940, issue 34844, page 2726]. Initially allotted 78522 but reverted to 01107. W/Cdr 10.02.54 Relinquished

A S BARRATT CMG MC [A] ACM 27.03.57 Retirement**

Air Chief Marshal Sir Arthur Barratt KCB CMG MC six time mentioned in despatches, died on Friday, 4th November 1966.

J R W SMYTH-PIGOTT DSO [A] G/Capt 08.10.34 Retired list

At his own request [LG 9 October 1934, issue 34094, page 6378]. His last position was an attachment to the Peruvian Government, effective from 15th March 1934 [LG 27 March 1934, issue 34036, page 2041].

D L ALLEN [SO] W/Cdr 26.09.33 Retired list

At his own request [LG 17 October 1933, issue 33987, page 6694].

J W CRUICKSHANK OBE [T] S/Ldr + 20.02.25

Squadron Leader Jasper Wallace Cruickshank DFC died from typhoid fever whilst on active service in Iraq.

H A VAN RYNEVELD DSO MC [A] Major 01.08.19 Cancelled

South Africa Recalled by Field Marshal Jan Smuts of South Africa to form the South African Air Force.

A SHEKLETON DSO [A] G/Capt + 01.03.41

Group Captain Alexander Shekleton CBE DSO is commemorated on the Ottawa Cremation Memorial. The circumstances of his death are recorded on the website 'The winter of their discontent - Harvards above' which reports the history of World War Two RAF [and] Fleet Air Arm training in Kingston & Ganaoque, Canada. The passage relevant to this appendix reads: *'Sadly, after months of coping with the problems of getting the station operational, Group Captain Alexander Shekleton collapsed and died of heart failure on March 1, 1941. His wife requested that his body be cremated and the ashes scattered over the open water of Lake Ontario.'*

E L GOSSAGE DSO MC [SO] AM 01.02.44 Retirement**

Air Marshal Sir Leslie Gossage KCB CVO DSO MC five times mentioned in despatches, died on Friday, 8th July 1949.

	Rank	Date	Reason
J E A BALDWIN DSO [A]	AM	15.08.39	Retirement

Air Marshal Sir John Baldwin KBE CB DSO KStJ four times mentioned in despatches, died on Monday, 28th July 1975. Between the 9th of January and 21st February 1942, as Air Officer Commanding No. 3 Group, Bomber Command, he was Acting Air Officer Commanding-in-Chief Bomber Command while waiting for the return from the United States of Air Chief Marshal Sir Arthur Harris.

	Rank	Date	Reason
C H K EDMONDS DSO OBE [A]	AV-M	03.10.45	Retirement**

Air Vice-Marshal Charles Humphrey Kingsman Edmonds CBE DSO twice mentioned in despatches, died on Sunday, 26th September 1954.

	Rank	Date	Reason
G R BROMET DSO OBE [SO]	AV-M	25.04.38	Retirement

Air Vice-Marshal Sir Geoffrey Bromet KBE CB DSO mentioned in despatches, died on Wednesday, 16th November 1983.

	Rank	Date	Reason
F E T HEWLETT DSO OBE [A & S]	G/Capt	15.03.34	Retired list

At his own request [LG 20 March 1934, issue 34034, page 1867]. During the course of his investigation, Paul McMillan has unearthed the fascinating detail from the website 'Grace's Guide to British Industrial History' that Group Captain Hewlett was taught to fly by his mother, Hilda Beatrice Hewlett who gained her Royal Aero Club Aviators' Certificate No. 122 on 29th August 1911, the first British woman to obtain a pilot's licence . Francis obtained his pilot's certificate No. 156 as a Sub-Lieutenant RN on 14th November 1911. Postwar Francis Esmé Theodore Hewlett and his mother settled in New Zealand and by May 1941, he was Station Commander at RNZAF Ohakea and by 1968, was patron of the Tauranga Aero Club, his rank now being recorded as Air Commodore. The website Auckland War Museum shows he was born on 21st January 1891, and died on Thursday, 7th November 1974.

	Rank	Date	Reason
R E C PEIRSE DSO AFC [A & S]	ACM	06.05.45	Retirement**

Air Chief Marshal Sir Richard Pierce KCB DSO AFC three times mentioned in despatches, died on Wednesday, 5th August 1970. After 'leaving' his appointment as Air Officer Commanding-in-Chief Bomber Command [he was succeeded by Air Arthur Harris], Sir Richard was appointed Air officer Commanding-in Chief Air Forces, India, where it is acknowledged he performed well. However, he rather 'blotted his copy book' when in 1944, he eloped with the wife of General Sir Claude Auckinleck.

	Rank	Date	Reason
A C WINTER OBE [SO]	G/Capt	01.06.37	Retired list

At his own request [LG 22 June 1937, issue 34410, page 4018].

	Rank	Date	Reason
J T BABINGTON DSO [A & S]	AM	18.02.44	Retirement**

Air Marshal Sir John Babington KCB CBE DSO, died on Tuesday, 20th March 1979. In order to avoid confusion with his younger brother, Air Marshal Sir Philip Babington [see next page], Sir John adopted his mother's maiden name of Tremayne.

	Rank	Date	Reason
E OSMOND CBE [A & S]	W/Cdr	21.11.37	Retired list

On account of ill-health [LG 23 November 1937, issue 34457, page 7353].

	Rank	Date	Reason
W D S SANDAY DSO MC [A]	Major	01.08.19	Cancelled
R B WARD [A & S]	W/Cdr	03.02.32	Retired list

Owing to ill-health. Seriously ill, Paul McMillan advises that Wing Commander Richard Barrington Ward died on Thursday, 18th May 1933, his death being reported in the *Bournemouth and Southampton Graphic*. He is buried in St. Mark Cemetery, Highcliffe.

	Rank		Date	Reason
R F STAPLETON-COTTON [T]	Major		01.08.19	Cancelled
E L CONRAN MC [A]	S/Ldr	+	06.01.24	No. 7 Group Andover

Australia Squadron Leader Eric Lewis Conran MC is buried in Hampstead Cemetery.

	Rank	Date	Reason
G BLATHERWICK [Ad]	S/Ldr	21.01.27	Retired list

On account of ill-health [LG 28 January 1927, issue 33243, page 584].

		Rank	Date	Reason
01080	L L GREIG MVO [Ad]	W/Cdr	26.11.45	Retired list**
	A H STEELE-PERKINS OBE [SO]	W/Cdr	08.08.33	Retired list

At his own request [LG 15 August 1933, issue 33969, page 5426].

	Rank		Date	Reason
T G HETHERINGTON CBE [SO]	G/Capt		11.07.43	Relinquished
R H HOWELL [SO]	Major		01.08.19	Cancelled
A B GASKELL DSC [S]	W/Cdr	+	15.09.27	30 Squadron

Wing Commander Arthur Bruce Gaskell was killed, and his passenger, Leading Aircraftman William Ronald Kittoe-Roberts, mortally injured when their Bristol F.2b H1632 crashed near Zam airfield in Iraq. A lenghty obituary to the Wing Commander was published in *The Times* on 17th September 1927, which states he was born on 7th September 1888, and following cadetship at the Britannia Naval College served in both the Mediterranean and Home Fleets before taking flying instruction and becoming an instructor at the Central Flying School, Upavon. His final year of service was on the Air Staff of Air Vice-Marshal Sir Edward Ellington, Air Officer Commanding in Iraq.

	Rank	Date	Reason
R L G MARIX DSO [S]	AV-M	06.12.45	Retirement**

Air Vice-Marshal Reginald Leonard George Marix CB DSO twice mentioned in despatches, died on Friday, 7th January 1966.

	Rank	Date	Reason
T O'B HUBBARD MC AFC [A]	W/Cdr	13.09.31	Retired list
E R C NANSON DSO AFC [S]	G/Capt	04.07.32	Retired list

At his own request [LG 5 July 1932, issue 33843, page 4385].

	Rank	Date	Reason
F K HASKINS DSC [A]	A/Cmdr	17.07.34	Retirement

Air Commodore Francis Knox Haskins DSC mentioned in despatches, died on Sunday, 15th June 1969.

	Rank	Date	Reason
A ap ELLIS [SO]	G/Capt	28.08.41	Retirement**
	G/Capt	20.0.45	Retired list**

Re-employed.

	Rank	Date	Reason
P BABINGTON MC AFC [A]	AM	01.12.45	Retirement**

Air Marshal Sir Philip Babington KCB MC AFC twice mentioned in despatches, died on Thursday, 25th February 1965, thus predeceasing his elder brother Sir John Babington [see previous page].

	Rank	Date	Reason
L A PATTINSON MC DFC [A]	AM	18.09.41	Retirement**

Air Marshal Sir Lawrence Pattison KBE CB DSO MC DFC mentioned in despatches, died on Monday, 28th March 1955.

	Rank	Date	Reason
R J BONE DSO [A & S]	G/Capt	15.04.34	Retired list

At his own request [LG 24 April 1934, issue 34044, page 2629].

	Rank	Date	Reason
S SMITH DSO AFC [A]	G/Capt	21.11.35	Retired list

At his own request. Paul McMillan has added that Group Captain Sidney Smith, formerly of the artillery, went to France at the beginning of March 1916, with 27 Squadron [Martinsyde G.100] as a Flight Commander and owing to an eye defect was prone to make rather heavy landings, thus gaining from his Commanding Officer the nick-name "Crasher". During the Second World War he was appointed Commandant of the London Command Air Traing Corps.

		Rank	Date	Reason
01210	B F MOORE [A]	W/Cdr	10.02.54	Relinquished
	H R NICHOLL [A]	AV-M	15.03.42	Retirement**

Air Vice-Marshal Sir Hazelton Nicholl KBE CB, died on Tuesday, 14th August 1956.

		Rank	Date	Reason
	A T WHITELOCK [A]	W/Cdr	25.03.38	Retired list
01199	P C MALTBY DSO [SO]	AV-M	02.10.46	Retirement**

Air Vice-Marshal Sir Paul Maltby KCVO KBE CB DSO AFC ON, died on Friday, 2nd July 1971. From April 1942, un til the surrender of Imperial Japanese forces in August 1945, he was a prisoner of war, his captivity commencing with the surrender of Java where he had been Air Officer Commanding. On his retirement he was appointed Sergeant at Arms in the House of Lords [Black Rod], holding the post until 1962.

		Rank	Date	Reason
02015	Hon. L J E TWISLETON-	F/O The Hon.	24.05.49	Resigned

WYKEHAM FIENNES [A] [He was now commissioned to the Royal Air Force Volunteer Reserve, Training Branch]. My co-author has discovered that the Honourable Twisleton-Wykeham-Fiennes service number has been duplicated with that given to Flight Lieutenant Frank Leonard Charmbury Butcher [see appointments *Gazetted* 26th September 1919, issue 31569, page 11919].

A CLEGHORN [T]	Major	01.08.19	Cancelled
C M MURPHY [A]	Major	01.08.19	Cancelled
E M MURRAY DSO MC [A]	G/Capt	31.07.33	Retired list

At his own request [LG 1 August 1933, supplement 33965, page 5119].

01179 A H JACKSON [A]	G/Capt	02.11.45	Retired list**
O T BOYD MC [A]	AM +	05.08.44	93 Group

Air Marshal Owen Tudor Boyd CB OBE MC AFC twice mentioned in despatches, died on Saturday, 5th August 1944. On 8th November 1940, he was appointed Deputy Air Officer Commanding-in-Chief, headquarters RAF Middle East and so it came about that he reported to Stradishall on 20th November, where he boarded Wellington IC T2873 of 214 Squadron Middle East Flight captained by Squadron Leader N P Samuels DFC. Heading for Luqa in Malta the crew forced-landed at Comiso in Sicily and all were taken prisoner, their details are recorded on page 31 of David Gunby and Pelham Temple's *Royal Air Force Bomber Losses in the Middle East and Mediterranean 1939 - 1942* which I have pleasure in acknowledging. During his time in captivity he made one near successful escape but was recaptured before, with others, succeeding a second time and reaching the United Kingdom in February 1944. Sadly, and possibly as the result of a stressful divorce, he died; his grave is in Mill Hill Cemetery.

B E SMYTHIES DFC [A]	W/Cdr +	17.06.30	29 Squadron

Killed while taking off from North Weald when his DH.60M Moth K1209 collied with lawn roller, over turned and burst into flames. At the time of his death he was forty-three years of age. His passenger, Aircraftman Frederick Reginald Stanley Holben was injured.

F H UNWIN [SO]	W/Cdr	27.03.32	Retired list
G LAING OBE [T]	AV-M	45	Retirement**

Air Vice-Marshal Sir George Laing KCB CBE, died Sunday, on 1st April 1956.

01191 A LEVICK [T]	W/Cdr	15.08.25	Retired list

In a Memorandum *Gazetted* 18th December 1919, supplement 31697, page 5740, the following Quartermasters and Captains, which included Captain Levick resigned their commissions on appointment to permanent commissions in the Royal Air Force. I strongly suspect that during the Second World War he was commissioned to the Royal Air Force Volunteer Reserve, Training Branch as a *Gazette* notice on 24th February 1942, issue 35467, page 915, confirms the appointment of Pilot Officer A Levick with effect from 11th September 1941.

T S IMPEY [A]	Major	01.08.19	Cancelled

LG 11 November 1919, issue 31637, page 13669. Appointed to a short servicer commission, ass notified in issue 31637, page 13669.

J C QUINNELL DFC [A]	A/Cmdr	11.12.44	Retirement**

Air Commodore John Charles 'Paddy' Quinnell CB DFC mentioned in despatches, died on Monday, 3rd January 1983.

G P GRENFELL DSO [T]	G/Capt	16.02.34	Retired list

Reserve of Air Force Officers - General Duties Branch: To be Group Captain in Class CC with effect from 1st February 1942 [LG 17 March 1942, issue 35491, page 1217].

01185 F C V LAWS OBE [T]	W/Cdr	01.09.33	Retired list

At his own request [LG 5 September 1933, issue 33975, page 5802]. Returned to service. G/Capt | 01.01.44 | Retired list**

C G SMITH OBE [T]	A/Cmdr	22.01.40	Retirement**

Re-employed. A/Cmdr | 11.02.46 | Retirement**

Air Commodore Charles Gainer Smith CB CBE, died on Wednesday, 13th October 1948.

01203 C E MAUDE [A & S]	W/Cdr	01.09.34	Retired list

At his own request [LG 4 September 1934, issue 34084, page 5607]. Returned to service. G/Capt | 21.04.46 | Retired list**

J H LIDDERDALE [SO]	W/Cdr	31.10.23	Retired list

On account of ill-health [LG 30 October 1923, issue 32875, page 7305]. AIR 1/2301/214/1 held at TNA Kew describes a personal reflection by J H Lidderdale for his time in 1915 at the Central Flying School. The record has not be digitised. Wing Commander John Henry Lidderdale's health continued to deteriorate and he died in Farnham, Surrey, on Saturday, 4th November 1933.

02012 E L TOMKINSON [A & S]	G/Capt	01.09.45	Retired list**
E T NEWTON-CLARE DSO [A]	Major	01.08.19	Cancelled
01157 A CORBETT-WILSON [T]	G/Capt	22.04.36	Retired list

At his own request. F/L | 23.01.54 | RAF[VR][T]

H STANLEY-ADAMS DSC [A]	Major	21.09.21	Resigned
D C S EVILL DSC [A & S]	ACM	15.01.47	Retirement**

Air Chief Marshal Sir Douglas Evill GBE KCB DSC AFC three times mentioned in despatches, died on Monday, 22nd March 1971.

01155 V GASKELL-BLACKBURN DSC [A & S]	G/Capt	21.08.41	Retired list**

Re-employed. | | .47 | Retirement

From Find a Grave website it is recorded that Group Captain Viviian Gaskell-Blackburn is buried in Dromod [St Michael and all Angels] Church, Waterville in Co. Kerry, Ireland., his death occurring on Saturday, 6th October 1956.

F C WILLIAMS OBE [SO]	G/Capt	01.11.38	Retired list

At his own request [LG 1 November 1938, issue 34566, page 6822].

A W TEDDER [A]	MRAF	30.05.51	Retirement**

Marshal of the Royal Air Force Lord Tedder Baron GCB twice mentioned in despatches, died on Saturday, 3rd June 1967. In a service career that lasted from the autumn of 1913, when he was commissioned as a 2nd Lieutenant to the Dorset Regiment [Special Reserve] to retirement from the Royal Air Force on 30th May 1951, Arthur William Tedder held some of the most prestigious posts in the Service. On 1st January 1941, he was appointed Air Officer Commanding-in-Chief, RAF Middle EastCommand during which he oversaw air operations throughout the North African campaign; Air Commander-in-Chief, Mediterranean Air Command from 15th February 1943, to the pinnacle of his Service when on 17th January 1944, he was appointed Air Commander-in-Chief and Deputy Supreme Allied Commander, SHAEF. During the war years he suffered two personnel tragedies; on 3rd August 1940, his son Flying Officer Arthur Richard Brian Tedder was killed on operations with 139 Squadron, and while in the Middle East and soon after the success of Operation *Torch* his wife was killed in an air accident when the aircraft in which she was a passenger overshot the runway at Cairo Airport, crashed and burst into flames.

F F MINCHIN DSO MC [A]	Major	01.08.19	Cancelled

It transpires, as Paul McMillan reports, Frederick Frank Minchin disappeared on the last day of August 1927, when attempting an Atlantic crossing in the company of Captain Leslie Hamilton and Princess Anne of Löwenstein-Wertheim-Freudenberg [see *Wikipedia* for a detailed account].

J H HERRING DSO MC [A]	G/Capt	02.07.42	Retirement**

Re-employed. G/Capt | 28.09.45 | Retired list**

A A WALSER MC DFC [A]	A/Cmdr	21.09.41	Retirement**

Air Commodore Andre Adolphus Walser MC DFC twice mentioned in despatches, died on Saturday, 26th February 1966.

J H S TYSSEN MC [A]	AV-M	21.02.42	Retirement**

Air Vice-MarshalJohn Hugh Samuel Tyson CB MC mentioned in despatches, died on 4th January 1953.

G HENDERSON [A]	Major	01.08.19	Cancelled
R F S MORTON [A]	A/Cmdr	25.10.37	Retirement

Air Commodore Rowland Francis Storrs Morton mention in despatches, died on 3rd April 1953.

R J F BARTON OBE [SO]*	G/Capt	01.01.31	Retired list

On account of ill-health [LG 6 January 1931, issue 33677, page 148].

G R M REID DSO MC [A]	AV-M	20.01.46	Retirement**

Air Vice-Marshal Sir Ranald Reid KCB DSO MC* mentioned in despatches, died on Sunday, 19th May 1991.

	Name	Rank		Date	Status
	E H M O'FARRELL [A]	Major		01.08.19	Cancelled
	S W SMITH [A]	A/Cmdr		21.09.41	Retirement**

Air Commodore Sydney William Smith OBE, died in December 1971.

| | C C MILES MC [A] | W/Cdr | | 06.06.37 | Retired list |
| | V O REES [T] | G/Capt | | 17.07.35 | Retired list |

At his own request [LG 5 November 1935, issue 34216, page 6978].

	C S DANBY MC [A]	Major		01.08.19	Cancelled
	M G LEE [A]	Major		01.01.19	Cancelled.
75371	A R STANLEY-CLARKE MC [A]	S/Ldr		08.11.47	Resigned**
	W J RYAN CBE [SO]	W/Cdr		18.03.31	Retired list

At his own request [LG 24 March 1931, issue 33701, page 1991].

| | G G A WILLIAMS [A] | S/Ldr | | 10.08.33 | Retired list |
| | T L LEIGH-MALLORY [A] | ACM | + | 14.11.44 | *en route* SEAC |

Air Chief Marshal Sir Trafford Leigh-Mallory KCB DSO three times mentioned in despatches, died on Tuesday, 14th November 1944, while *en route* with his wife, Lady Leigh-Mallory, to take up the post as Air Commander-in-Chief South East Asia Command when the 511 Squadron York I MW126 in which they were travelling flew into mountains above le Rivier d'Allemont [Isère], 20km east of Saint-Martin-d'Hères.. During the *Battle of Britain,* Air Vice-Marshal, as he was then ranked, was Air Officer Commanding No. 12 Group before progressing first to No. 11 Group in December 1940, and thence to Air Officer Commanding-in-Chief Fighter Command on 28th November 1942. As Air Chief Marshal he was made Commander-in-Chief, Allied Expeditionary Air Force with the task of coordinating the air elements tasked to support the D-Day landings in June 1944. He was the highest ranked Royal Air Force officer to be killed on active service during the Second World War. By a cruel irony of fate, his elder mountaineering brother, George Leigh-Mallory, disappeared during an attempt to scale Mount Everest [then unconquered] in 1924.

| | V A A ALBRECHT MC [A] | Major | | 01.08.19 | Cancelled |
| | Sir N A R D LESLIE CBE [SO] | W/Cdr | | 25.07.29 | Retired list |

At his own request [LG 22 October 1929, issue 33545, page 6693]. The following notice appeared in *The London Gazette* 21st October 1919, issue 31610, page 12893, under the heading 'Flying Branch': *'Squadron Leader Sir N A R D Leslie Bart CBE to be Squadron Leader [A], from Air Attaché,. 25th Sept. 1919.'* Sir Norman Leslie, 8th Baronet, died in London at the relatively early age of 48 on Wednesday, 16th June 1937.

	N M MARTIN CBE [A]	S/Ldr		10.09.24	Retired list
01222	G H P PADLEY [T]	G/Capt		19.05.43	Retired list**
	H F A GORDON [SO]	S/Ldr		19.01.29	Retired list
	B L HUSKISSON DSC [A]	W/Cdr		01.09.38	Relinquished

On appointment to RN and Captain[A] with seniority of 1st September 1938 [LG 4 October 1938, issue 34558, page 6203]. He was placed on the Retired list of the RN, ranked Captain, on 287h October 1945.

| 01144 | J A G de COURCY MC [A] | W/Cdr | | 20.02.38 | Retired list |

At his own request [LG 22 February 1938, issue 34486, page 1169]. Returned to the service in World War Two and was promoted Group Captain [temporary] with effect from 1st December 1940 [LG 10 December 1940, issue 35010, page 6984]. Sadly, before December was out Group Captain John Arthur Gerald de Courcy are not known. He is buried in Barton [St. Peter] Churchyard.

| | | G/Capt | + | 30.12.40 | 43 Group |
| | C F A PORTAL DSO MC [A] | MRAF | | 31.12.45 | Retirement** |

Marshal of the Royal Air Force Viscount Portal of Hungerford Baron KG GCB OM DSO* MC three times mentioned in despatches, died on Thursday, 22nd April 1971. Following a brief appointment as Air Officer Commander-in-Chief Bomber Command [April to October 1940], he was elevated to Chief of the Air Staff, the youngest officer to achieve this position. His ashes are interred in Funtington [St Mary's] Churchyard near Chichester in West Sussex.

| | J T WHITTAKER MC [A] | S/Ldr | + | 12.12.27 | RAF Poona |

Squadron Leader John Tudor Whittaker died in Jasmine Lodge Nursing Home, Fort Bombay.

| 01125 | N F D BUCKERIDGE [T] | S/Ldr | + | 26.04.40 | |

Died at his home from natural causes. Squadron Leader Norman Frank Dennis Buckeridge, aged 52, is buried in North Stoneham [St. Nicholas] Churchyard. During the *Great War* he was mentioned in despatches.

| 01174 | A F A HOOPER OBE [T] | W/Cdr | | 05.06.33 | Retired list |

A medal card for Major A F A Hooper, late of the North Staffordshire Regiment, can be accessed at TNA Kew under WO 372/10/28453.

| | C H B BLOUNT MC [A] | AV-M | + | 23.10.40 | AOC 22 Group |

Air Vice-Marshal Charles Hubert Boulby Blount CB OBE MC was killed in an air accident on Wednesday, 23rd October 1940, when the 24 Squadron aircraft in which he was a passenger crashed shortly after taking off from Hendon on a scheduled flight to Northern Ireland where he was to discuss with the General Officer Commanding Northern Ireland forthcoming army co-operation exercises. He is buried in the southwest corner of Essendon [St Mary] Churchyard, Hertfordshire.

| | A W H JAMES MC [A] | W/Cdr | | 21.05.25 | Retired list |

At his own request [LG 19 May 1925, issue 33048, page 3382]. Subsequently, and in the same year of his voluntary retirement, he was appointed to command No. 600[County of London] Squadron with effect from 17th November 1925 [LG 17 November 1925, issue 33103, page 7513]. However, his tenure in command was brief and he resigned his commission on 19th November 1926 [LG 23 November 1926, issue 33223, page 7582]. From 1931, Wing Commander James was Member of Parliament for Wellingborough.

| | C W ANSTEY [A] | S/Ldr | + | 03.05.20 | |

Squadron Leader Chisholm Wilfred Anstey is buried in Fleet [All Saints] Churchyard, Hampshire. He was formerly of the South Wales Borderers.

	H E M WATKINS [A & S]	W/Cdr		15.09.29	Retired list
01147	T W ELSDON [A & S]	S/Ldr		18.08.34	Retired list
	E V S WILBERFORCE DSC [S]	Lt-Col		13.09.21	Resigned
02023	R P WHITEHEAD [A & S]	S/Ldr		21.01.25	Retired list
01148	T H ENGLAND DSC [A & S]	G/Capt		14.06.44	Retirement**

At his own request [LG 14 July 1944, supplement 36612, page 3330].

| | F J RUTLAND DSC AM [A & S] | S/Ldr | | 19.09.23 | Retired list |
| | G S TREWIN AFC [O] | S/Ldr | | 17.06.30 | Retired list |

At his own request [LG 17 June 1930, issue 33616, page 3812].

| | R J MOUNSEY OBE [A] | G/Capt | + | 18.06.39 | |

Paul McMillan reports that Group Captain Roland James Mounsey OBE died in his sleep.

| | E W NORTON DSC [A] | Major | | 01.08.19 | Cancelled |

Appointed to a short service commission with effect from 1st August 1919 [LG 8 June 1920, issue 31933, page 6343]. This notification was subsequently cancelled and his appointed to a permanent commission reinstated [LG 14 November 1922, issue 32767, page 8038]. His rank in November 1922, was Squadron Leader.

| | | A/Cmdr | | 24.02.44 | Retirement** |

Air Commodore Ernest William Norton DSC, died on Monday, 23rd May 1966.

| | C E BRYANT DSO [A] | Major | | 01.08.19 | Cancelled |
| | S J GOBLE DSO OBE DSC [A] | | | | |

Australia According to his biography published by *Wikipedia,* Stanley James 'Jimmy' Goble, born in Croydon, Victoria on 21st August 1891, he travelled to the United Kingdom at his own expense and enlisted with the RNAS. He returned to Australia in November 1918, and on being informed that he had been appointed to a permanent commission in the Royal Air Force with the rank of Squadron Leader [honorary Wing

Commander] he was seconded to the Royal Australian Navy. Subsequently, he rose to the rank of Air Vice-Marshal and against his wishes was retired in February 1946. He died on Saturday, 24th July 1948, at the relatively early age of 56. For a complete assessment of his service, I recommend his *Wikipedia* entry.

L T N GOULD MC [A]	G/Capt	01.09.43	Retired list

Group Captain Lionel Thomas Nutcombe Gould was appointed to a temporary commission as Commander[A] with effect from 1st September 1943. Born 22nd November 1893, at Alveston, Stratford-on-Avon, Commander Gould died on Wednesday, 29th January 1947, at Radlett, Hertfordshire. The circumstances of his death, reported by Paul McMillan, were particularly tragic. While visiting his brother, Commander J G Gould RN, at 10 Radlett Road it is thought when after turning off the gas fire in his room he he pipe became disconnected for when found in the morning he had been asphyxiated by the fumes. He was laid to rest in Fulbeck Churchyard. Tragedy had also struck during the war when his son Flying Officer Auriol Stephen Nutcombe Gould was killed on 24th January 1943, when his 197 Squadron Typhoon [possibly DN365 recorded in Air-Britain's *'The Typhoon File'* compiled by C H Thomas and published in 1981, as being lost during a training sortie between Drem and Ayr] crashed into Queenside Hill, southeast Glasgow. Flying Officer Gould, 20 years of age, is buried in South Queensferry Cemetery.

A R C COOPER [SO]	W/Cdr	22.08.28	Retired list

At his own request [LG 7 September 1928, issue 33419, page 5898].

W L WELSH DSC [A & S]	AM	O1.12.44	Retirement**

Air Marshal Sir William Welsh KCB DSC AFC mentioned in despatches, died on Tuesday, 2nd January 1962.

R H PECK [A]	AM	02.04.46	Retirement**

Air Marshal Sir Richard Peck KCB OBE twice mentioned in despatches, died on Friday, 12th September 1952.

J B GRAHAM MC AFC [A]	G/Capt	01.07.39	Retired list

At his own request [LG 18 July 1939, issue 34646, page 4929].

01194	W D LONG OBE [SO]	G/Capt	03.01.46	Retired list**
	A G R GARROD MC [SO]	ACM	09.10.48	Retirement**

Air Chief Marshal Sir Guy Garrod GBE KCB MC DFC three times mentioned in despatches, died on Sunday, 3rd January 1965.

R A CHALMERS OBE AFC [A]	Major	01.08.19	Cancelled
T W MULCAHY-MORGAN MC [A]	W/Cdr	17.06.29	Retired list

At his own request [LG 21 June 1929, issue 33508, page 4123].

W J Y GUILFOYLE MC [A]	A/Cmdr	21.09.41	Retirement**

Australia. Air Commodore William James Yule Guilfoyle OBE MC six times mentioned in despatches, died on Sunday, 245h April 1948, as on result of burns sustained when a spirit stove exploded during a camping expedition with friends.

A L NEALE MC [A]	S/Ldr	20.11.20	Resigned

But was appointed a permanent commission as a Flight Lieutenant, with effect from 1st December 1920 [LG 30 November 1920, issue 32145, page 11823. Resigned for a second time [LG 27 March 1925, issue 33033, page 2117].

	F/L	25.03.25	Resigned

In the Second World War he received a commission in the Royal Regiment of Artillery, ranked Lieutenant with effect from 22nd December 1940 [LG 7 April 1941, supplement 35128, page 2019]. Albert Leslie Neale died on active service on Saturday, 3rd May 1941, and is buried in Brookwood Military Cemetery.

A C WRIGHT [A]	A/Cmdr	09.03.42	Retirement**

Air Commodore Arthur Claud Wright AFC, died on Saturday, 23rd April 1977.

J McCRAE MBE [T]	G/Capt	16.05.42	Retirement**

Re-employed.

	G/Capt	03.05.45	Retired list**
C H NICHOLAS [A]	A/Cmdr	12.11.44	Retirement**

Air Commodore Charles Henry Nicholas DFC AFC three times mentioned in despatches, died on Monday, 8th August 1966.

G W MURLS-GREEN DSO MC* [A]	G/Capt	24.03.42	Retired list

At his own request LG 5 May 1942, issue 35547, page 1973]. The Bar to his Military Cross was *Gazetted* 13th February 1917, supplement 29940, page 1539: *'For conspicuous gallantry in action. He brought down two enemy machines on successive days under adverse circumstances. He has displayed great dash and courage at every opportunity.'*

W J SHIELDS [T]]	G/Capt	09.01.42	Retired list**

02007	W V STRUGNELL MC [A]	A/Cmdr	07.06.45	Retirement**

Air Commodore William Victor Strugnell MC* mentioned in despatches, died in 1977.

J O ARCHER [A]	W/Cdr	22.09.35	Retired list

Returned to Service.

	G/Capt	01.05.46	Retired list**
C G TUCKER [T]	W/Cdr +	04.02.31	209 Squadron

On Wednesday, 4th February 1931, Wing Commander Charles Gilbert Tucker was commander of a Blackburn Iris III N238 seaplane of 209 Squadron, Mount Batten, which on landing in Plymouth Sound struck the water with considerable force and sank. From the crew of twelve only three were saved; Flight Lieutenants Maurice Hibbert Ely and Charles Ryley were pulled to safety suffering from injuries while Corporal William Manswell Barry was unhurt. Flying Officer Frederick Kingsley Wood was killed in the crash, the rest, including the Wing Commander, drowned: Sergeant Edmund Walter Harris Wilson, Leading Aircraftmen Cecil Gwilym Davies, Louis Charles Oates, Harold Corrie Ongley, William Sidney Ruttlidge, William Henry Stark and William George Stevens.

02003	J V STEEL [A]	W/Cdr	03.03.39	Retired list

At his own request [LG 7 March 1939, issue 34605, page 1552].

J SOWREY AFC [A]	A/Cmdr	17.08.47	Retirement**

Air Commodore William Sowery CBE DFC AFC twice mentioned in despatches, died on Thursday, 15th February 1968.

L F FORBES MC [A]	G/Capt	30.04.45	Retirement**
E H JOHNSTON OBE [A]	W/Cdr	01.10.32	Retired list

On account of ill-health [LG 4 October 1932, issue 33870, page 6252].

H J NEWTON-CLARE OBE [SO]	S/Ldr	31.03.20	Resigned
C W H PULFORD OBE AFC [A & S]	AV-M +	10.03.42	AOC Far East

Air Vice-Marshal Conway Walter Heath Pulford CB OBE AFC mentioned in despatches, died in tragic circumstances when in the company of two senior officers an attempt was made to avoid falling into Japanese hands by escaping in a motor boat. This ended when the craft was hit, presumably by enemy fire, and it was run aground on an island in the Juju group where several, including the Air Vice-Marshal, died from exhaustion, the date of his death being recorded as Tuesday, 10th March 1942. His remains are interred in Kranji War Cemetery.

B E SUTTON DSO OBE MC [A]	AM	07.06.45	Retirement**

Air Marshal Sir Bertine Sutton KBE CB DSO MC four times mentioned in despatches, died on Saturday, 28th September 1946. The cause of his death so soon after his retirement was attributed to the strain and stress of wartime service.

S G HODGES MC AFC [A]	S/Ldr	16.03.20	Resigned
F J ROBERTS [A]	Major	01.08.19	Cancelled

Paul McMillan adds: Major Frederick John Roberts was born in Buenos Aires on 15th September 1893, and died in Kenya on Friday, 25th February 1938. A partial Record of Service exists for him on Army Form B.103, which confirms his date of birth, and showing he was last of the Army Service Corps transferring to the Royal Flying Corps on 1st December 1915, and two days later on the 3rd, he was attached to 16 Squadron [BE.2s], on probation, at Chocques, returning home on 16th June 1916. On 14th February 1917, he returned to France, reporting to 59 Squadron [RE.8] at St. Omer. His second tour of duty ended with his posting back the United Kingdom on 18th September 1917.

K R BINNING MC [A]	Major	01.08.19	Cancelled

01182	J KEMPER [T]*	W/Cdr	+	18.12.45	

Wing Commander Joseph Kemper is buried in Willesden Jewish Cemetery; he was 59 years of age.

	R E SAUL DFC [A]	AV-M		29.06.44	Retirement**

Air Vice-Marshal Richard Ernest Saul CB DFC mentioned in despatches, died on Tuesday, 30th November 1965.

	F W STENT MC [A]	W/Cdr		15.01.36	Retired list

At his own request [LG 14 January 1936, issue 34242, page 311].

	E L MILLAR MBE [A]	S/Ldr		29.01.21	Retired list

On account of ill-health contracted in the Service [LG 24 June 1921, issue 32368, page 5014].

	P A O LEASK [A]	W/Cdr		31.07.31	Retired
	A G HORSLEY-CARR [T]	S/Ldr	+	12.02.26	RAF Old Sarum

Squadron Leader Alfred George Horsley-Carr was a passenger in a Vickers Vimy IV J7451 that had been attached to the Chemical Weapons Experimental Establishment at Porton Down for trials in laying smoke-screens and it was during one such test that the pilot became disorientated after the Vimy was enveloped in smoke. Seeking a suitable place to forced-land, Sergeant William Norman Pink, the pilot, failed to see a tree which was struck by one of the bomber's wings sending it our of control. Sergeant Pink was injured but Aircraftman Clifford Bartlett Cardall walked away without hurt. The location of the crash is reported as being near Winterslow some 3 miles or so ENE of Salisbury and almost a similar distance SE of Porton Down.

01127	P R BURCHALL [T]	W.Cdr		19.03.46	Retired list**

A non-digitised record for 2nd Lieutenant P R Burchell of the Royal Flying Corps is held at TNA Kew in Class WO 339/50712.

	H G DEAN [A]	G/Capt		16.05.38	Retired list

At his own request [LG 17 May 1938, issue 34511, page 3200]. It is known that he returned to the service in the Second World War and transferred from the General Duties Branch to the Technical Branch on 24th April 1940, retaining his rank [LG 13 September 1940 [issue 34945, page 5490].

	W G SITWELL DSC [A & S]				

The website 'Getty Images' has a photograph of Major W G Sitwell DSC who on the 8th August 1919, flew the flying boat F.5 from Felixstowe to Helsingfors, the capital of the new independent state of Finland. The 1,100 miles flight took sixteen hours to complete. Also featured in the photograph is General Kivekas, Chief of Staff of the Finnish Army, seated in the cockpit of the F.5 with Major Sitwell standing on the wing and pointing out items of interest to the General.

	E R MOON DSO* [A & S]	S/Ldr	+	29.04.20	230 Squadron

    Chevallier d'Honneur [see my summary for details].

	J S MILLS DSC [A & S]	Major		01.08.19	Cancelled
	R M FIELD [SO]	G/Capt		27.11.43	Retirement**

Beneath the heading Flying Branch in issue 31569 of *the London Gazette* published 26th September 1919, and on page 11919, the following appears: *'Squadron Leader R M Field to be Squadron Leader S from [SO]. 15th Sept, 1919.'*

	G F BREESE DSC [A]	S/Ldr		18.02.31	Retired list
02030	J C P WOOD [A & S]	W/Cdr		06.01.40	Cashiered

At the time Wing Commander James Conrad Peter Wood was on the staff of No. 1 Group, Abingdon. His dismissal from the service was published in *The London Gazette* on 19th January 1940, page 379.

01193	T V LISTER [A & S]	G/Capt		09.01.47	Retirement**
	R B B COLMORE OBE [A]	W/Cdr	+	05.10.30	Air Ministry

Killed when HM Airship R101 G-FAAW came down in bad weather near Beuvais in France during its maiden voyage to India. Wing Commander Reginald Blayney Bulteel Colmore, forty-three years of age, was Director of Airship Development. Along with others who perished in the crash, he is buried in Cardington [St. Mary's] Churchyard.

01145	B P H de ROEPER [A]	G/Capt		03.03.46	Retired list**
	K C BUSS [A & S}	G/Capt		03.11.40	Retirement**

Re-employed.

	F E SANDFORD AFC [A & S]	Major		01.08.19	Cancelled
	C W NUTTING DSC [T]	AV-M		30.08.42	Retirement**

Air Vice Marshal Charles William Nutting CBE DSC mentioned in despatches, died on Tuesday, 25th February 1964.

	J KILNER-WELLS [T]	W/Cdr		23.08.35	Retired list
01227	A E PETTINGELL [T]	S/Ldr		30.06.31	Retired list
	A J CURRIE [SO]	S/Ldr		30.12.29	Retired list
	E POWELL OBE [T]	Major		01.08.19	Cancelled
	E A B RICE MC [A]	A-VM		01.03.46	Retirement**

Air Vice-Marshall Sir Edward Rice KBE CB MC three times mentioned in despatches, died on Wednesday, 14th April 1948. During his short retirement of two years he was Director-General of Civil Aviation.

	A T HARRIS AFC [A]	MRAF		15.09.45	Retirement**

Marshal of the Royal Air Sir Arthur Harris Baronet GCB OBE AFC twice mentioned in despatches, died on Thursday, 5th April 1984. As Air Officer Commanding-in-Chief from February 1942 until the end of the war in Europe, Sir Arthur Harris oversaw the most prolonged night bombing campaign of the war. In carrying out the systematic destruction of Germany's industrial might, the campaign suffered the most appalling casualties which including accidents in training cost the lives of over 57,000 air and ground crew [see RAFBCL Roll of Honour for a breakdown of this terrible statistic]. A biography of Sir Arthur Harris, sensitively written by Henry Probert [late head of the Air Historical Branch] was published by Greenhill Books in 2001.

	F SOWREY DSO MC AFC [A]	G/Capt		26.05.40	Retirement

Group Captain Frederick Sowrey DSO MC AFC, died on Monday, 21st October 1968, at the age of 75, in Eastbourne, Sussex. Credited with thirteen aerial victories in the *Great War* notable, perhaps, was his first, the destruction of Zeppelin LZ-74 L.32 during the night of 23-24 September 1916.

01126	T F BULLEN OBE [T]	W/Cdr		10.02.54	Relinquished
	E R MANNING MC [A]	A/Cmdr		10.08.35	Retirement

Australia. Recalled to service in the Second World War, he rejoined the Royal Air Force in the Middle East, subsequently seeing active service in Malaya, Burma, India and the United Kingdom before retiring for a second time on

				20.05.45	Retired list**

Air Commodore Edye Rolleston Manning CBE DSO MC, died on Friday, 26th April 1957.

	M G P COPEMAN [A]	Lt-Col		29.11.22	Retired list

On account of ill-health while ranked Squadron Leader and permitted to retain the rank of Lieutenant-Colonel [LG 28 November 1922, supplement 32771, page 8416].

	F G D HARDS DSC DFC [S]	AV-M		03.06.43	Retirement**

Air Vice-Marshal Frederick George Darby Hards CBE DSC DFC mentioned in despatches, died on Wednesday, 10th July 1963.

01136	E R L CORBALLIS DSO [SO]	W/Cdr		08.02.32	Retired list
	G W WILLIAMSON MC [T]	W/Cdr		01.11.35	Ceased employment
01206	H A MICHELL [SO]	W/Cdr		30.10.43	Retired list**
01129	A J BUTLER MC [A]	W/Cdr		23.05.46	Retired list**
	F B BINNEY [A]	Major		01.08.19	Cancelled

01204   A C MAUND DSO [A]   AV-M   +   13.12.42   HQ TTC
Air Vice-Marshal Arthur Clinton Maund CB CBE DSO mentioned in despatches, died on natural causes on Sunday, 13th December 1942, during his tenure as Air Officer Administration, headquarters Technical Training Command. Aged 51, he is buried in Brookwood Military Cemetery.
          P C SHERREN MC [A]   W/Cdr   +   10.09.37   King's Cup Air Race
          Canada. During the race Wing Commander Sherren and the pilot Wing Commander E H Hilton reached the registration point over Scarborough Castle where their Miles Falcon became caught in turbulence and crashed onto a grassy knoll atop the cliffs. Wing Commander Sherren was thrown from the cockpit and rolled over the cliff to fall into the sea below. Both officers died on impact, a verdict of "accidental death" being returned at the inquest which was held in Scarborough.
          D R MacLAREN DSO MC DFC [A]   Major   01.08.19   Cancelled
          Canada Donald Roderick MacLaren was an outstanding fighter pilot during the *Great War* achieving fifty-four combat victories while flying Sopwith Camels with 46 Squadron, thus becoming the highest scoring Camel pilot. Returning to his country in late 1919, he returned, briefly, to England in 1920, where he resigned his commission with the Canadian Air Force. For further details, please refer to his biographical entry on *Wikipedia*.
          R LECKIE DSO DSC DFC [A & S]   AV-M   06.04.42   Retirement**
Air Vice-Marshal Robert Leckie CB DSO DSC DFC, died on Tuesday, 1st April 1975. On retirement from the Royal Air Force, Air Vice-Marshal Leckie transferred to the Royal Canadian Air Force, retiring on 1st September 1947.

                                                 CAPTAINS
                                                    294
          A A B THOMSON MC [A]   A/Cmdr   +   28.08.39   AOC 3 Group
On the 28th of August 1939, a Monday, he joined the crew of a 115 Squadron Wellington which had been tasked for a test flight, landing, I believe at Boscombe Down. On alighting, Air Commodore Arthur Ashford Benjamin ThomsonMC* AFC alighted and after inspecting the aircraft's bomb-bay walked forward and was struck by one of the propellers which was still windmilling. Grievously injured he died in the ambulance taking him to hospital. He had been appointed Air Officer Commanding 3 Group on the 14th of February 1938, at the time the youngest officer to have attained Air Commodore rank. He was succeeded by Air Vice-Marshal J E A Baldwin, summarised in the section of this appendix commenting on Majors.
          W B HARGRAVE [A]   G/Capt   17.04.46   Retirement**
          J R HOWETT [A]   Captain   01.08.19   Cancelled
          R S MAXWELL MC DFC [A]   Captain   To RN
I am reasonably certain that Captain Maxwell left the service between the wars but returned during the Second World War. An entry in *The London Gazette* 27th January 1942, issue 35435, page 448, shows Temporary Sub-Lt[A] R S Maxwell MC DFC AFC Promoted Temp. Lt[A] with effect from 15th January 1942.
          G ALLEN [A]   Captain   01.08.19   Cancelled
          E M POLLARD [A]   Captain   01.08.19   Cancelled
See Appendix E and entries for Flight Lieutenants granted short service commissions notified in LG 12 December 1919, issue 31685, page 15483.
          H V CHAMPION de CRESPIGNY MC DFC [A]   AV-M   06.11.45   Retirement**
Air Vice-Marshal Hugh Vivian Champion de Crespigny CB MC DFC mentioned in despatches, died on Friday, 20th June 1969.
          C H DIXON MC DFC [A]   Captain   01.08.19   Cancelled
          A S MORRIS OBE [T]   AV-M   10.05.46   Retirement**
Air Vice-Marshal Sir Samuel Morris KBE CB mentioned in despatches, died on Monday, 9th November 1964.
          E R PRETYMAN AFC [A]*   W/Cdr   01.07.37   Retired list
At his own request [LG 3 August 1937, issue 34423, page 4957]. There is some dispute regarding his second Christian name which appears variously as 'Radcliffe' and 'Radclyffe'. Born on 29th November 1894, Army Form B.103 shows enlistment to the Royal Flying Corps as August 1916. Served in Egypt and Salonika with 17 Squadron and in France with 19 Squadron following a spell on Home Defence duties with 78 Squadron.
          I T LLOYD [A]   A/Cmdr   31.07.39   Retirement
Re-employed.   A/Cmdr   29.03.46   Retired list**
Air Commodore Ivor Thomas Lloyd CB CBE four times mentioned in despatches, died on Friday, 28th October 1966.
          E J HODSOLL [S]   W/Cdr   01.05.35   Retired list
At his own request [LG 7 May 1935, issue 34158, page 2986].
          A J CAPLE [A]   A/Cmdr   03.11.45   Retirement**
Air Commodore Arthur John Capell CB DSO DFC three times mentioned in despatches, died on Wednesday, 18th April 1979.
          J R McCRINDLE OBE MC [A]   Major   01.01.22   Resigned
Army Form B.103 shows Major John Ronald McCrindle was born on 29th November 1894, and joined the Royal Flying Corps on 19th October 1914. By the early autumn of 1917, he was attached to 113 Squadron at Ismailia and briefly commanded the squadron while awaiting the return from leave of Major W H Primrose. Major McCrindle was formerly of the Gordon Highlanders.
02093   H COCKERELL [T]   S/Ldr   08.01.37   Retired list
          O G W G LYWOOD [T]   AV-M   29.03.46   Retirement**
Air Vice-Marshal Oswyn George William Gifford Lywood CB CBE mentioned in despatches, died on Sunday, 3rd February 1957.
          J C RUSSELL DSO [A]   A/Cmdr   06.01.43   Retirement**
Air Commodore John Cannan Russell DSO, died on Wednesday, 15th August 1956.
          C E H MEDHURST OBE MC [A]   ACM   19.04.50   Retirement**
Air Chief Marshal Sir Charles Medhurst KCB OBE MC twice mentioned in despatches, died on Monday, 18th October 1954.
          A R ARNOLD DSO DFC [A & S]   G/Capt   22.05.45   Retirement**
          C S MacNAB [SO]   Captain   01.08.19   Cancelled
          R H KERSHAW [A & S]   G/Capt   17.05.43   Retired list
          H STEWART [S]   S/Ldr   +   05.01.31   84 Squadron
Squadron Leader Harry Kershaw crashed while making a night landing at Shaibah. On touch down the Wapiti, serial not recorded, turned over and caught fire. Leading Aircraftman Henry Irving Wood was badly injured, but survived. As far as I can ascertain, Squadron Leader Stewart was not the squadron's Commanding Officer.
          N S DOUGLAS [Ad]   S/Ldr   16.12.37   Retired list
On account of ill-health [LG 21 December 1937, issue 34465, page 8002].
02229   J E B B MACLEAN DSC [S]   F/L   10.12.24   Retired list
          A S REDFERN [A]   Captain   01.08.19   Cancelled
02010   W THOMAS MC [T]   S/Ldr   23.02.32   Retired list
          R COLLISHAW DSO DSC DFC [A]   AV-M   29.10.43   Retirement**
          Canada Air Vice-Marshal Raymond Collishaw CB DSO* OBE [both military and civil] DSC DFC four times mentioned in despatches, died on Wednesday, 29th September 1976, in Vancouver. In 1999, the air terminal at Nanaimo Airport was re-named Nanaimo-Collishaw Air Terminal in his honour. His *great War* exploits as a fighter pilot, initially with the RNAS and then the RAF resulted in him becoming the highest scoring RNAS pilot and the second highest scoring Canadian fighter pilot with the RAF behind William 'Billy' Bishop. Assisted by A V Dodds, Raymond Collishaw wrote his biography in 1973, titled *Air Command - A Fighter Pilot's Story* which was published by William Kimber. Checking to see if copies are still available [2020] Amazon had two used on offer at £100 or over!

	C T MacLAREN OBE [A]	Captain	01.08.19	Cancelled
	F P HOLLIDAY DSO MC [A]	Captain	01.08.19	Cancelled
	E J L W GILCHRIST MC DFC [A]	Captain	01.08.19	Cancelled
03113	H E F WYNCOLL OBE MC [T]	S/Ldr	29.12.32	Retired list
	R GRAHAM DSO DSC DFC [S]	A V-M	29.06.48	Retirement**

Air Vice-Marshal Ronald Graham CB CBE DSO DSC* DFC mentioned in despatches, died on Friday, 23rd June 1967.

	C H C SMITH DSC [A & S]	Major	01.04.21	Resigned
02194	D S JILLINGS MC [T]	S/Ldr	01.10.26	Retirement

Returned to service. Granted a commission in the Reserve of Air Force Officers, General Duties Branch, Class C retaining Honorary Squadron Leader rank.

		G/Capt	01.01.46	

The London Gazette 1st January 1946, issue 37407, page 89, reporting the names of personnel honoured in the King's New Year's Honour List. His Army Form B.103 shows his birth date as 28th June 1891, and joining the Royal Flying Corps on the last day of December 1917. An obituary to this officer published in the *Eastern Daily Press* on Thursday, 23rd April 1953, states he was the first solder to be wounded in the *Great War* [this suggests he was an observer attached to 2 Squadron and was wounded by rifle fire from the ground while on patrol in a BE.2 of 2 Squadron piloted by Lieutenant W M Noel during the morning of 22nd August 1914. His rank is recorded as Sergeant-Major.

	V A H ROBESON MC [A]	S/Ldr +	17.10.23	

Squadron Leader Vyvyan Arthur Hemming Robeson MC mentioned in despatches, died after undergoing surgery in a hospital in Tewkesbury, Gloucestershire. Born on the 11th of February 1894, During the *Great War* he saw operational service with five squadrons, namely 12, 9, 10 , 46, with the latter he was a flight commander, before commanding 24 Squadron [SE.5A] from February 1918 through to the armistice and beyond.

	G H BOWMAN DSO MC* DFC [A]	W/Cdr	20.01.37	Retired list

At his own request [LG 26 January 1937, issue 34363, page 561]. Formerly of the Royal Warwickshire Regiment, Geoffrey Hilton Bowman gained his honours following transfer to the Royal Flying Corps, his MC being *Gazetted* 17th September 1917, supplement 30287, page 9564: *'For conspicuous gallantry and devotion to duty. He has taken part in many offensive patrols, which he led on twenty occasions, in the course of which four enemy aircraft were destroyed and twelve others driven down out of control. Although outnumbered by five to one on one occasion he handled his patrol of four machines with such skill and gallantry that after a very severe fight he was able to withdraw them without loss, having destroyed at least two enemy machines and driven down one out of control. His fearlessness and fine offensive spirit have been a splendid example to others.'* The award of a First Bar was published on 18th March 1918, supplement 30583, page 3418: *'For conspicuous gallantry and devotion to duty in leading twenty-five offensive patrols in two months, shooting down five enemy aircraft and showing marked skill as a leader.'* In the issue of 26th March 1918, supplement 30597, page 3743, appeared notice of his DSO and in the issue of 3rd June 1919, supplement 31378, page 7031, notification that he was awarded a DFC. His entry in *Wikipedia* [which I am pleased to acknowledge] shows he served with 29 Squadron and 56 Squadron. Born in Manchester on 2nd May 1891, he died, aged 78, on Wednesday, 25th March 1970, being cremated at Southwest Middlesex Crematorium. It is noted that he returned to the service on 1st September 1939, and retiring on on 15th December 1941.

	C G BURGE OBE [A]	S/Ldr	01.12.28	Retired list

At his own request [LG 11 December 1928, issue 33446, page 8173].

	N B TOMLINSON [T]	Captain	01.08.19	Cancelled
	H S POWELL MC [A]	W/Cdr	15.07.38	Retired list

At his own request [LG 19 July 1938, issue 34533, page 4682].

02032	W G P YOUNG OBE [SO]	W/Cdr	10.02.54	Relinquished
03074	A H STRADLING [SO]	A/Cmdr	20.12.45	Retired list**
10006	L AUKER OBE [T]	G/Capt	21.10.40	Retired list
03036	C A RIDLEY DSO MC [A]	S/Ldr	19.12.28	Retired list [at

At his own request [LG 18 December 1928, issue 33448, page 8330]. Returned to service.

		W/Cdr +	27.06.42	Stow Maries
	F W H LERWILL [T]	S/Ldr	30.06.31	Retired list

On account of ill-health [LG 30 June 1931, issue 33731, page 4252].

	R B MUNDAY DSC [A]	S/Ldr	05.05.32	Retired list

On account of ill-health. Squadron Leader Richard Burnard Munday was an extremely ill officer and just after two months following his release from the service he died on Monday, 11th July 1932. In addition to his DSC, he was awarded an AFC on 3rd June 1925 [LG 3 June 1925, supplement 33053, page 3781]. His entry on *Wikipedia* [which I have pleasure in acknowledging] shows his birth in Plymouth on the last day of January 1896, was to Mrs R C Munday, wife of Major-General Munday. Richard's operational success in the *Great War* was notable for his daring attacks on enemy observation balloons, one of which was the first to be destroyed at night in the Brebières sector,. He also sent down a trio of Albatros D.Vs and a reconnaissance machine, this being his final success which he achieved in the morning of 21st February 1918. Prior to his operational service, he was a flying instructor at Cranwell and then as a Flight Commander he was attached to No. 8 Squadron Royal Naval Air Service.

	G C PIRIE MC [A]	ACM	15.10.51	Retirement**

Air Chief Marshal Sir George Pirie KCB KBE MC DFC mentioned in despatches, died on Monday, 21st January 1980.

	J H D'ALBIAC DSO [A]	AM	14.04.47	Retirement**

Air Marshal Sir John D'Albiac KCVO KBE CB DSO mentioned in despatches, died on Tuesday, 20th August 1963.

02100	R J O COMPSTON DSC DFC [A]	W/Cdr	25.05.54	Relinquished
	G SOMERS-CLARKE [T]	Captain	01.08.19	Cancelled
	C F GORDON OBE MC [O]	G/Cpat	01.03.46	Relinquished
03096	C E WARDLE [SO]	W/Cdr	08.06.43	Retired list**
	T E LONGRIDGE [SO]	Captain	01.08.19	Cancelled
	H W STRATTON [Ad]	Lt-Col	14.07.211	Retired list
01138	D S K CROSBIE [A]	W/Cdr	08.12.28	Retired list

At his own request [LG 18 December 1928, issue 33448, page 8330]. Formerly of the Argyll and Sutherland Highlanders, Captain Dudley Stuart Kays Crosbie, observer to 2nd Lieutenant C A Gladstone became a prisoner of war on 30th April 1915, when their Avro 504 715 of 5 Squadron was hit by ground-fire from a machine-gun while reconnoitring the Ypres Salient, forced-landing near Inglemunster [West-Vlaaderen] where they set light to the Avro. Captain Crosbie, it seems, crossed into Holland where he was sheltered by villagers but surrendered when pursuing enemy troops threatened to start shooting civilians unless he surrendered - which he did [page 12, *'The Sky Their Battlefield'* which I acknowledge]. Ironically, in March 1918, Captain Crosbie was transferred, along with other prisoners, to Holland where he remaining interned until 18th November 1918, on which date he was repatriated to Hull.

	T L STEVENS [Ad]	S/ldr	20.02.23	Retired list
	W R READ MC AFC [A]	W/Cdr	17.05.32	Retired list

At his own request [LG 17 May 1932, issue 33826, page 3223].

	G T PORTER [A]	Captain	01.08.19	Cancelled
	H L REILLY DSO [A]	G/Capt	05.08.34	Retired list

At his own request [LG 7 August 1934, issue 34076, page 5057].

	C C DARLEY [A]	A/Cmdr	14.09.39	Resigned**

Air Commodore Charles Curtis Darley CBE AM, died on Sunday, 10th June 1962. Charles Darley is summarised on 27-28 September 1919, when the Vickers V/1500 piloted by his brother, Captain Cecil Hill Darley crashed north of Rome, bursting into flames. Despite valiant efforts by Charles he was unable to save his brother's life.

	T G BOWLER [Ad]	Captain	01.08.19	Cancelled

	E B GRENFELL MC AFC [A]	A/Cmdr		22.10.44	Retirement**

Air Commodore Eric Blake Grenfell MC AFC, died in September 1972.

	E C PERRIN OBE [SO]	F/L	+	05.07.21	Kirkee 1914-1918 Mem.
	F E HELLYER [Ad]	W/Cdr		01.01.46	Relinquished
	D R HANLON [A]	Captain		01.08.19	Cancelled
	C E H JAMES MC [A]	G/Capt		01.10.44	Retired list

At his own request.

03085	B D S TUKE [SO]	F/L		28.10.29	Retired list

Returned to service: Granted a commission in the General Duties Branch, Class C, as Flight Lieutenant, 1st December 1935 [LG 10 March 1936, issue 34263, page 1563].

		W/Cdr		12.04.48	Resigned**
	A McR MOFFATT [SO]*	S/Ldr		13.10.31	Retired list

Paul McMillan reports that Squadron Leader Alexander McRitchie Moffatt died on Saturday, 2nd December 1933, and was cremated at Darlington Crematorium. He is mentioned in Alastair Goodrum's book 'School of Aces - The RAF Training School That Won The Battle of Britain', copies of which are still available from Amazon.

01246	S C W SMITH [T]	S/Ldr		07.02.23	Retired list

On account of ill -health contracted on service [LG 6 February 1923, issue 32793, page 912].

	J W WOODHOUSE DSO MC [A]	G/Capt		08.06.41	Retired list

The private papers of Group Captain J W Woodhouse DSO MC are held at the Imperial War Museum. These include three flying log books covering flying with various squadrons and concluding in 1946, when he was a test pilot with Phillip and Powis Aircraft Limited.

	M HENDERSON DSO [A]	AV-M		29.04.45	Retirement**

Air Vice-Marshal Malcolm Henderson CB CIE CBE DSO, died on Tuesday, 7th March 1978.

	E A JACKSON [T]	Captain		01.0-8.19	Cancelled
	W J B CURTIS [T]	AV-M		31.07.47	Retirement**

Air Vice-Marshal Walter John Brice Curtis CB CBE mentioned in despatches, died on Saturday, 10th November 1973.

	E L OLIVER MC [A]	Captain		01.08.19	Cancelled
	C H ELLIOTT-SMITH [A]	G/Capt		06.10.42	Retirement**
		A/Cmdr		12.06.44	Retired list**

Re-employed. Attained Air Commodore rank.

Air Commodore Charles Henry Elliott-Smith AFC, died on Friday, 14th January 1994, aged 105, thus becoming the oldest officer of air rank appointed in August 1919, to pass away. He was born on Sunday, 6th October 1899.

	R B C M T de POIX [SO]	Captain		01.08.19	Cancelled
02052	E A BEAULAH [SO]	G/Capt		10.10.48	Relinquished
	L H T SLOAN [A]	Captain		01.08.19	Cancelled

Subsequently granted a short service commission; resigned with effect from 21st May 1921, on account of medical unfitness for flying duties [LG 20 December 1921, issue 32554, pages 10373 and 10374].

02176	W W HART MBE [T]	S/Ldr		15.07.37	Retired list

At his own request [LG 3 September 1937, issuue 34432, page 5561]. Returned to service: 24th April 1940, and transferred to the Technical Branch [LG 30 July 1940, issue 34910, page 4677], retaining Squadron Leader rank.

		S/Ldr		19.06.46	Retired list**
	E B BEAUMAN [A & S]	W/Cdr		21.03.38	Retired list

At his own request [LG 29 March 1938, issue 34497, page 2091].

	E R WHITEHOUSE [SO]	W/Cdr		05.08.31	Retired list

On account of ill-health.

	G B DACRE DSO [S]	A/Cmdr		26.06.44	Retirement**

Air Commodore George Bentley Dacre CB DSO twice mentioned in despatches, died on Thursday, 4th January 1962. In 1951, along with his wife he presented the Dacre Trophy to the Royal Air Force in memory of their son, Flying Officer Kenneth Fraser Baker DFC killed along with his navigator, Sergeant Sidney Rowland Didsbury DFM, during an a night intruder sortie over Germany 22-23 September 1943, flying 605 Squadron Mosquito IV HJ790 UP-R from Castle Camps.. Both are buried in Sage War Cemetery. The Dacre Trophy is awarded annually to the squadron judged to be the most efficient fighter squadron of the year.

	R C L HOLME MC [A]	F/L	+	04.10.22	1 Squadron

On the 4th of October 1922, a Wednesday, Flight Lieutenant Robert Charles Lyon Holme was a passenger in a 45 Squadron Vickers Vernon J6865, captained by Flight Lieutenant Alfred Lewis Messenger AFC, which crashed shortly after leaving Kirkuk and burst into flames. Flight Lieutenant Holme's was killed in the crash; Flight Lieutenant Messenger lingered for ten days before dying from his burns, while Aircraftman Albert Annott Milne died within hours of the accident. A brief description is reported by Wing Commander 'Jeff' Jefford on page 72 of his detailed history of 45 Squadron. This accident has been reported at various times in this appendix; additional information will appear in the fourth volume of this series.

03091	E R VAISEY [A]	W/Cdr		17.10.40	Retired list
	F W TROTT OBE MC [SO]	G/Capt		16.04.46	Retirement**
	F H SONGHURST MBE [T]				
	J H SIMPSON [A]	A/Cmdr		23.10.40	Retirement**

Air Commodore John Hilliard Simpson died on Friday, 10th February 1967.

02110	C J W DARWIN DSO [A]	S/Ldr	+	26.12.41	Golders Green

His son, Flight Lieutenant Christopher William Wharton Darwin, was killed on Friday, 7th August 1942, while attached to 274 Squadron [Hurricane]. He is buried in El Alamein War Cemetery.

05050	A C BOLTON MC [SO]*	W/Cdr		10.02.54	Relinquished
03053	P G SCOTT [A]	W/Cdr		02.04.45	Retired list**
	C B COOKE [A]	AM		12.11.49	Retirement**

Air Marshal Sir Cyril Cooke KCB CBE twice mentioned in despatches, died on Wednesday, 27th September 1972.

	G W ROBARTS MC [A]	Captain		01.08.19	Cancelled
02169	G H HALL AFC [A]	W/Cdr		22.01.44	Retirement**

At his own request [LG 8 February 1944, supplement 36365, page 675].

03035	C PORRI [T]	G/Capt		30.11.45	Retired list**
	R B MANSELL [A]	AV-M	+	02.01.45	RAF Deleg. Washington

Air Vice-Marshal Reginald Baynes Mansell CB CBE mentioned in despatches, died on Tuesday, 2nd January 1945, from heart failure. He is commemorated on the Ottawa Memorial, panel 4, column 1.

	F L ROBINSON DSO MC [A]	G/Capt		01.05.39	Retired list
	L J St. G BAYLY MC [A]	S/Ldr	+	23.10.27	Car accident

Bonhams Auctioneers in 2010 , sold for £2,702 including premium, a group of five medals that belonged to Squadron Leader Leonard Joseph St. George Bayly, injured in a road traffic accident in Rickmansworth in October 1927 [he died in Watford Peace Memorial Hospital]. Described as 'Court mounted as worn, although somewhat tatty', the Group the MC, 1914 Star, British War and Victory Medal with a mentioned in despatches Oakleaf and Croix de Guerre with Palme.

02233	C E H C MACPHERSON [A]	W/Cdr	+	18.07.44	Harrogate
	P B HUNTER [T]	W/Cdr		17.05.38	Retired list

At his own request.

Name	Rank		Date	Outcome
C COOPER [A]	Captain		01.08.19	Cancelled
R C HARDSTAFF [A]	W/Cdr		05.04.34	Cashiered

By sentence of General Court Martial [LG 17 April 1934, page 2472]. At the time of his Court Martial, Wing Commander Richard Cecil Hardstaff was commanding the School of Technical Training [Men] at Manston. His fall from grace was published in the *Dover Express* on Friday, 20th April 1934: *'The public examination took place on Tuesday at Canterbury Bankruptcy Court of Richard Cecil Harstaff, formerly Wing Commander, RAF, recently cashiered by sentence of court-martial. His liabilities were stated to be £537, and assets nil. Hardstaff, who is 40, and lives at Holm Croft, Manston, Thanet, stated that he joined the RNAS in 1915. He was subsequently promoted major and became squadron-leader on the formation of the RAF., when his income was £450 to £500 a year. He lived up to his income, as he more or less a position to keep up. He got into debt chiefly because of his wife's illness. While in Irak [sic] in 1929, his wife was taken ill, and in order to see her within the six weeks leave granted to him he travelled by Imperial Airways at a cost of £100, which he borrowed from a money-lender. When he was promoted Wing Commander in 1932, his income was £50 a month. He said he had had transactions with moneylenders since the war, but not all the time. The Officer Receiver said one money-lender was charging 192 per cent. Referring to tailors' bills of £76, he suggested nothing had been paid for eight years, and added, "Are you one of those people who believe being in debt to the tailor?" Hardstaff: "No, I do not think so." Debtor admitted borrowing another £20 last February, although his petition had been on file since last April, and incurring a new debt of £300 after his petition had been adjourned. He said that he expecting his gratuity of £1,500, which would clear the matter off. He had been collaborating with other airmen in the development of a new aero-engine on which had been spent £300. The public examination was adjourned until May 15th.* The case was subsequently followed up by the *Whitstable Times and Herne Bay Herald* on Saturday, 16th June 1934, in which the Official Receiver thought that it was almost a certainty [Hardstaff] would receive from the Air Ministry sufficient funds to settle his debts in full.

W D BUDGEN OBE [SO]	G/Capt		31.05.45	Retirement**

Re-employed. Rose in rank to Air Commodore.

	A/Cmdr		31.05.46	Retired list

Air Commodore William Douglas Budgen CBE, died on Wednesday, 19th March 1969.

J J BREEN [SO]	AM		02.05.46	Retirement**

Air Marshal John Joseph Breen CB OBE three times mentioned in despatches, died on Saturday, 9th May 1964.

G C BAILEY DSO [A]	A/Cmdr		25.09.44	Retirement**

Air Commodore George Cyril Bailey CB DSO twice mentioned in despatches, died on Thursday, 1st June 1972.

03068	A FITZ R P H SOMERSET-LEEKE [T]	W/Cdr	24.05.45	Retired list**
	P HUSKINSON MC [A]	A/Cmdr	25.01.42	Retirement**

Air Commodore Patrick Huskinson CB MC*, died on Thursday, 24th November 1966. During the night of 14th-15th April 1941, he was severely injured when a bomb exploded close to the flat where they were living. Taken to hospital, it was realised he had been blinded; however, his exceptional talents in regard to armaments led to him being appointed President of the Air Armament Board, a post that he held from January 1942, until the end of the war.

A S ELLERTON [SO]	A/Cmdr		14.06.49	Retirement**

On Monday 24th March 1930, Squadron Leader Alban Spencer Ellerton, was the pilot of Vickers Virginia IX J7709 which crashed while landing at night at Worthy Down. Squadron Leader Ellerton was injured, but two of his crew, Flying Officer Ernest Richard White and Pilot Officer Percy James Pratt, were killed. Leading Aircraftman Donald Angus Reich also required treatment for injuries. But Aircraftman Frederick Bernard Palmer escaped with little more than a severe shaking. Originally built as a Mk.VI J7709 was accepted by the squadron in 1927, and was brought up to Mk.IX standards soon after. Throughout its squadron service it carried the letter N, this being retained during a seven day attachment to RAE Farnborough in November 1929. Air Commodore Sir Edward Ellerton GCB CMG CBE four times mentioned in despatches, died on Tuesday, 13th June 1967.

	Name	Rank		Date	Outcome
	A P V DALY [A]	G/Capt		07.04.45	Retired list**
	C E W FOSTER [A]	S/Ldr	+	06.07.39	RAF Hospital Uxbridge
	Australia				
	D IRON [SO]	A/Cmdr		15.11.45	Retirement**

Air Commodore Douglas Iron CBE, died on Tuesday, 15th March 1983.

	Name	Rank		Date	Outcome
	A S MASKELL [A]	G/Capt		02.05.43	Retirement**

Re-employed.

		Rank		Date	Outcome
		G/Capt		10.01.44	Retired list**
03111	C H G WOOLLVEN MC [Ad]	G/Capt		15.09.47	Retirement**
	E de C HALLIFAX DSC [A & S]	Captain		01.08.19	Cancelled
	F P DON [SO]	AV-M		02.02.43	Retirement**

Air Vice-Marshal Francis Percival Don OBE mentioned in despatches, died on Friday, 18th September 1964.

	Name	Rank		Date	Outcome
	R St. C McCLINTOCK C [A]	F/L	+	22.06.22	S of TT [Men] Manston

Attached to the School of Technical Training [Men] at Manston, Flight Lieutenant Ronald St. Clair McClintock was flying a Sopwith 7F.1 Snipe F2409 practicing for a relay race which would feature in the forthcoming Hendon Pageant. Taking off from Northolt, the air was quite turbulent and Flight Lieutenant McClintock was thrown from the cockpit. His Military Cross was *Gazetted* on 21st June 1918, issue 30761, page 7418: *'For conspicuous gallantry and devotion to duty. On one occasion he shot down two enemy machines, and on the following day he attacked and shot down a hostile two-seater machine at a height of 100 feet. He has led upwards of forty patrols and has performed much valuable work on low-flying reconnaissance and bombing patrols. As a flight commander he has been untiring in his care of personnel and machines, and as a patrol leader he has displayed the greatest courage and resource.'*

	Name	Rank		Date	Outcome
	S N COLE [T]	S/Ldr		26.07.29	Retired list

On account of ill-health [LG 30 July 1929, issue 33521, page 4992].

	Name	Rank		Date	Outcome
	A T WILLIAMS [A]	W/Cdr	+	23.06.34	Air Ministry

Wing Commander Arthur Trafalgar Williams [he was Christened 'Trafalgar' as he was born on 'Trafalgar Day' 21st October 1894] died while serving on the Staff of Air-Vice Marshal Sir Edgar Ludlow-Hewlitt and was a consequence of being severely wounded in the chest, 1915, during active service in the *Great War*.

	Name	Rank		Date	Outcome
	L G S PAYNE MC [A]	A/Cmdr		21.04.45	Retired list**

Air Commodore Lionel Guy Stanhope Payne CBE MC AFC, died on Thursday, 11th February 1965.

	Name	Rank		Date	Outcome
	B E BAKER DSO MC AFC [A]	AM		10.05.50	Retirement**

Air Marshal Sir Brian Baker KBE CB DSO MC AFC mentioned in despatches, died on Monday, 8th October 1979.

	Name	Rank		Date	Outcome
	A W BIRD DSO [A]	Major		18.04.22	Resigned
02178	C H HAYWARD [A]	S/Ldr		22.07.25	Retired list

At his own request [LG 21 July 1925, issue 33068, page 4870].

	Name	Rank		Date	Outcome
	E D ATKINSON DFC AFC [A]	S/Ldr		18.01.32	Retired list
	G L HUNTING [T]	Captain		01.08.19	Cancelled
	C W MACKEY [A]	G/Capt		29.09.45	Retirement**
02082	A N BENGE [A]	S/Ldr		14.08.30	Retired list

At his own request [LG 4 November 1930, issue 33658, page 6959]. Returned to service.

		Rank		Date	Outcome
		G/Capt		23.10.45	Retired list**
02177	J C M HAY [Ad]	F/L		12.09.33	Retired list

Returned to service.

		Rank		Date	Outcome
		G/Capt		26.12.45	Retired list**
	C R COX AFC [A]*	A/Cmdr		14.07.46	Retirement**

Air Commodore Claude Russell Cox CBE AFC, died on Saturday, 19th August 1961.

	Name	Rank		Date	Outcome
	H G HUTCHINSON [SO]	F/L		21.12.21	Resigned
	H W G JONES MC [A]	Captain		01.08.19	Cancelled

No.	Name	Rank		Date	Status
03101	R WHITAKER MBE [SO]	W/Cdr		31.08.46	Retired list**
	G H A HAWKINS [SO]	Captain		01.08.19	Cancelled
	J F GORDON DFC [A]	S/Ldr		25.11.36	Retired
	C J Q BRAND DSO MC DFC [A]	AV-M		06.11.43	Retirement**

Air Vice-Marshal Sir Quinton Brand KBE DSO MC DFC, died on Saturday, 9th March 1968.

| | J M ROBB DFC [A] | ACM | | 26.11.51 | Retirement** |

Air Chief Marshal Sir James Robb GCB KBE DSO DFC AFC three times mentioned in despatches, died on Wednesday, 18th December 1968. By accessing the website Air of Authority - A History of RAF Organisation you will find a side view of Spitfire XVI SL721 bearing his personal code JM-R which he flew during his tenure as Air Officer Commanding-in-Chief Fighter Command - May 1945 to November 1957.

| | R G MACK [A] | F/L | | 19.02.21 | Retired list |

On account of ill-health contracted in the Service. [LG 4 October 1921, issue 32476, page 7765].

| | R S LUCY [A] | S/Ldr | | 01.08.35 | Retired list |

At his own request. Paul McMillan has unearthed the fascinating information that Squadron Leader Richard Spencer Lucy's wife succeeded to the Riccarton, Midlothian, on the death of her brother Lieutenant R J A Cuming Gibson Craig RN, and on succeeding Squadron Leader and Mrs Lucy wished to be known as Richard Spencer Gibson Craig Lucy. Subsequent to being placed on the Retired List, Squadron Leader Lucy obtained a commission in the Reserve of Air Force Officers, General Duties, Class CC which he later relinquished on 17th February 1940 [LG 16 April 1940, issue 34831, page 2248]. In November 1930, while on the Staff of No. 10 Group, Lee-on-Solent, he appeared in Court to face a charge of driving his motor car without displaying front and rear lights.

| | T H McDOWELL [A] | F/L | | 16.01.25 | Cashiered |

By sentence of Field General Court Martial [LG 24 March 1925, issue 33032, page 2051].

| | W E REASON [T] | S/Ldr | | 25.08.36 | Retired list |
| | F L J SHIRLEY MC [SO] | F/L | + | 30.11.20 | |

Flight Lieutenant Frank Lawrence James Shirley MC, educated at Reading School and Sandhurst, died from dysentery in Fitzjohn's Hospital, Rugby. He is buried in Rugby [Clifton Road] Cemetery. His MC was *Gazetted* in the Edinburgh edition on May 30th, 1917, issue 13097, page 1014: '*For conspicuous gallantry and devotion to duty. He displayed great courage and skill on many occasions in photographing the enemy's positions. On one occasion, although severely wounded, he completed his work and succeeded in landing his machine safely.*'

| | N H BOTTOMLEY AFC [SO] | ACM | | 01.01.48 | Retirement** |

Air Chief Marshal Sir Norman Bottomley KCB CIE DSO AFC four times mentioned in despatches, died on Thursday, 13th August 1970.

| | E B MASON [A] | F/L | + | 19.02.26 | Aden Flight |

Flight Lieutenant Eric Barnes Mason along with Aircraftman Jack Gwynne Cole died when their Bristol F2b [serial not recorded] came down at Nobat Dakim in Saudi Arabia.

| | S G FROST MBE [T] | F/L | | 01.11.22 | Retired list |

On account of ill-health contracted in the Service [LG 7 November 1922, issue 32764, page 7874].

| | H L H OWEN AFC [A] | Captain | | 01.08.19 | Cancelled |
| | E W HAVERS [T] | AV-M | | 26.01.46 | Retirement** |

Air Vice-Marshal Sir William Havers KBE CB mentioned in despatches, died on Wednesday, 28th February 1979.

| | J GILMOUR DSO MC [A] | Captain | | 17.12.19 | Resigned |
| | M L TAYLOR [A] | A-VM | | 19.05.46 | Retirement** |

Air Vice-Marshal Malcolm Lincoln Taylor CB AFC three times mentioned in despatches, died on Thursday, Christmas Eve 1970.

| | P E M LE GALLAIS AFC [A] | Captain | | 01.08.19 | Cancelled |
| | H A TWEEDIE AFC [SO] | S/Ldr | + | 17.04.26 | 14 Squadron |

Squadron Leader Harley Alec Tweedie OBE AFC and Flight Lieutenant Stanley Harry Wallage MC were killed when their DH.9A J7108 went out of control at 500 feet and spun to the ground at Amman. Squadron Leader Tweedie was *Gazetted* with his honours in the New Year Honours list for 1919, the AFC for services in India and the OBE in the honours granted by the King on 12th July 1920., the latter in the Edinburgh edition of Friday, July 16th, 1920, issue 13615, page 1665, and the former, also in the Edinburgh paper of January 6th, 1919, issue 13378, page 78. Flight Lieutenant Wallage won his gallantry award while serving as a 2nd Lieutenant. Published in *The London Gazette* supplement 30901, of 16th September 1918, page 11030, the citation reads: '*For conspicuous gallantry and devotion to duty. He personally destroyed seven enemy machines. He showed a fine spirit of dash and tenacity, and his skill and success as a fighting pilot was a fine example to others in his squadron.*' His entry on *Wikipedia* [which I acknowledge] shows he flew Bristol F.2bs with 22 Squadron and in total he was credited with the destruction of ten hostile machines between the afternoon of 10th February and the afternoon of 4th November 1918. His short service commission will be reported in the appendices for 1921. The DH in which the two officers lost their lives was one of twenty-five rebuilt airframes, the work being carried out by the RAF Packing Depot, Ascot, J7108 being shipped to Aboukir where it was reassembled and in February 1925, issued to 47 Squadron. The following April it was returned to Aboukir for repair, after which it was accepted by 14 Squadron.

| | H M PROBYN DSO [A] | A/Cmdr | | 29.04.44 | Retirement** |

Air Commodore Harold Melsome Probyn CB CBE DSO twice mentioned in despatches, died on Tuesday, 24th March 1992, at the grand age of 101.

| | E B GRENFELL [A] | A/Cmdr | | 22.10.44 | Retirement** |

Air Commodore Eric Blake Grenfell AFC, died in September 1972.

| | E E N BURNEY MC [A] | Captain | | 01.08.19 | Cancelled |

L L MacLEAN [A] Although recorded under the appointments for August 1st, 1919, Captain Lachlan Loudoun MacLean held a commission in the Indian Army, this being relinquished on his appointment to a permanent Commission in the Royal Air Force, which was effective from 22nd July 1920, although his air force service can be traced back to March 1915, when he commenced pilot training in Egypt with 4 Reserve Squadron. Paul McMillan has also located details of his birth on 5th September 1890, at Rawal Pindi, Bengal, India. Subsequently, he rose to the rank of Group Captain and was placed on the Retired list at his own request on 15th January 1939. He was, it seems, an outspoken officer and at one stage was placed under close arrest. Subsequent to his retirement, he was recalled on 25th August 1939, and served until reverting to the retired list on 2nd August 1944. Air Commodore Lachlan Loudoun MacLean MC twice mentioned in despatches died in 1978, or possibly at a later date.

| | O H FROST MC [SO] | F/L | | 01.01.21 | Resigned |
| | A HUNTER OBE [T] | Major | | 27.11.22 | Retired list |

On account of ill-health [LG 26 December 1922, issue 32780, page 9120].

21048	L A K BUTT [SO]	G/Capt		06.02.46	Retired list**
	G H COCK MC [A]	G/Capt		01.02.43	Retired list**
	L C KEEBLE [A]	G/Capt		01.07.39	Retired list

On account of ill-health [LG 4 July 1939, page 4581].

| | F W HUDSON [A] | F/L | | 22.12.20 | Retired list |

82057   Returned to service: Commissioned to the Administrative and Special Duties Branch with effect from 15th July 1940, as a Pilot Officer for the duration of hostilities [LG 6 August 1940, issue 34915, page 4815].

| | | P/O | | 08.08.41 | Resigned |
| | D F STEVENSON DSO MC [A] | AV-M | | 10.02.48 | Retirement** |

Air Vice-Marshal Donald Fasken Stevenson CB CBE DSO MC* three times mentioned in despatches, died on Friday, 10th July 1964.

| | F G STAMMERS OBE [SO] | G/Capt | | 29.05.45 | Retirement** |
| | T F HAZELL DSO MC DFC [A] | S/Ldr | | 20.07.27 | Retired list |

At his own request [LG 19 July 1927, supplement 33295, page 4649]. His entry on *Wikipedia* shows he was born in Ireland on 7th August 1892, and died at the relatively early age of 54 on 4th September 1946. He is buried at the Burrishoole Church of Ireland Cemetery. As his honours indicate, he was an outstanding airman and as a fighter pilot he was credited with the destruction of forty-three hostile machines, including observation balloons., thus becoming the third highest scoring Irishman behind the legendary Edward Mannock VC and George McElroy.

P R M DRUMMOND DSO MC [A] AM + 27.03.45 Air Member for Training

Air Marshal Sir Peter Drummond KCB DSO* OBE MC four times mentioned in despatches, was lost without trace on Tuesday, 27th March 1945, while *en route* to Canada with senior members of government to attend the official ceremony of the closing down of the Commonwealth Air Training Plan when their Liberator of 45 Group Communications Squadron disappeared off the Azores. Sir Peter is commemorated on the Runnymede Memorial panel 264.

A W F GLENNY MC* DFC [A] A/Cmdr 01.07.40 Retirement**

Air Commodore Arthur Willoughby Falls Glenny MC* DFC mentioned in despatches, died on Wednesday, 29th January 1947.

A G JONES-WILLIAMS MC [A] S/Ldr + 17.12.29 RAF Cranwell

Killed during an attempt to fly the Fairey Long Range Monoplane J9479 non-stop from Cranwell to Cape Town, accompanied by Flight Lieutenant Norman Hugh Jenkins [see Appendix E], both being killed when their aircraft came down near Zaghaouan in French Tunisia.

A C RANDALL DFC [A] F/L 23.12.26 Dismissed

Dismissed the service by sentence of General Court Martial [LG 4 January 1927, issue 33236, page 44]. A sad end for a very brave pilot whose DFC had been *Gazetted* on 2nd November 1918, supplement 30989, page 12971: '*A daring and skilful airman who during recent operations has accounted for six enemy aeroplanes. He is conspicuous for his determination and devotion to duty.*' Born in Paisley, Scotland on 6th February 1896, he was initially commissioned to the Border Regiment before transferring to the Royal Flying Corps on 27th August 1916. Attached to 32 Squadron, he scored two aerial victories, being wounded in the process of achieving his second in DH.2 A2548 while driving down an Albatros D.III in the vicinity of Bapaume on 11th March 1917. Recovered, he joined 85 Squadron and flying SE.5as he accounted eight hostiles between 18th June and 4th October 1918. Postwar he saw active service in the Baltic supporting the White Army in their conflict with the communists. Subsequently, he was posted to 210 Squadron and later 203 Squadron . At the time of his dismissal he may have been adjutant of the Inland Area Aircraft Depot. His entry in *Wikipedia* - which I acknowledge, indicates he was still alive in 1948, and living in Dominica.

A P M SANDERS [SO] ACM 29.01.56 Retirement**

Air Chief Marshal Sir Arthur Sanders GCB KBE twice mentioned in despatches, died on Friday, 8th February 1974.

L E PALMER [T] F/L 26.01.20 Relinquished
P F FULLARD DSO MC [A & S] A/Cmdr 20.11.46 Retirement**

Air Commodore Philip Fletcher Fullard CBE DSO MC* AFC mentioned in despatches, died on Tuesday, 24th April 1984.

R A COURTNEY MBE [T] F/L + 13.02.29 RAFC Cranwell
C C DURSTON [A] W/Cdr + 12.01.33 AHQ India

While attached to the Air Staff at Air Headquarters India, Wing Commander Cecil Campbell Durston was killed by a buffalo when indulging in big game hunting near Raipur.

G E LIVOCK DFC [S] G/Capt 24.06.45 Retirement**
A F F JACOB DSO [A] Captain 01.08.19 Cancelled
74522 Returned to the service: Administrative and Special Duties Branch S/ldr 25.01.45 Resigned**
W H DUNN DSC [S] A/Cmdr 29.06.44 Retirement**

Air Commodore Wilfred Henry Dunn CBE DSC* mentioned in despatches, died in June 1973.

03059 M A SIMPSON [A & S] S/Ldr 30.11.27 Retired list

On account of ill-health [LG 13 December 1927, issue 33337, page 7084].

02210 R F S LESLIE DSC DFC [A & S] W/Cdr + 11.07.43 267 Squadron

Wing Commander Reginald Frederick Stuart Leslie was killed when the Dakota I FD815 of 267 Squadron in which he was a passenger crashed at El Aouina, Tunisia. Prior to the crash the crew had been engaged in a dummy parachute drop over Sicily. The Wing Commander, who was 52 years of age, is buried in Medjez-El-Bab War Cemetery. At the time of the crash, 267 Squadron was based at Cairo West. Credit. Air-Britain [Historians] FA100-FZ999 serial register compiled by James J Halley MBE and published in 1989.

F J LINNELL [A & S] AM + 03.11.44 Air Ministry

Air Marshal Sir Francis Linnell KBE CB three times mentioned in despatches, died in a road traffic accident in Oxfordshire on Friday, 3rd November 1944. He was cremated at Charing [Kent County] Crematorium.

C J GALPIN DSO [A & S] Captain 01.08.19 Cancelled
C L SCOTT DSC [S] G/Capt 31.12.42 Retired list**
H G R MALET [A] S/Ldr 24.02.32 Retired list

At his own request [LG 1 March 1932, issue 33804, page 1423].

R B MAYCOCK OBE [SO] A/Cmdr 31.08.35 Retirement

Returned to service in December 1939, and from August 1941, was Air Attaché in Stockholm. 15.10.46 Retired list**

Air Commodore Richard Beauchamp Maycock OBE, died on Tuesday, 21st August 1951, having settled in Sweden and residing in Stockholm.

L D D McKEAN [A] AV-M 21.05.45 Retirement**

Air Vice-Marshal Sir Lionel McKean KBE CB mentioned in despatches, died on Saturday, 28th December 1963.

W B CUSHION [Ad] AV-M 10.02.47 Retirement**

Air Vice-Marshal Sir William Cushion KBE CB, died on Monday, 16th January 1978.

J L VACHELL MC [A] A/Cmdr 21.05.43 Retirement**

Air Commodore John Lyne Vachell MC, died on Friday, 11th July 1947.

H H McL FRASER [A] AV-M 20.12.45 Retirement**

Air Vice-Marshal Hugh Henry Macleod Fraser CB, died on Tuesday, 16th January 1962.

W P GROVES [SO] S/Ldr 26.09.23 Resigned
H W WOOLLETT DSO MC [A] W/Cdr 03.02.32 Resigned
65150 Returned to the service. Royal Air Force Volunteer Reserve Training Branch. P/O 10.02.42 Resigned**

Wing Commander Henry Winslow Woollett DSO MC* was born on the 5th of August 1895, and in the wake of active service with the 6th Battalion, Lincolnshire Regiment during which he survived the horrendous casualties in the ill-designed Gallipoli Campaign, he transferred to the Royal Flying Corps on 13th June 1916, distinguishing himself with 24 Squadron, initially flying DH.2 and later DH.5. With five aerial successes achieved, Henry returned to the United Kingdom. By March 1918, he had returned to the Western Front and flying Sopwith F.1 Camels was victorious in thirty aerial combats, his most famous achievement coming on 12th April when between his first patrol in the morning and the last in the late afternoon he sent down six hostile machines, all to the north of La Gorgue and as reported on The Aeroplane website the war's record. Included in his impressive tally of thirty-five victories was eleven balloons. His death at the age of 74, was reported from Southwold, Suffolk, on Friday, 31st October 1969.

F E P BARRINGTON [A] G/Capt 18.11.45 Retirement**
02136 J EVERIDGE MC [A] W/Cdr 10.02.54 Relinquished
C H DARLEY DSC DFC [A] Captain + 28.09.19 274 Squadron

See my summary for details.

H R H Prince Albert K G Personal ADC to HM The King [A]

02090 D CLOETE MC [A] S/Ldr 16.03.27 Retired list

At his own request [LG 15 March 1927, issue 33257, page 1699].

02205 J LEACROFT*MC [A] G/Capt 19.04.45 Retired list**

Group Captain John Leacroft MC* has an extensive biography on *Wikipedia* where the citations for his MC and First Bar are reported. Born in Derby on the 4th of November 1888, he died at Bexhill in Sussex on Thursday, 26th August 1971, aged 82.

| | H G SMART [A] | AV-M | | 01.09.45 | Retirement** |

Air Vice-Marshal Harry George Smart CBE DFC AFC mentioned in despatches, died on Friday, 28th June 1963.

| | J K WAUGH DSC [S] | S/Ldr | | 08.04.31 | Comm Flt Heliopolis |

Canada While flying Fairey IIIF SR1143 belonging to the Communications Flight at Heliopolis, Squadron Leader John Keith Waugh DSC stalled while approaching the airfield at Ismailia and crashed, the accident occurring on Easter Saturday, 4th April 1931. Alive when pulled from the wreckage, he died four days later. His two passengers, Aircraftsman David Golphin and James Alexander Shirreff Thomas were badly injured but, I believe, subsequently recovered. Squadron Leader Waugh's decoration was *Gazetted* on the 6th of January 1919; at the time of his death he was 39 years of age.

| | A DURSTON AFC [S] | AM | | 13.08.46 | Retirement** |

Air Marshal Sir Albert Durston KBE CB AFC twice mentioned in despatches, died on Saturday, 24 January 1959.

	G J C MAXWELL MC DFC AFC [A]	Major		14.02.21	Resigned
	A L McFARLANE [A]	Captain		01.08.19	Cancelled
03003	C S MORICE C [A]	G/Capt		22.01.45	Retired list**
	G M CLARKE [A]	F/L	+	14.04.21	208 Squadron

Flight Lieutenant George Malcolm Clarke AFC and his observer, Frank James Smith MC MM, died when their Bristol F.2b E2298 came into midair collision with another F.2b from the squadron, D7831, flown by Flying Officer William Ash Armstrong and Flying Officer Edward Blake Jones, both machines coming down near Bilbeis in Egypt. Details concerning the tragedy in which all four died will appear in the fourth volume of this series.

| | E R TEMPEST MC DFC [A] | F/L | + | 17.12.21 | 216 Squadron |

Flight Lieutenant Edmund Roger Tempest MC DFC was killed when the DH.10 E9084 of which he was in command swung and crashed out of control while attempting to take off for an air test from at Baghdad West. His observer, Flying Officer David D'Arcy Alexander Greig DFC was injured, but made a good recover. Full details will appear in the next volume.

| | T E SALT AFC [A] | S/Ldr | + | 14.10.31 | Aircraft Depot Karachi |

On Wednesday, 14th October 1931, Squadron Leader Trevor Edward Salt was air testing a Wapiti aircraft when he lost control and crashed into the bed of the Hubb River at Marud Khan near the airfield. His passenger, Leading Aircraftman Albert Emsley Parker survived. Squadron Leader Salt was 37 years of age.

| | E L P MORGAN [Ad] | S/Ldr | | 15.02.31 | Retired list |
| 03001 | Returned to service. | S/Ldr | | 01.03.44 | Relinquished |

On account of ill-health, ceasing to be employed LG 7 March 1944, supplement 36410, page 1111.

	D H M CARBERY MC DFC [A]	F/L		01.08.19	Cancelled
03060	W A SKEATE [A]	S/Ldr		15.12.43	Retired list**
	H A WHISTLER DSO DFC [A]	G/Capt	+	01.03.40	RAF India

Born in Theddlethorpe, Lincolnshire, on 30th December 1896, Harold Alred Whistler's military service began as a Sandhurst cadet and on graduation was commissioned as a 2nd Lieutenant in the Dorsetshire Regiment. On 9th July 1916, he transferred to the Royal Flying Corps, and six months later was wounded in action while attached to 3 Squadron. This has been recorded by Trevor Henshaw on page 67 of *The Sky Their Battlefield* as taking place during a photographic sortie, his Morane P A239 forced-landing near Mametz Wood on the Somme [forever associated with the 38th [Welsh] Division] during which his observer, Corporal E J Hare was injured. Subsequently, Harold flew with 80 Squadron [Sopwith F.1 Camel], achieving a total of twenty-three victories between 17th March and 2nd October 1918, his tally including an observation balloon destroyed near Etricourt on 15th September. At the time of his death he was Acting Air Commodore and returning to England as a passenger in an Imperial Airways Handley Page HP.42 G-AAGX *Hannibal* disappeared over the Gulf of Oman. Postwar, Group Captain Whistler had been award a First and Second Bar to his DFC.

02184	E H HOOPER [T]	W/Cdr		09.09.40	Retirement
Re-employed		G/Capt		31.05.46	Retired list**
	J S T FALL DSC AFC [A]	G/Capt		11.03.45	Retirement**
	G R A DEACON MC [A]	W/Cdr		16.11.35	Retired list

At his own request [LG 26 November 1935, issue 34223, page 7513].

| | E A FAWCUS [A] | G/Capt | | 10.01.40 | Retired list** |
| | K R PARK MC [T] | ACM | | 20.12.46 | Retirement** |

New Zealand Air Chief Marshal Sir Keith Park GCB KBE MC* DFC, died in New Zealand on Wednesday, 5th February 1975. One of the Royal Air Force's most ablest commanders, as Air Vice-Marshal he commanded No. 11 Group throughout the *Battle of Britain* and flying his personal Hurricane was a familiar sight to the airmen of the squadrons under his command. His differences of opinion with his opposite number in No. 12 Group, Air Vice-Marshal Trafford Leigh-Mallory have been well reported and need no further comment; suffice to say that having been posted to Malta in July 1942, the tactics that he employed in the *Battle of Britain* again paid dividends in repelling enemy air assaults on the island.

| | H I HANMER DFC [SO] | G/Capt | | 21.09.41 | Retired list |

At his own request [LG 19 September 1941, issue 35279, page 5423]. Army Form B.103 shows he was born on 5th February 1893, and transferred to the Royal Flying Corps on 4th June 1916. He embarked on the HM *Monis Queen* at Southampton on 9th June 1917, calling at Marseilles and arriving at Alexandria on 20th June 1917. Posted seven days later to 14 Squadron [BE.2s] at Deir-el-Belah, he was wounded in action 10th November 1917, and admitted to No. 66 Casualty Clearing Station for treatment to gunshot injuries. Trevor Henshaw on page 289 of his excellent *The Sky Their Battlefield* indicates that 2nd Lieutenant Hanmer had a fortunate escape from more serious injury in that when his BE.2e was hit, the bullet glanced off his cigarette case leaving his with only slight grazing to one of his ribs.

| | A L GREGORY MBE MC [T] | A/Cmdr | | 13.06.42 | Retirement** |

Air Commodore Arthur Leslie Gregory MBE MC mentioned in despatches, died on Wednesday, 24th February 1960.

	F NUTTALL MC DFC AFC [A]	F/L	+	18.09.20	30 Squadron
	New Zealand [See summary for details of his death].				
	R T NEVILL [T]	F/L		25.08.23	Resigned
	V BUXTON OBE [SO]	G/Capt		25.04.43	Retired list**
05051	W H CLOVER [T]	F/L		20.03.20	Retired list
	L J MacLEAN MC [A]	S/Ldr		01.04.35	Retired list

On account of ill-health [LG 2 April 1935, issue 34147, page 2237].

03047	C St. NOBLE [T]	S/Ldr		19.03.35	Retired list
02067	H M K BROWN [A]	F/O		16.09.54	Resigned**
	A E McKEEVER DSO MC [A]	Major	+	26.12.19	1 Squadron CAF
	Canada [See summary for details of his death].				
	H A SMITH MC [A]	W/Cdr	+	14.11.38	9 Squadron

The circumstances of Wing Commander Harry Augustus Smith's death in a flying accident are described on page 55 in my revision of Bomber Command losses, covering the period from July 1936 through to the outbreak of the Second World War.

| 03031 | J V READ MBE [T] | G/Capt | | 16.06.45 | Retired list** |
| | W E G BRYANT [SO] | A/Cmdr | + | 22.08.45 | AOC RAFCranwell |

Air Commodore Walter Edward George Bryant MBE, died on Wednesday, 22nd August 1945, after collapsing at the Collage while watching a play. Taken to Rauceby Hospital he died shortly after being admitted. He is buried in Cranwell [St. Andrew] Churchyard.

| | J A STONE [T] | AV-M | | 14.09.45 | Retirement** |

Air Vice-Marshal James Ambrose Stone CBE, died on Friday, 14th January 1966.

| 03081 | T C THOMSON [A] | G/Capt | | 09.04.40 | Retired list** |

	Name	Rank		Date	Status/Location
	A CHAPMAN [T]	F/L		01.11.26	Retired list
	L I BARKER [A]	Captain	+	16.09.19	7 Squadron
02199	M KEEGAN [T]	S/Ldr	+	19.02.44	Rathgarogue Catholic

Returned to the service in the rank of Flight Lieutenant 6th July 1938 [LG 20 October 1939, issue 34713, page 7044].   Churchyard

| 03112 | F WORKMAN MC [A] | S/Ldr | | 10.02.54 | Relinquished |
| | J McG GLEN MC [SO] | F/L | + | 17.07.24 | 5 FTS |

Flight Lieutenant John McGowan Glen died quite suddenly of heart failure at Bettwsycoed, Wales.

| 02117 | W H DOLPHIN [T] | G/Capt | | 05.08.41 | Retired list** |
| | B J SILLY MC DFC [A] | A/Cmdr | + | 07.12.43 | AOC RAF Base Batavia |

Air Commodore Benjamin James Silly MC DFC, died in captivity while being held by the Japanese on Tuesday, 7th December 1943. He is buried in Sai Wan War Cemetery, Hong Kong. His son, 20-year Lieutenant James Lovitt Silly, was killed in France on 22nd October 1944, while serving with 2nd Special Air Service Regiment AAC. He is the sole British service burial in Moyenmoutier Communal Cemetery, Vosges.

02037	J B P ANGELL [T]	S/Ldr		27.05.45	Resigned**
	F O SODEN DFC [A]	G/Capt		30.04.45	Retirement**
	L M LILLEY OBE [T]	Captain		01.08.19	Cancelled
02658	A G BOND AFC [A]	W/Cdr		24.07.42	Retired list**
	W B LAWSON [A & S]	Captain		01.08.19	Cancelled
03033	E B RICE [A]*	G/Capt	+	05.09.43	Sai Wan War

Prisoner of war February 1942: died in captivity. Mentioned in despatches 1st October 1946 [LG 1 October 1946].   Cemetery

| 02040 | C H AWCOCK [T] | S/Ldr | | 30.06.34 | Retired list |
| | J B FOX MC [A] | F/L | + | 03.03.22 | 20 Squadron |

Flight Lieutenant John Bertram Fox MC and his observer, Flight Sergeant Allen Benjamin Hemmings, died following a midair collision near Amritsar between his Bristol F.2b E2442 and Bristol F.2b H1548 flown by Flying Officer Joseph Buckley and Aircraftman Charles Reginald Richardson. Details of the tragedy will appear in the fourth volume.

| | G DONALD DFC [A & S] | Captain | | 01.08.19 | Cancelled |
| | J P COLEMAN AFC A & S] | A/Cmdr | | 21.05.46 | Retirement** |

Air Commodore John Patrick Coleman CBE AFC mentioned in despatches, died on Wednesday, 21st July 1976. Some papers show his first Christian name as 'Jack'.

| | W R MACKENZIE DSC [Ad] | Major | | 02.11.21 | Retired list |

On account of ill-health [LG 1 November 1921, issue 32504, page 8634].

| | A N GALLEHAWK [A & S] | A/Cmdr | | 11.03.42 | Retirement** |

Air Commodore Arthur Nobel Gallehawk AFC, died on Monday, 24th December 1945.

| | F W WALKER DSC AFC [SO] | A/Cmdr | | 30.10.45 | Retirement** |

Air Commodore Frederic William Walker DSC AFC, died on Saturday, 14th November 1970.

| 02201 | H S KERBY DSC AFC [A] | AV-M | | 28.06.46 | Retirement** |

Air Vice-Marshal Harold Spencer Kerby CB DSC AFC mentioned in despatches, died on Saturday, 8th June 1963.

| | A M WAISTELL DSC [SO] | F/L | | 10.07.20 | Retired list |

On account of ill-health caused by wounds [LG 24 June 1921, issue 32368, page 5014].

03092	N W WADHAM [A]*	S/Ldr	+	06.08.40	Cambridge Crematorium
02123	E DRUDGE MBE [T]	F/L		04.03.34	Retired list
	T GRAN [T]	Captain		01.08.19	Cancelled
	E V LONGINOTTO AFC [A]	F/L	+	31.12.26	Kranji Military Cemetery

The website Find a Grave, which I acknowledge, shows: *'In memory of a dearly loved second son who died at sea on board SS Khiua.'*

	P S JACKSON-TAYLOR [T]	G/Capt	+	01.02.45	Imtarfa Military Cemetery
	H V GERMAN [A & S]	F/L		26.08.30	Retired list
	L H SLATTER DSC DFC [A]	AM		01.02.49	Retirement**

Air Marshal Sir Leonard Slatter KBE CB DSC* DFC mentioned in despatches, died on Friday, 14th April 1961.

| | R M BAYLEY DFC [A] | G/Capt | + | 11.09.32 | Air Advisor Greek Govt. |

Group Captain Rene Maurice Bayley DFC died from 'sleepy sickness' in the Red Cross Hospital, Athens. He had been appointed as Air Advisor to the Greek Government as recently as 25th June 1932 [LG 5 July 1932, issue 33843, page 4385]. In recognition of his services in the *Great War*, and in addition to his DFC, Captain Bayley was mentioned in despatches [LG 21 September 1918, supplement 30913, page 11258] and Conferred by the Government of the French Republic the *Croix de Guerre, avec Palme* [LG 8 November 1918, supplement 30999, page 13199].

02152	V R GIBBS DSC [A]	W/Cdr		13.10.43	Retirement**
Re-employed.		W/Cdr		26.10.45	Retired list**
	W B CALLAWAY AFC [S]	A-VM		06.05.45	Retirement**

Air Vice-Marshal William Bertram Callaway CB AFC three times mentioned in despatches, died on Wednesday, 28th August 1974.

	F N HALSTED DSC [A & S]	F/L	+	03.10.20	Hollybrook Memorial
	T E B HOWE AFC [A]	Captain		01.08.19	Cancelled
	D G DONALD [A]	AM		24.05.47	Retirement**

Air Marshal Sir Grahame Donald KCB DFC AFC twice mentioned in despatches, died on Thursday, 23rd December 1976.

	E P HARDMAN DFC [A]	Captain		01.08.19	Cancelled
	W S NEWTON-CLARE [Ad]	Captain		01.08.19	Cancelled
	F M ROPE [T]	S/Ldr	+	05.10.30	Air Ministry

Killed in the crash of HM Airship R101 G-FAAW in bad weather at Beauvais in France. Squadron Leader Frederick Michael Rope, aged 42, was Assistant to Director of Airship Development/Technical]. Of the 54 crew and passengers on board, 48 died . The loss of the R.101, which was on its maiden flight overseas with Karachi as its destination, effectively ended British airship development in the 1930s.

| 03034 | G H REID DFC [A] | S/Ldr | | 21.06.27 | Retired list |

On account of ill-health. In February 1928, with Frederick Sigrist, he founded the Reid and Sigrist Engineering Company at New Malden, Surrey.

04190	C S RICHARDSON MBE [Ad]	G/Capt		25.05.45	Retired list**
02088	A S CHESHIRE MBE [T]	S/Ldr		08.12.41	Retired list**
	R W DAWES [Ad]	F/L		06.08.34	Retired list
	L J KILLMAYER MBE [SO]	S/Ldr		14.05.24	Retirement
	C F RASMUSEN [SO]	S/Ldr		29.12.31	Retired list
	R YOUNG [T]	G/Capt		17.01.46	Retirement**
	A J LONG [T]	F/L		14.07.34	Resigned
03048	J A SADLER [A & S]	G/Capt		01.01.42	Retired list**
	H A J WILSON [SO]	S/Ldr		10.05.31	Retired list

On account of ill-health [LG 12 May 1931, issue 33715, page 3072].

03010	S NIXON [SO]	S/Ldr		30.04.30	Retired list
	G M T ROUSE [A]	Captain		01.08.19	Cancelled
	E G HOPCRAFT DSC [A & S]	G/Capt.		17.12.41	Retired list**

R JOPE-SLADE DSC [O]	G/Capt	+	05.04.41	244 Squadron

Group Captain Robert Jope-Slade is commemorated on the Alamein Memorial, column 239. He lost his life when Vincent K6347 of 244 Squadron became lost in bad visibility during a communications flight from Shaibah and descended into the sea south of Bubiyan in the Persian Gulf. Sergeant Charles Trevor Dennett [Alamein Memorial column 243] also perished while Flight Lieutenant Dennis Crosby Wellburn was picked up uninjured but after returning to England and becoming a Lancaster pilot with 61 Squadronb was killed during operations to Berlin on 31st August-1st September 1943 [see RAFBCL 1943, page 300 for details].

02106	E J CUCKNEY DSC [SO]	A/Cmdr	06.05.50	Retirement**

Air Commodore Ernest John Cuckney CB CB DSC* mentioned in despatches, died on Monday, 8th November 1965.

03021	A H PEARCE DFC [S]	F/L	29.06.31	Retired list

Returned to service.

		G/Capt	22.09.45	Retired list**
	J A GLEN DSC [A]	F/L	12.03.28	Retired list

At his own request [LG 20 March 1928, issue 33368, page 2023].

	G D NELSON DSC AFC [T]	S/Ldr	01.01.31	Retired list

On account of ill-health [LG 6 January 1931, issue 33677, page 148].

	E O'D CREAN [SO]	F/L	09.05.28	Retired list

At his own request.

	G H KEITH [SO]	G/Capt	29.04.43	Retired list**
02236	B A MALET DFC [O]	W/Cdr	02.12.39	Retired list**

On account of ill-health [LG 5 December 1939, issue 34747, page 8106].

	M O F ENGLAND [O]	Captain	01.08.19	Cancelled
	H LEEDHAM [T]	A/Cmdr	09.07.45	Retirement**

Air Commodore Hugh Leedham CB OBE, died on Wednesday, 5th November 1947.

	A G BISHOP AFC [A & S]	A/Cmdr	22.12.49	Retirement**

Air Commodore Alan George Bishop CBE AFC mentioned in despatches, died in March 1969.

	L H COCKEY [A]	A/Cmdr	14.12.45	Retirement**

Air Commodore Leonard Herbert Cockney CB, died on Friday, 29th December 1978.

	H F DELARUE DFC [A & S]	Captain	01.08.19	Cancelled
	J W B GRIGSON DFC [S]	A/Cmdr	+	03.07.43	Rhodesian Air Trg Group

Air Commodore John William Boldero Grigson DSO DFC** twice mentioned in despatches, died on Saturday, 3rd July 1943, in an air accident near Bulawayo. At the time of his death he was Acting Air Officer Commanding Rhodesian Air Training Group. He rests in Harare [Pioneer] Cemetery

	W R D ACLAND [A]	W/Cdr	+	01.10.37	70 Squadron

The death of Wing Commander Wilfred Reginald Dyke Acland DFC AFC, Commanding Officer of 70 Squadron, received full coverage in *The Times* in its publication of 2nd October 1937. The first report, filed by the paper's Athens Correspondent the day previous, reads: *'The Imperial Airways flying-boat Courtier [G-ADVC] from Alexandria to Southampton, met with an accident when alighting in bad visibility at Phaleron Bay this morning, and three of her nine passengers lost their lives. They have been identified as:- Wing Command W R Dyke Acland DFC AFC commanding No. 70 [Bomber Transport] SquadronRAF in Iraq. Mr Raymond Henderson, an American and Mr Alexandre Elefterakis, a Greek. Four other passengers were slightly injured and are receiving treatment at the Greek Red Cross Hospital. They are:- Squadron Leader J Russey, also of No. 70 Squadron RAF.; Mrs Greer, who had booked from Basra to London; Mr M S Chronis, from Alexandria to Athens; and Mr J Dagge, from Basra to London, who is attached to the Anglo-Iranian Oil Company, Abadan, South Persia. The Rev. Richard Rees, RAF Chaplin attached to the Iraq Command; the pilot, Captain Poole, and four other members of the crew were unhurt. The flying-boat was seen to be circling normally preparatory to landing, but failed to flatten out and struck the glassy surface of the sea with great force. The victims were drowned in their cabin.* The second report, published in the same edition, under the banner 'An Authority on Deck Landing' continues: *Wing Commander W R Dyke Acland DFC AFC, whose death in the accident at Athens to the Imperial Airways flying-boat Courtier is reported on another page, had a distinguished career in the Royal Air Force, to which he was transferred from the Navy. He was on his way home from Iraq, where he was in command of No. 70 [BomberTransport] Squadron at Hinaidi. Born on June 26, 1894, Wilfred Reginald Dyke Acland was the son of the late Sir Reginald Dyke Acland KC who was the fifth son of the first baronet created in 1890 of St. Mary Magdalen, Oxford. After being educated at Winchester, where he was in Kingsgate House, he received a commission as sub-lieutenant RNVR. He went out to the Dardanelles in 1915, however, as an air mechanic, but in the following year was commissioned sub-lieutenant in the Royal Naval Air Service. After service in HMS Furious, flagship of aircraft carriers in the Grand Fleet, he became an authority on deck landing. During the war he was one of the early winners of the Dunning Cup [1918] for flights from and landings on the aircraft carrier Argus. In addition to two mentions in despatches he was twice decorated for service with coastal patrols in the Baltic. The Armistice having been signed, Dyke Acland decided to make his career in the recently formed Royal Air Force, and a few years later 1922-23] took the Staff College course, from which he was posted to Coastal Area Air Staff. After further service at Leuchars and Calshot he went, in 1928, to the Air Ministry in the Directorate of Operations and Intelligence, when he was appointed as instructor at the Staff College at Andover. When he had served in that capacity for three years he was selected for Staff Duties in the Iraq command, which he took up in the early part of last year, later being given the command he held at the time of his death. In 1921 he married Mary Strange, daughter of Mr. T Marshall of Trelawny, Lee-on-Solent, and had two daughters.'*

02144	S T FREEMAN [A & S]	W/Cdr	26.08.46	Retired list**
74839	C M CROWE MC DFC [A]	S/Ldr	09.07.554	Relinquished
02139	A FERRIS [SO]	S/Ldr	23.12.40	Retired list**
03106	G E WILSON [A]	A/Cmdr	31.10.43	Retirement**

Air Commodore George Edward Wilson OBE mentioned in despatches, died on Monday, 11th February 1963.

Note. Flight Lieutenant Arthur Francis Brooke [A] was appointed to a permanent commission, effective 1st August 1919 [LG 9 March 1920, issue 31816, page 2906]. Attaining Squadron Leader rank he was placed on the Retired list on account of ill health on 12th October 1932 [LG 11 October 1932, issue 33872, page 6418].

LIEUTENANTS
492

02141	F FOWLER DSC AFC [S]	W/Cdr	20.06.34	Retired list

On account of ill-health [LG 19 June 1934, issue 34061, page 3908]. His DSC was *Gazetted* on 12th May 1917, supplement 30066, page 4626: *'For conspicuous skill and gallantry during the last nine months, in reconnaissance, photographic and spotting machines. On the majority of occasions he has acted as pilot to Lieut. Gow RNVR his machine being constantly hit by anti-aircraft fire.'*

	D GILLEY DFC [A]	S/Ldr	12.10.28	Retired ;ist

At his own request [LG 11 December 1928, issue 33446, page 8173].

04021	Returned to service.	G/Capt	09.11.45	Retired list**
	T F N GERRARD DSC [A & S]	F/L	+	14.07.23	1 Squadron

Flight Lieutenant Thomas Francis Netterville Gerrard DSC, serving in Iraq, died as the result of an equestrian accident. Born on 13th August 1897, Kuala Kubu Bharu in the Malaya States, Gerrard enlisted at the outbreak of the *Great War* with the Royal Naval Air Service, gaining a DSC which was *Gazetted* on 20th July 1917, supplement 30194, pages 7425 and 7426: *'In recognition of his services during an air fight 4 June 1917. This officer led his flight against 15-20 hostile aeroplanes, and alone had ten engagements with these machines. He attacked one, and fired sixty rounds into its cockpit at point-blank range, the enemy machine rolling over and over for 3,000 feet, and then falling vertically out of control. He then attacked another enemy machine which had dived on to one of our machines from behind, and with the help of a Scout* [Captain Philip F Fullard] *he shot it down, the enemy being seen to crash to the ground. Another hostile Scout was then attacked by pilot, end-on, and received a long burst at very close range, the enemy going down in a spin, but apparently righting himself lower down. During this last encounter Flt. Cdr. Gerrard's machine was riddled with bullets, but, by fine piloting, he landed safely, although all but his lateral controls were shot away and his machine* [Sopwith Triplane N5440] *damaged to such an extent as to require return to Depot for complete rebuilding. This officer has now destroyed at least seven hostile aircraft. He was on active service in France and Belgium from April to September 1916, and during that period performed much valuable work.'* These actions took place while he was attached to 1 Squadron RNAS.

	F N HUDSON MC [please refer to Appendix E and the first table of Flight Lieutenants].				
	J H NORTON MC DFC [A]	Captain		17.09.20	Resigned
05017	H G WHITE [A]	AV-M		01.03.55	Retirement**

Air Vice-Marshal Hugh Granville White CB CBE, died on Friday, 23rd September 1983.

	C R ROBBINS MC DFC [A]	Lieutenant		01.08.19	Cancelled
03171	J H BUTLER [A]	G/Capt		18.02.46	Retirement**
	D S EVANS [A]	F/O	+	27.05.21	Delhi War Cemetery
03155	H F BRADLEY [T]	S/Ldr		29/.09.40	Retired list**
08121	R S SORLEY DSC [A]	AM		06.09.48	Retirement**

Air Marshal Sir Ralph Sorley KCB OBE DSC DFC, died on Sunday, 17th November 1974.

	H de V LEIGH DFC [S]	Lieutenant		01.08.19	Cancelled
	R G St. JOHN DSC [O]	Lieutenant		01.08.19	Cancelled
	E B C BETTS DSC DFC [O]	AV-M		10.03.46	Retirement**

Air Vice-Marshal Eric Bourne Coulter Betts CBE DSC DFC mentioned in despatches, died on Saturday, 30th October 1971.

	F L LUXMOORE [A]	F/L		03.08.29	Retired list

At his own request [LG 20 August 1929, issue 33527, page 5408].

04200	H V ROWLEY [A]	A/Cmdr		26.10.44	Retirement**

Air Commodore Herbert Victor Rowley mentioned in despatches, died on Saturday, 9th April 1966.

	C F BREWERTON DSC [A]	F/L	+	18.01.27	423 Flight HMS *Eagle*

Shortly after taking off from RNAS Hal Far in Avro Bison II N9972, Flight Lieutenant Cyril Fraser Brewerton DSC struck a cliff top and fell into the sea off Ghar Hasan, Malta. Flying Officer Edwin Chafe, a Lieutenant in the Royal Navy, Lieutenant Guy Owen Jones and LeadingTelegraphist George William Burton also perished. Flight Lieutenant Brewerton's DSC was *Gazetted* in supplement 30635 of the paper on 17th April 1918, page 4647, unfortunately without citation.

	G W R FANE DSC [A & S]	Captain		08.03.21	Resigned

Returned to army service. Under the heading Miscellaneous [LG 6 September 1939, supplement 34671, page 6116] his name appears, with others, in a long table of officers promoted Captain. However, in the collection of papers and documents held by the IWM his flying log book his flying log book is mentioned which identifies that in the *Great War* he flew coastal patrols from Great Yarmouth with 12 Squadron RNAS, subsequently becoming 212 Squadron of the Royal Air Force. Also in the collection, five photograph albums and one package, in all containing 444 prints.

	F J BAILEY [S]	Lieutenant		01.08.19	Cancelled
	W T S WILLIAMS DSC [SO]	F/Lt		03.02.26	Retired list

On account of ill-health [LG 2 February 1926, issue 33129, page 794].

74396	Returned to service: Commissioned Administrative and Special Duties Branch [LG 3 October 1939, issue 34700, page 6661].				
		S/Ldr	+	25.12.47	Cambridge City Cemetery
04222	L A C STAFFORD [T]	F/L		01.01.31	Retired list

On account of ill-health [LG 6 January 1931, issue 33677, page 148]. Returned to service. S/Ldr 12.04.42 Relinquished

04239	D R W THOMPSON [O]	G/Capt		26.05.44	Retired list**

At his own request.

03139	S S BENSON AFC [S]	A/Cmdr		24.12.44	Retirement**

Air Commodore Seymour Stewart Benson AFC, died in January 1990.

	E P M DAVIS AFC AM [A & S]	G/Capt	+	13.08.40	Runnymede Memorial

Group Captain Edward Peverell Meggs Davis lost his life when the *Luftwaffe* raided Detling on the 13th of August 1940. Born at Queenstown in Ireland on 20th October 1898, the eldest son of Edward Harry Meggs Davis CMG JP and a former Admiral on the RN, he served with distinction during the *Great War* during which he gained the Albert Medal. Although I have not been able to trace the relevant *Gazette* the citation for the award can be read on the website dedicated to holders of the Victoria & George Cross, which I respectfully acknowledge: *On the 3rd October 1917, whilst carrying out a practice flight, a seaplane, piloted by Flight Sub-Lieutenant James Douglas Grant, fell into the sea. The seaplane turned over and the pilot was enclosed in the boat under water. Flight Lieutenant Edward Peverell Meggs Davis immediately flew a seaplane to the position of the accident, made fast to the wreck, and dived under the wreck in uniform and endeavoured to extricate Flight Sub-Lieutenant Grant. To do this it was necessary for him to dive amongst and struggle through the mass of wires and broken parts of the wreck. Notwithstanding the imminent danger of being caught up amongst them, Lieutenant Davis continued his efforts to get Flight Sub-Lieutenant Grant out, until the emergency boat arrived on the scene. No other help was at hand until the arrival of this motor boat, which at the time of the accident was about a mile and a-half away. Flight Lieutenant Davis risked his life in endeavouring to save that of his brother officer, as there was every chance of his becoming caught under water in the wires of the wreck.'* Sadly, when recovered, Flight Sub-Lieutenant James Douglas Grant, 24 years of age, was dead; he is buried in Aberdeen [Allenvale] Cemetery. From one of many discussion websites, it seems that Group Captain David was in the operations block at Detling when the raid struck and he was killed by a shard of concrete striking his head. Although he is commemorated on the Runnymede Memorial, he was buried in Chelsea in St. Simon's Church.

	J R SWANSTON DFC [A]	F/O	+	28.06.20	60 Squadron

See summary for details concerning the air accident that claimed his life.

03240	A B ELLWOOD DSC [A]	AM		29.01.52	Retirement**

Air Marshal Sir Aubrey Ellwood KCB DSC mentioned in despatches, died on Sunday, 20th December 1992.

05034	P C WOOD [A]	W/Cdr		14.10.38	Retired list

At his own request [LG 25 October 1938, issue 34564, page 6637].

03178	C CHAPMAN DSC [O]	S/Ldr		16.05.38	Retired list

At his own request [LG 24 May 1938, issue 34513, page 3359].

	W F DICKSON DSO [A & S]	MRAF		16.07.59	Retirement**

Marshal of the Royal Air Force Sir William Dickson GCB KBE DSO AFC three times mentioned in despatches, died on Saturday, 12th September 1987. He attained the highest rank of those Lieutenants appointed to a permanent commission on the 1st of August 1919.

	D G McGREGOR AFC [O]	Lieutenant		01.08.19	Cancelled
04192	L RITSON [O]	S/Ldr		05.07.45	Resigned**
04042	B E HARRISON [O]	S/Ldr		27.05.37	Retired list
04032	J H GREEN [A & S]	G/Capt		26.11.46	Retirement**
04176	A J PRINCE- COX [T]	Captain		09.11.21	Retired list

On account of ill-health.

03210	E D DAVIS [A & S]	AV-M		06.02.46	Retirement**

Air Vice-Marshal Edward Derek Davis CB OBE, died on Monday, 19th September 1955.

Name	Rank		Date	Notes
W B FARRINGTON DSO [T]	G/Capt		09.02.46	Retirement**
04018 R A GEORGE MC [A]	AV-M		26.06.52	Retirement**

Air Vice-Marshal Sir Robert George KCMG KCVO KBE KStJ CB MC, died on Wednesday, 13th September 1967.

Name	Rank		Date	Notes
F M I WATTS [T]	Lieutenant		01.08.19	Cancelled
T L F BURNETT [T]	Major		10.05.22	Retired list

On account of ill-health contracted on active service [LG 9 May 1922, issue 32695, page 3626]. Ranked Flying Officer at the time, it is noted he had been awarded an MBE.

Name	Rank		Date	Notes
J F LAWSON AFC [A]	F/L	+	30.12.29	HQ Inland Area

Flight Lieutenant John Francis Lawson was fatally injured in a road traffic accident. His death, and that of his wife, along the rider of the motorcycle, William Albert Frederick Wild, was reported in *The Times* published on New Year's Eve. The collision occurred at Parkside on Wimbledon Common and so violent was the collision that both vehicles burst into flames and despite heroic efforts to reach Flight Lieutenant Lawson and his wife, and Mr Wild who was pinned against the side of the car, the intense heat from the flames made it impossible. Albert Richard Wild, brother of the deceased, was thrown from the pillion and was found some distance away badly injured and was taken to Wimbledon Hospital for treatment to burns on his head. A report issued from the hospital indicated he had improved slightly since admittance.

Name	Rank		Date	Notes
04159 F MacB PAUL [A]	F/L		10.02.54	Relinquished
C S T LAVERS DFC [A]	Lieutenant		01.08.19	Cancelled
10166 A B WIGGIN [T]	S/Ldr		21.12.31	Retired list

Returned to service: Commissioned to Equipment Branch and by 1st September 1940, promoted Wing Commander [LG 20 September 1940, issue 34949, page 5584].

Name	Rank		Date	Notes
	W/Cdr		12.02.45	Retired list**
03149 J A BORET MC AFC [A]	AV-M		13.04.48	Retirement**

Air Vice-Marshal John Auguste Boret CBE MC AFC twice mentioned in despatched, died on Sunday, 26th April 1964.

Name	Rank		Date	Notes
04185 G E RANSOM [A]	W/Cdr		11.02.45	Retired list**

An incomplete record for this officer exists in the form a Casualty Form - Officers showing that in 1917, he was posted to 42 Squadron on 26th March; 55 Squadron on 1st April; 70 Squadron on 30th May and to 10 Stationary Hospital on 3rd June, thence to 39 General Hospital from where he was discharged to duty on 30th June and posted on 7th July to 9th Wing [Special Duty Flight].

Name	Rank		Date	Notes
03182 A R CHURCHMAN DFC [A]	A/Cmdr		02.11.46	Retirement**

Air Commodore Allan Robert Churchman CB DFC, died on Tuesday, 13th January 1970.

Name	Rank		Date	Notes
H P LALE DFC [A]	G/Capt		08.04.41	Retirement**

Re-employed [LG 7 December 1943, supplement 36276, page 5340]. His *Wikipedia* entry [which I acknowledge] states Horace Percy Lale was born on 8th April 1886, in Nottingham, and was credited with twenty-three combat victories in the *Great War.* There is no indication of his re-employment. He died in Swindon on the 5th of April 1955, aged 68. Consulting *The London Gazette* his DFC was published on 3rd December 1918, supplement 31046, page 14323: *'A bold and courageous officer, who leads his patrol with marked skill and judgement. He has accounted for twelve enemy aeroplanes - five crashed, four shot down in flames, and three driven down out of control. On 6th September he led his patrol of nine machines to the assistance of some formations that were attacked by thirty or forty enemy aircraft; in the engagement he and his observer accounted for two Fokkers; eventually the enemy was driven off, five of their machines being destroyed and three shot down out of control.'* Subsequently, he added a First Bar and a DSO to his honours.

Name	Rank		Date	Notes
S B COLLETT [A]	Captain		30.03.21	Resigned

Returned to service:

Name	Rank		Date	Notes
	S/Ldr	+	30.06.34	600 Squadron AAF

During a display at Hendon on Empire Air Day, Saturday, 30th June 1934, Squadron Leader Stanley Beresford Collett, Commanding 600[County of London] Squadron was flying in the air gunner's seat of Hawker Hart K2983, piloted by Flying Officer Robert Francis Gordon Lea when it left the formation and in the ensuing forced-landing crashed, killing the Squadron Leader on impact. Flying Officer Lea was only slightly injured and was able to free himself from the cockpit before the machine caught fire. The accident received widespread press coverage, the report in *The Times* issued on Monday, 2nd July, stating that Squadron Leader Collett was the son of the then present Lord Mayor of London.

Name	Rank		Date	Notes
W DEANE MC [A]	F/O	+	20.03.20	20 Squadron

See summary for an explanation of his death in a flying accident.

Name	Rank		Date	Notes
G E GIBBS MC [A]	AM		28.06.54	Retirement**

Air Marshal Sir Gerald Gibbs KBE CIE MC** twice mentioned in despatches, died on Saturday, 10th October 1992. As recorded on the website Air of Authority - A History of RAF Organisation, Air Marshal Gibbs was the last Royal Air Force officer to be appointed Chief of the Air Staff and Commander-in-Chief, Indian Air Force, a position that he had great pleasure in handing over in the summer of 1954, to Air Marshal S Mukerjee whose own association with the Royal Air Force began when he reported to the Royal Air Force Collage at Cranwell with the September 1930 intake of Flight Cadets.

Name	Rank		Date	Notes
R D STARLEY MC [A]	G/Capt		04.05.42	Retirement**
P W S BULMAN MC AFC [A]	F/L		19.08.25	Resigned
B McENTEGART [A]	AV-M		09.11.45	Retirement**

Air Vice-Marshal Bernard McEntegart CB CBE mentioned in despatches, died on Saturday, 25th September 1954.

Name	Rank		Date	Notes
P WARBURTON [A]	W/Cdr		06.08.37	Retired list

At his own request [LG 6 August 1937, issue 34424, page 5043].

Name	Rank		Date	Notes
M MINTER [A]	Lieutenant		01.08.19	Cancelled
G W N R HAYNES [A]	Lieutenant		01.08.19	Cancelled
F G C WEARE MC [A]	F/L		30.01.24	Resigned
I D R McDONALD MC DFC [A]	F/O	+	22.09.20	84 Squadron

See summary outlining the death of this officer during air operations.

Name	Rank		Date	Notes
03175 E T CARPENTER [A]	W/Cdr		01.02.39	Retired list

At his own request.

Name	Rank		Date	Notes
03244 W B EVERTON [T]	W/Cdr		28.10.45	Retired list**
N LIDDALL [T]	F/L		13.07.28	Retired list

On account of ill-health [LG 1 January 1929, issue 33453, page 72].

Name	Rank		Date	Notes
D DROVER [T]	F/L		21.12.32	Retired list

On account of ill-health [LG 20 December 1932, issue 33894, page 8138].

Name	Rank		Date	Notes
05013 T W WARNE-BROWNE DSC [A]	AM		17.01.53	Retirement**

Air Marshal Sir Thomas Warne-Browne KBE CB DSC, died at the age of 64 on Saturday, 13th October 1962.

Name	Rank		Date	Notes
V S E LINDOP [A]	S/Ldr		25.02.35	Retired list

On account of ill-health [LG 7 May 1935, issue 34158, page 2986].

Name	Rank		Date	Notes
F H EBERLI [A]	Lieutenant		01.08.19	Cancelled
03098 A G WEIR [A]	W/Cdr	+	30.04.41	OC Troops

Wing Commander Archibald Graham Weir was a passenger aboard SS *Nerissa* which sailed from Halifax, Nova Scotia, on 21st April 1941, thus commencing her 40th wartime Atlantic crossing; aboard was a complement of 291 personnel. Stopping at St. John's, Newfoundland, SS *Nerissa* continued her crossing on the 24th, a Thursday, and was in the approaches to the British Isles when she was torpedoed and sunk by U-552 commanded by *Oberleutnant* Eric Topp. Loss of life was heavy and included eleven American Ferry Pilots *en route* to England to join the Air Transport Auxiliary. Wing Commander Weir, who had been serving as OC Troops in various troopships, is buried in Kilcommon Erris Church of Ireland Churchyard. His widow also bore the pain of losing two of their sons, Major Adrian John Anthony Weir MC, 1st Battalion, Scots Guards and

Flying Officer Archibald Nigel Charles Weir DFC of 145 Squadron who died on active service on 28th February 1944, and 7th November 1940, respectively. Adrian is buried in Beach Head War Cemetery, Anzio while Archibald has no known grave and is commemorated on panel 6 of the Runnymede Memorial. From Shaftesbury in Dorset both were exceptionally gifted academics and sportsmen. For a detailed account of the SS *Nerissa's* history and sinking, *Wikipedia* carries an excellent report.

	P A SIMMONS [SO]	G/Capt	28.12.45	Retirement**
	F PATERSON [Ad]	F/L	04.05.26	Retired list
04165	H V PENDAVIS DSO [A]	S/Ldr	01.01.39	Retired list

On account of ill health [LG 10 January 1939, issue 34588, page 219]. Late of the 3rd Battalion, Oxfordshire and Buckinghamshire Light Infantry, Lieutenant Hugh Valentine Pendavis resigned his commission on appointment to a permanent commission in the Royal Air Force [LG 17 May 1920, supplement 31902, page 5572]. Attached to the 2nd Battalion, he won the DSO early in the *Great War,* the citation appearing in *The Edinburgh Gazette* December 4th, 1914, issue 12746, page 1471: *'On 3rd November, conspicuous good work in advancing from his trench and assisting in driving away a party of the enemy who were commencing to dig a new trench within 30 yards of his own. Thirty of the enemy were shot down on this occasion.'* It is known that he rose in rank to Squadron Leader and on retirement left the United Kingdom in favour of Kenya where his wife, Ruth Margaret Pendavis died on 12th November 1956, whilst residing at Nakuru, Kenya [LG 8 May 1959, issue 41702, page 3061].

	W E SOMERVELL [A]	F/L	+	11.10.28	12 Squadron

Flight Lieutenant William Edmund Somervell AFC was killed on Thursday, 11th October 1928, when the tail section of his 12 Squadron Fairey Fox J7946, broke off during a dive over Hendon. Corporal Christopher John Loud also perished. Based at Andover in Hampshire, the crew had flown to Hendon where they were giving a demonstration of the Fairey Fox before His Highness the Sultan of Muscat.

	D W GRINNELL-MILNE [A]	F/O	14.10.25	Retired list

Lieutenant Duncan William Grinnell-Milne spent much of the *Great War* in captivity when with his observer, Captain C C Strong, his 16 Squadron BE.2c 4086 was forced down behind the lines near St. Quentin on the 1st of December 1915. A veritable thorn in the side of his captors, Duncan made numerous escape attempts, eventually succeeding in reaching neutral Holland in April 1918, where he was briefly interned before being allowed to return to England. He is frequently mentioned in John Lewis-Stempel's excellent treatise on British prisoners of war published under the title *The War Behind the Wire* [Weidenfeld & Nicholson, 2014]. It is further noted that he returned to action before the Armistice serving with 56 Squadron where he named his all-red painted SE.5a *'Schweinhnt'.* Postwar he served he served in Egypt and later as a test pilot at Farnborough.

85061   Returned to the service commissioned to the General Duties Branch 25th April 1939 [LG 2 May 1939, issue 34621, page 2926].

		F/O	20.07.44	Resigned**
04203	H B RUSSELL [A]	AV-M	09.05.49	Retirement**

Air Vice-Marshal Herbert Bainbrigge Russell CB DFC AFC three times mentioned in despatches, died on Saturday, 15th June 1963.

04026	A H GOLDIE [A & S]	F/L	12.05.30	Retired list
04114	K B LLOYD AFC [A]	AV-M	28.10.49	Retirement**

Air Vice-Marshal Kenneth Buchanan Lloyd CB CBE AFC twice mentioned in despatches, died on Wednesday, 8th August 1973.

	L J PEARSON [A]	Lieutenant	06.02.21	Resigned
	J L M de C HUGHES-CHAMBERLAIN [A]	G/Capt	06.03.46	Retirement**
04116	H O LONG [Ad]	G/Capt	01.07.44	Retirement**
	A T WYNYARD-WRIGHT [SO]	Lieutenant	01.08.19	Cancelled
	G M MOORE MC [A]	F/L	19.09.28	Retired list

At his own request [LG 18 September 1928, issue 33422, page 6097]. In addition to MC, Flight Lieutenant Guy Murton Moore was mentioned in a report from Air Vice-Marshal Sir Edward Leonard Ellington KCB CMG CBE, Air Officer Commanding British Forces in Iraq, *'For distinguished serves rendered in connection with the operations in the Penjwin area of Iraq during the period April-May 1927.'* [LG 23 March 1928, issue 33369, page 2136]. In addition to Flight Lieutenant Moore, also reported were Flight Lieutenant Richard Harris DFC, 86025 Sergeant [Pilot] Frederick William Newman and 335992 Leading Aircraftman Basil Henry Reeves.

04048	W A HARVEY [T]	F/L	14.08.35	Retired list
03135	F BEAUMONT [A]	A/Cmdr	18.01.49	Retirement**

Air Commodore Frank Beaumont CB, died on Friday, 27th December 1968.

	E J D TOWNESEND [SO]	A/Cmdr	27.11.46	Retirement**

Air Commodore Ernest John Dennis Townesend CBE, died on 13th October 1975, though a question mark as to the accuracy of this has been appended. His death occurred in the Bournemouth area.

03129	J C BARRACLOUGH [SO]	G/Capt	47	Retirement**
04052	F L B HEBBERT [A]	G/Capt	23.06.43	Retired list**
03217	D H de BURGH AFC [A]	A/Cmdr +	17.01.43	Director Telecomms.

Air Commodore Desmond Herlouin de Burgh AFC, died on Sunday, 17th January 1943, when the C-87 Liberator Express 41-11708, captained by Paul Bleecker, of Ferry Command, in which he was a passenger disappeared over the South Atlantic while on a flight from Brazil to Africa. For reasons best known to the authorities, Air Commodore de Burgh is commemorated on the Alamein Memorial, column 267, while Captain Bleecker and his nine-man crew are commemorated on the Ottawa Memorial.

	C R DAVIDSON MC [A]	S/Ldr	+	21.05.36	2 FTS Digby

Squadron Leader Charles Robert Davidson was the Chief Flying Instructor at No. 2 Flying Training School at Digby and in his spare time he had built for himself in the Station Workshops a Mignet HM.14 Pou de Ceil ['Flying Flea'] registered G-AEBC. Taking off it is believed he eased the control forward having sensed he was about to stall at which point the Pou de Ceil went into an uncontrollable dive - a fatal flaw in its design - and thus became the third pilot to be killed within a month flying these machines which, subsequently, were banned in the United Kingdom. Squadron Leader Davidson is buried in the Church of the Holy Cross at Scopwick; he was 39 years of age.

03230	L EARDLEY-WILMOT [Ad]	F/L		20.03.34	Retired list
04190	G T RICHARDSON [A]	W/Cdr		25.05.45	Retired list**
	L G WOOD [A]*	F/O	+	19.12.21	Home Establishment

While serving with 56 Squadron at Aboukir, Flying Officer Leslie Gronow Wood became ill with pulmonary tuberculous, a bacterial infection of the lungs, and was invalided home to Ipswich where, as Paul McMillan reports, he was born on 7th February 1898.

	B V S SMITH MC AFC [A]	W/Cdr		30.08.45	Retirement**
	L H BROWNING MC [A]	F/L	+	02.08.28	3 Squadron

Flight Lieutenant Lance Howard Browning MC DFC serving with 3 Squadron at Upavon lost his life when the squadron was detached to Sutton Bridge for air-firing practice over the Holbeach ranges. During one such exercise, the wings of his Hawker Woodcock failed and the aircraft dived into the ground within the confines of the ranges. [His DFC was gained while serving with 63 Squadron in Kurdistan [LG 12 July 1920, supplement 31974, page 7422].

04072	F H ISAAC [A & S]	W/Cdr	25.11.45	Retired list**
	A G B ELLIS [A & S]	F/O	26.09.23	Resigned
04202	G H RUSSELL DFC [A]	G/Capt	01.04.47	Retirement**
	G R TRAVIS [A]	Lieutenant	01.08.19	Cancelled
04106	B A S LEWIN [A]	S/Ldr	26.09.38	Retired list

At his own request [LG 27 September 1938, issue 34555, page 6082]. Returned to service and promoted Wing Commander, temporary, in the Technical Branch with effect from 1st December 1940 [LG 10 December 1940, issue 35010, page 6984]. W/Cdr 05.08.46   Retired list**

W H LONGTON DFC* AFC [A]   S/Ldr   +   06.05.27

Squadron Leader Walter Hunt Longton was killed on Monday, 6th June 1927 during the weekend of the Bournemouth Air Races when his Blackburn Bluebird G-EBKD came into collision at low altitude with Westland Widgeon G-EBPW flown by Laurence Openshaw, both aircraft coming down in the vicinity of Ensbury Park Racecourse, venue for the air race. On impact both machines caught fire and were totally destroyed. Squadron Leader Longton was buried in Upavon Cemetery, the funding for his headstone being supplied by his widow. A skilled and courageous pilot, his DFC was *Gazetted* on 2nd November 1918, supplement 30989, pages 12968 and 12969: *'On the 22nd August this officer led his formation of six machines to attack an equal number of enemy scouts. All the latter were accounted for, four being crashed and the remaining two driven down out of control. A brilliant performance, reflecting the greatest credit on this officer as leader, and all who took part in this engagement. During the last seven weeks Lieutenant Longton has destroyed seven enemy machines.' '[AFC gazetted 3rd June, 1918].'* A First Bar was published on 8th February 1919, issue 31170, page 2033: *'Between 29th September and 9th October this officer carried out twelve tactical reconnaissances, bringing back most valuable information; he also displayed great gallantry in attacking enemy troops on the ground. On 9th October, when on a low patrol, he observed a machine-gun nest which appeared to be the sole obstacle to our cavalry advance. Having informed the cavalry and field artillery of the situation, he co-operated with the former in their attack, and, after the enemy had been driven out, pursued them with machine-gun fire as they retreated.'*

H V PUCKRIDGE DFC [A]   F/O   10.05.22   Resigned

117797   Returned to the service commissioned to the Administrative and Special Duties Branch 31st December 1941 [LG 24 March 1942, supplement 35498, page 1337].   S/Ldr   24.08.54   Relinquished

N COMPER [A]   F/L   01.04.29   Retired list

At his own request [LG 5 April 1929, issue 33483, page 2284]. Army Form B.103 for this officer shows that in 1916, he was posted to 9 Squadron on 26th July, returned to Home Establishment on 28th April 1917, re-embarked on 20th December 1917, and joined 42 Squadron on Christmas Eve.

W F WILLIAMSON [A]   Lieutenant   01.08.19   Cancelled

04131   R E MEEK [Ad]   F/L   14.12.34   Retired list

Returned to service: date not traced.   S/Ldr   06.01.45   retired list**

D N THOMSON MC [SO]   Lieutenant   01.08.19   Cancelled

W L FENWICK [A]   F/L   +   27.05.28   84 Squadron

Flight Lieutenant William Longstaffe Fenwick, as Paul McMillan has discovered, was killed in a road traffic accident in Baghdad while attached to 84 Squadron from No. 5 Armoured Car Company. His passenger in the car, Flying Officer Edward Beresford Foster also died and both now rest in the RAF Cemetery at Ma'asker Al Raschid.

L J RIORDAN AFC [A]   F/L   03.04.29   Retired list

On account of ill-health [LG 12 April 1929, issue 33485, page 2437]. On the 28th of July 1936, Flight Lieutenant Leo James Riordan AFC was removed from the Retired List [LG 11 August 1936, issue 34313, page 5256].

W SUTHERLAND [T]   F/L   +   26.12.28   Armoured Car Wing

Flight Lieutenant William Sutherland died in RAF Hospital Hinaidi and is buried in Ma'asker Al Raschid RAF Cemetery. Paul McMillan also notes that in 1922, while attached to MAE Development Flight on the Isle of Grain, William was injured on 11th October in a motor cycle accident.

03160   L R BRIGGS [A]

Llewellyn Rolls Briggs retired from the Royal Air Force, on a date as yet untraced, in the rank of Flight Lieutenant. Subsequently, he was granted a commission in the Auxiliary Air Force and with the rank of Squadron Leader was appointed to command No. 502[Ulster][Bomber] Squadron on 1st July 1937 [LG 6 July 1937, issue 34415, page 4349].   G/Capt   10.02.54   Retirement**

Note. I am reasonably confident that during his *Great War* service he flew DH.2s with 24 Squadron, becoming a prisoner of war on 11th September 1916. The summary, as written by Trevor Henshaw in his indispensable *The Sky Their Battlefield* pinpoints the action to the Bapaume to Péronne road when the DH.2 7901 developed an engine fault but before Briggs could return to Bertangles he was intercepted by a trio of enemy scouts and in the uneven combat that followed Lieutenant Briggs was wounded in the shoulder and with his DH on fire he crash-landed in a shell hole. It seems that he was released to Switzerland on 9th December 1917.

04154   H G P OVENDEN [A]*   W/Cdr   27.07.54   Relinquished

H S F T JERRARD [Ad]   A/Cmdr   26.08.48   Retirement**

Air Commodore Henry Sam Francis Temple Jerrard , died on Sunday, 21st May 1961. To the best of my knowledge he held no decorations.

A B RAYMOND-BARKER [A]   F/L   21.09.21   Resigned

04170   C E V PORTER [A]   AV-M   27.12.46   Retirement**

Air Vice-Marshal Cedric Ernest Victor Porter CBE mentioned in despatches, died on Thursday, 17th April 1975.

W G MEGGITT MC [A]   F/L   +   28.01.27   41 Squadron

Flight Lieutenant William Geoffrey Meggitt MC lost control of Siskin III J7171 of 41 Squadron after encountering adverse weather and dived into the garden of a house in Beatrice Avenue in the Norbury district of London. He won his MC as an observer with 25 Squadron [FE.2b], the citation reading: *'For conspicuous gallantry and devotion to duty whilst one of a patrol engaging five hostile machines. He drove down one enemy machine and then attacked another, which was seen to go down vertically. He has previously brought down three hostile machines.'* [LG 17 April 1917, supplement 30023, page 3684]. Re-mustering to pilot, he returned to operations flying Bristol F.2b with 22 Squadron, only to be shot down on the 8th of November 1917, flying B1123. Wounded, he was subsequently repatriated on 2nd June 1918. His observer, Captain Francis Albert Durrad was hit by enemy fire twice during the combat and in the crash-landing was thrown from his cockpit and killed. His body was never recovered and he is commemorated on the Arras Memorial. The death of Flight Lieutenant Meggitt was reported in *The Times* where it is stated when extracted from the wreckage of his aircraft in the garden of No. 11 Beatrice Avenue he was unconscious, but died in the ambulance taking him to Croydon Hospital.

03219   J D S DENHOLM [SO]   G/Capt   13.10.45   Retirement**

C R KEARY [A]*   G/Capt   12.12.44   Retirement**

T S IVENS [A]   G/Capt   20.05.46   Retirement**

P L STEPHENS [Ad]   Lieutenant   01.08.19   Cancelled

C S FULTON [SO]   Lieutenant   01.08.19   Cancelled

04181   H C PYPER [Ad]   W/Cdr   10.02.54   Relinquished

04008   R M FOSTER DFC [A]*   ACM   05.02.54   Retirement**

Air Chief Marshal Sir Robert Foster KCB CBE DFC five times mentioned in despatches, died on Tuesday, 23rd October 1973.

04130   K A MEEK [Ad]   G/Capt   26.06.49   Retirement**

C M EASTLEY [A]   Lieutenant   01.08.19   Cancelled

03197   C CRAWFORD [A]   G/Capt   30.09.47   Retirement**

G C GARDINER DFC [A]   G/Capt   +   30.07.40   RAF Helwan

Group Captain George Cecil Gardiner DSO DFC died in Helmieh Hospital while serving as the Station Commander at RAF Helwan. He is buried in Cairo War Cemetery.

04167   P L PLANT [A]   G/Capt   20.08.46   Retired list**

R W REID MC [A]   Lieutenant   01.08.19   Cancelled

R B BOURNE [A]   Lt   +   06.11.19   Grangegorman Mil Cty

04194   J M J C J I ROCK [Ad]   G/Capt   01.01.46   Retired list**

H G W DEBENHAM [A]   Lieutenant   01.08.19   Cancelled

M MOORE [O] I am reasonably confident that this officer served with 45 Squadron and as an observer was shot down and made prisoner of war on 22nd July 1917. Trevor Henshaw records the squadron as losing four of their Sopwith Strutters during the morning of the 22nd, Lieutenant Moore's aircraft B2576, flown by Captain G H Cock MC, being forced down following interception from five hostile scouts.

	Name		Rank	Date	Status
	S G FROGLEY DSO DFC[A]		F/O	24.06.20	Retired list

09129   On account of ill-health caused by wounds [LG 20 August 1920, supplement 32025, page 8630]. Returned to service; commissioned to Administrative and Special Duties Branch on 1st February 1940 [LG 14 January 1941, issue 35042, page 285]. Simon Gilbert Frogley was obliged to relinquish his commission for a second time on account of medical unfitness for Air Force service and was permitted to retain his rank.

	Name		Rank	Date	Status
			S/Ldr	30.08.45	Relinquished
	J S GOGGIN [SO]		S/Ldr	14.02.28	Retired list
04241	E THORNTON [A]		G/Capt	27.03.45	Retirement**
	E O L BELL [Ad]		Lieutenant	01.08.19	Cancelled
	C F SMITH [A]		Lieutenant	01.08.19	Cancelled
03128	P J BARNETT MC [A]		W/Cdr	03.09.45	Retirement**
04172	J POTTER [A]		S/Ldr	31.12.52	Resigned
	F W DEANE DFC [A]	+	F/O	29.04.21	56 Squadron

Flying Officer Frederick William Deane DFC drowned following the crash of his Sopwith 7.F1 Snipe E7647 of 56 Squadron into the sea off Aboukir, Egypt. Additional information will be reported in the fourth volume.

C R W KNIGHT [A] An unusual occurrence where an appointment was made post-death for Lieutenant Clarence Raymond Wentworth Knight died on active service on Saturday, 21st June 1919, in Russia. First buried in Topsa Churchyard, he is now commemorated by a Special Memorial in Archangel Allied Cemetery. His entry to the Royal Flying Corps as a temporary 2nd Lieutenant from previous service as a private soldier with the Inns of Court Officers Training Corps was *Gazetted* on 19th March 1916, supplement 29521, page 3271. Army Form B.103 indicates that between April 1917 and October 1918, he was attached at various times to 56, 55, 101 and 151 Squadrons.

	Name		Rank	Date	Status
	H J Q CAMPBELL [Ad]		F/O	25.06.22	Dismissed

Canada Flying Officer Henry John Quick Campbell was dismissed the Service by sentence of General Court Martial [LG 22 September 1922, issue 32749, page 6778]. Formerly a Private with the Canadian Army Service Corps , he was seconded for duty with the Royal Flying Corps on 22nd November 1916 [LG 23 December 1916, supplement 29879, page 12574].

	Name		Rank	Date	Status
	F W W WILSON [A]		F/L	03.12.30	Dismissed

Flight Lieutenant Frederick William Walby Wilson was dismissed the Service by sentence of General Court Martial [LG 27 January 1931, issue 33684, page 607]. Formerly with the 5th Battalion, Liverpool Regiment, Territorial Force, relinquishing his commission on appointment to a permanent commission in the Royal Air Force [LG 12 May 1920, supplement 31897, page 5461]. Born on 19th April 1895, he transferred to the Royal Flying Corps in July 1916, and between 7th July and 2nd December 1917, flew Nieuport Scouts with 29 Squadron.

	Name		Rank	Date	Status
04024	B H GODFREY [SO]		W/Cdr	19.12.45	Retired list**
	W W GLENN MC [Ad]		Lieutenant	01.08.19	Cancelled
	D F COX [SO]		F/O	03.06.23	Resigned
	T G POLAND MC [A]		Lieutenant	01.08.19	Cancelled

Formerly resigned his commission [LG 9 March 1920, issue 31816, page 2906]

	Name		Rank	Date	Status
				10.03.20	Resigned
	N H LOCH [A]		Lieutenant	01.08.19	Cancelled
03191	M H COOTE [A]		F/L	12.12.28	Retired list

At his own request [LG 11 December 1928, issue 33446, page 8173]. Returned to service.

	Name		Rank	Date	Status
			S/Ldr	27.03.46	Retired list**
	C E WILLIAMSON-JONES DFC [A]		G/Capt	22.10.46	Retirement**
	K E WARD [A]		G/Capt	08.07.46	Retirement**
	T HUMBLE [O]		G/Capt	02.10.44	Retirement**
	W H DATE [SO]		Lieutenant	01.08.19	Cancelled
	R C JENKINS MBE [A]*	+	F/L	08.02.22	4 Squadron

Flight Lieutenant Robert Charles Jenkins MBE MC lost his life when on take off from Farnborough, accompanied by Observer Officer Allan Hesketh DFC, their Avro 504K H9829 came down within seconds of leaving the ground. An account of the accident appeared the next day in *The Times* beneath the banner: '*RAF Officer Killed - Biplane Strikes A Tree At Farnborough. Flight-Lieutenant R C Jenkins MC, died in Cambridge Hospital, Aldershot, yesterday afternoon as a result of an aeroplane accident which occurred at Farnborough at 11.30 a.m. Lieutenant Jenkins was piloting biplane H9829, which appeared to get up badly. Striking the telegraph wires on the Farnborough road, the machine swerved downward, struck its left wing against a pine tree, and collapsed nose downwards into the grounds of a house, opposite St. Fridewide, smashing an oak fence in its fall. Observer Officer A Hesketh jumped or fell from the aeroplane before the moment of impacxt and escaped with slight injuries, but the pilot's skull was fractured by contact with the engine.*' Late of the Devonshire and Cornwall Light Infantry, Lieutenant R C Jenkins relinquished his commission on appointment to a permanent commission in the Royal Air Force [LG 23 July 1920, supplement 31992, page 7825].

	Name		Rank	Date	Status
	J H RUTHERFORD [T]		Lieutenant	01.08.19	Cancelled
	R P M WHITHAM MC [A]	+	AV-M	23.03.43	Director-Gen. of War Org.

Returning to the UK by air from the Middle East Air Vice-Marshal Robert Parker Musgrave Whitham CB OBE MC died on Tuesday, 23rd March 1943, when his aircraft [Liberator II AL587 of 511 Squadron]was shot down over the Bay of Biscay. Air-Britain's AA100-AZ999 register indicates crew were *en route* Gibraltar to Lyneham; presumed ditched off the coast of Portugal. He is commemorated on the Runnymede Memorial, panel 118.

	Name		Rank	Date	Status
	H M COOMBS DFC [A]		F/O	+	08.06.21	216 Squadron

Flying Officer Herbert Milbourne Coombs DFC lost his life when the DH.10 39061, of which he was the sole occupant, spun while making a flat turn and crashed onto the Abbassia rifle range near Heliopolis. Additional details will be published in the fourth volume.

	Name		Rank	Date	Status
04103	J LAWSON [A]		W/Cdr	13.05.46	Retirement**
	G R O'SULLIVAN [A]		G/Capt	09.11.45	Retirement**
	C McM LAING MC [A]	+	F/L	21.11.34	58 Squadron

New Zealand Flight Lieutenant Charles McMenamen Laing MC died following an operation in the King Edward VII's Hospital for Officers in London. At the time of his death he was adjutant of the squadron which was based at Worthy Down. Paul McMillan has unearthed additional information, some of which can be found on the Kaplan Auctions site of South Africa.

	Name		Rank	Date	Status
	W G E HAYMAN [SO]		F/L	07.11.34	Retired list
	W SCOTT [T]	+	F/O	10.04.26	IAAD Henlow

Flying Officer William Scott, 49 years of age, died when Avro 504K H9535 of which he was the pilot, collided with Vickers Vimy F9184 over Henlow, both aircraft falling locked together. There were no survivors from the Vimy which was captained by Flying Officer Charles Victor Lacey AFC and crewed by Leading Aircraftman Reginald Richard Germain and Basil Henry Greene Young, and Aircraftman James William Simmons.

	Name		Rank	Date	Status
	S E TOOMER DFC [A]		AV-M	08.03.48	Retirement**

Air Vice-Marshal Sydney Edward Toomer CB CBE DFC twice mentioned in despatches, died on Monday, 22nd March 1954.

	Name		Rank	Date	Status
04230	C R STRUDICK [A]		W/Cdr	04.11.45	Retirement**
03216	C J S DEARLOVE [A]	+	G/Capt	30.11.41	

Group Captain Cuthbert Joseph Stanley Dearlove killed on Sunday, 30th November 1941, when Blenhiem IV Z7589 of WDCF hit by 'friendly fire' over Gialo, Libya. He is commemorated on the Alamein Memorial, column 239.

	Name		Rank	Date	Status
	W R CURTIS [A & S]	+	F/L	15.01.24	Air Ministry

Whilst testing Bristol F.2b C4721 for the Directorate of Research [Air Ministry], Flight Lieutenant William Reginald Curtis lost control while making a low-speed bank following engine failure. His observer, Squadron Leader Sidney Mechen Cleverly, aged 38, also died. Granted a shorty service commission on 22nd November 1920, in the rank of Squadron Leader [LG 30 November 1930, issue 32145, page 11823], this being made permanent on 10th October 1923 [LG 9 October 1923, issue 32869, page 6757]. *The Times*, in its issue of 16th January 1924, reported the crash: '*An aeroplane accident occurred during bombing practice at the Isle of Grain, Kent, experimental air stations yesterday. Two officers, Flight-Lieutenant W R Curtis and Squadron-Leader S M Cleverly, from the Air Ministry, were killed. The machine, a Bristol aeroplane, was piloted by Flight-Lieutenant Curtis. The machine crashed to the ground and the pilot was killed. Squadron-Leader Cleverly, who was a Senior Assistant in the Directorate of Research at the Air Ministry, was so badly injured that he died later.'*

04027	F C B SAVILE [A]	W/Cdr		07.04.45	Retired list**
	C BOUSFIELD [O]	F/O	+	02.10.24	14 Squadron

Flying Officer Colin Bousfield was killed near Heliopolis, Egypt, when his Bristol F.2b went into a spin from which he failed to recover. At the time he was flying solo.

03233	C N ELLEN DFC [O]	A/Cmdr		14.08.46	Retirement**

Air Commodore Cyril Norman Ellen DFC mentioned in despatches, died on Tuesday, 7th April 1981.

	E S ADES [S]	F/L		14.10.25	Resigned
03185	A St. H CLARKE AFC [A & S]	G/Capt		05.03.46	Retired list**
03234	G H ELLIOT [O]	F/O		08.08.26	Retired list

At his own request [LG 10 August 1926, issue 33190, page 5293]. Returned to service: Commissioned to the General Duties Branch and confirmed in his appointment as 'Pilot Officer' on 3rd September 1940 [LG 27 September 1940, issue 34954, page 5715]. He served throughout the Second World War eventually reverting to the Retired list on 13th October 1946, retaining the rank of Squadron Leader.

	F LEATHLEY MC [A]	F/L		27.01.25	Retired list
	M A BENJAMIN MC [SO]	Lieutenant		01.08.19	Cancelled
	J F NALDER [Sd]	Lieutenant		01.08.19	Cancelled
	A W SYMINGTON MC [SO]	F/L		20.03.32	Retired list
03126	G G BANTING [A]	AV-M		20.05.51	Retirement**

Air Vice-Marshal George Gaywood Banting CB CBE mentioned in despatches, died on Thursday, 27th December 1973.

	K C TILMAN [A & S]	F/L	+	11.03.24	442 Flight HMS *Argus*

At the time *Argus* was off Mallorca [Majorca] when Pilot Officer Richard Lewes took in Parnell Panther N7461, only to lose control and plunge over the side and into the sea. He survived, though badly injured, but Flight Lieutenant Kenneth Cromar Tilman lost his life. He was 27 years of age. From various reports in *The Times* the occasion was a large combined exercise involving the Atlantic and Mediterranean Fleets.

04138	R J MONTGOMERY-MOORE [Ad]	G/Capt		25.03.46	Retired list**
	G M CARTER [A]	F/O	+	17.01.20	North Stoneham Chyd
03099	F M F WEST VC MC [A]	A/Cmdr		29.03.46	Retirement**

EG 12 November 1918, issue 13350, page 4179: *'Captain West, while engaging hostile troops at a low altitude far over the enemy lines, was attacked by seven aircraft. Early in the engagement one of his legs was partially severed by an explosive bullet, and fell powerless into the controls, rendering the machine for the time unmanageable. Lifting his disabled leg, he regained control of the machine, and, although wounded in the other leg, he, with surpassing bravery and devotion to duty, manoeuvred his machine so skilfully that his observer was enabled to get several good bursts into the enemy machines, which drove them away. Captain West then, with rare courage and determination, desperately wounded as he was, brought his machine over our lines and landed safely. Exhausted by his exertions, he fainted, but on regaining consciousness insisted on writing his report.'* Air Commodore Ferdinand Maurice Felix West VC CBE MC twice mentioned in despatches died on Friday, 8th July 1988.

	D F LAWSON [A]	Lieutenant		01.08.19	Cancelled
	C E W LOCKYER [A]	AV-M		16.10.45	Retirement**

Air Vice-Marshal Clarence Edward Williams Lockyear CB, died on Wednesday, 7th August 1963.

	J H WINCH [T]	G/Capt		15.04.44	Retirement**
	F THOMPSON [A]	Lieutenant		01.08.19	Cancelled
03142	J A W BINNIE [A]	G/Capt		19.04.46	Retired list**
	J BUSSEY [A]	G/Capt		01.03.46	Retirement**
	M H FINDLAY DSC DFC [A]	F/O		01.10.20	Resigned
	R HALLEY DFC [A]	G/Capt		06.05.45	Retirement**
	*G E CREIGHTON [A]	Lieutenant		06.01.21	Resigned
	D R MULLAN [Ad]	F/O	+	01.03.22	5 FTS

Flying Officer Denis Richard Mullan was on approach to Shotwick in Avro 504K E3568 when he allowed the airspeed to drop to a critically low level resulting in the trainer stalling and diving nose first into the ground. Flying Officer Mullan was flying solo.

05018	V R S WHITE MC [Ad]	S/Ldr		10.02.54	Relinquished
04179	C D PYNE [A]	W/Cdr		10.02.54	Relinquished
04001	C FINDLEY DFC [A]	G/Capt		22.06.41	Retired list

Re-employed and, Paul McMillan advises, served for another five years.

04223	R L SWEENY [Ad]	F/L		13.05.39	Retired list

On account of ill-health.

03121	E R ARDLEY [Ad]	G/Capt		06.10.45	Retired list**
04041	A C B HARRISON MC [Ad	G/Capt		01.06.41	

Appointed Control Commission [B E] in Austria, Group Captain Anthony Cecil Boris Hamilton CBE MC died on Sunday, 8th June 1947. He is buried in Klagenfurth Cemetery. His lineage has Polish connections as is shown in the website 'Penrithbeacon,com'.

	H B MAUND [A]	Lieutenant		01.08.19	Cancelled
04070	W M M HURLEY [Ad]	G/Capt		14.11.46	Retirement
04246	C F Le P TRENCH [S]	G/Capt		01.03.41	
01421	H L MACRO DFC [S]	W/Cdr		06.10.45	Retired list**
	N B WARD [A & S]	F/L	+	18.06.23	216 Squadron

Flight Lieutenant Neville Byron Ward was a member of crew in Vickers Vimy FR3173 captained by Flying Officer Percy William Lingwood which crashed in the Mokattam Hills near the Egyptian capital, Cairo, killing everone on board. This included Mechanics William Jarvis and Frederick William Skuse. A report, filed by *The Times* Cairo correspondent on the morning of the accident, stated that the Vimy had taken off during the morning from Heliopolis and went out of control at three hundred feet. On impact it burst into flames; the bodies had been recovered and would be buried that same afternoon in the old Cairo cemetery.

	A W SIMON [A]	Lieutenant		01.08.19	Cancelled
	P J GARDINER [A]	F/O	+	31.01.22	60 Squadron

Australia Flying Officer Percy Justice Gardiner and Aircraftman George Fletcher Stewart, 19 years of age, perished when DH.10 E7839 lost engine power and spun out of control to crash near Risalpur aerodrome, the squadron's base.

05023	C A B B WILCOCK [A]	G/Capt		26.01.46	Retired list**
04096	G M KNOCKER [A]	G/Capt		30.12.46	Retirement**
	E R OPENSHAW [A]	G/Capt		12.03.46	Retirement**
	S P MARCUS [A]	F/O	+	15.08.21	6 FTS Manston

South Africa Flying Officer Stephen Percival Marcus died when he lost control of Bristol F.2b C761 while executing a low turn near the airfield having lost engine power.

	D W SIBLEY [A]	P/O	+	01.04.20	216 Squadron

See summary for the circumstances of his death.

No.	Name	Rank		Date	Notes
04162	N S PAYNTER [A]	A/Cmdr		15.01.47	Retirement**

Air Commodore Noel Stephen Paynter CB mentioned in despatches, died in March 1998, aged 99. His last service post was Deputy Director of Intelligence [Organisation and Security], which no doubt fitted him for his later role as Director of MI5.

No.	Name	Rank		Date	Notes
	A H G DUNKERLEY [A]	F/O		12.05.20	Resigned
	E G HILTON [A & S]	W/Cdr	+	10.09.37	King's Cup Air Race

See my report for Major [subsequently Wing Commander] P C Sherrin for details of the tragedy.

No.	Name	Rank		Date	Notes
	C H HARRISON [A]	S/Ldr	+	06.01.36	HAD Henlow

Squadron Leader Cecil Herbert Harrison took his own life while suffering from *'anxiety neurosis'* fearing that he was terminally ill with heart disease.

No.	Name	Rank		Date	Notes
	C H NOBLE-CAMPBELL AFC [A]	Lieutenant		01.08.19	Cancelled
03163	C P BROWN DFC* [A & S]	AV-M		15.03.54	Retirement**

Air Vice-Marshal Colin Peter Brown CB CBE DFC*, died on Tuesday, 19th October 1965.

No.	Name	Rank		Date	Notes
	R T B HOUIGHTON [A]	G/Capt		02.01.46	Retired list**
04076	L W JARVIS [A]	G/Capt			Retired**

Group Captain Louis William Jarvis [Retired] was appointed Commander of the Order of Polonia Restituta conferred by The President of the Republic of Poland [LG 24 September 1943, supplement 36813, page 4248].

No.	Name	Rank		Date	Notes
04151	G R OLIVER [Ad]	G/Capt		01.10.45	Retirement**
	H M MOODY MC [A]	F/L	+	23.04.31	24 Squadron

Born in 1898, at Welshampton in Shropshire, Henry Michael Moody was one of a twin, their father being the Reverend Henry Moody, vicar of the parish and Rural Dean of Ellesmere. Both boys joined the Royal Flying Corps and, tragically, Henry's brother, 2nd Lieutenant Charles Angelo Moody was killed in combat on the 21st of August 1917, when his 1 Squadron Nieuport 23 B1613 was shot down in the vicinity of Westroosebeke in Belgium's Flanders area. Eighteen years of age, he is buried in Tyne Cot Cemetery. Henry, meanwhile, flew Sopwith Camels with 45 Squadron, in France and Italy, finishing the war with eight confirmed victories. Additional details regarding his death will be published in the summary for 23rd April 1931.

No.	Name	Rank		Date	Notes
	D PRICE [A]	F/Lt	+	04.03.25	Boys Wing Cranwell
03169	E I BUSSELL [A]	A/Cmdr		04.04.46	Retirement**

Air Commodore Edward Irvine 'Peter' Bussell CBE twice mentioned in despatches, died on Wednesday, 3rd July 1968.

No.	Name	Rank		Date	Notes
03137	J R BELL DFC [A]	G/Capt		07.01.46	Retirement**
	J H DAND [A]	G/Capt		23.01.46	Retirement**
04071	A A C HYDE [A]	W/Cdr		12.03.45	Retirement**
	W J KING DCM [T]	G/Capt		29.04.43	Retired list**
02064	C J BROCKBANK MBE [T]	S/Ldr		22.05.29	Retired list

Army commission resigned on appointment to a permanent commission in the Royal Air Force [LG 17 May 1920, supplement 31902, page 5573].

No.	Name	Rank		Date	Notes
	J R M SIMPSON [A]	F/O		30.06.20	Resigned

72566   James Rounthwaite Moore Simpson returned to the Service and was commissioned to the Administrative and Special Duties Branch on 7th February 1939, as a Pilot Officer on probation [LG 14 February 1939, issue 34598, page 1073]. He was confirmed in his appointment on the last day of August 1939 [LG 26 September 1939, issue 34694, page 6507].

No.	Name	Rank		Date	Notes
		S/Ldr		24.08.54	Relinquished
72566		S/Ldr		24.08.54	Relinquished
21033	E N D WORSLEY [Ad]	G/Capt		25.02.46	Retirement**
06251	D d'H HUMPHREYS [A & S]	G/Capt		15.03.41	*En route*

Canada Group Captain Dudley d'Herbez Humphreys born 15th May 1895, and enlisted with the Royal Flying Corps on 20th June 1917. Army Form B.103 shows his father as Canadian and his mother French. His death occurred while *en route* to the Middle East aboard Wellington IC W5644 of No. 3 Group Training Flight, and captained by Sgt Ruchard Hugh Alington RNZAF. After taking off from a refuelling stop at Gibraltar the Wellington was intercepted by *Oberleutnant* Muncheberg of 7./JG26 northwest of Gozo and shot down. The crew were seen to get into the aircraft's dinghy but, sadly, were lost without trace. Their names are commemorated on the Runnymede Memorial [see page 46 of *Royal Air Force Bomber Losses in the Middle East and Mediterranean - Volume 1: 1939-1942* complied by David Gunby and Pelham Temple and published by Midland Publishing, 2006]. Prior to his air force service, Dudley d'Herbez Humphreys was commissioned to the 23rd Battalion, London Regiment.

No.	Name	Rank		Date	Notes
05005	G G WALKER MC [A]	W/Cdr		15.08.40	Retired list**
	J M BELL [SO]	Lieutenant		01.08.19	Short service
	W F WOOD [A]	Lieutenant		01.08.19	Cancelled
05015	J G WESTERN MBE [T]	W/Cdr		15.03.41	Retired list**

At his own request .

No.	Name	Rank		Date	Notes
	R L CROFTON [A]	G/Capt		22.03.45	Retired list**
03133	A H BEACH [A]	F/L		24.05.32	Retired list

Returned to service: Granted a commission in the General Duties Branch, Class CC, on 4th August 1938, retaining Flight Lieutenant rank [LG 13th December 1938, issue 34579, page 7921].

No.	Name	Rank		Date	Notes
		W/Cdr		10.02.54	Relinquished
	A W BEAUCHAMP-PROCTOR VC DSO MC DFC [A]	F/L	+	21.06.21	24 Squadron det. CFS

South Africa LG 29 November 1918, supplement 31042, page 14204: *'Between August 8th, 1918, October 8th, 1918, proved himself victor in twenty-six decisive combats, destroying twelve enemy kite balloons, ten enemy aircraft, and driving down four other enemy aircraft completely out of control. Between October 1st, 1918, and October 5th, 1918, he destroyed two enemy scouts, burnt three enemy kite balloons, and drove down one enemy scout completely out of control. On October 1st, 1918, in a general engagement with about twenty-eight machines, he crashed one Fokker biplane near Fontaine and a second near Ramicourt; on October 2nd he burnt a hostile balloon near Selvigny; on October 3rd he drove down, completely out of control an enemy scout near Mont d'Origny, and burnt a hostile balloon; on October 5th, the third hostile balloon near Bohain. On October 8th, 1918, while flying home at a low altitude, after destroying an enemy two-seater near Maretz, he was painfully wounded in the arm by machine-gun fire, but, continuing, he landed safely at his aerodrome, and after making his report was admitted to hospital. In all he has proved himself conqueror over fifty-four foes, destroying twenty-two enemy machines, sixteen enemy kite balloons, and driving down sixteen enemy aircraft completely out of control. Captain Beauchamp-Proctor's work in attacking enemy troops on the ground and in reconnaissance during the withdrawal following on the Battle of St. Quentin from March 21st, 1918, and during the victorious advance of our Armies commencing on August 8th, has almost been unsurpassed in its brilliancy, and as such has made an impression on those serving in his squadron and those around him that will not be easily forgotten. Capt. Beachamp-Proctor was awarded Military Cross on 22nd June, 1918, D.F.Cross on 2nd July, 1918, Bar to M.C. on 16th September, 1918, and Distinguished Service Order on 2nd November, 1918.'* The circumstances of his death will be summarised in Volume 4.

No.	Name	Rank		Date	Notes
	G R BARRY [T]	Lieutenant		01.08.19	Cancelled
04160	A H PAULL [A & S]	W/Cdr		28.04.46	Retirement**

At his own request [LG 6 August 1946, issue 37676, page 3985].

No.	Name	Rank		Date	Notes
04077	J K A JEAKES DFC [A & S]	S/Ldr		13.11.45	Retired list
04025	C B GODFREY [SO]*	F/L		31.12.24	Retired list
	B G H KEYMER DFC [A]	Captain	+	21.10.19	47 Squadron
04060	E J L HOPE [A & S]	G/Capt	+	06.08.41	87 Squadron

Group Captain Eustace Jack Linton Hope AFC was shot down while flying Hurricane IIB Z3224 during a *Rhubarb* sortie to Maupertus airfield [see page 131 RAFFCL 1939-1941 Revision, Norman L R Franks, Midland Publishing, 2008]. He is buried in Cherbourg Old Communal Cemetery.

No.	Name	Rank		Date	Notes
	P C CAMPBELL-MARTIN [O]	F/O	+	17.10.41	Reichswald
78357	Returned to service; commissioned Administrative and Special Duties Branch [LG 26 April 1940, issue 34838,				War Cemetery

page 2479]. Transferred to General Duties Branch [LG 8 October 1940, issue 34964, page 5910]. Missing from operations to Duisburg 16-17 October 1941, while flying as rear gunner in Wellington IC Z8862 BL-B of 40 Squadron. See RAFBCL 1941, page 163, for additional information/

J F G BOYLE [O]	Lieutenant		24.08.21	Resigned

Late of the King's Own Scottish Borders, Lieutenant John Francis George Boyle resigned his commission on appointment to a permanent commission in the Royal Air Force [LG 20 December 1920, supplement 32168, page 12477]. Born 17th June 1895, he enlisted with the Royal Flying Corps on the 1st June 1917, and served with 100 Squadron from 26th August 1917, until returning to the United Kingdom on 7th May 1918.

F T McELWEE [T]	F/L		21.09.27	Retired list
J DUNCAN [SO]	F/L		02.04.32	Retired list
J J WILLIAMSON AFC [A]	A/Cmdr		29.03.46	Retirement**

Air Commodore James John Williamson CBE AFC, died on Monday, 22nd December 1975.

G G G GRAVES [A]	Lieutenant		01.08.19	Cancelled
D S ALLAN [A]	G/Capt		12.12.45	Retirement**
L E M GILLMAN [SO]	F/L		08.02.33	Retired list

On account of ill-health [LG 7 February 1933, issue 33909, page 832].

04214 G S SHAW [A & S]	A/Cmdr		29.05.52	Retirement**

Air Commodore Gerald Stanley Shaw CB mentioned in despatches, died on Sunday, 14th November 1976.

R B T HEDGES [A]	Lieutenant		01.08.19	Cancelled
04038 R GRICE DFC [A]	A/Cmdr		23.01.50	Retirement**

Air Commodore Richard Grice OBE DFC, died on Monday, 27th September 1954. During the *Great War* he witnessed the shooting down of Manfred von Richthofen the *'Red Baron'* on 21st April 1918, and during the *Battle of Britain* he was commanding Biggin Hill when it was heavily bombed by the *Luftwaffe* on 6th September 1940. Some of the hangars, although damaged, were still standing and considering them to be a tempting target for further raids, he ordered their demolition . For this he faced a Court Martial but was exonerated.

03130 E L BARRINGTON MC [A & S]	F/L		01.09.25	Retired list

At his own request [LG 1 September 1925, issue 33080, page 5770].

Returned to service.	S/Ldr		09.11.45	Retired list**
N S DEWEY MC [A & S]	Lieutenant		01.08.19	Cancelled
03203 S D CULLEY DSO [A & S]	G/Capt		09.12.45	Retirement**
M M FREEHILL DFC [A]	S/Ldr	+	03.02.39	58 Squadron

Squadron Leader Maurice Michael Freehill DFC died in York Military Hospital. Subsequently his *Great War* medals and associated material was sold by Harland Military Antiques.

05007 C T WALKINGTON [A]	G/Capt		03.06.44	Retired list**

Mentioned in the Report Operations in Malaya and N E I 1941-2 [LG 26 February 1948, supplement 38216, page 1415].

04225 W E STATEN MC DFC [A]	AV-M		12.11.52	Retirement**

Air Vice-Marshal William 'Bill' Ernest Staton CB DSO* MC DFC* twice mentioned in despatches, died on Friday, 22nd July 1983. A larger than life character in every sense of the word, when the Second World War broke out he was commanding 10 Squadron [Whitley] and during his leadership he devised systems for illuminating targets that, subsequently, were employed by Path Finder Force. He is also mentioned in *Fly for Your Life* [pages 48 to 51] of Larry Foster's biography of Robert Stanford Tuck along with a photograph [opposite page 81] of Hawker Fury K2071 in which Wing Commander Staton overturned on landing at Grantham where he was the Chief Flying Instructor at 3 Flying Training School and at which time the young Tuck was undergoing flying instruction. While in the Far East as Senior Air Staff Officer West Group Java, William 'Bill' Ernest Staton was taken prisoner by the Imperial Japanese Army undergoing several bouts of torture at the hands of his captors for steadfastly refusing to answer their questions.

H O PROUT AFC [A]	F/O	+	04.11.20	24 Squadron

See summary for an explanation as to the circumstances of his death.

W E WINDOVER [A]	F/O		02.02.23	Dismissed

Flying Officer William Edward Windover was removed from the Royal Air Force, His Majesty [George V] having no further use for his services [LG 13 February 1923, issue 32795, page 1075]. During the *Great War* and ranked Captain his 110 Squadron DH.9A F1005 was forced down near Koblenz on Monday 21st October 1918, and with his observer, taken prisoner. For additional information, please refer to page 334 of my second volume in this series of Royal Air Force squadron losses.

E S ROBINS [A]	Lieutenant		22.03.22	Resigned

Similar to Lieutenant W E Windover, Lieutenant Eric Sanderson Robin's service is restricted to entries on his Army Form B.103, which indicates he was attached to 92 Squadron [he joined the squadron [SE.5A] while at Tangmere and deployed with them to Bray Dunes on the 2nd of July 1918]. Post-armistice and after several spells of leave, he was posted on 11th August 1919, to 1 BMTRD, thence to a Re-enforcement Park before returning to the United Kingdom on 24th September 1919.

S JONES DFC [A]	Lieutenant		01.08.19	Cancelled
C D SKINNER [A]	Lieutenant		01.08.19	Cancelled
10156 A SUTTON-JONES [Ad]	A/Cmdr		06.05.45	Retirement**

Air Commodore Arthur Elias Sutton-Jones CB mentioned in despatches, died in March 1958.

T ROBERTS [A]	Lieutenant		01.08.19	Cancelled
D G A BATTERBURY [A & S]	Lieutenant		01.08.19	Cancelled
S E S McLEOD [T]	Lt	+	11.08.19	4 Comms Squadron

Lieutenant Samuel Evans Smith McLeod was the sole fatality when when the Felixstowe Fury N123 crashed while taking off from the harbour at Harwich. The survivors are named as Lieutenant-Colonel Peregrine Forbes Morant Fellowes, an Australian, Major Edwin Rowland Moon DSO [see my summary for 29th April 1920], Captain Charles Langston Scott DSC, Captain John Ree, 2nd Lieutenant Joseph Francis Armitt, Warrant Officer John George Cockburn and Warrant Officer Harold Sant Locker. Lieutenant McLeod was laid to rest in Felixstowe [SS Peter and Paul] Churchyard

04229 S C STRAFFORD [A & S]	AM		09.06.54	Retirement**

Air Marshal Sir Stephen Strafford KBE CB DFC three times mentioned in despatches, died on Wednesday, 18th May 1966.

P J MURPHY [Ad]	S/Ldr		01.01.35	Retired list

At his own request [LG 8 January 1935, issue 34122, page 220]. Returned to the Service: Commissioned to the Equipment Branch as promoted Wing Commander [Temporary] on 1st September 1940 [LG 20 September 1940, issue 34949, page 5584].

03157 J D BREAKEY DFC* [A]	AV-M		10.05.54	Retirement**

Air Vice-Marshal John Denis Breakey CB DFC*, died on Friday, 8th January 1965.

04109 A E LINDON [T]	F/L		25.12.33	Retired list
C W H MOLLER [A]	F/L	+	28.03.36	Gibraltar

Flight Lieutenant Christopher William Henry Moller died in Gibraltar. He was late of Faldonside, Torquay and he is reported in *The London Gazette* 14th July 1936, issue 34304, page 4548, advising claims or demands to his estate should contact Bulcraig and Davis, Amberley House, Norfolk Street, Stand, London WC.2, Solicitors for the said Executors.

04189 E H RICHARDSON [A]	A/Cmdr		12.02.51	Retirement**

Air Commodore Eric Hardy Richardson CBE mentioned in despatches, died in January 1986.

04161 A L PAXTON [A]	AV-M		08.07.50	Retirement**

Australia Air Vice-Marshal Sir Anthony Paxton KBE CB DFC, died on Wednesday, 25th September 1957.

04195   R J RODWELL [A]   A/Cmdr   12.02.52   Retirement**

Air Commodore Robert John Rodwell CB, died in December 1970.

04123   A MacGREGOR DFC [A]   AV-M   09.09.49   Retirement**

Air Vice-Marshal Andrew MacGregor CB CBE DFC four times mentioned in despatches, died on Monday, 24th October 1983.

    H W L SAUNDERS MC DFC MM [A]   ACM   22.09.53   Retirement**

Air Chief Marshal Sir Hugh Saunders GCB KBE MC DFC* MM mentioned in despatches, died on Friday, 8th May 1987.

    G H H SCUTT MC [O]   F/L   +   15.02.24   25 Squadron

During a formation dive, Flight Lieutenant George Howard Homer Scutt's 7F.1 Snipe E7601 flew into the ground on the airfield at Hawkinge. His award of the MC was *Gazetted* in supplement 30761, page 7422: *'For conspicuous gallantry and devotion to duty. He has destroyed one hostile machine, and driven down three others out of control. He carried out an important single-machine reconnaissance, frequently descending to a height of 100 feet under heavy rifle and machine-gun fire, and obtained valuable information. While returning, he attacked 5 enemy machines, and ably assisted his pilot in driving them back over their lines. He has carried out many successful photographic reconnaissances, and has at all times proved himself to be a keen and daring officer.'* His death was reported in *The Times* where it is recorded he came from New Ross in Ireland.

    A O LEWIS-ROBERTS DFC [A]   G/Capt   22.01.46   Retirement**

    R C B BRADING DFC [A]   F/L   +   26.07.26   45 Squadron

Flight Lieutenant Reginald Carey Brinton Brading was part of the crew aboard Vickers Vernon II J7143 tasked for a mail run to Kirkuk and which crashed, killing the five crew, on take off from Hinaidi, coming down onto the roof of 1 Squadron's hangar. At the controls was Flying Officer Oswald Kempson Stirling Webb and in addition to Flight Lieutenant Brading he was accompanied by Squadron Leader Eric Miller Pollard, Sergeant Edgar Kennedy and Aircraftman Horace Leslie Davis. Wreckage and debris from the roof killed Aircraft Edgar Whittle and a civilian Mr Francis Crawford Inglis. A Pilot Officer Percy George Mee was injured, while Aircraft James Douglas Henderson escaped unhurt. A photograph of the crash appears on page 89 of *The Flying Camels*.

03125   J W BAKER MC [A]   ACM   17.12.56   Retirement**

Air Chief Marshal Sir John Baker GCB KCB MC DFC mentioned in despatches, died on Friday, 10th March 1978.

    R H W EMPSON [O]   F/L   15.08.39   Retired list

At his own request. [LG 15 August 1939, page 5610]. Army Form B.103 shows he was born on 25th April 1894, and following service with the 5th Battalion, Durham Light Infantry, transferred for observer training with the Royal Flying Corps on 24th August 1917, subsequently serving on the Western Front with 7 Squadron and later 6 Squadron. He died in 1967. His son, Lieutenant Patrick Brian Empson, serving with the Royal Artillery, died on 9th August 1943; he was cremated at Pontypridd Crematorium.

    B S WILCOX DFC [A]   Lieutenant   01.08.19   Cancelled

03134   H I T BEARDSWORTH [A]   A/Cmdr   23.09.46   Retirement**

Air Commodore Herbert Ivor Trentham Beardsworth CBE mentioned in despatches, died on Sunday, 9th August 1964.

    C L LEA-COX [A]   G/Capt   16.04.46   Retirement**

03181   L de V CHISMAN [A]   A/Cmdr   29.07.52   Retirement**

Air Commodore Leonard de Ville Chisholm CBE DFC mentioned in despatches, died on Sunday, 20th January 1974.

    J H DALE [T]   Lieutenant   01.08.19   Cancelled

Appointed to Short Service Commission with effect from 12th September 1919.

04143   P MURGATROYD [A]   G/Capt   10.02.54   Relinquished

    J W YOUNG [A]   F/L   07.09.27   Resigned

    F N S CREEK MC [O]   Lieutenant   01.08.19   Cancelled

    D E D TAYLOR MC [A]   Lieutenant   01.08.19   Cancelled

Returned to army duties and was restored to the Royal Fusiliers 9th March 1920 [LG 5 May 1920, supplement 31888, page 5207].

    F KEITH [A]   F/O   24.08.20   Resigned

Born on 7th October 1895, and accepted for observer training [ex-23rd Battalion, Royal Fusiliers] on 10th August 1917, and on completion of which served with 43 Squadron and 62 Squadron.

04029   J A GRAY [A]   AV-M   03.05.54   Retirement**

Air Vice-Marshal John Astley Gray CB CBE DFC twice mentioned in despatches, GM, died on Saturday, 6th June 1987.

    W A DUNCAN [A]   F/L   04.12.34   Retired list

    A W FRANKLYN MC [A]   G/Capt   30.08.48   Retirement**

    M G McL CAHILL-BYRNE [O]   F/L   31.03.26   Retired list

On account of ill-health [LG 30 March 1926, issue 33146, page 278]

    J S C ROBINSON [O]   Lieutenant   01.08.19   Cancelled

    E K BLENKINSOP [A]   F/L   23.09.29   Retired list

On account of ill-health [LG 1 October 1929, issue 33539, page 6249].

    M G S BURGER DFC [A]   F/O   24.01.20   Resigned

      South Africa Malcolm Graham Stewart Burger was born 14th September 1894, and enlisted in the Royal Flying Corps on 10th January 1918. Flew Sopwith F.1 Camels on the Western Front with 54 Squadron. His award was published in the Edinburgh edition of the *Gazette* February 11th, 1919, issue 13400, page 794: *'During the last battles this officer displayed marked gallantry and devotion to duty on low-flying bombing patrols, inflicting heavy casualties on numerous occasions. He has destroyed three enemy machines, and forced another to land.'*

04196   F H RONKSLEY MC [A]   F/L   26.08.34   Retired list

04113   H P LLOYD MC DFC [A]   ACM   04.06.53   Retirement**

Air Chief Marshal Sir Hugh Lloyd GBE KCB MC DFC mentioned in despatches, died on Tuesday, 14th July 1981.

    W D GAIRDNER DFC [A]   F/L   +   19.03.36   100 Squadron

While carrying out night practice attacks in the Johore Straits against HMS *Kent* Flight Lieutenant William Dalrymple failed to recover from a dive, his Vildebeest II K2927 of 100 Squadron plunging into the sea. Leading Aircraftman Thomas William Watson and Aircraftman Stephen Paul Jenner also perished. Additional information will appear in a forthcoming volume in this series.

04119   J McBAIN DFC [A]   S/Ldr   13.06.45   Retired list**

04098   A T LAING [Ad]   Lieutenant   01.08.19   Cancelled

Returned to service.   W/Cdr   26.09.45   Retired list**

03186   H W CLAYTON [SO]   S/Ldr   28.11.47   Retired list**

    E B WILSON [A]   Lieutenant   01.08.19   Cancelled

    G VERDEN [Ad]   F/O   05.04.22   Retired list

On account of ill-health contracted on active service [LG 4 April 1922, supplement 32661, page 2728]. A partial record of his service has survived on Army Form B.103 which shows he was posted from Mediterranean Group [269 Squadron] to Egypt Group 47 Squadron on 14th May 1920. It seems he was next posted to 202 Squadron [Mediterranean Group] before returning to 47 Squadron for administrative duties on 14th May 1920. Later in the year on 19th August, he was admitted to Moutazal Hospital from where he was discharged on 7th September 1920.

    R L McK BARBOUR DFC [A]   G/Capt   24.07.46   Retirement**

05012   E F WARING DFC [A]   A/Cmdr   06.04.49   Retirement**

Air Commodore Edmund Francis Waring CB DFC AFC mentioned in despatches, died in February 1987.

    E E PORTER DCM [A]   F/L   +   19.05.27   AC Depot Iraq

Flight Lieutenant Edward Ernest Porter was born at Merridge, a hamlet on Sedgemoor , WSW of Bridgwater in Somerset on 15th February 1890, and at the age of sixteen joined the army before being posted as a non-commissioned officer to the Royal Flying Corps on 25th July 1912, and attaining his Royal Aero Clubs Aviators' Certificate 549 on 9th July 1913, at CFS Upavon. He served with distinction throughout the *Great War*, being mentioned in despatches and awarded the DCM and MBE. Appointed as a stores officer, Flight Lieutenant Porter was *en route* to Karachi aboard the SS *Parsova* when he took his life by his own hand.

03220	O W de PUTRON [T]	A/Cmdr	04.07.51	Retirement**

Air Commodore Owen Washington de Putron CB CBE, died on Sunday, 17th February 1980.

	A G STRADLING [SO]	Lieutenant	01.08.19	Cancelled
04007	H E FORROW [A]	A/Cmdr	18.06.53	Retirement**

Air Commodore Henry Edward Forrow CB OBE, died on Wednesday, 2nd December 1959.

03045	A ROWAN [SO]	S/Ldr	01.01.36	Retired list
	J W NIXON [Ad]	F/O +	01.06.21	6 Squadron

John Walpole Nixon, described as a Flight Observer is believed to have died from natural causes for he is commemorated on the Brookwood 1914-1918 Memorial.

	W ELLIOTT DFC [A]	ACM	18.04.54	Retirement**

Air Chief Marshal Sir William Elliott GCVO KCB KBE DFC* ADC, died on Sunday, 27th June 1971.

	R E KEYS DFC [A]	F/O	08.11.21	Resigned
04084	J I T JONES DSO MC DFC MM [A]	S/Ldr	09.07.36	Retired list

At his own request [LG 14 July 1936, issue 34304, page 4512]. Returned to service. General Duties Branch and promoted Wing Commander [temporary] 1st September 1940 [LG 20 September 1940, issue 34949, page 5580], though he had been in uniform since August 1939, fulfilling the role of Chief Signals Officer, Training Command Head- quarters. His *Great War* exploits with 74 Squadron have been well publicised. He retired from the service in 1945, retaining the rank of Wing Commander.

04073	R IVELAW-CHAPMAN DFC [A]	ACM	29.10.57	Retirement**

The most senior Royal Air Force officer to be taken prisoner of war in World War 2. As Air Officer Commanding No 13 Base Elsham Wolds, Air Commodore [as he was then ranked] Ronald Ivelaw-Chapman, joined a 576 Squadron crew captained by Flight Lieutenant J M Shearer RNZAF and in Lancaster III ND783 UL-C2 took off from Elsham Wolds at 0015 on the 7th of May 1944, tasked to destroy an ammunition dump at Aubigné [Western France]. Shot down, he, along with the aircraft's bomb aimer, Sergeant J A Ford RAAF, were the sole survivors. Both set off to evade capture and in this Sergeant Ford was successful, but the Air Commodore was apprehended forty-eight hours after the Normandy invasion was launched. Unbeknown to him, the prime minister, Winston Churchill, was so alarmed that the Air Commodore, privy to the invasion plans, might fall into the hands of the Germans authorised his execution; fortunately, with his capture coming after the invasion his knowledge became of less importance and Ronald, after spending several months in hospital undergoing treatment for his injuries, sat out the remainder of the war in a prison camp until released by American forces in April 1945 [see my RAFBCL 1944 page 212 for additional information]. Air Chief Marshal Sir Ronald Ivelaw-Chapman GCB KBE DFC AFC mentioned in despatches, died on Friday, 28th April 1978. [See Addendum for additional information].

	E E P SMITH [A & S]	F/O +	25.06.24	MAEE

F.lying Officer Edward Ewart Paul Smith was drowned while in the process of testing Supermarine Sea Lion III N170 when during the take off run off Felixstow, and travelling at high-speed, the boat commenced porpoising and out of control crashed violently. For the Schneider Trophy contest the previous year, N170, then registered G-EBAH, was test flown by Henry Biard [credit '**flickr.com**'].

	S S A TURNER MBE [T]	F/L	28.04.35	Retired list
	C J SIMS DFC [A]	F/L +	30.12.29	Farnborough

Flight Lieutenant Charles John Sims died in his room at Farnborough from a self-inflicted gunshot wound to the head. From information gleaned by Paul McMillan, whom I gratefully acknowledge, Flight Lieutenant Sims had recently undertaken work of a secret nature in Iraq and had only recently returned to the United Kingdom. Prior to going to Iraq he was attached to the School of Photography, Biggin Hill. His entry on *Wikipedia* shows he was born in Bournemouth of 20th December 1899, and during the *Great War* he achieved nine combat victories, including the destruction of a balloon during the morning of 9th November 1918. Throughout this period he was based at Bergues flying Sopwith F.1 Camels with 213 Squadron.

03117	C E H ALLEN DFC [A]	AV-M	15.03.54	Retirement**

Air Vice-Marshal Charles Edward Hamilton Allen CB DFC, died on Monday, 27th October 1975.

	F F GARRAWAY [A]	G/Capt +	12.05.41	Linton-on-Ouse

Group Captain Frederick Frank Garraway OBE was killed along with twelve members of the station's ground staff while fighting fires from a night raid by the *Luftwaffe* on the station. As they fought the blaze another bomb dropped in their vicinity and perished in the blast. A veteran of the *Great War*, Group Captain Garraway had only been in post for a day. He is buried in Newton-on-Ouse [All Saints] Churchyard. In September 2014, a new memorial commemorating the thirteen airmen was unveiled at Linton-on-Ouse, the occasion being reported by *The Post* a Yorkshire newspaper.

	C R PITHEY DFC [A]	F/O +	22.02.20	2 Squadron

South Africa [See summary for details concerning his death].

04035	V E GROOM DFC [A]	AM	26.09.55	Retirement**

Air Marshal Sir Victor Groom KCVO KBE CB DFC* twice mentioned in despatches, died on Thursday, 6th December 1990.

	G S PEFFERS DFC [A]	Lieutenant	01.08.19	Cancelled
04231	J F V SUGARS [O]	W/Cdr	10.02.54	Relinquished
	A V SHEWELL [T]	Captain	14.06.22	Retired list

On account of ill-health contracted on active service [LG 13 June 1922, issue 32719, page 4478].

04111	K A LISTER-KAYE [A]			

Under the main heading Special Reserve of Officers and sub-heading Reserve Units. Captain K A Lister-Kaye of the 3rd West Yorkshire Regiment, relinquished his commission on appointment to a permanent commission in the Royal Air Force [LG 22 April 1920, supplement 31974, page 4686]. He features in my first volume of this work, page 102, when he was wounded during operations with 84 Squadron and was evacuated to England by way of HMHS *Panama*. Following retirement he was knighted, returning to the service in the General Duties Branch and promoted Squadron Leader on the 1st of March 1942 [LG 27 March 1942, issue 35503, page 1387].

	C HARRISON [A & S}	2Lt +	03.05.19	186 Squadron

See summary for details regarding his death in a flying accident.

04205	W SANDERSON DFC [O]	G/Capt	15.09.42	Retirement**
	C A HOY MC [T]	G/Capt	13.02.46	Retirement**
Re-employed.		G/Capt	15.02.47	Retired list**
	F R HOCKNEY [A]	F/O	01.10.20	Resigned

76075   Returned to the service: commissioned 16th November 1939, as Pilot Officer in the Administrative and Special Duties Branch [LG 12th December 1939, issue 34752, page 8257].

		S/Ldr	09.07.54	Relinquished
03249	EJ FFOULKES-JONES [A]	W/Cdr	27.10.45	Retirement**
04038	R H HANMER MC [A]	G/Capt	14.02.46	Retirement**
03212	R M DAVY [T]	W/Cdr	28.08.42	Retirement**
Re-employed.		W/Cdr	01.01.46	Retired list**
	R R EVANS [A]	Lieutenant	01.08.19	Cancelled
	W A HANCOCK [T]	F/L	27.06.41	Retired list**
	F EVERETT [T]	Lieutenant	01.08.19	Cancelled
04004	W F FLOYD [T]	F/L	27.07.25	Retired list

03119	J C ANDREWS MBE [T]	F/L		10.10.31	Retired list

Returned to the service: commissioned 12th September 1939, as Pilot Officer in the General Duties Branch [LG 31 October 1939, issue 34721, page 7275]. Relinquished on account of medical unfitness.

		S/Ldr		24.09.48	Relinquished
10108	M J JAMES MBE [T]	A/Cmdr		16.01.47	Retirement**

Air Commodore Maurice Jewison James MBE, died in December 1987.

10096	H J GILBERT [T]	S/Ldr		20.01.44	Retired list**
	O S WAYMOUTH [T]	Lieutenant		01.08.19	Cancelled
04226	E S STEDDY [T]	W/Cdr		10.02.54	Relinquished
03132	C C BAZELL [T]	G/Capt		24.05.49	Retirement**
04054	H W HESLOP [A]	AV-M		06.02.55	Retirement**

Air Vice-Marshal Herbert William Heslop CB OBE, died on Monday, 27th December 1976.

	W G STAFFORD MC DCM [T]	F/O		05.02.27	Retired list

Hon. M H R KNATCHBULL-HUGESEN MC [SO] *The London Gazette* 6 November 1931, issue 33769, page 7140, beneath the heading 'Crown Office, House of Lords, 4th November 1931, listing Members returned to service in Parliament following the recent election shows: 'County of Kent, Ashford Division, Captain Michael Herbert Rudolf Knatchbull [commonly called Captain the Hon. Michael Herbert Rudolf Knatchbull] MC.' He was placed on the Retired list on account of ill-health 1st October 1920 [LG 8 October 1920, issue 32078, page 9815].

	F GRAVE MBE [T]	S/Ldr		21.03.29	Retired list

Army Form B.103 shows he was accepted, on probation, for employment with the Royal Flying Corps as an Equipment Officer with effect from 8th January 1918. He was formerly of 2/11th London Regiment.

03117	R F CASEY DFC [O]	F/O		01.04.27	Retired list

At his own request [LG 5 April 1927, issue 33263, page 2215]. His DFC [LG 3 December 1918, supplement 31046, page 14319] was heroically won: 'On 25th September the machine in which this officer was an observer on a long-distance bombing raid was attacked by a number of enemy aeroplanes. In the engagement Lt. Casey, having shot down two enemy scouts, was wounded in the thigh; he, however, continued the action until he fainted. At this time four enemy machines were firing at close range. The pilot roused LKt. Casey, who, with fine determination, brought his gun into action and shot down two of the attacking aeroplanes out of control; the remaining two then broke off the engagement. Exhausted by the effort, Lt. Casey again fainted, and was landed in a French aerodrome. A very fine example of skill, courage and devotion to duty on the part of Lt. Casey.' Army Form B.103 shows he was attached to 110 Squadron and following admittance to a French hospital he was evacuated to England aboard HMHS *Carisbrook Castle*. On the 9th of October 1918, he recommended for the award of the DFC. Turning to Trevor Henshaw's *'The Sky Their Battlefield'* identifies the target as Frankfurt and that Lieutenant Casey's DH.9A F993 was flown by Lieutenant R P Brailli. On page 249 of my second volume, I record details of the four 110 Squadron machines lost from the raid.

	R N ESSELL [A]	F/O	+	09.12.20	6 Squadron

See summary for the circumstances of his death.

	J C BELFORD [A]	F/L		13.05.32	Retired list

At his own request [LG 31 May 1932, issue 33830, page 3503].

	E C DELAMAIN MC [O]	S/Ldr		01.08.36	
	A GARRITY [T]	A/Cmdr		18.04.47	Retirement**

Air Commodore Arthur Garrity CBE, died in December 1978.

	H A L PATTISON [A]	S/Ldr		01.12.37	Retired list

At his own request [LG 21 December 1937, issue 34465, page 8002].

	F WHITTAKER [Ad]	F/L		12.07.24	Retired list
	G B BOOTH [Ad]	Lieutenant		01.08.19	Cancelled
03131	C F B BASIL [T]	F/O		25.11.24	Retired list

On account of ill-health.

	T L JONES [O]	O/O		30.07.21	Dismissed

Observer Officer Thomas Lewis Jones was dismissed the service by sentence of General Court Martial [LG 20 September 1921, issue 32461, page 7384]. Formerly of the 4th Battalion, The Welch Regiment, Lieutenant Thomas Lew Jones relinquished his commission in the Territorial Forces on appointment to a permanent commission in the Royal Air Force [LG 4 June 1920, supplement 31930, page 6312]. Army Form B.103 shows he was born on the 10th of May 1895, transferring to the Royal Air Force on 29th April 1918.

	W MYERS MC DCM [SO]	Lieutenant		01.08.19	Cancelled
	W F WOOD [T]	Lieutenant		01.08.19	Cancelled
04235	V H TAIT [T]	AV-M		29.01.46	Retirement**

Air Vice-Marshal Sir Victor Tait KBE CB, died on Sunday, 27th November 1988.

	J M McENTEGART [T]	Lieutenant		01.08.19	Cancelled
03183	J F CLARK [T]	S/Ldr		10.02.54	Relinquished
	H G ROWE [O]	G/Capt		10.03.46	Retirement**
	A McC GODDARD [Ad]	F/L		27.02.29	Retired list

At his own request [LG 12 March 1929, issue 33476, page 1753]. In 1940, Flight Lieutenant Arthur McCallum Goddard was granted a commission in the Administrative and Special Duties Branch with effect from 1st September [LG 5 November 1940, issue 34986, page 6400], and with a new Service No. 86450.

		S/Ldr		14.09.45	Resigned
	S T KEMP [T]	F/O		17.01.26	Retired list
	A LEDGER [T]	F/O	+	04.12.23	55 Squadron

Flying Officer Aubrey Ledger was killed and his Indian Officer passenger injured when their DH.9A H173 went into a flat=spin shortly after take off from Hinaidi. The DH.9A had been with the squadron since the 22nd of May 1923.

04003	M B FITZGERALD MBE [T]	F/O		01.08.23	Retired list

On account of ill-health.

	R G FUSSELL [T]	F/O		29.05.29	Dismissed

By sentence of General Court Martial [LG 4 June 1929, issue 33503, page 3694]. Army Form B.103 shows he was born on 17th December 1894, and was a direct entry to the Royal Flying Corps on the 1st of February 1915.

04058	B T HOOD [T]	F/L		26.11.34	Retired list

Returned to the Service.

		W/Cdr		27.02.48	Retired list**
O3236	J A ELLIOTT [T]	G/Capt		01.07.47	
10106	F J W HUMPHREYS [SO]	G/Capt		01.02.46	Retired list**
03166	J BULLOCK [T]	F/L		08.06.30	Retired list
	J A ALLEN [SO]	Captain		12.04.22	Retired list

On account of ill-health contracted on active service [LG 11 April 1922, issue 32668, page 2935].

	D R MITCHELL [T]	F/L		17.03.36	Retired list
	N B HEMSLEY MBE [T]	F/O	+	31.03.21	Biggin Hill

Flying Officer Noel Butler Hemsley, attached to the Instrument Design Establishment, Biggin Hill, was killed along with Mr Edward Fenton Terry, a civilian technical assistant, when their DH.4 D8393 stalled shortly after take off from Biggin Hill. According to Air-Britain's *DH.4/DH.9 File* the accident occurred during a flight to test a 'drift sight' and it was while turning at low altitude that control was lost. Edward Terry survived the crash but died from his injuries. Noel Butler Hemsley's entry on the CWGC website indicates his unit as No. 1 Group; he is buried in the southeast corner of Keston Churchyard. The DH in which the crew died was first issued in October 1918, to 217 Squadron at Varssenaere and shortly before the squadron returned to the United Kingdom it was passed on 17th March 1919, to Alquines and 98 Squadron. However, '98' headed for home four days later having deposited D8393 with 1 Aeroplane Supply Depot who oversaw its ferry to England on 23rd March.

	W J RICHARDS [T]	F/L	+	12.05.31	Iraq

Flight Lieutenant William Joseph Richards, a Signals Officer, died in RAF Hospital Hinaidi and is buried in Ma'asker Al Raschid RAF Cemetery.

	C J POOLE [T]	F/O		10.09.24	Retired list
03250	C A C FIDLER DCM [T]	F/L		19.02.33	Retired list

Returned to the service in the Technical Branch and promoted Squadron Leader 1st September 1940 [LG 14 February 1941, issue 35076, page 903].

		W/Cdr		31.12.47	Retired list**

Appointed to a commission as Flying Officer in the Royal Air Force Volunteer Reserve, Training Branch, 29th September 1948. [LG 21st December 1948, supplement 38483, page 6610].

		F/O		30.06.49	Resigned
10076	H T H COPELAND [Ad]	S/Ldr		16.04.45	Retired list**
10111	R D LAMBERT [T]	W/Cdr		10.02.54	Relinquished
10240	M R PREECE [T]	F/L		10.02.54	Relinquished
03123	F H ASTLE [T]	F/L		18.09.34	Retired list

On account of ill-health [LG 18 September 1934, issue 34088, page 5907].

63213	W R DAY [T]	G/Capt		07.01.46	Retirement**
05003	F S WAINSCOT [T]	S/Ldr		10.02.54	Relinquished
	C V LACEY AFC [A]	F/O	+	10.04.26	IAAD Henlow

Flying Officer Charles Victor Lacey AFC was the captain of Vickers Vimy F9184 of the Inland Area Aircraft Depot, Henlow when it came into collision with an Avro 504K H9535 of the same unit, both aircraft falling locked together. See my entry in the appendix for Flying Officer William Scott for details.

	H HACKNEY [S]	F/L		23.07.30	Retired list

On account of ill-health [LG 25 July 1930, issue 33628, page 4644].

03232	R W EDWARDS [T]	W/Cdr		10.02.54	Relinquished
	G J DAVIES [T]	F/O		17.05.29	Retired list
04149	H NORRINGTON [A]	W/Cdr		27.02.45	Retirement**
04078	J W JEAN DSM [T]	G/Capt		23.12.45	Retirement**
10114	W LINIKER [T]	W/Cdr		11.01.46	Retired list**
04063	J W HOSKING MBE [T]	S/Ldr		26.11.45	Retired list**
	G ATTRILL MBE [T]	F/L		17.11.25	Retired list
	R L HARTLEY AFC [T]	F/O	+	23.08.22	8 Squadron

Flying Officer Robert Lionel Hartley AFC, along with Aircraftman Alfred Glasby, died when their DH.9A E9913 stalled at 1,000 feet during an air test and spun to the ground near Hinaidi airfield. On impact the DH burst into flames. Flying Officer Hartley's AFC was *Gazetted* in a supplement [31378] to the paper on 3rd June 1919, page 7033.

	C F CHINERY [T]	G/Capt		01.03.45	Retirement**
04201	E H RUNDLE [T]	W/Cdr		10 02 54	Relinquished
04173	C H POTTS DSM [T]	S/Ldr		09.09.36	Retired list

On account of ill-health [LG 22 September 1936, issue 34325, page 6078].

04209	H H S SCOTT DSM [T]	W/Cdr		27.05.45	Resigned**
05021	E WHITTLESEA [T]	S/Ldr		18.04.44	Relinquished

On ceasing to be employed in the Administrative and Special Duties Branch [LG 25 April 1944, supplement 36483, page 1891].

	S T LITTLETON [T]	F/O		17.11.26	Resigned
03164	H J BROWN [T]	F/L		21.02.33	Retired list

Returned to service; commissioned in the rank of Flight Lieutenant in the Equipment Branch on 5th March 1938 [LG 14 November 1939, issue 34733, page 7646].

		W/Cdr		10.02.54	Relinquished
	P COYLE [T]	F/L		01.03.31	Retired list
	J NOONAM DSM [T]	F/L		16.01.33	Retired list

On account of ill-health [LG 24 January 1933, issue 33905, page 526]. He was awarded the MSM in recognition of his services in North Russia [LG 22 December 1919, supplement 31703, page 15841].

	T S JOBLING [T]	F/O		02.07.24	Resigned
04046	R D McE HART [T]	W/Cdr		19.05.44	Retirement**
Re-employed.		W/Cdr		27.12.46	Retired list**
	R G GORE [T]	F/L		30.10.30	Retired list
05016	A P WHITE [T]	W/Cdr	+	27.02.41	

During the early afternoon of Thursday, 27th of February 1941, the Parnall Aircraft Factory at Yate, Bristol, was attacked by a single *Luftwaffe* He111 captained by *Oberleutnant* Herman Lohman released seven 250kgs bombs with such accuracy that over fifty persons, including Wing Commander Alfred Percival White who was visiting the works, perished. He is buried in the extension to Chipping Sodbury [St. John the Baptist] Churchyard. For additional information regarding the raid, I recommend the websites World War II Today and South Gloucestershire War Memorials.

	C O TOWLER DSM [T]	F/L		11.04.33	Retired list
	C E WHINNEY [T]	F/O		11.03.25	Retired list
04204	H W St. JOHN DFC [O]	S/Ldr		14.10.35	Retired list
04204	Returned to the service and transferred to the Technical Branch 24th April 1940 [LG 7 March 1941, 35097, page 1371].				
		W/Cdr		15.04.46	Retired list**
	W A CORYTON [A]	ACM		15.05.51	Retirement**

Air Chief Marshal Sir Alec Coryton KCB KBE MVO DFC, died on Tuesday, 20th October 1981.

	A G QUINNELL [Ad]	F/O		05.07.22	Retired list

On account of ill-health [LG 4 July 1922, issue 32726, page 5039].

04180	R PYNE [A]	A/Cmdr	+	17.05.44	SASO HQ 10 Group

Took off from RAF Bolt Head in Hurricane I W9118 of the Group's Communication Flight, intending to visit units within his command but flew into a balloon cable and crashed near Dartmouth. At the time of his death he had been honoured with the DFC and mentioned in despatches. He was cremated in Golders Green Crematorium.

	H K GOODE DSO DFC [A]	G/Capt		15.12.41	Resigned**
	J GLOVER [O]	F/L		03.04.34	Retired list
04093	H E KING [A]	W/Cdr		18.02.43	Retired list**
04134	W J MILLEN [A]	W/Cdr		26.11.45	Retirement**
03184	E S B CLARKE [A]	G/Capt		13.09.45	Retirement**
At his own request.					
04236	G S TAYLOR [A]	W/Cdr		26.02.48	Retired list**
	C S GRAY [A]	F/O		15.03.22	Retired list

On account of ill-health contracted on active service.

04133	R MENZIES [A]		C/Capt	01.06.41	
03153	J BRADBURY [A]		G/Capt	20.05.49	Retired list**
	D A COX [O]		O/O	23.08.22	Retired list

On account of ill-health contracted on active service [LG 22 August 1922, issue 32740, page 6163].

04144	G A R MUSCHAMP [A]		G/Capt	28.02.53	Retirement**
	H G McKECHNIE [T]		F/O	15.02.22	Resigned
	W K ROSE [A & S]		F/O	21.12.21	Retired list

On account of ill-health [LG 20 December 1921, issue 32554, page 10374]

05022	R A WHYTE [A & S]		S/ldr	17.01.45	Retirement**
Re-employed.			W/Cdr	26.05.46.	Retired list**
	A E GOOCH [T]		F/O	05.06.20	Resigned

On account of physical unfitness for flying [LG 4 June 1920, issue 31929, page 6189].

10146	F A SKOULDING [T]		A/Cmdr	19.06.49	Retirement**

Air Commodore Francis Arthur Skoulding CBE, died on Thursday, 16th May 1974.

	R JONES MC [A]		Lieutenant	01.08.19	Cancelled
04085	R REAY-JONES as notified on 23rd January 1935.		G/Capt	20.01.48	Retirement**
04090	J E KENDRICK DFC [O]		Lieutenant	08.01.21	Resigned

Almost certain to be John Eversleigh Kendrick whose DFC was *Gazetted* on 3 December 1918, supplement 31046, page 14323: *'This officer has acted as Observer on numerous occasions in co-operation with out artillery and in photographic reconnaissance. By his coolness and skill under all circumstances he has gained the complete confidence of all the pilots with whom he has served, enabling them to carry out their observations and photography with full assurance that their safety from surprise attacks is insured.'* His Army Form B.103 shows he joined the Royal Flying Corps on 25th March 1918, and was attached to 16 Squadron with effect from 7th April 1918. He returned to the service in 1940, and was granted a commission as a Pilot Officer under probation within the Administrative and Special Duties Branch on 14th March [LG 9 April 1940, issue 34826, page 2075, but his commission was terminated on 29th August [LG 27 September 1940, issue 34954, page 5722].

05019	J WHITFORD [A]		AV-M	05.03.49	Retirement**

Air Vice-Marshal Sir John Whitford KBE CB twice mentioned in despatches, died on Friday, 12th August 1966.

04050	R H HAWORTH-BOOTH DFC [A]		W/Cdr	14.08.45	Retirement**
04049	J A G HASLAM MC DFC [O]		W/Cdr	25.12.45	Retired list**
04045	J S HARRISON [O]		S/Ldr	31.10.38	Retired list

At his own request [LG 1 November 1938, issue 34566, page 6821]. Granted a commission in Class CC of the Reserve of Air Force Officers, within the General Duties Branch, as an Honorary Squadron Leader with effect 31st October 1938 [LG 26 December 1939, issue 34760, page 8550]. Subsequently transferring to the Administrative and Special Duties Branch, with effect same date, as notified in LG 5 January 1940, issue 34767, page 90] with same issue on page 88 notifying relinquishment of his Class CC commission on appointment to a commission in the Royal Air Force Volunteer Reserve, with effect from 1st September 1939, and reverting to Flight Lieutenant.

			F/L	26.12.40	Dismissed

By sentence of General Court Martial [LG 7 January 1941, issue 35057, page 154].

	E G GAFF [A]		F/O	07.01.22	Resigned
	V CROOME [A]		G/Capt	20.01.44	Retirement**
	F G PRINCE [A]		2Lt	+ 17.05.19	58 Squadron

See summary for the circumstances of his death.

03236	J A ELLIOTT [T]		G/Capt	08.01.51	Retirement**
04032	O G GREGSON [A]		F/L	18.11.28	Retired list

At his own request [LG 20 November 1928, issue 33440, page 7556]. Returned to the service in the Second World War and is named in Appendix C of the Report of RAF Operations in Malaya and NEI 1941-2 [LG 26.02.48, supplement 38216, page 1415]. Between February 1942 and late summer 1945, he was a prisoner of the Japanese. After leaving the service, and having settled in Australia, he lived until 13th August 1979; Oswald Gordon Gregson is buried in Karrakatta Cemetery, Perth. He is commemorated on the Australian War Memorial, where his rank is recorded as 'Acting Wing Commander'.

	C A HORN [O]		G/Capt	27.09.45	Retired list**
	J BLACKFORD [A]		G/Capt	28.04.45	Retired list**
04110	J W LISSETT [A]		G/Capt	19.07.48	Retirement**
	W E DIPPLE [A & S]		G/Capt	02.06.45	Retired list**
03245	H E FALKNER [O]		W/Cdr	31.03.45	Retired list**

75906   This service number is recorded against his name when reverting to the Retired List; however, 75906 belongs to Herbert Joe Knevitt, a Pilot Officer on probation with effect from 2nd October 1940, within the Technical Branch[LG 16 May 1941, issue 35165, page 2820], who subsequently retired, at his own request, while ranked Wing Commander on 10th March 1962 [LG 6 April 1962, supplement 42644, page 2930].

03229	F T EADES [O]		S/Ldr	10.02.54	Relinquished
04102	G M LAWSON MC [O]		A/Cmdr	21.12.45	Retirement**

Air Commodore George Maxwell Lawson CBE MC mentioned in despatches, died on Saturday, 21st August 1965.

	D S ROBERTSON [O]		Lieutenant	01.08.19	Cancelled
03118	W S ALLEN [T]		F/L	01.07.35	Retired list

At his own request [LG 9 July 1935, issue 34178, page 4440].

	B F DEANE [O]		F/O	+ 15.04.21	SAC Old Sarum

Flying Officer Bernard Frederick Deane and Aircraftman Philip Frederick Elliott died when their Bristol F.2b F4933 stalled while making a turn with a failing engine, coming down near the village of Mouxton [sic] in Hampshire. Additional information will be reported in the fourth volume.

04017	J V GASCOYNE DFC [A]		Lieutenant	25.10.21	Resigned

Returned to service; commissioned in the Technical Branch as a Pilot Officer on 4th September 1940 [LG 4 October 1940, issue 34960, page 5838].

			G/Capt	29.09.46	Retired list**
	L B DUGGAN [A & S]		G/Capt	29.09.46	Retirement**
	J PARSONS [T]		F/O	06.03.31	Retired list
	H J BRADLEY [A & S]		F/O	+ 06.02.23	216 Squadron

Flying Officer Harold Joseph Bradley died when Vickers Vimy F9165 nosed over in a forced-landing on soft sand at Zisa, some 20 miles south of Amman in Trans-Jordan. The pilot, Flying Officer Arthur Reginald Jones and Aircraftman Percy Leonard Leavesley were injured.

	J S NICHOL [O]		S/Ldr	+ 24.11.38	1 E&WS Cranwell
	R H F de V S SOMERSET [A & S]		Lieutenant	01.08.19	Cancelled
	D WOOD [A]		Lieutenant	01.08.19	Cancelled
03143	G W BIRKINSHAW [A & S]		A/Cmdr	22.12.47	Retirement**

Air Commodore George William Birkinshaw CB, died on Saturday, 22nd October 1977.

03159	E BREWERTON [A & S]		S/Ldr	14.05.46	Retired list**
	G McCORMACK [O]		F/L	+ 28.03.28	14 Squadron

Flight Lieutenant George McCormack and his observer/air gunner, Leading Aircraftman James Kimberley died when their DH.9A crashed near Amman, Trans-Jordan.

03§76	G P H CARTER [A]	A/Cmdr	29.08.50	Retirement**

Air Commodore Gerald Paul Halliley Carter CBE, died on Sunday, 17th September 1989.

05004	C WALKER [A]	F/L +	08.05.44	

Flight Lieutenant Cecil Walker, 51 years of age, is buried in Kearsley New Church Burial Ground.

	K L HARRIS [A]	F/L	14.01.31	Retired list

On account of ill-health [LG 13 January 1931, issue 33680, page 307].

02111	H DAWES MBE [SO]	G/Capt	26.08.46	Retired list**
	S C BLACK [A]	F/L	18.11.28	Retired list

At his own request [LG 11 December 1928, issue 33446, page 8173].

	R J WILLSON [O]	F/O +	31.03.26	28 Squadron

Flying Officer Reginald John Willson and Leading Aircraftman Arthur John Burgess died during an air exercise in wireless telegraphy, their Bristol F.2b coming down near Quetta.

03172	J P CAFFERKEY [A]	S/Ldr	10.02.54	Relinquished
	M C TRENCH [O]	F/O +	24.04.23	39 Squadron

Flying Officer Maurice Crosbie Trench and Pilot Officer Frederic Samuel Harris were killed when their DH.9A E8489 spun-in from 100 feet shortly after taking off from Spittlegate. On impact a fire broke out, completely destroying the bomber.

03206	F K DAMANT [A]	W/Cdr +	16.05.41	RAFC SFTS

Wing Commander Frederick Korsten Damant DFC and his passenger, Leading Aircraftman Alan Neil Pearce died during a test flight in Oxford I P1881 from Cranwell when the elevators broke away and out of control the twin-engined trainer dived into the ground. The crash occurred within seconds of the aircraft leaving the ground. Both airmen are buried in Cranwell [St. Andrew] Churchyard. Alan Pearce was aged 18, and was the sone of Colonel Stanley Arthur Coxon Pearce and Ivy Pearce of Salisbury, Rhodesia. The tragedy is reported in 'Aircraft Accidents in Lincolnshire during the Second World War' complied, produced and edited by Graham J Platt. Frederick Korsten Damant's DFC was awarded for his services in Iraq during 1920-1921 [LG 10 October 1922, issue 32754, page 7134]. His service number has been misreported by CWGC as '63206'.

	F J SMITH MC MM [O]*	O/O +	14.04.21	208 Squadron

Observer Officer Frank James Smith MC MM and his pilot, Flight Lieutenant George Malcolm Clarke AFC died when their Bristol F.2b E2298 came into midair collision with Bristol F.2b D7831 flown by Flying Officer William Ash Armstrong and Flying Officer Edward Blake Jones over Bilbeis, Egypt. Additional remarks will be reported in the fourth volume.

	C A SPENCE [A]	Lieutenant	01.08.19	Cancelled
04030	E B GREEN MC [O]	S/Ldr	27.03.46	Retired list**
04217	S J SMETHAM [S]	W/Cdr +	17.12.40	

Wing Commander Stanley James Smetham was cremated in Oxford Crematorium. A Memorial Plaque carries the inscription *Where Your Treasure Is There Will Your Heart Be Also.* He is also commemorated on Emmanuel College, Cambridge, Roll of Honour.

	P N MELITUS [O]	Lieutenant	01.08.19	Cancelled
	E H SEARLE [A & S]	F/L +	10.04.34	47 Squadron

Flight Lieutenant Edmund Henry Searle was carrying out a local reconnaissance of the Rumbek region which was situated roughly 20 miles north of Rumbek in Sudan when his Fairey Gordon I K2624 crashed. Flight Lieutenant Searle died on impact and Leading Aircraftman Arthur George Woolley died from his injuries the next day. Also flying in the Gordon was the District Commissioner for Rumbek, Mr. Frank C S Lorimer who, although injured, recovered. As an illustration of how such accidents were regarded, the wreck, which I can only assume was fairly intact, was considered worthy of repair and continued in squadron service. On 12th February 1937, while taxying at Khartoum and undercarriage leg gave way but, again, repairs were carried out on site and K2624 soldiered on until October 1939, when it was struck off charge. Air-Britain's *The K File - The Royal Air Force of the 1930s* admirably compiled by James J Halley MBE and published in 1995, shows the Gordon as being shipped to Aboukir where it was reassembled and test flown in readiness for delivery to 47 Squadron. At the time of his appointment to a permanent commission, Lieutenant Searle was attached to 1 Aeroplane Supply Depot, returning to Home Establishment on 13th October 1919.

	L SMITH [Ad]	F/L	31.08.32	Resigned
04237	A G THACKRAY [S]	W/Cdr	29.12.46	Retirement**
	C S MILLER [O]	F/O	01.09.20	Resigned
	H W PEARSON [A]	Lieutenant	01.08.19	Cancelled

Canada Ceased employment with the RAF with effect from 12th August 1919 [LG 27 August 1919, supplement 31524, page 10841].

03146	E A BLAKE [A]	G/Capt	02.03.44	Retirement**
	B A FOORD MC [O]	F/L +	18.10.22	

Flight Lieutenant Basil Arthur Foord MC died in the Central Royal Air Force HospitaL, Finchley. In addition to his MC, he was awarded the DFC for distinguished service in Waziristan between the years 1919-1920 [LG 29 April 1921, issue 32307, page 3440]. His MC was gained while with the 7th Battalion, London Regiment, Territorial Forces, and was *Gazetted* 16th September 1918, supplement 30901, page 10950: *'For conspicuous gallantry and devotion to duty while in charge of the right attacking platoon in a raid on the hostile lines. He displayed a fine fighting spirit and powers of leadership, personally accounting for many of the enemy. When the time for withdrawal came, he remained behind to assured himself that all his casualties were brought back, assisting to carry some of them himself. He was the only surviving officer, and his gallant behaviour throughout was a fine example to all ranks. '.*

10070	W H BOWDEN [Ad]	F/O	15.07.30	Retired list
	A G PEACE [A]			

To the General List 16th June 1916, formerly Sapper attached Canadian Divisional Signal Corps [LG 18 July 1916, Canada issue 29671, page 7102]. Born 16th July 1891; Royal Flying Corps 19th September 1916; during 1917 attached 9 Squadron.

04005	J D FODEN AFC [A]	G/Capt	20.06.46	Retirement**
	C B DICK-CLELAND [SO]	F/L	24.01.27	Retired list

On account of ill-health [LG 28 January 1927, issue 33243, page 584].

L H I BELL [A] Although his release from the Royal Air Force is untraced it transpire that by 1931 he was a ground engineer working at Gatwick. On Sunday, 25th January 1931, he was one of two passengers taken up from Gatwick in Avro 504K G-AACW piloted by Mr. W J Martin and which had been modified in that the control column had been removed from the rear cockpit, now occupied by Lawrence Herbert Irving Bell and and Mr. S J W Meathrel. The flight appears to have been of a demonstration nature in company with other machines, but instead of landing as the other aircraft had done, Mr. Martin climbed to around 1,500 to 2,000 feet and, according to eyewitnesses, attempted to make a barrel roll but seemed to abort the attempt. The Avro then began to spin, twice seeming to recover to a straight gliding altitude only to spin again and crash to the ground near Horley [ASN Wilibase Occurrence 27503, which I acknowledge]. *The Tines* reported the accident the following day, identifying the pilot as James Martin, 24, of Station Hotel, Ponshurst, Joseph Leathrell, 21, of Holmsdale-road, Bromley, Kent and L H Irving Bell, aged about 40, ground engineer of Tonbridge, Kent. The Avro, belonging to Home and Counties Aircraft Services, fell into a field about a quarter of a mile from Balcombe-road near Horley. All three were killed in the crash and all were described as competent pilots.

	L G MAXTON [A]	G/Capt	12.09.44	Retirement**
	A H E LINDOP [O]	Lieutenant	01.08.19	Cancelled
04238	A S THOMPSON [Ad]	W/Cdr	11.03.40	Retirement**

Re-employed [LG 7 December 1943, supplement 36276, page 5340].

	C R FENTON [Ad]	Lieutenant	08.12.20	Resigned
	C F FALKENBERG DFC [A]	Lieutenant	01.08.19	Cancelled
	R W RAYN [A]	Lieutenant	01.08.19	Cancelled

COLONELS
2

H R M BROOKE-POPHAM CB CMG DSO AFC		ACM	06.03.37	Retirement

In 1939, he was appointed Head of the RAF Training Mission in Canada and in 1940 he took up a similar post in South Africa before bing appointed Commander-in-Chief, Far East Command. On return to the United Kingdom he was made Inspector-General of the Air Training Corps. Air Chief Marshal Sir Robert Brooke-Popham GCVO KCB CMG DSO AFC KSt.J four times mentioned in despatches, died on Tuesday, 20th October 1953.

B C H DREW CMG CBE [SO]		A/Cmdr	15.11.29	Retirement

Air Commodore Bertie Clephane Hawley Drew CMG CVO CBE mentioned in despatches was granted a commission in Class CC of the Reserve of Air Force Officers, effective from 25th July 1938, but relinquished this commission on 8th March 1939. He died on Thursday, 2nd January 1969.

LIEUTENANT-COLONELS
6

A D WARRINGTON-MORRIS CMG OBE [SO]		A/Cmdr	03.07.33	Retirement

Air Commodore Alfred Drummond Warrington-Morris CB CMG OBE mentioned in despatches, died on Saturday, 24th March 1962. Similar to Air Commodore Drew, he was granted a commission in Class CC of the Reserve of Air Force Officers and between Boxing Day 1942 and retirement on 8th November 1944, served as Deputy Director of the Air Training Corps./

R E M RUSSELL CBE DSO [SO]		Lt-Col	22.08.19	Cancelled
J L FORBES [AP[T]]		A/Cmdr	13.05.32	Retirement

Air Commodore James Louis Forbes OBE, died on Wednesday, 8th September 1965.

F RANKEN [AP[T]]				
C T MacLEAN DSO MC [A]		AV-M	27.12.40	Retirement**

New Zealand   Air Vice Marshal Cuthbert Trelawder MacLean CB DSO MC twice mentioned in despatches, died on Tuesday, 25th February 1969.

O H K MAGUIRE DSO [A]		Lt-Col	22.08.19	Cancelled

MAJORS
10

R H VERNEY OBE [AP[T]]		A/Cmdr	01.08.38	Retirement

Air Commodore Reynell Henry Verney CBE, died on Sunday, 27th October 1974.

A H W E WYNNE OBE [SO]		W/Cdr	01.07.25	Retired list

At his own request [LG 30 June 1925, issue 33062, page 4370].

A J MILEY OBE [AP[T]]		G/Capt	29.03.45	Retired list**
R HILTON-JONES OBE [SO]				
R M HILL MC AFC [A]		ACM	01.07.48	Retirement**

Air Chief Marshal Sir Roderic Hill KCB MC AFC*four times mentioned in despatches, died on Wednesday, 6th October 1954.

G H NORMAN [A]		S/Ldr +	18.08.21	RAE Farnborough

Squadron Leader Geoffrey Hamilton Norman died from natural causes at his home in Aldershot and is buried in Savoy Chapel Westminster.

H J F HUNTER MC [A]		A/Cmdr	15.06.39	Retirement

Returned to service on the outbreak of the Second World War serving mainly as Air Officer Commanding various overseas Groups before reverting to the Retired List on 18th January 1946. Air Commodore Henry John Francis Hunter CBE MC three times mentioned in despatches, died on Monday, 12th September 1966.

V S BROWN [AP[T]]		A/Cmdr	30.11.37	Resigned

Air Commodore Sir Vernon Brown Kt CB OBE, died on Tuesday, 26th August 1986. During the Second World War, and as a civil servant, he was Chief Inspector of Accidents, and as Malcom Barrass records on his website Air of Authority - A History of RAF Organisation he discovered why so many Stirling bombers failed to recover from a dive; it seems the pilots' safety harness was so uncomfortable that many pilots released it once airborne and on refastened it in time for landing. Thus, if in flight the aircraft went into a dive, the pilot fell forward onto the control column, thereby making it near impossible for recovery.

F W SCARFF MBE [AP[T]]		Major	31.12.21	Retired list

Major Frederick William Scarff MBE died on 1st May 1931.

W A McCLAUGHRY DSO MC DFC [A]		AV-M +	04.01.43	AOC AHQ Egypt

For details reporting Air-Vice Marshal Wilfred Ashton McLaughry CB DSO MC DFC three times mentioned in despatches death on Monday, 4th January 1943, please refer back to the entry for Major A W Tedder and the death of his wife, Lady Tedder. Air-Vice Marshal McClaughry is buried in Heliopolis War Cemetery where his headstone bears the inscription 'A Man of Valour, Forceful, Skilled, Yet Human, Modest, Kind.'

CAPTAINS
17

R ADDENBROOKE-PROUT OBE MC [SO]		S/Ldr	23.04.24	Resigned
A S C MacLAREN MC* AFC [A]		S/Ldr	01.06.30	Retired list

On account of ill-health. 2nd Lieutenant Archibald Stuart Charles McLaren was *Gazetted* with the MC on 27th July 1916, supplement 29684, page 7439: *'For conspicuous gallantry. On approaching an enemy aerodrome he observed a hostile aeroplane on the ground preparing to start, with pilot and observer in their seats and mechanics holding on to the wings. He descended to 100 feet, dropped a bomb squarely into the machine and blew it up, together with pilot, observer and mechanics. He then attacked and set fire to a Fokker which was in a hangar.'*

02206	K M St. C G LEASK MC [A]		AV-M	01.12.49	Retirement**
	O M SUTTON MC [A]		F/L +	16.08.21	AAE Martlesham Heath

Flight Lieutenant Oliver Manners Sutton MC was killed while testing the Bristol Braemar C4297 when it swung taking off from Martlesham Heath and crashed against a hangar. Aircraftman Charles Sheridan also died, while Corporal Cecil Stanley Ellison was injured and Aircraftman Barman escaping with no more than a shaking. Flight Lieutenant Sutton is buried in Withyham [St. Michael] Churchyard. Additional information will be provided in the next volume.

	J NOAKES [A]		G/Capt	27.03.45	Retirement**
	O STEWART MC AFC [A]		Major	22.12.22	Resigned
	G S M INSALL VC [A]		G/Capt	30.07.45	Retirement**
02129	H J EDGAR [A]		F/L	01.07.25	Retired list

At his own request [LG 30 June 1925, issue 33062, page 4370].

02045	G BARRETT AFC [A]		F/L	01.11.22	Retired list

On account of ill-health contracted in the service.

	G L GODDEN OBE [T]		Captain	22.08.19	Cancelled
78320					

Returned to service; commissioned as a Pilot Officer on 1st April 1940, to Administrative and Special Duties Branch [LG 26 April 1940

issue 34838, page 2479].	S/Ldr	22.06.54	Relinquished
C TURNER AFC [A]	A/Cmdr	21.05.44	Retirement**

Air Commodore Cresswell Turner AFC, died on Friday, 19th October 1951.

J F ROCHE [A]	F/L +	12.25	70 Squadron

Flight Lieutenant John Francis Roche died while performing the duties of an Intelligence Officer, attached to 70 Squadron. He is buried in Ma'asker Al Raschid RAF Cemetery.

02070 M F BROWNE [T]	S/Ldr	04.03.36	Retired list

On account of ill-health [LG 3 March 1936, issue 34261, page 1386].

R F L DICKEY DSC [A & S]	F/L	14.01.25	Resigned
W J de SALIS DSC [A & S]	Captain	22.11.22	Resigned

76508   Returned to service; commissioned as a Flying Officer on 18th September 1939, to General Duties Branch [LG 5 January 1940, issue 34767, page 90].

	S/Ldr	10.02.54	Relinquished
G T R HILL [A]	Captain	22.08.19	Cancelled
02080 J G S CANDY [A]	W/Cdr	26.01.46	retired list**

LIEUTENANTS
6

02082 R S CAPON [A]	F/L	08.11.25	Retired list

At his own request. Service number '02082' also allotted to Captain [subsequently Group Captain] A N Benge - see list of Captains appointed on 1st August 1919. In retirement Flight Lieutenant Robert Stanley Capon became Superintendent of Scientific Research, Royal Aircraft Establishment, Air Ministry and in the New Year's Honours List of 1931, was appointed MBE [LG 1 January 1931, supplement 33675, page 9].

A G JARVIS [A]	Lieutenant	22.08.19	Cancelled

Re-appointed short service commission [LG 12 September 1919, issue 31548]. Though this was duly cancelled [LG 10 October 1919, issue 31593, page 12554]. I have, however, retained his service record against his entry in Appendix E.

J W D LEIGH MC [A]	Lieutenant	22.08.19	Cancelled
T C LUKE MC [A]	S/ldr +	01.07.35	

As Temporary 2nd Lieutenant Thomas Carlyon Luke was *Gazetted* with a MC on 25th August 1917, supplement 30251, page 8812: *'For conspicuous gallantry and devotion to duty in aerial combats. On several occasions he attacked hostile formations and dispersed them, although they were in superior numbers, showing great dash and fearlessness in engaging them at close range. He has taken part in thirty-five offensive patrols, at all times setting a fine example of courage and devotion to duty.'* An AFC was *Gazetted* on 3rd June 1935, supplement 34166, page 3618. Within weeks of receiving his AFC, Squadron Leader Thomas Carlyon Luke MC AFC died in RAF Hospital Halton. Paul McMillan reports that since 13th March 1935, Squadron Leader Luke was non-effective sick, thus indicating he had been taken terminally ill.

70452 C G MATHEW [A]	F/L	01.09.23	Resigned

But granted a commission in Class C of the Reserve of Air Force Officers, retaining Flight Lieutenant rank, with effect from 1st September 1923 [LG 4 September 1923, issue 32859, page 5994]. Subsequently transferred to the Administrative and Special Duties Branch. With effect from 1st September 1939 [LG 27 October 1939, supplement 34718, page 7184] and retaining his rank.

	S/Ldr	22.06.43	Relinquished

On account of ill-health [LG 13 July 1943, supplement 36089, page 3164]. Squadron Leader Cecil George Mathew, 53 years of age, died on Saturday, 30th August 1947, and was cremated in Woking [St. John's] Crematorium. His name is commemorated on panel 4.

J H JEPHSON [A]	Captain	02.11.21	Resigned

Note. Probably without exception, those named above had an appointment date of 1st August 1919.

LG 26 September 1919, issue 31569, page 11919. The following additions to officers appointed to permanent commissions was published, all with seniority from 1st August 1919.

GROUP CAPTAIN

E M MAITLAND CMG DSO AFC	A/Cmdr +	24.08.21	AOC RAF Howden

Air Commodore Edward Maitland CMG DSO AFC DFM[US] died when the Airship R.38 broke up over the Humber river on Wednesday, 24th August 1921, killing forty-four of the forty-nine personnel on board. At the time of his death he was Air Officer Commanding RAF Airship Base, Howden. He is buried in Hull Western Cemetery along with some of the crew who perished. An impressive Memorial upon which the names of those who died are mounted on a panel fixed to the Memorial. The tragedy was widely reported in the papers, *The Times* carrying seven separate reports in its edition published on the 25th.

WINGS COMMANDERS
5

01059 T R CAVE-BROWNE-CAVE CBE	W/Cdr	01.07.31	Retired list

At own request [LG 30 June 1931, issue 33731, page 4252]. Returned to service and transferred from the General Duties Branch to the Technical Branch, retaining Wing Commander ran, with effect from 24th April 1940 [LG 13 August 1940, issue 34920, page 4942].

A D CUNNINGHAM OBE	AV-M	19.07.38	Retirement

Recalled to service on 2nd November 1939, serving Deputy Senior Air Staff Officer, Headquarters Fighter Command. Air Vice-Marshal Alexander Duncan Cunningham CB CBE twice mentioned in despatches, died on Tuesday, 3rd February 1981.

01066 J W O DALGLEISH OBE	W/Cdr	09.10.20	Retired list

On account of ill-health [LG 8 October 1920, issue 32078, page 9815].

J N FLETCHER AFC	W/Cdr	01.06.31	Resigned

Late of the Corps of Royal Engineers, Captain J N Fletcher AFC resigned his commission on appointment to a permanent commission in the Royal Air Force [LG 16 June 1920, supplement 31994, page 6672]. On leaving the air force he was commissioned to the General List, Officer Training Corps, subsequently resigning his commission as Lieutenant-Colonel and Officer Commanding Berkhampsted School Contingent, Junior Division on 1st June 1931 [LG 30 June 1931, issue 33731, page 4249]. He was awarded the Royal Aero Club Aviators' Certificate 229 on 4th June 1912.

SQUADRON LEADERS
3

D HARRIES AFC	AV-M	19.08.46	Retirement**

Air Vice-Marshal Sir Douglas Harries KCB AFC mentioned in despatches, died on Wednesday, 6th December 1972.

W C HICKS AFC	G/Capt +	26.06.39	

Group Captain William Charles Hicks AFC was, according to a report in the *Daily Mirror,* in charge of the barrage balloon defences of London at the time of his death. He was living at Dorney Common, Windsor and was 48 years of age. Paul McMillan adds that Group Captain Hicks was born at Portsea in Hampshire on 19th August 1890.

E H SPARLING	W/Cdr	19.02.37	Retired list

At his own request.

| 02047 | J A BARRON | F/L | | 21.10.25 | Retired list |

At his own request [LG 20 October 1925, issue 33094, page 6777].

| 02059 | R S BOOTH AFC | W/Cdr | | 20.01.45 | Retirement** |
| | C W C BROWNE | Captain | | 30.11.21 | Resigned |

Paul McMillan reports that on the 12th of June 1919, by deed-poll he was to be referred to as Chetwode William Caulfield-Browne, his third Christian name now being incorporated into his surname. He was born at Teddington, Middlesex on 23rd September 1895, and died on 29th October 1973, in Hampshire.

| 02015 | F L C BUTCHER | S/Ldr | | 15.04.26 | Retired list |

At his own request.

| | R A COCHRANE AFC | ACM | | 29.11.52 | Retirement** |

Air Chief Marshal The Honourable Sir Ralph Cochrane GBE KCB AFC four times mentioned in despatches, died on Saturday, 17th December 1977. During the Second World War , apart from two years as Director of Flying Training, he was one of the principal architects of carrying out the 'bombing campaign' from September 1942 to February 1943, he was Air Officer Commanding No. 3 Group, and thence Air Officer Commanding No. 5 Group until February 1945, when he departed for duties as Air Officer Commanding-in-Chief Transport Command.

| | J B COLE HAMILTON | AV-M | + | 22.08.45 | AOC 11 Group FC |

Air Vice-Marshal John Beresford Cole-Hamilton CB CBE twice mentioned in despatches, succumbed to cancer at the age of 51, and was laid to rest in Bradford-on-Tone [St. Giles] Churchyard.

	G G H COOKE DSC AFC	W/Cdr		28.03.34	Retired list
	H V DREW	G/Capt		03.11.45	Retirement**
	T W ELMHIRST AFC	AM		29.06.50	Retirement**

Air Marshal Sir Thomas Elmhirst KBE CB AFC KStJ four times mentioned in despatches, died on Saturday, 6th November 1982. I have mentioned this on a number of occasions in my writings, but it is worth repeating here that Sir Thomas Elmhirst when commanding 15 Squadron [June 1934 - August 1935] adopted the form for the squadron's 'number-plate' as XV Squadron which it has been known as ever since.

| | R V GODDARD | AM | | 08.04.51 | Retirement** |

Air Marshal Sir Victor Goddard KCB CBE twice mentioned in despatches DFM[U], died on Wednesday, 21st January 1987.

| 02168 | J H HAGON | S/Ldr | | 14.02.46 | Retired list** |
| | I C LITTLE AFC | F/L | + | 24.08.21 | Air Ship Base Howden |

See Air Commodore Edward Maitland on the previous page for details. Flight Lieutenant Little, too, is buried in Hull Western Cemetery.

| | P E M MAITLAND AFC | AV-M | | 12.08.50 | Retirement** |

Air Vice-Marshal Percy Eric Maitland CB CBE MVO AFC twice mentioned in despatches, died on Thursday, 22nd August 1985.

| | R S MONTAGU DSC | F/L | + | 24.08.21 | Air Ship Base Howden |

See Air Commodore Edward Maitland on the previous page for details. Flight Lieutenant Rupert Samuel Montagu is buried in Hull Western Cemetery

| 02250 | T P Y MOORE | S/Ldr | | 11.02.31 | Retired list |

On account of ill-health [LG 10 February 1931, issue 33688, page 932].

| | A W MYLNE | A/Cmdr | | 21.05.45 | Retirement** |

Air Commodore Athol Wordsworth Mylne, died on Wednesday, 11th April 1979. One of only a few who reached and retired with air rank without receiving a decoration.

| | P G N OMMANNEY | F/L | | 04.08.23 | Resigned |

Strongly suspect Flight Lieutenant Patrick Gream Nelson Ommanney transferred to the Royal Navy for on 8th May 1946, an officer with the name and initials 'P G N Ommanney' was promoted from Lieutenant-Commander to Commander [LG 23 August 1946, issue 37699, page 4246].

| | H L RUTTY | F/L | | 26.09.19 | Cancelled |
| 03055 | H S SCROGGS | G/Capt | + | 29.09.41 | OC Thorney Island |

On the 15th of April 1916, the Admiralty published a list of promotions which included Acting Sub-Lieutenant Henry Sydney Scroggs to the rank of Sub-Lieutenant in His Majesty's Fleet [LG 18 April 1916, issue 29552, page 4022]. Subsequently transferred on 1st April 1918, to the Royal Air Force and a permanent commission on August 1st, 1919, he was mentioned in despatches on 24th September 1941 [LG 24 September 1941, supplement 35284, page 5570]. Five days later, while ranked Group Captain and commanding the Coastal Command airfield at Thorney Island he was killed when 59 Squadron Hudson V AM867 TR-G captained by Squadron Leader Paul Draycott Dear swung while taking off, crashed and exploded, killing the three crew which included Aircraftman Arthur Gamston whom Ross McNeill records as belonging to 415 Squadron RCAF [see *Royal Air Force Coastal Command Losses - Volume 1 1939-1941* page 154. Squadron Leader Dear and Group Captain Henry Sydney Scroggs , who perished during the attempted rescue of the Hudson's crew, are buried in West Thorney [St. Nicholas] Churchyard, their ages being 27 and 45 respectively.

| 03075 | R S SUGDEN AFC | G/Capt | | 25.05.46 | Retirement** |

Known to have received a commission in the Training Branch of the Royal Air Force Volunteer Reserve from which he resigned as a Flying Officer on 3rd April 1951 [LG 22 May 1951, supplement 39232, page 2808].

| | G M THOMAS | F/L | + | 24.08.21 | Air Ship Base Howden |

See Air Commodore Edward Maitland on the previous page for details. Flight Lieutenant Thomas is buried in Hull Western Cemetery.

	E F TURNER AFC	G/Capt		09.11.45	Retirement**
	W UNDERHILL DSC	G/Capt		21.11.45	Retirement**
	A H WANN	A/Cmdr		02.11.46	Retirement**

Air Commodore Archibald Herbert Wann twice mentioned in despatches, died in France on Monday, 11th October 1948.

FLYING OFFICER

| | S B HARRIS AFC | G/Capt | | 17.04.46 | Retirement** |

LG 3 October 1919, issue 31581, page 12141. The following three officers were appointed to permanent commissions, with effect from 1st August 1919.

WING COMMANDER

| 05045 | W D BEATTY CBE AFC | W/Cdr | | 01.01.20 | Retired list |

At his own request.
Late of the Corps of Royal Engineers, Major William Dawson Beatty CBE AFC resigned his commission on being appointed to a permanent commission in the Royal Air Force [LG 30 March 1920, supplement 31842, page 3986]. Wing Commander William Dawson Beatty OBE AFC died in Egypt on 9th June 1941, and is buried in Cairo War Cemetery; he was no longer serving with the Royal Air Force. It is noted that His Majesty through the prerogative of his Royal License permitted Wing Commander Beatty to wear the Order of Military Merit, Class II, as conferred by the King of Spain [LG 23 November 1920, issue 32133, page 11388].

SQUADRON LEADER

| 01163 | B H N H HAMILTON DSO | S/Ldr | | 05.08.25 | Retired list |

At his own request [LG 18 September 1925, issue 33085, page 6089]. Returned to the service in the Second World War and transferred from the General Duties Branch to the Technical Branch 24th April 1940 [LG 12 September 1940, issue 35273, page 5295]. In addition to the award of the DSO he was mentioned in despatches [EG 6 January 1919, issue 13378, page 82].　　S/Ldr　　17.03.45　　Retired list**

FLIGHT LIEUTENANT

	R D OXLAND		AV-M	10.05.46	Retirement

Air Vice-Marshal Robert Dickinson Oxland CB CBE, died on Tuesday, 27th October 1959.

LG 8 October 1920, issue 32078, page 9815. The following officer was appointed with seniority of commission from 1st August 1919.

FLYING OFFICER

05038	ATTWOOD	Charles William	G/Capt	15.05.45	Retirement**

LG 28 October 1919, issue 31620, pages 13138 and 13139

SQUADRON LEADERS
4

	FAITHFULL OBE	George Ferdinand Hay	S/Ldr	15.02.22	Retired list
	LOWE	John Claude Malcolm	W/Cdr	21.02.38	Retired list
	SHEPHERD	Philip Alfred	W/Cdr	24.02.29	Retired list
	WRIGHT	Maurice Edward Arthur	S/Ldr	01.08.28	Relinquished

FLIGHT LIEUTENANTS
41

	AITKEN MC AFC	Robert Stanley	AV-M	20.07.46	Retirement**

Air Vice-Marshal Robert Stanley Aitken CB CBE MC AFC, died on Thursday, 21st January 1982.

02036	ANDREWS DSO MC*	John Oliver	AV-M	17.04.45	Retirement**

Air Vice-Marshal John Oliver Andrews CB DSO MC*, died on Monday, 29th May 1989.

	BAILEY AFC	Lionel Mundy	W/Cdr	01.05.36	Retired list
	BAKER MC	George Brindley Aufrere	AV-M	28.07.46	Retirement**

Air Vice-Marshal George Brindley Aufrere Baker CB CBE MC twice mentioned in despatches, died on Wednesday, 23rd October 1968.

	BILES DFC	George William	G/Capt	24.03.46	Retirement**

By deed poll dated 26th December 1926, abandoned the name George William Biles and adopted the name George William Bentley [LG 12 January 1926, issue 33123, page 339].

	BROWN DSC AFC	Leslie Oswald	AV-M	23.01.49	Retirement**

Air Vice-Marshal Sir Leslie Brown KCB CBE DSC AFC three times mentioned in despatches, died on Wednesday, 28th June 1978.

02085	CHANDLER MBE	Charles Kingsley	G/Capt	10 10 43	Retirement**
	CHAPPELL MC	Roy Williamson	A/Cmdr	29.09.46	Retirement**

Air Commodore Ray Williamson Chappell MC, died on Sunday, 7th February 1982.

	COLYER DFC	Douglas	AM	14.07.46	Retirement**

Air Marshal Douglas Colyer CB CMG DFC mentioned in despatches, died on Thursday, 23rd February 1978.

	CONINGHAM DSO MC	Arthur	AM	07.11.47	Retirement**

Australia Air Marshal Sir Arthur Coningham KCB KBE DSO MC DFC AFC four times mentioned in despatches, died during the night of Thursday-Friday, 29th-30th January 1948, while flying between the United Kingdom via Lisbon to South America. The aircraft in which he was a passenger, Avro Tudor IV G-AHNP *Star Tiger* of British South American Airways departed Santa Maria in the Azores and was lost without trace. Sir Arthur 'Mary' Coningham is best remembered for his drive and expertise when commanding the Western Desert Air Force and his time as commander of the tactical air forces in the Normandy fighting of 1944.

02113	DAY AFC	John Forbes Andre	F/L	03.01.36	Retired list

Returned to service: transferred to Technical Branch in the rank of Flight Lieutenant, effective 24th April 1940 [LG 28 February 1941, issue 35090, page 1209].　　S/Ldr　+　30.10.42　　24 Squadron

Squadron Leader John Forbes Andre Day AFC died in the crash of Hudson III V8983 captained by Flying Officer Raymond Cook which flew into a hillside at Baldwins Wood near Wendover in Buckinghamshire. There were no survivors. Squadron Leader Day is buried in Brookwood Military Cemetery. At the time of his death he was 52 years of age.

02118	DON	David Sigismund	S/Ldr	23.09.31	Retired list

At his own request [LG 22 September 1931, issue 33755, page 6109]. In the New Year's Honours List for 1930, it was announced that Squadron Leader David Sigismund Don was appointed to be a Member of the Fourth Class of the Royal Victorian Order [LG 1 January 1930, supplement 33566, page 6]. Awarded Aviator's Certificate No. 802 by the Royal Aero Club on 2nd June 1914, when ranked Midshipman.

	EVENS	Harold Walter	G/Capt	01.11.44	Retirement**
	FULLER MBE	Norman Berwick	Captain	28.10.19	Cancelled
02148	FULLJAMES MC	Reginald Edgar Gilbert	G/Capt	23.04.45	Retirement**
	GODSAVE	George Elliot	S/Ldr	01.02.35	Retired list

On account of ill-health [LG 5 February 1935, issue 34130, page 846].

02167	GWYER MBE	Percy Edward	S/Ldr	06.05.33	Retired list

Returned to service: resumed service 24th April 1940, and transferred in his rank to the Technical Branch [LG 30 July 1940, issue 34910, page 4677].　　W/Cdr　　30.09.45　　Retired list**

	HOOPER	Frederick James	F/L	04.10.22	Retired list
	JENNINGS MC AFC	Montague Righton Nevill	F/L	28.10.19	Cancelled

82822					

Returned to service: commissioned to Administrative and Special Duties Branch, ranked Pilot Officer, 22nd July 1940 [LG 20 August 1940, supplement 34927, page 5096].　　F/L　　20.07.54　　Relinquished

02198	KEEBLE DSC	Noel	W/Cdr	31.10.45	Retired list**
	LEES	Alan	AM	26.11.49	Retirement**

Air Marshal Sir Alan Lees KCB CBE DSO AFC five times mentioned in despatches, died on Tuesday, 14th August 1973.

	MacKAY MC DFC	Charles Joseph	W/Cdr	+	09.12..30	Staff College Andover

Wing Commander Charles Joseph Mackay MC DFC died from a brain haemorrhage. At the time of his death he was an instructor at the Staff College.

	MACKENZIE	Andrew Ronald	S/Ldr	28.01.35	Retired list
	MAGRATH	Walter Stanley	F/L	+	11.12.23	RAF Amman

Flight Lieutenant Walter Stanley Magrath died from a fractured skull after being thrown from his horse; he is buried in Ramleh War Cemetery.

	MAYNARD AFC	Forster Herbert Martin	AV-M	12.11.45	Retirement**

Air Vice-Marshal Forster Herbert Martin Maynard CB AFC four times mentioned in despatches, died on Monday, 26th January 1976.

	MORGAN MC	Whitworth Archibald Cecil	G/Capt		

Divisional Accident Prevention Organiser, Eastern Division, Royal Society for the Prevention of Accidents [LG 31.12.60, supplement 42231, page 8905]. His MC was gained as a 2nd Lieutenant, formerly of the 2nd Battalion, Welsh Regiment and *Gazetted* 27th July 1916, supplement 29684, page 7440: *'For conspicuous gallantry and skill. With other pilots he attacked an enemy reconnaissance of nine machines. Under heavy machine-gun fire he got within twenty yards of one of them, shot the Observer and brought the machine down in our lines.'*

03005	MULHOLLAND AFC	Denis Osmond	G/Capt	23.07.46	Retired list**
	ORDE	Michael Amyas Julian	F/L +	05.08.20	1 FTS

Flight Lieutenant Michael Amyas Julian Orde died after his Bristol F.2b C4870 spun-in off a tight turn over Netheravon airfield. A second member of crew, Flying Officer Burton Ankers DCM survived, though badly injured. Flight Lieutenant Orde is buried in Beaulieu Cemetery.

	ORLEBAR	Augustus Henry	AV-M +	04.08.43	DC Combined Ops.**

Air Vice-Marshal Augustus Henry Orlebar CB AFC* mentioned in despatches, died on Wednesday, 4th August 1943 in Westminster Hospital after being taken ill in June 1943. In 1929, he held for a while the air speed record and, appropriately in the spring of 1931, he commanded the RAF High Speed Flight. Air Vice-Marshal Orlebar is buried in Podington [St. Mary] Churchyard.

03022	PEARCE OBE	Joseph Laurence Kevin	F/L	14.02.29	Retired list

At his request. He returned to the service in the Second World War, serving until 16th August 1946, when as a Squadron Leader he revetted to the Retired list on account of medical unfitness [LG 27 August 1946, supplement 37700, page 4290].

	ROBERTSON AM	Paul Douglas	G/Capt	31.12.45	Retirement**

Group Captain Paul Douglas Robertson was born in Willesden, Middlesex, on the last day of April 1891, and after seeing many parts of the world joined the RNAS in February 1916, and by early 1918, he held the rank of Acting Flight Commander and was commanding the Hornsea Mere Sub-Station and it was here on 28th February 1918, that he won the Albert Medal [subsequently converted to the George Cross], the circumstances being recorded on the website The Comprehensive Guide to the Victoria & George Cross: *'On 28th February 1918, a seaplane got out of control and spun to the ground. Robertson, the observer, jumped from the machine just before he hit the ground and landed safely, as the ground was marshy. The pilot, Flight Lieutenant H C Lemon, was imprisoned in the seaplane, which, on striking the ground, immediately burst into flames, and notwithstanding that the vicinity of the seaplane was quickly a furnace of burning petrol, and that heavy bombs, a number of rounds of ammunition, and the reserve petrol tank were all likely to explode, Robertson returned and endeavoured to extricate the pilot, and only desisted when he had been so severely burned in the face, hands and leg that his recovery was for some time in doubt. Robertson's injuries were severe enough that he lost an eye in the incident. He was invested with his Albert Medal at Buckingham Palace by King George V on 31st October 1918.'* Following the death of his first wife, he re-married and in 1967, emigrated to New Zealand where he died at the age of 84, on Monday, 4th August 1975. Cremated, his ashes are interred in Purewa Cemetery. Hs medals are now in a private collection following sale by auction by Glendinning's on 10th November 1999. Flight Lieutenant Hubert Charles Lemon whom he valiantly tried to save is buried in Tooting [St. Nicholas] Churchyard; he had been mentioned in despatches.

03044	ROUTH	Eric John Daubeny	W/Cdr	06.10.45	Retired list**
	SAUNDBY MC AFC	Robert Henry Magnus Spencer	AM	22.03.46	Retirement**

Air Marshal Sir Robert Saundby KCB KBE MC DFC AFC four times mentioned in despatches, died on Thursday, 25th September 1971. During the Second World War, which from the end of July 1943, he was Deputy Air Officer Commanding-in-Chief at Bomber Command and right-hand man to Sir Arthur Harris with whom he had served in the early '20s as a flight commander on 45 Squadron.

	SCRIVEN AFC	Victor Reginald	S/Ldr +	05.04.34	HQ Wessex Area

Squadron Leader Victor Reginald Scriven's death was reported in *The Adelaide Mail* probably in remembrance of his time, on loan to the Australian Air Force, during which time he commanded the seaplane carrier *Albatross*. Paul McMillan adds that at the time of his death he was performing engineering duties at HQ Wessex Area. The cause of his passing is not known.

	SHEARER	Ambrose Bernice	F/L	28.10.19	Cancelled

Canada My co-author recording that Flight Lieutenant Ambrose Bernice Shearer was born in Ontario on 8th May 1893, and died in British Columbia on Friday, 5th September 1952.

	SLATER MC* DFC	James Anderson	F/L +	26.11.25	3 Squadron

Flight Lieutenant James Anderson Slater MC* DFC and 20-year old passenger, Pilot Officer Pilot Officer William John Reginald Early, when their dual controlled Sopwith Snipe dived into the ground shortly after taking off from Upavon. His MC was *Gazetted* on 4th February 1918, supplement 30507, page 1606, the award citation being omitted., but I believe this omission was rectified in the Edinburgh edition of 8th July 1918, issue 13285, page 2396: *'For conspicuous gallantry and devotion to duty. When returning from a patrol he attacked enemy infantry, silenced a field gun and fired on transport. On another occasion he silenced a battery in very difficult weather conditions fired on ammunition wagons and enemy infantry, and brought back his patrol safely. He Alsop led a patrol of twelve machines in very bad weather to attack a wood held by the enemy. His patrol dropped over thirty bombs, fired 3,000 rounds and drove the enemy from the wood with heavy casualties. In the course of this flight six enemy scouts were engaged and driven off. Later, he led a similar patrol with great success. He showed splendid courage and determination.'* A First Bar, with citation, was published on 22nd June 1918, supplement 30761, page 7400" *'For conspicuous gallantry and devotion to duty. On one occasion during recent operations he attacked a large formation of hostile scouts, one of which he drove down in flames. Later, during the same flight, he took part in a general engagement, in which he drove down another enemy machine completely out of control. Two days later he attacked two enemy scouts, causing one of them to crash to earth. In eighteen days he has engaged in twenty-five combats at close quarters, shooting down eight hostile machines. His great gallantry and fine offensive spirit have inspired all ranks to a very high degree.'* The citation for his DFC appeared in the London paper, supplement 30827, page 9204: *'This officer has led numerous offensive patrols with the utmost skill and determination, and it is entirely due to his fine leadership that many enemy aircraft have been destroyed with the minimum of casualties to his formation.'* His operational flying commenced with 1 Squadron, during which he was credited with two aerial victories while with 64 Squadron he gained a further twenty-two. Along with Pilot Officer Early he is buried in Upavon [St. Mary the Virgin] Churchyard at Upavon.

	SUMMERS MC	John Kenneth	G/Capt	01.03.43	Retirement**
	THOM DFC	William Dorian	F/L	28.10.19	Cancelled
	THOROLD DSC AFC	Henry Karslake	AV-M	08.09.47	Retirement**
	WALMSLEY MC	John Banks	F/L	28.10.19	Cancelled
05008	Reinstated as Flying Officer.		AM	01.08.52	Retirement**

Air Marshal Sir Hugh Walmseley KCB KCIE CBE MC DFC five times mentioned in despatches, died on Monday, 2nd September 1985.

	WOOLLARD AFC	Felix St. John	F/L +	22.11.26	24 Squadron

Flight Lieutenant Felix St. John Woollard AFC and Flying Officer Frederic Laing Collison perished when their DH.9A J7310 stalled and crashed while taking off from Kenley, bursting into flames on impact with the ground.

FLYING and OBSERVER OFFICERS
43

	ARNISON MC	Charles Henry	F/O	06.10.20	Retired list

Owing to injuries and permitted to retain his rank [LG 5 October 1920, issue 32074, page 9695].

	BEALE DSO	Clive Oliver Bertram	F/O	28.10.19	Cancelled
03141	BILNEY	Christopher Neil Hope	AV-M	27.03.54	Retirement**

Air Vice-Marshal Christopher Neil Hope Bilney CB CBE mentioned in despatches, died on Sunday, 3rd July 1988.

	BLACK	Charles Thomas	F/O	28.10.19	Cancelled
03161	BROADBERRY MC	Edric William	G/Capt	21.12.47	Retirement**
	BROCKMAN	Frank George	G/Capt	25.03.49	Relinquished
	CHICK AFC	Arthur Leslie	F/L	14.05.29	Retired list

At own request [LG 21 May 1929, issue 33497, page 3405].

	CRIPPS	Sydney Trevor Brander	F/L		05.02.29	Retired list
	CULLEN	Ian	S/Ldr		15.10.37	Retired list

Returned to service: Commissioned to the Reserve of Air Force Officers, General Duties Branch, in the rank of Flight Lieutenant [Honorary Squadron Leader] in Class C, 1st April 1938 [LG 16 August 1938, issue 34542, page 5294].

			F/L		01.09.39	Relinquished
03205	DALZELL	William Arthur Kirkpatrick	G/Capt		12.07.45	Retirement**
03224	*DOUGALL DFC	Norman Stewart	F/O		10.01.23	Retired list

Owing to ill-health contracted on active service [LG 9 January 1923, issue 32785, page 225]. Returned to service: Commissioned to the Administrative and Special Duties Branch in the rank of Pilot Officer on 6th March 1940 [LG 26th March 1940, issue 34817, page 1782].

	FINDLAY MC	James Lloyd	Captain		31.08.21	Resigned
04062	HORRY DFC	Thomas Stanley	G/Capt		16.11.44	Retirement**
	JONES	Edward Blake	F/O	+	14.04.21	208 Squadron

See my entry in Appendix E for Flying Officer William Ash Armstrong.

	KING MC DFC	Charles Ley	A/Cmdr		17.-2.44	Retirement**

Air Commodore Charles Ley King MC DFC AFC mentioned in despatches, died on Sunday, 22nd April 1956.

	KINKEAD DSO DFC	Samuel Marcus	F/L	+	12.03.28	RAF High Speed Flight

South Africa Flight Lieutenant Samuel Marcus Kinkead DSO DSC* DFC while carrying out a high-speed flight in Supermarine S.5 N221 flew into the sea off Calshot. Born in Johannesburg on 25th February 1897, Samuel Kinkead had a distinguished operational career in the *Great War* eventually achieving thirty-three confirmed victories. Postwar he added three more aerial victories whilst attached to 47 Squadron supporting the White Russians against the Bolsheviks. In 1927, he joined the High Speed Flight and was in command when he was killed near the Calshot Lightship. His body was recovered and laid to rest in Fawley [All Saints] Churchyard.

	LOYD	Eric Edward Foster	F/O		18.02.20	Resigned
04124	MACKWORTH DFC	Philip Herbert	AV-M		26.09.50	Retirement**

Air Vice-Marshal Philip Herbert Mackworth CB CBE DFC mentioned in despatches, died on Saturday, 30th August 1958.

04128	MASSEY MC	Herbert Martin	A/Cmdr		21.06.50	Retirement**

Prisoner of war 1st-2nd June 1942, after being shot down while flying as second pilot to Flight Lieutenant N E Winch of 7 Squadron in Stirling I N3750 MG-D during operations to Essen. Became Senior British Officer at Stslag-Luft III Sagan until repatriated on medical grounds 22nd May 1944 [see RAFBCL 1942 page 109]. At the time he held the rank of Group Captain. Air Commodore Herbert Martin Massey CB DSO MC three times mentioned in despatches, died on Monday, 29th March 1976.

	McEWEN	Ian Howard Potter	F/O		28.10.19	Cancelled
	*MULLEN	John Wilfrid	F/O		28.10.19	Cancelled
65913						

Returned to service: Commissioned Training Branch as Acting Pilot Officer 1st May 1941 [LG 30 May 1941, issue 35176, page 3109]. Resigned [LG 8 June 1943, supplement 36044, page 2621].

			P/O		11.05.43	Resigned**
04145	NELSON	Hugh	G/Capt		28.05.45	Retirement**
04151	O'DONNELL DFC	Godfrey Cathbar	F/L		07.09.34	Retired list

Paul McMillan has partially traced his Second World War service during which he rose to the rank of Wing Commander [temporary]

	PARK MC DFC	Walter Henry	S/L	+	19.10.28	OC RAF Hawkinge

Squadron Leader Walter Henry Park MC died, following an operation, in Shorncliffe Military Hospital. His MC was *Gazetted* on 22nd June 1918, supplement 30761, page 7420: *'For conspicuous gallantry and devotion to duty. He undertook a long-distance reconnaissance under the most adverse conditions, and though several other machines were compelled to abandon the attempt he by persistence completed his task and returned with valuable information. He is a patrol leader of the highest order, and his consistent gallantry and valuable services cannot be too highly praised.'*

	PARRY	Palmer John	F/O	+	11.02.22	100 Squadron

Flying Officer Palmer John Parry was mortally injured when his Bristol F.2b D7856 crashed shortly after taking off from Baldonnel the previous day, His passenger, Aircraftman James Ernest Harris died in the crash.

	PENNINGTON	George Arthur	F/O		02.06.23	Resigned
	POOLE AFC MM	William Henry	W/Cdr			
	*PORTER	Frederick Grenville	F/O	+	15.06.23	4 FTS
	RANDELL DFC	James Rupert Francis	F/L		03.03.28	Retired list

At own request [LG 6 March 1928, issue 33363, page 1583].

04186	RAPLEY	Cyril	G/Capt		26.01.50	Retirement**

Commissioned to the Royal Air Force Reserve of Officers, Class J, in the rank of Flight Lieutenant 15th January 1951 [LG 20 February1951, supplement 39152, page 917].

			F/L		01.07.51	Relinquished
	ROUGH DFC	Herbert Leonard	S/Ldr		01.08.39	Retired list

At his own request [LG 1 August 1939, issue 34650, page 5324].

	SCHOLEFIELD DCM	Edward Rodolph Clement	F/L		28.08.25	Retired list

At own request [LG 25 August 1925, issue 33078, page 5633].

	SHARP	Harold Hodgson	F/O		07.01.25	Retired list

On account of ill-health [LG 6 January 1925, issue 33009, page 142].

	SHARPE AFC	William	F/O		28.10.19	Cancelled
03227	STEELE DFC	Charles Ronald	AM		26.02.52	Retirement**

Air Marshal Sir Charles Steele KCB DFC mentioned in despatches, died on Wednesday, 14th February 1973.

	STEVENS MC*	Cecil Alfred	AV-M		....11.54	Retirement**

Air Vice-Marshal Cecil Alfred Stevens CB CBE MC* twice mentioned in despatches, died on Sunday, 30th November 1958.

	*TURTON-JONES	John Wyntoun	G/Capt		26.01.46	Retirement**
05001	TYRRELL DFC	Guy Yelverton	G/Capt		07.04.45	Retired list**
05006	WALKER MC DFC	Henry Edward	A/Cmdr		01.03.51	Retirement**

Air Commodore Henry Edward Walker MC DFC, died in 1958.

05008	WALMSLEY MC	Hugh Sydney Porter	AM		01.08.52	Retirement**

Air Marshal Sir Hugh Walmsley KCB KCIE CBE MC DFC five times mentioned in despatches, died on Monday, 2nd September 1985.

	WILLIAMS MC DFC	Frederick	Captain		07.12.21	Retired list

On account of ill health contracted in the Service. It appears, as reported by my co-author, that Frederick Williams MC DFC was serving in Mesopotamia when he contracted severe paralytic poliomyrlitis which led to his discharge. He lived in Devon for the remainder of his life and died from a stroke in Exeter in 1964. He wrote a memoir *Don't Let Them Bag the Nines: the First World War Memoir of a de Havilland Pilot*. It is still available from Amazon.

	WILLIAMS MC	John Jordan Lloyd	F/L		23.06.34	Retired list
05036	WRAY MC AFC	Arthur Mostyn	A/Cmdr		10.05.46	Retirement**

Air Commodore Arthur Mostyn Wray DSO MC DFC* AFC three times mentioned in despatches, died on Tuesday, 6th April 1982.

CAPTAIN

	EMMETT MC DFC	Edwin Cheere	G/Capt		28.03.45	Retired list**
		South Africa				

* Observers

LG 2 December 1919, issue 31669, page 14924

FLIGHT LIEUTENANTS
5

*BRYSON MC DFC AM	Oliver Campbell	G/Capt		15.08.43	Retired list**
*EARP	David Shearman	S/Ldr		05.05.37	Retired list
GRAY MC	Alexander	AV-M		27.03.49	Retirement**

Air Vice-Marshal Alexander Gray CB MC twice mentioned in despatches, died on Friday, 16th May 1980.

MacNAB	John Alexander	F/L		26.10.33	Retired
02242 *MAURICE DFC	Alfred Price	S/Ldr		18.04.37	Retired

Granted the honorary rank of Wing Commander 11th May 1939 [LG 11 July 1939, issue 34644, page 4769].   Retired
Rejoined the service General Duties Branch and promoted Wing Commander 1st May 1940 [LG 12 March 1940, issue 34810, page 1472].

FLYING OFFICERS
12

*BOCKETT-PUGH	Henry Charles Edward	F/O	+	22.09.20	84 Squadron

See summary for the circumstances of his death.

03150 BOUCHIER DFC	Cecil Arthur	AV-M		26.06.49	Retirement**

Air Vice-Marshal Sir Cecil Boucher KBE CB DFC twice mentioned in despatches, died on Friday, 15th June 1979.

04037 HAINES DFC	Harold Alfred	A/Cmdr		17.07.48	Retirement**

Air Commodore Harold Alfred Haines CBE DFC, died on 26th June 1955.

*HILTON	Louis Massey	F/L		22.04.31	Retired list

At own request [LG 21 April 1931, issue 33709, page 2580].

HOOTTON MC	Lionel Conrad	F/O	+	16.05.22	6 Squadron

He is buried Ma'asker Al Raschid RAF Cemetery.

04101 *LANG	Albert Frank	AV-M		28.05.46	Retirement**

Air Vice-Marshal Albert Frank Lang CB MBE AFC, died on Monday, 20th June1977.

JERRARD VC	Alan	F/L		24.08.33	Retired list

On account of ill-health [LG 29 August 1933, issue 33973, page 5668].
LG 1 May 1918, issue 30663, page 5287: *'When on an offensive patrol with two other officers he attacked five enemy aeroplanes and shot one down in flames, following it down to within one hundred feet of the ground. He then attacked an enemy aerodrome from a height of only fifty feet from the ground, and, engaging single-handed some nineteen machines, which were either landing or attempting to take off, succeeded in destroying one of them, which crashed on the aerodrome. A large number of machines then attacked him, and while thus fully occupied he observed that one of the pilots of his patrol was in difficulties. He went immediately to his assistance, regardless of his own personal safety, and destroyed a third enemy machine. Fresh enemy aeroplanes continued to rise from the aerodrome, which he attacked one after another, and only retreated, still engaged with five enemy machines, when ordered to do so by his patrol leader. Although apparently wounded, this very gallant officer turned repeatedly, and attacked single-handed the pursuing machines, until he was eventually overwhelmed by numbers and driven to the ground. Lt. Jerrard had greatly distinguished himself on four previous occasions, within a period of twenty-three days, in destroying enemy machines, displaying bravery and ability of the highest order."*

04127 MASON DSC DFC	John Melbourne	A/Cmdr		13.05.46	Retirement**

Air Commodore John Melbourne Mason CBE DSC DFC four times mentioned in despatches, died on Sunday, 17th September 1950.

RANDALL DFC	George Ebben	F/L		22.11.22	Resigned
TREVETHAN MC	Richard Michael	S/Ldr		03.07.34	Half-pay
*VAN der BYL South Africa	Albert Lawrence Montague	F/O		09.09.19	Cancelled
WAUCHOPE	Charles Lancelot	F/O		28.02.20	Relinquished

On return to army duty with the `Northamptonshire Regiment. Paul McMillan adds that he retired, with a gratuity on 11th June 1921, departing the United Kingdom for South Africa on 22nd July 1921. Subsequently, he moved to Rhodesia from where on 6th October 1922, he applied to the Royal Aero Club on the subject of medals.

* Subject to proving their medical fitness; seniority backdated to the 1st of August 1919

Addendum to the appendix. 1st August 1919, section concerning Majors, second page headed E L Gossage, 17th entry Group Captain Thomas Gerard Hetherington CBE was placed on the retired list on the last day of March 1935, on account of ill-health [LG 2 April 1935, issue 34147, page 2237]. I can only assume his health improved and at some point re-joined the service.

LG 7 January 1921, issue 32185, page 184, the following officer is appointed to a permanent commission with seniority as at 1st August 1919.

FLYIMG OFFICER

BOWEN	George	F/L	14.02.32	Retired list

** Indicates active service in both World Wars.

Appendix 2E - Short Service Commissions

A significant number of the officers here named had their commission amended to permanent but rather than transfer their details to Appendix D, I have left them in situ, placing an asterisk ahead of their surname. Service numbers, where reported, have been appended, but a note of caution. It is not unknown for instances of duplication; for example, Gilbert Latham Ormerod was allocated 08230 as was Flying Officer Frank Wright CBE, though in most cases duplication occurred within other arms of the military. Again, I pay tribute to my co-author, Paul McMillan, for his input regarding this appendix. Also to be observed the many final service dates reported in 1954, in practically every case the officer concerned had served during the Second World War and remained thereafter in the service until relinquishing his commission under the provisions of the Navy, Army and Air Force Reserve Act of 1954. An example of this procedure being Flying Officer Arthur Cecil Haywood Groom DFC named below.

LG 12 September 1919, issue 31548, pages 11468, 11469 and 11470

SQUADRON LEADERS
3

MEYER	Thomas Bernard		S/L	17.06.35	Relinquished
SOWREY AFC	William		A/Cmdr	21.09.42	Retirement**

Air Commodore William Sowery CBE DFC AFC twice mentioned in despatches, died on Thursday 15th February 1968.

*WILLOCK	Robert Peel		AV-M	02.08.46	Retirement**

Air Vice-Marshal Robert Peel Willock CB, died on Thursday, 22nd March 1973.

FLIGHT LIEUTENANTS
32

06025	BARNABY	Hazen Ottis		F/L	14.06.31	Relinquished

TNA Kew has a document for this officer under AIR 76/23/3.

	BELFIELD	Arthur Geoffrey Nevill		W/Cdr	11.03.36	Retired list

At his own request [LG 17 March 1936, issue 34265, page 1743].

	BURLING DSC DFC Edward James Poynter			G/Capt	22.01.42	Retirement**
Re-employed				G/Capt	27.05.46	Retired list**
06039	*CLAPPEN	Donald William		A/Cmdr	23.06.49	Retirement**

Air Commodore Donald William Clappen CB, died on Saturday, 30th November 1978.

	COX	Henry		F/L	24.04.20	Resigned
	EDGAR	Herbert James		F/L	01.07.25	Retired list

At his own request [LG 30 June 1925, issue 33062, page 4370].

10179	ETHERIDGE	Harold Gaul		S/Ldr	12.09.30	Relinquished

A document for this officer is held by TNA Kew under AIR 76/152/223.

	*FELLOWES	Henry Owen		F/O	18.12.29	Cashiered

Stationed at RAF Training Base, Leuchars, Fife in Scotland, he was declared bankrupt [LG 30 August 1929, issue 33530, page 5690].

	FERRIS-SCOTT	Leycester Percy		F/L	12.09.19	Cancelled
87206	GROOM DFC	Arthur Cecil Haywood		F/O	09.07.54	Relinquished
06072	HETHERINGTON MBE Charles Goldby			F/L	22.01.29	Relinquished

A document for this officer is held by TNA Kew under AIR 76/224/4.

	HUDSON MC	Frank Neville		F/L	+	06.06.22	6 Squadron

Flight Lieutenant Frank Neville Hudson MC was critically injured when his Bristol F.2b D7844 crashed while attempting to land with engine failure at Suleimaniyeh in Iraq, on 31st May 1922, lingering until Tuesday, 6th June. His passenger, Flight Lieutenant Ernest Drudge MBE was injured. Buried in the RAF Cemetery at Ma'asker Al Raschid on the outskirts of Baghdad, Flight Lieutenant Hudson's *Great War* service was first with XV Squadron, winning the MC which was *Gazetted* on 30th March 1916, supplement 29528, page 3429: *'For conspicuous gallantry and skill on several occasions, notably when, although severely wounded in the head, he successfully completed his aerial reconnaissance. After recrossing the line and landing at an aerodrome, he at once lost consciousness. This young officer is only 18 years of age, but has many times driven off enemy machines and twice forced them to the ground.'* Army Form B.103 indicates he was struck by shrapnel on 29th February 1916, and was taken to the 7th Stationary Hospital, and thence to England on 5th March aboard HMHS *St. David*. Recovered, he joined 54 Squadron at Leffrinckhoucke on 17th July 1916 and was shot down a year later on 15th July 1917, while on a special reconnaissance in Sopwith Pup A6240. As a prisoner he was held at Karlsruhe.

	*JOHNSON AFC	Eric Digby		A/Cmdr	21.04.44	Retirement**

Air Commodore Eric Digby Johnson AFC three times mentioned in despatches, died on Saturday, 16th January 1971.

	KEEBLE DSC	Noël		F/L	04.08.34	Retired list
	*KEMP AFC	Walter Horace Ernest		F/L	+	11.04.24	84 Squadron

Flight Lieutenant Walter Horace Ernest Kemp lost his life along with his passenger Aircraftman Arthur Lee Adams when their DH.9A J552 stalled on take off from Jalibah. On its arrival in the Middle East J552, fitted with dual controls, was issued to 8 Squadron but may well have reverted to a standard DH.9A during a rebuild at the Aircraft Depot Hinaidi between October and December 1923. His short service commission was converted to that of a permanent commission, with effect from 12th September 1919 [LG 7 January 1921, issue 32185, page 184].

06090	KING	Dudley Warr		F/L	12.09.36	To Class C
Returned for service in the Equipment Branch.				W/Cdr	05.08.45	Resigned**
	*LUCKING	David Frederick		G/Capt	14.12.45	Retirement**
	McDOUGALD	Leslie Alfred		Captain	25.12.20	Relinquished

On account of ill-health contracted on active service [LG 24 December 1920, issue 32173, page 12602].

	*MESSENGER	Alfred Lewis		F/L	+	04.10.22	45 Squadron

Please refer to Appendix D and the entry for Flight Lieutenant Robert Charles Lyon Holme.

	*MURRAY	Charles Geoffrey		G/Capt	01.11.42	Retirement**
06110	OAKEY	Wesley Howard		F/L	12.09.30	Relinquished

TNA Kew holds a document for this officer under AIR 76/378/18.

11063	*OSBORNE	Richard Francis		A/Cmdr	28.04.47	Retirement**

Air Commodore Richard Francis Osborne died on Wednesday, 13th December 1950, at the comparatively early age of 60; he was undecorated.

	PYNCHES	Thomas Lé Gee		F/L	31.08.28	Relinquished

On account of ill-health [LG 7 September 1928, issue 33419, page 5898].

REA AFC	Cecil Arthur	S/Ldr		23.01.38	Resigned
15142 RICHARDSON	Gurth Alwyn	F/O	+	10.10.20	RAF Wireless Section

Flying Officer Gurth Alwyn Richardson was born on the 5th of June 1890, and following enlistment in the *Great War* was commissioned as a temporary Sub-Lieutenant RNAS specialising in wireless telegraphy. Subsequently, he was attached to No. 1 Wing RNAS at Dunkirk and while on aerial patrol in Sopwith 1 ½ Strutter N5154 of 2 Squadron RNAS [piloted by Flight Sub-Lieutenant N Von L Tapscott] as an observer on 12th May 1917, his aircraft forced-landed in neutral Holland where the crew were interned. Gurth Richardson was repatriated on 8th September 1918, and as indicated was granted a short service commission. By 1920, he was serving in Northern Ireland overseeing the erection of wireless aerials and telephone stations. On the 9th of October, he was part of a military patrol which following an inspection of a public house in the village of Newceston the patrol, consisting of two Crossley cars, one of which was being driven by Flight Lieutenant Richardson, came under attack during which he was shot in the head and mortally wounded. Returned to his home city of Norwich, he was buried with full military honours, the cortegé preceded by a band from the Hampshire Regiment and attended by officers, including Squadron Leader Arthur Tedder, from the airship station at Pulham. A detailed account of the ambush and its consequences can be found on the website The Irish Revolution and similar sites.

*ROBERTSON	James Leask	G/Capt		02.04.42	Retired list**
SIDDONS-WILSON	Albert Edgar	F/L		12.09.19	Cancelled
SPIERS	Alexander Donaldson	S/Ldr		09.06.20	Resigned
*VINCENT	Francis John	F/L		12.09.19	Cancelled

Subsequently, he returned to the service and was appointed to a permanent commission.   A/Cmdr   08.02.46   Retirement**
Air Commodore Francis John Vincent CBE DFC twice mentioned in despatches, died on Sunday, 15th October 1967.

*WALDRON	Ernest Noel Edward	S/Ldr		13.12.34	Retired list

On account of ill-health [LG 18 December 1934, issue 34115, page 8207].

WILLIAMS MC	Trevor Lotherington	F/L		12.09.19	Cancelled
WORRALL DSC	Henry Vernon	F/L		12.09.26	Relinquished

FLYING OFFICERS [from FLIGHT LIEUTENANTS]
2

HEMMING DSC	Geoffrey Wilson	F/L	+	26.02.26	480 Flight Calshot

Geoffrey Wilson Hemming DSC was killed shortly after taking off from Calshot in a Fairey IIID of 480 Flight [airframe serial not reported]. His passenger, Flying Officer Robert Collins died two days later from his injuries. A detailed report of the crash appeared the following day in *The Times* which read: '*Flight-Lieutenant Hemming DSC, who lived at The Grove, Fawley, Hampshire, lost his life yesterday afternoon in a seaplane accident at Calshot. He was accompanied in the machine by Flying-Officer Robert Collins, who was seriously injured and taken to Haslar Hospital. The machine was a Fairey seaplane. The machine had just taken off from the water and, on reaching a height of 100ft suddenly banked, and the next moment nosedived, crashing to the ground between the slipway and the hangars. The officers were taken immediately to the sick bay at Calshot, but Mr. Hemming lived only a few moments. Mr. Collins, in addition to the head, received a fractured arm and a compound fracture of the leg. Mr. Collins had a narrow escape from death last August, when, following night flying in connection with the naval manoeuvres, his machine [Felixstowe F.5 N4039 of 480 Flight captained by Flight Lieutenant Norbert Marie Sackville Russell which came down in the water on 16th August 1925] crashed near Calshot and became a mass of flames. On that occasion the wireless operator lost his life, and Mr. Collins was rescued in a semi-conscious condition as the flames were leaping about him.*'

08095 *SAVERY DFC	Robert Churton	F/L		31.10.37	Retired list

On 29th November 1937, Flight Lieutenant Robert Churton Savery was granted a commission in Class C [LG 11 January 1938, issue 344572, page 195, amended on 7th May 1938, by transfer from Class C to Class CC [LG 15 November 1938, issue 34570, page 7198]. Subsequently, he reverted to the Retired list, retaining the rank of Squadron Leader, on 27th July 1945.

FLYING OFFICERS
208

06175 ADAMSON	Bertie Charles	F/L		12.09.30	Relinquished
13054 ADKINS	Hubert John	F/L		27.05.33	Retired list

Granted a commission in the Reserve of Air Force Officers as Flight Lieutenant Class C, 7th October 1935 [LG 28 April 1936, issue 34278, page 2700].   W/Cdr   28.03.45   Resigned**

10189 ALGER	Henry Sewell	F/L		12.09.27	Relinquished

A document pertaining to Flight Lieutenant Henry Sewell Alger is held by TNA Kew under AIR 76/4/215.

10213 ALLAN	Alexander Henry	F/O		12.09.19	Cancelled

Reappointed as Flying Officer to the Stores Branch on 17th June 1920 [LG 17 June 1921, issue 32360, page 4826]. He died from natural causes on Sunday, 20th October 1940, and is buried in the extension to Torquay Cemetery.   W/Cdr   +   20.10.40   2 Sig. School Yatesbury

06178 ALLEN	Ralph Eric Herbert	F/L		12.09.32	To Class C

Flight Lieutenant Ralph Eric Herbert Allen was fatally injured after being struck by a motor-van in Parliament Street. At the time of his death, which was reported in the *Western Daily Press*, he was employed by Scotland Yard as Assistant Mechanical Engineer. A brief biography of this officer can be found on the website Grace's Guide to British Industrial History. As will be noted, he was still in the Reserve.

*ALLEN	William Richard Percy	S/Ldr		10.10.32	Retired list
AMOORE	Charles Edward	Captain		30.10.20	Resigned
*ANDREWARTHA	Ernest Victor Emerson	F/O	+	15.05.34	Home Establishment

Returning from Iraq, where he had been serving as a stores officer at the Aircraft Depot, in April 1933, Flying Officer Ernest Victor Emerson Andrewartha fell serious ill and was diagnosed as suffering from cancer. Subsequently admitted to a specialist cancer hospital in Chelsea, he passed away on Tuesday,15th May 1934.

06195 AYSCOUGH	Frederick John Harvey	F/O		12.09.26	Relinquished

A document for this officer is held by TNA Kew under AIR 76/15/224.

BAKER	Alfred Henry	F/O		01.10.32	Retired list
10177 BAKER	Edward Savery	F/L	+	30.08.24	To Class C

While still in the Reserve, Flight Lieutenant Edward Savery Baker died on Friday, New Year's Day 1926.

*BAKER	George	F/L		12.12.31	Retired list

My co-author, however, identifies Flight Lieutenant George Baker as becoming a stores officer with the Auxiliary Air Force and, subsequently, was commissioned, with effect from 1st February 1933, in his rank to 601[County of London] [Bomber] Squadron. Resigning his commission in 1939, at which point he was granted a commission in Class CC of the Reserve of Air Force Officers, 13th March 1939, but relinquished his Class CC commission on 1st September 1939, on transfer to the Royal Air Force Volunteer Reserve and a commission in the Administrative and Special Duties Branch. He is known to have been promoted Squadron Leader and served until at least July 1945.

10220 *BAMBER	Harry John	F/O		01.08.29	Retired list

At own request [LG 13 August 1929, issue 33525, page 5279]. Returned to service: Commissioned Equipment Branch and promoted Flight Lieutenant 1st September 1940 [LG 20 September 1940, issue 34949, page 5584].   F/L   +   09.05.41   Harlington Cemetery

06202 BARNARD	Alfred Hawgood	F/O		07.08.29	To Class C

A document for this officer can be accessed at TNA Kew under AIR 76/23/10.

BARNARD	Franklyn Leslie	F/O		12.12.19	Cancelled

Note. Granted a commission in the Reserve of Air Force Officers on 28th December 1923, Franklyn Leslie Barnard was killed on 28th July 1927, during a test flight of Bristol 99A Badmington G-EBMK in preparation for the forthcoming King's Cup Air Race. At the time of his death, Franklin was chief pilot of Imperial Airways. It is believed the crash occurred shortly after taking off from Filton Aerodrome, Bristol. From eyewitness reports the engine appeared to fail at 200 feet and while gliding down to forced-land the aircraft stalled in a turn at approximately eighty feet after which it dived into the ground. ASN Wikibase Occurrence report 56867. A document for Flying Officer Barnard is held at TNA Kew under AIR 76/23/19.

No.	Surname	Forename(s)	Rank		Date	Status
06206	BASEDEN	Maurice William	F/O		12.09.26	Relinquished

A document for this officer is held by TNA Kew under AIR 76/26/140.

No.	Surname	Forename(s)	Rank		Date	Status
	BELL	James William	F/L		01.01.36	Retired list

At his own request [LG 31 December 1935, issue 34237, page 8408].

No.	Surname	Forename(s)	Rank		Date	Status
11162	*BENNETT	Vyvian George Anthony	G/Capt		23.09.54	Retirement**
10068	*BERRY	Alfred Sidney	F/L		10.12.31	Retired list
10190	BINGHAM	Samuel	S/Ldr	+	13.12.39	

Died in hospital from natural causes. Squadron Leader Samuel Bingham is buried in Egypt in Alexandria [Chatby] Military and War Memorial Cemetery. He was 47 years of age and married to Martha McBlain McIntosh Bingham of Bedford.

No.	Surname	Forename(s)	Rank		Date	Status
06219	*BIRD	Thomas George	G/Capt		07.04.50	Retirement**
	BIRTLES	Henry James	Lieutenant		11.04.21	Resigned
06222	BITTLES	George Henry	Lieutenant		11.04.21	Resigned

A document for this officer is held at TNA Kew under AIR 76/40/182.

No.	Surname	Forename(s)	Rank		Date	Status
06225	BLAKE	Gilbert Lawrence	W/Cdr		10.02.54	Relinquished
10025	*BRIDGES	Herbert Peggford	Captain		01.01.22	Resigned

A document for this officer is held by TNA Kew under AIR 76/54/134.

No.	Surname	Forename(s)	Rank		Date	Status
08239	BRIE	Reginald Alfred Charles	W/Cdr		10.09.52	Retirement
	BRIGHT	Reginald Harry	F/O		12.09.19	Cancelled
03162	BROCKMAN	Frank George	G/Capt		25.03.49	Relinquished
	*BROOMFIELD DFC	Albert James Ernest	F/L		29.10.30	Retired list

At his own request [LG 28 October 1930].

No.	Surname	Forename(s)	Rank		Date	Status
	*BROWN MM	Hilton Oscar	F/L		09.06.26	Retired list

On account of ill-health [LG 8 June 1926, issue 33170, page 3755].

No.	Surname	Forename(s)	Rank		Date	Status
06238	BROWN	Lee Roy Lowerison	W/Cdr		15.01.46	Resigned**
	BRUCE	Edward Roy	F/O		12.09.19	Cancelled
06241	BRYANT	Rupert Chandos	F/L		12.09.26	To Class B

Granted a commission in Class CC as Flight Lieutenant 4th November 1938 [LG 24 January 1939, issue 34592, page 547].
On account of ill-health [LG 28 November 1944, supplement 36814, page 5450].

No.	Surname	Forename(s)	Rank		Date	Status
			S/Ldr		01.09.44	Relinquished
	BURMANN	Alexander Henry	F/O		12.09.19	Cancelled
	CARD	John Stephen	F/O		12.09.26	Relinquished
	CARDWELL	Fred	P/O	+	25.10.19	HMS *Vindictive*

Shot down Krasnaya Gorka, Petrograd Bay, Russia. Aircraft type not identified. He is commemorated on the Archangel Memorial.

No.	Surname	Forename(s)	Rank		Date	Status
07003	CAREY	Denis Holcombe	W/Cdr		25.07.43	Retired list

At his own request [LG 31 August 1943, supplement 36152, page 3871].

No.	Surname	Forename(s)	Rank		Date	Status
11009	CARTWRIGHT	Harry	F/L		03.02.33	Retired list

Granted a commission 19th May 1938, in Class CC of the Equipment Branch in existing rank [LG 13 December 1938, issue 34579, page 7922].

No.	Surname	Forename(s)	Rank		Date	Status
	CHAPMAN	William	Captain		18.08.20	Resigned
10221	*CLEASBY	William Joseph	W/Cdr		31.05.45	Retired list**
	COURTENAY-DUNN	Adrian Lancelot	F/O	+	19.03.20	99 Squadron

See summary for an account of his death.

No.	Surname	Forename(s)	Rank		Date	Status
10244	*CURTIS	George Arthur	W/Cdr		29.08.44	Retired list**
11027	DAINTY	Norman	F/L		16.05.32	Retired list

Returned to service: Commissioned to the Equipment Branch ranked Squadron Leader with effect from 1st June 1940 [LG 7t June 1940, issue 34866, page 3438].

No.	Surname	Forename(s)	Rank		Date	Status
10080	*DALE	John Henry	S/Ldr		05.08.35	Retired list

Returned to the service: Commissioned to the Equipment Branch in the rank of Wing Commander with effect from 1st December 1940 LG 10th December 1940, issue 35010, page 6984].

No.	Surname	Forename(s)	Rank		Date	Status
			W/Cdr		16.02.45	Retired list**
	DAMPIER	Ernest Patrick	Captain		23.12.22	Retired list

Owing to ill-health [LG 22 December 1922, issue 32779, page 9044]. Returned to service: Commissioned to the Stores Branch in the rank of Flight Lieutenant with effect from 18th May 1936 [LG 22nd September 1936, issue 34325, page 6080].

No.	Surname	Forename(s)	Rank		Date	Status
			F/L		06.05.40	Relinquished
	DAY	Henry Brunner	F/O		12.09.19	Cancelled
11010	DENMAN	James Lemoine	F/L		27.09.31	Retired liat

Returned to service: Commissioned to the Equipment Branch in the rank of Squadron Leader with effect from 1st June 1940 [LG 7th June 1940, issue 34866, page 3437].

No.	Surname	Forename(s)	Rank		Date	Status
	de PENCIER	John Dartnell	F/O	+	17.05.20	12 Squadron

Canada See summary which explains the cause of his death.

No.	Surname	Forename(s)	Rank		Date	Status
	de WAAL	Hubert John	F/O		12.09.26	Relinquished

My co-author, Paul McMillan, reports that Flight Lieutenant [Rtd] Hubert John de Waal died in Perth, Australia, on Saturday, 15th March 1941.

No.	Surname	Forename(s)	Rank		Date	Status
13153	DICKISON DFM	William	F/O		12.09.19	Cancelled

Re-employed; date not known. Promoted Flight Lieutenant 1st July 1930 [LG 1 July 1930, issue 33621, page 4113]. Promoted Squadron Leader he was transferred from the General Duties Branch to the Technical Branch 24th April 1940 [LG 20 December 1940, issue 35019 20th December 1940].

No.	Surname	Forename(s)	Rank		Date	Status
			W/Cdr		27.12.44	Retired list**
	DICKSON	Denys Newson	F/O	+	23.03.22	6 FTS Manston

Flying Officer Denys Newson Dickson overshot his approach to Manston in DH.10A E5497, and while banking to go round again stalled and crashed to the ground. Amazingly, his passenger, Leading Aircraftman Joseph McCausland suffered no more than a bad shaking from the accident.

No.	Surname	Forename(s)	Rank		Date	Status
	*DROWLEY	Thomas Edward	AV-M		29.09.49	Retirement**

Air-Vice Marshal Thomas Edward Drowley CBE, died on Saturday, 2nd March 1985.

No.	Surname	Forename(s)	Rank		Date	Status
	DUFF	William Ferguson	F/O		12.09.19	Cancelled
	*DUFFIELD	Edwin Ivan Thomas	F/L		31.01.33	Retired list

Placed on the retired list [LG 31 January 1933, issue 33907, page 676].

No.	Surname	Forename(s)	Rank		Date	Status
			F/L		31.01.33	Retired list
	DUNLOP	Frederick	F/O		11.05.20	Relinquished

On account of ill-health contracted on active service [LG 11 May 1920, issue 31894, page 5362].

No.	Surname	Forename(s)	Rank		Date	Status
	EATON	Charles	F/O		23.07.20	Resigned
	EDGAR	Ian Grant Gibson	F/O		26.09.31	Relinquished
10087	*ELLIOTT	Christopher John	F/L		03.02.34	Retired list

Granted a commission in the rank of Flight Lieutenant in Class C with effect from 27th January 1937 [LG 12 March 1937, issue 34379, page 1646].

Returned to service: Commissioned in the Equipment Branch in the rank of Squadron Leader with effect from 1st June 1940 [LG 7th June 1940, issue 34866, page 3438].

No.	Surname	Forename(s)	Rank		Date	Status
			S/Ldr		28.02.45	Retired list**
	*FAIRBAIRN	William Ross	F/L		25.11.25	Resigned
10245	*FARLEY	William Charles	W/Cdr	+	09.05.41	16 MU Stafford

Wing Commander William Charles Farley, having his short service commission amended to that of a permanent officer, effective from 12th September 1919, was killed during a *Luftwaffe* raid on Friday, 9th May 1941. He is buried in Burwash [St. Bartholomew] Churchyard.

| | FENN | Charles | F/L | | 28.04.30 | Relinquished |

Returned to the service in the Second World War and was granted a commission in Class CC on 29th July 1940, retaining his rank.

| | FENWICK | Horace Edgar | F/O | + | 04.11.20 | 24 Squadron |

See summary for information regarding his death in a flying accident.

| | FINCH | Albert Ernest Wilford | F/O | | 12.09.26 | Relinquished |
| | FLETCHER | Henry Douglas | F/O | | 12.09.30 | Relinquished |

Transferred from the General Duties Branch to the Stores Branch on 15th July 1922 [LG 19 September 1922, issue 32748, page 6715].

| 07089 | *FLINN | Charles Henry | A/Cmdr | | 19.06.50 | Retirement** |

Air Commodore Charles Henry Flinn CBE mentioned in despatches, died in December 1978.

| | FRANCIS | William Bertie | F/O | | 12.09.30 | Relinquished |
| | *FREEMAN- | John | F/L | + | 27.11.31 | 6 Squadron |

FOWLER At the time of his death from septicaemia Flight Lieutenant John Freeman-Folwler was serving as the Stores Officer attached to 6 Squadron. He is buried in Ismailia War Memorial Cemetery.

| | FYFIELD | Albert John | F/O | + | 29.04.20 | Felixstowe |

Killed when the Felixstowe F.5 flying boat in which he was flying crashed [see summary for details].   Churchyard

| | *GAGE | John Woodward | F/L | | 31.12.21 | Retired list |

On account of ill-health [LG 30 December 1921, issue 32561, page 10656].

07098	*GEMMEL	Henry James	G/Capt		02.02.47	Retirement**
	GIBSON	Gordon Alfred Frederick	F/O		03.12.19	Unemployed
	GODFREY	Reginald William	F/O		30.10.20	Resigned
	*GOLDSWORTHY	William Alfred George	F/O		06.08.31	Retired list

At his own request [LG 18 August 1931, supplement 33745, page 5402].

| | GOODALL | MacDonald | F/O | | 12.09.36 | Relinquished |
| | *GREIG | D'Arcy David Alexander | A/Cmdr | | 23.11.46 | Retirement** |

Air Commodore D'Arcy David Alexander Greig DFC AFC, died in July 1986.

| | *GREY | Trevlyn Lionel | F/O | | 09.06.26 | Retired list |

On account of ill-health [LG 8 June 1926, issue 3170, page 3756].

	GRIMSHAW	Albert	F/O		12.09.19	Cancelled
	HAMMOND	John Edward Clancy	F/O		20.06.20	Resigned
07136	HARVEY	Leslie Gordon	AM		14.02.56	Retirement**

Air Marshal Sir Leslie Harvey KBE CB mentioned in despatches, died on Saturday, 14th October 1972.

| 13089 | HAYNES | Richard John Efford | W/Cdr | | 27.07.44 | Relinquished |

On ceasing to be employed; retaining the rank of Wing Commander [LG 1 August 1944, supplement 36633, page 3562].

	HAYWOOD-	Harold Charles	F/O		12.09.30	Relinquished
	GIBBONS					
	HIGGS	Thomas Arthur	F/O		14.09.23	Relinquished

On account of ill-health [LG 25 September 1923, issue 32865, page 6429]. Subject of a Receiving Orders under the Bankruptcy Act 1914, [EG 17 June 1924, issue 14032, page 835].

07162	HORREX	Charles Edwin	G/Capt		27.07.46	Retirement**
	HOWARTH	George Harry	F/O		04.05.20	Relinquished
	HOWELL	William Harold	F/O		16.01.24	Relinquished

On account of ill-health [at the time Flying Officer William Harold Howell was in Class A of the Reserve].

	HOWSAM MC	George Roberts	F/O		09.05.21	Resigned
	HUSBAND	Ernest Wilfrid	F/O		12.09.30	Relinquished
13091	HUTCHINS	John William	W/Cdr		14.12.44	Retirement**
11050	*IRONMONGER	John Joseph	G/Capt		17.06.43	Retired list**
04075	*JARVIS	Arthur Gordon	F/L		10.06.29	Retired list

Granted a commission in Class CC 13th July 1938. Thence to General Duties Branch.   G/Capt   10.02.54   Relinquished

| | *JENNINGS | James Henry | F/L | | 12.09.27 | Relinquished |
| 10222 | *JOLLEY | Thomas Henry | F/L | | 25.05.34 | Retired list |

On the 4th June 1934, Flight Lieutenant [Retd] Thomas Henry Jolley was appointed MBE and by the summer of 1940, he had returned to the service and was promoted Squadron Leader in the Equipment Branch [LG 7 June 1940, issue 34866, page 3437]. W/Cdr 31.07.43   Retired list
At his own request [LG 14 September 1943, supplement 36170, page 4081].

| | KANN | Raymond Victor | F/O | | 12.09.19 | Cancelled |
| | KELLY | Edward Caulfield | Lieutenant | | 18.02.20 | Resigned |

Born in Ireland on 23rd February 1896, Edward Caulfield Kelly first served with the Royal Dublin Fusiliers before transferring to the General List on 21st May 1917, though he was already operational as an observer with 45 Squadron and with his pilot assisted in the destruction of five hostile aircraft between the 9th and 28th May 1917, being wounded in the thigh while securing their fifth success, his pilot 2nd Lieutenant W A Wright landing the Sopwith Strutter A8269 safely. After leaving the Royal Air Force he moved, by 1926, to New Guinea and by the time of Japan entering the war he was employed as an Agricultural Inspector at Kavieng in New Ireland. Interned, initially, as a civilian prisoner at Rabaul he was selected with others for forced-labour and was embarked on the SS *Montevideo Maru* bound for Hainan when it was torpedoed on 1st July 1942.

| | KING | Ernest George | F/O | | 22.11.26 | Relinquished |
| | KINGSTON | Edward Colston Kenyon | F/O | | 28.01.25 | Relinquished |

On account of ill-health [LG 27 January 1925, issue 3015, page 596].

	KIRK DCM	Harry Ernest	F/O		12.09.30	Relinquished
11039	KNIGHT MBE	Alfred George	G/Capt		27.05.46	Retirement**
	KNIGHT	Charles Edwin	F/O		22.01.21	Resigned
	KYTE	William Alfred	F/O		12.09.30	Relinquished
07201	*LANGFORD-	Thomas Audley	AV-M		15.05.49	Retirement**
	SAINSBURY AFC					

Air Vice-Marshal Thomas Audley Langford-Sainsbury CB OBE DFC AFC** mentioned in despatches, died on Wednesday, 21st June 1972.

	LINGHAM DFC	George Alexander	F/O		12.09.19	Cancelled
	LEE-BARBER	George Welham	F/O		12.09.19	Cancelled
	*LINSSEN	Sydney Glanvill	F/L		24.11.26	Retired list

On account of ill-health. As Paul McMillan has discovered, Flight Lieutenant Sydney [sometimes spelt Sidney] Glanvill Linssen was removed from the Retired list on, he suspects, account of being declared bankrupt. The notification refers to him being a Captain in His Majesty's army.

11155	LOBLEY	Arthur Cecil	W/Cdr	25.07.45	Retirement**

Canada On account of medical unfitness for Air Force service.

	*LONGHURST	Claud Arthur	F/O	19.06.20	Relinquished

Owing to ill-health contracted on active service [LG 18 June 1920, issue 31946, page 6703]. His commission had been made permanent.

	LUCAS	Herbert James	F/O	21.01.29	Relinquished
	*MAHONEY	John	F/O	01.08.25	Retired list
	MAILLARD	George Clement	F/O	22.01.21	Resigned
	MARSHALL DFC	Keith Douglas	Lieutenant	27.11.20	Relinquished

On account of ill-health caused by wounds contracted on in the Service.

	MARTIN	Albert James	F/O	12.09.30	Relinquished
10118	*McCARTHY	John	F/L	14.11.31	Retired list

Returned to the service until reverting to the Retired list.

			S/Ldr	16.05.44	Retired list**
	McCONNACHIE	William Whitefield	F/L	12.09.30	Relinquished
	McDONALD	Hugh Crichton	F/O	12.09.24	To Class A

Killed 5th May 1925, in a flying accident during annual training at Brough, Yorkshire, when the Blackburn Kangaroo G-EAIT crashed shortly after becoming airborne. The aircraft belonged to North Sea Aerial & General Transport Limited based at Brough. Prior to its civilian registration it carried the serial B9978 of the Royal Air Force. Two unnamed passengers escaped with their lives.

	MILES	John Lambert	F/O	12.09.34	Relinquished
	MILNER	John William	F/O	12.09.19	Cancelled
	MULLETTE	Robert George	F/O	12.09.33	To Class C
	NEWPORT	Sydney George	F/O	12.09.32	Relinquished
	NICHOLL	Harry Wynne	F/O	12.09.30	Relinquished
08015	NOLAN	Martin William	F/O	28.01.25	Retired list

On account of ill-health [LG 27 January 1925, issue 33015, page 595]. His health recovered and on 3rd December 1940, he was granted war substantive rank of Flight Lieutenant [LG 14 January 1941, issue 35042, page 274] effective from 3rd December 1939. He reverted to the Retired list having served throughout the war in the General Duties Branch.

			G/Capt	06.01.46	Retired list
08023	ORMEROD	Gilbert Latham	F/O	17.12.33	Retired list

On account of ill-health. Returned to service: Commissioned Administration and Special Duties Branch in the rank of Flight lieutenant with effect from 1st September 1939, issue 34738, page 7805]. This entry indicated his service number as 08230 but this had been issued to Frank Wright [Group Captain with effect from 1st July 1940] and, subsequently, his [Ormerod] number was corrected to 08023. On 1st December 1941, he was promoted Squadron Leader [Temporary] after which there is no further trace. However, he is not named on the CWGC data base. An entry under his full name, on the internet, shows he was private soldier in the *Great War* serving as 32796 in the Loyal North Lancashire Regiment before transferring to the Royal Flying Corps on 28th December 1916. Army Form B.103, shows he was posted 22 Squadron [Bristol F.2b] on 13th October 1917, and was so attached until he returned home on 16th June 1918, serving as a Flight Commander since 13th April.

08026	*PAINE	James Theodore	G/Capt	01.10.49	Retirement**

At own request [LG 4 April 1950, supplement 38877, page 1654].

	*PARK	Stanley Miles	G/Capt	08.10.46	Retirement**
	PARRETT	Ernest	F/L	01.01.32	Retired list
	PEIRCE	Harold Claude	F/O	12.09.26	Relinquished
08036	*PERRY-KEENE	Allan Lancelot Addison	AV-M	03.08.49	Retirement**

Air Vice-Marshal Allan Lancelot Addison Perry-Keene CB OBE mentioned in despatches, died on Monday, 16th March 1987.

	PITCHER	Arthur Edwin	F/O		12.09.30	Relinquished
	*PLENDERLEITH	William Noble	W/Cdr	+	09.12.38	210 Squadron

Wing Commander William Noble Plenderleith collapsed and died as he entered his office at Pembroke Dock on Friday, 9th December 1938.

11160	*POLDEN	Charles Joseph	F/L	01.11.32	Retired list

Returned to service: Commissioned to Equipment Branch in the rank of Squadron Leader with effect from 1st June 1940 [LG 7th June 1940, issue 34866, page 3437].

			W/Cdr	01.05.45	Retired list**
11082	*POOLE	Sidney Raymond Lawrence	W/Cdr	22.04.54	Retirement
	POWELL	Doctor Raymond Leonard	F/O	12.09.27	Relinquished
	POWELL	Robert Arthur William	F/O	18.10.21	Cashiered

By sentence of General Court Martial [LG 16 December 1921, issue 32551, page 10276].

11041	*POWNALL	Charles Herbert	W/Cdr	18.01.48	Retirement**
	PUDNEY	Walter Godfrey	F/O	12 09.19	Cancelled
	PUNNETT	Lionel Schuyler	F/O	12.101.30	Relinquished
10224	*RANFORD	Valentine Beaconsfield	A/Cmdr	02.04.47	Retirement**

Air Commodore Valentine Beaconsfield Ranford CBE, died on Thursday, 9th October 1980.

	RAVENHILL	George William Charles	F/O	12.09.30	Relinquished
21072	*REIDY	Alphonsus Michael	W/Cdr	01.08.44	Retired list**

On account of medical unfitness [LG 23 November 1948, supplement 38462, page 6125].

	ROBINS	Percy Donald	F/O	12.09.19	Cancelled
08071	*ROBINSON	Frank Grenville Argyle	G/Capt	28.11.46	Retirement**

Group Captain Frank Grenville Argyle Robinson was appointed Deputy Lieutenant County of Warwick 22nd October 1965.

	ROBINSON	Geoffrey William	Lieutenant	18.08.21	Relinquished

On account of ill-health [LG 16 August 1921, issue 32424, page 6492].

	ROGERSON	John Thomas	F/O	20.03.23	To Class C

As my co-author has discovered, Flying Officer John Thomas Rogerson emigrated aboard the SS *Metegama* to Canada, departing Liverpool on 30th December 1922. He then joined the Canadian Air Force. Subsequently, he settled in the United States of America where after several moves he joined the Curtiss Florida Aviation Camp on New Year's Day 1926. He remained active in aviation throughout the Second World War. Much additional information may be found on the website Early Aviators.

08078	ROLFE	Basil Raynham	F/O	+	05.03.40	Blackburn Aircraft

Flying Officer Basil Raynham Rolfe, employed as a test pilot for Blackburn Aircraft, was testing Botha L6129 on Tuesday, 5th March 1940, when during a routine test flight control was lost and the aircraft dived into the ground some 300 yards north of Sheardowne Farm. Flying Officer Rolfe, a holder of the Royal Order of the Phoenix [Greece] is buried in Elloughton [St. Mary] Churchyard extension; he was 45 years of age. His flight test observer, John Johnson BSc died from his injuries.

	ROSE	Sidney Charles	F/O	12.09.26	Relinquished
70932	ROSE DFC	Thomas	F/L	10.02.54	Relinquished
	RUSSELL	James Mellanby	F/O	12.09.19	Cancelled
10232	*SARGENT	Leonard Nathan	W/Cdr	26.02.46	Retired list**
08092	SAUNDERS	Harold Edgar Fellgate	F/O	12.09.30	Relinquished

Returned to the General Duties Branch and was promoted Squadron Leader on 15th July 1939 [LG 8 September 1939, supplement 34674, page 6134], serving until 1st March 1944, when he relinquished his commission on account of ill-health. W/Cdr 01.03.44 Relinquished

On 16th July 1952, he was granted a commission in the Secretarial Branch, terms of service for five years, in the rank of Flight Lieutenant [LG 19th August 1952, supplement 39625, page 4415]. His service number was now 192085, and as such he was promoted Squadron Leader on 4th November 1954 [LG 11 January 1955, supplement 40379, page 216].

	SCAIFE	Alfred Hunting	F/O		15.09.26	Retired list

On account of ill-health [LG 17 September 1926, issue 33202, page 6035].

	*SHARP	Harold Hodgson	F/O		07.01.25	Retired list

On account of ill-health [LG 6 January 1925, issue 33009, page 142].

11024	*SHAW	Archibald Thomas	F/L		04.09.31	Retired list

Returned to service: Commissioned Equipment Branch in the rank of Squadron Leader effective 1st June 1940 [LG 7 June 1940, issue 34866, page 3437]. W/Cdr 19.04.45 Retired list**

	SHEPARD AFC	Frederick Hubert Guy	F/O	+	02.10.19	1 Comms. Squadron

Flying Officer Frederick Hubert Guy Shepard AFC was killed when the DH.4 F5783 of No 1 Communications Squadron based at Kenley, crashed low on fuel in Strawberry Lane, Newcastle. His passenger, Lieutenant Albert Page, escaped injury. Engaged on a mail delivery flight, the crew experienced mist and low cloud and had descended to low-level seeking a suitable field in which to forced-land. Sighting a sports field, the DH landed only to crash into a goal post. Flying Officer Shepard is buried in Cowley Churchyard.

	SILLS	Thomas Henry	Lieutenant		11.01.21	Resigned
10226	*SIMS	Reginald Gordon	F/L		17.06.38	Retired list

Returned to service: Commissioned Equipment Branch as Squadron Leader effective 1st June 1940 [LG 7 June 1940, issue 34866, page 3438].

	SIVEWRIGHT	William John	F/O		12.09.26	Relinquished
	SLATER	Joseph Benjamin	F/O		12.09.26	Class C

Flying Officer Joseph Benjamin Slater died on Tuesday, 11th December 1928, while still retained in Class C of the Reserve.

	SOMERS	Albert James	F/O		23.01.20	Relinquished

On account of ill-health. As a Civil Servant, Flying Officer Albert James Somers [Retd] was attached to the Air Ministry as an Inspector of Warders, as notified in LG 5 October 1928, issue 33427, page 6426.

	SOUTHALL	Arthur William	Lieutenant		31.08.21	Resigned
	STANDISH	William Joseph	F/L	+	03.05.22	

Flight Lieutenant William Joseph Standish died from a cerebral haemorrhage on Wednesday, 3rd May 1922.

	*STEVENSON	Leslie George	F/O		04.10.22	Retired list

On account of ill-health [LG 3 October 1922, issue 32752, page 6990].

	*STEVENSON	Richard William	F/L	+	31.07.31	
10228	*STEWART	Reginald Wyndham	F/L		24.05.37	Relinquished
08132	STOCKBRIDGE	John Bell	G/Capt		31.08.54	Relinquished
	STROUD MBE	George John	F/O		01.12.26	Retired list

At own request [LG 30 November 1926, issue 33225, page 7817].

	*STRUBEN	Harry Marinus	F/O	+	24.06.21	25 Squadron

Flying Officer Harry Marinus Struben was practising landings when he lost control of 7F.1 Snipe E6156 and spun into the ground near Caesar's Camp, Folkestone. He was buried with full military honours in Hawkinge [St. Michael} Churchyard.

	*STURMAN	George William	F/O		07.12.24	Retired list

On account of ill-health [LG 9 December 1924, issue 33000, page 8981]. His short-service commission had been made permanent.

	SULLIVAN	Humphrey Gerald	F/O		29.02.24	Relinquished

On account of ill-health contracted on active service [LG 26 February 1924, issue 32912, page 1727].

74232 Returned to service: Commissioned Administrative and Special Duties Branch as Pilot Officer with effect from 19th September 1939 [LG 26 September 1939, issue 34694, page 6507]. W/Cdr 24.08.54 Relinquished

	SUSANS MBE	Frank	Major		04.09.20	Retired list

13044 Returned to service: Commissioned Administrative and Special Duties Branch as Flight Lieutenant with seniority from 1st January 1930 [LG 20 October 1939, issue 34713, page 7043]. W/Cdr 01.01.46

	SWEETING	Alan Ernest	F/O		12.09.19	Cancelled
	TAYLOR	Henry Foster Joseph	F/O		12.09.26	Relinquished
13169	*THORPE	Edward Frederick	W/Cdr		18.09.44	Retirement**
	VINER	John Scotchford	F/O		12.09.30	Relinquished
	VOSPER	Roy Atcherley	F/L		12.09.30	Relinquished
08171	*WALSER MC	John Gustave	W/Cdr		26.04.46	Retirement**
	WALTER	Richard Noel	F/O		12.09.19	Cancelled
	WALTERS	Albert	F/O		12.09.19	Cancelled
	WALTHO	Nevill Charles	F/O	+	28.08.23	CFS Upavon

Flying Officer Nevill Charles Waltho was the first person to be killed in the United Kingdom as the result of a glider accident since the death of Percy Pilcher in 1899. Flying Officer Waltho wast test flying the 'Brokker' glider [it had no official name] when it stalled and crashed onto Milton Hill near the village of Pewsey some six miles south of Marlborough, Wiltshire. For a description of the glider and additional information regarding the accident, please refer to the description provided by *Wikipedia*.

	WARNER	Arthur Frederick	F/O		12.09.26	Relinquished
	WARNER	Reginald William	F/O		12.09.26	Relinquished
	WATSON	George Louis Gordon	F/O		19.09.26	Relinquished
	WAY	Hal Arthur Leonard	F/O		12.09.26	Relinquished
	WEBB	Harry Frederick	F/L		18.03.32	Retired list

On 1st February 1933, he was granted a commission in the Auxiliary Air Force and appointed as a Civilian Stores Officer attached to No.603 [City of Edinburgh] [Bomber] Squadron with Flight Lieutenant rank [LG 31 January 1933, issue 33907, page 677]. On 31st July 1939, he was granted a commission, in his rank, to the Equipment Branch, Class CC [LG 10 October 1939, issue 34705, page 6799]. Commission relinquished in Class CC [LG 5 March 1940, issue 34805, page 1318]. F/L 01.09.39 Relinquished

10162	*WELLS	Albert Thomas	S/Ldr		25.08.40	Retired list

Owing to ill-health.

10229	*WILLIAMS	Herbert Arthur	F/O		28.11.31	Retired list

Returned to service: Commissioned Equipment Branch as Squadron Leader with effect from 1st June 1940 [LG 7 June 1940, issue 34866, page 3437]. S/Ldr 18.11.46 Retired list**

08196	WILSON	Cecil Frederick Charles	F/L		14.09.54	Relinquished
10170	*WOOLLETT	Archibald Pharaoh	G/Capt		01.09.46	Retirement**
	*WOOLVERIDGE	Harry Leonard	A/Cmdr		08.01.47	Retirement**

Air Commodore Harry Leonard Woolveridge CB OBE, died on Tuesday, 29th March 1960.

	*WORTON	Frederick Charles	F/O		11.01.22	Retired list

On account of ill-health [LG 13 January 1922, issue 32576, page 375].

	WRATHALL	John Sydney Garston	F/O	12.09.26	Relinquished
	WRIGHT	Robert Lancelot Gerrard	F/O	12.09.19	Cancelled
08159	*WYNNE-TYSON	Lynden Charles	F/L	18.06.29	Retired list

At his own request [LG 25 June 1929, issue 33509, page 4195]. Flight Lieutenant Lynden Charles Wynne-Tyson was initially short service commissioned as Lynden Charles Tyson but, as my co-author reports, adopted the surname WYNNE-TYSON by deed poll dated 26th September 1919, enrolled in the Central Office of the Supreme Court of Judicature. The 22nd day of October 1919, Lynden Charles Tyson of 32 Connaught Mansions, Battersea Park, London, has abandoned his former surname Tyson and has adopted and assumed the name of Lynden Charles Wynne-Tyson. In the Second World War he returned to the service but reverted to the Retired list on 25th October 1941, retaining the rank of Wing Commander.

21040	*YOUNG	John Frederick	A/Cmdr	28.11.50	Retirement**

Air Commodore John Frederick Young CBE MM, died on Sunday, 9th June 1991. Born on 3rd March 1895, at the time of his death he was one of the oldest officers of air rank to have seen active service in the *Great War* having begun his service with the 12th Battalion, Royal Fusiliers [City of London Regiment]. Ahead of his transfer to the Royal Air Force, he rose in rank to Company Sergeant Major. My co-author, who has supplied much of the above, points out that on 14th January 1924, a Pilot Officer John Frederick Young was appointed to a short service commission, his terms of engagement being for five years. During his service and while in training he survived a serious air accident when his Avro 504K F8945 of 2 FTS Duxford came into midair collision with a Bristol F.2b from the same FTS. Sadly, the pilot of the Bristol, Pilot Officer Eric Martin MC was killed.

OBSERVER OFFICERS
6

	BONIFACE	Henry Andrew	F/O	12.09.34	Relinquished
75187	Granted a commission in Class C as a Flight Lieutenant [LG 16 March 1937, issue 34380, page 1751. LG 26 October 1954, supplement				
40309, page 6064.			S/Ldr	26.10.54	Relinquished
08239	BRIE	Reginald Alfred Charles	F/O	12.09.22	To Class A
Returned to service, date not established.			W/Cdr	10.09.52	

LG 7 October 1952, supplement 39663, page 5273. Appointed to a short service commission in the rank and date shown above. I cannot be certain, but I suspect he reverted to the Retired list on 10th September 1952.

09040	LANGAN DFC	Richard Stafford	F/L	07.09.54	Relinquished

Note. At some point the *Gazette* corrected his entry to John Richard Stafford-Langham DFC.

	RUTLEDGE AFC MM	Wilfred Lloyd	O/O	01.01.20	Relinquished
	Canada	At own request [LG 9 March 1920, issue 31816, page 2906].			
	WALLACE	James Campbell	O/O	12.09.19	Cancelled
	WISNEKOWITZ MC	Harry	F/O	08.11.26	Relinquished

LG 16 September 1919, issue 31554, page 11588

SQUADRON LEADERS
2

	*BRADLEY OBE	John Stanley Travers	AM	27.10.45	Retirement**

Air Marshal Sir John Bradley KCB CBE mentioned in despatches, died on Wednesday, 6th January 1982.

	HEWITT	Harold Edward James	S/Ldr	11.08.26	Retired list

On account of ill-health [LG 10 August 1926, issue 3190, page 5293].

FLIGHT LIEUTENANTS
23

06022	BAILEY	Charles William	F/L	26.04.47	Resigned

Flight Lieutenant Charles William Bailey, Paul McMillan reports, while in Class C of the Reserve was attached in a civilian capacity to the Air Ministry and in 1938, was sent to the Far East as Inspector of Landing Grounds. By 1940, he was under the aegis of AHQ Burma advising on the the the extension of facilities at established airfields and the construction of new sites. Subsequently, he was commissioned on 25th March 1944, to the Administrative and Special Duties Branch. On Monday, 15th March 1954, he was one of thirty-three fatalities when BOAC Lockheed L-749A Constellation G-ALAM *Belfast* crashed at Kallang Airport, Singapore, while *en route* from Sydney to London Heathrow. The pilot, Captain Trevor Hoyle was among those who died and though the accident was attributed to pilot error, it was recognised that Captain Hoyle had been on duty for over twenty-one hours; the airport's fire service also came in for criticism for the tine it took them to reach the scene of the crash. Additional information can be read on *Wikipedia's* account of the tragedy.

	BAWN	Leslie Francis Palmer	F/L	16.09.32	Relinquished

In the Second World War, Flight Lieutenant Leslie Francis Palmer Bawn obtained a commission with the Royal Army Service Corps.

	BLAKE AFC	Alfred Montague	F/L	+	16.10.37	Blackburn Aircraft

While in Class C of the Reserve, to which he had been placed on 16th September 1933, and while fulfilling the duties of Chief Test Pilot for Blackburn Aircraft, Flight Lieutenant Alfred Montague Blake AFC was found dead from carbon monoxide poisoning in the garage of his home, the engine of his car still running. At the inquest into his death an open verdict was returned. Consulting *Blackburn Aircraft since 1909* by A J Jackson and published by Putnam's in 1968, Flight Lieutenant Blake's last first flight of a prototype took place on Tuesday, 9th February 1937, when he flew the Blackburn B-24 Skua K5178. At the Hendon display on 26th June of that year, he demonstrated the Skua prototype and two days later flew K5178 at the SBAC show held at Hatfield.

	BURKE	James Michael	F/L	03.12.24	Relinquished

On account of ill-health [LG 2 December 1924, issue 32998, page 8783].

	CAMERON	Dudley Keith	F/L	16.09.30	Relinquished
74882	Returned to service: Commissioned Administrative and Special Duties Branch in the rank of Flight Lieutenant, effective from 22nd May				
1939 [LG 20 October 1939, issue 34713, page 7044].			S/Ldr	10.02.54	Relinquished
	CATCHPOLE MC DFC.	Basil Everard	F/L	16.09.19	Cancelled
	*CRICHTON MBE	Henry Lumsden	A/Cmdr	01.04.47	Retirement**

Air Commodore Henry Lumsden CB MBE, died on Thursday, 2nd October 1952.

	DEXTER	Frederick Reginald Parkes	F/L	16.09.30	Relinquished
15104	*FRY MC	William Mayes	W/Cdr	15.07.45	Retired list**
	JAMES	Harold Hindle	F/L	16.09.19	Permanent
	McCANN	Charles William	F/L	16.09.19	Cancelled
03005	*MULHOLLAND AFC	Denis Osmond	W/Cdr	06.09.40	Retirement
Re-employed.			G/Capt	23.07.46	Retired list**
	*RHODES	George Cecil	S/Ldr	09.02.36	Retired list

Granted a commission in Class C as Squadron Leader [LG 24 March 1936, issue 34267, page 1902, S/Ldr   30.04.36   Relinquished

	*ROBERTSON	Paul Douglas	G/Capt		23.12.45	Retired list**
	STEPHENSON-	William George	F/L	+	23.04.21	
	PEACH	Died from pneumonia in the British Station Hospital, Karachi.				
	*STEVENS OBE	George	G/Capt		10.2.42	Retirement**

| 09113 | TAYLOR | Charles Arthur | F/L | | 05.06.20 | Relinquished |

On account of physical disability [LG 4 June 1920, issue 31929, page 6189].

| | TOOKE | Benjamin Cecil | F/L | + | 11.07.24 | |

Flight Lieutenant Benjamin Cecil Tooke succumbed to pancreatitis in the RAF Combined Hospital, Basra.

| | TRURAN AFC | Cyril Jameson | F/L | | 08.08.25 | Cashiered |

By sentence of General Court Marshal [LG 29 September 1925, issue 33088, page 6280]. This was as a consequence of an air accident near Shaibah on 17th April 1925, in which his observer Flying Officer Thomas Thomson was killed. Both officers were attached to 84 Squadron. An entry on *WikiTree* which I have pleasure in acknowledging, indicates that he emigrated to Southern Rhodesia where he died in the capital, Salisbury, on the 8th of April 1965, at the age of 72. Another website, which I acknowledge, The Peerage, shows Cyril Jameson Truran as being born at Stoke Newington, London, on 24th April 1892, with the additional information that his son, Anthony John Jameson Truran, issue of his first wife, was killed in a flying training accident on 25th November 1940. Anthony, aged 20 and commissioned Pilot Officer, was attached to 615 Squadron AAF. He was cremated at Woking [St. John's] Crematorium.

	*WATKINS AFC	Siegfried Richards	W/Cdr		17.05.35	Retired list
	*WILSON	Donald William	F/L		03.08.31	Retired list
	WORTHINGTON MC	Percy	F/L		01.02.36	Relinquished
	YOUNG	Thomas Kenneth	F/L		16.09.19	Cancelled

FLYING OFFICERS
36

| 06173 | *ADAMS | Cyril Douglas | A/Cmdr | | 17.11.49 | Retirement** |

Air Commodore Cyril Douglas Adams CB OBE six times mentioned in despatches, died on Friday, 19th August 1988. When commanding RAF Oakington, Group Captain Adams was in his car on the airfield observing the Stirlings of 7 Squadron taking off for a raid on the port of Kiel. As he watched he noticed that one of the Stirling's [W7445 MG-V] was failing to become airborne and moments later it overshot the runway and crashed into an orchard where it caught fire. He immediately drove to the scene and his subsequent actions resulted in the award of the OBE, *Gazetted* on the last day of March 1942, supplement 35507, page 1449: *'One night in November 1941, an aircraft fully laden with petrol, bombs and several thousand rounds of ammunition, crashed shortly after taking off and came to rest in an orchard, where it burst into flames. Long grass in the vicinity became ignited from burning petrol and some trees caught fire. Group Captain Adams, who was in his car on the aerodrome at the time, immediately drove to the scene and was the first to arrive there. With complete disregard of his personal safety he entered the aircraft and searched for survivors, while so doing, ammunition was exploding in profusion and Group Captain Adams was well aware of the presence of a number of heavy bombs under the floor on which he stood. Despite the growing intensity of the heat and the imminent danger from the bombs, he extricated and took to a place of safety an airman who was seriously injured and then extinguished the flames on the airman's clothing. Group Captain Adams then covered the casualty with his own overcoat. Returned to the aircraft and, finding no other survivors, successfully removed the body of a dead airman. By his gallant action, this officer undoubtedly saved the life of the injured airman.'* My RAFBCL 1941, page 182, identifies the captain of the Stirling as Sgt I H Hunter RNZAF who died from his injuries shortly after the crash, while the deceased airman pulled from the bomber was Sgt A C Bennett RAAF.

| | *ADAMS | James Michie | G/Capt | | 04.07/49 | Retirement |
| | ATKIN | Hubert Clare | F/O | | 16.09.22 | To Class C |

While still in the Reserve, Flying Officer Hubert Clare Atkin died in Persia at Abadan on Friday, 11th May 1928.

| | AULIFF | Harry | F/O | | 16.09.22 | To Class C |

Flying Officer Harry Auliff died while still in the Reserve on Sunday, 2nd September 1928; his funeral was held five days later.

| | AUSTEN | Valentine George | F/O | | 26.09.19 | Cancelled |
| 74997 | | Returned to service: Commissioned Administrative and Special Duties Branch with effect from 1st September 1939, initially as Lieu- |

tenant [LG 20 October 1939, issue 3471, page 7045].

			W/Cdr		18.05.54	Relinquished
10236	BALLANTYNE	Hector Bell Smith	W/Cdr		19.06.43	Retirement**
06204	*BARRETT	John Francis Tufnell	G/Capt	+	03.09.41	North Luffenham

During the night of 2nd-3rd September 1941, Bomber Command raided Berlin and Group Captain Barrett, then Station Commander at North Luffenham, accompanied 61 Squadron's Commanding Officer, Wing Commander George Engebret Valentine in Manchester I L7388. It is known that the crew reached the target area where their aircraft was shot down with complete loss of life. For additional information, please refer to page 136 of RAFBCL1941.

| 06208 | BATTLE | Henry Frederick Vulliamy | A/Cmdr | | 13.10.46 | Retirement** |

Air Commodore Henry Frederick Vulliamy Battle OBE DFC mentioned in despatched, died on Sunday, 4th October 1981, at Thorpeness, Suffolk.

| 06214 | BENNETT-BAGGS | James Leonard Neville | F/O | | 16.09.22 | To Class A |

At TNA Kew under AIR 76/16/128 a document exists for this officer; his date of birth is recorded as 31st July 1898. TNA Kew also has a medal card under WO 372/1/171351. Employed by Armstrong Whitworth as Chief Consultant Pilot.

| | | | S/Ldr | | 04.06.54 | Relinquished |
| | *BEST | William | F/L | + | 08.03.34 | RAF Depot ME |

Flight Lieutenant William Best died following an operation. At the time of being taken ill he was fulfilling the duties of Stores Officer.

| | *COOPER | Arthur Thomas | S/Ldr | | 29.06.32 | Retired list |
| 07043 | DAVIES | Edward Dayrell Handley | A/Cmdr | | 27.10.50 | Retirement |

Air Commodore Edward Davrell Handley 'Peter' Davies CBE, died on Thursday, 21st March 1974.

| 10083 | *DEAN | David Wingrave | W/Cdr | | 16.10.45 | Retired list |

On account of medical unfitness for Air Force service.

| | *EVANS | Thomas Henry | G/Capt | | 21.01.46 | Retirement** |
| 07084 | FIDDAMENT | Arthur Leonard | AV-M | | 25.03.49 | Retirement** |

Air Vice-Marshal Arthur Leonard Fiddament CB CBE DFC, died on Thursday, 5th August 1976.

| | *GREEN MC | Wilfred Charles | W/Cdr | | 04.07.44 | Retired list** |
| | HEWETT | James Duff | Lieutenant | | 08.09.21 | Resigned |

New Zealand Subsequent joined the Royal New Zealand Air Force and, as reported by my co-author, suffered the loss of his son, Leading Aircraftman James Duff 'Peter' Hewett who died with his flying instructor at 2 SFTS Woodbourne while practicing instrument take offs in Oxford II NZ1243 and coming into collision with Oxford II NZ1257. Both aircraft came down near Renwick, roughly a mile from the airfield. There were no survivors from this accident which occurred during the morning of Wednesday, New Year's Eve 1941. Full details of the crash are reported on page 165 of Errol Martyn's tribute to his country's airmen *For Your Tomorrow - Volume One: Fates 1915-1942.* All were laid to rest in Wellington [Karori] Cemetery.

	*HOGAN	Reginald Victor John Somerville	S/Ldr		26.08.35	Retired list
10105	HOLMES	Albert	W/Cdr		10.07.45	Retired list**
	LUNNON	Walter Edward	F/O		16.09.30	Relinquished
10124	*MASTERS	Charles Herbert	G/Capt		13.09.46	Retirement**
	MEDCALF	James Victor	F/O	+	07.09.27	

Presumed killed during an attempt to cross the Atlantic from Harbour Grace in Newfoundland in a Stinson SM-1 Detroiter *'Sir John Carling'* registered to Carling Brewers. Accompanying Flying Officer James Victor Medcalf, who at the time was still in Class A of the Reserve, was Canadian born Captain Terence Bernard Tulley AFC. A report in *The Times* published on September 10th, filed the previous day from their Toronto correspondent, was heavily critical of the advisability of these flights *"which take a toll of human life while serving no scientific or other useful purpose."*

	MILLER	Walter Davis	Lieutenant		01.04.21	Resigned
08005	MOULE	Eric John	W/Cdr		10.02.54	Relinquished
	PROCKTER	Henry William	F/O		16.09.26	Relinquished
04186	RAPLEY MSM	Cyril	G/Capt		26.01.50	Retirement**
	ROBERTSON	Douglas Blanchard	F/O		16.09.19	Cancelled
	ROCHELLE	William Aubry	F/O		16.09.26	Relinquished

117541   Returned to service: Commissioned Administrative and Special Duties Branch as Pilot Officer with effect from 25th February 1942 [LG 24 March 1942, supplement 35498, page 1337].

			S/Ldr		17.08.54	Relinquished

10142	*SANDERSON DSM Leonard Thomas		F/L		25.12.32	Retired list

Returned to the service during the Second World War and as a Wing Commander died in a military hospital on Saturday, 20th November 1943. He is buried in Oxford [Botley] Cemetery.

	SANT	Philip Leighton	F/O		25.07.28	Relinquished

On account of ill-health.

08162	VERNON	James Tassie	S/Ldr		21.05.45	Resigned
08190	WHITEHEAD	Walter William	W/Cdr		21.09.54	Relinquished
	WILSON	Richard Fraser	F/L		23.09.31	Retired list

On account of ill-health [LG29 September 1931, issue 33757, page 6239].

	YARNOLD	Walter Keith	F/O		16.09.19	Cancelled
	*WEST	Richard William Gordon	F/L		16.04.24	Retired list

On account of ill-health [LG 15 April 1924, issue 32927, page 3102]. Granted a commission in Class C, General Duties, in the Reserve of Air Force Officers with effect from 28th July 1937, ranked Flight Lieutenant [LG 2 November 1937, issue 34450, page 6824]. Subsequently granted a commission in Class CC of the Reserve of Air Force Officers.

			S/Ldr		05.04.56	Relinquished

OBSERVER OFFICERS
2

	GORDON DFC	Robert Bisset	O/O	+	20.03.20	20 Squadron

See summary for the circumstances of his death.

	HUNTER	Robert Bruce	Lieutenant		14.06.22	Retired list

On account off ill-health contracted on active service [LG 13 June 1922, issue 32719, page 4478].

LG 24 October 1919, issue 31616, pages 13032, 13033 and 13034

SQUADRON LEADERS
3

	ATKINSON OBE	Harold Gordon	S/Ldr		24.10.19	Cancelled
	BETTINGTON OBE	Egerton Mitford	S/Ldr		10.10.20	Resigned
	FULLER	Hugh Clarence	S/Ldr		24.10.31	Relinquished

06005   LG 10 May 1938, issue 34509, page 3026, granting a commission in the Auxiliary Air Force, General Duties Branch, in the rank of
73501   Flight Lieutenant [Honorary Squadron Leader] effective from 4th April 1938. An administrative entry [LG 28 March 1939, issue 34611, page 2100] states relinquishment of his commission with effect from 27th September 1938, on appointment to a commission in the Royal Air Force Volunteer Reserve and is reappointed to the Auxiliary Air Force with effect from 12th October 1938. On the 1st of September 1939, relinquished his Auxiliary Air Force commission and in the rank of Flight Lieutenant was accepted into the Equipment Branch of the Volunteer Reserve [LG 26 April 1940, issue 34838, page 2481]. At some stage he transferred to the Administrative and Special Duties Branch and relinquished his commission on 17th April 1940, owing to ill-health [LG 26 April 1940, issue 34838, page 2479]. A most unusual sequence of service.

FLIGHT LIEUTENANT from SQUADRON LEADER

	HOWETT	John Reginald	S/Ldr		24.10.30	Relinquished

FLIGHT LIEUTENANTS
77

06018	*ALFORD MC Canada	Francis Reginald	G/Capt		26.10.44	Retirement**
	ATHERLEY	Jack Erskine Munro	F/L		25.10.22	Relinquished

On reappointment to the Manchester Regiment. On 15th June 1937, he was granted a commission in the Reserve of Air Force Officers, Class C and by the 19th of August 1948, he was in Class CC and attached to the Secretarial Branch. My co-author has traced his final entry to 9th November 1948, which amended his rank to Flying Officer.

	ATKINSON	John Clifford	F/L		24.10.30	Relinquished
	BAKER MC AFC	Valentine Henry	Captain		01.10.21	Resigned
	*BOUMPHREY	Colin	S/Ldr		08.07.39	Retired list

On account of ill-health [LG 18 July 1939, issue 34646, page 4929].

	*BOWEN	Horace George	A/Cmdr		01.02.44	Retirement**

Air Commodore Horace George Bowen MBE, died on Monday, 1st November 1971.

21077	*BOWLER	Thomas Geoffrey	AV-M		06.04.51	Retirement**

Air Vice-Marshal Thomas Geoffrey Bowler CB CBE twice mentioned in despatches, died on Thursday, 5th September 1974.

	*CASTER MC	William Samuel	G/Capt		13.03.46	Retirement**
	*COLEMAN	Francis Henry	A/Cmdr		29.10.45	Retirement**

Air Commodore Francis Henry Coleman DSO, died in the June of 1975.

	COOK DSC	Norman Richard	F/L		24.10.19	Cancelled
	COOPER DSC	Edward John	F/L		10.12.24	Relinquished

On account of ill-health [LG 27 January 1925, issue 3015, page 596].

	*CROKE	Lewis George Le Blount	A/Cmdr		09.10.45	Retirement**

Air Commodore Lewis George Le Blount Croke CBE mentioned in despatches, died on Tuesday, 16th February 1971.

	*CROSS DFC	Bernard Charles Henry	F/L		15.10.28	Retired list

At own request [LG 30 October 1928, issue 33434, page 7019].

	*DALISON AFC	Charles Beauvoir	G/Capt		30.10.47	Retirement**
	DANIEL	Robert Elletson Herbert	F/L		28.10.30	Relinquished
	*DAWSON	Grahame George	AV-M	+	14.11.44	SASO Mediterranean

Air Vice-Marshal Grahame George Dawson CB CBE twice mentioned in despatches, died on Tuesday, 14th November 1944. He is buried in Choloy War Cemetery. According to the website Air of Authority, Air Vice-Marshal Dawson was Senior Air Staff Officer Mediterranean Air Command, a post that he took up on 17th February 1943. The website, Key Aero, which I gratefully acknowledge, reports he was a passenger aboard Liberator II AL584 of 144 Maintenance Unit *en route* from the Middle East to Lyneham when in crashed into the side of a mountain near Autun [Saône-et-Loire] resulting in the deaths of eight personnel.

No.	Name	Forename	Rank		Date	Status
06050	DEANS DSC	Ernest Edward	F/L		24.10.30	Relinquished

Returned to service: Commissioned Administrative and Special Duties Branch in the rank of Flight Lieutenant, effective 1st September 1939 [LG 28th November 1939, issue 34742, page 7966].

No.	Name	Forename	Rank		Date	Status
			S/Ldr		01.06.54	Relinquished
	DICKSON DFC	John Charles Oswald	F/L		04.05.32	Relinquished

On account of ill-health.

No.	Name	Forename	Rank		Date	Status
	DUFFUS	James Logie Lyall	F/L		24.10.22	Relinquished

On account of ill-health.

No.	Name	Forename	Rank		Date	Status
	ERRINGTON	George Henry	Major		31.12.21	Relinquished

On account of ill-health [LG 30 December 1921, issue 32561, page 10656].

No.	Name	Forename	Rank		Date	Status
	FITZHERBERT DSC	Evelyn Cecil Walter	F/L		24.10.32	Relinquished
06057	*FLETCHER AFC	Albert William	G/Capt	+	05.08.43	

Group Captain Albert William Fletcher OBE DFC AFC is buried in Sussex in Lancing [St. James the Less] Churchyard extension.

No.	Name	Forename	Rank		Date	Status
	FORSYTH	William Edward Charles Blaxland Codrington	F/L		23.10.30	Relinquished
	*FREW AFC DSO MC	Matthew Brown	AV-M		19.12.48	Retirement**

Air Vice-Marshal Sir Matthew Frew KBE CB DSO* MC* AFC twice mentioned in despatches, died on Tuesday, 28th May 1974.

No.	Name	Forename	Rank		Date	Status
	FROST	Stanley	F/L		15.02.31	Relinquished
	GARDNER DSC	William Edward	F/L		24.10.19	Cancelled
	HACKMAN	Trevor Ratcliff	F/L		30.04.26	Relinquished
	HEMMING AFC	Harold	F/L		04.06.31	Relinquished
	HERVEY	Lionel Arthur	F/L		24.10.21	Resigned
	*HOWE AFC	Thomas Edward Barham	A/Cmdr		19.08.41	Retirement**

Air Commodore Thomas Edward Barham Howe CBE AFC* twice mentioned in despatches, died on Friday, 2nd January 1970.

No.	Name	Forename	Rank		Date	Status
	IRELAND DFC	Harold Mervyn	F/L		01.08.29	Relinquished

During the Second World War Flight Lieutenant Harold Mervyn Ireland was granted a commission as a Pilot Officer in the Royal Air Force Volunteer Reserve Training Branch. As my co-author reports, it was effective from the 1st of February 1941.

No.	Name	Forename	Rank		Date	Status
			F/O		31.12.48	Resigned
	*IRWIN AFC	Herbert Carmichael	F/L	+	05.10.30	Air Ministry

Flight Lieutenant Herbert Carmichael Irwin was captain of the ill-fated HM Airship R101 G-FAAW registered to the Air Ministry and which crashed in bad weather with heavy loss of life on its maiden voyage to India, coming down near Beauvais in France.

No.	Name	Forename	Rank		Date	Status
	JENNER-PARSON	Charles Hugh Beresford	Captain		13.09.22	Relinquished

On account of ill-health [LG 12 September 1922, issue 32746, page 6582].

No.	Name	Forename	Rank		Date	Status
	*JONES	John Hugh Oscar	G/Capt		30.04.45	Retirement**
	LANDER AFC	Frederic Charles	F/L		12.12.21	Resigned
	*LATIMER	Archibald	F/L		08.11.26	Dismissed

By sentence of General Court Martial [LG 23 November 1926, issue 33223, page 7581].

No.	Name	Forename	Rank		Date	Status
	*LAURENCE MC	Frederic Hope	G/Capt		31.12.45	Retirement**
	*LEE MC	Arthur Stanley Gould	AV-M		21.01.46	Retirement**

Air Vice-Marshal Arthur Stanley Gould Lee MC mentioned in despatches, died on Wednesday, 21st May 1975.

No.	Name	Forename	Rank		Date	Status
	LINGARD	Aubrey Lawrence	F/L		24.10.27	Relinquished
	*MACKENZIE AFC	William Herbert	S/Ldr		03.02.26	Retired list

At own request [LG 2 February 1926, issue 33129, page 794].

No.	Name	Forename	Rank		Date	Status
	MAN DFC	William	Major		08.12.21	Resigned
	MONSON-FITZJOHN	Gilbert John	F/L		17.11.21	Resigned

Paul McMillan reports that Flight Lieutenant Gilbert John Monson-Fitzjohn died in Lancashire on Sunday, 28th June 1936.

No.	Name	Forename	Rank		Date	Status
	NEWBURY	Alfred Donald	F/L		24.10.26	Relinquished
	*NEWTON DSC	Thomas Henry	S/Ldr		31.12.30	Retired list

On account of ill-health [LG 13 January 1931, issue 33680, page 307].

No.	Name	Forename	Rank		Date	Status
06111	*O'BRIEN DSC	Garrett Michael Farrelly	F/L		28.04.34	Retired list

LG 27 April 1937, issue 34392, page 2738. Granted a commission in Class C with effect from 21 January 1937, as Flight Lieutenant. LG 20 October 1939, issue 34713, page 7041. Commission in Class CC relinquished on appointment to a commission in the Royal Air Force Volunteer Reserve, retaining the rank of Flight Lieutenant.

No.	Name	Forename	Rank		Date	Status
	*PECK DSO MC	Arthur Hicks	G/Capt		25.04.42	Retirement**

Re-employed but, subsequently, reverted to the Retired list at his own request.

No.	Name	Forename	Rank		Date	Status
06116	PIPON DSC	Arthur Roach Thomas	F/L		22.02.40	Resigned
	POWELL	William Archer	F/L		24.10.19	Cancelled
	PRITCHARD	Edward Randall	F/L		24.10.19	Cancelled
	*PRYOR	Arthur Deen	A/Cmdr		27.11.41	Retirement**

Air Commodore Arthur Deen Pryor, died on Tuesday, 20th July 1982. His sole honour was the *Croix de Guerre* [France].

No.	Name	Forename	Rank		Date	Status
	PURSER MC	Phillips Charles	F/L		24.10.19	Cancelled
	REES	Herbert George Powell	F/L		24.10.31	Relinquished
	RIDLEY DSC	Cyril Burfield	F/L	+	17.05.20	12 Squadron

See summary for the circumstances of his death in an air accident.

No.	Name	Forename	Rank		Date	Status
	ROBERTS	Arthur	F/L		24.10.26	Relinquished
	ROBERTS MC DCM	Elmer Peter	F/L		24.10.30	Relinquished
	ROULSTONE MC	Alexander	F/L		24.10.19	Cancelled
	RUSHFORTH MC	Henry Philip	F/L		24.10.19	Cancelled
06130	SHOPPEE DSC	Lionel Conrad	S/Ldr		08.03.47	Relinquished

On account of medical unfitness for Air Force service [LG 23 November 1948, supplement 38462, page 6126].

No.	Name	Forename	Rank		Date	Status
06131	SIMPSON	Ewen Watson	W/Cdr		22.03.43	Relinquished
06135	SNOW	Arthur Courtenay	S/Ldr		21.09.54	Relinquished
	*STEVENSON MBE	Robert Little	W/Cdr	+	21.11.37	

Wing Commander Robert Little Stevenson MBE died suddenly at Leysdown, Sheerness, on Sunday, 21st November 1937.

No.	Name	Forename	Rank		Date	Status
	*STEWART AFC	Douglas	W/Cdr		27.11.34	Retired list

On account of ill-health.

No.	Name	Forename	Rank		Date	Status
06139	*STUDD DFC	Theodore Quintus	G/Capt		23.05.45	Retirement**

LG 28 April 1953, supplement 39837, page 2355. Commissioned as Flying Officer in the Training Branch of the Royal Air Force Volunteer Reserve, with effect from 1st December 1952.

No.	Name	Forename	Rank		Date	Status
			F/O		01.12.59	Relinquished
	TATTERSALL MBE	Tom Whitaker	F/L		24.10.19	Cancelled
	*THOMAS AFC	Meredith	AV-M		18.04.46	Retirement

Air Vice-Marshal Meredith Thomas CSI CBE DFC AFC twice mentioned in despatches, died on Sunday, 20th May 1984.

*THOMPSON	Thomas Frederick Wailes	W/Cdr		30.06.38	Retired list

At his own request.

TURNER	Ernest Frederick	F/L		24.10.19	Cancelled
WALKER	George Harry	F/L		04.08.20	Resigned
*WALLER AFC	William Hastings De Warrenne	W/Cdr		07.09.35	Retired list.
WARD	David Ernest	F/L		24.10.32	Relinquished

76167   LG 13 April 1937, issue 34388, page 2381. Granted a commission in Class C , ranked Flight Lieutenant, with effect from 15th February 1937. Relinquished Class CC commission on appointment to a commission in the Royal Air Force Volunteer Reserve, General Duties Branch, with effect from 1st September 1939 [LG 19 December 1939, issue 34756, page 8403], but immediately transferred to the Administrative and Special Duties Branch, as notified on page 8404.   W/Cdr   +   12.07.45

Wing Commander David Ernest Ward was cremated in Nottingham Crematorium where is commemorated on panel 5.

*WARREN	George Fitzgerald Penrose	F/O		27.12.28	Retired list

At own request [LG 1 February 1929, issue 33462, page 775].

WHITWORTH AFC	Lloyd	F/L		24.10.26	Relinquished
WIGGLESWORTH DSC	Horace Ernest Philip	AM		07.05.48	Retirement**

Air Marshal Sir Philip Wigglesworth KBE CB DSC three times mentioned in despatches, died on Saturday, 31st May 1975.

WILLIAMS MBE	Frederick Thomas	F/L	+	18.01.22	RAE Farnborough

While flight testing the BAT FK.23 Bantam II F1653 on the 10th of January 1922, Flight Lieutenant Frederick Thomas Williams MBE crashed on to a hut in Marlborough Lines in the Aldershot Barracks complex. Critically injured, Flight Lieutenant Williams, who was thirty years of age, died eight days later in Connaught Military Hospital, Farnborough.

WOOD	Ernest Alfred Edward	Captain		15.11.22	Relinquished

On account of ill-health contracted in the service [LG 14 November 1922, issue 32767, page 8039].

WOODCOCK	William Percy	F/L		24.10.22	To Class B
	LG 7 December 1926, issue 33227, page 8004.	F/L		24.10.26	Relinquished
11062 *YOUNG	Robert Alexander	A/Cmdr		22.10.46	Retirement**

Air Commodore Robert Alexander Young, died on Saturday, 2nd March 1974.

FLYING OFFICERS [from FLIGHT LIEUTENANT]
4

*MELLERSH AFC	Francis John Williamson	AV-M		28.09.54	Retirement**

Air Vice-Marshal Sir Francis Mellersh KBE AFC twice mentioned in despatches, died on Wednesday, 25th May 1955, in tragic circumstances. A member of the Itchenor Yacht Club, Sir Francis had planned a trip to Cherbourg in his yacht and invited his friend Lieutenant-Commander Baring to join him. The Commander, who was a serving officer, arranged to fly, as a passenger, down to the yacht club by helicopter and as the helicopter hovered to allow him to alight so the rotor blades clipped a mast of one of the yachts moored nearby and rolled onto its side. Sir Francis was struck on the head by a blade and the Commander was hit by the still spinning tail rotor. Both were killed instantly while a very shocked pilot was assisted from the wreckage unhurt

08039 *PIDCOCK	Geoffrey Arthur Henzell	AV-M		23.04.51	Retirement**

Air Vice-Marshal Geoffrey Arthur Henzell Pidcock CB CBE, died on Thursday, 12th February 1976.

PINDER DFC	John William	F/L		24.10.19	Cancelled
*WAKEFIELD	William Wavell	F/L		03.10.23	Resigned

FLYING OFFICERS
159

ADDIS	Philip Edward Dansey	F/O		08.08.23	Relinquished

On account of ill-health [LG 7 August 1923, issue 32851, page 5432].

AKEHURST	Bernard Charles	F/O		26.06.20	Relinquished

On account of ill-health. Flying Officer Bernard Charles Akehurst died on Friday, 19th August 1921, in Staffordshire.

ALEXANDER	Alan Finlay	F/O		01.09.20	Resigned
06185 *ANDERSON DFC	Charles Torr	G/Capt		125.07.42	Retired list**

On account of ill-health [LG 20 October 1942, supplement 35750, page 4543].

06188 ARMSTRONG	Malcolm Heath	F/O		12.07.43	Resigned**
BAILLIE	George	F/O		24.10.26	Relinquished
71696	In 1940, he returned to the service as an Honorary Squadron Leader.	S/Ldr		01.08.45	Relinquished
06209 *BAYLEY	Arthur Cyril	W/Cdr		13.04.40	Retired list**

On account of ill-health [LG 26 April 1940, issue 34838, page 2475].

06216 BENTLEY DFC	William	S/Ldr		10.2.54	Relinquished
06223 BLACK	Howard Charteris	F/O		28.10.30	Relinquished

Returned to service: Commissioned Administrative and Special Duties Branch with effect from 13th March 1940, in the rank of Pilot Officer [LG 9th April 1940, page 34826, page 2075].   P/O   16.05.41   Terminated**

BLENNERHASSETT MC	Giles Noble	Captain		22.01.21	Resigned
*BOYCE AFC	George Harold	A/Cmdr		14.08.46	Retirement**

Air Commodore George Harold Boyce CB AFC mentioned in despatches, died on Monday, 22nd December 1975, at Alcester in Warwickshire.

BREWIN	Thomas	F/O		24.10.30	Relinquished
BROWNE DFC	Reginald Frederick	F/O		11.03.25	Relinquished

On account of ill-health [LG 10 March 1925, issue 33028, page 1701].

*BRYER AFC	Gerald Mornington	G/Capt		30.07.46	Retirement**

LG 3 May 1946, issue 37553, page 2127. Conferred by His Majesty the King of the Hellenes 'Gold Cross' 3rd May 1946, ranked Group Captain.

BURDEN	Joseph	F/O		24.101.19	Cancelled
BURGESS AFC	Vernon William	F/O		02.02.26	Resigned
BURNLEY	Frank Oswald	F/O		01.09.29	Relinquished
BURR MC DCM MM	William John	F/O		17.12.26	Relinquished
BUTLER DFC	Maurice Henry	F/L		24.10.28	Relinquished
	On account of ill-health [LG 30 October 1928, issue 33434, page 7019].				
CANNON	Samuel Lawrence	F/O		24.10.26	Relinquished
07001 CANTLE	Roy Llewellyn	F/O		24.10.22	To Class A

LG 12 December 1939, issue 34752, page 8254. Transferred from General Duties Branch to Administrative and Special Duties Branch. LG 30 June 1942, issue 35615, page 2879. Transferred to RAF Regiment.   F/L   01.02.42

Recorded in the Air Force List, October 1944; no further trace; believed to have left the service by January 1945.

07004 *CARNEGIE AFC	David Vaughan	AV-M		12.06.54	Retirement**

Air Vice-Marshal David Vaughan Carnegie CB CBE AFC, died on Monday, 3rd August 1964.

	CARTER	Basil Royston	F/L	+	25.09.25	29 Squadron

Flight Lieutenant Basil Royston Carter AFC died in a midair collision over the Essex village of Elmdon, some 6 miles ESE from Royston in Hertfordshire, when his Gloster Grebe II J7385 came into midair collision with a fellow 29 Squadron aircraft piloted by Sergeant Thomas James McGrath who was flying J7395, both airmen being killed. The report in *The Times* is worth recording in full for it illustrates the growing concern the number of air accidents to service aircraft: *'Another fatal collision involving to Royal Air Force machines occurred yesterday. Flight-Lieutenant Royston Carter of North Finchley, and Pilot-Sergeant Thomas James McGrath of Devizes, both of 29 [Fighter] Squadron [Duxton [sic]], came into collision in the air and crashed near Royston, Cambridgeshire. Both were killed instantly. Three machines were engaged in fighting practice over Elmdon, a village four miles west of Saffron Walden and nine miles north of Duxford, two of them flying together and another apparently attacking them. They were being watched by a number of the villagers and by women and children gleaning [collecting loose grain and anything of use following harvest] in the fields in the neighbourhood when two of them suddenly came into collision. One machine fell into the trees of a wood, and the other, after steadying itself for a few moments, crashed in a field a hundred yards away. The third machine at once flew back to Duxford Aerodrome to report. Both airmen were found dead in their wrecked machines. The total number of air accidents in the Royal Air Force during the year at home and abroad now numbers 32, involving the death of 41 men. Eighteen of the accidents have been at home and 14 abroad. The death roll at home numbers 25 and that abroad 16. For the same period last year there were 41 accidents to machines, and the deaths numbered 57. Of these 26 accidents were at home and 15 abroad, while 35 of those killed met their deaths in this country. To this year's figures should be added the death of three officers of the Royal Air Force Reserve. The number of accidents this year is fewer than last year, although there are now more squadrons and more hours have been flown.'*

07010	*CARTER MC	Oliver Eric	AV-M		07.06.46	Retirement**

Air Vice-Marshal Oliver Eric Carter CBE MC AFC, died in the March of 1977.

07011	*CASSIDY	John Reginald	A/Cmdr		27.05.46	Retirement**

Air Commodore John Reginald Cassidy CBE, died on Sunday, 8th December 1974.

	CAVE MC	Thomas Walford	Lieutenant		24.10.22	Relinquished

On account of ill-health contracted in the Service [LG 7 November 1922, issue 32764, page 7874].

07016	*CHICK MC	John Stanley	A/Cmdr		27.12.47	Retirement**

Air Commodore John Stanley Chick MC AFC, died on Thursday, 21st January 1960.

07021	CLARKE	Frederick Wellesley	S/L		08.06.54	Relinquished
	*CLAYSON MC DFC	Percy Jack	F/L		16.04.29	Retired list

On account of ill-health [LG 23 April 1929, issue 33488, page 2698].

116122	Returned to service: To be Flying Officer [emergency] with effect from 20th December 1941, in the Administrative and Special Duties					

Branch [LG 3 March 1942, issue 35476, page 1020].

			F/L		10.02.54	Relinquished
	CLOWES	Richard	F/O		24.10.19	Cancelled
08207	COOPER MC	John Henry	Lieutenant		01.02.21	Resigned

Returned to the service: Commissioned Royal Air Force Volunteer Reserve.

			S/Ldr		01.06.54	Relinquished
	*COX MC AFC	Wilfred Reseigh	G/Capt		14.05.46	Retirement**
	CREAMER DFC	Reginald Cyril	F/O	+	26.06.24	HQ Trans-Jordan

On Thursday 26th June 1924, Flying Officer Creamer, accompanied by Leading Aircraftman Frank Charles Perrin took off from Amman in DH.9A H151 and almost immediately spun out of control, crashed and burst into flames with fatal consequences for both airmen. Reginald Cyril Creamer's award was *Gazetted* on 3 Jun 1919, supplement 31378, page 7031. No citation appended.

	CUMMINGS DFC	Philip Hildersley	G/Capt		11.07.44	Retirement**
	DAGG AFC	Charles Canada Kirby	F/O		23.12.30	Relinquished
73144	Commissioned as a Pilot Officer on probation to Administrative and Special Duties Branch, 25th April 1939 [LG 2 May 1939, issue					

34621, page 2926].

			F/O		21.06.41	Resigned**
1459273			AC2	+	18.02.42	RAF Driffield

Aircraftman Charles Canada Kirby Dagg is buried in Driffield Cemetery. At the time of his death he was on RAF Driffield strength and he is commemorated on page 102 left hand column of RAFBCL Volume 9 the Roll of Honour. Research by my co-author has revealed that on Friday, 2nd September 1927, he appeared before Marylebone Magistrates Court charged with striking an off-duty policeman. Found guilty as charged he was fined £10 and ten shillings. By the summer of 1936, he was employed as a motor car salesman when again he was in trouble, this time for striking a Bailiff's assistant for which he was fined £1 with fifteen shillings costs. Although conjecture on my part, these two civil offences may have precipitated his resignation in on 21st June 1941.

07041	*DALY	George Dermot	AV-M		29.09.49	Retirement**

Air Vice-Marshal George Dermot Daly CB DFC, died on Saturday, 12th October 1974.

	DAWES	Arthur James	Major		22.12.20	Resigned

Most likely to take up employment as secretary to the Flight Cadets' Mess at Cranwell from where his death at the age of 61, was reported on 20th July 1930.

	DAWSON DFC	Samuel	Lieutenant	+	17.09.19	HMS *Vindictive*

New Zealand Lieutenant Samuel Dawson DFC failed to return from an operational sortie and is commemorated on the Archangel Memorial.

07051	*DICK	Matthew Crawford	W/Cdr		01.05.39	Retirement
07060	*DOWN AFC	Harold Hunter	A/Cmdr		15.11.45	Retirement**

Air Commodore Harold Hunter Down CBE AFC mentioned in despatches, died on Thursday, 20th June 1974. On the 7th of October 1930, a Tuesday, Flying Officer Down, attached to 448 Flight aboard the carrier HMS *Eagle* escaped uninjured when his aircraft, Fairey IIIF S1324 collied with S1731 over Aboukir Bay, Egypt. Both machines landed safely, but tragically Corporal Leslie Arthur Knight was thrown out of S1324 and fell to his death.

	DRUDGE	George Frederick	F/O		01.10.24	Relinquished

On account of ill-health [LG 3 October 1924, issue 32979, page 7189].

07062	DRY	William Frederick	G/Capt		16.02.46	Retirement**

Re-employed [LG 19 March 1946, supplement 37504, page 1433] omitting mention of his CBE [LG 16 April 1946, supplement 37534, page 1904].

97076	*EVANS MC DFC	Dudley Lloyd	W/Cdr		10.09.45	Retired list**
	FITZGERALD-	Neale	F/O	+	14.06.20	14 Squadron

EAGAR Accompanied by Aircraftman Percy William Thacker, Flying Officer Neale Fitzgerald-Eagar took off from Ramleh in Bristol F.2b E2293 with the intention of transiting to Ismailia but tragically strayed well off course, eventually coming down in the Sinai desert where on the 20th of September 1920, a Camel Corps patrol came across their aircraft. Subsequently, their remains were found - Flying Officer Fitzgerald-Eagar is believed to have died from exposure some seven days after the forced-landing while the body of Aircraftman Thacker was discovered in mountains near Nekhel. Both were brought to Suez War Memorial Cemetery where they now rest side-by-side.

	FLOOK DFC	Sidney Samuel	F/O		24.10.19	Cancelled
07090	*FLOWER	Arthur Hyde	G/Capt		16.05.45	Retired list**
	FOWLER AFC	Gordon James	F/O		24.10.19	Cancelled
	FOX-RULE DFC	Gordon	Captain		29.06.21	Relinquished

On account of ill-health contracted in the Service. The citation for his award was *Gazetted* in supplement 30913, page 11251, and reads: *'Whilst on a bombing raid this officer dived to 100 feet and obtained a direct hit on a bridge, completely destroying it. Seeing a body of the enemy on the bank of the river he attacked them, causing them to disperse in disorder. He was then attacked by five biplanes; these he drove off, though his observer had been hit twice, and he landed safely at a French aerodrome. In all, he has taken part in thirty bomb raids and ten photographic reconnaissances, invariably displaying a marked offensive spirit.'*

FULTON	Cecil Sutherland	F/O		24.10.19	Cancelled
GASH	Albert Victor	F/O		24.10.26	Relinquished
07102 *GLAISHER DFC	John Malcolm	G/Capt	+	19.10.45	

Group Captain John Malcolm Glaisher DFC is buried in Algeria in Dely Ibrahim War Cemetery; he was 51 years of age.

07109 *GRAHAM MC	Strang	A/Cmdr		29.03.46	Retirement**

LG Tuesday 13 July 1943, supplement 36089, page 3155, of the second supplement: the award of the George Medal: *'In March 1943, a Wellington aircraft overshot when landing and crashed into another aircraft. The impact carried both aircraft against a hangar, where they burst into flames. Group Captain Graham was on the scene immediately. Disregarding the danger from exploding ammunition, petrol tanks and oxygen bottles, and although he was aware of 1 of the aircraft carried a 250-lb bomb, he led the rescue party in extracting 3 members of crew from the blazing aircraft. Group Captain Graham then led the fire fighting party in an endeavour to save the burning hangar. He was attacking the fire, which had spread to the offices of the hangar, when the bomb on the aircraft, less than 8 feet away, exploded. With his face badly cut by splintered glass and flying debris, and bleeding profusely, he was persuaded to go to the station sick quarters, where he made light of his injuries and inspired others who had been injured by the explosion. After receiving first aid treatment, he returned to the scene of the accident and directed operations until the fire had been subdued.'* Air Commodore Strang Graham MC GM mentioned in despatches, died on Wednesday, 21st September 1994, six months short of his 100th birthday. The occasion of his award occurred on the last day of March 1943, the two Wellington bombers being ICs X9944 which was struck by AD628 captained by Flight Sergeant R W Humphrey RAAF. For additional information, please refer to my RAFBCL OTU losses, page 209.

GREEN MC	Ernest George	F/O	+	24.05.22	2 Squadron

Flying Officer Ernest George Green MC and Sergeant Walter John Stivey died when their Bristol F.2b J6673 stalled off a tight turn while making a low pass over the airfield and spun to the ground. A former observer, Flying Officer Green's MC was *Gazetted* on 26th May 1917, supplement 30095, page 5181: *'For conspicuous gallantry and devotion to duty as an observer. He has on several occasions brought down hostile machines, and has carried out many successful photographic reconnaissances. He has at all times set a fine example of courage and initiative.'*

GRUBB	Lewis William Richardson	F/O		24.10.19	Cancelled
07119 HALFORD DFC	Wallis	F/L		24.10.30	Relinquished

LG 19 September 1939, issue 34687, page 6354. Granted a commission in Class CC in the rank of Flight Lieutenant with effect from 27th July 1939. Transferred 26th July 1939, to the Administrative and Special Duties Branch [LG 21 November 1939, issue 34738, page 7805.

		S/Ldr		01.07.54	Relinquished
07121 HALL	Robert	S/Ldr		09.06.45	Resigned**
HALLIWELL	John Hassell	F/O		24.10.19	Cancelled
HALLIWELL	Wilfrid	F/O		24.10.26	Relinquished
HAMILTON DFC	Leslie	F/O		28.11.19	Relinquished

At his own request and transferred to the Unemployed list.

HAMILTON	Wallace Ferrier	F/O		24.10.19	Cancelled

Reinstated as a Flying Officer and granted a short service commission on 23rd February 1922 [LG 7 March 1922, issue 32631, page 1953].
LG 4 June 1929, issue 33503, page 3694. On account of ill-health.

		F/O		04.06.29	Relinquished
07126 *HAMPTON DFC	Herbert Nind	G/Capt		25.06.46	Retirement**
HARRIS	Percival	F/O		26.01.27	Relinquished

On account of ill-health [LG 28 January 1927, issue 33243, page 585].

HARRISON	Leslie George	F/O		04.09.26	Relinquished
07133 HARRISON DFC	Richard	AV-M		25.04.46	Retirement**

Air Vice-Marshal Richard Harrison CB CBE DFC AFC four times mentioned in despatches, died on Saturday, 18th May 1974. For the greater part of the Second World War he filled senior appointments in Bomber Command; from 7th December 1940, to 15th January 1942, he was Senior Air Staff Officer at No. 1 Group, and this was followed by a similar role at Headquarters Bomber Command, before taking over the duties as Air Office Commanding No. 3 Group on 27th February 1943, a position he held for the next three years. Photographs [one in colour] of Air Vice-Marshal Harrison are recorded on the Air of Authority website.

*HARVEY MM	John Robert Rowland	F/L		05.10.36	Retired list

At own request [LG 6 October 1936, issue 34329, page 6367].

HAVELOCK-	George Henry	F/O	+	30.07.20	

SUTTON MC Flying Officer George Havelock-Sutton MC died in RAF Hospital Halton from acute nephritis [inflammation of the kidneys]. He is buried in Halton [St. Michael] Churchyard.

HAYWARD MC	George Searle Lomax	F/O	+	15.08.24	2 FTS

While giving instruction to Pilot Officer Charles Victor Brearley at No. 2 Flying Training School, Digby, on Friday, 15th August 1924, their Avro 504K H9863 lost engine power and dived to the ground at Metheringham Heath some four miles NNE of the airfield. Both were killed but the Avro was salvaged and by October 1929, was reported to be with Headquarters 23 Group at Spittlegate. During the *Great War* in which he enlisted as a private soldier, serving with the 3rd Hussars, George Searle Lomax Hayward was commissioned to the Royal West Kent Regiment in the early autumn of 1916, transferring to the Royal Flying Corps late 1917. Trained as an observer he was posted to 22 Squadron [Bristol F.2b] and between 29th November 1917 and 22nd April 1918, accounted for twenty-four enemy aircraft. His MC was *Gazetted* on 23rd July 1918, supplement 30813, page 8807: *'For conspicuous gallantry and devotion to duty. On three separate occasions when engaged with large hostile formations, he has attacked and sent crashing to earth two hostile machines on each occasion. He has displayed consistent skill, courage and determination in dealing with hostile aircraft.'* Postwar, he spent a few months on the Unemployed list before being granted a short service commission. Prior to becoming a flying instructor he saw service in India.

HEMPEL	Arthur Ernest	F/O		24.02.27	Relinquished.
HILL	Vernon Francis Roland	F/O		24.10.28	Relinquished
07153 *HODSON AFC	George Stacey	AV-M		07.09.51	Retirement**

Air Vice-Marshal George Stacey Hodson CB CBE AFC, died on Friday, 1st October 1976.

HOLLAND	Horace Lloyd	F/O	+	21.02.20	100 Squadron

See summary for details regarding his death.

07159 HOOD	Roland	F/L		09.07.54	Relinquished
07164 *HOWARD DFC	George Vivian	G/Capt		23.08.46	Retirement**
HUMPHREYS	Gordon Noel	F/L		24.04.27	Relinquished
07168 HUSTINGS	Norman William	F/O	+	07.04.23	

Flying Officer Norman William Hustings lost his life in a road traffic accident, details being reported in the *Chelmsford Chronicle*. My co-author, while researching AIR 76 documents at TNA Kew came across his service number in AIR 76/246/61 and he believes this was the first reference prior to the Second World War that an officer's service number is quoted, the allocation being made circa March 1920.

21076 *HUSTWAITE	John Walter	W/Cdr		03.01.46	Retirement**
JOHNSON	Ralph Mortimer	F/O		24.10.19	Cancelled
JONES	Albert Leslie	F/O		24.10.26	Relinquished
JONES	Bernard Collier	F/O		24.10.19	Cancelled
07188 JONES-LLOYD	Owen John Frederick	F/O		05.11.30	Relinquished

LG 2 May 1941, issue 35151, page 2514. General Duties Branch. Granted a commission for the duration of hostilities in the rank of Pilot

Officer, with effect from 31st March 1941. Initially, he served with 63413 as his service number.

No.	Surname	Forename	Rank		Date	Disposal
			F/L		20.07.54	Relinquished
	KIDD	Geldart	F/O		24.10.26	Relinquished
	LAMPLUGH	Alfred Gilmer	F/O		24.10.19	Cancelled
	*LATHAM	Raymond Hugh	F/L		27.01.37	Retired list

LG 9 February 1937, issue 34369, page 896. On account of ill-health.

No.	Surname	Forename	Rank		Date	Disposal
07202	LEACH MC	Anthony	G/Capt		09.06.46	Retirement**
	LING	Edward Matthew	F/O		24.10.28	Relinquished
	LIPSCOMB	Lancelot Jennings	F/O		24.10.26	Relinquished
07210	*LOCK	Henry George Watts	G/Capt		25.04.46	Retirement**
07213	LOWEN	Lionel William	S/Ldr		26.05.44	Relinquished

On account off ill-health.[LG 6 June 1944, supplement 36459, page 2693 and LG 19 June 1945, supplement 37135, page 3180].

No.	Surname	Forename	Rank		Date	Disposal
	LOWRIE	William Edward	F/O		24.101.9	Cancelled
07216	*LYDFORD AFC	Harold Thomas	AM		16.04.56	Retirement**

Air Marshal Sir Harold Lydford KBE CB AFC, died on Thursday, 20th September 1979.

No.	Surname	Forename	Rank		Date	Disposal
07228	*MACKAY	Edward Percy	G/Capt		16.01.48	Retirement**
	MACKENZIE	Ian Campbell Ross	F/O		24.10.19	Cancelled
	McENTEGART	James Mathews	F/L		24.10.30	Relinquished
07226	McFARLANE MC	John	G/Capt		07.05.46	Retirement**
	McKENZIE-MARTIN	Edward Charles	F/O		10.03.20	Resigned
	McLAREN MC	James Alexander	F/O	+	17.01.25	208 Squadron

Flying Officer James Alexander McLaren MC lost his life near Ismailia while flying Bristol F.2b HR1636 [though there is a question mark as to the accuracy of the airframe serial]. Formerly of the Liverpool Regiment it was while serving with his regiment that he gained his MC [LG 17 September 1917, supplement 30287, page 9578 and 9579]: *'For conspicuous gallantry and devotion to duty when in command of a wiring party. The work was urgent, and continuously interfered with by heavy enemy bombing, but by his personal example and total disregard of danger he impressed his men with the importance of the task, and completed it successfully. He has for a long time being in charge of wiring parties. On the whole front of his brigade, and on all occasions he has proved himself a very gallant and capable officer.'*

No.	Surname	Forename	Rank		Date	Disposal
07232	McLOUGHLIN	Eugene Joseph	S/Ldr		26.02.48	Retired list**
	McQUISTAN DFC	Finlay	F/O		20.03.22	Removed

Note. The entry in LG 23 June 1922, issue 32722, page 4728 reads: *'Flying Officer Finlay McQuistan DFC is removed from the RAF.'*

No.	Surname	Forename	Rank		Date	Disposal
07235	*McSWINY	Philip Myles	G/Capt		11.07.41	Retirement**
	*MARTINGELL AFC	Gilbert Henry	S/Ldr	+	20.02.36	RAFC Cranwell

ASN Wikibase Occurrence 206954 [which I gratefully acknowledge] which quotes from *Almost a Boffin* by E E Vielle states that Squadron Leader Martingell had taken from the College in Tutor I K3201 to give instruction to Aircraftman Robert Tomlinson and fifteen minutes or so later dived headlong into the garden of Squadron Leader Martingell's married quarter. Reports vary; one suggests failure to recover from a spin, while E E Vielle, acknowledging that the cause was never fully established, writes *'One theory to the cause was that the pupil pilot's parachute had become jammed against the control column, another that the pupil pilot had become 'frozen' at the controls.'* I note that E E Vielle refers to eighteen year old Robert Tomlinson as a Flight Cadet, but this is not supported by entries in *The List of Graduates*.

No.	Surname	Forename	Rank		Date	Disposal
07249	*MERCER	William Kinnear	G/Capt		21.06.44	Retirement**
	MOODY	George Frederick	F/L		14.12.32	Retired list

At his own request [LG 13 December 1932, issue 33891, page 7932].

No.	Surname	Forename	Rank		Date	Disposal
	MORGAN AFC	George Alfred	F/O		24.10.19	Cancelled
	MURCHIE	Charles Plowman	F/O		02.08.26	Relinquished

During the Second World War, as discovered by my co-author, Charles Plowman Murchie was granted a commission in the Royal Army Service Corps with effect from 27th March 1940.

No.	Surname	Forename	Rank		Date	Disposal
	MURRAY	William Grant	Captain		22.12.20	Resigned
	NIGHTINGALE	Charles Esmond	Captain		01.05.21	Resigned

73315 Returned to service: Commissioned as an Honorary Squadron Leader in the Royal Air Force Volunteer Reserve, Administrative and Special Duties Branch, on 25th April 1939 [LG 2 May 1939, issue 34621, page 2926].

No.	Surname	Forename	Rank		Date	Disposal
			F/O		24.09.44	Relinquished
	NORTON	Martin John	F/O		02.07.23	Dismissed

The Service by sentence of General Court Marshal [LG 17 July 1923, issue 32845, page 4926].

No.	Surname	Forename	Rank		Date	Disposal
	PACKHAM	Alfred John	F/O		24.10.26	Relinquished
08027	PAKENHAM-WALSH DFC	Louis Henry	F/L		24.10.26	Relinquished

Returned to service: Granted a commission in the Reserve of Air Force Officers, General Duties Branch, Class C as a Flying Officer [LG 28 February 1939, issue 34603, page 1396]. Transferred to the Administrative and Special Duties Branch, as Flight Lieutenant, on 1st September 1939 [LG 31st October 1939, issue 34721, page 7276].

No.	Surname	Forename	Rank		Date	Disposal
	PAPENFUS DFC	Marthinus Theunis Steyn	Lieutenant		10.11.19	Unemployed
	PEATY	Leonard Frederick	F/O		24.10.19	Cancelled

72713 Returned to service: Commissioned to the Administrative and Special Duties Branch, 21st February 1939, in the rank of Pilot Officer [LG 28 February 1939, issue 34603, page 1396].

No.	Surname	Forename	Rank		Date	Disposal
			P/O		10.02.54	Relinquished
08034	*PENDRED DFC	Lawrence Fleming	AM		13.10.55	Retirement**

Air Marshal Sir Lawrence Pendred KBE CB DFC three times mentioned in despatches, died on Friday, 19th September 1986.

No.	Surname	Forename	Rank		Date	Disposal
08040	PILKINGTON AFC	Christopher	F/L		24.10.31	To Class C

While still in the Reserve, Flight Lieutenant Christopher Pilkington AFC died from pneumonia while being treated in Hertfordshire and Bedfordshire Hospital on Wednesday, 29th August 1934.

No.	Surname	Forename	Rank		Date	Disposal
08046	*POPE MC	Sydney Leo Gregory	A/Cmdr		02.03.46	Retirement**

Air Commodore Sydney Leo Gregory Pope CBE MC DFC AFC mentioned in despatches, died on Wednesday, 5th November 1980.

No.	Surname	Forename	Rank		Date	Disposal
08055	PRESTON DFC	Walter George	F/L		24.10.26	To Class A

Returned to service: Commissioned to the Royal Air Force Reserve, General Duties Branch, in Flight Lieutenant rank, with effect from 29th August 1939 [LG 12 December 1939, issue 34752, page 8254].

No.	Surname	Forename	Rank		Date	Disposal
			W/Cdr		12.09.46	Relinquished

On account of medical unfitness for Air Force service [LG 8 October 1946, supplement 37749, page 4987].

No.	Surname	Forename	Rank		Date	Disposal
08062	*QUINE MC	Sylvester Lindsay	G/Capt		31.01.45	Retirement**
08665	READ	Reginald James	F/L		08.08.41	Resigned
	*RICKARDS	Aubrey Robert Maxwell	W/Cdr	+	30.10.37	84 Squadron

ASN Wikibase Occurrence 209225 [which I have pleasure in acknowledging], reports the death of Wing Commander Rickards in a flying accident on Saturday, 30th October 1937. Taking off from Khor Gharim in Vickers Vincent K6346 of 84 Squadron, presumably to return to Shaibah, the aircraft stalled and dived to the ground. In addition to the Wing Commander, Pilot Officer Robert Henry McClatchey, a Canadian, and Aircraftman Leslie George O'Leary perished. The location of the crash is reported to have been in one of the most desolate areas of Oman. The bodies of the crew were buried in situ, but a determined effort to find their remains resulted in a search conducted in 1997. This was successful and they are now resting in the Christian Cemetery at Muscat.

| | *ROBINSON MC | Harry Noel Cornforth | F/L | + | 02.06.26 | A & GS Eastchurch |

Born in West Hartlepool, Co. Durham on Christmas Day 1898, Flying Robinson was commissioned to the Royal Flying Corps on 10th May 1917 [LG 29 May 1917, supplement 30100, page 5309] and on completion of his training went to the Western Front where he flew Sopwith Camels, first with 46 Squadron and then with 70 Squadron, achieving in total ten aerial combat victories. Postwar, and having relinquished his rank of Acting Captain and obtaining a short service commission, subsequently made permanent [as shown above] he served in Iraq. Sadly, his health failed and following an illness that lasted for several months he died on the 2nd of June 1926. At the time of his death he had been awarded a DFC for gallantry in Iraq, while the French government had conferred on him a *Croix de Guerre*.

| | RODGER MC DCM | Robert Cruden | F/O | | 09.12.26 | Relinquished |

Born on the 7th of June 1895, at Largs in Ayrshire, he enlisted with the Royal Flying Corps on 29th December 1915, and was accepted for observer training on the 7th of March 1917, returning to Home Establishment on the 13th. Returning to the Western Front on 8th of May, he joined 2 Squadron at Hesdigneul two days later. On the 26th, flying in an unidentified FK.8, believed piloted by Captain F Fernihough, the crew came came under sustained machine-gun fire from the ground and 2nd Lieutenant Rodger received a painful wound to his left leg. His death, recorded on one of the many ancestry websites, is reported to have occurred while undergoing surgery for lung cancer on the 1st of June 1961. He is buried in Bognor Regis.

| 08214 | ROWAN | Fred Harris | F/O | | 25.12.20 | Relinquished |

On account of ill-health contracted on active service [LG 24 December 1920, issue 32173, page 12602].

| | ROY MC | Hugh St. Clair | F/O | | 26.07.22 | To Class B |

Flying Officer Hugh St. Clair Roy MC died in Strabane District Hospital, Northern Ireland, on Saturday, 12th November 1927, possibly while still in the Reserve.

| 11075 | SCARROTT | George | A/Cmdr | | 28.09.53 | Retirement** |

Air Commodore George Scarrott CBE mentioned in despatches, died on Saturday, 24th June 1961.

| | SEARSON DFC | Harold Ernest | F/L | | 19.10.28 | Retired list |

At own request [LG 30 October 1928, issue 33434, page 7109].

| 08103 | *SHALES | Francis Harbroe | S/Ldr | | 22.07.40 | Retired list** |

LG 30 July 1940, issue 34910, 4677. On account of ill-health.

| | SHIELDS DFC | Thomas MacMillan | F/O | | 26.11.24 | Resigned |
| | SIDEBOTTOM DFC | William | F/O | + | 08.12.20 | 30 Squadron |

See summary for a description of his death while flying an operational mission.

| 20002 | *SIMS | Francis Henry | A/Cmdr | | 17.04.46 | Retirement** |

Air Commodore Francis Henry Sims CBE, died on Sunday, 1st March 1970.

| | SMITH | Walter Morgan | F/L | | 18.02.25 | Relinquished |

On account of ill-health [LG 17 February 1925, issue 33021, page 1172].

| 75899 | Returned to service: Commissioned as a probationary Pilot Officer for the duration of hostilities in the Administrative and Special Duties | | | | | |

Branch with effect from 13th November 1939 [LG 5 December 1939, issue 34747, page 8108].

| | | | F/L | | 17.08.54 | Relinquished |

LG 17 August 1954, supplement 40255, page 4751.

| 08123 | *SPACKMAN DFC | Charles Basil Slater | AV-M | | 04.04.50 | Retirement** |

Air Vice-Marshal Charles Basil Slater Spackman CB CBE DFC* mentioned in despatches, died on Tuesday, 7th December 1971.

| | STEWART MC DFC | David Arthur | F/L | | 30.08.24 | Ceased employment |

On becoming an airline pilot employed by Imperial Airways. Tragically, as Paul McMillan reports, his career as a civilian pilot was brief for on Christmas Eve 1924, he took off from Croydon Airport in DH.34 G-EBBX with seven passengers bound for Paris, but soon after becoming airborne the airliner stalled and crashed on Castle Hill, Purley where the Kingsdown housing estate is under construction. On impact the DH overturned and burst into flames. There were no survivors.This was the first fatal air accident involving an Imperial Airways aircraft since its formation in the March and as such this led to a very protracted inquest and Public Inquiry which, with adjournments, lasted until 18th February 1925, when the jury returned a verdict of death by misadventure. For a very detailed account of the Public Inquiry proceedings, please refer to the *Wikipedia* entry dealing with the loss of this aircraft.

	STUBBS DFC AFC	John Stevenson	F/O		24.10.19	Cancelled
08140	SYMONDS	Sydney	F/L		24.10.39	Relinquished
	THOMPSON	Arthur Robert	F/O		24.10.19	Cancelled
	TOWNEND AFC	Algernon Cyril	F/O		24.10.19	Cancelled
	TOWNSEND	William Elliott	F/O		24.10.27	Relinquished
	*TURNER DSC DFC	Edward Eric	F/O	+	28.12.22	27 Squadron

Flying Officer Edward Eric Turner DFC and his wireless operator and air gunner Aircraftman James Frederick Sly were engaged with other DHs on an operational sortie in the Waziristan area of the North West Frontier when their aircraft E8468 was struck on the port mainplanes by a bomb dropped from the machine above them. Out of control their DH dived and crashed at, or close to, Palose [possibly now referred to as Palosi].

	TWEEDY	Robert Hall	Captain		04.05.21	Resigned
	URMSTON	Edward Arthur Brabazon	F/O		07.08.20	Resigned
	*USHER	Ernest Caizley	F/O		24.10.19	Cancelled
08161	*VENN	George Oswald	A/Cmdr		03.10.45	Retirement**

Air Commodore George Oswald Venn CBE twice mentioned in despatches, died on Sunday, 11th March 1984.

| | VILLERS | Thomas Vernon | F/O | | 13.11.20 | Relinquished |

On account of ill-health contracted on active service [LG 12 November 1920, issue 32122, page 1003].

| 08165 | VINE | Leslie Edward | F/O | | 24.10.22 | To Class B |

LG 21 September 1954, supplement 40281, page 5379.

			S/Ldr		21.09.54	Relinquished
	WAGNER	Alwyn Warwick Stockwell	F/O		24.10.26	Relinquished
	WALLER	Hardress de Warranne	F/O	+	21.02.20	2 Squadron

See summary for the circumstances of his death.

| | WALLWORK MC | John Wilson | F/O | + | 18.12.22 | AEE |

Sent to Brockworth to test the Gloucestershire Nightjar J6930, Flying Officer Wallwork was killed trying to regain the airfield after the aircraft's engine failed at 200 feet. Enlisting with the Royal Flying Corp as a Flight Cadet, John Wilson Wallwork, born in Manchester on the 6th of May 1898, joined 40 Squadron at Bruay on the 13th of August 1917, and following a long spell of incapacitation proved himself as an SE.5a scout pilot by his tenacity in offensive patrolling. His MC was *Gazetted* on 26th July 1918, supplement 30813, page 8853: '*For conspicuous gallantry and devotion to duty. During recent operations he participated in many offensive low-flying and bombing attacks, and carried them out with great courage and determination. From very low altitudes he bombed enemy troops and transports, inflicting heavy casualties. He caused, while on an offensive patrol, more than one enemy machine to crash, and brought down others out of control. He set a magnificent example of courage and skill.'* He is mentioned many times in David Gunby's history of the squadron, published in 1994, by The Pentland Press under the title *Sweeping the Skies*.

| | WATERTON | Edmund Alfred Mary | F/O | | 24.10.19 | Cancelled |
| | WHITELEY | Francis Norman | F/O | | 20.07.20 | Resigned |

LG 21 June 1940, supplement 34877, page 3771. Royal Army Pay Corps. Commissioned as a Lieutenant with effect from 9th February 1940, noting he was *'late RAF'* and allotted the service number 119045.

	WHITTON	George William Mahony	F/O		24.10.30	Relinquished
08193	*WIGGLESWORTH AFC Cecil George		A/Cmdr		12.10.46	Retirement**

Air Commodore Cecil George Wigglesworth CB AFC, died on Tuesday, 8th August 1961.

08195	*WILLIAMS MC DFC Thomas Melling		AM		07.02.53	Retirement**

Air Marshal Sir Thomas Williams KCB OBE MC DFC* twice mention in despatches, died on Sunday, 10th June 1956.

	WINCH	Hubert Edward	F/O		24.10.26	Relinquished
	WOODBRIDGE	Albert Edward	F/L		01.11.26	To Class A

Ceased Royal Air Force Employment [LG 7 February 1928, issue 33354, page 858].

					01.02.28	Imperial Airways

As captain of DH.66 Hercules G-ABMZ *'City of Jerusalem'* Imperial Airways he stalled and crashed during a night approach to Jask Airport in Persia on Friday, 6th September 1929. The heavy landing collapsed the undercarriage and the port wing was forced back against the fuselage where the wing-mounted flares ignited petrol that had spilled from ruptured fuel tanks. In addition to Flight Lieutenant Woodbridge [RAFO] two of his crew perished and two were saved; the aircraft was carrying mail from the United Kingdom to India.

	WRIGHT	Ernest Chumley Bruce	F/O		29.12.23	Relinquished

On account of ill-health [LG 28 December 1923, issue 32892, page 9112].

	WYBROW	Sidney George	F/O		24.10.27	Relinquished
08233	*YOOL	William Munro	AV-M		27.06.49	Retirement**

Air Vice-Marshal William Munro Yool CB CBE, died on Tuesday, 19th September 1978.

	YOUNG DFC	Horace Norman	F/O	+	13.07.21	12 Squadron

Died, probably from natural causes, and is buried in Prees [St. Chad] Churchyard, Shropshire. Additional to his DFC and First Bar he had been Mentioned in Despatches, as has been recorded on Army Form B.103c on 20th May 1918. Although incomplete, the Form shows he was born on 27th December 1898, and joined the RFC on 15th June 1917. On the 7th of December 1917, he reported to Mons-en-Chaussée where he was attached to 8 Squadron. On the 10th of August 1918, he was wounded [see my second volume of squadron losses, page 136 for details, which notes his death on 13th July 1921].

	ZINK	Edmund Leonard	F/O		03.11.20	Resigned

OBSERVER OFFICERS

11

	BRADLEY	Patrick Joesph	F/O		24.10.26	Relinquished
	*CAILLARD	Camille Percy Maurice Benjamin	F/O	+	05.03.26	AD Karachi

On Friday, March 5th, 1926, Flying Officer Caillard, accompanied by Leading Aircraftman Andrew Barron, took off from Karachi for bombing practice in an unidentified Bristol F.2b and crashed with fatal consequences for both airmen during the sortie. Formerly of the Wiltshire Regiment, Camile Caillard was born in Hove, Sussex on the 14th of November 1898, and attached to 22 Squadron for the last few months of the *Great War* flew Bristol F.2bs. In the spring of 1919, he was attached, briefly, to 99 Squadron, thence to 25 Squadron before returning to 22 Squadron on 13th May.and remaining with '22' until 23rd August 1919, when he joined 12 Squadron at Heumar.

	COCKERAM MC	Percy Allbutt	F/O		24.10.26	Relinquished
	GARNER AFC	Ernest James	O/O	+	18.10.20	HMS *Pegasus*

During a test flight in Fairey IIIC N9257 on Monday, 18th October 1920, his pilot, Flying Officer Frederick Henry Isaac lost control and spun into the sea off Feneraki near Constantinople. Flying Officer Isaac was picked up, though in an injured state, but Ernest Garner drowned before help arrived. Subsequently, his body was recovered and taken for burial in Haidar Pasha Cemetery.

09008	GAYFORD DFC	Oswald Robert	A/Cmdr		...08.44	Retirement**

Air Commodore Oswald Robert Gayford CBE DFC* AFC twice mentioned in despatches, died on Friday, 10th of August 1945. The website Air of Authority has a wealth of information pertaining to Air Commodore Gayford who post *Great War* re-mustered as a pilot and was much involved with setting long-distance flying records which led to his award of the Air Force Cross. In retirement, which, sadly, was short-lived, he held the position of Regional Controller for the Eastern Region of the Ministry of Fuel and Power. He has been afforded a CWGC headstone over his grave in Naughton [St. Mary] Churchyard, Suffolk, where he is the sole Second World War casualty.

	HAMILTON MC	Robert	F/O		24.10.30	Relinquished
	JENKINS DFC DSM Norman Hugh		F/L	+	17.12.29	

Killed during an attempt to fly non-stop in a Fairey Long Range Monoplane from Cranwell to Capte Town, piloted by Squadron Leader Arthur Gordon Jones-Williams OBE MC, both officers perishing in the crash near Zaghaouan in French Tunisia. See also my entry in Appendix D for Squadron Leader Jones-Williams.

	SMITH DFC	Harold				
09041	STEVENS	Alick Charles	AM		14.12.53	Retirement**

Air Marshal Sir Alick Stevens KBE CB mentioned in despatches, died on Thursday, 2nd July 1987.

	TRULOCK	John Camilo	Lieutenant		06.02.20	Relinquished

Of Spanish descent and born 24th June 1892, his Army Form B.103 for 1917, shows he was permitted to to travel on leave to Villagarcia*on 23rd June 1917, and a month later on 22nd July was posted missing with his pilot 2nd Lieutenant C C Knight when his 55 Squadron DH.4 A7508 engaged on bombing enemy positions near Ghent suffered engine failure and forced-landed near Terneuzen [Zeeland]. Both officers were taken prisoner, but not before they managed to set light to their aircraft. * Probably Villagarcía de Arousa in the Province of Pontevedra, Galicia.

	WATSON	William Stanley	F/L		24.10.30	Relinquished

FLYING OFFICERS [from PILOT OFFICERS]

62

	*ADAMS	Albert Jabez	F/L		19.05.32	Retired list
	ADAMS	Frank	F/O		24.10.19	Cancelled
	ALLEN MC	Laurence Wilfred	F/O		01.09.26	Relinquished
	ANDERSON	Alex Thomas James	F/O	+	17.07.22	205 Squadron

Flying Officer Alex Thomas James Anderson was killed and his passenger Flying Officer Robert Dyet Lambert injured when their Parnall Panther N7509 went into a sideslip and crashed near the airfield at Leuchars. By awful coincidence, near a rock-crowned mound of the Niederbarr and close to the ruins of Flohbarr castle, a French passenger aeroplane on a flight from Strasbourg to Paris with four English passengers sideslipped and crashed. The details of the accident can be read in *The Times* published on 18th July 1922.

	BAGNALL	William	F/O		24.10.19	Cancelled
	BARRON	Augustus Alfred Ward	F/O		24.10.31	Relinquished
	BROWN	Ernest Amedee Jellicorse	F/O		24.10.26	Relinquished
	BRYAN	Bernard Gordon	F/L		25.08.20	Resigned
	BUIST MC	Alexander Charles Seaton	Lieutenant		27.01.20	Relinquished

On account of ill-health contracted on active service [LG 3 February 1920, issue 31765, page 1427].

73112	Returned to the service as a Pilot Officer on probation, commissioned to the Administrative and Special Duties Branch, 2nd May 1939					

[LG 9 May 1939, issue 34624, page 3114].

			S/Ldr		06.05.44	Relinquished

LG 23 May 1944, supplement 36524, page 2346. On account of ill-health.

| | CARPENTER | Sydney David | | Lieutenant | 10.03.21 | Relinquished |

On account of ill-health contracted in the Service [LG 22 March 1921, issue 32265, page 2304].

| | CASE | Albert Edward | | F/O | 24.10.19 | Cancelled |
| 07018 | CHRISTOPHERSON Paul | | | F/L | 10.01.44 | Dismissed |

Dismissed the Service by sentence of General Court Marshal, 10th January 1944 [LG 6 June 1944, supplement 36549, page 2697]

| | CLARK | Clifford Claude | | F/O | 16.11.37 | Resigned |
| | COLMAN | Esca Houghton | – | F/O | 24.10.19 | Cancelled |

Born 19th July 1891, a document exists for this officer at TNA Kew under AIR 76/99/89.

| | DAVIS | Frank Howard | | F/O | 24.10.19 | Cancelled |
| | FFRENCH | Harold Harris | | F/O | 29.09.21 | Removed |

Also known as Harold Harris French, a document for this officer is held at TNA Kew under WO 339/124524. Paul McMillan has discovered via one of the many ancestry websites the following: '*No. 5785 in Canadian Militia, Sergeant, 17th March 1918, discharged to join the RAF, assumed the second 'F', became Ffrench. Discharged for embezzlement of £1566-12s-7d; cashed a cheque for £700 on which he forged a signature, 1920. He risked all to spend one last Christmas at home with Laura and his son John [Laura pregnant with James]: police knocked on front door, he jumped from the upstairs bedroom window and escaped. That was the very first time that Laura knew anything was wrong; she never saw Harold again. Harold phoned Laura's brother Jim, asked to meet him on Liverpool Street Station, gave him a left luggage ticket and said it was to look after Laura. Jim went to the left luggage office and retrieved a suitcase, full of money which he took to the police! Harold turned up in Canada at his sister Olive's house in Peterborough, but Olive claimed that they refused to help him.* RAF Records show Harold was never caught. Nevertheless, the following appeared in *The London Gazette* 22nd July 1921, issue 32398, page 5881: '*In the High Court of Justice - King's Bench Division [King's Remembrance] 1921 No.8 - Between His Majesty's Attorney-General, Informant, and Harold Harris Ffrench, Defendant. To the above named Defendant, Harold Harris Ffrench, late of the Royal Air Force Record Office, Blandford, in the county of Dorset. Take notice, the proceedings by way of information have been commenced against you in the High Court of Justice, King's Bench Division [King's Remembrance Department], by His Majesty's Attorney-General, on behalf of His Majesty, in which the Informant's claim is for the recovery of the sum of £866 18s 7d, payable by you for monies received by you to and for the use of His Majesty, together with the sum of £1 13s 11d costs. And take notice, that the Court has, by Order dated the 18th day of July 1921, ordered that personal services upon you by Writ of Subpoena in the said proceedings shall be dispensed with, and that service of the same be effected by sending prepaid post letters, each containing a copy of the said writ and of the said Order, addressed respectively to you at the Record Office of the Royal Air Force, Blandford, in the county of Dorset, and at No. 1 Wyfold-road, Fulham, in the county of London, and by the insertion of this notice once in the London Gazette, the Times and Daily Mail newspapers. And further take notice, that in default of your entering an appearance at the The King's Remembrances's Department of the King's Bench Division, Royal Courts of Justice, Strand, London, within 14 days after the insertion of this advertisement, inclusive of the day of such insertion, according to the exigency of the said writ, an information may be filed and Judgement signed thereon and execution issued on such Judgement, together with costs, at the expiration of 14 days from the day of signing such Judgement. Treasury Solicitor, Law Courts Branch, 705, Royal Courts of Justice, Strand, WC2.*' Additional research by my co-author reveals a letter written by his grandson, Anthony Ffrench, to the Disclosures Team at Cranwell in which a date of birth of 31st December 1891, is given along with emigration to Canada circa 1909, where on 23rd September 1914, Harold attested and going to serve with the Canadian Signal Corps and Pay Corps. Miscellaneous detail pertaining to his *Great War* service was also sent. A Record of Service, stamped with a date July 1989 [or 1999 it is extremely blurred] indicates service with the Middle East Communications Flight between 22nd November 1918, and 7th November 1919, at which date he came under the aegis of the Records Office at Blandford. The date of his absconding from the service was 21st January 1921.

| 10091 | *FREDERICK | William Bernard | | F/L | 20.06.32 | Retired list |

LG 7 April 1936, issue 34272, page 2285. Granted a commission in the Auxiliary Air Force, Stores Branch, retaining his rank. LG 22 September 1936, issue 34325, page 6080, relinquishes his commission in the Auxiliary Air Force upon being granted a commission in Class C of the Reserve of Air Force Officers, 14th July 1936, retaining his rank. Promoted Squadron Leader, William Bernard Frederick died at the age of 54 on Sunday, 2nd March 1941. He rests in Lacey Green [St. John] Churchyard, Buckinghamshire.

| 03122 | GOLDER DSM | William Henry | | W/Cdr | 06.09.41 | Retirement |

Re-employed as per entry in LG 7 December 1943, supplement 36276, page 5341.

				W/Cdr	13.03.45	Retired list**
	GORRINGE	Kingsley Charles Lee		F/O	24.10.26	Relinquished
	GOWLER	George Alfred		F/O	08.12.26	Relinquished
	GWYNNE-TIMOTHY	Gordon Roland St. Cyr		F/O	05.05.20	Resigned
07137	HAZELL	Oswald Theobald		F/O	24.10.24	To Class A

Returned to service: Commissioned within the Reserve of Air Force Officers, General Duties Branch, and promoted Flight Lieutenant with effect from 3rd September 1939 [LG 20 December 1940, issue 35019, page 7119]. LG 1 September 1942, supplement 35686, page 3811. Awarded the Air Force Cross; rank Squadron Leader.

				S/Ldr	09.07.54	Relinquished
	HERBERT DCM	Bert Edgar		F/O	24.10.34	Relinquished
07142	HERBERT	Sydney		S/Ldr	09.07.54	Relinquished
	HERD	James Fleming		F/O	29.08.32	Relinquished
	HERON DFC	Oscar Aloysius Patrick		F/O	07.11.26	Relinquished
	HUMPHREYS	Walter Ebenezer		F/O	24.08.20	Resigned
07170	HUXLEY DFC	Joseph Harold		F/O	04.08.26	Relinquished

Returned to service: Commissioned to the Royal Air Force Volunteer Reserve, Training Branch, in the rank of Pilot Officer, effective from 2nd April 1941 [LG 9 May 1941, issue 35158, page 2681] as 67170 but, subsequently, reverted to his original service number. LG 14 October 1947, supplement 38095, page 4801.

				P/O	19.09.47	Resigned**
	JACKSON	John Daniel		F/O	24.10.26	Relinquished
07193	KING	Patrick John Richardson		G/Capt	01.01.45	

LG 6 March 1951, supplement 39163, page 1168. Appointed to a commission in the Royal Air Force Reserve of Officers, Class J in the rank of Group Captain [Retired]. LG 5 April 1966, supplement 43941, page 3931.

| | | | | F/L | 01.10.64 | Relinquished |
| 07196 | KIRK | Fred | | A/Cmdr | 12.01.48 | Retirement** |

Air Commodore Fred Kirk OBE, died Friday, 11th July 1980.

	LACEY	George		F/O	24.10.19	Cancelled
	LOWRIE	William Edward		F/O	24.10.19	Cancelled
	MAGEE	Frank Joesph		F/O	24.10.26	Relinquished
07239	MARSDEN	Eric		F/O	16.02.27	Relinquished

TNA Kew holds a document for this officer under AIR 76/334/82.

| | McERLEAN | Michael Henry | | F/O | 08.11.26 | Relinquished |
| | MICHAELSON | Ralph Charlesson | | F/O | 01.12.20 | Resigned |

TNA Kew has a record for this officer under AIR 76/345/140. My co-author has discovered some interesting facts concerning Flying Officer Michaelson who was born in Kensington on the 17th December 1899. He was of Swedish extraction and his first Christian name was Knut, though he was later to be known as Ralph Charles Michaelson. Subsequent to his resignation as a short service commission officer, he obtained a commission in Auxiliary Air Force which was terminated on 16th October 1939. However, as 74538 he re-entered the service, confirmed in his appointment on 4th September 1940, and served until:-

| | | | | W/Cdr | 15.10.54 | Relinquished |
| 21079 | *MITCHELL | James Wason | | G/Capt | | Retired list** |

LG 13 March 1951, supplement 39169, page 1296. Royal Air Force Reserve of Officers. James Wason Mitchell G/Capt [Retd] appointed to a commission in Class J, with effect from 19th Febuary 1951, in the rank of Flight Lieutenant.

	MORRIS	Leslie Grenville	F/O		24.10.19	Cancelled
	NORTH	Frederick Charles	F/O		24.10.27	Relinquished
	O'BRIEN	Francis Albert	F/O	+	08.06.31	AST Hamble

Killed while attempting to loop Siskin III G-ABHT, his aircraft coming down near Sarisbury, a village below the present M.27 and roughly midway between Southampton and Fareham on the northwest side of Portsmouth Harbour. According to ASN Wikibase Occurrence 202429 [which I am pleased to acknowledge], it is believed Flying Officer O'Brien attempted the manoeuvre at too low an altitude and before he could recover his aircraft flew into the ground. An inquest into to his death was held on Wednesday, 10th June.

| 08022 | OSBORN | Edwin Stanley | S/Ldr | | 17.03.48 | Relinquished |

Note. On 24th October 1928, he was transferred to Class B of the Reserve, but with effect from 7th May 1938, he was granted a commission in Class CC as a Flight Lieutenant with seniority dated 13th January 1937, in the Administrative and Special Duties Branch, later being transferred to the Technical Branch, ranked Squadron Leader, with effect from 30th January 1941. On 26th May 1946, he returned to the Administrative and Special Duties Branch [Class CC] and appears to have been allocated 192348 as his service number.

	OWEN DFC MM	James	F/O		24.10.19	Cancelled
13068	PACK	George Thomas Harvey	G/Capt		24.06.44	Retirement**
	PARKER	Leonard Arthur	F/O		24.10.32	Relinquished
08047	POTTER	Stephen Holsworth	F/O		24.10.26	To Class A
LG 20 August 1929, issue 33527, page 5409.			F/L		26.07.29	To Class C
LG 28 February 1933, issue 33916, page 1363.			F/L		01.12.32	To Class A
LG 29 October 1935, issue 34214, page 6790.			F/L		24.10.35	To Class C
LG 13 April 1937, issue 34388, page 2381.			F/L		24.10.36	To Class A
LG 31 August 1954, supplement 40266, page 5014.			W/Cdr		31.08.54	Relinquished
	ROPER	Charles	Lieutenant		23.11.21	Relinquished

On account of ill-health [LG 22 November 1921, issue 32525, page 9257].

| | SEWELL | John | F/O | | 05.02.29 | Relinquished |
| | SLATER | Ian Cecil | F/O | + | 15.08.21 | 208 Squadron |

Taking off from Heliopolis with General Charles Richard Newman CMG DSO, Chief of the General Staff, Egypt, as his passenger, Flying Officer Slater stalled while banking and moments later the Bristol F.2b F4926 struck the ground. Help arrived quickly and General Newman was pulled from the wreckage with very serious injuries. A report of the accident, filed that day from Cairo, appeared in *The Times* on the 16th: *"An aeroplane from Ismailia, conveying General Newman, Chief of the General Staff in Egypt, crashed at Heliopolis this morning. The pilot was killed and General Newman received such injuries that his recovery is considered very doubtful."* - Reuter. However, the general did recover and under the heading *'Commissions signed by the Lord Lieutenant of the County of Devon'* he is recorded as Major-General Charles Richard Newman CB CMG DSO of New Park, Axminster, Devon [LG 10 May 1938, issue 34509, page 3025].

| | SLATER MBE | James Henry | F/O | | 24.10.19 | Cancelled |
| 08117 | SMITH | Henry Allan | S/Ldr | | 30.08.41 | Relinquished |

On account of ill-health [LG 5 September 1941, issue 35266, page 5159].

| | SMYTH | Geoffrey Robert Basil | F/O | | 24.10.28 | Relinquished |

Note. On 17th April 1931, his surname became 'Smyth-Homewood' [LG 19 May 1931, issue 33717, page 3273].

| | STEGGALL DCM | Francis Ronald | F/O | | 24.10.22 | To Class C |

Note. Held at The National Archives is a record for this officer, reference WO 339/128675 covering the period 1914-1922, his rank being recorded as 2nd Lieutenant, Royal Flying Corps. I believe he may have emigrated to South Africa where on 26th April 1930, he married Cynthia Campbell, the ceremony coming within the jurisdiction of Johannesburg. Paul McMillan, my co-author, reports Flying Officer Steggall served in the Royal Navy during the Second World War.

| | STORRS | Harold Heywood | F/O | | 23.06.26 | To Class C |
| 80658 | | | | | | |

Returned to service: Commissioned to the Administrative and Special Duties Branch, 13th June 1940, for the duration of hostilities in the rank of Pilot Officer [LG 2 July 1940, issue 34887, page 4022].

			P/O		24.08.41	Terminated**
	TADMAN CGM	Frederick John	F/O		24.10.19	Cancelled
	TAYLOR	Albert Jesse Hanchet	F/O		24.10.26	Relinquished

Note. In the Third Supplement to *The London Gazette*, Tuesday 14 November 1944, supplement 36793, page 5205, under the heading CENTRAL CHANCERY OF THE ORDERS OF KNIGHTHOOD and appointment to the Most Excellent Order of the British Empire. *To be an Additional Officer of the Military Division of the Said Most Excellent Order*. Group Captain Albert Jesse Hanchet-Taylor [C.1775] Royal Canadian Air Force.

| 08145 | TAYLOR | Ernest | S/Ldr | | 24.08.54 | Relinquished |
| 21035 | *THOMAS | Richard Maelor | W/Cdr | | 22.01.46 | Retirement** |

Note. LG 13 June 1964, supplement 43343, page 4956, under the heading *'Most Excellent Order of the British Empire, Ordinary Members of the Civil Division* Wing Commander Richard Maelor THOMAS, Chairman Bath, Wells and District War Pensions Committee.

| | UPTON | Sidney | F/O | | 24/10.19 | Cancelled |
| 08181 | WEBB | Henry | F/L | + | 16.07.44 | |

Flight Lieutenant Henry Webb, 58 years of age, died in RAF Hospital St. Athan; he is buried in Bath [Haycombe] Cemetery.

| | WHITMORE DSC | Frank Henry | F/O | | 24.10.19 | Cancelled |

Note. It seems he returned to the service for on the 3rd of June 1927, Flying Officer Frank Henry Whitmore DSC was appointed to the Most Excellent Order of the British Empire [Military Division] [LG 3 June 1927, supplement 33280, page 3611].

| | LG 1 March 1938, issue 34488, page 1351. | | S/Ldr | | 02.03.38 | Retired list |

On account of ill-health.

| | WILLIAMS | Harold Boswarick | F/O | | 03.05.30 | Relinquished |

OBSERVER OFFICERS [from PILOT OFFICERS]
8

| | BLOY | Anthony Wollam | O/O | | 10.08.21 | Dismissed |

By sentence of General Court Martial [Air Force List 3053 - 3055 October 1921].

| 08246 | *COLLINS | Harold John | A/Cmdr | | 10.04.48 | Retirement** |

Air Commodore Harold John Collins CBE, died on Sunday, 27th July 1969.

| | DAY MC | William Conway | F/L | + | 24.07.24 | 84 Squadron |

On Thursday, 24th July 1924, Flight Lieutenant Day, now a qualified pilot, accompanied by Flying Officer Donald Ramsay Stewart, forced-landed his DH.9A H147 of 84 Squadron in the desert south of Jalibah, Iraq. William Day, as a 2nd Lieutenant with the Middlesex Regiment, was *Gazetted* with the MC on 6th April 1918, supplement 30614, page 4211: *'For conspicuous gallantry and devotion to duty in leading his company through two heavy barrages to a position where he beat off several counter-attacks. Later, when in command of the battalion, after all the senior officers had become casualties, his reports, which were sent back regularly, were of the greatest value to the higher command.'* I suspect this award was in recognition of actions in what many historians refer to as *'The Kaiser's Battle'*.

| | GRAY | John Harold | O/O | | 11.06.24 | Relinquished |

On account of ill-health [LG 10 June 1924, issue 32944, page 4609].

JONES	Thomas Percy Taylor		P/O	+	29.04.24	5 FTS Shotwick

Pilot Officer Thomas Percy Taylor Jones and Aircraftman Cyril Sydney Richards died when their Bristol F.2b F4954 spun and crashed on the airfield.

PAGET	Bernard James	F/O		24.10.26	Relinquished
09043	THOMASSON DFC MM Frederick	F/L		24.10.28	To Class B

LG 28 October 1930, issue 33656, page 6599. Re-employed with the Regular Air Force for a further year, with effect from 24th October 1930, retaining Flight Lieutenant rank. LG 15 November 1938, issue 34570, page 7196. Under the heading RESERVE OF AIR FORCE OFFICERS, General Duties Branch, Squadron Leader Frederick Thomasson was granted a commission in Class CC as a Flight Lieutenant [Honorary Squadron Leader] with effect from 7th December 1936, Honorary rank effective 5th November 1937. LG 20 October 1939, issue 34713, page 7043. Granted a commission in the Administrative and Special Duties Branch with effect from 1st September 1939, in the rank of Flight Lieutenant, seniority 7th December 1936. Service number 192835 allocated. LG 8 February 1949, supplement 38532, page 683. Secretarial Branch. Appointed to a commission [Class B], as Flight Lieutenant with effect from 6th December 1948.

		F/L	30.04.52	Relinquished
THOMSON DFC	George Irving	F/L	04.08.34	Relinquished

LG 11 November 1919, issue 31637, pages 13668 and 13669.

SQUADRON LEADER
2

IMPEY	Thomas Smith	S/Ldr	11.11.26	Relinquished

LG 22 October 1935, issue 34210, page 6636. *'The permission granted to Squadron Leader Thomas Smith Impey to retain his rank is withdrawn on his conviction by the civil power. 10th [sic] Sept. 1935.'* This was an unusual case of conspiracy to defraud an 84-year old Mrs Harriet Eyre-Williams of Thurloe Place, South Kensington, by implying several million pounds of money was held in an American Trust Fund and was reported in *The Times* in their edition of 14th September 1935. In addition to Squadron Leader Thomas Smith Impey, described at the opening of the trial before Judge Dodson at the Central Criminal Court, as being a former major in his Majesty's service, and now a company director, Richard Lindsay Rogers, a secretary and Lilian Amelia Burton, an authoress, were also charged. At the opening of the trial, Mr G D Roberts prosecuting described Impey as being treated almost like a son by Mrs Eyre-Williams who had parted with £34,000. The trial lasted for over a week, concluding in guilty verdicts against all three defendants; Squadron Leader Impey, described by Judge Dodson as having acted in a treacherous manner, was sentenced to five years penal servitude, Mrs Burton to four while Rogers, the secretary, was sent to prison for 12-months.

LOWE	John Cecil Mansfield	S/Ldr	28.10.19	Cancelled

FLIGHT LIEUTENANTS
10

	BELT MC MBE DCM Charles Burnley	Captain		25.04.20	Unemployed
	*GREENWOOD Vincent	S/Ldr		06.12.35	Retired list
	HOBBS DSO DSC Basil Deacon	Captain		03.06.19	Unemployed

According to *Wikipedia* Basil Deacon Hobbs, born 20th December 1894, at Arlington in Berkshire, moved to Canada in 1915, undergoing flying instruction in America at the Wright Flying School in Dayton, Ohio. Returning to England, he joined the Royal Naval Air Service. It appears he returned to Canada in 1920, joining the RCAF and retiring in 1927, holding the rank of Major. On the outbreak of the Second World War he rejoined the RCAF and rose to Group Captain rank. His death was reported in 1963.

06114	PAYN	Harold James	S/Ldr	10.02.54	Relinquished
	PIZEY	Edmund May	Captain	25.04.22	Relinquished

On account of ill-health contracted in the Service [LG 25 April 1922, issue 32680, page 3236].

06144	TODD	Henry Cuthbert	S/Ldr	13.09.43	Relinquished

On account off ill-health [LG 28 September 1943, supplement 36187, page 4312].

	WAIN	William Donston	F/L	+	01.02.20

CWGC indicates he was married and was aged 30 at the time of his death and was buried in Marlow Cemetery. Flight Lieutenant Wain died, according to the Marlow Society website, which I acknowledge, in a Berlin hospital. His military unit was given as No. 1 School of Bomb Dropping and Navigation at Stonehenge in Wiltshire. Although he qualified as a pilot with the Royal Naval Volunteer Reserve, for most of his service he was a munitions officer.

WAITE MBE	Robert Bruce	F/L	11.03.25	Relinquished

On account of ill-health. Flight Lieutenant Robert Bruce Waite, as discovered by my co-author, was born in Devizes on 23rd September 1868, and in 1890, enlisted in 1st Royal Dragoons, his regimental number being 3219. His death in the Chelsea Hospital, London, occurred on 12th June 1928. His widow subsequently received a pension as recorded in World War One Pension Records Cards and Ledgers.

WILKINSON	Frank Campbell	F/L	11.11.34	Relinquished
WILLIAMS	Frederick Raban	S/Ldr	17.06.20	Relinquished

On account of ill-health contracted in the Service [LG 2 July 1920, issue 31962, page 7127].

FLYING OFFICERS
9

11076	BURRIDGE	Edward Alfred	A/Cmdr	25.06.48	Retirement**

Air Commodore Edward Alfred Burridge mentioned in a despatch, died in the late spring or early summer of 1982.

	JONES	William	F/L	11.11.30	Relinquished
	LONG	Walter Meriton	F/L	11.11.26	Relinquished
	MACASKIE	Donald Stuart Calthorpe	F/O	11.11.19	Cancelled
10130	*NICHOLL	William Greville MacDonald	G/Capt	30.09.45	Retirement

On account of medical unfitness for Air Force service.

	TERRY	Ernest Pollden	F/L	11.11.30	Relinquished
10160	*TOTTLE	Ernest Alfred	S/Ldr	29.01.49	Retired list

On account of medical unfitness for Air Force service.

	TURNER	Bertrand	F/O	11.11.19	Cancelled
	WALTERS	Leslie Allan	F/O	11.11.32	Relinquished

OBSERVER OFFICER

09047	UMPLEBY	William John	F/O	11.11.26	To Class A

LG 14 May 1929, issue 33495, page 3242.

	F/L	05.01.29	To Class C

LG 21 June 1929, issue 3508, page 4123.

	F/L	09.06.29	To Class A

LG 14 November 1933, issue 33995, page 7375.

	F/L	11.11.33	To Class C

LG 5 February 1935, issue 34130, page 846.

	F/L	11.11.34	To Class B

LG 12 December 1939, issue 34752, page 8254. Transferred to the Administrative and Special duties Branch, 29th August 1939.
LG 2 January 1945, supplement 36871, page 50.

	F/L	19.12.44	Resigned

FLYING OFFICERS [from PILOT OFFICERS]

*ELLIOTT	Ernest Frank	F/O		06.07.27	Retired list

On account of ill-health [LG 5 July 1927, issue 33291, page 4328].

*HOLBROOK	Vincent Stanley	F/O		08.08.23	Retired list

On account of ill-health [LG 7 August 1923, issue 32851, page 5432].

LANGRIDGE	Arthur Bracy	S/Ldr	+	12.11.26	Uxbridge

Squadron Leader Arthur Bracy Langridge, a Barrister serving in the Office of the Judge Advocate-General suffered a seizure and died at Cranwell where he intended to present a lecture on Royal Air Force Law. From a report in the *Uxbridge & West Drayton Gazette* of 19th November, 1926, he had been feeling unwell but decided to go ahead with his planned visits to Digby and Cranwell. He was buried with full Service honours in Cranwell [St. Andrew's] Churchyard. At TNA Kew under WO 339/116933 a document exists for this officer [1914-1922].

NEWMAN	Edwin James	F/O		11.11.30	Relinquished
NUNN	Charles Henry Napier	F/L		10.11.30	Relinquished
*THOMSON	Thomas	F/O	+	17.04.25	84 Squadron

While flying as observer to Flight Lieutenant Cyril Jameson Truran AFC their DH.9A [airframe serial not recorded] crashed near Shaibah injuring the pilot; Flying Officer Thomas Thomson is buried in Basra [Makina] Royal Air Force Cemetery. Please refer to Flight Lieutenant Truran's entry for information regarding his dismissal from the Service which was a direct consequence of the accident that killed Flying Officer Thomson.

LG 28 November 1919, issue 31663, page 14702

SQUADRON LEADER

*CORDINGLEY OBE John Walter	AV-M		01.03.47	Retirement**

Air Vice-Marshal Sir John Cordingley KCB KCVO CBE mentioned in a despatch, died on Wednesday, 5th January 1977.

FLIGHT LIEUTENANTS
8

BOUMPHREY	Geoffrey Maxwell	F/L		28.11.19	Cancelled

Note. At TNA Kew under WO 339/14799 a document exists for this officer [1914-1918]. Formerly of the 8th Battalion, South Lancashire Regiment, as Captain Geoffrey Maxwell Boumphrey he made his mark in the history of 46 Squadron when accompanied by Captain F Findley and flying Nieuport 12 A3274 together engaged and shot down an Albatros east of Ypres on 5th February 1917, thereby scoring the squadron's first aerial combat success since arriving on the Western Front the previous October. At the time '46' was based at Droglandt; additional detail is provided by Trevor Henshaw in his classic *The Sky Their Battlefield.* Meanwhile, Army Form B.103 indicates Captain Boumphrey was wounded in the left leg and following treatment at No. 7 Stationary Hospital was evacuated to England on HMHS *Princess Elizabeth* on February 10th. Paul McMillan shows a birth date of 7th August 1894, at Lymm, Cheshire and death occurring in Chardstock, Devon, on 29th November 1969.

CLARKE	Henry Harold	F/L		28.11.28	Relinquished

LG 31 May 1935, issue 34165, page 3555. Notified death of Henry Harold Clarke, late of Stoke Court, Stoke Pogis, Buckinghamshire, who died on 6th April 1935, noting he was late Captain, Royal Welsh Fusiliers and Flight Lieutenant, Royal Air Force.

GOODWIN AFC	Edwin Spencer	AV-M	09.03.48	Retirement**

Air Vice-Marshal Edwin Spencer Goodwin CB CBE AFC* three times mentioned in despatches, died on Friday, 17th May 1991.

*HAIG	Rollo Amyatt de Haga	S/Ldr		03.03.26	Retired list

At own request [LG 2 March 1926, issue 33138, page 1570].

21078	*HIRST	Lewis Vere	W/Cdr	+	11.03.42

Died on active service; Wing Commander Lewis Vere Hirst is buried in Harrogate [Stonefall] Cemetery.

06108	NIGHTINGALE	Alfred James	F/L	28.11.26	To Class C
			F/L	07.09.31	To Class B
			F/L	28.11.34	To Class C

LG 15 September 1931, issue 33753, page 5969.
LG 11 December 1934, issue 34113, page 8058.
LG 15 November 1938, issue 34570, page 7198. Transferred from the Stores Branch to General Duties Branch, Class C, with effect from 1st November 1938, retaining the rank of Flight Lieutenant. Subsequently transferred to the Administrative and Special Duties Branch. Thence to a Class CC commission in the Secretarial Branch in the rank of Squadron Leader and allocated service number 192440 [LG 5 August 1947, supplement 38035, page 3671].

06109	NUNN DSC DFC	Harry Laurence	W/Cdr	31.08.54	Relinquished
	STEPHENSON-PEACH MBE	Robert Louis	F/L	01.11.34	Relinquished

FLYING OFFICERS [from FLIGHT LIEUTENANTS]
2

08121	*SORLEY DSC	Ralph Squire	AM	06.09.48	Retirement**

Air Marshal Sir Ralph Sorley KCB OBE DSC DFC, died on Sunday, 17th November 1974.

	*SIMONS	William Vazie	F/L	11.12.29	Retired list

LG 10 December 1929, issue 33559, page 8027. At own request.

FLYING OFFICERS
7

CAMERON MBE	Donald Phillips	F/O	28.11.22	To Class A
		F/O	07.02.28	To Class C
		F/O	10.09.28	To Class A
		F/O	29.01.30	Relinquished

LG 7 February 1928, issue 33354, page 858.
LG 25 September 1928, issue 33424, page 6219.

On account of ill-health [LG 4 February 1930]. I have shown the various movements between classes of the Reserve [and in the case of Alfred James Nightingale above] as examples of how numerous were the *Gazette* notifications for officers granted short service commissions.

07019	CLAPP	Owen Wilson	W/Cdr	11.09.44	Resigned**
07046	DEANE	Laurence Archibald William	F/L	09.12.33	To Class C

The website Lancing College War memorial, which I gratefully acknowledge, has a profile on the life of Flight Lieutenant Laurence Archibald William Deane who was born in the Nottinghamshire town of Towcester on 21st April 1899. Following his education at Lancing College he enlisted with the Royal Flying Corps and saw service in France with 38 Squadron. During his time in the Reserve he attended refresher flying training with the Bristol Central Flying School [sic] by which time he was a civilian technical officer at Halton. Mobilised during the Second World War, the website notes that from 1946 to 1951, he was a Wing Commander at Halton until his death in a walking accident near the summit of Mount Snowden. A memorial service commemorating his life was held at St. George's Chapel, RAF Halton, on Sunday, 30th September 1951.

FINDLAY MC New Zealand	James Lloyd	Captain	31.08.21	Resigned

Note. *Wikipedia* carries a fairly comprehensive account of the life of James Lloyd Findlay, born in Wellington, New Zealand, on 6th October 1895. When war was declared in August 1914, he was in England and on volunteering his services was granted a commission in the East Surrey Regiment. In France he saw action in *The Battle of Loos* [1915] and on the Somme in 1916, at which time he was wounded. Decorated with the Military Cross and mentioned in despatches, James Findlay transferred to the Royal Flying Corps [I have accessed the file for surviving Royal Flying Corps officers records, but can find no supporting evidence of his air force service]. His gallantry award, I suspect, was *Gazetted* on 3rd June 1916 [LG 3 June 1916, supplement 29608, page 5573], while his appointment to the *Legion d'Honneur - Croix de Chevalier* appeared in the *Gazette* [Edinburg edition] supplement 13085, page 840, of May 3rd, 1917. Returning to his entry in *Wikipedia*, it is reported that he returned to New Zealand in 1921, having married in London during the August. In June 1923, he was one of the first officers to enlist in the New Zealand Air Force and in 1938, returned to the United Kingdom for attachment to the Royal Air Force as an exchange officer. During this time he commanded 48 Squadron and, later, RAF Hooton Park before returning to New Zealand where he rose to the rank of Air Commodore and retiring in 1954, after ten years of service as his country;s Air Attaché in Washington DC. In the course of his military career tragedy struck in the *Great War* when his eighteen year old brother, 2nd Lieutenant Ian Calcutt Findlay of the 2nd Battalion, Yorks and Lancashire Regiment succumbed to wounds on the 10th of August 1915, and in the Second World War his son, Flying Officer Ian Thompson Findlay RNZAF was killed flying Spitfires with 241 Squadron over Yugoslavia on the 12th of January 1944. He is buried in Belgrade Cemetery and his profile is recorded in Errol Martyn's second volume *'For Your Tomorrow'* page 183, and page 190 of the biographical volume of the series. Air Commodore James Lloyd Findlay died in Richmond, Surrey, on Thursday, 17th March 1983.

	HOLDING	Brian	F/O	+	07.03.22	5 FTS

Presumed killed when his Avro 504K D4542 went down in the Irish Sea off the north coast of Wales. At the time of his death, Flying Officer Holding was twenty-two years of age.

	ROGERS	William Roland	F/O		28.11.28	Relinquished
08098	SCALES	Edgar Athol	S/Ldr		24.05.42	Relinquished

Army Form B.103 raised for Lieutenant E A Scales of the Royal Air Force shows:-

	13.02.19	O/C 31 Wing	Assumed command of 72 Squadron [Cadre]	Field	13.02.19	31 Wing Orders No 13 of 15.02.19
	24.02.19	O/C 31 Wing	Relinquished command of 72 Squadron [Cadre]	Field	24.02.19	31 Wing Orders No 15 of 24.02.19
	24.03.19	O/C 31 Wing	Posted from 72 Sqd to Aircraft Pk 25.3.19	Field	25.03.19	31 Wing Orders No 22 of 24.03.19
	27.03.19	O/C 31 Wing	Posted from Aircraft Park to & assumed command of 72 72 Sqd [Cadres]	Field	27.03.19	31 Wing Orders No. 23 of 27.03.19
	24.04.19	O/C 31 Wing	Assumed command of 30 Squadron [Cadre] in addition to 72 Squadron [Cadre] on 30 Sqd occupying the same camp as 72 Squadron	Field	24.04.19	31 Wing Orders No 30 of 24.04.19
		Effective with unit [72 Sqd Cadre]			03.05.19	Census
	08.09.19	O/C 31 Wing	Posted to Aircraft Park	Baghdad	04.09.19	31 Wing Orders No 68 of 08.09.19

An earlier Army Form B.103 for this officer, with dates between 28th October 1916 and 12th June 1917, indicates service with the 14th King's Hussars, the final entry stating he was invalided to India from Busrah by a Hospital Ship.

OBSERVER OFFICER

ROBINSON	Jack Senir Clarke	O/O		28.11.19	Cancelled

FLYING OFFICERS [from PILOTS OFFICERS]
3

	BAYES	Archibald William Clayton	O/O		01.01.27	Relinquished
07229	*McKEEVER	Stephen	W/Cdr	+	08.10.40	

Wing Commander Stephen McKeever is buried in Haidar Pasha Cemetery, Turkey.

WINCKWORTH	George Hardman	F/O		08.12.30	Relinquished

LG 5 December 1919, issue 31674, pages 15061 and 15062

SQUADRON LEADERS
2

SEWELL OBE	John Percy Claude	W/Cdr		05.12.29	Relinquished
WRIGHT AF	Maurice Edward Arthur	S/Ldr		01.08.28	Relinquished

FLIGHT LIEUTENANTS
6

	BAKER OBE	Allan Hugh Bancroft	S/Ldr		05.12.26	Relinquished
11079	*BROWNE	James Stark	A/Cmdr		25.02.48	Retirement**

Air Commodore James Stark Browne AFC, died in October 1985.

HUGHES	Hywel Ivor	F/L		05.12.19	Cancelled

74134 Returned to Service. Commissioned to the Administrative and Special Duties Branch for the duration of hostilities as a Pilot Officer on probation 19th September 1939 [LG 26 September 1939, issue 34694, page 6506]. LG 21 February 1941, supplement 35083, page 1085. Transferred to the Technical Branch.

	24.04.40		S/Ldr	03.11.44	Relinquished

On account of ill-health [LG 21 November 1944, supplement 36801, page 5442].

MEATES	Bernard Crossley	F/L		22.03.26	Relinquished

Paul McMillan notes that in the Second World War Bernard Crossley-Meates was commissioned to the Royal Navy Volunteer Reserve. TNA Kew hold a document for Barnard Crossley-Meates under ADM 273/28/24

MUSGRAVE AFC	Christopher	F/L		05.12.31	Relinquished
SNELL AFC	Percy William	F/L		05.12.19	Cancelled

FLYING OFFICERS
47

	*ADAMS	Francis Percy	S/Ldr		07.08.34	Retired list
	AYLING	Christopher	F/L		30.08.26	Relinquished

On account of ill-health.

BANKES-JONES	The Reverend Ralph Myddleton	F/L		07.09.22	Terminated

On appointment to Chaplin [LG 5 September 1922, issue 32744, page 6445].

06203	*BARRACLOUGH	Charles Edward	G/Capt		21.09.49	Retirement**
	BIRD DFC	Clarence Oscar	F/O	+	27.05.20	70 Squadron

See summary for details surrounding his death in an air accident.

	BIRD	Stanley Wooldridge	F/O		05.12.19	Cancelled
	BIRKETT	George	F/L		05.12.34	Relinquished
06227	BLIGH	Harry	F/L		05.12.26	To Class A

LG 33891, issue 33891, page 7932.

15 November 1938, issue 34570, page 7196. Grant a commission in Class CC, retaining his rank, with effect from 4th January 1937.

		W/Cdr		18.05.54	Relinquished
BOULLE	Vincent Adolph	F/O		05.12.19	Cancelled
BROWN	William Joseph	F/O		15.12.30	Relinquished
CARPENTER	Frank	F/L		22.09.28	Retired list

At his own request [LG 25 September 1928, issue 33424, page 6219].

COX	Pierse Joseph	F/O	+	14.04.21	14 Squadron

On Thursday, 14th April 1921, while operated from Ramleh and flying Bristol Fighter H1533, Flying Officer Pierse Joseph Cox crashed and was killed, his passenger, Flying Officer Christopher Pilkington AFC being gravely injured. Flying Officer Cox is buried in Jerusalem Protestant Cemetery. Flying Officer Pilkington [see the Short Service Commission table for 24th October 1919] recovered from his injuries.

07037	*DADDO-LANGLOIS	William James	G/Capt		22.12.43	Retirement**
	DALE	Charles Brodrick Mitcalfe	F/O		05.12.25	To Class B
	DICKINSON	Francis Gilbert Conynghame	F/O		05.12.19	Cancelled
	de NEVERS	Bernard Albert	F/O		05.12.26	To Class C
07077	*FAIRWEATHER	James MacGregor	W/Cdr	+	28.05.40	

Reported to have been lost when the SS *Aboukir* was sunk on Tuesday, 28th May 1940. This day is remembered by the people of Belgium as the day when their king, Leopold III against the advice of his minsters, surrendered his country to the Germans. This caused dismay throughout his kingdom and abroad, subsequently leading to his abdication on 16th July 1951. As to the fate of SS *Aboukir*, Captained by Rowland Morris-Woolfenden, the vessel eluded the first attack by E-boats but was sunk in a second attack, thus becoming the first Allied ship to be torpedoed by an E-boat. Of a complement of over 500 passengers and crew which included military personnel as well as civilians, only between twenty-six or thirty-two [different accounts vary] were saved. For a detailed account of the sinking, please refer to the ship's history as reported on *Wikipedia*. Wing Commander James MacGregor Fairweather is commemorated on the Runnymede Memorial panel 3.

	*GILES	Frederick Alexander	F/O		12.09.23	Resigned
	GOMPERTZ	Arthur Vincent Howard	F/L		17.12.23	Resigned
	HANNON	William Ignatius	F/O		05.12.26	Relinquished
07140	*HENWOOD DFC	Francis Herbert Donald	G/Capt		27.10.46	Retirement**
	*HOBSON DFC	Eric Ralph Carrington	S/Ldr	+	09.04.38	6 Squadron

Born in San Fernando, Trinidad, on 12th February 1895, the young Eric Hobson was schooled in the United Kingdom, where between January 1910 and December 1913, he was a pupil at Sherborne School in Dorset. Returning to Trinidad he spent the next two years as a member of the island's constabulary. Following enlistment to the British West Indies Regiment, he transferred to the Royal Flying Corps in 1918, and was serving in Egypt with 47 Squadron when the Armistice was signed in November 1918. By May 1933, he was attached to 601 Squadron AAF at Hendon where he was greatly traumatised when one of a flight of three Hawker Harts that he was leading on a practice flight crashed with fatal consequences for its crew. At the subsequent inquest, Flight Lieutenant Hobson tried to take the blame for the accident, but this was dismissed by the Coroner who in his summing up praised Hobson for his *"very generous and sportsmanlike action"*, a verdict of *"death by misadventure"* being returned. There is, I suggest, little doubt that this terrible accident from time to time played on his mind and despite serving with great distinction in the Middle East where he was honoured with the Distinguished Service Order he took his own life on Saturday, 9th of April 1938. An immensely tragic end to a very gifted officer. Squadron Leader Hobson is buried in Ramleh War Cemetery. During his air force service he was *Gazetted* with the DFC [Somaliland] on 12th July 1920, and the DSO on 6th May 1938 for operations in Palestine. In Preparing these notes I am indebted to 601[County of London] Squadron - Squadron Historical Database and the official website for Sherborne School Archives.

07155	*HOLLAND	Robert John Hayne	F/L		11.03.34	Retired list

Returned to service: Commissioned Accountant Branch: Squadron Leader [temporary] 1 Sept. 1941 [LG 9 September 1941, issue 35270, page 5221].

			S/Ldr		18.04.45	Retired list**
07160	HOPPS AFC	Frank Linden	AV-M		24.03.50	Retirement**

Air Vice-Marshal Frank Linden Hopps CB CBE AFC mentioned in a despatch, died on Sunday, 10th October 1976.

	HUMPHREYS	William Rolwand Spottiswoode	W/Cdr		16.12.43	Resigned**
	JAQUES MC	John Barclay	F/O	+	01.04.20	216 Squadron

See summary for details concerning his death in an air accident.

	JONES	Arthur Reginald	F/L	+	05.08.31	208 Squadron

On Wednesday, 5th August 1931, while flying in an Atlas, the airframe serial being omitted, Flight Lieutenant Arthur Reginald Jones lost control having encountered fog and crashed near Almaza aerodrome in Egypt. On impact the Atlas burst into flames; Leading Aircraftman Edgar Giles Clive Henry also perished.

	JONES	Kenneth Foxcroft	F/O		05.12.26	Relinquished
	LAMB	Robert	F/O		30.04.31	Relinquished
	LITTLEJOHN	Robert	F/O		26.05.20	Unemployed
	LONGHURST	Eric Randall	F/O		19.06.20	Relinquished

On account of ill-health. TNA Kew has a record for this officer under AIR 76/306/18.

11174	METCALFE	Robert Frederick Charles	W/Cdr		10.02.54	Relinquished
07237	MAILER AFC	Stewart Earl	F/L	+	25.03.25	

Australia   The website Billion Graves, which I acknowledge, records Flying Officer Stewart Earl Mailer as being buried in Brighton General Cemetery in the State of Victoria. Additional to this, my co-author has discovered the circumstances in which Flight Lieutenant Stewart Earl Mailer AFC was killed. It seems he returned to Australia in 1923, and in the November of '24, enlisted as a Flying Officer in the Royal Australian Air Force and at the time of his death was flying instructor at Commonwealth Government Service Flying School at Point Cook. On the fateful day he was instructing in Avro 504K A3-28 [ex-E3743] with Cadet Officer Alan Moorhouse Charlesworth as his pupil. Taking off at around 0915, the exercise proceeded smoothly with three good landings being performed by Cadet Officer Charlesworth and it was while approaching the landing area for the fourth landing that events went terribly wrong. With the engine 'off' and banking at forty-five degrees, nose down, the Avro went out of control at 300 feet and despite a desperate effort by Flying Officer Mailer to recover the situation, the Avro crashed just a few hundred yards from one of the hangars. Amazingly, Cadet Officer Charlesworth emerged from the wreckage with facial injuries, a sprained ankle and severe shock, but Flying Officer Mailer was killed by the impact. He was buried with full Service honours, the funeral service being conducted by the Reverend R West Scott. Subsequently, Charlesworth recovered and over the next thirty years rose to the rank of Air Commodore before retiring on the last day of December 1955, his final posting being Commander of Australia's North West Area.

	PAGET AFC	Louis George	F/L		05.12.30	Relinquished
21080	*PARK	Leslie Woodland	W/Cdr		13.08.47	Retirement**
	PRESTON AFC	Raphael Chevallier	F/L		20.09.27	Resigned

205390   His commission in Class A on appointment to a commission in the Special Reserve [LG 20 September 1927, issue 33313, page 6003]. LG 18 April 1950, supplement 38887, page 1869. Appointed to a commission in the Training Branch of the Royal Air Force Volunteer Reserve in the rank of Flying Officer, with effect from 8th March 1950.

			W/Cdr		09.03.58	Relinquished
	PRUDEN	William Colin	F/O		09.12.26	Relinquished
	ROBINSON MC	Geoffrey	F/O	+	10.02.22	Farnborough

Taking off from Farnborough on Friday, 10th February 1922, in DH.14 Okapi [c/n E.44], Flying Officer Geoffrey Robinson MC, accompanied by a civilian technical assistant, John Seymour Mitchell, had the awful misfortune when flying near Burnham Beeches to the west of Farnham Common, Buckinghamshire, to collide with the top of a tree in Dropmore Park. Out of control, the DH crashed and burst into flames killing both occupants.

RUDD	John Alexander	F/O		05.12.32	Relinquished
SAUNDERS	William Waldron	F/O		20.12.23	Relinquished

On account of ill-health [LG 22 January 1924, supplement 32900, page 689].
LG 10 March 1925, issue 33028, page 1701. Granted a commission in Class B, General Duties Branch, retaining Flying Officer rank, with effect from 10th March 1925.

		F/O		10.03.29	Relinquished
SAVAGE	John Aubrey Hoggarth	F/O		23.10.28	Relinquished
TANCRED MBE	Christopher Humphrey	F/L		03.12.28	Relinquished
TEAGLE	Cyril Hollis	F/O	+	12.09.21	55 Squadron

While on a contact patrol supporting local levies on Monday, 12th September 1921, flying DH.9A H153 and accompanied by Aircraftman Stanley Sydney Stephen Cox, the DH came under ground-fire from rebels, several bullets striking Flying Officer Cyril Hollis Teagle who, having flown clear of the area, forced-landed at Catas, near Desht-i-Harir, some 20 miles SW from Rowanduz, Iraq. Despite his serious wounds, together with Aircraftman Cox who was also injured, Flying Officer Teagle managed to set their machine alight in order that it would be of no value to the rebels. Very sadly, he succumbed to his wounds four days later. Happily, Stanley Cox made a full recovery.

	THORNTON	Thomas Alfred	F/L		10.01.35	Relinquished
08154	TRAVERS DFC	Frederick Dudley	F/O		05.12.39	To Class C

Note. This was not the end of his flying career as an entry in *The London Gazette* supplement 36547, page 2682, of 10th June 1944, shows him as a recipient of the King's commendation for valuable services in the air at which time he was a Captain flying with British Overseas Airways Co-operation. This commendation was in respect of the King's birthday honours awards. Notification of his DFC [Salonika] appeared in the *Gazette* [Edinburgh edition] December 5th, 1918, issue 13363, page 4478: *'A gallant and able officer who has displayed on many occasions boldness in attack, never hesitating to engage the enemy as opportunity occurs. On June 1st he, in company with two other pilots, attacked a hostile formation of twelve machines; four of these were shot down and the remainder driven off.'* It is further noted that he was formerly of the Hertfordshire Yeomanry.

	WELSH	Stanley Frederick Aubrey	F/O		05.12.26	Relinquished
11066	YOUNG MBE	Hugh Joseph	W/Cdr		23.01.43	Retired list**

OBSERVER OFFICERS
4

	BULTEEL	John Crocker	F/O		31.03.26	Relinquished

On account of ill-health [LG 30 March 1926, issue 33146, page 2279].

21050	*ESSEX	Bertram Edward	AV-M		29.06.56	Retirement**

Note. Air Vice-Marshal Bertram Edward Essex CB CBE mentioned in despatches, born on 13th October 1897, died on Friday, 5th of June 1959.

09023	*LEDGER	Arthur Percy	AV-M		17.05.52	Retirement**

Not. Air-Vice Marshal Arthur Percy Ledger CB CBE mentioned in despatches, born in Canterbury, 29th August 1897, died on Wednesday, 6th May 1970, at Bridge, Kent. His service biography appears in RAF Commands - A History of Royal Air Force Organisation and an entry in *Wikipedia*.

09055	WYATT MC	Montague James	F/O		05.12.22	To Class B

LG 26 May 1925, issue 33050, page 3554.

			F/O		26.05.25	To Class C

LG 7 December 1926, issue 33227, page 8004.

			F/O		05.12.26	To Class B

LG 15 March 1932, issue 33808, page 1770.

			F/O		05.12.30	To Class C

LG 15 November 1938, issue 34570, page 7197. Granted a commission in Class CC of the Reserve of Air Force Officers, General Duties Branch, ranked Flying Officer, with effect from 1st June 1937. LG 5 December 1939, issue 34747, page 8108. Transferred to the Administrative and Special Duties Branch, with effect from 1st September 1939, retaining rank and seniority.

			W/Cdr		17.09.54	Relinquished

FLYING OFFICERS [from PILOT OFFICERS]
26

	ATTWOOD	Ernest Henry	F/L		01.01.26	

Flight Lieutenant Ernest Henry 'Tich' Attwood, born Birmingham on 6th March 1899, was still in Class A of the Reserve at the time of his death. He had joined Imperial Airways in November 1926, and was killed twelve years later on Sunday, 27th November 1938, when the Empire Flying Boat G-AETW *Calpurnia* encountered bad weather and came down on Lake Ramadi, Iraq, just fifteen miles short of its destination, the Imperial Airways station at Habbaniya. Reports of the accident were reported in *The Times* in their issues of 29th and 30th November 1938. Claims on his estate were advertised in *The London Gazette* in its issue [34598] of 14 February 1939, page 1100. He lived at 'Quobleigh', Fair Oak, Hampshire.

	BAILEY	Philip	F/L		10.08.37	Relinquished
	BILLINGS	Clarence Henry	Lieutenant		23.11.20	Resigned
	BIRD	Ernest	F/O	+	30.11.23	AEE Martlesham Heath

Flying Officer Ernest Bird and Corporal George Roger Budd died in the crash of Short Springbok J6975 which Flying Officer Bird was testing when at 1,500 feet, and shortly after take off, it went into an uncontrolled spin, crashed and burst into flames near the airfield. Second of two aircraft, J6975 flew for the first time on 24th July 1923 and as recently as 31st October, had new wings fitted by Short's who returned the Springbok to Martlesham Heath on 7th November. The accident was reported the next day in *The Times* noting that Corporal Budd came from Anstruther in Fife.

07007	CARROLL	Albert Daniel Leo	S/Ldr		08.06.54	Relinquished
	COOKE	William Joseph	F/O		05.12.27	Relinquished
	DUFTY	George Clifton Watson	F/O		05.12.32	Relinquished
07065	*DUMINY	John	W/Cdr		05.09.41	Retirement**

Re-employed.

			W/Cdr		04.11.45	Retired list**
07073	EDMUNDS	John	F/O		05.12.26	Relinquished
07101	GISSING	Charles Cunningham	S/Ldr		05.11.45	Relinquished

On account of medical unfitness for Air Force service [LG 20 November 1945, supplement 37356, page 5649].

	HELPS	Victor William	P/O		24.06.21	Unemployed

My co-author, Paul McMillan, reports that on 23rd July 1921, a month after leaving the service, Victor William Helps was riding his motorcycle between Bridgwater and Taunton in Somerset when, it is believed, a tyre burst causing him to be thrown from his machine and sustaining fatal head injuries. His death was reported in the *Western Morning News*.

	HOBBY MC	Harold Spurgeon	F/O		05.12.19	Cancelled
	ILES	Harry William	F/O		28.01.25	Cashiered

By sentence of General Court Martial [LG 17 February 1925, issue 33021, page 1172].

07217	MACARTHUR	Donald Michael Ian	F/O		26.07.26	Removed from Service

TNA Kew hold a document for this officer under AIR 76/312/26

	NOEL	Harry Norris Victor Le Vavasseur	F/O		05.12.30	Relinquished
	OXLAND	William Henry Lionel	F/O		21.08.20	Unemployed
	POTTER	Sydney Hugh	F/O	+	14.08.21	47 Squadron

Spun and crashed near Heliopolis, Egypt, on Sunday, 14th August 1921, after losing control of DH.9A E9900. His passenger, Corporal Horace Merilion Lake also perished.

08056	PRETTY	Reginald Charles	W/Cdr		10.02.54	Relinquished
	PRICE	Harold Chadwick	F/O		05.12.19	Cancelled
	RIGDEN	Cecil Osborne	F/O	+	29.11.20	216 Squadron

See summary for the circumstances leading to his death in a flying accident.

	SHAW	John Hudson	F/O		05.12.19	Cancelled
08110	SILVESTER	James	A/Cmdr		15.01.46	

Retirement**Air Commodore James Silvester CBE twice mentioned in despatches, died ten years later on Thursday, 5th of January 1956. It is recorded on the Air of Authority - A History of RAF Organisation website that when the *Great War* was declared in August 1914, he joined the Royal Warwickshire Regiment [City of Birmingham Battalion] in the September at the tender age of sixteen and a half.

21075	*TOMKINS	Mark Frank	W/Cdr		26.09.47	Retired list**
	TRUNDLE	Guy Marcus	F/O		03.01.31	Relinquished

LG 24 September 1935, issue 34201, page 6008. Reserve of Air Force Officers, General Duties Branch, granted a commission in Class C with effect from 30th August 1935, in the rank of Flying Officer. LG 23 August 1938, issue 34544, page 5419. Relinquished on appointment to a commission in the Auxiliary Air Force, 5th July 1938, and given the service number 90441.

			W/Cdr		21.09.54	Relinquished
08156	TURNBULL	Edgar Albert	F/L		08.02.37	Relinquished
	WILSON	Grenville Wainwright	F/O		05.12.26	Relinquished

OBSERVER OFFICERS [from PILOT OFFICERS]
10

	ARMSTRONG	William Ash	F/O	+	14.04.21	208 Squadron

Killed in a midair collision near Bilbeis, Egypt, when his Bristol F.2b D7831 struck Bristol F.2b E2298, claiming the lives of four airmen. Flying with Flying Officer William Ash Armstrong was Flying Officer Edward Blake Jones, a permanent officer named in Appendix D. All are rest in Ismailia War Cemetery.

08218	*BARNES	Eric Delano	A/Cmdr		20.12.49	Retirement**

Air Commodore Barnes CB AFC three times mentioned in despatches, died on Wednesday, 4th of December 1957.

08241	BUGGÉ	Fawcett Hagbert	F/O		05.12.30	Relinquished

LG 8 October 1935, issue 34205, page 6303, granted a commission in Class A of the Reserve of Air Force Officers, ranked Flying Officer.
Traced to *The London Gazette* 14th June 1945, supplement 37119, page 2992, and the extensive list of officers mentioned in despatches. His rank at the time was Squadron Leader and he had been honoured with the AFC.

			S/Ldr		10.02.54	Relinquished
	BYRNE	Brennan Claude Sydney	O/O	+	03.09.20	47 Squadron

See summary for information regarding his death in an air accident.

11235	*CARTER	Rodney Thomas	W/Cdr		28.05.44	Retired List**
	COGGAN	George Sydney	F/O		05.12.26	Relinquished
11238	*DRAKE	Bruce Gerdyne	W/Cdr		06.05.50	To reserve**
	HOLLEY	Kenneth Herbert	F/O		20.09.27	To Class C

On the 1st of May 1928, Flying Officer Kenneth Herbert Holley was granted a commission in the Territorial Army joining the 5th Battalion, Durham Light Infantry as a Lieutenant.

	KITT	Leslie Watson	F/O		05.12.26	Relinquished
	LOWE	Theodore Linley	F/L	+	25.05.25	84 Squadron

Flight Lieutenant Theodore Linley Lowe died in a non-air related accident and is buried in Basra [Makina] RAF Cemetery. Prior to going out to Iraq he played rugby football for the Harlequins who report he was *"bustling forward and a beautiful place-kicker."* This notice appeared in the 14th September 1925, issue of *Athletic News*.

LG 12 December 1919, issue 31685, pages 15483 and 15484

FLIGHT LIEUTENANTS
6

	*HOOPER MC DFC	Geoffrey Herbert	F/L		13.06.23	Resigned

LG 28 June 1927, issue 33289, page 4143.

			F/L		13.06.27	Relinquished
	LALLY MC AFC	Conrad Tolendal	F/L		12.12.19	Cancelled
	PICKTHORN MC	Charles Edward Murray	F/L		12.12.19	Cancelled

LG 27 February 1925, issue 33025, page 1424. *'The King has been pleased to give and grant unto the undermentioned gentlemen, late of the Royal Air Force, His Majesty's Royal licence and authority to wear Decorations of the Order Al Merito which have been conferred upon them by the President of the Republic of Chile, in recognition of valuable senders rendered by them to the Chilean Government:- Insignia of the Second Class. Major Edward Charles Murray Pickthorn MC.'*
LG 23 March 1926, issue 33144, page 2112. Reserve of Air Force Officers, General Duties Branch, a commission in Class A as Flying Officer on probation, with effect from 23rd March 1926.

			S/Ldr		23.03.34	Relinquished

His entry in *Wikipedia* records he was born in Ilford on 20th September 1896, and died at the age of 41 at Orford, Suffolk, on 3rd March 1938. During the *Great War* he was credited with five combat victories, the fourth resulting in the death of Prince Friedrich Karl of Prussia. The biography goes on to report that he was first commissioned to the Army Service Corps and on transfer to the Royal Flying Corps he qualified as an observer and as such flew with 8 Squadron. Subsequently, he underwent pilot training and by the end of 1916, was flying DH.2s with 32 Squadron.. 2nd Lieutenant Pickthorn features in Trevor Henshaw's *The Sky Their Battlefield* where on page 41, while flying with 2nd Lieutenant C T H Vaisey on 29th June 1916, he not only fought off a trio of enemy aircraft, but then flew the BE.2d 5763 back to Bellevue as his pilot had been critically wounded. Sadly, Charles Thomas Hinton Vaisey died on the 1st of July 1916, and was laid to rest in Warlincourt Halte British Cemetery, Saulty.

	*POLLARD	Eric Miller	S/Ldr	+	26.07.26	45 Squadron

Squadron Leader Pollard was killed in an horrendous flying accident at Hinaidi, Iraq, when the Vickers Vernon II J7143 of 45 Squadron crashed on take off, coming down onto the roof of a hangar. Please refer to Appendix D and Lieutenant [Flight Lieutenant] Reginald Carey Brinton Brading DFC for additional information.

	POWELL MC	Frederick James	F/L		05.06.31	Relinquished
74207	Returned to the service.		W/Cdr		07.09.54	Relinquished
SMITH		Ronald Sinclair	Major		10.08.22	Relinquished

On account of ill-health contracted in the Service.

FLYING OFFICERS
35

	ALLISON	George Henry	F/L		12.12.35	Relinquished
06200	BALLARD	Maurice	S/Ldr	+	12.09.42	

Squadron Leader Maurice Ballard is commemorated on the Alamein Memorial, column 247.

	BLADON	Graham Clarke	A/Cmdr		22.02.59	Retirement

Air Commodore Graham Clarke Bladon CB CBE twice mentioned in despatches, died on Wednesday, 11th October 1967.

| 06245 | BURBIDGE | Maurice | F/L | | 12.12.30 | Relinquished |

A record for this officer is held at TNA Kew under AIR 76/66/74

	CLELLAND	Robert	F/O		12.12.19	Cancelled
07031	*COTTLE DFC	Jack	G/Capt		21.06.44	Retired list**
	DAVIES MC	Frederick Harry	F/O		12.12.19	Cancelled
07049	DESOER	Noël Lloyd	AV-M		01.07.49	Retirement**

Air Vice-Marshal Noël Lloyd Desoer CBE three times mentioned in despatches, died on Monday, 21st August 1978. In retirement he spent seventeen very productive years in assisting the team writing the Official History of the Second World War against Japan. Having served for the best part of the war in India and Burma, he was well qualified to lend his knowledge of the conflict.

| | DODKINS | Lionel Claud | F/O | + | 12.06.21 | 31 Squadron |

Flying Officer Lionel Claud Dodkins is buried in Wallington [Bandon Hill] Cemetery. Prior to his air force service, he served with the cyclist battalion of the 25th London Regiment, their website recording that Flying Officer Dodkins had seen active service in Egypt, India and Afghanistan.

	ELLIOTT	Charles Allen	F/O		14.12.36	Resigned
	ELLIS	Eric Thomas Haulton	F/O		12.12.19	Cancelled
	GRANT	William Valentine Newby	F/O		05.04.22	Relinquished

On account of ill-health contracted on active service [LG 11 April 1922, issue 32668, page 2935].

| | HARRIS | Bertrand Reginald | F/O | + | 10.12.22 | A&GS Eastchurch |

Flying Officer Bertrand Reginald Harris died from pleurisy while being treated in RN Hospital, Chatham.

| | *HOLLINGHURST DFC | Leslie Norman | ACM | | 27.12.52 | Retirement** |

Air Chief Marshal Sir Leslie Hollinghurst GBE KCB DFC twice mentioned in despatches DFC [US], died on Tuesday, 8th June 1971, while returning to England from Normandy where he had attended the D-Day commemorations.

| | HUGHES | John Sydney | F/O | | 03.11.26 | Relinquished |

On account of ill-health [LG 2 November 1926, issue 33217, page 7051].

| | JONES DFC | Simon | F/O | | 12.12.19 | Cancelled |
| | JUNOR DFC | Hugh Robert | F/L | 19.08.26 | + | Farnborough |

Flight Lieutenant Hugh Robert Junor DFC lost his life while conducting a flight test of Gloster Gamecock I J7906 near the maker's Hucclecote facility. Eyewitnesses to the crash state the pilot baled out, but at too low an altitude for his parachute to deploy; on impact, wreckage of the Gamecock injured two people on the ground, fortunately both survived. An inquest was held on Friday, 27th August, the proceedings being reported in the *Gloucestershire Chronicle,* which was adjourned after hearing evidence from witnesses. Flight Lieutenant Hugh Robert Junor DFC is buried in Byfleet [St. Mary's] Churchyard. During the *Great War* he had served in Egypt, winning his award in this theatre, the citation reading: *'On 17th September* [1918] *this officer performed an act of conspicuous merit and gallantry. Single-handed, he engaged five enemy machines, and so protected the Arab force from aerial attack at a most critical time when they were engaged in destroying a railway. Lieut. Junor continued the combat till he was driven down by force of numbers, his petrol supply being practically exhausted.'* LG 8 February 1919, issue 31170, page 2041].

| 11049 | *KEEPING | Eustace George | G/Capt | | 31.05.45 | Retired list** |
| 07195 | *KIRBY | John Lawrence | A/Cmdr | | 04.03.46 | Retirement** |

Air Commodore John Lawrence Kirby CB CBE, died on Wednesday, 20th February 1980.

	McINTYRE AFC	Ivor Ewing	Lieutenant		20.06.23	Resigned
07230	McKENNA DCM	Hugh Walter	S/Ldr		10.02.54	Relinquished
	*MARTYN	Gilbert	S/Ldr	+	28.10.36	Air Ministry

Squadron Leader Gilbert Martin died while undergoing treatment in the Princess Mary Hospital at RAF Halton. At the time of his death, as discovered by my co-author, Squadron Leader Martyn was serving with the Directorate of Operations and Intelligence.

| | MILLER | Albert | F/O | | 12.12.19 | Cancelled |

A document for this officer is obtainable from TNA Kew by quoting AIR 76/347/79.

	MONTGOMERY	James Lome	F/O		12.12.19	Cancelled
08017	*NORTON	Frederick Arthur	G/Capt		26.06.48	Retirement**
08021	ODDIE	Gerard Stephen	A/Cmdr		26.04.44	Retirement**

Air Commodore Gerard Stephen Oddie DFC AFC, died on Thursday, 3rd May 1984.

| 72923 | RANKIN | Robert Munro | W/Cdr | | 24.08.54 | Relinquished |
| 08087 | *RUSSELL | Norbert Marie Sackville | W/Cdr | | 28.05.45 | Retired list** |

An interesting entry in *The Edinburgh Gazette* October 26th, 1928, issue 14490, page 1159, lists a Flight Lieutenant N M S Russell of 69 Cambridge Mansions, Cambridge Road, Battersea Park, London, as one of many notified of a 'Receiving Orders' under the Bankruptcy Acts, 1914 and 1926.

| | SAUNDERS DFC | Alfred William | F/O | | 05.02.27 | Relinquished |

During pleasure flying on Wednesday, 21st May 1930, in New Zealand in DH.60G Moth G-EBZY [ZK-ABV] registered to Bryant House Airways, Te Rapa, Alfred William Saunders failed to recover from a spin and crashed at Te Awamutu in New Zealand's North Island. Critically injured he subsequently died; his passenger, Alfred Trench Minchin was killed on impact. The Moth, although substantially damaged, was repaired. Alfred Saunders was of Irish descent and during the *Great War* secured a dozen combat victories, two shared, while flying SE.5as with 60 Squadron, his DFC being *Gazetted* on 2nd August 1918, supplement 30827, page 9203.

| 08101 | SEWARD | Walter John | AV-M | | 31.05.54 | Retirement** |

Air Vice Marshal Walter John Seward CB CBE mentioned in despatches, died on Saturday, 9th September 1972.

| | SHAPRE | Orwell Egbert | F/O | | 16.02.27 | Relinquished |
| | SMITH | Bryan Evers Sharwood | F/O | | 12.12.19 | Cancelled |

There are a number of entries in *The London Gazette* referring to Bryan Evers Sharwood Smith, the last being *Gazetted* on 28th September 1954, issue 40288, page 5512, referring to the appointment of Sir Bryan Evers Sharwood Smith KBE CMG ED to the Governorship of Northern Rhodesia on 1st October 1954.

| | STEDMAN | Raymond de Lacy | F/L | | 09.07.29 | Retired list |

At his own request [LG 16 July 1929, issue 33517, page 4705].

| 08151 | *TOOGOOD | Charles Francis | G/Capt | | 24.11.46 | Retirement** |
| 08232 | *WYNNE | Frederick Robert | G/Capt | | 17.08.45 | Retirement** |

OBSERVER OFFICERS
15

| | COOPER MC | Horace Arthur | O/O | | 12.12.19 | Cancelled |
| | *COX | Albert John | S/Ldr | + | 06.04.38 | RAF Depot Uxbridge |

Squadron Leader Albert John Cox was serving as a stores officer at the time of his death.

| | GREENSLADE | Richard Samuel | F/L | + | 08.01.30 | 4 FTS |

Killed at Abu Sueir in a midair collision between Avro 504Ns J8716 and J8981 in which four airman, including Flight Lieutenant Richard Samuel Greenslade perished, the others being New Zealander, Flying Officer Charles Edson Galpin, Corporal William Henry Chilman ans Leading Air-craftman Leonard Vincent Green. Air Britain's J1 - J9999 register, notes J8716 had undergone a rebuild and when destroyed was flying as JR8716.

GREENWOOD	Eric Major		F/O		23.12.26	Relinquished
HANTON	William George		Lieutenant		23.12.20	Resigned
HARDY MC	Philip		F/O		12.12.19	Cancelled

Subsequently placed on the Unemployed list, TNA Kew holds a record for this officer under AIR 76/208/185.

JAMISON DFC	Robert McKinley		F/O		28.12.26	Relinquished
NESBIT	Charles Henry Fletcher		F/O		12.12.26	Class C

Australia On returning to Australia, Flying Officer Charles Henry Fletcher Nesbit became the managing director and chief instructor of Wings Limited and as reported in *The Sydney Morning Herald* of Wednesday, October 15th, 1930, was killed during the course of a navigational instruction flight with two pupils which departed in a Puss Moth during the morning of Monday, the 13th, and failed to return. Subsequently, the wreckage was sighted from the air some 29 miles from Perth on the eastern goldfields railway. On reaching the scene of the crash, a thickly timbered hill, it seems a landing was being attempted but the Puss Moth clipped the top of a sapling and then struck a tree stump and overturned, the engine being broken off and finishing up beneath the tailplane. The two pupils were names as William Robert Bell, a pupil pilot and a nurse, Miss Haidee Rae, a pilot from Wilgro, Bullsbrook. The cause of the tragedy was attributed to engine failure. The loss of the DH.80A Puss Moth is recorded on page 269 of A J Jackson's *De Havilland Aircraft* [Putnam, 1962] and is identified as VH-UPC

NICHOLSON	Gordon Lawrence		O/O		01.10.20	Resigned
NICHOLSON DFC	Jaffray John Walter		F/O		15.12.34	Relinquished
REYNOLDS	Arthur Edward		F/L		12.12.26	To Class A

My co-author after hours of searching discovered that Flight Lieutenant Arthur Edward Reynolds emigrated to Canada where he enlisted with the Royal Canadian Air Force. Ranked Flying Officer, he was killed in a flying accident at Camp Borden in Ontario on the 1st of November 1928, when the DH.60X Moth RCAF 58 in which he was flying with Major William Harvey Currie MC MM crashed, his passenger being seriously injured. Making a good recovery Major Currie subsequently joined the Ottawa Militia and was working as an insurance agent when he collapsed and died in a local hospital where he was being treated for a Cerebral Hemhora

SINCLAIR	Alexander Douglas		O/O		12.12.19	Cancelled
TAYLOR	Harold		O/O		12.12.19	Cancelled
TERRY	Geoffrey Rouse		O/O		12.12.22	To Class C

Australia My co-author reports that Observer Officer Geoffrey Rouse Terry, late of the Northumberland Hussars and Royal Flying Corps and Royal Air Force returned to Australia embarking on the SS *Diogenes* sailing from London to Sydney on the 3rd of January 1923.

WYNNE	Arthur Francis		F/O		21.02.28	Resigned

FLYING OFFICER [from PILOTS OFFICERS]
15

06233	*BRITTON	Edmund Arnold Courtney	G/Capt		07.12.46	Retirement**
		LG 4 July 1961, supplement 42403, page 4936. Class J.	F/L		08.01.61	Relinquished
	DINNAGE	Harry Alexander	F/O		12.12.31	Relinquished
07070	EASON	Frederic Robert	F/O		23.12.30	Relinquished
	*EASTWOOD	Douglas Donald MacAlister	S/Ldr	+	16.07.38	

Squadron Leader Douglas Donald MacAlister Eastwood died in RAF Hospital Halton following a long illness

07080	FENTON	Edward Norman	F/O		12.12.22	To Class A
		LG 7 October 1924, issue 32980, page 7255.	F/O		03.10.24	To Class C
		LG 18 July 1933, issue 33961, page 4805.	F/O		26.05.33	To Class A

 LG 15 November 1938, issue 34570, page 7196. Reserve of Air Force Officers, General Duties Branch, granted a commission in Class CC with effect from 7th May 1938, as Flying Officer with seniority as at 3rd January 1938.

		LG 5 March 1940, issue 34805, page 1318.	F/O		03.09.39	Relinquished

97080   LG 22 October 1940, issue 34976, page 6142. Transferred to the Administrative and Special Duties Branch with effect from 10th October 1940, retaining the rank of Flying Officer. Service number subsequently reverted to original issue.

		LG 17 February 1948, supplement 38209, page 1125.	F/L		22.09.54 +	

Believed to have died while still in the Reserve of Air Force Officers.

	GILL	Herbert William	F/O		12.12.19	Cancelled
74510		Returned to the service with effect from 5th November 1939.	S/Ldr		06.08.54	Relinquished

Note. Another example of duplication of service numbers in that 74510 was also issued to Major Evelyn David Vereker Prendergast MBE DFC.

	HALL	Donald Ernest	F/L		12.12.38	Relinquished
07146	HEWITT	Edward Norman	F/O		12.12.28	Relinquished

Returned to service. Commissioned to the Administrative and Special Duties Branch as Pilot Officer on probation 20th March 1940, initially as 81088

[LG 16 July 1940, issue 34898, page 4368]. Reverted to his original service number.			F/L		12.6.45	Resigned**
	HOWLEY	Charles Edmund	F/O		12.12.19	Cancelled
	LORD	Douglas Gerald Rabson	F/O		01.05.36	Relinquished
07222	*McDONALD	John Alexander	G/Capt		14.01.47	Retirement**
07250	*MERER	John William Frederick	A-VM		11.05.55	Retirement**

Air Vice Marshal John William Frederick Merer CB mentioned in despatches, died on Saturday, 31st October 1964, in the General Hospital at Amersham, Buckinghamshire.

	PARKINSON	William	F/O		30.12.31	Relinquished
08061	*PURDIN	William Edmund	G/Capt		11.02.46	Retirement**
08085	*RUSSELL	Barnabas Henry Cross	A/Cmdr		28.02.53	Retirement**

Air Commodore Barnabas Henry Cross Russell CBE twice mentioned in despatches, died on Monday, 2nd October 1989.

OBSERVER OFFICERS [from PILOT OFFICERS]
14

	ALEXANDER	Harry	F/O		12.04.27	Resigned
	BECK	Lionel William	F/O		12.12.30	Relinquished
	BOOTHROYD DFC	Clement Graham	F/O		12.12.26	Relinquished
08240	BROWN	Frederick William	F/O		31.07.54	Relinquished
	BRUNTON MC	Raymond Alexander	Lieutenant		16.12.20	Resigned
	DARNBROUGH	Albert Harold	O/O		12.12.19	Cancelled
11078	DAVISON	Joe	W/Cdr		09.11.45	Relinquished

On reversion to Southern Rhodesian Forces.

	HOARE	Lawrence James	F/O		12.12.26	Relinquished
	McGOWAN	William	F/O		21.12.29	Relinquished
	MALYAN	Bernard James	F/O	+	28.05.28	

Flying Officer Bernard James Malyan died at Hardwick, Marsh Lane, Stanmore while still in the Reserve.

	MURRAY	Douglas Hugh	F/O		12.12.31	Relinquished

11035	RICH	Richard Thomas	W/Cdr		26.11.47	Retired list**
	TAYLOR MC	Harold	O/O		12.12.19	Cancelled
	WILLCOX	Arthur Leslie	F/O		12.12.27	Relinquished

LG 19 December 1919, issue 31698, page 15746.

FLIGHT LIEUTENANT

| | WATTS | Frederick James | F/L | | 19.12.30 | Relinquished |

75214   Returned to service. Commissioned to the Administrative and Special Duties Branch with effect from 1st September 1939, in the rank of Flight Lieutenant [LG 27 October 1939, supplement 34718, page 7183].

| | | | W/Cdr | | 14.09.54 | Relinquishe |

FLYING OFFICERS
7

| | BERNARD | James Lawrence | F/O | | 12.12.19 | Cancelled. |
| 06247 | BURKE | Edward Joseph Augustine | F/L | + | 20.11.30 | |

Flight Lieutenant Edward Joseph Augustine Burke, as my co-author has discovered, died in the most harrowing circumstances after forced-landing with his two companions in the frozen wastes of the northern reaches of the Yukon. The full story of his last flight, which began on10th October, is related in an issue of *The Royal Air Force Quarterly* and is reproduced on the Find a Grave website. The aircraft which he was piloting was a Junkers F.13 CF-AMX. His mechanic, Emil Kading and passenger Bob Martin eventually made it to safety.

| 07028 | COPLEY | Reginald James | F/O | | 19.12.30 | Relinquished |

LG 25 February 1936, issue 34259, page 1241. Reserve of Air Force Officers. General Duties Branch. Granted a commission as Flight Lieutenant in Class C, on re-employment 6th January 1936. On 7th May 1938, he was transferred to Class CC [LG 15 November 1938, issue 34570, page 7197]. With effect from 1st September 1939, he relinquished his commission in Class CC on appointment to a commission in the Royal Air Force Volunteer Reserve and was immediately commissioned to the Administrative and Special Duties Branch [LG 27 October 1939, supplement 34718, pages 7182 and 7183]. His service number was now 75185 but subsequently reverted to 07028.

			S/Ldr		17.09.54	Relinquished
	GRIFFITH DFC	John Sharpe	F/O		03.11.20	Resigned
07204	*LESTER	Hugh Lewis Pingo	W/Cdr		22.12.43	Retirement**
	*RANSON	Hubert Everitt	F/O	+	09.10.22	5 FTS

While flying in Avro 504K H2482 of 5 FTS Shotwick, and accompanied by Pilot Officer Victor John Hatton, Flying Officer Hubert Everitt Ranson lost control when at the top of a loop, spun and crashed. He had been *Gazetted* on 13th January 1922, issue 32576, page 375, appointing him to a permanent commission with seniority as at 19th December 1919. Pilot Officer Hatton's short service commission had been promulgated as recently as 2nd Sept- ember 1922 [LG 19 September 1922, issue 32748, page 6715. He made a good recovery from his injuries and served until resigning his commission, and now ranked Flying Officer, on 1st April 1928 [LG 3 July 1928, issue 33400, page 4503].

| | WATERS | Charles Bernard | F/O | | 19.12.26 | Relinquished |

OBSERVER OFFICERS
2

| 08248 | CRAIK | David | F/L | | 19.12.30 | Relinquished |

LG 13 September 1940, issue 34945, page 5493. Returned to service. Commissioned to the Administrative and Special Duties Branch, 9th August 1940, as a Pilot Officer on probation.

| | | | S/Ldr | | 01.06.54 | Relinquished |
| 10233 | *TRUSS | Josiah Edward | W/Cdr | | 13.07.46 | Retired list** |

FLYING OFFICERS [from PILOT OFFICERS]
6

07059	DORMOR	Ronald Bertram	F/L		04.06.54	Relinquished
	GYE	Herbert James	Lieutenant		06.04.21	Resigned
	MASON	Stanley James	F/O	+	28.08.24	19 Squadron

Flying Officer Stanley James Mason was killed when his 7F.1 Snipe F2444 failed to pull out of a half-roll.

| 08164 | *VINCENT | Claude McLean | AV-M | | 29.08.52 | Retirement** |

Air Vice-Marshal Claude McLean Vincent CB CBE DFC* AFC twice mentioned in despatches, died on Tuesday, 8th August 1967. The Air of Authority website notes he was born in Trinidad on 21st January 1896, and on leaving the service returned to the West Indies.

| 08182 | WEBSTER | Sidney Norman | A/Cmdr | | 12.08.50 | Retirement** |

Air Commodore Sidney Norman Webster CBE AFC* Twice mentioned in despatches, died on Thursday, 5th April 1984. In 1927, he was one of the pilots chosen for to represent the Royal Air Force in the Schneider Trophy competition.

| | WHITFIELD | Lawrence | F/O | + | 17.09.31 | |

An amateur jockey, and while still in Class A of the Reserve, Flying Officer Lawrence Whitfield sustained fatal injuries while riding in a meeting at Hurst Park. Taken to the Star and Garter Home at Petersham, Surrey, he passed away while undergoing treatment.

OBSERVER OFFICERS [from PILOT OFFICERS]
4

| | CUTHBERT | Edwin | F/O | | 25.03.25 | Relinquished |

On account of ill-health [LG 27 March 1925, issue 33033, page 2117].

| | de MOYES-BUCKNALL | Silvio Paul Bernini | F/O | | 12.12.26 | Relinquished |

79389   Returned to service. Commissioned to the Administrative and Special Duties Branch, with effect from 10th April 1940, ranked Pilot Officer on probation [LG 112 June 1940, issue 34870, page 3523].

| | | | F/L | | 23.10.45 | Resigned** |
| | ROSS | Maurice St. John | O/O | | 12.10.22 | Relinquished |

On account of ill-health [LG 10 October 1922, issue 32754, page 7135].

| | WATSON | John Spencer Fletcher | O/O | | 09.10.23 | Relinquished |

On enlistment in the army [LG 30 October 1923, issue 32875, page 7305].

Note. Flight Lieutenant Geoffrey Ward Robarts MC was appointed to a permanent commission on 10th October 1919 [LG 8 March 1921, issue 32250, page 1899]. It is noted, however, that his appointment to a permanent commission on 1st August 1919, as a Captain was later cancelled, but it appears he was granted a short service commission on 10th October 1919.

Appendix 2F - The Roll of Honour 1st January - 31st December 1919

The influenza pandemic continued to rage across the world until the summer of 1919, and there can be no doubt whatsoever that a high percentage of non-related air accident deaths were caused by the virulent strain of the virus identified as H1N1. Easily the worse month was February 1919, with 322 Royal Air Force deaths recorded, a high percentage owing to the pandemic; however, by April air force deaths had reduced significantly and this downward trend would continue throughout the remaining months of the year. A surprising amount of casualties occurred in North Russia, though none, as far as I can tell, involved operational squadrons. The asterisk placed in front of a surname indicates death as a result from an air accident; I am aware that the daily tables of casualties reported on the CWGC website contains information that may be missing details of squadrons, while other entries show the casualty as belonging to a squadron that on the date of his death had been disbanded. These discrepancies, invariably, can be laid at the door of the reporting authority. Thanks to the input of my co-author, Paul McMillan, names recorded on the CWGC website where only the initials have been reported, e.g. BAIN R T, have now been fully resolved.

By October, Record Offices were notifying officer deaths using the recently promulgated ranks of Pilot Officer, Flying Officer et al, though the previous system of retention of army ranks continued in many instances.

The three squadron casualties notified in November were non-air accident related.

ROYAL AIR FORCE

Mechanic	ADAM	David Smith	15 March 1919	25 Squadron
Mechanic	ADAMS*	Amos	27 March 1919	114 Squadron
Captain	ADAMS*DFC mid	Allen Percy	6 March 1919	30 Squadron
AC1	ALEXANDER	Donald William	11 March 1919	98 Squadron
2Lt	ALLEN* South Africa	Charles Arthur	12 March 1919	48 Squadron
Captain	ATKINSON MC DFC *Croix de Guerre* Belgium	Rupert Norman Gould	7 March 1919	90 Squadron

Identified only by his initials on the CWGC website, through *Wikipedia* I have been able to identify not only his Christian names, but that he was born in Shanghai, China, on the 17th of July 1896. His death, like so many here recorded, was from pneumonia following influenza while on leave from his squadron. He is buried in Great Berkhampsted [St. Peter] Church Cemetery. Turning to *The London Gazette* the following in respect of citations has been published. Supplement 30561, page 2904, of 7th March 1918, that for his MC: *'For conspicuous gallantry and devotion to duty. This officer has done a large amount of successful artillery work, has taken part in many night bombing raid, and has continually distinguished himself by his fearlessness and determination in descending to low altitudes in order to attack hostile infantry and machine guns. On one occasion, also, he successfully attacked and drove down a hostile balloon.'* Supplement 30989, page 12961, of 2nd November 1918: *'A gallant and determined officer whose services over the lines since May last in long-distance and photographic reconnaissances, and as leader of bomb raids, have been of a very high order. On a recent occasion, when on solitary photographic reconnaissance at 15,000 feet, his machine was attacked by eight Fokker biplanes; one of these he shot down.'* The award conferred on him by His Majesty King of the Belgians was *Gazetted* on 15th July 1919, supplement 31457, page 8987. Although attached to 90 Squadron at the time of his death, his operational service on the Western Front was with 10 and 98 Squadrons.

Mechanic	BAIN	Robert Taylor	22 February 1919	25 Squadron
Lt	BANNERMAN*	Gilbert Gunn	8 June 1919	110 Squadron
Captain	BANNISTER*	Edward Gentleman	14 February 1919	111 Squadron
Mechanic	BARBER	James	7 February 1919	207 Squadron
2Lt	BARCLAY*	John George	10 May 1919	25 Squadron
Captain	BARKER*	Leslie Ivan	19 May 1919	7 Squadron
AC2	BATEMAN	John Newman	14 February 1919	73 Squadron
Mechanic	BENJAMIN	David	4 March 1919	166 Squadron
Sgt	BENT	William Ernest	10 March 1919	25 Squadron
AC2	BERRY	William Arthur	1 November 1919	206 Squadron
Sgt	BILLING MSM	Bertie	16 February 1919	20 Squadron

Paul McMillan has traced the service of Sergeant Bertie Billing MSM and this reveals he transferred from the the 59th Company, Royal Engineers to the Royal Flying Corps and posting to 1 Squadron on 4th July 1912. Subsequently, he served with 6 Squadron before being attached to 20 Squadron and in addition to his MSM he was posthumously mentioned in despatches. His military service commenced on the 3rd of June 1908.

Corporal	BISCOE MM	Frederick Albert	25 February 1919	5 Squadron
Lt-Col	BODDAM- WHETHEM*DSO	Arthur Courtney	22 June 1919	Staff HQME 111 Squadron
F/Sgt	BOHRINGER	Frederick George	22 January 1919	139 Squadron
AC2	BORTHWICK*	James	9 May 1919	25 Squadron
F/Sgt	BOTT	Albert Edward	1 November 1919	99 Squadron
Mechanic	BOTTOMLEY	William Russell	15 June 1919	19 Squadron
Lt	BRODIE*	Eric Brownlee	11 February 1919	43 Squadron
Corporal	BROOKER	William Henry	6 November 1919	221 Squadron
Mechanic	BROWN	George Atkinson	12 January 1919	207 Squadron
LAC	BUCKLEY	George	24 February 1919	25 Squadron
Corporal	BUNNING	Fred	18 February 1919	4 Squadron
Lt	BURNAY*	Percy Samuel	6 March 1919	57 Squadron
Private	BURTON	Thomas	29 December 1919	2 Squadron
2Lt	CARTLON-SMITH*	Beavan	6 February 1919	100 Squadron
Mechanic	CARLYON	Edward Henry	27 January 1919	207 Squadron
Mechanic	CAYGILL	George	7 July 1919	106 Squadron
AC2	CHALLENOR	Ewart Oswald	28 February 1919	57 Squadron
LAC	CHEADLE	Edward	14 March 1919	53 Squadron
Lt	CHRISTIE Canada	Donald Murdoch	23 February 1919	3 Squadron
2Lt	CLARK*	Harry Thomas	16 June 1919	84 Squadron
2Lt	CLARKE*	Fred	5 June 1919	105 Squadron

	Surrey Yeomanry [Queen Mary's Regiment]			
P/O	CLARKE*MC	Joseph	1 October 1919	99 Squadron
	17th Lancers and Worcestershire Regiment			
Sgt	COCKERILL*	Thomas Wray	21 April 1919	66 Squadron
F/O	COCKMAN	Charles Burton Blenheim	10 December 1919	111 Squadron
	B Battery Honourable Artillery Company			
Lt	COLLINGE*	Charles Ingham	25 July 1919	216 Squadron
	Royal Tank Corps			
AC1	COOPER	Gerald Alfred	6 July 1919	20 Squadron
Sgt	COPE	Francis Edward	28 February 1919	29 Squadron
2Lt	COTTERELL*	Robert James	13 January 1919	236 Squadron
Mechanic	COX	Joseph Butler	5 October 1919	63 Squadron
Private	CROSSLEY	Fred William	26 June 1919	94 Squadron
Lt	CROUDACE*	Harold	13 January 1919	36 Squadron
Lt	CUMMING*	Charles Linnaeus	31 January 1919	206 Squadron
Mechanic	DANGERFIELD	Percy Frederick	3 January 1919	74 Squadron
Captain	DARLEY*DSC* DFC Cecil Hill		28 September 1919	274 Squadron
	Cross of Military Merit Spain			
Lt	DAVIES DFC*	Edgar George	6 February 1919	29 Squadron
	Croix de Guerre Belgium			
Mechanic	DAVIS	Edward Blayney	25 February 1919	54 Squadron
2Lt	DAVIS*MM	Harry	20 May 1919	59 Squadron
	3/Royal Warwickshire Regiment			
Sgt Major	DEELEY	Arthur	3 March 1919	99 Squadron
Lt	DEVONSHIRE*	Feray Vulliamy	11 July 1919	31 Squadron
	7/[Queen's Own] Hussars			
Corporal	DIX	Alfred Fred	19 September 1919	12 Squadron
AC1	DRINKWATER	Neville	3 March 1919	149 Squadron
Private	ESCRITT	Robert	7 January 1919	246 Squadron
Lt	EVANS*	Richard Ralph	20 August 1919	5 Squadron
AC2	EVERARD	Charles	26 April 1919	12 Squadron
Captain	EVERSDEN	Robert Ernest	15 August 1919	47 Squadron
	3/Suffolk Yeomanry			
Sgt	FISHER	George	16 June 1919	29 Squadron
Mechanic	FITT	Edgar Henry	22 March 1919	55 Squadron
Corporal	FLINTOFF*	Elton Humphreys	10 July 1919	214 Squadron
Mechanic	FORD	Henry Thomas	15 January 1919	19 Squadron
Lt	FORDER*	Ernest George	25 February 1919	75 Squadron
Corporal	FOREHEAD	Charles Russell	15 March 1919	211 Squadron
AC1	FORREST	Christopher Thomas	13 February 1919	5 Squadron
Private	FOSTER	Frederick Charles	24 February 1919	101 Squadron
AC1	FRANKLIN	William Proctor Dowdeswell	16 February 1919	79 Squadron
AC2	FREEMAN	Frank Oliver	27 December 1919	47 Squadron
Sgt	GAILLARD*	Paul	25 April 1919	88 Squadron

Belgium An artillery sergeant acting as an interpreter for the squadron at Nivelles. A casualty card was raised by the Royal Air Force naming him incorrectly as Sergeant 'R Guillard'.

Lt	GARDNER*	John Harrison	9 January 1919	100 Squadron
Sgt	GARDINER	Harry Victor	18 February 1919	51 Squadron
Lt	GARROD	Basil Rahere	4 February 1919	149 Squadron
	1/The Loyal North Lancashire Regiment			

One of three sons of Colonel Sir Archibald E Garrod [late of AMS], Regius Professor of Medicine in the University of Oxford, to loses their lives. Lieutenant Thomas Martin Garrod, aged 20, of the 3rd Battalion, The Loyal North Lancashire Regiment, fell on the 10th of May 1915, and is now buried in Bethune Town Cemetery, as his elder brother, Lieutenant Alfred Noel Garrod, aged 28, who died on 25 January 1916, while serving with the 100th Field Ambulance, RAMC. Thomas's epitaph has been taken from verse 5 of Psalm 130; *'I Look For The Lord My Soul Doth Wait For Him In His Word Is My Trust'* while Basil Garrod, aged 21, who is buried in Cologne's Southern Cemetery has a line from the Hymn 'Now The Laborer's Task is O'er' written by John Ellerton in 1871 and, I assume, amended in 1875 by John B Dykers; *'Father In Thy Gracious Keeping Leave We Here They Servant Sleeping.'* For reasons known only to the family, Alfred's headstone has no inscription. Lieutenant Basil Garrod's Record of Service shows he was born on the 29th of December 1897, and he died in 36 Casualty Clearing Station from Lobar Pneumonia. His funeral was conducted by the Reverend C D R B Bankes, attached 70 Squadron, on the 7th of February 1919.

Lt	GATTENS*mid	Charles	15 June 1919	63 Squadron
	South Africa			
Mechanic	GIBBONS	Henry Frank Leslie	1 March 1919	103 Squadron
Lt	GIBBS*	Stanley	14 May 1919	206 Squadron
Mechanic	GILLON	William Gillespie	5 April 1919	49 Squadron
AC1	GLEED	Albert John	17 February 1919	60 Squadron
2Lt	GONDRE	Jean	20 July 1919	48 Squadron
	France			

Nineteen year old 2nd Lieutenant Jean Gondre, born on the 29th of July 1899, in Paris, joined the RFC on 7th November 1917. He is summarised on page 73 of my second volume. He is commemorated on the Archangel Memorial, thus it is almost certain he was no longer on the nominal roll of the squadron, now in India and settling at Quetta.

Corporal	GOULDING	George Montague	16 February 1919	203 Squadron
Lt	GRAHAM*	Edward William	3 January 1919	56 Squadron
	Canada Canadian Army Service Corps			
2Lt	GRANT*	Paul Thomas	21 January 1919	65 Squadron
	Canada			
2Lt	GREEN*	Smith	18 February 1919	70 Squadron
Corporal	GREGORY	Thomas Hayden	28 February 1919	8 Squadron
AC1	GROOME	Edward Alfred	14 March 1919	103 Squadron
Mechanic	HAIGH	James	7 March 1919	79 Squadron
Lt	HALL*	Clifford	9 July 1919	214 Squadron
Sgt	HALL	Henry John	23 July 1919	221 Squadron

Rank	Surname	Forename(s)	Date	Squadron
Sgt	HALLAM	Edward Leslie Earnshaw	22 February 1919	10 Squadron
2Lt	HAMMOND*	Harry Charles	11 February 1919	70 Squadron
Sgt	HARRIS	Albert Charles	7 October 1919	20 Squadron
AC2	HARRIS	John James	9 February 1919	79 Squadron
Mechanic	HARRISON	Aylmer Russell	27 February 1919	60 Squadron
2Lt	HARRISON*	Cuthbert	3 May 1919	186 Squadron
AC1	HASEMORE	Arthur Sydney	18 June 1919	31 Squadron

Aircraftsman Arthur Sydney's casualty form gives his unit as 114 Squadron based at Quetta and showing the cause of his death as 'Heatstroke.' Both squadrons were India based, 31 Squadron being at Risalpur.

Rank	Surname	Forename(s)	Date	Squadron
Corporal	HARVEY	Stanley Frank	27 March 1919	59 Squadron
Lt	HARWOOD*AFC	Gerald	1 May 1919	97 Squadron
	3/Suffolk Regiment			
Mechanic	HAWKER	Alfred George	6 January 1919	70 Squadron
Captain	HAYES*	George William Norman Risdale	30 May 1919	11 Squadron
	6/Royal Munster Fusiliers			
Lt	HEMSWORTH*	Gore William	15 August 1919	1 Squadron
AC1	HERRIOTT	Frederick	23 February 1919	20 Squadron
Lt	HEWETT*	Leonard Stanley	6 February 1919	100 Squadron
Private	HIGGINS	Matthew	22 January 1919	39 Squadron
Major	HILL	Alan Purdie Dunlop	8 February 1919	59 Squadron
	Royal Garrison Artillery			

A non-digitised record for Major Alan Purdie Dunlop Hill is held by TNA Kew under WO 339/9715. A service record exists for him showing he was born on the 11th of December 1893, transferring to the RFC on the 1st of June 1916; unfortunately, information ceases with his posting to 8 Squadron on 3rd May 1917.

Rank	Surname	Forename(s)	Date	Squadron
Lt	HILL	Stafford Norman	2 March 1919	101 Squadron
AC2	HINTON	William	17 February 1919	12 Squadron
2Lt	HITCHCOCK*	Albert Edward	29 January 1919	28 Squadron
AC2	HOUGH	Charles	17 December 1919	12 Squadron
AC1	HUMPHREYS	Wallace Gilbert	20 February 1919	8 Squadron
Lt	HUNT*	Cyril Frank	23 April 1919	97 Squadron
2Lt	HUTCHISON	Harry	27 March 1919	149 Squadron
	Canada			
Lt	HUTTON	William Douglas Campbell	27 March 1919	149 Squadron
Lt	ILLINGWORTH	Frederick William	6 February 1919	23 Squadron
	Twice mentioned in a despatch. Camerons [Scottish Rifles]			

Army Form B.103 shows Lieutenant Frederick William Illingworth was posted to 23 Squadron at Auchel on the 28th of May 1917, and within 24-hours of his arrival he transferred with the squadron to Bruary from where on June 7th, the day the *Battle of Messines* opend, he was posted 'missing'. Turning to Trevor Henshaw's *'The Sky Their Battlefield,'* this shows he was flying Spad VII B1524/1 and was shot down circa 0715 near Menin, and was wounded in the engagement. He is buried in Edinburgh [Portobello] Cemetery. At the time of his death 23 Squadron was based at Clermont and its possible he was no longer of the squadron's establishment.

Rank	Surname	Forename(s)	Date	Squadron
LAC	JACKSON	Thomas Douglas	13 February 1919	52 Squadron
Lt	JACOB	John Victor Reed	16 March 1919	25 Squadron

Lieutenant John Victor Reed Jacob's service record shows he was admitted to 14 Stationary Hospital at Wimereux on the 4th of March 1919, seriously ill with Cerberus- Spinal Meningitis and died on the 16th. He was buried with full military honours in Terlincthun British Cemetery, Wimille, by the Reverend E T Kirby who was attached to the Boulogne Base. John Jacob's father, Major J E F Jacob, was formerly of the 1st Battalion, South Lancashire Regiment.

Rank	Surname	Forename(s)	Date	Squadron
Corporal	JAFFE*	Louis Hyman	10 July 1919	214 Squadron
Captain	JEFCOATE*MBE mid	Frank	14 February 1919	111 Squadron
	Suffolk Regiment South Afric			
2Lt	JEMMESON*	George Edwin	15 May 1919	221 Squadron
Captain	JOHN	Francis Ernest	26 February 1919	204 Squadron
	Croix de Guerre France			

Captain Francis Ernest John was posted home, presumably in good health, six days prior to his death. Aged 30, he is buried in Hampstead Cemetery.

Rank	Surname	Forename(s)	Date	Squadron
Mechanic	JOHNSON	Thomas William	26 February 1919	52 Squadron
AC2	JONES	John Edward	10 July 1919	207 Squadron
AC2	JORDAN*	Alexander James Siddons	23 December 1919	48 Squadron
Lt	KELLOUGH*	William Roy	3 March 1919	88 Squadron
	Canada			
Lt	KEMP	Sidney Albert	21 February 1919	3 Squadron
	Attached No. 1 Aerial Range			

Born on the 8th of December 1899, Lieutenant Sidney Albert Kemp joined 3 Squadron at Valhereux on 12th July 1918. Admitted to 20 General Hospital, he succumbed to a combination of Influenza and Septicaemia.

Rank	Surname	Forename(s)	Date	Squadron
Mechanic	KEMP	William Robert	2 March 1919	12 Squadron
2Lt	KENNEDY*	William	12 March 1919	48 Squadron
Mechanic	KEMP	William	17 February 1919	33 Squadron
Captain	KEYMER*DFC*	Basil Graham Homfray	24 October 1919	47 Squadron
	Croci di Guerre [Italy]			
2Lt	KIME MM	Gilbert Henry Ernest	12 May 1919	10 Squadron
	Essex Regiment			

Born on 17th November 1894, 2nd Lieutenant Gilbert Kime joined 10 Squadron at Droglandt, as an observer, on 10th June 1918, and was seriously wounded on the 1st of October [see page 276 of my second volume]. He was first treated at 2 Canadian Casualty Clearing Station at Mouvaux before being transferred to Wimereux and admittance to 14 General Hospital. His left leg and been fractured by bullets, and he was sent to England aboard HMHS *Princess Elizabeth*. My summary of 1st October, I now believe to be slightly in error; at the time I did not have a copy of his service records and I'm now of the opinion that he may not have been on the squadron's nominal strength at the time of his death. He rests in Woodgrange Park Cemetery, East Ham.

Rank	Surname	Forename(s)	Date	Squadron
Sgt	KING	George Thomas	23 February 1919	25 Squadron
AC2	KINSELLA	Gerald	5 April 1919	42 Squadron
LAC	KRALL	Karl	28 February 1919	211 Squadron
2Lt	KRETMAR*	William Forrest King	7 May 1919	141 Squadron
AC2	LAVILLE	William	27 June 1919	8 Squadron
Captain	LAWRENCE	Percival William Bernard	27 February 1919	149 Squadron

Sgt	LEADBETTER	Nicholas	18 February 1919	107 Squadron
AC2	LEESON	Charles	4 March 1919	80 Squadron
2Lt	LEWIN	Percival Lionel Thomas	9 September 1919	66 Squadron
Lt	LIMERICK*	Victor	20 August 1919	5 Squadron

Royal Field Artillery

Sgt	LINDLEY*	Hirst	15 June 1919	63 Squadron
2Lt	LINKLETTER	Silas Montague	27 August 1919	2 Squadron

USA

2Lt	LLOYD*	Frank	1 February 1919	61 Squadron
2Lt	LYON MM*	Lloyd Diets St. Aubyn	28 February 1919	54 Squadron

Jamaica

LAC	LUCAS	Stanley	18 February 1919	205 Squadron
AC1	MACE*	Alfred	23 April 1919	6 Squadron
AC2	MARSHALL	James	24 February 1919	115 Squadron
Lt	MARTIN	Bruce	1 March 1919	105 Squadron

5/Royal Berkshire Regiment attached 35th T M B.

An incomplete Record of Service for this observer officer exists which shows he was born on the 30th of August 1892, and enlisted with the RFC on the 11th of November 1917. The son of the Reverend J J and Mrs M E Martin of The Hut in North Road, Selsey, he is buried here in St. Peter's Church Cemetery. Knowing of his background, his epitaph reads: *'He Of The "Merry Heart" Proverbs 17.22'.*

AC1	MASSON	Samuel	8 February 1919	7 Squadron
Lt	McEACHRAN*	Niall	20 May 1919	59 Squadron

3/Higland Light Infantry

Lt	McLEOD	Samuel Evans Smith	11 August 1919	4 Squadron
Captain	McLENNAN MC	John Lawrence	28 August 1919	47 Squadron

Canada

Mechanic	McQUARRIE mid	Thomas Emmett	24 October 1919	14 Squadron
Mechanic	MEE	George Irwin	9 January 1919	3 Squadron
Private	MILLETT	Ernest	16 August 1919	38 Squadron
Lt	MILLS*AFC mid	John McFarlane Denholm	22 June 1919	111 Squadron
Captain	MINORS	Ronald Towers	27 March 1919	18 Squadron

Worcestershire Regiment

Sgt	MITCHELL	Edward George	3 December 1919	58 Squadron
2Lt	MITCHELL*	John Thomas	24 January 1919	112 Squadron

Canada

AC2	MORGAN	Frank	25 September 1919	48 Squadron
Lt	MORRIS*	John Clarke	3 January 1919	19 Squadron

3/Duke of Wellington's [West Riding Regiment]

2Lt	NEWETH	William Bernard	25 February 1919	60 Squadron
LAC	NICHOLLS	Eernest Joseph	19 September 1919	31 Squadron
AC2	NICKLESS	John	11 February 1919	79 Squadron
AC2	OATES	James	30 January 1919	22 Squadron
AC1	O'BRIEN	Patrick	5 February 1919	21 Squadron
Sgt	O'FLYNN	Patrick Joseph	12 February 1919	98 Squadron
Mechanic	O'NEILL	William Francis	18 April 1919	7 Squadron
Sgt	PAGE*	Arthur Baden	14 May 1919	206 Squadron
Captain	PATEY DFC	Herbert Andrew	18 February 1919	210 Squadron

RMLI 'Howe' Battalion, RN

Captain Herbert Andrew Patey, born on 29th September 1898, transferred to the RNAS on the 4th of August 1917, and from the 12th of June 1918, until he was shot down and made a prisoner of war on the 5th of September [see page 210 on my second volume] was carrying out the duties of a Flight Commander on the squadron. Dying from Pneumonia, he is buried in Hampstead Cemetery. The citation for his DFC appeared in *The London Gazette* of 21st September 1918, supplement 30913, page 11253: *'While leading his flight on an offensive patrol eight enemy machines were encountered. Captain Patey was cut off from his patrol by two of the enemy who got on his tail, and continued in that position until within 2,000 feet of the ground, at which point his machine was hit in the petrol tank. Notwithstanding his serious handicap, he turned four times on his pursuers, destroying one, and driving the remainder away. On previous occasions this officer has destroyed two enemy and brought down two more out of control, and, in company with other pilots, he has assisted in destroying or bringing down out of control five additional enemy aircraft.'*

Captain	PAYNE*MC mid	Lawrence Allan	19 February 1919	48 Squadron

South Africa

AC1	PEPLOE*	Charles Reginald	23 April 1919	6 Squadron
F/L	PERCIVAL mid	John Frederick Spencer	1 March 1919	206 Squadron

John Percival is summarised on page 112 of my second volume, at which time he was ranked Second Lieutenant. Looking at Army Form B.103c, here it is recorded that he was evacuated to England aboard HMHS *St. Denis* on 1st September 1918, having sustained multiple wounds. In my summary I suggested his death might be attributed to the influenza pandemic, but this was written before I had access to surviving officers' records, and in light of the entry 'multiple wounds', it is a possibility that his war injuries were the cause of his death at the age of 29; he rests in St. Pancras Cemetery. Interestingly, his rank is now recorded as Flight Lieutenant.

Mechanic	PLUMB	William Ernest	20 January 1919	207 Squadron
Mechanic	POLLICOTT	George William	27 February 1919	107 Squadron
2Lt	PORTER	William	28 February 1919	83 Squadron
Lt	PREECE	Charles Evered	18 February 1919	2 Squadron

Queen's Own Worcestershire Hussars [Worcester Yeomanry]

2Lt	PRINCE*	Frederick George	17 May 1919	58 Squadron
2Lt	RAW	Wilfred Addison	14 March 1919	78 Squadron

South Africa

AC2	REEVE	Herbert George	3 February 1919	9 Squadron
LAC	REIDSMA	Thomas	28 February 1919	59 Squadron
Mechanic	ROBINSON	David Miller	19 February 1919	99 Squadron
Lt	ROBINSON	Ernest Charles	20 January 1919	10 Squadron
Major	ROBINSON*	Hugh Huntley	3 May 1919	25 Squadron

RAMC

Corporal	ROBINSON	Lambert	14 February 1919	202 Squadron
Captain	RUSSELL	Cyril Ernest Shaftesbury	5 March 1919	149 Squadron

Unfortunately Captain Cyril Ernest Shaftesbury Russell's Record of Service is incomplete, the last entry being made on 21st September 1918, showing he had proceeded on leave on the 20th and was due to return to duty on the 4th of October. He was born on the 4th of April 1898, and enlisted with the RFC on 18th March 1916.. He is buried in Cologne's Southern Cemetery.

2Lt	SALMON *	Frederick Charles	1 May 1919	97 Squadron
AC1	SCHLAMP	Stanley Charles	9 March 1919	25 Squadron
LAC	SHAW	Christopher James	19 February 1919	59 Squadron
Sgt	SHAW	Fred William	24 February 1919	5 Squadron
AC2	SHIRLEY	Walter	26 June 1919	63 Squadron
Mechanic	SHUTTLEWORTH	Harry	7 January 1919	3 Squadron
2Lt	SIMMONS*	Arthur Donald	26 February 1919	44 Squadron
2Lt	SINCLAIR*	Robert	24 January 1919	70 Squadron
2Lt	SMITH*	Algernon Sydney	20 March 1919	57 Squadron
2Lt	SMITH*	Hugh Cassillis	15 May 1919	78 Squadron
Corporal	SMITH	John Allen	4 February 1919	73 Squadron
Mechanic	SPARROW	Charles Herbert	6 January 1919	142 Squadron
Sgt	SPONG*	Maynard George	2 October 1919	99 Squadron
2Lt	SPRATT*	Sidney	17 May 1919	58 Squadron
2Lt	STACE*	Arthur Howard Bartlett	3 May 1919	25 Squadron
Sgt	STACEY	Herbert Walter	3 February 1919	13 Squadron
2Lt	SULLIVAN*	Frank Harrington	29 March 1919	216 Squadron
	USA			
Lt	SUMNER*	Francis Cyril	9 July 1919	214 Squadron
Captain	SUTTLE	William Parker	2 February 1919	215 Squadron

Captain William Parker Suttle was admitted to 3 Canadian Stationary Hospital on 26th January 1919, where his condition slowly deteriorated until his death eight days later from Lobar Pneumonia. He was buried with full military honours at Longuenesse[St. Omer] Souvenir Cemetery by the Reverend A Harden, Chaplin attached to 3 Canadian Stationary Hospital. William Suttle had been on the Nominal Roll of the squadron since the 3rd of July 1918.

LAC	TAIT	Leonard Henderson	12 October 1919	47 Squadron
AC2	TAYLOR	Charles William Chamberlain	3 May 1919	70 Squadron
AC1	TAYLOR	James Roach	5 September 1919	11 Squadron
Mechanic	TAYLOR	Joseph William	22 February 1919	65 Squadron
Sgt	THOMPSON	Arthur Stanley	1 March 1919	102 Squadron
Lt	THOMPSON*	Douglas Blaxland	24 October 1919	47 Squadron
	Royal Field Artiller			
LAC	THOMPSON	James Easton	4 March 1919	5 Squadron
Lt	THOMPSON	Sidney	26 January 1919	27 Squadron
Lt	THORNTON*	Frank Oswell	6 March 1919	57 Squadron
P/O	TISDALL*	Michael Henry	23 December 1919	48 Squadron
2Lt	TODD	Leslie Graham	26 February 1919	99 Squadron
	14/London Regiment			
Captain	TONKS DFC*	Adrian James Boswell	14 July 1919	80 Squadron
Lt	TRATMAN	Leslie William Thomas Draycott	13 March 1919	38 Squadron

Lieutenant Leslie William Thomas Draycott Tratman is featured on page 63 of my second volume, where he is shown as being taken prisoner of war. Army Form B.103c shows he was born on the 1st of November 1898, and he was repatriated on the 23rd of December 1898. From Forest Hill, London, he is buried in Ladywell Cemetery where the register notes he was a night flying pilot. At the time of his death 38 Squadron had returned from France and as a cadre was based at Hawkinge. I am unable to say for certainty if Lieutenant Tratman had rejoined the squadron.

AC1	TRICKER*	Ernest James	6 May 1919	8 Squadron
2Lt	TURKINGTON*	Ivan	23 June 1919	79 Squadron
Lt	TURNER*	Bertram Eric Nelson	15 May 1919	221 Squadron
Lt	TWILTON*	Reginald John	25 April 1919	88 Squadron
Mechanic	VAUGHAN	Llaurence	5 February 1919	79 Squadron
Sgt	WALKER	Herbert	20 February 1919	108 Squadron
2Lt	WALLIS	Frank	13 February 1919	18 Squadron
Mechanic	WALLS	Thomas	24 February 1919	99 Squadron
Corporal	WAPLES	John William	3 January 1919	74 Squadron
2Lt	WARD	Lewis John Beer	2 January 1919	55 Squadron
Captain	WARMAN DSO MC mid	Clive Wilson	12 May 1919	81 Squadron

A partial Record of Service exists for Captain Clive Wilson Warman, this showing that on 18th of June 1917, he was posted to 23 Squadron at La Lovie and while on an offensive patrol on 20th August 1917, he was wounded. Trevor Henshaw records this on page 112 of *The Sky Their Battlefield* noting that Clive Warman had a dozen aerial victories to his credit. The airframe serial of his Spad VII has not been recorded. I have, however, traced the citation for his MC which, oddly, was not *Gazetted* until 9th January 1918, supplement 30466, page 650, by which time he had been *Gazetted* with the DSO [LG 26 September 1917, supplement 30308, page 9969] which records he already had been honoured with the MC. No citation appended for his DSO, but that for his MC reads: *'For conspicuous gallantry and devotion to duty. He has on all occasions proved himself to be an exceptionally skilful and gallant pilot, having in the space of six weeks brought down six machines and destroyed a hostile balloon. He has also driven down five other enemy machines, displaying a consistent determination to attack at close range regardless of personal danger.'* His mention in a despatch is recorded on Record of Service, indicating this was published circa 7th December 1917. Another point, or two, of interest is that although shown as being attached to 81 Squadron, I very much suspect he was on the nominal roll of 1 Squadron CAF which was based at Shoreham [81 Squadron formed at Gosport on 7th January 1917, but disbanded 4th July 1918, its numberplate being transferred to 1 Squadron CAF]. Of Shoreham in Sussex, he is buried in Brookwood Military Cemetery where his headstone is inscribed: *'Loved By All That Knew Him Most Of All By Father & Mother.'*

2Lt	WATERS*	Andrew John	31 January 1919	206 Squadron
Lt	WEAVER*	Herbert John	6 May 1919	8 Squadron
	6/Queen's Own Regiment, West Kent Regiment			
LAC	WEBB	Bernard Percy Norley	19 August 1919	10 Squadron

Although 10 Squadron was in existence as a cadre based at Ford in Sussex, Leading Aircraft Bernard Percy Norley Webb is buried in Egypt at Alexandria [Hadra] War Memorial Cemetery.

Lt	WEBSTER*	Alexander	24 January 1919	70 Squadron
Mechanic	WEEKS	William Cecil	22 August 1919	114 Squadron
2Lt	WELLS	Sydney	26 March 1919	48 Squadron
2Lt	WESTALL*	Arthur	29 March 1919	216 Squadron
Corporal	WHARTON	Thomas Stanley	10 June 1919	207 Squadron
AC1	WHITE	Ernest Frederick George	10 July 1919	20 Squadron

2Lt	WHITELAW Canada	Frederick John	28 February 1919	148 Squadron
Mechanic	WILLIAMS	Richard Emrys	18 March 1919	99 Squadron
Lt	WILLIAMS*	Trevor Lewis	1 January 1919	72 Squadron
Mechanic	WILSON	John Hudson	4 March 1919	8 Squadron
Lt	WILSON*	William Nichol	8 June 1919	110 Squadron
Sgt	WITHERS	Ernest William	27 June 1919	20 Squadron
2Lt	WOOD*	James	9 January 1919	100 Squadron
2Lt	YOKUM* Canada	Chester Frank	10 February 1919	59 Squadron
Lt	YORKE* Cheshire Regiment	Frederick	13 January 1919	36 Squadron

CANADIAN AIR FORCE

Major	CARTER*DSO*	Albert Desbrisay	22 May 1919	2 Squadron CAF
	Croix de Guerre [Belgium] Three times mentioned in despatches			
Major	McKEEVER DSO MC* DFC	Andrew Edward	26 December 1919	1 Squadron CAF
	Queen's Own Royal Rifles of Canada			

Born on the 21st of August 1894, Major Andrew Edward McKeever like so many of his countrymen who served with distinction in the RFC and Royal Air Force began his military service as a private soldier in the militia before being accepted by the RFC in November 1916, sailing for England that same month. Qualifying as a pilot he went to France where he joined 11 Squadron at Izel-lez-Harmeau but within days moved with the squadron to La Bellevue where flying Bristol F.2bs he and his air gunner between them destroyed thirty-one enemy aircraft. Along with William Bishop VC and Raymond Collishaw, he helped with the formation of the Canadian Air Force and to Andrew fell the honour of commanding 1 Squadron CAF but the war ended before the squadron became operational and in their short-sighted wisdom the government of Canada dissolved the air force. Technically, therefore, Major McKeever was no longer serving when he died from complications following a road traffic accident which left him with a fractured leg, but in recognition of his invaluable contribution to the *Great War's* victory, I hereby honour his name with the Roll of Honour. Andrew Edward McKeever is buried in Listowel [Fairview] Cemetery, Ontario.

JANUARY
1920

Any lingering hopes that the huge reduction of operation squadrons, as witnessed in the previous year was at an end were quickly dispelled, though with the reorganisation of the air force a handful would re-emerge either through the process of being reformed or by taking over the 'number plate' of an existing squadron.

It was not, however, all despair. Trenchard's outstanding ability to organise to the best advantage with what few resources he had at his disposal were wisely used and the foundations of a professional Royal Air Force emerged which has stood our nation in good stead for over century.

Among his lasting achievements was in ensuring that training to the highest standard would be the bedrock on which the force would be built and to this end an apprenticeship scheme was established for ground tradesmen, and for the officer corps commissions would follow the twin-paths of permanent and short service. As will be seen from the appendices reported at the end of 1919, a strong force of senior and middle-ranked officers had been established, while at the Cadet College at Cranwell, provision was made for twice-yearly intakes of flight cadets who on successful graduation would be appointed to permanent commissions.

The short service commission officer, appointed to the General List, would serve terms of service that might vary between three and five years, followed by placement on the reserve list and be liable for recall in the case of dire emergency.

In time, other types of commission would be offered, and these will be reflected through the appropriate appendices.

Tuesday 20 January 1920
Five squadrons were relieved of their duties during the day, 1 Squadron, which for the best of a year had existed as a cadre, disbanded at Uxbridge, 2 Squadron at Weston-on-the-Green, 5 Squadron at Bicester - all three had first come into existence before the *Great War* though 1 Squadron initial role between May 1912 and April 1914 was the operation of balloons, airships and kites. By April 1914, it had received its first aeroplanes, though on the outbreak of war in August 1914, those types on establishment were shared out to those squadrons accompanying the British Expeditionary Force to France. Thus, it then had to re-equip and train before deploying to St. Omer in March 1915.

At Duxford, 8 Squadron disbanded and 28 Squadron was stood down at Eastleigh.

Thursday 22 January 1920
The disbanding process of the 20th resulted this day with five more squadrons ceasing to exist; two Shotwick units were disbanded, 27 Squadron and 55 Squadron. 56 Squadron and 60 Squadron disbanded at Bircham Newton, and at Spittle-gate time was called on 70 Squadron.

Friday 30 January 1920
84 Squadron disbanded

Saturday 31 January 1920
25 Squadron disbanded.

FEBRUARY
1920

In my preamble for the year, I remarked that some of the disbanded squadrons would be reborn through taking over the 'number plate' of an existing squadron and the first examples of this now came about. At Suez 142 Squadron whose war time duties had been tactical reconnaissance and artillery observation for which it was equipped with a mixture of aircraft types, though since January 1919, predominately DH.9s became 55 Squadron under the command of Flight Lieutenant C H Elliott-Smith. A rather truncated Record of Service for the month of May and June 1916, exists for this officer. It is part handwritten and part typed:-

				Embarked England 22.11.15	
				Disembarked Alexandria 11.12.15	
25.5.16	17 Sqdn	*Placed on sick leave*		*22.5.16*	*B.213*
24.6.16	"	*Proceeded to Alexandria en route*		*16.6.16*	"
		to England [on duty]			
"	"	*Proceeded to England &*		*17.6.16*	"
		struck strength of No 17 Squadron			
15.6.16	"	*Appointed Flight Commander &*		*1.6.16*	"
		to be tempy. Capt.			
		[W.O. Cablegram 7035 dated 10.6.16 [A.O.2]			
17.6.18	NR	*Emb. Per H.T. "Transylvania"*		*17.6.16*	
		for U.K. [to report to W.O.]			

56 Squadron which had disbanded at Bircham Newton as recently as 22nd January under Captain D W Grinnel-Milne, reformed at Aboukir when the 'number plate of 80 Squadron [Major C M Leman] was handed over to Squadron Leader P Babington MC AFC.

Considerable coverage to the life of Captain Duncan Grinnell-Milne during his time in captivity is provided by John Lewis-Stempel in his quite absorbing work regarding British prisoners of war. Published under the title *The War Behind the Wire,* Duncan is first mentioned on page 193 followed by seven more mentions, the last on page 289. The first entry on his Record of Service indicates he was reported missing on 16th May 1916, at which time he was a Flight Commander attached to 25 Squadron. With his observer, Corporal D McMaster, his FE.2b 6341 was shot down by the combined efforts of four Fokker scouts in the vicinity of Fournes [probably Fournes-en-Weppes [Nord] as the crew were operating to the west of Lille]. The remainder of the form reads:-

8.7.16   DAAG   *Officially reported prisoner of war*   W.O. List No X 19426 0103/8141

The next entry indicating he had escaped and was being sent to England has been lined through.

Re Eng. 25.2.19 W.O. List 1/3/19

30.7.19 1 ASD   *Posted to No 1 ASD*   3.3.19   B.213

12.8.19 214 Sq   *To Egypt & SoS of BEF France*   21.6.19

The form is then stamped in red *DECEASED 22/11/73*

Major C M Leman is shown as holding the DFC and MC, his service records being copied from the summer of 1919:-

Embarked Marseilles   11.6.19

HT "Calidonia" Disembarked Alexandria   13.6.19

17.6.19 *Joined Base Depot from B E F*   14.6.19 BDRO 144

4.7.19 *To 'X' E R D for temp. Duty*   3.7.19   " 158

10.7.19 *Posted to Training Brigade*   8.7.19   MERO 165

From 'X' E R D Base Depot on completion 9.7.19 BDRO 167
of temp. Duty

To retain Acting Rank [A/Major] pending   10.6.19 80 Sqdn RO128
Air Ministry sanction

Posted to 80 Squadron   10.6.19 IBRO 225

On appointment d 10.6.19 & to be Act/Major 10.6.19 HQME RO 223
whilst so employed

Cyril Mountain Leman was *Gazetted* with the MC on 22nd June 1918, supplement 30761, page 7416: *'For conspicuous gallantry and devotion to duty. Whilst on a low-flying bombing patrol he, by a direct hit from a bomb, put out of action a hostile battery and silenced another by machine-gun fire. The enemy fire was so intense that he was forced to land in front of the enemy's advanced line, whence he returned to make his report after leaving his machine a total wreck. He has on many occasions created great havoc as a result of bombing and attacking with machine-gun fire batteries in action, enemy transport and infantry, inflicting very heavy casualties on them. His skill and gallantry have been most marked.'* It is almost a certainty that the forced-landing referred to in the citation took place on the 21st of March 1918, the first day of the German Spring Offensive. At the time he was a Flight Commander attached to 3 Squadron at Warloy Baillon, and on the day in question he was flying Camel B9155; *The Camel File* records his aircraft was shot up in combat near Vaux and that he crashed-landed at around 1600 on heavily shelled ground.

His DFC was *Gazetted,* without a citation, in the Edinburgh edition on the 5th of June 1919, issue 13458, page 2048. Prior to the outbreak of the Second World War he returned to the service and was granted a commission, with effect from the 16th of May 1939, in the Administrative and Special Duties Branch, serving until relinquishing his commission under the provisions of the Navy, Army and Air Force Reserves Act, 1954. He was now ranked Squadron Leader and had been conferred with the MBE [LG 24 September 1941, supplement 35284, page 5568].

The third officer identified, Squadron Leader Philip Babington, was born on the 25th of February 1894, and following cadet service with the Inns of Court, Officer Training Corps, was commissioned to the 9th [Cyclist] Battalion of the Hampshire Regiment. However, before Christmas 1914, he had transferred to the RFC, after which his service was even by the standards of the *Great War* meteoric. From June 1916 to January 1918, he commanded 46 Squadron on the Western Front and during the tenure of his command oversaw the transition from Nieuport 12s of French design to Sopwith's amazingly versatile Camel. Then, on handing over to Major R H S Mealing, he was appointed to 141 Squadron on its formation on the 1st of January 1918, and for the next six months immersed himself in working up the squadron to proficiency as a Home Defence unit.

From the summer of '18 to that of 1919, he commanded No 50 [Home Defence] Wing with his headquarters at The Vineyards at Great Baddow near Chelmsford in Essex. This was followed with commands of 37 Squadron and on its renumbering 39 Squadron, bot formations being cadres.

On handing over command of 56 Squadron in October 1921 to Squadron Leader G C A Williams, Philip Babington, now a permanent officer since August 1919, served in a number of Staff appointments before taking command of an operational squadron for the last time - 19 Squadron at Duxford where he was 'in the chair' from July 1924 to July of the following year. During those twelve months '19 divested themselves of Snipes of *Great War* vintage and converted to Gloster Grebes.

Now of air rank, his final appointment, commencing in August 1942, was as Air Officer Commanding-in-Chief of Flying Training Command.

Air Marshal Sir Philip Babington KCB MC AFC twice mentioned in a despatch retired on the 1st of December 1945. His death was announced on the 25th of February 1965, thereby predeceasing his elder brother, Air Marshal Sir John Babington KCB CBE DSO who died on the 20th of March 1979.

Similarly, another re-numbering ceremony took place during the day when at Heliopolis, where 58 Squadron was still in the process of ferrying Vickers Vimys from England, their new identity became 70 Squadron.

Meanwhile, at home 24 Squadron disbanded at Uxbridge, and I Ireland 141 Squadron was stood down, its duties being taken over by 100 Squadron.

Saturday 21 February 1920
2 Squadron   F/O C R Pithey DFC*   +   Hollybrook Memorial, Southampton
Bristol F.2b H1567   South Africa
T/o Shotwick to transit to Baldonnel but failed to arrive. Croye Rothes Pithey, aged 27, came from Sheepersnek in the Natal. His Record of Service shows he was born on the 19th of August 1895, and enlistment to the RFC on the 8th of May 1917. His operational tour began on the 7th of March 1918, with 52 Squadron [RE.8] at Bonneuil, but a spell in hospital quickly brought this to an end and following his discharge he was posted to 12 Squadron on the 17th of April to 12 Squadron, also equipped with RE.8, at Soncamp, and it was '12' that he gained his awards.

The first was *Gazetted* on the 3rd of August 1918, supplement 30827, page 9202: *'While on reconnaissance, 8,000 yards behind enemy lines he saw a hostile balloon on the ground; descending to 1,700 feet, he and his observer engaged and destroyed it. He then completed his reconnaissance. On another occasion, while on photograph work, he was attacked by nine hostile scouts. By skilful manoeuvring he enabled his observer to shoot down three; the remaining six dispersed. He displays the greatest courage and determination in photographic and reconnaissance work.'*

I suspect his observer may have been 2nd Lieutenant Hervey Rhodes DFC, for he is shown as a joint recipient with Croye Pithey in the First Bar citation published on 3rd December 1918, supplement 31046, page 14317: *'Lieut. Pithey and his observer, have crashed five enemy aeroplanes and driven down five out of control; in addition, they have shot down two balloons in flames, displaying conspicuous courage and skill on all occasions. On 1st September they attacked an enemy two-seater on contact patrol; this machine at first retired east but returned, accompanied by six scouts, to the attack; after a short engagement they were driven off, and Lieut. Pithery, although his machine was badly shot about, continued his patrol and brought back a most valuable and accurate report.'*

His commission to the General List was published in the issue of 5th October 1917, supplement 30327, page 10394, showing his seniority as being from 13th September 1917. He was appointed to a permanent commission on the 1st of August 1919 [LG 1 August 1919, issue 31486, page 9870].

On the Aerodrome website, which I gratefully acknowledge, this shows a total of ten aerial victories, which included two kite balloons, between the 3rd of May and the 3rd of September 1918. It is noted that Hervey Rhodes was of the Yorkshire Regiment, their partnership eventually being broken when Croye was wounded on the 27th of September, a day of fierce ground fighting in *The Battle of the Canal du Nord* [see my Second Volume and pages 256 to 262 for details of the losses incurred this day].

2 Squadron   F/O H de W Waller   +   Hollybrook Memorial, Southampton
Bristol F.2b H1621
T/o Shotwick similarly charged and presumed to have suffered the same fate. Hardress de Warrenne Waller's entry on the CWGC website has no information regarding his next of kin. Hardress Waller was granted a short service commission on the 24th of October 1919 [LG 24 October 1919, issue 31616, page 13034]. Although no next of kin has been appended, I have little doubt his father [or possibly his uncle] was Major James Hardress de Warranne Waller DSO who in 1920 was Senior Technical Assistant, Reinforced Concrete Construction, Controller-General of Merchant Ship-building Department, Ministry of Shipping.

100 Squadron   F/O H L Holland   +   Hollybrook Memorial, Southampton
Bristol F.2b H1612
T/o Shotwick also instructed for the transit to Baldonnel and lost over the sea. Administrative details regarding Horace Lloyd Holland had yet to record his posting to 100 Squadron, and his entry on the CWGC website records him as being attached to B Flight, 141 Squadron, '141' having disbanded on the 1st of the month. Horace Lloyd Holland received his short service commission on the same day as that for Hardress Waller, his entry appearing on page 133.

Sunday 29 February 1920
After working up at Stirling and Cramlington, 63 Squadron sailed for the Middle East in June 1917, and by mid-August was established in Mesopotamia, first at Basra but when disbanding on this day had been at Baghdad for the past year. During this time it had operated a variety of aircraft types ranging from scouts to bombers. At the time of ceasing its duties it was equipped with RE.8, the last of their fighter types having been pensioned off in December 1919.

MARCH
1920

During the month Royal Air Force support for the White Russians in their fight against the Bolsheviks in South Russia ceased. It was not the most satisfactory of campaigns though this is no reflection on the dedication and resolve of the airmen who were operating in an environment hostile in weather and whose political masters were facing up to the fact that defeating Bolshevism by force was no longer feasible - a pill bitter to swallow for Churchill whose reputation was once again the subject of press condemnation.

Many of the arrows of condemnation drew analogies between his handling of operations in South Russia to his close involvement in the Gallipoli campaign of 1915 [in which my father, Private William Thomas Chorley, fought with West

Somerset Yeomanry], and its humiliating outcome which left thousands dead on the slopes of this inhospitable peninsular.

There are a myriad of reasons behind the decision taken to rundown the Russian operation, not least, perhaps, the undeniable fact that much of the aid sent at considerable cost to the nation's tax payers had been siphoned off into the hands of profiteers, while tons of supplies were either abandoned to the Bolsheviks or were not used effectively.

Thus, a staged withdrawal to the port of Novorossiysk on the Black Sea was set in train. Throughout these final days operations continued in order not to be overrun by a triumphant Bolshevik army eager to press their advantage home and inflict as many casualties as possible.

Friday 19 March 1920
An interesting item filed under *Imperial and Foreign News Items* in *The Times,* reported the departure from Antwerp of the *Lapland* carrying seven hundred and fifty emigrants from *"the devastated regions of Belgium"* indicative of the slow rebuilding in areas shattered by the recent war..

99 Squadron	F/O A L Courtenay	Injured
DH.9A *H4387*	Dunn	
	Sgt W J Palmer DFM	Injured

T/o Mianwali and reported to have descended onto a dry river bed whereupon one of the bombs exploded. Adrian Lancelot Courtenay-Dunn was critically injured and died two days later.

To the best of my knowledge this was the final accident reported by the squadron ahead of giving up its 'number plate' to 27 Squadron on the 1st of April 1920.

The citation for William James Palmer's award reads: *'A first-class observer, who has taken part in fifteen bomb raids, displaying at all times great courage and determination. On a recent raid, his formation was repeatedly attacked by hostile aircraft; he nevertheless under very difficult circumstances succeeded in taking eighteen good photographs, and also collected much valuable information. In the course of the several engagements, he shot down an enemy machine in flames.'* [LG 2 November 1918, supplement 30989, page 12977]. This engagement took place on the 4th of September, 1918, while flying with his regular pilot, Second Lieutenant F T Stott, their DH being D1049 of 107 Squadron, which with another crew came to grief on 28th October 1918 [see my second volume, page 359].

Saturday 20 March 1920
| 20 Squadron | F/O W Deane MC | + | Delhi Memorial [India Gate] |
| Bristol F2b F4447 | O/O R B Gordon DFC | + | Delhi Memorial [India Gate] |

T/o Bannu for bombing operations over the Sherani district; reported as *'crashed'*. Robert Bissett Gordon was *Gazetted* as an Observer Officer on 24th August 1918 [LG 27 August 1918, issue 30868, page 100009]. As yet I have not traced details for his award, or that for William Deane.

William Deane's name appears in Appendix D for permanent officers appointed in August 1919.

Sunday 28 March 1920
During the day 'A' Squadron operated for the last time, carrying out attacks on rail targets - including an armoured train - and harassing cavalry.

Monday 29 March 1920
One sortie was flown this day. Appropriately this was made by Squadron Leader Raymond Collishaw who had been in South Russia since July 1919, where he took command of 47 Squadron and, subsequently, 'A' Squadron. It was a ranging sweep over territory known to be in 'enemy' hands and, no doubt, to access the advance of their forces.

Born in British Columbia on the 22nd of November 1893, Raymond Collishaw underwent pilot training in February 1916, at RNAS Redcar and subsequently flew as a scout pilot on the Western Front where he excelled in aerial combat, gaining a DSO and First Bar, a DSC and following the merger of the air arms in 1918, the DFC.

The citation for the DSC appeared in the *Gazette* of 20th July 1917, supplement 30194, page 7426: *'In recognition of his services on various occasions, especially the following: On June 1st, 1917, he shot down an Albatross Scout in flames. On 3rd June, 1917, he shot down an Albatross Scout in flames. On 5th June, 1917, he shot down a two-seater Albatross in flames. On the 6th June, 1917, he shot down two Albatross Scouts in flames and killed the pilot in a third. He has displayed great gallantry and skill in all his combats.'*

A richly deserved DSO was *Gazetted* on 11th August 1917, supplement 30227, page 8206: *'For conspicuous bravery and skill in successfully leading attacks against hostile aircraft. Since the 10th of June, 1917, Flt. Lieut. Collishaw has himself brought down four machines completely out of control and driven down two others with their planes shot away. Whilst on an offensive patrol on the morning of the 15th of June, 1917, he forced down a hostile scout in a nose dive. Later, on the same day, he drove down one hostile two-seater machine completely out of control, one hostile scout in a spin, and a third machine with two of its planes shot away. On the 24th June, 1917, he engaged four enemy scouts, driving one down in a spin and another with two of its planes shot away; the latter machine was seen to crash.'*

A year on he was honoured with a the DFC, this being *Gazetted* on 3rd August 1918, supplement 30827, page 9199: *'This officer is an exceptionally capable and efficient squadron commander, under whose leadership the squadron has maintained a high place in the Army Wing. He has carried out numerous solo patrols and led many offensive patrols, on all occasions engaging the enemy with great bravery and fearlessness. Up to date he has accounted for forty-seven enemy machines, twenty-two in the last twelve months.'*

The citation for the First Bar to his DSO I have copied from the Air of Authority website, which I dutifully acknowledge: *'A brilliant squadron leader of exceptional daring, who has destroyed fifty-one enemy machines. Early one morning he, with another pilot, attacked an enemy aerodrome. Seeing three machines brought out of a burning hangar he dived five times, firing bursts at these from a very low altitude, and dropped bombs on the living quarters. He then saw an enemy aeroplane descending over the aerodrome; he attacked it and drove it down in flames. Later, when returning from a reconnaissance, he was attacked by three Albatross Scouts, who pursued him to our lines, when he turned attacked on, which fell out of control and crashed.'*

At the time of the operations in South Russia he had been appointed to a permanent commission. During the 1920s he commanded 41 Squadron from October 1923 to May 1924, and July 1925 through to November 1927 he led 23 Squadron. The early part of Second World War service was spent in Egypt where he held posts as Air Officer Commanding Egypt Group, 202 Group and 204 Group respectively, before returning to the Uk to take up his final appointments as Air Staff at Fighter Command headquarters and thence Air Officer Commanding No 14 [Fighter] Group.

Air Vice-Marshal Raymond Collishaw CB DSO* OBE [both military and civil] DSC DFC and four times mentioned in a despatch retired on the 29th of October 1943, and immediately took up the post as Regional Air Liaison Officer, Civil Defence.

Returning to Canada his death in West Vancouver was signalled on the 28th of September 1976.

Tuesday 30 March 1920
On reaching Novorossysk, 'A' Squadron set about the task of destroying as much of their equipment as possible in order to deny its future use by the Bolsheviks. Tanks were used to crush the remaining Sopwtih Camels while other supplied were handed to the White Russians which had accompanied the retreat.

Their duties over, the remaining personnel went to Theodosia and embarked on a waiting British transport vessel and sailed for Constantinople and home.

APRIL
1920

The second anniversary of the the formation of the Royal Air Force. I have remarked on several occasions operations carried out in various regions of Russia in support of forces opposed to the Bolsheviks, 47 Squadron coming in for attention, even following its official re-titling as A Squadron.

In parallel to these operations was another which Chaz Bowyer in *RAF Operations 1918 - 1938* title's *The Mad Mullah.*

At Mianwali 99 Squadron [DH.9A] handed over its 'number plate' to 27 Squadron.

Thursday 1 April 1920

216 Squadron	F/O J B Jaques MC AFC	+	Khartoum War Cemetery
HP O/400 F302	P/O D W Sibley	+	Khartoum War Cemetery
	Sgt E W Wadey DFM	+	Khartoum War Cemetery
	AC2 R C Meldrum	+	Khartoum War Cemetery

T/o Khartum with the intention of returning to Cairo but crashed at Dagash near Abu Hamad, Sudan. John Barclay Jaques was one of hundreds *Gazetted* as a Second Lieutenant on the 22nd of September 1914 [LG 22 September 1914, issue 28910, page 7486]; many, I suspect, are now commemorated in cemeteries and memorials along the length of the Western Front where the British Expeditionary Force fought from August 1914 to November 1918. His MC was promulgated, with a citation, on 3 June 1916 [LG 3 June 1916, supplement 29608, page 5574]. He was granted a short service commission in the rank of Flying Officer on 5th December 1919 [LG 5 December 1919, issue 31674, page 15062], and his AFC was *Gazetted* posthumously on 12th July 1920 [LG 12 July 1920, supplement 31974, page 7422].

Desmond Wilkie Sibley is named in the August 1919 table of permanent officers. He was London born, as was Sergeant Wadey and Aircraftman Meldrum. The headstones of John Jaques and Edmund Wadey are inscribed: *He Did His Duty* and *In Loving Memory* respectively. Sergeant Wadey's award was published on 2nd November 1918, in supplement 30989 of the *Gazette*, page 12977: *'This non-commissioned officer has taken part in forty-three night bombing raids as Gunlayer, and has rendered most consistent and excellent service, deserving of high praise. He sets a fine example to other NCO Observers.'*

Reginald Meldrum appears to have lost his father as only his mother is recorded by CWGC and in her epitaph to her son is most poignant: *"Rest In Peace My Beloved Son May We Meet In Eternity, Mother."*

Saturday 3 April 1920
An amusing item appeared in *The Times* under the heading *GERMAN AIRMAN'S APPLICATION* the report reading; *"A former German flying officer recently applied to Handley Page, Limited, for a position as a pilot. He enclosed recommendations from German squadron commanders under whom he had served on the Western Front, and stated that he was familiar with English territory, having flown over the eastern counties on many occasions! No vacancy was found for him."*

Friday 16 April 1920

| 5 Squadron | F/O R Pughe | + | Delhi Memorial [India Gate] |
| Bristol F.2b F4627 | | | |

T/o Loralai landing ground and lost control while attempting to turn without applying sufficient bank. Robert Pughe was buried in Loralai Cemetery 14.

Thursday 29 April 1920

230 Squadron	S/Ldr E R Moon DSO*	+	Southampton Old Cemetery
Felixstowe F.5	*Chevalier d'Honneur*		
N4044	F/O A J Fyfield	+	Felixstowe [SS Peter and Paul] Churchyard
	Sub-Lt G J d'A Fonseca	+	
	Portugal		
	F/L C O Modin	Injured	
	F/O L H Pakenham-Walsh	Injured	
	AC2 G T Bass	+	Hollybrook Memorial Southampton

T/o Felixstowe for, in the words of the Air Ministry *"was engaged in an instructional cruise."* The Times in its issue the next day, having reported the Air Ministry's statement and the names of the crew, continues; *"A Felixstowe correspondent telegraphs that the crew of the Venture, a divers' boat working on a wreck, saved Observer-Officer Walsh, and Lieutenant Modin was rescued by Mr Little, a fisherman, and his son. Squadron Leader Moon, who was a well-known Felixstowe officer, had a very narrow escape when pilot of the Felixstowe Fury when she started on a voyage to the Cape, which ended disastrously a few minutes after she left Felixstowe. The bodies of Squadron Leader Moon and Flying Officer Fyfield were recovered in the afternoon.*

'The weather was sunny with a light breeze and a calm sea at the time of the accident, and several witnesses state that the machine was about 1,700ft above the sea when it went into a spin."

Edward Rowland Moon's service began prior to the outbreak of the *Great War* and was *Gazetted* with the DSO on 15th September 1917 [at the time he was being held prisoner in East Africa]; *'Since April 1916, has carried out constant flights over the enemy's coast, including reconnaissance, bomb-dropping and spotting for gun fire in all weathers. Has shown great coolness and resource on all occasions.'* [Supplement 30133, page 5959, 15 June 1917]. A First Bar was *Gazetted* on the 16th of March 1918, issue 30581, page 3395: *'In recognition of the resource and gallantry displayed by him in the following circumstances:-*

'On the 6th January 1917, whilst on a reconnaissance flight over the Rufji Delta with Cdr. The Hon. Richard O B Bridgeman DSO RN as observer, he was obliged by engine trouble to descend in one of the creeks, where it became necessary to destroy the seaplane to avoid the possibility of its being captured.

'For three whole days the two officers wandered about the delta in their efforts to avoid capture and to rejoin their ship. During this time they had little or nothing to eat, and were continually obliged to swim across the creeks, the bush on the banks being impenetrable. On the morning of the 7th January they constructed a raft of three spars and some latticed window-frames. After paddling and drifting on this for the whole of the 7th and 8th January, they were finally carried out to sea on the morning of the 9th, when Cdr. Bridgeman, who was not a strong swimmer, died of exhaustion and exposure. In the late after Flt. Cdr. Moon managed to reach the shore, and was taken prisoner by the Germans. He was released from captivity on the 21st November 1917. He displayed the greatest gallantry in attempting to safe the life of his companion.'

Squadron Leader Moon was appointed to a permanent commission on the 19th of August 1919 [see Appendix D, 1919] and had survived the crash of the Felixstowe Fury on 11th August 1919, in which Lieutenant Samuel Forbes Smith McLeod was killed killed [see Appendix D, 1919]. The body of Commander, The Hon. Richard Orlando Beaconsfield Bridgeman, serving aboard HMS *Hyacinth,* was recovered and he is now buried in Dar Es Salaam War Cemetery in Tanzania.

Louis Henry Pakenham-Walsh was short service commissioned on 24th October 1919 [see Appendix E, 1919].

**MAY
1920**

Monday 17 May 1920

| 12 Squadron | F/L C B Ridley DSC | + | Cologne Southern Cemetery |
| Bristol F.2b D8059 | | | |

T/o Bickendorf and over the Lindenthal district of Köln came into collision with the Bristol summarised below. Cyril Burfield Ridley is recorded in Appendix E 1919, for short service commissioned officers *Gazetted* on 24th October 1919.

| 12 Squadron | F/O J D de Pencier | + | Cologne Southern Cemetery |
| Bristol F.2b H1566 Canada | | | |

T/o Bickendorf and lost in the circumstances described above. John Dartnell de Pencier's father, the Most Reverend Adam Urias de Pencier DD OBE was of the See House in Nanton Avenue, Vancouver. Commissioned to the General list of the RFC on 21st June 1917 [LG 6 July 1917, supplement 30170, page 6787], John de Pencier was short service commissioned on 12th September 1919, issue 31548, page 11469.

Thursday 27 May 1920

70 Squadron	F/O C O Bird DFC	+	Cairo New British Protestant Cemetery
Bristol F.2b D7927	A/Cmdr R M Groves	+	Cairo New British Protestant Cemetery
	CB DSO AFC *Legion d'Honneur*		

T/o Almaza but with seconds of becoming airborne the engine cut and the Bristol spun to the ground. Clarence Oscar Bird was short service commissioned on 5th December 1919 [see Appendix E 1919]. In addition to his DFC, he was *Gazetted* with the AFC [posthumously] on 12th July 1920 [LG 12 July 1920, supplement 31974, page 7422]. As yet I have not traced the citation for his DFC.

Air Commodore Robert Marsland Groves was Acting Air Officer Commanding RAF Middle East Area at the time of his death. Born on the 3rd of January 1880, his service, with the Royal Navy, can be traced back to 1908, when he was appointed Staff Officer for wireless telegraphy duties with the 2nd Cruiser Squadron and was attached to HMS *King Edward VII.* He was appointed to a permanent commission on 1st August 1919, his details appearing in Appendix D for that year. Throughout his brief time as a senior permanent officer Robert Groves served in the Middle East.

JUNE
1920

Monday 14 June 1920

14 Squadron	F/O N Fitzgerald-Eager	+	Suez War Memorial Cemetery
Bristol F.2b E2293	New Zealand		
	AC1 P W J Thacker	+	Suez War Memorial Cemetery

T/o Ramleh intending to transit to Ismailia but came down in the Sinai desert. Neale Fitzgerald-Eager and Percy William James Thacker met the cruelest of deaths, as explained the historian and author, Errol Martyn: *"flew off course and forced-landed in the Sinai desert, where the pilot's body was later located 30 miles west of Nekhl, some 70 miles west of Suez. A court of inquiry found that he had died of exposure, accepting that this had occurred a week after the landing, on the 21st. The body of his passenger, AC1 P W J Thacker, was found by the Camel Corps on the mountains near Nekhl after the inquiry, his date of death being accepted as that of the day of the flight. Apparently no trace of the aircraft had been found up to the time of discovery of the two bodies."* Errol adds a footnote explaining that Flying Officer Fitzgerald-Eager was born in Australia but emigrated to New Zealand prior to 1912, and enlisted with the New Zealand Expeditionary Force and sailed with the Main Body of the force, subsequently transferring to the RFC and from the 1st of April 1918, to the Royal Air Force. He was thirty-two years of age. Percy Thacker was twelve years his junior.

Monday 28 June 1920

60 Squadron	F/O J R Swanston DFC	+	Karachi 1914-1918 War Memorial
DH.10 E9081	AC2 F C Oliver	+	Karachi 1914-1918 War Memorial

T/o Risalpur for an air test during which the DH spun out of control, crashed and caught fire. John Romilly Swanston's entry in the records has no information regarding his next of kin. He was a permanent officer, so named in Appendix D of August 1919. The citation for his award was published in the Edinburgh edition of the *Gazette* [issue 13346, page 4064, on 4 November 1918]: *'A very capable flight commander. On a day last month he led a formation of twenty machines on a low bombing raid on an enemy aerodrome, and by skilful management succeeded in effecting a complete surprise, which resulted in great damage being done. Capt. Swanston has carried out twenty-two valuable reconnaissance flights over the line, has personally obtained a direct hit on an enemy aerodrome, set fire to a railway truck containing enemy anti-aircraft guns, destroyed two enemy aeroplanes, and helped to destroy another. During his three periods of employment on active service he has been in the air 310 hours.'*

His surviving Army Form B.103 shows he was posted to 213 Squadron [Camel] at Bergues on the 25th of July 1918, with the added annotation '5th Group'. Meanwhile, the *Edinburgh Gazette* published on 3rd May 1921, issue 13703, page 719, reports the the award of a First Bar to his DFC and this is reflected in the Roll of Honour.

Frank Cecil Oliver, aged 19, was of Dartford in Kent.

JULY
1920

Monday 5 July 1920

12 Squadron	F/O A J Macqueen	+	Cologne Southern Cemetery
Bristol F.2b H1594			

T/o Bickendorf for local flying and crashed, heavily, at Heumar. An unnamed airman passenger survived, though, I suspect, seriously injured. Alexander John Macqueen's entry in the register is devoid of detail regarding his parents. He had been short service commissioned as recently as 4th May 1920 [LG 4 May 1920, issue 31886, page 5104].

His Record Service is interesting; born on the 11th of April 1889, the entries read:-

17.08.18	*53 Sq*	*Posted to 53 Sqd*	*10.08.18*	*B.213*
21.09.18	*18 CCS*	*Admitted [Tonsilitis]*	*10.09.18*	*A.36*
14.09.18	*18 CCS*	*Admitted [Tonsilitis]*	*11.09.18*	*A.36*
21.09.18	*18 CCS*	*Dis to duty*	*16.09.18*	*A.36*
09.11.18	*53 Sq*	*Leave 5.11.18 - 19.11.18*		*B.213*
08.03.19	*59 Sq*	*Posted to 59 Sq*	*02.03.19*	*B.213*
18.04.19	*"*	*Leave 17.4 - 1.5.19*		*"*
08.08.19	*7 Sq*	*Posted to 7 Sq*	*24.07.19*	*"*

15.08.19	"	Leave 14.8.19 to 24.8.19		"
20.10.19	12 Sqdn	Posted to No 12 Sqdn	09.09.19	NR
06.03.20	"	To Lille of T/Duty	02.03.20	B.213

Apart from the first entry, the rest appear to have been entered by the same hand.

Monday 12 July 1920

| 24 Squadron | F/O V O Reynolds | + | Wallington [Bandon Hill] Cemetery |
| DH.9A F1646 | AC2 P Braithwaite | + | Coventry [St. Paul's] Cemetery |

T/o Kenley and while in the process of banking and low speed near the airfield lost control and spun to the ground. On impact the DH went up in flames. Victor Oliver Reynolds, formerly of the Hampshire Regiment, was one of a number of army officers re-seconded for duty with the Royal Air Force with effect from the 1st of August 1919, their new terms of engagement being for two years [LG 27 April 1920, issue 31879, page 4851].

His headstone carries the inscription: *"One Of The Old Contemptibles"* and it would be remiss of me not to mention, briefly, the probability of Victor's service that earned him the right to be referred to as an Old Contemptible. It is highly likely that in August 1914, he was a private soldier serving with the 1st Battalion of the Royal Hampshire Regiment and that he saw action within twenty-four hours of de-training on the 25h near Le Cateau. At the time the British Expeditionary Force, commanded by Field Marshal Sir John French, were retiring in a south-easterly direction having given the German army a hot reception in front of Mons. Coming under the aegis of General Horace Smith-Dorrien's II Corps, the Hampshires fought a stiff action with 11th Brigade around the village of Ligny. Unlike Mons where the accuracy of the British rifle fire cut swathes in the ranks of the German infantry, Le Cateau is remembered mainly as an artillery battle which for many soldiers was their baptism of coming under sustained shell fire.

That Victor survived this and the brutal years that followed, both as a solider and airmen, it seems ironic that a basic flying error brought his life to an all too early end.

AUGUST
1920

Monday 2 August 1920

| 6 Squadron | F/O R D C Palmer DFC | + | Baghdad [North Gate] War Cemetery |
| Bistol F.2b H1462 | F/O H Hutchinson | + | Baghdad [North Gate] War Cemetery |

T/o Baghdad tasked for a reconnaissance sortie. Flying at 3,000 feet [this suggests other aircraft were in the vicinity] spun out of control and crashed before recovery could be effected. Robert Daniel Cecil Palmer, formerly a cadet, was commissioned on 17th November 1917 [LG 23 November 1917, supplement 30395, page 12126] and it would seem his service had been unbroken since. His DFC was *Gazetted* on 12th July 1920 [no citation] in supplement 31974, page 7422 of the paper issued on that date. TNA Kew has a non-digitised record for Flying Officer Palmer under WO 339/ 120627. Harold Hutchinson's simple epitaph reads: *"Loved And Remembered."*

Saturday 28 August 1920

| 2 Squadron | F/O N H Dimmock AusFC | InJured | |
| Bristol F.2b F4528 | Major H F Chads MC | + | Castlebar Church of Ireland Cemetery |

T/o Castlebar where the Bristol had been detached but collided, at speed, with a trestle and crashed out of control. Harry Francis Chads was commissioned as a Second Lieutenant from The Royal Military College to the The Border Regiment on 9th March 1910 [LG 8 March 1910, issue 28346, page 1684].

SEPTEMBER
1920

Friday 3 September 1920

| 47 Squadron | *Not known* | | |
| DH.9 'D9824' | O/O B C S Byrne | + | Cairo War Memorial Cemetery |

T/o Almaza with the intention of returning to Helwan only to spin in off a climbing turn. Observer Officer Brennan Claude Sydney is recorded on the CWGC website as having been educated at Newport Grammar School, Essex. He was short service commissioned on 5th December 1919, issue 31674, page 15062. His headstone is inscribed with the Latin inscription: *"Requiescat In Pace."*

Saturday 18 September 1920

30 Squadron	F/L F Nuttall MC DFC AFC	+	Tehran War Cemetery
RE.8 D4698	Twice mention in a despatch New Zealand		
	LAC L A Dellow	+	Tehran War Cemetery

T/o Kazvin for operations over Enzeli but turned back owing to adverse weather and on nearing base, and making ready to land, it spun out of control and crashed. Both airmen were first buried at the squadron's detached base at Kazvin.

A pilot of outstanding ability, the following citations have been traced, commencing with that for his MC [LG 24th August 1918, supplement 30862, page 9916]: *'For conspicuous gallantry and devotion to duty. Seeing another machine driven down by hostile fire in the enemy's lines, he glided to the ground under heavy fire, and dispersed the enemy with his machine gun. He took the stranded pilot on board and got safely away. By his prompt and courageous action he saved his comrade from being taken prisoner.'*

Tuesday, 15th July 1919, supplement 31457, page 8985, for his DFC: *'A gallant flight leader, who has rendered valuable services in carrying out the most arduous duties in action, and has commanded his flight with great skill under exceptionally difficult conditions. On the 27th April, 1918, near Kirkuk, whilst engaged in attacking enemy troops from a low altitude, he was shot down, wounded.'*

The award of the AFC was *Gazetted* on 10th October 1919, supplement 31592, page 12527, in recognition of distinguished service during the *Great War.* His epitaph reads: *'God Be With You Till We Meet Again'.* Leonard Alfred Dellow's service number 60764 indicates he enlisted with the RFC between 1916 and March 1917, either as a direct entry from civilian life, or by transferring from another arm of the services. His headstone carries the words: *"Even Me, Even Me Let Thy Mercy Fall On Me"* which is taken from the hymn *"Lord, I hear of showers of blessing."*

* This episode is recorded on page 50 of John Hamblin's excellent telling of 30 Squadron's history. The pilot who was brought down was Lieutenant A P Adams, the fuel tank of his BE.2c having been shot through. Frank Nuttall was flying one of the squadron's Martinsyde machines. He is mentioned on numerous pages, thereby reflecting his influence on the squadron. Interestingly, in recording his death, John Hamblin refers to him as Captain Nuttall.

Wednesday 22 September 1920
84 Squadron   F/O H C E Bockett-Pugh DFC*   +   Basra Memorial
DH.9A F2838   F/O I D R McDonald MC DFC   +   Basra Memorial
T/o Shaibah for operations connected with the relief of Samawah and loaded with supplies to be released over a defence ship on the Euphrates Bar. Fell to rebel gunfire, landing in a river at Dangatore near Samawah in Mesopotamia. Taken alive from their aircraft, they were subsequently executed by their captors.*

Henry Charles Edward Bockett-Pugh was a permanent officer, commissioned as such on 2nd December 1919, but with his seniority effective from 1st August of that year [LG 2 December 1919, issue 31669, page 14924]. The First Bar to his DFC was *Gazetted* on 12th July 1920, supplement 31974, page 7422. As shown on the Herts at War website, he was born in Dover on the last day of December 1898.

Ian Donald Roy McDonald is named in Appendix D of the permanent commissions list of 1st August 1919. His MC, with citation, was *Gazetted* on 16 September 1918, supplement 30901, page 10986: *'For conspicuous gallantry and devotion to duty. With seven scouts he attacked eighteen enemy machines, of which three were destroyed and one driven down completely out of control. When driven down to within 200 feet of the ground by two enemy machines owing to a choked engine, he turned on them and drove one down. He has in all destroyed eleven enemy aircraft and carried out valuable work in attacking enemy troops on the ground.'* Oddly, the citation for his DFC predates that for his MC, appearing in the Edinburgh edition on 7th August 1918, issue 13300, page 2815: *'A dashing fighting pilot. In the past two months he had destroyed five enemy machines and brought down two others out of control. At all times he shows a fine offensive spirit and complete disregard of danger.'*

* The Imperial War Museum website, which I am pleased to acknowledge, in their section regarding lives remembered, has an extract from Charles Brockett-Pugh, who wrote: *"My uncle, Henry Charles Edward Brockett-Pugh, was shot down and killed by Iraqis on 22nd September 1920, He was trying to drop supplies to HMS Greenfly, which was stuck aground in the Tigris Delta. Apparently, the bomb doors failed to open, leaving the plane too heavy to climb away from some Arabs, who shot the plane down and then killed the navigator Flying Officer Ian MacDonald. Uncle Charles tried to buy his freedom, which was a common policy at the time, but the headman came up and shot him dead."*

NOVEMBER
1920

Monday 1 November 1920
84 Squadron   DH.9A E779   While being attended to at Nasiriyah in Mesopotamia by armourers Air-craftman Alexander Langton Marshall and Wallace Wallwork a 112lb bomb exploded killing both airmen and destroying the DH. Their ages were nineteen and twenty respectively.

Thursday 4 November 1920
24 Squadron   F/O H O Prout AFC   +   Croydon [Mitcham Road] Cemetery
Bristol F.2b F4852   F/O H E Fenwick   +   St. Albans [Hatfield Road] Cemetery
T/o Kenley and on return the crew were faced with trying to land on an airfield masked by fog and while making their approach flew into a tree. Harold Oliver Prout held a permanent commission as per Appendix D of August 1st, 1919.

Horace Edgar Fenwick's short service commission is recorded in Appendix E under those officers so granted on 12th September 1919. His epitaph is: *"Jesu Mercy, Mary Pray, R.I.P."*

Monday 29 November 1920
216 Squadron   F/O C O Rigden   +   Cairo War Memorial Cemetery
DH.10 E9062   F/O S T B Cripps   Injured   Retired list 5 February 1929
                AC1 A L Goodhill   +
T/o Heliopolis and in the course of making a turn at low altitude lost control and came down heavily. Cecil Osborne Rigden, short service commissioned and listed in Appendix E for 1919, was initially commissioned on 7th March 1918 [LG 16 March 1918, supplement 30580, page 3377]. A Record of Service form has been raised, but it has no useful detail appended apart from his name, rank and initials.

His parents requested, and was granted the following inscription: *"I Hope To See My Pilot Face To Face When I Have Crossed The Bar."*

Sydney Trevor Brander Cripps made a good recovery from his injuries and served until 5th February 1929, when at his own request he was placed on the retired list, at which time he was ranked Flight Lieutenant and had been awarded the DFC. He held a permanent commission, his name appearing in Appendix D for officers *gazetted* on 28th October 1919, issue 31620, page 13139.

DECEMBER
1920

Wednesday 8 December 1920

| 30 Squadron | F/O W Sidebottom DFC | + | Tehran Memorial |
| DH.9A E780 | AC2 A Liston | Safe | |

T/o for operations against Bolshevik forces near Enzeli and forced-landed some distance from Rostamabad in NW Persia. William Sidebottom attempted to escape but was shot while doing so. Aircraftman Liston appears to have been unharmed. Although mentioned by John Hamlin in his history of the squadron, details of William's attempt to escape receives no mention, neither is the name of Aircraftman Liston recorded.

Thursday 9 December 1920

| 6 Squadron | F/O R N Essell DFC | + | Baghdad [North Gate] War Cemetery |
| Bristol F.2b D7867 | Mr C C Garbett CIE | Injured | |

T/o and crashed in a desert landing at Tauq in Mesopotamia. Colin Campbell Garbett was Secretary to the High Commissioner of Mesopotamia. Robert Narcissus Essell was a permanent officer whose name is recorded in Appendix D naming officers to appointed on the 1st of August 1919. The citation for his honour was promulgated in both the London and Edinburgh editions of the *Gazette* for 28th October 1921 [London], issue 32501, page 8495: *'For great gallantry and devotion to duty. This officer has flown over 125 hours and carried out 50 bomb raids. He is a very keen and daring pilot, who on two occasions has been shot down by hostile action.'*

From a military family, his headstone bears the words: *"Beloved Son Of Col. F K Essell CMG & Mrs Essell Bevere, Worcester."*

Colin Campbell Garbett is reported on at least six occasions in *The London Gazette* spanning the years 1905 to 1941.

Appendix 3A - Squadron Losses Table and Losses by Aircraft Type

With the significant reduction in aircraft accidents, losses by squadron and aircraft type for the year 1920 have been combined.

Column 1 - Squadron
Column 2 - Aircraft type
Column 3 - Total number destroyed
Column 4 - Fatalities
Column 5 - Remarks

2 Squadron	Bristol F.2b	3	3	1 airman injured
5 Squadron	Bristol F.2b	1	1	
6 Squadron	Bristol F.2b	2	3	1 civilian injured
12 Squadron	Bristol F.2b	3	3	
14 Squadron	Bristol F.2b	1	2	
20 Squadron	Bristol F.2b	1	2	
24 Squadron	Bristol F.2b	1	2	
	DH.9A	1	2	
30 Squadron	DH.9A	1	1	
	RE.8	1	2	1 airman safe
47 Squadron	DH.9	1	1	
60 Squadron	DH.10	1	2	
70 Squadron	Bristol F.2b	1	2	
84 Squadron	DH.9A	2	4	1 destroyed in a ground accident resulting in two deaths
99 Squadron	DH.9A	1		2 airmen injured
100 Squadron	Bristol F.2b	1	1	
216 Squadron	DH.10	1	2	1 airman injured
	HP O/400	1	4	
230 Squadron	Felixstowe F.5	1	4	2 airmen injured
Totals		25	41	
	Bristol F.2b	14	19	
	DH.9	1	1	
	DH.9A	5	7	
	DH.10	2	4	
	HP O/400	1	4	
	RE.8	1	2	
	Felixstowe F.5	1	4	
Totals		25	41	

Appendix 3B - Squadron Locations as at 31st December 1920

This appendix identifies squadrons that were extant as at 31st December 1920, disbandment information having been reported in the monthly reports for 1920. As with previous volumes, the information here presented has been taken from Air-Britain's *The Squadron of the Royal Air Force & Commonwealth 1918-1988* compiled by James J Halley and published in 1988. The table illustrates the role for the still fledgling service; policing the Empire with the emphasis in maintaining a strong presence in 'The Jewel of the Crown', India as well as in Iraq and Egypt. It is interesting to note that the fighter defence of the United Kingdom rested on the shoulders of 25 Squadron.

Squadron	Location	Date	Notes
1 Squadron	Risalpur	21January 1920	Reformed in India with Sopwith 7F.1 Snipe. One Nieuport
	Bangalore	11 May 1920	Nighthawk received for evaluation.
2 Squadron	Oranmore	1 February 1920	Reformed in Ireland and equipped with Bristol F.2b.
3 Squadron	Bangalore	1 April 1920	Reformed in India with Sopwith 7F.1 Snipe.
4 Squadron	Farnborough	30 April 1920	Brought up to establishment with Bristol F.2b from its
	Aldergrove & Baldonnel		cadre status. Detachments to Ireland in November 1920.
5 Squadron	Quetta	1 April 1920	Reformed in India with Bristol F.2b.
6 Squadron	Baghdad West	in situ	Exchanged RE.8 for Bristol F.2b in July 1920.
8 Squadron	Helwan	18 October 1920	Reformed in Iraq with DH.9A.
12 Squadron	Heumar	in situ	Supporting the Allied occupation of the Rhineland and
	Bickendorf	17 November 1920	equipped with Bristol F.2b.
14 Squadron	Ramleh & Amman	1 February 1920	Reformed by 111 Squadron renumbering as 14 Squadron with Bristol F.2b for patrol duties in Palestine and Trans Jordan.
20 Squadron	Bannu	in situ	North West Frontier duties; equipped with Bristol F.2b
	Parachinar	18 July 1920	
	Tank	5 November 1920	
24 Squadron	Kenley	1 April 1920	Reformed for communication duties; various types.
25 Squadron	Hawkinge	1 February 1920	Reformed and equipped with 7F.1 Snipe.
27 Squadron	Mianwali	1 April 1920	Reformed by 99 Squadron renumbering as 27 Squadron equipped with DH.9A for North West Frontier duties.
28 Squadron	Ambala	1 April 1920	Reformed by 114 Squadron renumbered as 28 Squadron equipped with Bristol F.2b for North West Frontier duties.
30 Squadron	Baghdad	1 February 1920	Brought up to establishment from a cadre; DH.9A.
31 Squadron	Risalpur	in situ	Equipped with Bristol F.2b for North West Frontier duties.
	Mhow	15 April 1920	
	Cawnpore	26 November 1920	
39 Squadron	Biggin Hill	in situ	Remaining as a cadre.
47 Squadron	Helwan	1 February 1920	Reformed by 206 Squadron renumbering as 47 Squadron equipped with DH.9 with DH.9A arriving in December.
55 Squadron	Suez	1 February 1920	Reformed by 142 Squadron renumbering as 55 Squadron
	Maltepe	12 July 1920	equipped with DH.4 replaced by DH.9 in February which
	Baghdad West	30 September	were phased out in September. DH.9A from June.
56 Squadron	Aboukir	1 February 1920	Reformed by 80 Squadron renumbering as 56 Squadron equipped with Sopwith 7F.1 Snipe.
60 Squadron	Lahore	1 April 1920	Reformed by 97 Squadron renumbering as 60 Squadron
	Risalpur	1 April 1920	and moving to Risalpur equipped with DH.10.
70 Squadron	Heliopolis	1 February 1920	Reformed by 58 Squadron renumbering as 70 Squadron equipped with HP O/400 and Vimy.
84 Squadron	Baghdad West	13 August 1920	Reformed with DH.9A for policing duties over Iraq.
	Shaibah	20 September 1920	Based here for the next twenty years.
100 Squadron	Baldonnel	in situ	Absorbed the cadres of 117 Squadron and 141 Squadron.
202 Squadron	Alexandria	9 April 1920	Equipped with Short 184 for naval duties.
203 Squadron	Leuchars	1 March 1920	Equipped with Sopwith F.1Camel as a fleet fighter unit.
205 Squadron	Leuchars	15 April 1920	Equipped with Parnall Panther for fleet reconnaissance.
207 Squadron	Bircham Newton	1 February 1920	Reformed and equipped with DH.9A.
208 Squadron	Ismailia	1 February 1920	Reformed by 113 Squadron renumbering as 208 Squadron and equipped with RE.8 which were phased out in November 1920, with the arrival of Bristol F.2b.
210 Squadron	Gosport	1 February 1920	Reformed by 186 Squadron renumbering as 210 Squadron and equipped with Sopwith Cuckoo.
216 Squadron	Qantara	in situ	Equipped with HP O/400 and DH.10.
230 Squadron	Felixstowe	in situ	Equipped with F.2a, F.3, F.5, Fairey IIIB and Fairey IIIC.
238 Squadron	Cattewater	in situ	Aircraft storage facility.

Appendix 3C - Permanent Commissions

Although the 147 officers named in this appendix are shown beneath their respective *Gazette* dates, their seniority in rank was frequently back dated, many to the 1st of August 1919. Consequently, for which I apologise, some of those named may have been duplicated with the initial list of permanent commission appointees reported in Appendix D for 1919.

LG 20 January 1920, issue 31743, page 837

			FLIGHT LIEUTENANT			
	WATSON AM	Victor Albert		F/L	20.02.20	Cancelled
			FLYING OFFICER			
04044	HARRISON DFC	George Henry		G/Capt	18.03.46	Retirement

LG 23 January 1920, issue 31751, page 983

GENDLE OBE	Albert Edgar	F/L	+	07.12.23

On the proviso that he learns to fly within the next twelve months. It seems likely that he did; tragically, however, and having been promoted Flight Lieutenant, he was murdered by dissident Arabs outside of Baghdad, a fellow officer, Flight Lieutenant Arthur H Pearce, being injured in the same attack. Paul McMillan also reports that Flight Lieutenant Gendle specialised in meteorology and had carried out weather observations in connection with the transatlantic "R" Class airships. The incident which took his life was reported in *The Times* on 12th December: *'Flight-Lieutenants Gendle and Pearce, who were walking after dusk along the Kadhimain high road, were attacked by five Arabs armed with knives and sticks, on Friday, half-a-mile to the west of Baghdad railway station. Flight-Lieutenant Gendle was stabbed in the heart and lungs, and succumbed. Flight-Lieutenant Pearce was injured in the arm and left unconscious, but revived and was able to crawl to the railway station and inform the police. Then, in spite of his injuries, he returned to the scene of the attack hoping to save his friend's life, but found that he was already dead. Flight-Lieutenant Pearce has been sent to hospital, and is progressing favourably. It is believed that the motive for the outrage was robbery only.'*

LG 30 January 1920, issue 31761, page 1265

		FLIGHT LIEUTENANT		
BARTLETT DSC*	Charles Phillips Oldfield	Major	27.12.22	Retired list
		S/ldr	26.08.32	Retirement

On account of ill-health. Subsequently rescinded.

During his service, which began with the Royal Naval Air Service, Squadron Leader Charles Phillips Oldfield DSC struggled with health problems. His well deserved award of a First Bar to his DSC was *Gazetted* on 17th May 1918, supplement 30687, issue 5856: *'For conspicuous bravery and devotion to duty in carrying out bombing raids and in attacking enemy aircraft. On the 28th March 1918, he carried out three bombing raids. Whilst returning from one of these missions he was attacked at a height of about 2,500 feet by three enemy triplanes, and five other scouts. One of these he drove down, attacking it with his front guns, whilst his observer shot down out of control a second. Observing that two of the triplanes were diving on him, he side-slipped his machine away with the result that the two enemy machines collided and fell to the ground together, where they burst into flames. He has carried out very many bombing raids, and brought down several enemy machines, invariably showing the greatest skill and determination.'* The action referred too was carried out in DH.4 N6000 of 5 Squadron RNAS. Despite being dogged by ill-health, he lived to the grand age of 98, his death in February 1987, being reported from Cheltenham in Gloucestershire. I am pleased to acknowledge *Wikipedia* for the information here reported.

6 February 1920, issue 31770, page 1564

		FLIGHT LIEUTENANT		
O'NEILL MC	William Hickley Lovell	S/Ldr +	05.10.30	DD Civil Aviation India

Squadron Leader William Hickley Lovell O'Neill MC, Deputy Director of Civil Aviation in India, was one of the many fatalities when the Airship R.101 G-FAAW crashed near Beauvais in France.

LG 20 February 1920, issue 31788, page 2073

		FLYING OFFICER		
LAING	Alexander Thomas	F/L	20.10.29	Retired list

At his own request [LG 10 December 1929, issue 33559, page 8027].

LG 9 March 1920, issue 31816, page 2906

		FLIGHT LIEUTENANT		
BROOKE	Arthur Francis	S/Ldr	12.10.32	Retired list

On account of ill-health [LG 11 October 1932, issue 33872, page 6418].

LG 30 March 1920, issue 31841, page 3901

			FLYING OFFICER		
04205	TRAILL DFC	Thomas Cathcart		AV-M	21.09.54	Retirement

Air Vice-Marshal Thomas Cathcart Traill CB OBE DFC twice mentioned in despatches, died on Monday, 1st October 1973. As with many of his contemporaries Thomas Cathcart Traill commenced his service with the Royal Navy and as at 2nd August 1914, he was a Midshipman at HMS *Lord Nelson*. On 11th June 1917, he is reported as being a Cadet with the Royal Flying Corps. For an appreciation of his long service, please refer to the website Air of Authority - A History of RAF Organisation.

LG 14 May 1920, issue 31900, page 5487

CHAPLAINS BRANCH

3

KEYMER OBE MA	Bernard William	Reverend	29.10.23	Resigned
67568	McCALMAN MC MA Hugh	Reverend	01.07.22	Resigned

His award of the Military Cross was *Gazetted,* without the citation appended, on 18th January 1928, supplement 30482, page 957.

| COLLIER | George Henry | | G/Capt | 12.08.34 | |

Promoted to the relative rank of Group Captain [LG 2 October 1934, issue 34092, page 6180].

LG 1 June 1920, issue 31924, page 6087

SQUADRON LEADER

| STODART DSO DFC David Edmund | | | S/Ldr | 01.03.31 | Retired list |

CHAPLAINS BRANCH
4

BEAUCHAMP MC	H				
BLACKBURN	D F				
FIRTH MC	J				
McHARDY MA MC	Archibald				

His award of the Military Cross was *Gazetted*, without the citation appended, on 3rd June 1919, issue 31370, page 6830. The Reverend Archibald McHardy MC MA Staff Chaplain, Royal Air Force, appointed Honorary Chaplain to the King, 1st September 1942 [LG 30 October 1942, supplement 35768, page 4755]. In the summer of 2960, with the approval of Her Majesty the Queen on the recommendation of Sir Ian A Johnson-Gilbert CBE LL.D former Lord Lieutenant, The Reverend Archibald McHardy CB CBE MC KHC was made Deputy Lieutenant of the County of the City of Edinburgh [EG 3 June 1960, issue 17827, page 344].

LG 15 June 1920, issue 31942, page 6587

FLIGHT LIEUTENANT - MEDICAL BRANCH

| PORTER MC MB | Joseph Herbert | | S/ldr | 09.12.23 | Dismissed |

Squadron Leader Joseph Herbert Porter MC MB dismissed the service by sentence of Field General Court Martial [also dismissed, Flight Lieutenant Patrick Joseph Flood], a sad end to their service, particularly for Squadron Leader Porter whose gallantry in action earned him the Military Cross, *Gazetted* 6th April 1918, supplement 30614, page 4224: *'For conspicuous gallantry and devotion to duty. He was in charge of the divisional collecting post during an action, and by his example and thoroughness did much to encourage all ranks in the discharge of their duties. He went forward in charge of bearers, and by his untiring energy succeeded in getting his communications re-established in the face of great difficulties.'* That their dismissal was by a Field General Court Martial suggests their offences took place overseas in an area where operations were underway.

LG 22 June 1920, issue 31949, page 6794

FLIGHT LIEUTENANT

| 10029 | COATES | Frank Edwin John | | W/Cdr | 26.07.40 | Retired list |

Re-employed until reversion to Retired list at his own request.
| | | | | W/Cdr | 22.09.43 | Retired list |

LG 2 July 1920, issue 31962, page 7127

FLIGHT LIEUTENANT
2

| WILLIAMS | Frederick Hubert | | F/L | 07.06.28 | Retired list |
| ELLISON | William Harry | | F/L | 07.10.25 | Retired list |

On account of ill-health [LG 6 October 1925, issue 33090, page 6421].

LG 9 July 1920, issue 31972, page 7355

FLYING OFFICER

| ELLISON | William Harry | | F/L | 07.10.25 | Retired list |

On account of ill-health [LG 6 October 1925, issue 33090, page 6421].

LG 13 July 1920, issue 31978, page 7458

WING COMMANDERS - MEDICAL BRANCH
7

| COOPER DSO BA | Henry | | G/Capt | 03.01.32 | Retired list |
| FLACK CBE | Martin William | | G/Capt + | 16.08.31 | |

Group Captain Martin William Flack CBE died following a long illness in RAF Hospital Halton.IREDELL   Alfred William

| IREDELL | Alfred William | | AV-M | 01.03.38 | Retired list |

At his own request. Air Vice-Marshal Sir Alfred William Iredell KBE CB MRCS LRCP at his own request relinquished his rank on re-employment with the Royal Air Force and was appointed Group Captain, 7th September 1939 [LG 31 October 1939, issue 34721, page 7275]. His death was announced on

| McINTYRE MC MA MB | John | | AV-M | 01.03.34 | Retirement |

Air Vice-Marshal Sir John McIntyre KBE CB MC MB B.Ch at his own request relinquished his rank on re-employment with the Royal Air Force and was appointed Group Captain, 7th September 1939 [LG 31 October 1939, issue 34721, page 7275]. His death was announced on Saturday, 7th October 1950. During the Second World War, Sir John McIntyre was Commandant of the RAF Psychiatric Hospital at Rockside Hydro in the Derbyshire town of Matlock where aircrew suffering from the strain of bombing operations underwent treatment.

| RICHARDSON | Albert Victor John | | AV-M | 01.03.41 | Retirement |

OBE MB BA Air Vice-Marshal Albert Victor John Richardson CB OBE MB BCh DPH KHS, died on Friday, 16th September 1960.

STANFORD DSO	Charles Edward Cortis		G/Capt	20.03.29	Retired list
MB BSc					
WELLS CBE	Hardy Vesey		A/Cmdr	30.01.34	Retired list

Air Commodore Hardy Vesey Wells CBE MRCS LRCP, died on Sunday, 30th December 1956. His military service was initially with the Royal Navy and in 1913, qualified as a pilot under the tutelage of the Naval Wing of the Royal Flying Corps.

SQUADRON LEADERS - MEDICAL BRANCH
14

| CLEMENTS OBE | Edward Cecil | | G/Capt | 05.08.34 | Retired list |

Group Captain Edward Cecil Clements CBE MRCS LRCP, died on Wednesday, 19th May 1965. His CBE, described as being in perfect condition, was auctioned by Worth Point via eBay UK.

| DUCK OBE | William Agar Scholefield | | A/Cmdr | 11.01.41 | Retirement |

Re-employed and voluntary relinquished his rank: served until:
| | | | W/Cdr | 24.03.46 | Retirement |

Air Commodore William Agar Scholefield Duck OBE MRCS LRCP DPH, died on Sunday, 15th January 1978.

HEWAT MB	Harry Aitken	A/Cmdr		21.11.45	Retirement

Air Commodore Harry Aitken Hewat CBE MB Ch.B DTM & H, died on Saturday, 4th April 1970.

KNOWLES MD	Reginald Herbert	A/Cmdr		01.01.43	Retirement

Re-employed and served until:

		A/Cmdr		02.08.43	Retirement

Air Commodore Reginald Herbert Knowles MD MB Ch.B, died in Worthing on Saturday, 13th July 1974.

MacGREGOR MC MD	James	G/Capt		23.11.34	Retired list

Group Captain James MacGregor MC MD CM LRCP & S, emigrated to Australia where he died at Chiselwood in New South Wales on Wednesday, 16th June 1954.

PLAYNE DSO MB BA	Basil Alfred	A/Cmdr		01.09.38	Retired list

At his own request [LG 6 September 1938, issue 34548, page 5680]. Air Commodore Basil Alfred Playne, DSO MB B.Ch MRCS LRCP returned, briefly, to the service but reverted to the Retired list on 23rd March 1940 [LG 6 August 1940, issue 34915, page 4813], he died in Pontypridd on Sunday, 6th February 1944.

PORTEOUS MB	Harold Burnet	W/Cdr		17.06.35	Retired list
RANKEN MB BS FRCS	David	G/Capt		07.09.38	Retired list
RIPPON OBE	Thomas Stanley	W/Cdr		19.05.35	Retired list
SHORTEN FRCS	William Wood	W/Cdr	+	27.12.33	RAF Hospital Halton
SMARTT MB BA	Frank Naugle Bury	G/Capt		24.12.39	Retirement

Re-employed and served until:

		G/Capt		19.11.45	Retirement
TREADGOLD	Henry Asbourne	G/Capt		01.07.36	Retired list

CBE MD BS MRCS MRCP On account of ill-health [LG 30 June 1936, issue 34300, page 4165].

TURNER MBE	Harry Moreton Stanley	W/Cdr		22.09.30	Retired list

Wing Commander Harry Moreton Stanley MBE MD MRCS LRCP DTM & H was born in Hanley, Staffordshire on 2nd December 1876, and died in London on Monday, 5th February 1951.

WHITTINGHAM MB	Harold Edward	AV-M		01.03.46	Retirement

Air-Vice Marshal Harold Edward Whittingham CBE MB Ch.B FRCP[E] FRFPS[G] FRCP[London] DPH DTM & H KHP, died on Saturday, 16th July 1983.

FLIGHT LIEUTENANTS - MEDICAL BRANCH
24

BIGGS MC	Kenneth	AV-M		02.11.47	Retirement

Air Commodore Kenneth Biggs MC MRCS LRCP DPH emigrated to Australia and in 1988, was living in Brisbane and may have died there in that year. He was born in Hendon on 4th March 1890. His MC was *Gazetted* on 9th January 1918, supplement 30466, page 587: *'For conspicuous gallantry and devotion to duty in leading and organising his stretcher-bearers under intense fire of every description, in such a manner that our wounded were rapidly evacuated. He worked unceasingly in the open for 24 hours, until he was severely wounded, by his admirable courage and determination saving many lives.'*

CRAIG MC MB	Eric William	A/Cmdr		12.08.44	Retirement

At his own request. His MC was *Gazetted* on 16th August 1917, supplement 30234, page 8363: *'For conspicuous gallantry and devotion to duty. During the night he repeatedly led the bearers beyond the front line under heavy fire. By his example and courage he was the means of rescuing many wounded.'* Air commodore Eric William Craig MC MB B.Ch, died on Tuesday, 28th December 1965.

14101	ELLIOTT MB BA	Robert Andrew George	G/Capt	16.11.42	Retired list

At his own request [LG 15 December 1942, supplement 35822, page 5459].

14102	FLOOD	Patrick Joseph	F/L	09.12.23	Dismissed

By sentence of General Court Martial. During the Second World War was commissioned 11th October 1939, in the Royal Army Medical Corps as a Lieutenant and allotted 125108 [LG 16 April 1940, supplement 34830, page 22287]. Major 19.11.43 Relinquished
On account of ill-health [LG 19 November 1943, supplement 36253, page 5069].

14103	FORBES	John Turnbull Thomson	W/Cdr	05.10.46	Retired list
	GLYNN MB	Arthur Samuel	A/Cmdr	01.07.40	

Paul McMillan reports, Air Commodore Arthur Samuel Glynn was born on 29th June 1885, at Bareilly, Uttar Pradesh, India and died Malindi, Coast, Kenya on Saturday, 15th April 1967.

KEANE	Percival Maurice	W/Cdr		28.02.33	Retired list
KELLY MC MB BA	Thomas James	AV-M		18.10.47	Retirement

Air Vice-Marshal Thomas James Kelly CBE MC MD Ch.B, died on Thursday, 25th May 1967, at the age of 77, while being treated in RAF Hospital Wroughton after a long illness. Between 1941 and 1942, he was principal medical officer in Bomber Command. In addition to his Military Cross, he was also conferred by Russia with the Order of St. Stanislas, 3rd Class [with swords] [LG 14 January 1918, supplement 30476, page 828].

KYLE	James	G/Capt		26.11.43	Retired list

Re-employed and served until:

		A/Cmdr		21.01.46	Retirement

Air Commodore James Kyle MRCS LRCP, died on Saturday, 8th October 1949. My co-author adds, in retirement he was appointed Assistant Medical Director for British Overseas Airways Corporation. During his *Great War service* he survived he was badly gassed, returned to medical school at the end of 1916, and obtaining his MRCS and LRCP.

LIVINGSTON	Philip Clermont	AM		26.08.51	Retirement

Air Marshal Sir Philip Clermont Livingston KBE CB AFC FRCS LRCP DPH DOMS, died on Friday, 12th February 1982.

MARSHALL OBE	Gerald Struan	G/Capt		27.03.44	Retirement

At his own request.

MORTON MB	Terence Charles St. Clessie	AV-M		25.09.51	Retirement

At his own request. Air Vice-Marshal Terence Charles St. Clessie Morton CB OBE MD Ch.B FRCP DPH DPM DTM & H, died on Wednesday, 16th October 1968, at Truro in Cornwall.

14110	OVERTON	Robert Sydney	W/Cdr	11.05.41	Retirement

Re-employed same day and served until:

			G/Capt	13.07.47	Retirement
14109	O'NEILL MB	Christopher Thomas	A/Cmdr	18.01.52	Retirement

Air Commodore Christopher Thomas O'Neill OBE MB Ch.B, died on Thursday, 8th April 1971, while undergoing treatment in RAF Hospital Wroughton. His medals, which included a rare 1923 Chanak Crisis OBE group were auctioned by DNW in December 2017, the catalogue recording the citation for the OBE: *'This officer has shown great ability and zeal as a medical officer, and he has accomplished splendid work for the Greek refugees at the concentration camp at San Stefano. Owing to the prevalence of typhus and other diseases in the camp, this service was rendered at very great risk to his own life. His work among the refugees not only resulted in many lives being saved but also enhanced greatly the prestige of the British service.'* The guide price of £700-£900 pounds was well exceeded, the gavel coming down at £2,000.

PANTER BA	Arthur Edward	AV-M		06.10.46	Retirement

Air Vice-Marshal Arthur Edward Panter CB MA MRCS LRCP KHS, died on Wednesday, 12th March 1969, at the age of 79.

POWER MC	D'Arcy	AV-M		12.01.46	Retirement

Air-Vice Marshal D'Arcy POWER CBE MC MRCS LRCP, died on Boxing Day 1958.

ROTHWELL MB	John	W/Cdr		26.02.36	Retired list

At his own request [LG 25 February 1936, issue 34259, page 1241].

ROOK	Alan Filmer		AV-M	03.07.48	Retirement

Air-Vice Marshal Sir Alan Filmer Rook KBE CB FRCP MRCH DPH, died on Friday, 26th August 1960. An excellent tribute to his service, compiled by Richard R Trail, may be read on the website Royal College of Physicians.

SCOTT BA	Henry Wakeman		G/Capt	15.04.32	Retired list

On account of ill-health [LG 19 April 1932, issue 33818, page 2566].

14115 THOMAS MB BS	Thomas John		G/Capt	06.01.44	Retired list
Re-employed and served until:			G/Capt	10.08.46	Retirement
14116 THOMPSON MB	Thomas Rolland Stuart		S/Ldr	08.06.40	Retired list
Re-employed and served until:			S/Ldr	06.11.41	Retirement

His career ended in some controversy in that he was the guilty party in divorce proceedings brought by Major Wallace Henry Glydd Drake-Brockman against his wife, a Section Officer in the Women's Auxiliary Air Force coming under the influence of Squadron Leader Thomas Rolland Stuart Thompson, her superior officer. A sum of £1,500 pounds in damages against the aforesaid Squadron Leader is mentioned.

14117 TOPHAM MB	Richard Stanley		F/L	01.05.27	Retired list

At his own request [LG 3 May 1927, issue 33271, page 2879]. Returned to the service during the Second World War and promoted Wing Commander 1st June 1941 [LG 10 June 1941, issue 35187, page 3324].

			W/Cdr +	10.03.44	

His death occurred in St. Mary's Abbey Hospital, Kensington. He is commemorated on panel 3 at Golders Green Crematorium.

14118 WIGMORE MB	Arthur John Ormsby		S/Ldr	20.07.34	Retired list

On account of ill-health. Squadron Leader Arthur John Ormsby Wigmore MB Ch.B MRCS LRCP, died on Sunday, 29th August 1948.

14119 YOUNG MB	Peter Hutchison		G/Capt	06.08.44	Retired list

LG 8 October 1920, issue 32078, page 9815

FLIGHT LIEUTENANT

GRAN MC	Tryggve		F/L	06.08.21	Relinquished

His MC was *Gazetted* on 24th August 1918, supplement 30862, page 9910: *'For conspicuous gallantry and devotion to duty. He bombed enemy aerodromes with great success, and engaged enemy searchlights, transport and other targets with machine-gun fire. He invariably showed the greatest determination and resource.'*

FLYING OFFICER

05038 ATTWOOD	Charles William		G/Capt	01.09.41	Retirement
Re-employed.			G/Capt	15.05.45	Retirement

My co-author reports that Group Captain Charles William Attwood was born on the 1st of September 1891, and died in Surbiton in January 1973. His medals were put up for auction by DNW with an estimate of between £280 to £320, the gavel coming down at £480. A biography of his military service makes interesting reading, noting he attested at the age of eighteen as a sapper with the Corps of Royal Engineers, transferred in in July 1912, to the Royal Flying Corps, subsequently gaining his Royal Aero Club Aviators' Certificate [No. 4259] as a Sergeant Pilot on 17th February 1917. His *Great War* flying was on the Western Front, initially with 8 Squadron and later with 35 Squadron. His interwar service mirrored that of numerous permanent officers, during which he specialised in signals and following command of 102 Squadron switched to Coastal Command as Chief Signals Officer at Headquarters No. 16 [Reconnaissance] Group at Lee-on-Solent.

LG 16 November 1920, issue 32125, page 11119

WING COMMANDER

KIRBY VC OBE DCM Frank Howard			G/Capt	08.12.26	Retired list

Group Captain Frank Howard Kirby, born at Thame in Oxfordshire on 12th November 1871, was a Corporal in the Corps of Royal Engineers and taking part in the Second Boer War when he won the Victoria Cross, the citation being published in *The London Gazette* published on 5th October 1900, issue 27235, page 6126: *'On the morning of the 2nd June 1900, a party sent to try to cut the Delagoa Bay Railway were retiring, hotly pressed by very superior numbers. During one of the successive retirements of the rearguard, a man, whose horse had been shot, was seen running after his comrades. He was a long way behind the rest of his troop and was under brisk fire. From among the retiring troop Corporal Kirby turned and rode back to the man's assistance. Although by the time he reached him they were under a heavy fire at close range, Corporal Kirby managed to get the dismounted man up behind him and take him clear off over the next rise held by our rearguard. This is the third occasion on which Corporal Kirby has displayed gallantry in the face of the enemy.'* Subsequently, he was awarded the Distinguished Conduct Medal for his services in South Africa and prior to his transfer to the Royal Flying Corps had been granted a commission as an honorary Lieutenant. Group Captain Frank Howard Kirby VC died at Sidcup, Kent, on Sunday, 8th July 1956, at the age of 84; he is buried in Streatham Park Cemetery. His Victoria Cross is on display at the Lord Ashcroft VC Gallery in the Imperial War Museum. Additional information regarding his service is available on *Wikipedia*.

SQUADRON LEADERS
4

BRUCE OBE	William Robert		G/Capt +	21.01.32	

Group Captain William Robert Bruce OBE died in Netley Hospital on Thursday, 21st January 1932, where he is buried in the military cemetery.

LYONS OBE	Thomas Owen		W/Cdr +	01.02.26	

Wing Commander Thomas Owen Lyons OBE died from the effects of the *Great War* and his recent service in Iraq. He is buried St. Giles Churchyard at Ickenham in the London Borough of Hillingdon.

PARKIN MBE	James Edward		W/Cdr	12.03.24	Retired list

Wing Commander James Edward Parkin returned to the service and was granted a commission in Class C of the Reserve of Air Force Officers, ranked Flight Lieutenant [honorary Wing Commander] 12th July 1937 [LG 10 August 1937, issue 34425, page 5123]. Granted a commission in Class CC of the Reserve of Air Force Officers, ranked Wing Command, 15th April 1940 [LG 18 June 1940, issue 34876, page 3706]. Subsequently served in the Administrative and Special Duties Branch.

			W/Cdr	01.05.45	Relinquished
WILFORD	James Henry		W/Cdr	07.11.25	Retired list

FLIGHT LIEUTENANTS
14

ARCHBOLD	Cuthbert Leopold		A/Cmdr	25.04.46	Retirement

Air Commodore Cuthbert Leopold Archbold CBE, died on Tuesday, 22nd May 1962.

AYLWIN OBE	William Edgar		G/Capt	25.04.42	Retired list
BALDWIN	Frederick Alfred		G/Capt	01.07.38	Retired list

At his own request [LG 5 July 1938, issue 34528, page 4334].

CLARK	William Charles		G/Capt	27.12.45	Retirement
FULLER	Nevill Ross		G/Capt	26.02.46	Retirement
MASON	Cecil		S/Ldr	20.12.25	Retired list
MATON MBE	William Henry George		S/Ldr	11.09.26	Retirement
10430 McBIRNEY	David		S/Ldr	08.08.26	Retired list

Squadron Leader David McBirney returned to the service, Administrative and Special Duties Branch, 1st September 1939, retaining his rank [LG 21st November 1939, issue 34738, page 7805].

			S/Ldr	08.08.44	Relinquished

MILLETT	William	G/Capt		20.09.40	Retired list

On account of ill-health [LG 27 September 1940, issue 34954, page 5717].

RYLANDS	Joseph	A/Cmdr	+	04.04.45	Air Member for Personnel

Air Commodore Joseph Rylands CBE mentioned in despatches, died in RAF Hospital Uxbridge on Wednesday, 4th April 1945.Since 7th September 1942, he had filled the position of Senior Service Accountant in the Department of Air Member for Personnel, and was due to leave the service. He is buried in Watford North Cemetery where his headstone is inscribed *Till We Meet Again*.

SKEATS	Thomas George	A/Cmdr	+	01.12.44	AOC 56[Maint.] Wing

Air Commodore Thomas George Skeats CBE, died on 1st December 1944, in RAF Hospital Northallerton following an operation. He was appointed Air Officer Commanding No. 56[Maintenance] Wing as recently as September 1944. He is buried in Annan Cemetery.

THOMAS OBE	Rudall Woodliffe	A/Cmdr		13.04.44	Retirement

Air Commodore Rudall Woodliffe Thomas OBE, died on Monday, 9th July 1973.

WADDINGTON OBE	William James	S/Ldr		29.10.28	Retirement
WILLIAMS	Basil Winstanley Michael	G/Capt		13.08.40	Retirement

Paul McMillan, my co-author, reports Groupn Captain Basil Winstanley Michael Williams, died on Tuesday, 6th March 1951.

FLYING OFFICERS
48

10021	ANDERSON	Frank	S/Ldr		31.03.32	Retired list

Squadron Leader Frank Anderson returned to the service on 1st November 1939, and at his own request reverted in rank to Flight Lieutenant. He continued to serve throughout the Second World until:

			W/Cdr		01.04.46	Retired list
	BAXTER	James	F/O		26.02.21	Retired list
	BEERE	Thomas Francis	F/O		13.12.22	Retired list

On account of ill-health contracted on active service [LG 12 December 1922, issue 32776, page 8799].

	BELL MM	Thomas	S/Ldr		2509.32	Retired list
10071	BULLEN	Ernest Stanford	F/L		27.04.31	Retired list

Flight Lieutenant Ernest Stanford Bullen MBE returned to the service and was granted a commission in Class CC, retaining his rank, on 8th May 1939 [LG 18 July 1939, issue 34646, page 4932].

			S/Ldr		06.11.41	Retired list
	CARTER DCM	Lewis Edward	F/L		28.03.28	Retirement

Flight Lieutenant Lewis Edward Carter features in several websites, the most informative being **ms-my.facebook.com** [which I have pleasure in acknowledging] which displays an excellent photograph of him when he was a Sergeant [possibly taken following his transfer from the Lancers to the Royal Flying Corps]. His military service was extensive when at the age of nineteen and eight months he attested for the Lancers of the Line in Birmingham, where he was born on 5th March 1880, on 28th November 1899. During his time with the Lancers he improved his education and subsequently was permitted to extend his terms of engagement in order to complete 21 years with the colours. However, on 19th July 1912, he transferred to the Royal Flying Corps, reporting to 1 Squadron at Netheravon as an Air Mechnic 1st Class, where within six months he regained his Sergeant rank and in 1913, qualified for his Royal Aero Club Aviators' Certificate [No. 32] on 2nd September. His next posting was to 6 Squadron and thence to France where he was attached to the 3rd Aircraft Park. On the 13th of February 1917, he was *Gazetted* with the Distinguished Conduct Medal; *'For conspicuous gallantry and devotion to duty. He has shown great courage initiative throughout the campaign, and has been in continuous service since the commencement of hostilities.'*His commission was *Gazetted* on 30th May of that year. In the 1960s he was Branch Honorary Secretary of the Lewisham Branch of The Old Contemptibles' Association. Known as 'Chum' Lewis Carter, he died on Tuesday, 7th June 1977.

10073	COLLIER	Kenneth Dowsett Gould	A/Cmdr		25.02.47	Retirement

Air Commodore Kenneth Dowsett Gould Collier CBE BSN, died in June 1971.

	COMFORT	Alfred Horace	S/Ldr		03.11.35	Retired list

On account of ill-health [LG 5 November 1935, issue 34216, page 6978].

10077	CRAIG	Robert	F/L		09.06.32	Retired list
	CRICHTON	John Pender	F/O		28.11.23	Retired list

On account of ill-health [LG 1 January 1924, issue 32894, page 54].

	CULLEN	Charles Edward	F/L		30.10.27	Retired list
	DANN	Henry James	F/O		30.06.24	Dismissed

Flying Officer Henry James Dann was dismissed the service by sentence of General Court Martial [LG 19 August 1924, issue 32966, page 6275].

10082	DAVIS	Clarence Tremaine	S/Ldr		18.07.40	Retired list

Re-employed.

			S/Ldr		16.04.42	Retired list

My co-author reports Clarence Tremaine Davis was born on 23rd July 1890, and died on Wednesday, 6th April 1966.

10084	DENNIS	Stanley David	W/Cdr		07.12.43	Retired list

At his own request

10089	FARMAN	Edward Crisp	A-VM		29.04.53	Retirement

Air Vice-Marshal Edward Crisp Farman CB CBE, died on Wednesday, 27th July 1966.

	FELSTEAD DCM	George	F/O		06.41.21	Retired list
10094	GARDINER	John Roland	F/L		19.02.31	Retired list

Flight Lieutenant John Roland Gardiner returned to the service and promoted Squadron Leader [Temporary] [LG 7 June 1940, issue 34866, page 3437], remaining in the Equipment Branch.

			W/Cdr		09.09.44	Retired list

Born, Paul McMillan, reports on 19th February 1896, John Roland Gardiner died on Sunday, 22January 1961.

10101	HARRISON	William Herbert	F/L		21.04.35	Retired list

Flight Lieutenant William Herbert Harrison returned to the service by September 1941.

			S/Ldr		29.10.43	Retired list
	JONES	Hugh	F/L	+	10.05.32	RAF Tangmere

Paul McMillan reports that Flight Lieutenant Hugh Jones had been non-effective, sick, since February 1932, and died in RAF Hospital, Halton.

10109	JUKES	Alfred	F/L		24.06.29	Retired list

Flight Lieutenant Alfred Jukes MBE was granted a commission in Class CC as Squadron Leader on 24th January 1939 [LG 9 May 1939, issue 34624, page 3114].

			S/Ldr		01.09.39	Relinquished

Continuing in service until:

			S/Ldr		12.09.45	Retired list
10110	KINGSTON	William Arthur	W/Cdr		01.09.44	Retirement
10113	LAWRENCE	Ernest William	F/L		31.07.32	Retired list

Flight Lieutenant Ernest William Lawrence returned to the service and was promoted Squadron Leader 1st December 1940 [LG 10 December 1940, issue 35010, page 6984].

			S/Ldr	+	23.04.44	RAF Thorney Island

Squadron Leader Ernest William Lawrence is buried in Portsmouth [Milton] Cemetery where his headstone bears the words *Whosoever Believeth In God Shall Not Perish, But Have Everlasting Life*. He was 55 years of age.

10116	LITTLEWOOD	Wallis St. John	W/Cdr	+	25.10.42	151 Squadron

Wing Commander Wallis St. John Littlewood died when the Luftwaffe carried a hit and run raid on the South Devonshire resort of Torquay, some of the gunfire from their strafing run scoring hits on the Palace Hotel which had been requisitioned for use as a hospital and, in accordance with the Geneva convention, a red cross had been painted on its roof. According to the Devon Heritage website, which I have pleasure in acknowledging, nineteen service personnel were killed and forty-five injured. The hotel was hit again during a similar raid on 30th December 1942, sustaining serious structural damage. Wing Commander Wallis St. John Littlewood OBE is buried in the extension to Torquay Cemetery; he was 51 years of age.

10122	MACROSTIE	Reginald David Gorrie		S/Ldr	01.01.40	Retired list
	Re-employed.			W/Cdr	21.04.48	Retired list

My co-author has unearthed some useful information regarding Wing Commander Reginald David Gorrie Macrostie MBEwho was born on New Year's Day 1890. Apparently he is mentioned in *Flying Fury* by James McCudden VC which the author completed just a few days before his death on the 9th of July 1918 [see my second volume, page 35, for details].

10125	MAYGOTHLING	George John	F/L	07.07.33	Retired list

Flight Lieutenant George John Maygothling, as a civilian, was granted a commission as Flight Lieutenant with No. 600[City of London] [Fighter] Squadron Auxiliary Air Force, 19th November 1934 [LG 4 January 1935, issue 34121, page 137]. On 1st September 1939, he relinquished his commission in Class CC [LG 5 March 1940, issue 34805, page 1318]. He was promoted Squadron Leader in the Equipment Branch on 1st June 1940 [LG 7 June 1940, issue 34866, page 3438].

S/Ldr +	20.11.40	B Maintenance Unit

Squadron Leader George John Gothling, 52 years of age, is buried in Harrow Cemetery. His widow Emily Beatrice Maygothling was dealt another blow when she was informed that their son, Pilot Officer Gordon James Maygothling, serving with 109 Squadron, Tempsford, was missing while on active service on 29th March 1942. Details of his loss during a raid to Lübeck on 28th-29th March 1942, are reported in my RAFBCL 1942, page 55.

	MITCHELL	Charlie Young	F/L	06.04.27	Retired list

On account of ill-health [LG 5 April 1927, issue 33263, page 2215].

	MOORE	Alick James	G/Capt	11.08.46	Retirement

Group Captain Alick James Moore was born in Sidcup, Kent, on 8th August 1891, and died in Bournemouth on Sunday, 5th August 1962.

	NICHOLLS	John Robert	F/L	19.11.24	Retired list

On account of ill-health. Prior to his Royal Air Force service, John Robert Nicholls, as my co-author has discovered, served with distinction in the army having enlisted in 1898, when he was twenty years of age. In April 1916, he was was awarded his Long Service and Good Conduct medal; the following year being commissioned 2nd Lieutenant as an equipment officer in the Royal Flying Corps.

	OLIVER	George	F/L	03.11.25	Retired list

During the Second World War Flight Lieutenant George Oliver was granted a commission in the Training Branch of the Royal Air Force Volunteer Reserve, ranked Flying Officer and allotted the service number 100850.

			F/O	27.08.49	Resigned
10132	ORGAN	Thomas James	F/L	19.12.32	Retired list

Flight Lieutenant Thomas James Organ returned to the service and was promoted Squadron Leader [temporary] on 1st June 1940 [LG 7 June 1940, issue 34866, page 3437].

			S/Ldr	26.06.43	Retired list
10134	PARKER	Herbert	F/L	28.02.31	Retired list

Flight Lieutenant Herbert Parker returned to the service and was promoted Squadron Leader in the Equipment Branch on 1st June 1940 [LG 7 June 1940, issue 34866, page 3438]. Paul McMillan reports Squadron Leader Parker retiring at some point between September and November 1943. During his first term of service, commencing 30th December 1912, and attachment to 2 Squadron, and following his commission as a permanent officer, he served aboard the seaplane carrier HMS *Argus*. During a spell ashore he was injured on 17th February 1922, when his motorcycle came into collision with a civilian car. Subsequently, from 12th October 1928, he was a stores officer at No. 4 Stores Depot, Ruislip, Middlesex.

10137	POWELL MBE	Frank James Bickley	F/L	04.11.32	Retired list

Flight Lieutenant Frank James Bickley Powell MBE as a civilian was granted a commission, retaining his rank, as a Stores Officer with the Auxiliary Air Force and attached to No. 600[City of London] [Bomber] Squadron on 1st February 1933 [LG 31 January 1933, issue 33907, page 677]. On 5th December 1934, he transferred to No. 605[County of Warwick] [Bomber] Squadron [LG 1 January 1935, issue 34120, page 65]. His Auxiliary Air Force commission was relinquished on 12th September 1939 [LG 26 April 1940, issue 34838, page 2481] and returning to the Equipment Branch he was made Squadron Leader [temporary] on 1st June 1940 [LG 7 June 1940, issue 34866, page 3437]. He continued to serve throughout the Second World War until:

			W/Cdr	22.05.45	Retired list
10138	POWELL	Frederick William	F/O	03.08.21	Retired list

Flying Officer Frederick William Powell served in the Second World War.

			S/Ldr	17.05.48	Retired list
	PRATT	Frank	F/O	01.04.25	Retired list

Flying Officer Frank Pratt while serving at Uxbridge changed his surname by Deed Poll to Battey-Pratt [LG 5 March 1920, issue 31809, page 2820].

	ROBERTSON	Norman	F/L	20.01.31	Retired list

On account of ill-health.

	SAYWOOD	Arthur Mrytle		S/Ldr	14.03.32	Retired list
	SLADDEN MBE DCM	Robert John		Captain	02.11.21	Retired list
10148	SLEIGH	Horatio		F/L	18.11.34	Retired list

Flight Lieutenant Horatio Sleigh returned to the service and was promoted Squadron Leader [temporary] on 1st June 1940, issue 34866, page 3438]. Retired at his own request [LG 5 December 1944, supplement 36823, page 5558].

			W/Cdr	10.10.44	Retired list
	SMITH	Karl Anastasia	F/L	13.01.26	Retired list

On account of ill-health [LG 12 January 1926, issue 33123, page 301].

	STONE	Oliver Thornton		F/O +	12.11.22	2 Armoured Car Company

Flying Officer Oliver Thornton Stone died in Jerusalem's Military Hospital from diptheria.

	STROUD MBE	George Thomas	F/L	13.11.27	Retired list
	THORNE	Walter	AV-M	14.05.47	Retirement

Air Vice-Marshal Walter Thorne CB CBE, is thought to have died on Wednesday, 5th October 1960.

	TURNER DCM	Arthur William	S/Ldr	01.12.33	Retired list
10167	WILKINS	Frederick Ralph	W/Cdr	19.06.43	Retirement
	WILSON	George Clarence	F/L	05.01.35	Retired list
10169	WOOD	Ernest Richard	G/Capt	20.04.48	Retirement

LG 30 November 1920, issue 32145, page 11823

FLIGHT LIEUTENANTS
3

10026	BRYANT	Walter Frank	W/Cdr	11.09.31	Retired list

On account of ill-health [LG 15 September 1931, issue 33753, page 5969[. Re-employed and at his own request relinquishes the rank of Wing Commander to that of Squadron Leader [LG 4 April 1941, issue 35127, page 1961].

			W/Cdr	27.10.46	Retired list
	FAWDRY MBE	Thomas	A/Cmdr	01.06.46	Retirement

Air Commodore Thomas Fawdry CB CBE mentioned in despatches, died in September 1968. He held the distinction of holding the post of Senior Equipment Staff Officer in three Commands, Maintenance, Technical Training and from 15th July 1942, Bomber Command.

	HILLIAR	George Arthur	W/Cdr	01.05.37	Retired list

LG 1 December 1920

FLIGHT LIEUTENANT

	BURKINSHAW	William	F/L	03.01.23	Retired list

On account of ill-health [LG 5 January 1923, issue 32784, page 141].

LG 17 December 1920, issue 32166, page 12400

FLIGHT LIEUTENANTS

3

| | BURKINSHAW | William | | F/L | 03.01.23 | Retired list |

On account of ill-health [LG 5 January 1923, issue 32784, page 141].

| 10102 | HAWLEY | Thomas Alec Gordon | | F/L | 05.04.30 | Retired list |

At his own request [LG 15 April 1930, issue 33597, page 2424]. Returned to the service and commissioned as Squadron Leader in the Equipment Branch by 1 June 1940 [LG 7 June 1940, issue 34866, page 3437].

| | | | | F/L | 01.01.48 | |
| 10039 | JACOBS | Vere Julius Bethel | | S/Ldr | 29.12.37 | Relinquished |

Returned to the service and commissioned as Squadron Leader in the Equipment Branch by 1 June 1940 [LG 7 June 1940, issue 34866, page 3437].

| | | | | S/Ldr | 14.09.43 | Retired list |
| | SHAW DSO | Cecil Arthur | | F/L | 28.06.22 | Retired list |

On account of ill-health [LG 27 June 1922, issue 32723, page 4834].

LG 7 January 1921, issue 32185, page 184

FLYING OFFICER

| | OSBORN MM | Fredrick Alfred | | F/O | 02.09.24 | Retired list |

FLYING OFFICERS

4

10119	McDONALD	John Kinloch		W/Cdr	25.10.44	Retirement
	MEYNELL DCM	Edward		S/Ldr	05.01.36	Retired list
10135	PAYNE	Herbert James		G/Capt	18.10.45	Retirement
10163	WHILTON DCM	Frederick		F/L	31.03.31	Retired list

On account of ill-health [LG 31 March 1931, issue 33703, page 2141. Returned to the service and commissioned as a Flight Lieutenant in the Reserve of Air Force Officers, General Duties Branch, Class CC with effect from 17th May 139 [LG 1 August 1939, issue 34650, page 5325].

| | | | | W/Cdr | 25.07.45 | Retired list |

FLYING OFFICER [from PILOT OFFICER]

| 10100 | GRIFFIN | Frederick Carlton | | W/Cdr | 20.09.41 | Retired list |

On account of medical unfitness for Air Force service [LG 30 June 1950, supplement 38955, page 3361].

Appendix 3D - RAF [Cadet] College Cranwell

On the 1st of November 1919, Air Commodore Charles Alexander Holcombe Longcroft was appointed as the first Commandant of the Royal Air Force [Cadet] College, Cranwell, where as shown in this appendix the first entries of flight cadets assembled in the form of three intakes in 1920.

February 1920 [Naval] entry   15

The Naval entry consisted of midshipmen, thirteen of which had graduated from the Britannia Royal Naval College at Dartmouth, the exceptions being Henry Wells Foote [Tonbridge] and Cecil George Hancock [Osborne].

16001	BEATTY	Henry Longfield	F/L	+	15.02.35	210 Squadron

Flight Lieutenant Henry Longfield Beatty was the captain of Short Singapore III K3595 which with other Singapores departed Pembroke Dock bound for Basrah in Iraq. While in transit their aircraft, flying in bad weather, crashed into the side of Mount Beloritania near Messina in Sicily. There were no survivors from the crew of nine which included 41 year old Mr Reginald John Penn, a Senior Technical Officer attached to RAE Farnborough. A full account of this terrible accident will appear in a future volume.

16002	BROOKMAN	Herbert Geoffrey	F/L	+	22.04.36	

Flight Lieutenant Herbert Geoffrey Brookman contracted septicaemia and died while being treated in Peshawar Military Hospital.

16003	COLLINGWOOD	Cuthbert John	G/Capt		28.04.48	Retirement
16004	D'AETH	Narborough Hugh	AV-M		25.06.56	Retirement

Air Vice-Marshal Narborough Hugh D'aeth CB CBE Polar Medal three times mentioned in despatches, died on Tuesday, 21 January 1986. On retiring from his final service appointment, Senior Air Staff Officer, Headquarters Home Command, he entered Lincoln Theological College to train for Holy Orders and was ordained Deacon in December 1957. By 1960, he was holding an a position in Tasmania.

16005	DAVID	Edward Hugh Markham	G/Capt		29.05.50	Retirement

Group Captain Edward Hugh Markham David OBE, died on Saturday, 10th August 1957. My co-author has discovered, via Scotland's War - Orkney's War website, that a young 18-year old Sub-Lieutenant Edward David serving aboard HMS *Revenge*, flagship of Admiral Sir Sydney Fremantle, he witnessed the aftermath of the scuttling of the interned German High Seas Fleet at Scapa Flow on Sunday, 21st May 1919.

16006	DRABBLE	John Edward Layward	F/L		14.12.32	Retired list

At own request [LG 13 December 1932, issue 33891, page 7932].

16007	FOOTE	Henry Wells	F/O		09.04.27	Resigned
16040	GARNONS-WILLIAMS	Miles Herbert	G/Capt		22.04.45	Retirement

Group Captain Miles Herbert Garnons-Williams died in the War Memorial Hospital, Brecon, on Monday, 29th September 1952.

16008	HANCOCK	Cecil George	F/L		01.08.29	Dismissed

By sentence of General Court Marshal [LG 13 August 1929, issue 33525, page 5278].

16009	HARE	Bertram William Trelawney	F/L		15.06.35	Retired List

At his own request [LG 18 June 1935, issue 34171, page 3930].

16010	PECK	Jasper Godfrey	F/O	+	03.03.24	111 Squadron

Flying Officer Jasper Godfrey Peck was killed in a midair collision between his 7F.1 Snipe E6617, a dual control version, and an Avro 504K H3071 from 2 FTS which shared Duxford airfield with 111 Squadron. Flying Officer Peck's passenger, Flight Vauldrey Adolph Albrecht was injured, while Sergeant George Thomas Bond died in the Avro and his pupil, Pilot Officer William Alfred Tattersall survived, though injured. The accident occurred as the two aircraft were preparing to land.

16011	PRANCE	Dennis Caldwell	W/Cdr		06.08.42	Retirement
16012	SPENCER	Geoffrey Roger Cole	AV-M		10.07.56	Retirement

Air Vice-Marshal Geoffrey Roger Cole Spencer CB CBE twice mentioned in despatches, died on Sunday, 7th December 1969.

16013	WEEDON	Colin Winterbottom	AM		02.09.52	Retirement

Air Marshal Sir Colin Winterbottom Weedon KBE CB, died on Sunday, 16th February 1975.

16014	YALE	William Corbet	F/L	+	04.09.36	31 Squadron

Flight Lieutenant William Corbet Yale was killed and Leading Aircraftman John Mumbray injured when their Wapiti V J9730 collided with telegraph wires and crashed near Fort Sandeman in what was then the North West Frontier region of India. Today it is Zhob in Pakistan. Despite the damage J9730 was recovered and returned to the squadron's base at Drigh Road where it was repaired and returned to service. However, on 28th January 1937, it came to grief at Drigh Road and this time the damage was deemed terminal.

February 1920 [Schools] entry   32

16018	AKERMAN	Walter Joseph Martin	AV-M		14.03.56	Retirement

Air Vice-Marshal William Joseph Martin Akerman CB CBE three times mentioned in despatches, died on Wednesday, 9th December 1964.

16016	BARRETT	James Burnley	W/Cdr		23.04.43	Retirement

Wing Commander James Burnley Barrett died in Westminster Hospital on Saturday, 16th January 1954.

16025	BERNARD-SMITH	George Christopher Bernard	F/O		06.06.26	Resigned

[LG 15 June 1926, issue 33172, page 3901]. Flying Officer George Christopher Bernard Bernard-Smith was commissioned to the Reserve of Air Force Officers, retaining his original service number, on 22nd September 1936 [LG 13 October 1936, issue 34331, page 6541]. Rising to the rank of Wing Commander he was killed in a flying accident on the 10th of December 1941, whilst commanding 254 Squadron [Blenheim IVf V5801 QY-P], and is buried in Montrose [Sleepyhillockl] Cemetery [see RAFCCL 1939-1941, pages 168 and 169]

16027	BONHAM-CARTER	David William Frederick	A/Cmdr		27.02.53	Retirement

Air Commodore David William Frederick Bonham-Carter CB DFC mentioned in despatches, died on Friday, 17th May 1974.

16029	BROOK	William Arthur Darville	AV-M	+	17.08.53	AOC No 3 Group

Air Vice-Marshal William Arthur Darville Brook CB CBE twice mentioned in despatches was killed on Monday, 17th August 1953, while undergoing a jet conversion course at RAF Coningsby. Taking off in Meteor F.4 VT290 it was concluded that the Air Vice-Marshal lost consciousness and on coming too was unable to prevent his aircraft hitting a hedge and cartwheeling into a haystack at Litteywood Farm near Bradley-in-the-Moors, 5 miles NW of Uttoxeter, Staffordshire. At the time of his death he was Air Officer Commanding No. 3 Group, but had been notified he was to take up an appointment as Vice Chief of the Air Staff in September 1953.

| 21038 | BROWN | John Redvers | G/Capt | | 07.02.55 | Retirement |

I suspect Flying Officer J R Brown was allotted 21038 on his transfer from the General Duties Branch to the Stores Branch on 19th January 1925 [LG 27th January 1925, issue 33015, page 596].

| 16033 | COMBE | Gerald | AV-M | | 01.04.55 | Retirement |

Air Vice-Marshal Gerald Combe CB mentioned in despatches, died on Saturday, 15th December 1979.

| | CONNOLLY | Sylvanus George | F/L | + | 27.01.36 | 35 Squadron |

Flight Lieutenant Sylvanus George Connolly, Flight Lieutenant Philip Vaughan Edwards and Leading Aircraftman Frank Campling died when their Gordon IIIF K1776 of 35 Squadron spun out from cloud and crashed at Atbara near Gebeit airfield [now Port Sudan International Airport]. According to Air Ministry Form 1180, the Gordon was seen to pass behind some clouds from which it emerged in a spiral dive, partially recovered before spinning out of control. Flight Lieutenant Connolly managed to bale out but at too low an altitude for his parachute to deploy. All three airmen are buried in Khartoum War Cemetery.

| | DESMOND | Thomas Joseph | G/Capt | | 28.01.50 | Retirement |
| 16032 | FALCONER | Colin Logan | A/Cmdr | | 01.04.49 | Retirement |

Air Commodore Colin Logan Falconer CBE twice mentioned in despatches, died on Monday, 7th November 1994.

| | FORSTER | Edward Beresford | F/O | + | 26.05.28 | 84 Squadron |

Flying Officer Edward Beresford Forster was fatally injured in a motor car accident.

| 16035 | GAY | George William | S/Ldr | | 26.09.46 | Retirement |

On account of medical unfitness for Air Force service [LG 8 October 1946, supplement 37749, page 4985].

| 11074 | GORE | Charles William | A/Cmdr | | 15.10.56 | Retirement |

Air Commodore Charles William Gore OBE mentioned in despatches, died in June 1975. As a Pilot Officer he transferred from the General Duties Branch to the Stores Branch, thus having his service number amended. I have little doubt that his transfer was occasioned by losing his flying fitness; he was posted as a supernumerary non-effective owing to sickness to the Royal Air Force Depot on 22nd August 1922, from 31 Squadron in India. His photograph on the website Air of Authority shows him in Air Commodore dress, less his flying badge.

| 16041 | HAWTREY | John Gosset | AV-M | | 26.10.54 | |

Air Vice-Marshal John Gosset Hawtry CBE mentioned in despatches, died in San Remo, Italy, while returning overland to England from Iraq where he had handed over command as Air Officer Commanding, Air Headquarters Iraq to Air Vice-Marshal Hugh Hamilton Brookes. Air Vice Marshal Hawtrey was accompanied by his *Aide d'Camp* Flying Officer Rupert Holmes.

| | HAYTER | Matthew Charles | P/O | + | 24.10.22 | 24 Squadron |

Pilot Officer Matthew Charles Hayter was killed after losing control of Bristol F.2b F4831 while approaching RAF Kenley, the squadron's base. A detailed account of the accident, which occurred during the afternoon of Tuesday, the 24th October, was published in the Friday's edition on the *Surrey Mirror* in which an eyewitness gave evidence to the Coroner that Pilot Officer Hayter turned at 2,000 feet but with insufficient air speed and as a consequence the Bristol stalled and spun to the ground.

| | HAYTER- | Noel Cecil | F/O | + | 21.03.25 | 27 Squadron |

HAMES Flying Officer Noel Cecil Hayter-Hames was acting as observer to Flying Officer Edward John Dashwood during an operational bombing sortie during which Flying Officer Dashwood dived too low in DH.9A E8792 and ran into concentrated and accurate ground fire. With the bombs still attached the DH crashed and burst into flames near Torra Tukka in the Waziristan area of the North West Frontier. A detailed account of these operations, as submitted on 30th October 1925, from the India Office, can be read in supplement 33104, pages 7595 to 7601 of *The London Gazette* published on 20th November 1925.

| 16055 | HUXHAM | George Herbert | G/Capt | | 01.04.51 | Retirement |
| | LACEY | Ernest Vair Sleigh | F/L | + | 24.11.31 | Station Flight Kenley |

Flight Lieutenant Ernest Vair Sleigh Lacey and his passenger, Pilot Officer John Edward Shrimpton, were killed when their DH.60M Moth K1210, came into collision with a 23 Squadron Bristol Bulldog IIA K1677 flown by Pilot Officer Edmund Stokes who managed to land safely, though his fighter, which turned over, was sufficiently damaged that it was struck off charge on 7th February 1932. A report of the accident appeared the next day in *The Times* where it was stated that both aircraft were preparing to land and it is though neither pilot was aware of the other's presence, the Moth passing beneath the Bulldog and removing its undercarriage. Flight Lieutenant Lacey is buried in Whyteleafe [St. Luke's] Churchyard.

16021	MACKAY	Malcolm Bruce	G/Capt		02.05.50	Retirement
16023	MANGLES	Roland Arthur Ross	G/Capt		27.09.48	Retirement
16015	MILLS	George Holroyd	ACM		18.09.62	Retirement

Air Chief Marshal Sir George Mills GCB DFC twice mentioned in despatches, died on Wednesday, 14th April 1971. From June 1963, until his retirement in 1970, Sir George Mills held the position of Black Rod in the Houses of Parliament; he was also a Trustee of the Imperial War Museum.

| 16028 | MITCHELL | Frederick George Stewart | AV-M | | 29.07.58 | Retirement |

Air Vice-Marshal Frederick George Stewart Mitchell CB CBE, died on Wednesday, 13th February 1974.

| | PONTIFEX | Rupert William | F/O | + | 18.04.25 | 6 Squadron |

Flying Officer Rupert William Pontifex and Aircraft Edward Barber died when their Bristol F.2b F4961 was hit by rifle fire during a bombing mission, and crashed near Mirkhan-Sinjar in Iraq. On impact the Bristol burst into flames and was reduced to charred scrap.

| 16019 | REVINGTON | Arthur Patrick | A/Cmdr | | 04.01.54 | Retirement |

Air Commodore Arthur Pethick Revington CB CBE three times mentioned in despatches, died on Monday, 21st April 1986.

| 16026 | ROWE | Francis Charles Thorn | F/L | | 14.08.33 | Retirement |

Flight Lieutenant F C T Rowe returned to the service in the Second World War and took up a post in the Technical Branch on 24th April 1940, retaining his service number. Subsequently rising to Wing Commander rank he retired for a second time on 14th November 1945.

| 16042 | SHEPHERD | Gordon Carruthers | G/Capt | | 09.06.54 | Retirement |
| 16088 | SPAIGHT | Robert Henry Seymour | A/Cmdr | | 21.08.50 | Retirement |

Air Commodore Robert Henry Seymour Spaight CBE, died on Saturday, 20th November 1993. The Air of Authority website notes that as a Flight Cadet he was involved in a motorcycle accident which nearly resulted in the loss of a leg. However, the surgeon who operated him was able to save the limb and Flight Cadet Spaight graduated with a permanent commission on 21st April 1923 [LG 19 June 1923, issue 32835, page 4279].

| | SPRINGFIELD | Cecil Montague Oakes Osbourne | P/O | | 10.01.23 | Retired list |

On account of ill-health [LG 9 January 1923, issue 32785, page 225].

| | STONE | Cecil John | F/O | | 12.06.29 | Relinquished |

Flying Officer Cecil John Stone relinquished his permanent commission on transferring to the army [LG 21 June 1929, issue 33508, page 4123]. He served as a Lieutenant with the East Surrey Regiment [LG 11 June 1929, issue 33505, page 3860].

| 16031 | STONE | Ralph Ashinhurst Bird | G/Capt | | 13.12.46 | Retirement |
| 16017 | WAITE | Reginald Newnham | A/Cmdr | | 19.09.53 | Retirement |

Air Commodore Reginald Newnham Waite CB CBE mentioned in despatches, died on Wednesday, 7th May 1975.

| | WHELAN | Robert Darley | F/O | + | 03.12.27 | 12 Squadron |

Flying Officer Robert Darley Whelan and Aircraftsman Arthur Henry Lacy died after encountering fog while flying in Fairey Fox I J7941. Seeking to make a precautionary landing, Flying Officer Whelan flew into a tree on The Ridgeway near Enfield, Middlesex. J7941 was the first production Fox and flew for the first time on 10th December 1925. Later converted to dual control configuration it was delivered to the squadron in July 1927. A poster print of this aircraft can be obtained from *Flight Global*.

| 16043 | BARNES | Leonard Kelly | | A/Cmdr | + | 14.12.48 | EANS Shawbury |

Air Commodore Leonard Kelly Barnes CBE mentioned in despatches, died on Tuesday, 14th December 1948, during his tenure as Commandant of the Empire Air Navigation School, Shawbury where he had endeared himself to staff and pupils alike by substituting his pilots' flying badge for a navigator's half-wing. As a Flight Cadet in 1922, he was awarded the Abdy Gerrard Fellows Memorial Prize.

| 16044 | BENNETT | Victor Bruce | | A/Cmdr | | 22.10.47 | Retirement |

Air Commodore Victor Bruce Bennett DFC twice mentioned in despatches, died on Wednesday, 9th May 1973.

| | BETT | David Lindsey Gordon | | F/L | + | 17.01.33 | |

Flight Lieutenant David Lindsey Gordon Bett died in RAF Halton Hospital following an operation.

| | CAITHNESS | James Ernest Stewart | | P/O | | 02.05.23 | Resigned |
| | CHARLTON | John Sills | | P/O | | 24.10.23 | Resigned |

LG 23 October 1923, issue 32873, page 7118. Although having resigned his commission, it was not until 24th July 1945, that his name was removed from the Royal Air Force [LG 4 August 1925, issue 33072, page 5219]. John Sills Charlton returned to the service in the Second World War and as a Flight Lieutenant was commissioned to the Administrative and Special Duties Branch with effect from 18th September 1939, and given the service No. 75503 [LG 14 November 1939, issue 34733, page 7645].

| | | | | S/Ldr | | 01.04.42 | Resigned |
| | COVENTRY | Edward Bernard | | P/O | + | 29.09.23 | 39 Squadron |

Pilot Officer Edward Bernard and Corporal William Wardle died within minutes of taking off from Spittlegate in DH.9A E8695/9 after control was lost causing the DH to dive to the ground and burst into flames.

| 16050 | DAWSON | Walter Lloyd | | ACM | | 06.05.60 | Retirement |

Air Chief Marshal Sir Walter Dawson KCB CBE DSO, died on Friday, 10th June 1994.

| 16066 | GUPPY | Cecil | | W/Cdr | | 03.02.45 | Retirement |
| 24070 | HANCOCK | Richard Claude | | F/O | | 19.03.32 | To Class A |

Notification cancelled [LG 30 September 1932, issue 33868, page 6178]. Granted Acting Squadron Leader rank, 2nd May 1936, whilst employed with the Indian Air Force [LG 30 June 1936, issue 34300, page 4164].

| | | | | W/Cdr | + | 10.06.41 | |

Wing Commander Richard Claude Hancock mentioned in despatches, is buried in Lustleigh Church Cemetery, Devon.

16053	HEALY	Ernest Alton		G/Capt		02.11.46	Retirement
16054	HODGSON	Edgar Arnott		G/Capt		01.07.50	Retirement
	JOHNSON	Anson Geoffrey Stewart		P/O		17.05.24	Removed

'Pilot Officer Anson Geoffrey Stewart Johnson is removed from the RAF, His Majesty having no further use for his services.' [LG 30 May 1924, issue 32940, page 4313].

| | KEEY | Edward Charles | | P/O | + | 15.10.23 | CFS Upavon |

Pilot Officer Edward Charles Keey was approaching to land at RAE Farnborough in Bristol F.2b J6665 when he lost flying speed, stalled and crashed.

| | KEEY | Montague William | | F/L | + | 15.07.37 | |

Flight Lieutenant Montague Willian Keey died on Thursday, 15th July 1937. He was the brother of Pilot Officer Edward Charles Keey, tabled above, who predeceased him. Both were educated at Imperial Service College and on their arrival at Cranwell, Edward was placed in A Squadron and Montague in B Squadron.

| 16057 | KING-LEWIS | Arthur | | G/Capt | | 04.02.48 | Retirement |
| 16058 | MACFADYEN | Douglas | | AM | | 29.04.59 | Retirement |

Air Marshal Sir Douglas Macfadyen KCB CBE mentioned in despatches, died on Friday, 26th July 1968. Flight Cadet Macfadyen graduated in August 1922, with the Sword of Honour for his entry. His son, Ian David Macfadyen, born 19th February 1942, also entered RAFC Cranwell, rising to the rank of Air Marshal.

| 16059 | MATURIN | Charles Bagot Beaumont Maturin | | F/O | | 24.06.24 | Resigned |

Returned to the service as a Pilot Officer on 26th September 1939, within the Administrative and Special Duties Branch [LG 3 October 1939, issue 34700, page 6662], service No. 74534 amended to 84534.

| | | | | W/Cdr | | 20.07.54 | Relinquished |
| 16060 | PELLY | Claude Bernard Raymond | | ACM | | 13.11.59 | Retirement |

Air Chief Marshal Sir Claude Pelly GBE KCB MC ADC three times mentioned in despatches, died on Saturday, 12th August 1972.

| | RATCLIFFE | Charles Harrington | | F/O | | 26.09.28 | Resigned |
| | REID | Ellis | | F/O | + | 12.11.24 | 1 Squadron |

Flying Officer Ellis Reid was flying a dual controlled 7F.1 Snipe F2499, accompanied by Lieutenant William Henry Edwin Cotter, when he lost control and spun into the ground near the airfield at Hinaidi. The impact killed Flying Officer Reid but Lieutenant Cotter survived, though very seriously injured. At RAFM Hendon records for Flying Officer Reid show that as a Flight Cadet he forced-landed at 1300 hours, without injury, in Avro 504K E3320, but at midday on 14th February 1923, while flying solo in 2 Squadron Bristol F.2b J6593 he spun in off a turn at Farnborough and was seriously injured [J6593 was repaired and by January 1926, was on the strength of 14 Squadron in Trans-Jordan].

16062	RICCARD	Cecil Stanley		G/Capt		01.01.51	Retirement
16085	SEALY	Charles Forbes		G/Capt		25.12.54	Retirement
16063	STEVENS	Charles Herbert		G/Capt		12.01.48	Retirement
11072	VALLANCE	Roper Guy Aymer		W/Cdr		04.09.49	Retirement
	VINTCENT	Neville		F/O			Resigned

In the King's Birthday Honours list 1938, Neville Vintcent Esq. DFC, Manager of Tata's Aviation Department in Bombay, was honoured with the MBE [LG 9 June 1938, supplement 34518, page 3703].

| | WALLER | Robert Richard Studdert | | F/O | + | 10.05.25 | 31 Squadron |

Flying Officer Robert Richard Studdert died on 10th May 1925, from injuries received in a night flying accident at Ambala 24-hours previously, the identity of his Bristol F.2b not being recorded. Like so many pilots of this age, he had survived several mishaps while serving with the squadron. On 11th January 1924, a problem with the petrol feed on Bristol F.2b J6647/K obliged him to make a forced-landing at Dardoni during which the starboard wheel dropped into a ditch, damaging the airframe. Repaired, it was issued to 20 Squadron where it was first coded F and later D before returning to 31 Squadron and another crash, this time at Hyderabad on 26th November 1928. Meanwhile, on 2nd December 1924, Flying Officer Waller was tasked to go to the Aircraft Park at Lahore and pick up Bristol F.2b D8097. On return to Ambala he misjudged his approach and crashed-landed. Damage was slight and squadron returns show D8097 being on charge between January and April 1925.

Appendix 3E - Short Service Commissions

Paul McMillan has unearthed a most useful item regarding short service commissioned officers and the Reserve of Air Force Officers and though the item has been taken from the Air Estimates for 1923-1924, some of the detail relates to the situation facing the Royal Air Force in its formative years. The Air Estimates for 1923-1924, sanctioned a force comprising of seven hundred pilots supported by twelve thousand airmen, the majority of pilots to be short service commissioned. The concept for the short service commission officer had been formulated in July 1919, which set the terms of engagement as three years service followed by four years reserve service. At the time when many of these officers commissioned in 1919, was reaching the end of their three year term of service, the establishment of the Reserve of Air Force Officers [RAFO] had been conceived and it was envisaged that around a hundred or so would join the Reserve which would be open to ex-wartime and commercial pilots. Royal approval for the RAFO had been granted in December 1921, but over twelve months would elapse before it featured in the compilations of the Air Force List, by which time [1920] the three year term of service for short service commissioned officers, initially optional, was set at four years. An asterisk ahead of a surname indicates appointment to a permanent commission. Entries showing relinquishment of a commission in 1954, invariably falls within the provisions of the Navy, Army and Air Force Reserves Act of 10th February 1954. Remarks appended to officers who served with the Medical Branch have in the main been condensed from their obituary notices in the *British Medical Journal* which I have pleasure in acknowledging.

LG 6 January 1920, issue 31720, pages 200 and 201 - 9 appointees

FLIGHT LIEUTENANT
2

BOURN	Dudley George	F/L		06.01.20	Cancelled
PRITCHARD OBE	John Edward Maddock	F/L	+	24.08.21	Air Ministry

Flight Lieutenant John Edward Maddock Pritchard was killed in the loss of HM Airship R.38 [ZR.2] which broke up in flight over the River Humber. Of the forty-nine persons aboard R.38, forty-four were killed, two were injured, including the pilot Flight Lieutenant Archibald Herbert Wann ans, miraculously, three escaped without physical hurt but were obviously very shocked. As my co-author reports, Flight Lieutenant Pritchard, who was included in the crew as the Air Ministry's representative, was highly experienced in airship operations and had commanded non-rigid airships duuring his RNAS service and later as an air force officer. Born in Leighton Buzzard, Bedfordshire in 1889, a biography of his life can be read on *Wikipedia*.

FLYING OFFICERS
4

07238	MANN DFC	William Edward George	A/Cmdr		18.04.45	Retirement

Air Commodore Edward George Mann CB CBE DFC twice mentioned in despatches, died on Wednesday, 4th May 1966. Prior to his appointment he had been transferred to the Unemployed List on 27th August 1919, following his initial RNAS service and subsequent attachment to 208 Squadron with which he was a Flight Commander, appointed on 27th August 1918. During his long service he specialised in communications.

	MUDGE	Lorenzo Alfred	F/O	+	05.05.25

Died from heart failure in RN Hospital Chatham where he was being treated for a fractured left femur and shock.

PHILLIPS	Francis John	F/O	06.01.39	Relinquished

As Captain Francis John Phillips he is mentioned in the New Year's Honours List for 1941, when he was Deputy Controller and Air Raid Precautions Officer, Southampton and appointed MBE [LG 1 January 1941, supplement 35029, page 14].

WALE	Norman Walter	F/O	18.09.31	To Class B

Granted a commission in Class CC, General Duties Branch, 1st January 1936, retaining his rank [LG 15 November 1938, issue 34570, page 7197] and allotted service No. 70701.

	F/L	01.05.44	Relinquished

On ceasing to be employed [LG 9 May 1944, supplement 36503, page 2116].

FLYING OFFICER [from PILOT OFFICER]

11040	*McCREARY	Albert Edward Frederick	F/L	05.07.34	Retired list
			W/Cdr	30.07.46	Retired list

Returned to the service and served until reverting to the Retired list.

OBSERVER OFFICER

HOLLIS	John Augustus	O/O	06.01.20	Cancelled

See Short Service Commission officers for 10th August 1920.

OBSERVER OFFICER [from PILOT OFFICER]

ANDERSON DFC	Alexander Melvin	O/O	05.10.21	Resigned

Granted a commission, on probation, in the Reserve of Air Force Officers, 22nd May 1923, in the rank of Flying Officer [LG 22 May 1923, issue 32825, page 3617].

	F/O	15.11.33	Relinquished

On account of ill-health [LG 14 November 1933, issue 33995, page 7375].

LG 20 January 1920, issue 31743, page 836

FLIGHT LIEUTENANT

HINSHELWOOD	Thomas	Major	11.04.22	Relinquished

DSC DFC On account of physical unfitness for full flying duties [LG 2 May 1922]. Paul McMillan, my co-author, reports that Major Thomas Hinshelwood DSC DFC died at Billesdon in Leicestershire on Saturday, 16th June 1928.

FLYING OFFICERS
5

	BAXTER	Eric Gordon	F/O		20.01.20	Cancelled
07009	*CARTER	Guy Lloyd	A/Cmdr	+	18.07.44	AOC HQ Balkan AF

Air Commodore Guy Lloyd Carter DSO AFC three times mentioned in despatches, is buried in Bari War Cemetery, Italy. He was 44 years of age. While ranked Group Captain he was awarded the DSO [LG 19 February 1943, supplement 35911, page 883]; *'This officer has commanded the fighter force in the Western Desert with conspicuous success. Despite the magnitude of his task, Group Captain Carter has flown on numerous sorties. He has displayed high powers of leadership and great courage throughout.'*

07057	*DIXON AFC	Noel Parker	G/Capt	03.07.45	Retired list

	*PYNE	George Henry Ernest	F/O	14.01.29	Retired list

Granted a commission in Class C, retaining his rank, with effect from 4th August 1936 [LG 2 March 1937, issue 34376, page 1418]. Transferred to Class CC 7th May 1938, and whilst in Class CC died on 5th November 1938, as reported in the *Biggleswade Chronicle* published on 11th November 1938. Flight Lieutenant George Ernest Pyne was 54 years of age, and died following an illness of three weeks duration. The article went on to say that his military service was spread over four decades from the Royal Fusiliers, secondment to the Royal Army Service Corps and later the Royal Air Force and, it seems, at the time of his death he was Adjutant at Henlow. My co-author adds that two sons, Flight Lieutenant Derrick Joseph Oswald Pyne died [by one of the quirks of fate] on 5th November 1943, and is commemorated on panel 2, column 2, of the Ottawa Memorial, and an older brother, Sergeant Thomas Basil George Pyne serving with 73 Squadron was shot down and killed on 14th May 1940. His Hurricane [either P2856 as recorded in squadron records or N2334 in an official postwar report] crashing in the Bois de Voncq. First laid to rest in Voncq French National Cemetery, Sergeant Pyne now rests in Choloy War Cemetery. See page 268 of Peter D Cornwell's *The Battle of France Then and Now - Six Nations Locked in Aerial Combat September 1939 to June 1940* [After the Battle, 2007].

10052	*SMITH	Arthur William	G/Capt	18.11.47	Retirement

OBSERVER OFFICER [from PILOT OFFICER]

MUNSON	Edward James			

Granted a commission in the Administrative and Special Duties Branch for the duration of hostilities in the rank of Pilot Officer with effect from 19th September 1939, allotted service No. 74189 [LG 26 September 1939, issue 34694, page 6506]. F/L   07.09.54   Relinquished

LG 30 January 1920, issue 31761, page 1264

FLIGHT LIEUTENANT [from HON. FLYIMG OFFICER]

HEDGCOCK	Frederick Joseph Warr	F/L	30.02.20	Cancelled

FLYING OFFICERS
8

	BOTTOMS	Arthur but by 12th December 1922, as per entry in the *Gazette* on that date, issue 32776, page 8799, now known as:			
	*CUDDEN-DAVIS	Arthur Wilfred			
07024	COLBECK MBE	Paul	F/O	17.09.28	Relinquished

A document for this officer is held at TNA Kew under AIR 76/96/72. Paul Colbeck was born on 17th September 1878, and died on 22nd May 1970.

FRITH	Charles Victor	F/O	10.12.23	Resigned
GREBBY DFC	Reginald John Patrick	F/O	03.05.33	Relinquished

On account off ill-health contracted on active service [LG 9 May 1922, issue 32695, page 3626].

LEECH	Edgar James	F/O	22.08.23	Resigned
PALMER	Robert Daniel Cecil	F/O +	02.08.20	6 Squadron

See my summary for details of his death.

STERLING DFC	Robert	F/O	06.12.21	Relinquished

On account of physical unfitness for flying duties.

08023 WRIGHT	Frank	G/Capt	01.09.40	

On 17th September 1956, and having retired from the Royal Air Force, Group Captain Frank Wright CBE was granted a commission in the Royal Air Force Volunteer Reserve, Training Branch in the rank of Flying Officer. F/O   17.09.62   Relinquished

FLYING OFFICERS [from PILOT OFFICERS]
2

KNOX	Arthur	F/O	30.01.27	Relinquished

TNA Kew has a document for this officer under AIR 76/281/99.

TISDALL	Michael Henry [See my summary for 48 Squadron recording his death on Tuesday, 23rd December 1919].			

OBSERVER OFFICER

HUTCHINSON	Harold	F/O +	02.08.20	6 Squadron

See my summary for the circumstances of his death.

OBSERVER OFFICERS [from PILOT OFFICERS]
2

MORTIMORE	William Beresford	F/O	30.01.27	Relinquished
VICKERS	John Harold	Lieutenant	20.04.23	Relinquished

On account of ill-health contracted in the Service [LG 18 May 1923, issue 32824, page 3533].

LG 9 March 1920, issue 31816, page 2906.

FLIGHT LIEUTENANT
2

06133	*SLESSOR MC	John Cotesworth	MRAF	31.12.52	Retirement

Marshal of the Royal Air Force Sir John Slessor GCB DSO MC three times mentioned in despatches, died on Thursday, 12th July 1979. Born on the 3rd of June 1897, John Cotesworth Slessor's childhood was marred when he contracted polio which left him lame in both legs. Nevertheless, he overcame his disability and on 6th July 1915, succeeded in obtaining his Aviators Certificate [No. 1447]. Leaving the service in 1919, he pursued a number of occupations including ferrying Bristol F.2bs to the Middle East and assisting in keeping open a power house during the General Strike. In 1920, he accepted a short service commission which almost immediately became permanent. In retirement he wrote *The Central Blue* [Cassel, 1956].

TAYLOR MBE	Lester Edward			

FLYING OFFICER [from PILOT OFFICER]

HARPER MC	William Eardley	F/O	01.05.20	Relinquished

On account of ill-health [LG 4 May 1920, issue 31886, page 5106].

LG 30 March 1920, issue 31841, pages 3900 and 3901

SQUADRON LEADER

	*DOUGLAS MC	William Sholto	MRAF	01.11.47	Retirement

Marshal of the Royal Air Force Lord Douglas of Kirtleside Baron, GCB MC DFC three times mentioned in despatches, died on Friday, 31st October 1969. Similar to Marshal of the Royal Air Force Slessor, William Sholto Douglas left the service in 1919, and, briefly, was a civilian pilot in the employment of Hadley Page during which he accomplished a number of aviation 'firsts' including the first cross-Channel commercial flight to Brussels in July 1919. Becoming disenchanted with civilian flying, he left Handley Page and it was only in a chance meeting with Trenchard that he decided to return to the Royal Air Force. He is remembered most as Sir Hugh Dowding's successor as Air Officer Commanding in Chief Fighter

Command, a post that he held from November 1940 to January 1943. In 1963, he penned two autobiographies *Years of Combat* and *Years of Command* both being published by Collins.

FLYING OFFICERS
6

	ASHBY	Gordon Doré	F/O	30.03.32	Relinquished

Returned to the service and granted a commission as a Pilot Officer in the Administrative and Special Duties Branch, effective from 28th February 1939 [LG 7 March 1939, issue 34605, page 1553] with service No. 72601.

			W/Cdr	18.05.54	Relinquished
	CRAIGEN	John Samuel James	F/O	26.03.34	Relinquished

Returned to the service and granted a commission in the General Duties Branch, Class C, effective 245h July 1939, seniority 24th July 1925 [LG 1st August 1939, issue 34650, page 5325] with service No. 70937.

			F/L	26.03.45	Resigned
	LOGSDAIL	Edward William	F/O +	07.07.23	24 Squadron

Flying Officer Edward William Logsdail who was being instructed by Flying Officer Marcel Gustavo Louis Trapagna-Leroy AFC in DH.9A H3431 died when the tail section of their aircraft broke away during recovery from a steep dive, initiated at 1,500 feet, and out of control crashed onto a house in Kenley, bursting into flames on impact. Not surprisingly, in view of the magnitude of the tragedy, the crash was given widespread press coverage and a detailed account will appear in the next volume of this work.

08088	*SAKER	Harold John	S/Ldr	08.01.38	Retired list

At his own request [LG 11 January 1938, issue 34472, page 194]. Returned to the service and was promoted Wing Commander 12th March 1940 [LG 12th March 1940, issue 34810, page 1472].

			G/Capt	11.03.46	Retired list
08113	*SINCLAIR DFC	Findlay Willard	W/Cdr	13.07.44	Retirement

On account of ill-health [LG 25 July 1944, supplement 36622, page 3449].

08227	WORMELL	Eric	F/O	30.03.35	To Class C

Transferred from the General Duties Branch to the Administrative and Special Duties Branch, 29th August 1939 [LG 12 December 1939, issue 34752, page 8254].

			S/Ldr	21.09.54	Relinquished

FLYING OFFICERS [from PILOT OFFICERS]
3

	HOLTHOUSE	John	F/O	24.01.21	Resigned

Joined the South African Air Force.

	O'BRIEN-SAINT	James Terence	F/O	15.01.28	Resigned
	STAFFORD	Ernest Robert	F/O	02.09.28	Relinquished

LG 20 April 1920, issue 31870, pages 4575 and 4576

FLIGHT LIEUTENANT
3

	*McLAREN MB	Duncan	AV-M	06.02.50	Retirement

Paul McMillan reports Air Vice-Marshal Duncan McLaren CBE MB Ch.B, died at Cobham in Surrey, on Saturday, 1st November 1980.

	*SIMPSON	Sturley Philip	AV-M	27.03.47	Retirement

Air-Vice Marshal Sturley Philip Simpson CB CBE MC twice mentioned in despatches, died on Thursday, 28th April 1966.

	*WISEMAN	Percy John	A/Cmdr	09.02.46	Retirement

Air Commodore Percy John Wiseman CBE, died on Saturday, 16th October 1948. During the Second World War he held the position of Command Accountant in Ballon Command, Fighter Command, Allied Expeditionary Force and Air Defence Great Britain, and Fighter Command.

FLYING OFFICERS
5

	COOK	Brian Herbert	F/O	20.04.31	Relinquished
08086	RUSSELL	Herbert John Tuson	F/L	20.04.31	Relinquished

Flight Lieutenant Herbert John Tuson Russell was granted a commission in Class C of the Reserve of Air Force Officers with effect from 9th November 1937, retaining his rank [LG 23 November 1937, issue 34457, page 7353]. On 1st October 1938, his commission was amended to Class CC [LG 13 December 1938, issue 34579, page 7921].

			W/Cdr	20.10.45	Relinquished

On account of medical unfitness for Air Force service [LG 6 November 1945, supplement 37336, page 5390].

	SPRINGETT	Bernard Penfold	F/O	26.10.21	Dismissed

Flying Officer Bernard Penfold Springett was dismissed the service by sentence of General Court Martial. There is little doubt, as Paul McMillan has discovered, that Flying Officer Springett was something of a rogue. An extract from the *Police Gazette* published on Wednesday, October 4th, 1922, under Apprehensions - Surrey, reads: *'Walton-on-Thames [Co.] - By obtaining £5 by false pretences. Bernard Penfold Springett, b. 1892, 5ft. 8ins., medium build, c.fresh, h.ginger [dull], e.grey [piercing], clean shaven: dress, grey lounge suit, brown or grey trilby hat. In possession of cheque book on the London County Westminster & Parr's Bank, Kingston-on-Thames Branch, Nos, D24514 onwards, and cheques are drawn on the Hon. G Savile's No. 2 a/c, and signed B P Springett.. Has cashed several cheques, generally through hotel keepers. Last heard of on South Coast. Warrant issued.'* Apprehended, his case was reported in the *Sunday Mirror* published on 29th October 1922: *'Bernard Penfold Springett, thirty, was sentenced at Bow-street yesterday to four months' imprisonment in the second division for obtaining £6 by means of a worthless cheque from Mr. Samuel Bennett Sharp, a Covent Garden fruit merchant. In two other cases where warrants had been granted against him for obtaining money at Esher and Ramsgate were also taken into consideration. Springett was acquitted of two further charges of embezzling £612s from Captain the Hon. George Savile of Thames Ditton, by whom he had been employed as secretary, and of obtaining credit for food and lodging by fraud at a Covent Garden hotel. Mr. Leyeester [the Magistrate] accepted his explanation that he used Captain Savile's money for petty disbursements.'* Bernard Springett next turns up over a decade later in Australia, again the subject of interest to the police, having deserted from the Royal Australian Air Force station at Laverton, Victoria, on 3rd July 1940. A note in the Police Gazette for 1945, indicates he had been *"Recovered"*. Australian records show he was born on 3rd April 1895, and was discharged from the service on 2nd October 1940.

	WEEKS	Reginald Victor	F/O	20.04.31	Relinquished

Flying Officer Reginald Victor Weeks was granted a commission in the Balloon Branch, ranked Flight Lieutenant, on 8th February 1937 [LG 15 June 1937, issue 34408, page 3862]. Appointed Adjutant [LG 27 July 1937, issue 34421, page 4818]. His death at 17 Cranleigh Parade, Stanstead, Surry, was announced on Tuesday, 5th October 1937.

	WEST MC	Theodore James	F/L	19.04.27	Relinquished

On account of ill-health [LG 2 August 1927, issue 33299, page 5001]. His MC was *Gazetted* on 25th November 1916, supplement 29837, page 11546: *'For conspicuous gallantry in action. He attacked an enemy machine and brought it down, displaying great courage and ability.'*

FLYING OFFICER [from PILOT OFFICER]

	ARMITAGE	Henry John	F/O	08.12.26	Relinquished

On account of ill-health [LG 7 December 1926, issue 33227, page 8004].

AIKEN   Lawrence William   F/O   +   01.06.25   60 Squadron

Flying Officer Lawrence William Aiken, serving at Miranshah, died in Nowshera Hospital where he had been admitted with Enteric fever.

WHIPPEY DFC   Frederic Arthur   F/O   20.04.39   Relinquished

My co-author reports Flying Officer Frederic Arthur Whippey DFC was born in Dulwich on 21st May 1893, and died at Richmond on Tuesday, 13th February 1973.

LG 4 May 1920, issue 31886, page 5104

FLIGHT LIEUTENANT

GRIBBEN MC   Edward   F/L   04.05.20   Cancelled

Returned to army duties.

FLYING OFFICER [from FLIGHT LIEUTENANT]

*BALFOUR MC   Harold Harington   F/L   22.08.23   Resigned

Permitted to retain the rank of Captain [LG 24 August 1923, issue 32856, page 5768]. Entering politics, he was unsuccessful in gaining Stratford in 1924, but in 1929, was elected as Member of Parliament for Isle of Thanet. Subsequently, he was held the post of Under-Secretary of State for Air. His biography can be accessed on *Wikipedia* which records his *Great War* service, first with the 60th Rifles and later with the Royal Flying Corps where he flew scouts with 60 and 43 Squadrons, achieving nine combat successes.

FLYING OFFICERS
3

MACQUEEN   Alexander John   F/O   +   05.07.20   12 Squadron

Please refer to the summary for information concerning his death.

PRITT MC   Walbanke Ashby   F/O   08.12.20   Resigned

ROBERTSON   James   F/O   09.06.27   Relinquished

FLYING OFFICER from PILOT OFFICER

MITCHELL   Harold John   F/O   04.05.27   Relinquished

OBSERVER OFFICER [from PILOT OFFICER]

LOCHNER   John Tobias Albert   F/O   +   21.11.24   208 Squadron

South Africa Flying Officer John Tobias Albert Lochner died from pneumonia and is buried in Ismailia War Memorial Cemetery. He was born in 1892, at Moorseesburg in Cape Colony and had served since 13th March 1918.

LG 14 May 1920, issue 31900, page 5487

CHAPLAINS BRANCH
4

CRAWSHAW   Aubrey Aitken   S/Ldr   12.10.20   Relinquished

Permitted to retain Honorary Chaplin to the Royal Air Force [LG 12 September 1920, page 9892].

DAVIES BA   George Anthony   G/Capt   15.01.38   Retired list

At his own request [LG 25 January 1938, issue 34476, page 529]. His promotion to the relative rank of Group Captain was promulgated on 28th June 1935 [LG 23 July 1935, issue 34182, page 4776].

LAW   John Talbot Skinner   Reverend   01.04.23   Relinquished

Appointed Honorary Chaplin to the Royal Air Force [LG 30 March 1923, issue 32810, pages 2420 and 2421].

STILL MA   John Henry Pelllatt   S/Ldr   01.11.37   Retired list

At his own request [LG 2 November 1937, issue 34450, page 6824]. His promotion to the relative rank of Squadron Leader was promulgated in *The London Gazette* 13th August 1920, issue 32017, page 8410.

LG 18 May 1920, issue 31904, page 5609

FLIGHT LIEUTENANT

06140   TAYLOR AFC   Alfred George   F/L   23.02.28   To Class C

Returned to the service and commissioned, retaining his rank effective 1st September 1939, in the Administrative and Special Duties Branch [LG 28th November 1939, issue 34742, page 7966].   W/Cdr   22.08.42   Relinquished

On account of ill-health [LG 1 September 1942, supplement 35686, page 3816].

FLYING OFFICER [from FLIGHT LIEUTENANT]

08089   *SANDERSON DFC Alfred Clifford   AM   14.02.55   Retirement

Air Marshal Sir Clifford Sanderson KBE CB DFC twice mentioned in despatches, died on Wednesday, 28th January 1976. Born on 19th February 1898, he flew as pilot in the *Great War* with 16 Squadron and was wounded in his right hand on 6th May 1917, when his RE.8 A4596 was shot about by hostile aircraft during a photographic reconnaissance mission. His observer, Lieutenant P A B Lytton escaped without injury [as per report by Trevor Henshaw, page 87, *The Sky Their Battlefield*]. Treated in 42 Casualty Clearing Station before transfer to No. 8 General Hospital, Second Lieutenant Sanderson was evacuated to England aboard HMHS *Panama*. In September 1918, he returned to the Western Front as a Flight Commander attached to 46 Squadron [Camel]. Prior to his granting of a short service commission, he had been on the Unemployed list since 22nd January 1919. According to the website Air of Authority, Air Marshal Sir Clifford Sanderson retired in order to facilitate advancement for younger officers.

FLYING OFFICERS
8

DANIEL   Frank Charles   Lieutenant   13.10.20   Unemployed

HAWKINS   Harold Clive   Lieutenant   11.02.20   Unemployed

07171   *HYDE   William Vincent   W/Cdr   15.11.46   Retirement

ILES AFC   Leslie Millington   AV-M   04.11.48   Retirement

Air Vice-Marshal Leslie Millington Iles CBE AFC twice mentioned in despatches, died on Friday, 13th December 1974.

07242   *MARTIN   Leon   G/Capt   06.12.47   Retirement

*MILNE   Robert Ernest   F/L   27.02.31   Dismissed

Canada Flight Lieutenant Robert Ernest Milne was dismissed the service by sentence of General Court Martial. Paul McMillan, my co-author, has established that Flight Lieutenant Milne served with 28 Squadron in India during 1928. His dismissal from the service was picked up by and reported in the *Western Morning News*. It seems that by 1939, he was in the employment of Air Service Flying Limited at Hamble as a flying instructor and referred to as Flight Lieutenant Robert Ernest Milne. Born in Saskatchewan on 23rd January 1899, he died in England at Gosport, Hampshire on Friday, 27th August 1976.

PEMELL	Harold Thomas		Captaain	30.03.21	Resigned
SAWYER	Herbert Gifford		S/Ldr	01.03.37	Retired list

At his own request [LG 12 March 1937, issue 34379, page 1646].

FLYING OFFICERS [from PILOTS OFFICERS]
3

	ATEN DFC	Marion Hughes	F/O	18.05.31	Relinquished
	BLYTHE	Percy Robert	F/O	18.05.20	Cancelled
07095	FULFORD	Edgar	F/O	18.05.33	To Class C

Continued in service during the Second World War. S/Ldr 08.06.54 Relinquished

OBSERVER OFFICERS [from PILOT OFFICERS]
2

09013	*HESKETH DFC	Allan	A/Cmdr	08.07.54	Retirement

Air Commodore Allan Hesketh CB CBE DFC twice mentioned in despatches, died on Friday, 9th March 1973. On 24th February 1921, he was injured in the crash of Avro 504K F8751 of 4 Squadron, Farnborough, which spun in near Cove in Hampshire, killing the pilot, Flying Officer William Leslie Gordon Spinney.

11064	*REDMAN DFC	Albert James	G/Capt	26.03.49	Retirement

Group Captain Albert James Redman DFC was granted a commission in the Royal Air Force Volunteer Reserve, Training Branch, effective from 9th January 1950 [LG 17 October 1950, supplement 39043, page 5163]. F/O 31.07.53 Resigned

LG 1 June 1920, issue 31924, page 6087

CHAPLAINS BRANCH
6

DUNNE MC	M J			
GILLAN MA BD	David Hedley	G/Capt	11.02.21	

The Reverend David Hedley Gillan MA BA is granted the relative rank of Group Captain for the purpose of precedence, discipline and administration [LG 11 February 1921, issue 32224, page 1190].

JONES MC	Sydney J			
HALL OBE	Richard			
HOBSON	James Sydney	Reverend	31.08.22	Resigned
MOFFATT MA BD	William	G/Capt	13.08.20	

The Reverend William Moffatt MA BD is granted the relative rank of Group Captain whilst employed as Staff Chaplin [LG 13 August 1920, issue 32017, page 8410].

LG 8 June 1920, issue 31933, page 6343

FLYING OFFICER [from FLIGHT LIEUTENANT]

BIRKBECK DFC Robert Alexander Amended - See LG 15 June 1920, issue 31942, page 6587].

FLYING OFFICERs
4

21045	*BOURNE	William	W/Cdr	26.08.42	Retirement

Re-employed. W/Cdr 04.04.47 Retired list

06243	BUDGE	Arthur Stanley	F/O	10.10.31	Relinquished

Commissioned in theGeneral Duties Branch of the Royal Air Force Volunteer Reserve with effect from 1st September 1939, as an Acting Flight Lieutenant [LG 20 October 1939, issue 34713, page 7042] but immediately transferred to the Administrative and Special Duties Branch [LG 20th October 1939, issue 34713, page 7045]. S/Ldr 13.04.45 Resigned

HOLMES	George Barker	F/L	31.05.31	Relinquished

Granted a commission in the Reserve of Air Force Officers, General Duties Branch, Class C, retaining his rank, 6th March 1935 [LG 19 March 1935, issue 34143, page 1907]. Flight Lieutenant George Barker Holmes, along with his wireless operator Gwyn Evans Langman and Charles Francis Wolley Dod OBE, died when the DH.86 G-ACVZ *Jupiter* of Imperial Airways crashed into a pine wood near Elsdorf [Nordrhein-Westphalia], some 22km west of Köln on Tuesday, 16th March 1937. The crew had taken off at 2130 on a combined mail and passenger flight from Croydon Airport for Butzweilerhof [where the author was stationed between 1956 and 1958]. Contact was lost at 2318 when the DH was over Belgium and in the vicinity of Hasselt. Following a search the wreckage was found in a wood where it had collided with an elm tree that had been broken in half by the impact. Watches worn by the deceased had all stopped at 0024, indicating the severity of the crash. A J Jackon's indispensable *De Havilland Aircraft* [Putnam 1962] shows G-ACVZ as a single-pilot aircraft, construction number 2303, and making its first flight on 7th December 1934.

08147	*THEAK	William Edward	AV-M	17.03.54	Retirement

Air Vice-Marshal William Edward Theak CB CBE twice mentioned in despatches, died on Friday, 28th January 1955. His death was reported in *The Times* which stated Air Vice-Marshal Theak died suddenly at his home at Woodbridge, Suffolk.

OBSERVER OFFICERS
2

09037	ROGERS AFC	Alfred Douglas	A/Cmdr	10.07.48	Retirement

Air Commodore Alfred Douglas Rogers CBE AFC twice mentioned in despatches, died Monday, 11th November 1974. Fifty-seven years earlier to the date, and when he was an observer Sub-Lieutenant in the RNAS, the Short 184 N9047 in which he was flying ditched 45 miles south of Start Point on the South Devon coast. By good fortune, although injured, along with his pilot he was rescued. His appointment to a short service commission came within weeks of his placement on the Unemployed list, 26th March 1920.

WALKER	Alfred Charles	F/O	08.06.28	Relinquished

LG 15 June 1920, issue 31942, page 6587

FLIGHT LIEUTENANT [from SQUADRON LEADER]

POWELL MC	Frederick James	F/L	05.06.31	Relinquished

FLIGHT LIEUTENANT

*BRADY DSM	Bernard John William	F/L	28.11.29	Retired list

At his own request [LG 3 December 1929, issue 33557, page 7868].

FLYING OFFICER [from FLIGHT LIEUTENANT]

BIRKBECK DFC	Robert Alexander	F/L	12.05.31	Relinquished

According to his entry of *Wikipedia* Flying Officer Robert Alexander Birkbeck had a distinguished *Great War* service with 1 Squadron and flying Nieuport scouts secured a total of ten aerial combat victories. After leaving the Royal Air Force he worked as a shipbroker until his death at Oxted in

Surrey on Sunday, 9th of January 1938, at the comparatively early age of 39. Paul McMillan has traced his obituary to the *Sevenoaks Chronicle and Kentish Advertiser* published on 14th January 1938; *'We regret to announce the death which took place on Sunday of Mr Robert Alexander Birkbeck of Stackhouse, West Hill, Oxted. Mr Birkbeck, who was 39 years of age, was best known as stage manager for a number of plays for the Chrichton Dramatic Club. In this role he succeeded Mr R H Yates, upon the latters resignation, and continued to the time of his death. He was stage manager for 'Call it a Day', presented by the Society a few weeks ago. Mr Birkbeck served with the Colours in the Great War and was awarded the Distinguished Flying Cross, He leaves a widow and two children. The funeral took place Tandridge yesterday [Thursday], the vicar, Canon Roland H Gragg officiating.'*

FLYING OFFICER
5

*GIBBONS DFC	Frank George		F/L	+	21.05.32	204 Squadron

Flight Lieutenant Frank George Gibbons DFC who flew Bristol F.2bs with 22 Squadron, securing, with his observer, fourteen combat victories between the last day of May and 27th September 1918, died when his Spartan G-ABTT belonging to Spartan Aircraft Limited flew into a tree and crashed at Stanton, a village on the A143 northwest of Bury St. Edmunds, Suffolk and southwest of the Norfolk market town of Diss.. At the time of his death, he was a participant in an air race being flown over several laps commencing from Heston Airport. According to the report in *The Times* thirty-one competitors took off at around 10.30 on Saturday morning, but only eight remained when the race ended just after 6 o'clock that evening. The weather, it is reported, was extremely poor and Flight Lieutenant Gibbons death was attributed to poor visibility. The race was won by Mr F R Walker in a Puss Moth. Sponsored by the *Morning Post* the race set the competitors a challenging test in their navigational skills.

HORSEY	Herbert John	F/O	12.06.35	Relinquished
MAWBEY MC	Lawrence Walter	Lieutenant	08.01.21	Relinquished

On account of ill-health contracted in the service [LG 15 February 1921, issue 32227, page 1283]. His MC was *Gazetted* on 26th July 1918, supplement 30813, page 8823: *'For conspicuous gallantry and devotion to duty while engaged on low flying and bombing attacks overt the hostile lines, when, on many occasions, he dropped bombs on the enemy personnel, horses, transport and camps, and engaged enemy troops with his machine gun from very low altitudes. At all times he displayed a fine fighting spirit and a determination to get at close quarters with his opponents which was deserving of the highest praise.* 'Born on 27th March 1899, Army Form B.103 records his service with 1 Squadron as being between 7th November 1917 and 8th June 1918, with his award of the MC dated 22nd April 1918.

08133 *STORRAR	Sydney Ernest		AV-M	09.09.47	Retirement

Air Vice-Marshal Sydney Ernest Storrar CBE, died in March 1969.

*TRAPAGNA	Marcel Gustave Louis		F/O	+	07.07.23	24 Squadron

LEROY AFC See my remarks for Flying Officer Edward William Logsdail who was short service commissioned in the issue of 30th March 1920.

FLYING OFFICER [from PILOT OFFICER]

PHAROAH-BAND	Lawrence Claud	Lieutenant	25.01.22	Resigned

Returned to the service in the Second World War, his name being recorded as Lawrence Claude Pharorah-Band, and commissioned to the Royal Air Force Volunteer Reserve as 72917.

		S/Ldr	16.06.45	Resigned

On account of medical unfitness for Air Force service

OBSERVER OFFICER [from PILOT OFFICER]

MITCHELL DSO DFC	John	F/O	05.06.29	Relinquished

LG 2 July 1920, issue 31962, pages 7127

FLIGHT LIEUTENANT

COURT-TREATT	Chaplin	Major	22.04.21	Resigned

FLYING OFFICERS
11

*BURTON	Eric		G/Capt	24.03.46	Retirement
*CALVEY	Harold Charles		F/L	+	01.07.28	23 Squadron

Flight Lieutenant Harold Charles Calvey and Flight Sergeant William Charles Hollier, whose trade was that of carpenter/rigger, died when their Avro 504N H2534 dived without any warning sign of trouble into the ground at Clifton near Henlow while on a practice flight from the Armament Practice Camp at Sutton Bridge where the Kenley based squadron had been detached for armament training. The tragedy received extensive coverage in the press with *The Times* correspondent filing from Biggleswade: *'An Avro Lynx two-seater aeroplane piloted by Flight Lieutenant H C Calvey, stationed at Kenley Aerodrome, crashed in a hay field which adjoins the parish church at Clifton, near Biggleswade, at 6.45 this evening. The pilot and his passenger, who could not be established tonight, were both killed instantly. The machine approached the village flying in a northerly direction at an altitude of about 1,000 feet and a speed of about 100 miles an hour. It appeared to be flying perfectly. Suddenly it nose-dived and struck the ground near a house in which the pilot lived when he was stationed at the Henlow Aerodrome. The crash was heard by the congregation in All Saints' Church, Clifton, the aeroplane having past over the church during the reading of the first lesson. The rector's wife, who was not in the church, saw the machine pass over and heard the crash. After learning of the death of the occupants she summoned the pay reader from the church and he conveyed the news to the rector, who made the announcement to the congregation just before the blessing. Special prayers were offered. The service had not been disturbed, but the congregation, having heard the crash, sat with uncomfortable feelings during the latter part of the service. Mr Frank Humphries of the Clifton Lodge residential boarding-house, a friend of the dead pilot, said: "We cannot understand what caused the crash. Flight Lieutenant Calvey was formerly stationed at Henlow Aerodrome, where he was a very popular officer. He spent yesterday at the Royal Air Force Display with several other officers from Henlow, who are staying with me, and it is thought he was coming to give them a friendly greeting. He has flown over the house hundreds of times. Directly I heard the crash I rushed to the scene. Calvey was almost unrecognisable, but I knew him by parts of his clothing. He leaves a widow and one son. I believe he was on the staff at Kenley." An eye-witness of the accident, Mr G W Secker of Whiston Farm, Clifton, said he was out for a walk when he noticed a machine coming from the direction of London. It seemed to be up over 1,000 feet and he judged its speed to be 100 miles per hour. It was flying perfectly, when it suddenly nose-dived. "We are used to stunting" said Mr Secker, "as we are so near the Henlow Aerodrome, and I thought this machine was stunting. I watched for it to rise from the other side of the trees, but instead there was a crash. I ran to the spot, but two RAF officers who live near by were already there. We tried to move the wreckage, but we could see that the airmen were dead. I telephoned to Henlow Aerodrome and a fire-engine and an ambulance were on the scene within five minutes. The machine was smashed to match-wood. It fell with such force that it embedded itself in the ground."'*

07087 *FLEMING	Donald Malcolm		G/Capt	22.08.46	Retirement
HILL	Hepworth Ambrose Vyvian		F/O	+	25.02.21	100 Squadron

The son of Lieutenant-Colonel H A Hill of the West India Regiment and Mrs Hill, Flying Officer Hepworth Ambrose Vyvian Hill is buried in Belfast City Cemetery. He died in the most tragic circumstances in that he was shot by a sentry on Aldergrove Aerodrome on Friday, 25th February 1921. He had served with 100 Squadron since 9th November 1920, prior to which he had been on duty in the Middle East. Transferring from the Army Service Corps to the Royal Flying Corps and qualifying as an observer, he was wounded on 145h July 1926, while flying in BE.2c 2500 of 9 Squadron, piloted by Captain John Upton Kelly. The circumstances of the action were connected to the Somme offensive which had begun two weeks earlier. Taking off early in the morning, tasked for a contact patrol, the RE was flying at 500 feet near Longueval when an anti-aircraft shell burst in their vicinity. Captain Kelly was temporarily blinded and was assisted in making his forced-landing near Maricourt by his wounded observer. Additional material appears on page 44 of Trevor Henshaw's *The Sky Their Battlefield*. Admitted to a casualty clearing station, 2nd Lieutenant Hill was returned to England the next day aboard HMHS *St. Denis*. A photograph of his headstone, taken by Helena Herd, can be seen on the FindA Grave website.

07161	HORNE	John Gaylor	F/L	09.11.27	Relinquished

On account of ill-health [LG 8 November 1927, issue 33327, page 7119]. During the Second World War he returned to the service and was granted a commission in the Royal Air Force Volunteer Reserve, General Duties Branch, as a Pilot Officer with effect from 16th December 1941 [LG 31 March 1942, issue 35508, page 1462] and given the service number 114338, but subsequently reverted to his original number. On 7th September 1945, and now ranked Flight Lieutenant, he was awarded an AFC [LG 7 September 1945, supplement 37256, page 4485]. His health again failed and he relinquished his commission [LG 11 November 1947, supplement 38120, page 5312].

			F/L	29.10.47	Relinquished
07223	*MACDONALD DFC	Somerled Douglas	A/Cmdr	15.03.54	Retirement

Air Commodore Somerled Douglas Macdonald CB CBE DFC mentioned in despatches, died on Friday, 23rd November 1979.

	PENNYCOOK	Matthew	F/O	04.07.22	Dismissed

By sentence of General Court Martial [LG 11 July 1922, issue 32738, page 5208].

08118	SMITH DCM	Sydney	F/L	10.02.54	Relinquished

But with no retention of rank [LG 21 June 1955, supplement 40516, page 3591]. A most unusual announcement. My co-author has traced to the Edinburgh edition of the *Gazette* August 13th, 1915, page 1247, the citation for his award of the DCM, gained in the service of 10th [Scottish] Battalion, Liverpool Regiment [Territorial Force]: *'For conspicuous gallantry and marked ability at Hooge on 16th June 1915. With a small party he worked up a German trench, killed thirty of the enemy with bombs, including a machine-gun team, and captured the gun, Corporal Smith subsequently found his way into the fourth line of German trenches and remained there until ordered to retire, and, later, he repulsed with complete success a counter-attack made by the enemy.'* In addition, Paul McMillan has unearthed numerous newspaper and casualty cards where Sydney Smith is mentioned, including reference to an injury sustained in the United Kingdom on 5th August 1916, while undergoing training at 13RS when he misjudged a landing in BE.2c 2674. Casualty Card reference 285745 22262 Smith. Also, reference to his capture on 27th January 1917, on the Bulgarian front. Turning to my copy of Trevor Henshaw's *The Sky Their Battlefield* Part VI and page 278 of the reports concerning casualties in Macedonia and The Aegean, the entry for the day in question shows he was serving with 17 Squadron and flying BE.2d 4533 on a bombing sortie he crossed the lines, experiencing heavy anti-aircraft fire, and was some 60 miles inside hostile territory when the engine 'cut' thus necessitating a forced-landing between Drama and Cavalla. Casualty Card reference 285746 22263 indicates his release and arrival in Salonika on 16th February 1919. The newspaper reports all feature articles in the *Manchester Evening News*.

08138	*SUTHERLAND DFC	Robert Bruce	G/Capt	25.09.47	Retirement
	Canada				
07185	*WHITWORTH-JONES	John	ACM	29.05.54	Retirement

Air Chief Marshal Sir John Whitworth-Jones GBE KCB mentioned in despatches, died on Wednesday, 4th February 1981.

	*WOOLLEY DFC	Frank	A/Cmdr	06.08.54	Retirement

Air Commodore Frank Woolley CBE OBE DFC mentioned in despatches, died on Tuesday, 23rd June 1981.

FLYING OFFICER [from PILOT OFFICER]

	TATTAM	Francis Frederick	F/O	06.12.22	Relinquished

On account of ill-health contracted on active service [LG 5 December 1922, issue 32774, page 8616].

LG 9 July 1920, issue 31972, page 7355

FLIGHT LIEUTENANT

	GOODWIN	Alfred Sebastian	F/L	22.09.26	Relinquished

On account of ill-health [LG 21 September 1926, issue 33203, page 6101].

LG 13 July 1920, issue 31978, pages 7458 and 7459

SQUADRON LEADERS - MEDICAL BRANCH
3

14123	HARVEY	Henry	S/Ldr	01.08.29	Relinquished
	JOBSON	Frederick Cuthbert	S/Ldr	01.08.23	To Class D.2
	ROE OBE MB	Robert Lloyd	Major	22.03.22	Relinquished

On account of ill-health [LG 21 March 1922, issue 32645, page 2330]. This was the second time that he had relinquished his commission owing to ill-health, the previous being when as a temporary Captain RAMC on 15th November 1915 [LG 17 November 1915, supplement 29370, page 11436].

FLIGHT LIEUTENANT - MEDICAL BRANCH
27

	AHERNE	Richard John	G/Capt	30.11.44	Retired list
14127	*BARR-SIM MB	Albert Edward	W/Cdr	07.09.45	Retirement

Re-employed and served until:

			G/Capt	14.01.46	Retirement
14128	*BELL MB	Robert Ernest	S/Ldr	23.04.32	Retired list

At his won request [LG 3 May 1932, issue 33822, page 2891].

14129	*BODDIE MB	Donald George	A/Cmdr	25.10.46	Retirement

On account of medical unfitness for Air Force service [LG 5 November 1946, supplement 37776, page 5413]. Air Commodore Donald George Boddie MB Ch.B was Chief Medical Officer in the Far East at the time when Japan entered the Second World War in December 1941. Based in Singapore, he was seriously injured during a Japanese air raid on the city and was evacuated first to Indonesia and thence to India and South Africa. Within months of returning to the United Kingdom he was invalided from the service and died less than a year later in Twickenham on Monday, 18th August 1947. He was cremated in Martlkae Crematorium, his name being commemorated on panel 2. I am grateful to the website WikiTree which I freely acknowledge.

14130	*BRISCOE MB	Abraham	A/Cmdr	26.01.52	Retirement

Air Commodore Abraham Briscoe CBE MB Bc.H BAO, died on Friday, 5th December 1969. During his twenty years of service, he held senior positions in India where he was attached to Air Headquarters, and South Africa where he was involved with aircrew training for SAAF personnel. His final appointment was honorary physician to King George VI. In retirement he was employed as a ship's surgeon with the Ellerman and Bucknall Line. Abraham Briscoe never married.

14131	*CANTON MB	Thomas Joseph Xavier	W/Cdr	03.03.45	Retirement

Re-employed and served until;

			G/Capt	04.03.54	Retirement
14132	*DANIEL MB	Herbert McWilliams	S/Ldr	09.10.36	Retired list

At his own request [LG 13 October 1936, issue 34331, page 6541].

14133	*GRAY	Edwin Noel Hillman	W/Cdr	01.04.38	Retired list

At his own request [LG 5 April 1938, issue 34499, page 2251].

14134	*HALL MB MA	Philip Augustus	G/Capt	07.04.47	Retirement

Re-employed and served until:

			G/Capt	20.03.48	Retirement

HOSFORD	John Perceval		F/L	13.07.20	Cancelled

Paul McMillan has traced Flight Lieutenant John Perceval Hosford's death of Poole Farm, Biedford, Devon as occurring on Wednesday, 22nd September 1953. He was formerly of the city of Bath.

*LUMLEY MC MB	Eric Alfred		A/Cmdr	29.03.50	Retirement

Air Commodore Eric Alfred Lumley CBE MC MD Bc.H DPH DTM & H, died on Monday, 6th August 1979, at Walmersley, Lancashire.

MALONE	William Aloysius		F/L	13.07.26	Relinquished

Flight Lieutenant William Aloysius Malone was subject to a Receiving Order under the Bankruptcy Act 1914, but the petitioning creditors were unable to ascertain his address [EG 15 February 1924, issue 13997, page 260].

14140	*MONTGOMERY	Thomas	F/L	22.08 & 28.10.41	Retirement

MB BA His precise date of retirement remains untraced but between the two dates here shown. However, he volunteered to continue in service and rose to the rank of Group Captain,.

			G/Capt	01.06.42	Retirement

Wing Commander Thomas Montgomery MD Bc.H DPH, died at his Devonshire home of Belstone on Monday, 21st March 1966.

MUGLISTON	Reginald		Captain	02.02.21	Resigned

Captain Reginald Mugliston MD became a ships' surgeon and died at sea from peritonitis on Friday, 20th October 1939.

*MURPHY MB	Frederick John		AV-M	13.05.51	Retirement

Air Vice-Marshal Frederick John Murphy CB CBE MB, died on Thursday, 22nd May 1969. During his long military service which began as a Lieutenant in the Royal Army Medical Corps, Frederick Murphy was a gifted sportsman whose prowess ranged from hockey and tennis to golf.

PUNCH	Edward Philip		S/Ldr	13.07.28	Relinquished
O'GORMAN MB	Edward Gerald		F/L +	29.04.22	4 FTS Abu Sueir

Flight Lieutenant Edward Gerald O'Gorman MB died when Bristol F.2b H1647 overshot while trying to land at Heliopolis and crashed out of control.

O'MULLANE MB	Jerome John		F/L	13.07.20	Cancelled
SAUNDERS	Frederick Joshua Page		S/Ldr	04.09.34	Relinquished
SHEIL MB	William Francis		F/L	13.07.20	Cancelled
14148	SMYTH	James Coulter	F/L	26.08.22	To Class D.2

Subsequently transferred to Class D.1 [LG 5October 1926, issue 33208, page 6375]. Returned to the service, and the Medical Branch, and promoted Squadron Leader LRCP & S, LM LDS [LG 9 September 1941, issue 35270, page 5223].

			G/Capt	05.10.54	Relinquished
THOMPSON	Charles Henry Burton		F/L	13.07.28	Relinquished
*TROUP	Howard Branston		S/Ldr	03.02.32	Retired list

Squadron Leader Howard Branston Troup MRCS LRCP was placed on the Retired list on account of ill-health [LG 2 February 1932, issue 33795, page 710]. Squadron Leader Troup died in March 1951, at the Harefield Sanatorium, as reported in *The British Medical Journal*.

WATSON MB	Andrew		F/L	13.07.20	Cacelled
WELLS BA	Jack Pascoe		F/L	13.07.22	To Class D.2
14152	*WILSON MC MB	William Fothergill	W/Cdr	16.08.42	Retirement

Re-employed and served until retiring at his own request.

			W/Cdr	21.04.45	Retirement
YOUNG MB	Charles Henry		F/L	13.07.22	To Class D,2

FLIGHT LIEUTENANT

04069	HARDMAN DFC	Edmund Parfitt	F/L	30.06.40	Relinquished

Re-employed.

			S/Ldr	01.07.54	Relinquished

FLYING OFFICERS
3

ALLEN	James Bernard		F/L +	05.12.33	

Flight Lieutenant James Bernard Allen died while still in Class A of the Reserve; his death occurring while in the employment of Mary du Caurroy, Her Grace, the Duchess of Bedford. On the day in question, he was flying with the Duchess in her recently acquired GAL Monospart ST.4 G-ACKT when he narrowly missed a line of high tension cables only to lose control and crash near Thrupps Farm, Thrupp End, Station Road, Lidlington some 3 miles southeast of Cranfield, Bedfordshire. The Duchess was only slightly injured, but Flight Lieutenant Allen's injuries were mortal and he died the same day. They had taken off from Woburn Abbey's private strip.

07078	*FEATHER	Vincent Percy	G/Capt	30.08.47	Retirement

Granted a commission in Class J of the Royal Air Force Reserve of Officers, 15th January 1951, in the rank of Flight Lieutenant [LG 27 February 1951, supplement 39158, page 1044].

			F/L	15.01.55	Relinquished
TALBOT	John		Lieutenant	25.06.21	Resigned

On account of ill-health [LG 28 June 1921, issue 32372, page 5139].

OBSERVER OFFICER

08225	BRADFORD	Wilfred Wyles	F/O	28.06.27	Relinquished

On account of ill-health [LG 19 July 1927, supplement 33295, page 4649]. His health recovered, Flying Officer Wilfred Wyles Bradford was granted a commission in the Administrative and Special Duties Branch on 12th December 1940 [LG 14 January 1941, issue 35042, page 283] and was initially allotted 89172 as his service number, subsequently reverting 08225.

			S/Ldr	09.09.49	Relinquished

LG 23 July 1920 issue 31991, pages 7776 and 7777

FLIGHT LIEUTENANTS
3

*ANDERSON DSO DFC	Walter Fraser		F/L	06.04.27	Retired list

At his own request [LG 12 April 1927, issue 33265, page 2411].

GROVES	John Osborn		Captain	20.04.21	Resigned

Granted a commission as a Flying Officer in the Reserve of Air Force Officers, Class A, General Duties Branch, 20th April 1923 [LG 20 April 1923, issue 32816, page 2892].

			F/O	07.10.25	Relinquished

On account of ill-health. Born 28th May 1893, at Lymm, Cheshire, Flying Officer John Osborn Groves died in Shenley Hospital, Barnet, Hertfordshire, on Monday, 15th January 1962.

HILL	Gerard Robert		Captain	17.02.21	Resigned

FLYING OFFICER [from FLIGHT LIEUTENANT]

07054	DIMMOCK AFC	Norman Herford	W/Cdr	28.05.54	Relinquished

FLYING OFFICERS
8

BRAGG	Charles Willie		F/O +	28.03.22	39 Squadron

Flying Officer Charles Willie Bragg was killed when he stalled off a climbing turn, downwind, in DH.9A E967 shortly after becoming airborne from Spittlegate. His passenger, Leading Aircraftman Wialter Wren also died when the DH burst into flames on impact.

	COSGRAVE	Arthur Michael George	Lieutenant	12.07.22	Relinquished

On account of physical unfitness for full flying duties. Born in Aldershot on 28th September 1897, he emigrated to Australia where he died in the State of Western Australia on Friday, 29th March 1968.

	FERRELL	Clifton Gordon	F/O	19.07.27	Relinquished
	*HAMILTON DFC	Leslie	F/O	19.09.25	Resigned

Flying Officer Leslie Hamilton joined Imperial Airways and was last reported on the last day of August 1927, when in the company of a fellow company pilot, Frederick F R Minchin and their passenger Princess Anne of Löwenstein-Wertheim-Freudenburg, their Fokker F.VIIa G-EBTQ disappeared while attempting to fly nonstop from RAF Upavon to Ottawa. A detailed report can be read on the Aviation Safety Netwoork Occurrence Report 59882.

07128	*HARGROVES	Joseph Henry	W/Cdr	+	05.07.40	101 Squadron

Commanding No 101 Squadron, Wing Commander Joseph Henry Hargroves IGSM lost his life on the squadron's second day of operations, having previously being consigned to a training role. Flying Blenheim IV N6140 to attack a target in northwest Germany he is reported to have come down in the sea. His body, along with that of his observer Sergeant Ewart William Smith IGSM, was recovered; both now rest in Kiel War Cemetery. That of the crew's wireless operator/air gunner, Sergeant Robert Mark Livermore who had been mentioned in despatches, was never found and he is commemorated panel 16 at the Runnymede Memorial. Additional information can be found in my RAFBCL 1939-1940 revision, page 162, though reference to this being the squadron's first operational sortie is incorrect.

	HYSLOP	Maitland	F/O	+	30.09.21	84 Squadron

Taking off from Nasiriyeh, Iraq, for a bombing sortie one of the bombs fell and exploded, destroying DH.9A H66 and instanly killing Flying Officer Maitland Hyslop and Aircraftman Edward Plummer.

08049	POTTER	Samuel Lewis Hope	S/Ldr	24.05.45	Resigned

FLYING OFFICERS [from PILOT OFFICERS]
5

06181	ALLIOTT	Eric Herbert	F/O	10.08.31	Relinquished

Granted a commission in the Reserve of Air Force Officers, Class A, General Duties Branch and retaining his rank [LG 24 September 1935, issue 34201, page 6008]. Transferred to the Technical Branch 17th January 1941 [LG 13 June 1941, issue 35190, page 3383]. Subsequently, relinquished his commission under the provisions of the Navy, Army and Air Force Reserves Act 1954.

			F/L		30.07.54	Relinquished
	CHIPPER	Arthur Albert Bamford	F/O		20.07.31	Relinquished
	DUDDING	Maynard Cecil	F/L	+	12.04.35	

TNA Kew has a record for Maynard Cecil Dudding, born 30th November 1893, under AIR 76/142/54. While still in Class C of the Reserve, Flight Lieutenant Dudding was killed onFriday, 12th April 1935, when the Miles M.2 Hawk G-ACNX which he was piloting with the passenger, and owner, Mr Peter Conley Pitt, flew into a tree and crashed at The Worthies, near Malmesbury, Wiltshire. Additional information is available on the Aviation Safety Network Occurrence Report 191358.

	DUNBAR	John Campion	F/O	22.07.28	Relinquished
	HALE	Marcus Samuel	F/O	14.06.21	Dismissed

By sentence of General Court Martial [LG 28 June 1921, issue 32372, page 5139]. In the New Year's Honours List for 1946 [LG 28 December 1945, supplement 37412, page 279] Commander Marcus Samuel Hale, Officer Commanding, No 1 Ferry Pool, Air Transport Auxiliary, was made an MBE in the Civil Division of the Most Excellent Order. I suspect he is the same person dismissed the service in June 1921.

OBSERVER OFFICER

09045	*TITMAS	John Francis	A/Cmdr	07.06.54	Retirement

Air Commodore John Francis Titmas CB mentioned in despatches, died on Saturday, 28th April 1973.

LG 10 August 1920, issue 32012, page 8278. Twenty-one officers named with various dates indicated for seniority ranging between 6th January and 9th August 1920.

FLIGHT LIEUTENANT

	*GARDNER DSC	Richard Gregory	A/Cmdr	01.02.46	Retirement

Air Commodore Rigard Gregory Gardner CBE DSC mentioned in despatches, died on Wednesday, 5th April 1961.

FLYING OFFICER [from FLIGHT LIEUTENANT]

	DALY DSC DFC	Rowan Heywood	F/O	+	05.06.24	39 Squadron

Flying Officer Rowan Heywood Daly DSC DFC mentioned in despatches, his observer Sergeant William Henry Brewer and the crew of DH.9A J7087 of 39 Squadron crewed by Flying Officer Leslie Gordon Lucas and Aircraftman Leslie Coppleston, died in a midair collision over the airfield. Flying Officer Daly was flying in DH.9A E8654 which was burnt out in the crash. His biography can be read on *Wikipedia*.

FLYING OFFICERS
12

11239	*CARDWELL AFC	Harold Edmund	G/Capt	29.06.49	Retirement
07012	CASWELL	Bruce Bernard	G.Capt	18.02.46	Retirement
07056	DIVERS	Rowland John	G/Capt	11.09.45	Retirement
	GOODALL	John Henry Warwick	F/O	07.09.21	Resigned
	*HALLIDAY	Christopher George	F/L	27.06.29	30 Squadron

Flight Lieutenant Christopher George Halliday died when his Wapiti IIA J9408 crashed and turned over near Luqait, Iraq. His passenger, Leading Aircraftman John Laverty was injured. J9408 is mentioned on page 304 of John Hamblin's *Flat Out - The Story of 30 Squadron Royal Air Force* [Air-Britain, 2002] but apart from noting it bore the letter A no other remarks are appended. However, the same publisher's J1-J9999 register is more forth-coming and notes the airframe was repaired at Hinaidi and returned to the squadron on 3rd September 1929. Subsequently, it went on to serve with 84 and 55 Squadrons before being declared beyond economical repair at Hinaidi and struck off charge on the 1st of May 1936.

07129	HARKER	Seymour Caley	F/L	19.02.28	To Class C

Flight Lieutenant Seymour Caley Harker was granted a commission in Class CC of the Reserve of Air Force officers on 7th May 1938 [LG 13th December 1938, issue 34579, page 7921].

			S/Ldr	28.04.45	Resigned
	HARTUNG MM	Charles Stanley	F/O	08.04.25	Resigned
	McCLEAN	Charles Malachy	F/O	05.08.27	Relinquished
08069	*RITCHIE AFC	Alan Patrick	AV-M	28.12.45	Retirement

Air Vice-Marshal Alan Patrick Ritchie CBE AFC three times mentioned in despatches, died on Thursday, 17th August 1961.

08169	WALKER	John Charles			

Flying Officer John Charles Walker was granted a commission in the Equipment Branch, with the rank of Flight Lieutenant, with effect from 8th February 1937 [LG 15 June 1937, issue 34408, page 3862].

			S/Ldr	12.05.43	Relinquished
	WILTON	Guy Nöel	F/O	24.07.27	Relinquished

OBSERVER OFFICER

	HOLLIS	John Augustus	F/L	23.01.34	Relinquished

FLYING OFFICERS [from PILOT OFFICERS]
4

	BAKER	Cecil Henry	F/O		03.08.27	Relinquished
	*BEILBY	Arthur Edward	S/ldr	+	09.05.37	

Flight Lieutenant Arthur Edward Beilby died in the Nuffield Guys Hospital, St. Thomas Street, Southwark.

07029	CORDINGLEY	Vollrath Christian	F/O		29.07.28	To Class C

Subsequently adopted the Christian name Victor in lieu of Vollrath and with effect from 29th August 1939, transferred from the General Duties Branch in the Reserve of Air Force Officers to the Administrative and Special Duties Branch [LG 12 December 1939, issue 34752, page 8254]. Following several extensions of service and transfer to the Secretarial Branch:-

			F/L		07.03.59	Relinquished
	ELLIOT MC	Gerald Augustus	F/O		10.08.31	Relinquished

TNA Kew holds a record for this officer under ADM 273/27/64.

LG 27 August 1920, issue 32032, page 8793

FLIGHT LIEUTENANT

	CLARK	Cecil Christian	Captain		01.04.22	Resigned

Rejoined the service and granted a commission in Class A of the Reserve of Air Force Officers as a Flying Officer on probation, with effect from 23rd July 1929, in the General Duties Branch [LG 23 July 1929, issue 33519, page 4854].

			S/Ldr	+	30.11.39	2 AACU

Squadron Leader Cecil Christian Clark was killed during the afternoon of 30th November 1939, when the Blackburn Skua L2981 in which he been exercising with HMS *Fraser* off Eastney ranges plunged into shallow water in the upper reaches of Portsmouth Harbour. Extremely poor visibility was a contributory factor. Although searches commenced immediately, it was not until 20th April 1940, that his body was found in Porchester Creek, a mere half mile or so from where he had crashed. Aged 42, is buried in Gosport [Ann's Hill] Cemetery.

FLYING OFFICERS
12

06235	*BROUGHALL MC	Herbert Seton	G/Capt		15.3.46	Retirement
	CHANDLER	Guy Pretor Worsley	F/O		23.08.31	Relinquished
07023	CLINTON	Arnold Cadman	F/O		14.08.27	To Class C

With effect from 14th August 1932, his Reserve commitment was extended by five years, followed by wartime employment. A record for this officer is held at TNA Kew under WO 339/105526 and AIR 76/92/207.

			F/O		10.02.54	Relinquished

Paul McMillan adds; Arnold Cadman Clinton born Walthamstow, Essex, in October 1896, and died October 1967, St. Pancras, Middlesex.

	COLLEY	Reginald Thomas	F/O		06.07.21	Resigned

Flying Officer Reginald Thomas Colley returned to the service and as a Pilot Officer on probation, 28th March 1939, in the Administrative and Special Duties Branch [LG 4 April 1939, issue 34613, page 2266] as 72803.

			S/Ldr		25.05.54	Relinquished
07113	GREENE	Frederick Charles Boughton	F/L		10.08.33	To Class C

Transferred from the General Duties Branch of the Reserve of Air Force Officers to the Administrative and Special Duties Branch [LG 12 December 1939, issue 34752, page 8254].

			W/Cdr		24.10.45	Relinquished

On account of medical unfitness for Air Force service [LG 6 November 1945, supplement 37336, page 5388].

07175	INGRAM	Arthur Ferguson	F/L		15.01.28	Resigned

Flight Lieutenant Arthur Ferguson Ingram is granted a commission in Class C of the Reserve of Air Force Officers, 20th April 1936 [LG 26 May 1936, issue 34287, page 3375].

			F/L		01.09.39	Relinquished

On appointment to a commission in the Royal Air Force Volunteer Reserve, retaining his rank [LG 20 October 1939, issue 34713, page 7041].

			W/Cdr		09.07.54	Relinquished
	JACKSON	Cecil	F/L		29.04.36	Relinquished

On account of ill-health [LG 28 April 1936, issue 34278, page 2700].

	*LEGUEN de LACROIS	Aleth Thomas Septimus	F/L		27.05.34	Retirement
	*PLAYFORD	Evan Randal Bruce	F/L		19.06.26	Retired list

At his own request. Paul McMillan reports, Flight Lieutenant Evan Randal Bruce Playford served as a pilot in the Second World War, his service number being 74206, and on 1st June 1942, ranked of Squadron Leader. Released 1945, and died in Cheltenham on Wednesday, 26th March 1947.

	RUSSELL	Arthur Leslie	F/L		23.08.31	Relinquished
08108	SHOOSMITH	William Matthew	F/O		29.07.30	To Class C

Retained in the Reserve; served throughout the Second World War.

			F/O		10.02.54	Relinquished
08189	WHITE	Aubrey Freeland	S/Ldr		10.02.54	Relinquished

FLYING OFFICERS [from PILOT OFFICERS
6

11068	*BATES	Leslie John Vernon	AV-M		02.10.55	Retirement

Air Vice-Marshal Sir Leslie Bates KBE CB twice mentioned in despatches, died on Friday, 18th November 1966.

	GANDELL MM	William Ernest	F/O		27.01.33	Relinquished
	McMANUS	Walter Frank	F/O		28.03.23	Relinquished

On account of ill-health [LG 27 March 1923, issue 32809, page 2320].

08004	*MORETON	Noel Vivian	G/Capt		01.07.50	Retirement
	PRATT	George Edward	F/O	+	14.09.23	To Class A

Flying Officer George Edward Pratt, still in Class A of the Reserve, joined Daimler Airway as a commercial pilot and on 14th September 1923, after taking off from Croydon on a scheduled flight to Manchester in DH.34 G-EBBS with a crew of two and three passengers crashed at Ivinghoe in Buckinghamshire. At the subsequent inquest, commencing at 17th September at Ivinghoe Town Hall, held before the Coroner and from evidence provided by eye witnesses it seems the DH encountered a storm which appeared to stop the engine. However, it restarted and at around 1805 the pilot attempted to make a precautionary landing but stalled. On impact the aircraft turned over and all on board perished. A verdict of "Accidental death" was returned at the conclusion of the inquest on 24th September.

70916	WARDLE	Harry Downing	F/O		18.08.31	Relinquished

Flying Officer Harry Downing Wardle was granted a commission in Class C of the Reserve of Air Force Officers, General Duties Branch, retaining his rank, with effect from 12th April 1938 [LG 22 November 1038, issue 34573, page 7355]. Later transferred to the Administrative and Special Duties Branch [LG 20 October 1939, issue 34713, page 7044], 15th March 1939, as 74875.

			S/Ldr		15.02.54	Relinquished

FLIGHT LIEUTENANT [from SQUADRON LEADER]

| 06171 | SHIELD MC | Horace Scott | F/L | 19.11.28 | Relinquished |

As Temporary 2nd Lieutenant Horace Scott Shield his award was *Gazetted* in the Edinburgh edition of 5th October 1915, issue 12859, page 1513:
'For conspicuous gallantry and skill when on patrol duty with Corporal T Bennett on 13th September 1915. When over Bois de Biez, at about 10,000 feet, he sighted a German Albatross, and at once dived and attacked it at about 7,000 feet, being subject at the time to heavy anti-aircraft gun fire. The German Albatross used a machine-gun very conveniently mounted, but Corporal Bennett handled his gun with such skill that he disabled the German machine, which side-slipped and then nose-dived to the ground in our lines.Second Lieutenant Shield has been exceptionally keen in pursuing German machines whenever seen, and on this occasion he manoeuvred his own machine with admirable skill and judgement.' Referring to Army Form B.103c, this identifies his squadron as 16 Squadron, a Tactical reconnaissance unit equipped with BE.2 and operating from Merville. On the 1st of January 1916, he was mentioned in despatches and later in the month, the 25th, posted to 10 Squadron [BE.2] at Chocques. It is further noted that he was born on 14th February 1895, and prior to transferring to the Royal Flying Corps, served with the 14th Battalion, Durham Light Infantry and later with the North Staffordshire. Come the Second World War Flight Lieutenant Horace Scott Shield MC, and with effect from 4th April 1940, was granted a commission in the General Duties Branch as a Pilot Officer on probation [LG 26 April 1940, issue 34838, page 2477]., serving until:

| | | | S/Ldr | 01.02.44 | Resigned |

FLIGHT LIEUTENANT
3

21071	*HANSON-ABBOTT Clifford		W/Cdr	31.03.41	Retirement
Re-employed.			G/Capt	23.02.46	Retired list
	*MacLAREN	Archibald Stuart Charles	S/Ldr	01.06.30	Retired list
	OBE MC AFC				

On account of ill-health. There are a number of websites devoted to this officer, the majority focusing on his attempt with Flying Officer William Noble Plenderleith and Flight Sergeant W H Andrews, a flight engineer, to circumnavigate the world in 1924, in competition with teams from America, Argentina, France, Italy and Portugal. The attempt by the British team was made in a Vickers Vulture VI amphibia G-EBHO which after a series of mishaps came to grief when attempting to take off from Akyab Island off Burma. With generous assistance from the Americans [subsequent winners who completed this marathon journey in 175 days, landing home on 25th September 1924], a second Vulture arrived at Akyab, this being G-EBGO but this, too, was lost following a landing by Flying Officer Plenderleith on 4th August 1924, after encountering heavy fog in the Commander Islands in the Bering Sea. By good fortune they were to beach their aircraft and, subsequently, they were picked up by HMCS *Thiepval*. This epic attempt had begun at Calshot on 25th March 1924 [the date of which Squadron Leader MacLaren was placed on half-pay, Scale B [LG 8 April 1924, issue 32925, page 2924].

| 14139 | *MAXWELL MB | George Henry Hope | G/Capt | 14.01.48 | Retirement |

FLYING OFFICERS
10

| | BENSTEAD | Frederick Edward Clark | F/L | 12.05.32 | Resigned |

Most likely brought about by the entry in the Edinburgh edition of the *Gazette* April 19th, 1932, issue 14853, page 326, under the Bankruptcy Acts 1914 and 1926: *'Frederick Edward Clark Benstead, residing at 117 Sturton Street, Cambridge, in the County of Cambridge, Officer in the reserve of H M Air Force, now of no occupation.*

| 07122 | *HALLAWELL | Charlton | A/Cmdr | 15.10.48 | Retirement |

Air Commodore Charlton Hallawell mentioned in despatches, died on Tuesday, 29th December 1981.

| | HICKS DFC | George Rhensburg | F/L | 01.07.31 | Relinquished |

On 10th July 1936, Flight Lieutenant George Rhensburg Hicks DFC was granted a commission in Class C of the Reserve of Air Force Officers [LG 8th September 1936, issue 34321, page 5794] and was transferred to Class A on 18th December 1936 [LG 12 January 1937, issue 34359, page 269]. He relinquished his commission on completion of service 10th January 1939, as an Honorary Squadron Leader [LG 14 March 1939, issue 34607, page 1773]. It appears, however, that he continued to serve in the Reserve of Air Force Officers and on 15th March 1948, was appointed to a commission [Class CC] in the Secretarial Branch in Squadron Leader rank as 192768 [LG 1 June 1948, supplement 38305, page 3245]. It seems he was still active as at January 1950, as an entry in the *Gazette* published on 24th January 1950, reporting relinquishment of his commission was subsequently cancelled in supplement 38838, page 769, of the edition issued on 14th February 1950.

07179	JAMES	Amos Francis	G/Capt	09.08.46	Retirement
	SHEPPARD	Robert Hugh McCoubrie	F/L	01.09.35	Relinquished
	SUTCLIFFE	Sextus Edward	F/O	02.09.27	Relinquished
	SMITH	Arthur Charles	F/O	14.07.31	Relinquished
08175	*WARE	Sidney Herbert	A/Cmdr	15.03.48	Retirement

Air Commodore Sidney Herbert Ware, died on Friday, 22nd October 1982.

| | WESTAWAY | Horace William | F/O | 27.08.31 | Relinquished |
| 21081 | *WHELLOCK | Capel Stanley | G/Capt | 09.06.50 | Retirement |

On account of medical unfitness for Air Force service [LG 13 June 1950, supplement 38941, page 3046].

FLYING OFFICERS [from PILOT OFFICERS]
5

	ANSON	Cyril Okeover	Lieutenant	01.02.22	Relinquished
On account of ill-health.					
	DURRANT	Charles Edward	Lieutenant	04.04.23	Relinquished
On account of ill-health					
	LINGWOOD	Percy William	F/O +	18.06.23	216 Squadron

Flying Officer Percy William Lingwood was killed in the crash of Vickers Vimy IV F3173, which came down in hilly country known as the Megattom [or Mokattam] Hills southeast of Cairo; he is buried alongside other members of the crew in Cairo New British Protestant Cemetery. A photograph showing his grave can be viewed on the Find a Grave website which I dutifully acknowledge. Also named are Flight Lieutenant Neville Byron Ward and Air Mechanics William Jarvis and Frederick William Skuse.

| | SPOONER MM | John | F/O | 27.08.29 | Relinquished |
| | SWANTON | Sidney Hugh Hamilton | F/O | 11.09.37 | Relinquished |

FLIGHT LIEUTENANTS
2

| 09058 | CLEMSON DSC | Alfred William | F/L | 18.08.31 | Relinquished |

On 28th October 1938, Flight Lieutenant Alfred William Clemson OBE DSC was granted a commission in Class C of the Reserve of Air Force Officers [LG 28 February 1939, issue 34603, page 1395]. This was relinquished on 1st September 1939, on being appointed to a commission in the

Royal Air Force Volunteer Reserve [General Duties Branch] [LG 31 October 1939, issue 34721, page 7275]. He served throughout the Second World War, and beyond until:

| | | S/Ldr | 01.06.54 | Relinquished |
| *ROACH AFC | Harold Jace | A-VM | 01.01.51 | Retirement |

Air Vice-Marshal Harold Jace Roach CB CBE AFC mentioned in despatches, died on Tuesday, 21st June 1977.

FLYING OFFICER [from FLIGHT LIEUTENANT]

| GOSSIP | George Hatfeild Dingley | F/O | +_ | 24.04.23 | 56 Squadron |

Australia Formerly of the Royal Naval Air Service, Flying Officer George Hatfeild Dingley Gossip, born in Sydney, New South Wales, on 6th January 1897, flew Sopwith F.1 Camels with 4 Squadron RNAS [subsequently 204 Squadron] scoring six combat victories spread between 1st October 1917 and 30th July 1918. His death came in a flying accident when his Sopwith 7F.1 Snipe F2487 of 56 Squadron Detached Flight, San Stefano, spun and crashed on or close to the airfield. He is buried in Turkey at Istanbul. Information regarding his arial victories are reported on the Aerodrome Website, which I have pleasure in acknowledging.

FLYING OFFICERS
23

| APPLEFORD | Walter Alexander Nelson | F/O | | 28.03.22 | Resigned |

It is noted that Alexander Nelson Appleford as a 2nd Lieutenant commissioned to the Army Service Corps had to relinquish his commission owing to ill-health on 8th October 1915 [LG 7 October 1915, supplement 29319, page 9870], though he recovered sufficiently to be accepted as a 2nd Lieutenant [probation] to the military wing of the Royal Flying Corps on 11th May 1916 [LG 13 June 1916, supplement 29621, page 5831].

| | ATKINSON | William Roberts Kempton | F/O | | 16.11.27 | Resigned |
| | *BAGGS | Humphrey William | F/L | + | 16.06.27 | CFS Wittering |

Flight Lieutenant Humphrey William Baggs and Flying Officer Sydney Fleetwood Bell died when their Sopwith 7F.1 Snipe DC spun into the ground near Wothorpe, a village roughly 2 miles SW of Stamford and about 3 miles NW from their airfield.

| | BARTON | Frank Henry | F/O | + | 13.01.22 | 8 Squadron |

Flying Officer Frank Henry Barton lost his life in a midair collision over Hinaidi when the formation of DH.9As broke in readiness to land and his aircraft H102 came into collision with that flown by Flight Lieutenant Albert Grounds Peace AFC. Both machines fell to the ground; the two pilots were killed, as was Aircraftman Walter William Stephen Brown in E8473. By a miracle Aircraftman Eric Pattinson, who was accompanying Flying Officer Barton, survived

| 09063 | BIRD | Clifford Harrold | F/O | | 15.09.29 | Relinquished |

Returned to the service and granted a commission in the Reserve of Air Force Officers in Class CC, with effect from 25th September 1944, and served until relinquishment.

| | | | W/Cdr | 20.05.46 | Relinquished |
| 09064 | *BOND | Frank Edgar | G/Capt | 27.01.42 | Retired list |

At his own request [LG 10 February 1942, issue 35451, page 665].

| 09065 | *BOSWELL | Kenneth Lenton | A/Cmdr | 24.12.45 | Retirement |

Air Commodore Kenneth Lenton Boswell OBE, died on Saturday, 19th November 1977.

	BRIGGS	Cyril Ferdinand	F/L		20.09.29	Relinquished
	BERNEY	James Charles	F/O		25.09.27	Relinquished
	CUMMING Subsequently changed his name to:				

BURNEY=CUMMING James Charles and returned to the service on 16th May 1939, with a commission in the Reserve of Air Force Officers as a probationary Pilot Officer [73516].

| | | | S/Ldr | 25.05.54 | Relinquished |
| | GILBERT | Christopher Guy | F/O | | 08.01.21 | Resigned |

Returned to the service and received a commission in the Administrative and Special Duties Branch on 14th February 1939, and allocated the service number 72663 [LG 21 February 1939, issue 34600, page 1217].

| | | | W/Cdr | 05.10.54 | Relinquished |
| 09071 | *HAMERSLEY MC | Harold Alan | G/Capt | 13.06.44 | Retirement |

Australia Group Captain Harold Alan Hamersley's award, gained as temporary Captain, was *Gazetted* on 22nd June 1918, supplement 30761, page 7412: *'For conspicuous gallantry and devotion to duty. On one occasion whilst leading his patrol he attacked a formation of six enemy planes. In the ensuing fight he destroyed two of these machines, one falling flames and the second crashing to earth, and during the same engagement assisted another officer in destroying a third. In addition to these he has destroyed five hostile machines and driven down three out of control. He is a magnificent pilot, displaying at all times an utter disregard of fear.'* His *Wikipedia* biography shows he was born on 6th February 1896, in Guildford, Western Australia, and prior to his transfer to the Royal Flying Corps fought in Gallipoli Campaign where he was wounded. Following his transfer, he flew SE.5as with 60 Squadron.

| | JACKSON | Edwin | F/O | | 19.11.24 | Relinquished |

On account of ill-health [LG 18 November 1924, issue 32994, page 8347].

| 11073 | *LEWIS | Wilfred Thomas | | | |

Granted his commission as a stores officer, Flying Officer William Thomas Lewis was transferred to the General Duties Branch on 10th December 1923 [LG 4 March 1924, issue 32915, page 1931]. However, he appears to have reverted to the Stores Branch by 1st November 1931, on which date he was promoted Flight Lieutenant [LG 10 November 1931, issue 33770, page 7248].

| | | | S/Ldr | 28.11.46 | Retired list |
| 09077 | *PARKER | Vivian Steel | G/Capt | 08.08.46 | Retirement |

Group Captain Vivian Steel Parker rose to notice in the post war years of the Royal Air Force and was *Gazetted* with the DFC and AFC, *Gazette* references 15th March 1929, issue 33477, page 1822, and 1st January 1935, supplement 34119, page 17. The DFC was in recognition of his gallant and distinguished service rendered in connection with operations against the Akhwan in the southern desert regions of Iraq. From the RAF Commands website, which I acknowledge, it is known that while performing test pilot duties at A&AEE Martlesham Heath he baled out of the Vickers 151 Jockey J9122 on 15th July 1932, which according to Air-Britain's J File crashed into an orchard at Woodbridge, Suffolk. The month previous J9122 had appeared at the Hendon Display sporting the digit '1'.

| 09078 | *PEARCE | Frederick Laurence | A/Cmdr | 17.03.52 | Retirement |

Air Commodore Frederick Laurence PEARCE CBE DSO DFC three times mentioned in despatches, died on Wednesday, 3rd December 1975.

| 09079 | POWELL | Walter Baldwin Eyer | F/L | | 13.09.34 | To Class C |

Flight Lieutenant Walter Baldwin Eyer Powell, while still in the Reserve, was transferred from the General Duties Branch to the Administrative and Special Duties Branch on 29th August 1939 [LG 12 December 1939, issue 34752, page 8254].

| | | | W/Cdr | 31.08.54 | Relinquished |
| 09080 | *RANKIN | Archibald James | A/Cmdr | 13.05.51 | Retirement |

Air Commodore Archibald James Rankin OBE AFC three times mentioned in despatches, died on Friday, 8th February 1974. He is mentioned in John F Hamlin's excellent history of 30 Squadron, published by Air-Britain in 2002, with the title *Flat Out - The story of 30 Squadron Royal Air Force*.

	RICHARDSON MC	Herbert Brian	F/O		18.05.21	Resigned
	SIMPSON	Ian Charles Grant	F/O		28.09.27	Relinquished
09084	*SMYTHE	Cyril Richard	W/Cdr	26.08.46	Retirement
	SPIERS	Cyril Douglas	F/L		13.09.31	Relinquished
	SPINNEY	William Leslie Gordon	F/O	+	24.02.21	4 Squadron

Flying Officer William Leslie Gordon Spinney was killed when his Avro 504K F8751 of 4 Squadron, Farnborough, spun in near Cove, Hampshire; he is buried in Wembley [St. John] Churchyard. Observer Officer Allan Hesketh DFC survived, though badly injured.

| 09087 | *SWANN | Walter English | W/Cdr | 28.01.42 | Retired list |

FLYING OFFICER [from PILOT OFFICERS]
5

| | CHALMERS | Colin Ward Silvester | F/O | 20.09.31 | Relinquished |

Returned to the service and granted a commissions in the Administrative and Special Duties Branch as Pilot Officer [probation] and allotted the service number 82064 on 16th July 1940 [LG 6 August 1940, issue 34915, page 4815].   F/O   13.02.45   Resigned

| | MACMILLAN | Harry | F/O | 27.09.30 | Relinquished |
| 09075 | MEREDITH | Alfred Cuckson | S/Ldr | 27.07.54 | Relinquished |

While still on the Reserve Class C, Flying Officer Alfred Cuckson Meredith was transferred from the General Duties Branch to the Administrative and Special Duties Branch with effect from 29th August 1939 [LG 12 December 1939, issue 34752, page 8254]. An entry in the *Gazette* reporting his promotion to Squadron Leader [temporary] on 1st January 1943 [issue 35855, page 218] shows his original service number, but the entry recording his relinquishing of commission on 27th July 1954, shows 88257 [LG 27 July 1954, supplement 40240, page 4391].

| | NEWNHAM | Sidney Allan Charles | F/O | 24.01.23 | Resigned |
| 09082 | ROSE | Robert Harold | F/O | 20.09.31 | Relinquished |

Flying Officer Robert Harold Rose was granted a commission in Class A of the Reserve of Air Force Officers, General Duties Branch, with effect from 21st September 1937 [LG 28 September 1937, issue 34439, page 6021]. On 25th November 1943, he was transferred from the General Duties Branch to the Administrative and Special Duties Branch [LG 7 December 1943, supplement 36276, page 5342]. My co-author, Paul McMillan, believes Flight Lieutenant Robert Harold Rose may have died while still in Royal Air Force Service. The precise date is not known, but one of the many ancestry websites suggests October 1949.

LG 8 October 1920, issue 32078, page 9815

SQUADRON LEADER

| | DRAPER DSC | Christopher | S/Ldr | 06.10.21 | Resigned |

Squadron Leader Christopher Draper DSC, frequently referred to as *The Mad Major* was one of the Royal Naval Air Service's and, subsequently, Royal Air Force, most colourful characters. He gained his nickname after, according to his extensive entry on *Wikipedia,* when in 1918, and commanding 208 Squadron, he "accidentally" flew under a bridge in full view of a body of soldiers who cheered him most heartily, and so the penchant for repeating the exercise was born. Released from the Air Force he became a second-hand car salesman, but in April 1919, was appointed Chief Test Pilot for the British Aerial Transport Organisation during which he made the first flight of the FK.26 which was specifically designed as a passenger carrying aircraft. Surviving a crash at Hendon while flying the BAT Bantam on 23rd March 1920, he sought an interview with Sir Hugh Trenchard which resulted in a short service commission. Posted to the Central Flying School he led the School's aerobatic team at the Hendon Air Pageant in July 1921, but as indicated above, he resigned his commission soon after. His life thereafter was a mix of highs and lows, much being recounted in his memoirs *The Mad Major* published in 1982, by Aero Publishers. Christopher Draper died at the age 86, in Camden, on Tuesday, 16th January 1979.

FLYING OFFICERS
4

| | BUCKLEY | Joseph | F/O | + | 03.03.22 | 20 Squadron |

Flying Officer Joseph Buckley and Aircraftman Charles Reginald Richardson died when their Bristol F.2b H1548 came into collision with Bristol F.2b E2442 from the squadron, and piloted by Flight Lieutenant John Bertram Fox MC and with Flight Sergeant Allen Benjamin Hemmings as his observer/air gunner. Both machines came down some 23 miles from Lahore during their return flight to Ambala [this corrects the information shown on the website A list of fatal accidents to British aircraft overseas 12 Nov 1918 - 1929 which reports the two aircraft as coming down near Amritsar while returning to Quetta]. Certainly, 20 Squadron was Ambala based at the time, moving to Quetta on 24th October 1922.

| | HEAVEN MC | Archibald Cecil | F/O | 30.09.29 | Relinquished |
| | PETT MC | Henry Basil | F/L | 06.04.26 | Resigned |

On appointment to a commission in the Auxiliary Air Force [LG 6 April 1926, issue 33148, page 2436]; the same page showing he joined No. 601 [County of London] Bombing Squadron.   F/L   11.01.28   Resigned

| 09095 | RIVETT- | Wilfred John | F/O | 12.11.24 | Relinquished |
| | CARNAC MBE | On account of ill-health. | | | |

FLYING OFFICERS [from PILOT OFFICERS]
5

| 09057 | *BLACKFORD | Douglas Leslie | A/Cmdr | 12.02.46 | Retirement |

Air Commodore Douglas Leslie Blackford twice mentioned in despatches, died in December 1953.

| 09092 | DUNNING | Robert William Ferguson | F/L | 06.10.31 | Relinquished |

Returned to the service and was granted a commission in the Administrative and Special Duties Branch as a Pilot Officer [probation] on 26th August 1940, initially as 84463 [LG 27 September 1940, issue 34954, page 5720].   P/O   28.05.41   Resigned

| 21128 | *HESKETH | Richard Norman | W/Cdr | 07.04.50 | Retirement |
| | USHER-SOMERS | Cronan Edmund | F/O | + | 16.05.24 | 20 Squadron |

Flying Officer Cronan Edmund Usher-Somers was killed when his Bristol F.2b D7821 stalled shortly after departing Quetta with Lieutenant Edward Charrington Mackenzie, Adjutant with the 25th Pack Artillery Brigade, based at Quetta. Flying Officer Usher-Somers medals, which included an India General Service 1908-35, with Waziristan Clasp 1919-21 [He was attached to 20 Squadron] was auctioned in 2011 by Dix Noonan Webb in March 2011, selling for £330. Lieutenant Mackenzie is commemorated on the Lancing College War Memorial.

| | WILSON | Leslie Talbot | Lieutenant | 19.01.21 | Resigned |

OBSERVER OFFICER

| 09043 | THOMASSON DFC MM | Frederick | F/L | 30.04.52 | Relinquished |

Squadron Leader Frederick Thomasson DFC MM received a commission in the Secretarial Branch on 6th December 1948, reverting to Flight Lieutenant and adopting the service number 192835 [LG 8 February 1949, supplement 38532, page 683].

LG 12 October 1920, issue 32081, page 9892

CHAPLAINS BRANCH

| | ELAND | Mackenzie James | S/Ldr | 15.02.27 | Resigned |

LG 15 October 1920, issue 32086, page 10000

FLIGHT LIEUTENANT

| | *INGPEN | Donald Lane | W/Cdr | 11.08.33 | Retired list |

On account of ill-health [LG 15 August 1933, issue 33969, page 5426]. Wing Commander Donald Lane Ingpen of the Legal Branch had been on half-pay since 16th November 1932, owing to problems with his health [LG 15 November 1932, issue 33883, page 7265].

LG 26 October 1920, issue 32096, page 10306

FLIGHT LIEUTENANT

09098   DABBS   Douglas Hammond   F/L   20.08.28   Relinquished
Returned to the service and was commissioned to the Administrative and Special Duties Branch as a Pilot Officer on probation 1st November 1940, initially given a new service number 88082 [LG 20 December 1940, issue 35019, page 7121] but subsequently reverted to 09098 on promotion to Flying Officer 2nd March 1941 [LG 8 August 1941, issue 35241, page 4581].   W/Cdr   08.06.54   Relinquished

FLYING OFFICERS
8

09099   *CAHILL   Charles Howard   G/Capt   16.11.46   Retirement
09101   *CHAMBERLAYNE Paul Richard Tankerville James   A/Cmdr   12.08.46   Retirement
         AFC Michael Isidore Camille Austrian by birth Air Commodore Paul Richard Tankerville James Michael Isidore Camille Chamberlayne CB AFC, died on Wednesday, 3rd May 1972. Known as 'Tanks', in early life he was appointed as a page at the court of Emperor Franz Joseph in Vienna. On 4th February 1916, he was attached to 11 Squadron [Bristol Scout] but was badly injured when he crashed taking off from Bertangles on 29th April 1916. On 5th May, he was evacuated to England aboard HMHS *Stad Antwerpen*. On 4th August 1932, he took over command of 30 Squadron [Wapiti IIA] at Mosul and is mentioned several times in John F Hamlin's history of the squadron published by Air-Britain in 1932, titled *Flat Out The story of 30 Squadron Royal Air Force*.
         LELEU   Lionel Louis   F/O   19.10.23   To Class A
While still on the Reserve, Flying Officer Lionel Louis Leleu joined Imperial Airways and was killed on Tuesday, 28th March 1933, when a fire broke out in the cabin of AW Argosy II G-AACI *City of Liverpool* resulting in a terrible crash at Eessen near Diksmuide [West Vlaanderen], Belgium. Including Captain Leleu, fifteen perished, the youngest of the passengers being a young German girl, *Fräulein* Lotte Voss, aged sixteen. The oldest passenger is believed to have been 54 year old Sir John Thomas Podger Rowland. As reported on the Aviation Safety Network, which I dutifully acknowledge, Captain Leleu had taken off from Brussel-Haren on a scheduled flight to Croydon and eyewitnesses to the accident report seeing the Argosy descended, trailing smoke from the rear section, when at approximately 200 feet the tail section parted company with the fuselage. An unproven theory suggested the fire was deliberately started either in the toilet or luggage area by a passenger intent on committing suicide. If it was deliberate, then this was the first time that a civil airliner had been destroyed by sabotage.
         LITTLEWOOD   John Edward Harry   F/O   12.10.35   Relinquished
         SANDIFORD   Henry Spear   F/L   +   10.05.35   30 Squadron
Flight Lieutenant Henry Spear Sandiford [often referred to as Harry Spear Sandiford] was killed when his Wapiti IIA J9853 collided with an armoured car on the musketry range near Mosul. Aircraftman John Gilbert Plevey, who was in the armoured car died, while Leading Aircraftman Jack Woledge Rogers who was the Wapiti's air gunner, survived, though was gravely injured. Leading Aircraftman Harold Gilbert Keattch who was in the car escaped with only minor injuries. Flight Lieutenant Sandiford and Aircraftman Plevey, attached to No. 1 Armoured Car Company, were buried with full military honours in Ma'asker Al Raschid RAF Cemetery. The tragedy, it seems, was not reported in the squadron's operations record book. Air-Britain's J1-J9999 register reports the Wapiti as coming into collision with two armoured cars.
         SMITH   Graham Stuart   F/O   09.11.27   Relinquished
On account of ill-health [LG 20 December 1927, issue 33339, page 8144].
         VEEVERS CARTER George   F/L   06.08.38   Relinquished
Flight Lieutenant George Veevers-Carter had, meanwhile, been granted a commission in Class C of the Reserve of Air Force Officers on 18th October 1937 [LG 7 December 1937, issue 34461, page 7662], subsequently commissioned on 18th September 1939, within the Administrative and Special Duties Branch with the service number 75510 [LG 14 November 1939, issue 34733, page 7645]. S/Ldr   11.09.54   Relinquished
09109   *VINCENT AFC   Stanley Flamank   AV-M   06.02.50   Retirement
Air Vice-Marshal Stanley Flamank Vincent CB DFC AFC, died on Saturday, 13th March 1976. His biography published on the Air of Authority website is extensive; he is credited as destroying the first enemy aircraft for 60 Squadron in the *Great War* while in the Second World War as Commanding Officer of Northolt during the *Battle of Britain* he is reputed to have attacked a formation of Dorniers head-on, shooting down five, though these were never credited. Thus, according to the biography, he was the only pilot to shoot down enemy aircraft in both wars. Among his other notable attributes was the establishment during the *Great War* of a standard pattern of verbal instructions to trainee pilots.

FLYING OFFICERS [from PILOT OFFICERS]
3

         SAGON   Colin   F/O   12.10.35   Relinquished
         SHAW   Cyril Raymond Laurence   F/O   +   25.06.34   Bristol RFS Filton
Flying Officer Cyril Raymond Laurence Shaw was killed while giving dual instruction in DH.82 Tiger Moth G-ACBE when it came into collision with DH.82 Tiger Moth G-ACBB. Both aircraft had taken off from Filton, G-ACBB being flown with Flying Officer Hamish McKenzie Kerr instructing Flying Officer Geoffrey Paul French Hills who died when the trainer fell into a wheat field near the village of Nibley on the west side of Yate, Gloucestershire. Flying Officer Kerr parachuted and his life was saved as he fell into a deepish quarry which gave him those few precious extra feet of heigh to allow his parachute to deploy, plus the fact that he came down in water that cushioned his landing. Flying Officer Shaw also baled out but at too low an altitude to allow his parachute to fully open. His pupil, Flying Officer John Macphee Darroch, sadly, did not survive.
09108   TURNER MM   Arthur   F/O   12.10.27   Relinquished
Returned to the service and served until.   S/Ldr   11.09.54   Relinquished

LG 29 October 1920, issue 32105, page 10456

PILOT OFFICER

08011   NEWTON   George Ewart   F/L   18.10.31   Relinquished
Returned to the service and granted a commission in Class CC of the Reserve of Air Force Officers with effect from 20th June 1938, retaining his rank [LG 13 December 1938, issue 34579, page 7921].   W/Cdr   26.10.54   Relinquished

LG 12 November 1920, issue 32122, page 11003

FLIGHT LIEUTENANTS
5

         ADAMS OBE   Paul   S/Ldr   17.06.33   Relinquished
         FOXEN   Harry Thomas   S/Ldr   17.06.27   Relinquished
On account of ill-health [LG 12 July 1927, issue 33293, page 4497].
10180   GALLOWAY   Ernest Douglas   S/Ldr   17.06.32   To Class B
Still in the Reserve of Air Force Officers, Squadron Leader Ernest Douglas Galloway was granted a commission in Class CC of the Equipment Branch as a Flight Lieutenant [Honorary Squadron Leader], 12th May 1939 [LG 8 September 1939, supplement 34674, page 6135]. His Class CC commission was relinquished on 1st September 1939 [LG 30 December 1941, issue 35398, page 7380]. S/Ldr   15.03.45   Resigned
         GORDON MBE   Thomas Grove   S/Ldr   17.06.31   Relinquished
         *STEVENS   George   G/Capt   10.02.42   Retired list

286

	BAMBER	Robert Quarm		F/O	17.06.31	Relinquished
10189	BASSETT	Richard		F/O	17.06.39	Relinquished
	BLACKITH	Robert		F/O	09.04.24	Relinquished

On account of ill-health. Paul McMillan, my co-authors, reports Flying Officer Robert Blackith died on Sunday, 27th April 1930.

10193	BOREHAM	Charles Henry		F/O	17.06.27	Relinquished

Granted a commission in Class C of the Reserve of Air Force Officers, General Duties Branch, retaining his rank on 28th October 1938 [LG 28TH February 1939, issue 34603, page 1396]. Thence to a commission in the Administrative and Special Duties Branch, 23rd June 1938, ranked Flight Lieutenant [LG 31 October 1939, issue 34721, page 7276].

				F/L	24.05.42	Relinquished

On ceasing to be employed and retain his rank [LG 2 June 1942, issue 35580, page 2383].

	CLARKE	Harry William		F/L	17.07.29	Relinquished
	FINZEL	Francis Edward Charles		F/O	17.06.27	Relinquished
10182	HARVEY	Charles		S/Ldr	17.06.30	Relinquished
	HAWKER	Harry Bartlett		F/L	17.06.31	Relinquished
10201	ORMEROD	Francis Albert		F/O	17.06.31	Relinquished

A file for this officer is held by TNA Kew under AIR 76/382/103.

10202	PEIRCE	Leonard Reginald		S/Ldr	10.08.54	Relinquished
10204	PLUNKETT	John Augustus		F/L	17.06.27	To Class C

Flight Lieutenant John Augustus Plunkett died while still in the Reserve, his son notifying the authorities by letter on 2nd November 1930, that his father, who was Postmaster at RAF Halton, had died on Saturday, 20th September 1930. My co-author also adds that a file for Flight Lieutenant Plunkett is at TNA Kew under AIR 76/406/142.

	ROBERTS	John		F/L	17.06.31	Relinquished
10205	SHAW MBE	Walter Langston		S/Ldr	17.06.31	Relinquished

Returned to the service, relinquishing a commission in Class CC, with effect from 1st September 1939 [LG 28 November 1939, issue 34742, page 7964]. Served until.

				W/Cdr	17.08.54	Relinquished
	STEER	Elias George		F/O	11.10.27	Relinquished
	STOKES	Frederick Samuel		F/O	17.06.27	Relinquished
	SURR	Thomas		F/L	17.06.31	Relinquished
	VAUGHAN	Charles St. John		F/O	17.06.31	Relinquished

LG 16 November 1920, issue 32125, page 11119

FLIGHT LIEUTENANT [from SQUADRON LEADER]

	NICOLL	Reginald Eycott		F/L	15.10.29	Relinquished

FLYING OFFICERS
6

	GARDNER	Harold William		F/O	+	10.03.21	AEE Martlesham Heath

Flying Officer Harold William Gardner lost his life while test-flying DH.10 F8423, crashing from an uncontrolled spin at Hasketon, a mile or so WNW from the centre of Woodbridge, Suffolk. He is buried in Croydon [Mitcham Road] Cemetery.

	HUMPHREY	Wilfred Beresford Joe		F/O	21.03.23	Relinquished

On account of ill-health [LG 20 March 1923, issue 32807, page 2170]. However, his health improved and he was granted a commission in Class C [Equipment Branch], in the rank of Flight Lieutenant, on 16th February 1938 [5 July 1938, issue 34528, page 4335], subsequently transferred from Class C to Class CC [LG 15 November 1938, issue 34570, page 7198]. On 1st September 1939, he was commissioned within the Royal Air Force Volunteer Reserve with the service number 75876 [LG 5 December 1939, issue 34747, page 8107], transferring to the Administrative and Special Duties Branch.

				W/Cdr	09.07.54	Relinquished
	KLYNES	Alexander Henry		F/O +	08.04.24	

Flying Officer Alexander Henry Klynes died on Tuesday, 8th April 1924, in RAF Hospital Finchley. Creditors or claimants on his his estate were advised to contact Charles Everett, Solicitors at 5 Arundel Street, Strand, London WC.2 [LG 27 June 1924, issue 32950, page 5033].

	LANGLEY DFC	Matthew John		F/O	23.01.23	Remove

His Majesty having no further occasion for his services as an officer [LG 6 February 1923, issue 32793, page 912], a sad conclusion for an officer Who served with distinction in South Russia and was *Gazetted* with the DFC [EG 26 December 1919, issue 13543, page 4139]. Note. A Sapper Matthew John Langley [114359] was commissioned to the Royal Engineers, Territorial Army, as a Lieutenant on 20th January 1940 [LG 19 January 1940, supplement 34775, page 350].

	NICHOLSON	Ernest William		F/L	+	14.01.24	Isle of Grain

Admitted to St. Bartholomews Hospital, Flight Lieutenant Ernest William Nicholson died on Monday, 14th January 1924, from diabetes and pleurisy.

09163	*WARWICK	Alwyn John		G/Capt	02.03.45	Retirement

PILOT OFFICERS
4

09154	*GAUNTLETT	Francis Vincent		F/O	29.10.29	Relinquished

By 1938, Flying Officer Francis Vincent Gauntlett had returned to the service [General Duties Branch] and with effect from 7th May 1938, was transferred from Class C to Class CC in the rank of Flight Lieutenant [LG 15 November 1938, issue 34570, page 7197]. His service was extended on 1st March 1947, for a further four years on the active list, and as a Squadron Leader was transferred from Administrative and Special Duties Branch to the Secretarial Branch, and with allocation of a new service number 192860 [LG 2 May 1947, supplement 37947, page 2013]. He was appointed to a commission in Class CC of the Branch on 29th April 1949 [LG 2 August 1949, supplement 38679, page 3751]. He continued to serve until 1960 [LG 8th March 1960, supplement 41975, page 1725].

				S/Ldr	01.03.60	Relinquished
09156	KOHLER	Eric Frank		P/O	07.09.22	Relinquished

On account of ill-health contracted in the Service [LG 3 October 1922, issue 32752, page 6989]. He returned to the service on 1st September 1939, as a Pilot Officer, in the Administrative and Special Duties Branch [LG 7 November 1939, issue 34727, page 7503], retaining his original service number. Subsequently appointed OBE he served until.

				W/Cdr	13.07.54	Relinquished
	ROBERTSON MM	Cecil Duncan		F/O	29.10.28	Relinquished
	RUSH	Edward Arthur		P/O +	19.08.21	2 FTS Duxford

Pilot Officer Edward Arthur Rush, accompanied by Pilot Officer Eric Raven Lush, took off from Duxford in Bristol F.2b H1419, authorised for a cross-country flight which appears to have proceeded satisfactorily until engine failure occurred and while attempting to turn, presumably to make a forced-landing, the Bristol stalled and spun in at Croxton a mile to the NNE from the centre of Thetford, Norfolk. Both officers perished, Edward Arthur Rush being just nineteen years of age.

LG 30 November 1920, issue 32146, page 11823

SQUADRON LEADER

*CLEVERLY	Sidney Mechen		S/Ldr	+	15.01.24	Isle of Grain

On Tuesday, 15th January 1924, Squadron Leader Sidney Mechen Cleverly was an observer in Bristol F.2B C4721, which took off from the Isle of Grain with Flight Lieutenant William Reginald Curtis at the controls. Soon after take off the engine failed and while attempting to turn, control was lost and the aircraft spun to the ground with fatal consequences for both officers. The Bristol was attached to the Directorate of Research at the Air Ministry.

FLYING OFFICERS
4

	PIDSLEY	George William	F/O	+	09.04.22	203 Squadron

Flying Officer George William Pidsley while attached to 203 Squadron at Donibristle was involved in a motorcycle accident and died from a fracture to his skull. He was off duty at the time.

	PIGGOTT	John	F/O	17.06.27	Relinquished
	WALLAS	Robin Fraser	Lieutenant	11.01.22	Resigned
09169	*WARDLE	Alfred Randles	Air Cmdr	02.12.52	Retired

Air Commodore Alfred Randles Wardle CBE AFC, died on 31st July 1989.

FLYING OFFICER [from PILOT OFFICER]

JOHNS	William Earl	F/O	15.10.31	Relinquished

LG 17 December 1920, issue 32166, page 12401

FLIGHT LIEUTENANT
2

*FERNIHOUGH MC Frank		G/Capt	16.10.45	Retirement
*HENDERSON MC AFC Thomas		F/L	01.11.27	Resigned

As my co-author reports, a document for Flight Lieutenant Thomas Henderson is held at TNA Kew under AIR 76/221/124. After leaving the service he married into the Dechars Brewing family. Born on 22nd May 1894, he served as an observer with 10 Squadron during the *Great War.*

FLYING OFFICERS
9

	BOWYER	Stanley Arthur Hamilton	Captain	08.02.22	Resigned

Believed returned to the service; commissioned to the Administrative and Special Duties Branch as a Pilot Officer on probation, 1st August 1939, as Stanley Arthur Hamilton-Bowyer [LG 8 August 1939, issue 34652, page 5486], as 73815. Transferred to the General Duties Branch 3rd October 1940 [LG 14 February 1941, issue 35076, page 911].

			S/Ldr	01.07.54	Relinquished
	CHAUNCY	Peter	F/O	24.11.27	Relinquished
	CLARK	Clifford Claude	F/O	16.11.37	Resigned
	DURWARD	John	F/L	07.12.29	Relinquished
09176	*HILL	Cedric Waters	G/Capt	05.01.44	Retirement

Australia Paul McMillan reports that on leaving the service, Group Captain Cedric Waters Hill continued flying as a ferry pilot with Air Transport Auxiliary, further adding that during the *Great War* he was taken prisoner by the Turks and was held at Yozgad prisoner of war camp from where he escaped in the company of Lieutenant Elias Henry Jones. A detailed account of their ingenious escape can be read on the website Australian Dictionary of Biography. Turning to Trevor Henshaw's *The Sky Their Battlefield* and Part VII operations in Egypt and Palestine, Second Lieutenant Hill's capture is reported on 3rd May 1916, when his 14 Squadron BE.2c 4419 was hit by file fire during a photographic reconnaissance to El Arish. Forced-landing on the Bardawill Peninsula he was captured following a mammoth seven hour engagement with Arabs, whom he tried to bribe for the the then considerable sum of fifty pounds for his freedom, but to no avail. Born in Warwick, Australia on 3rd April 1891, he died in England at Windsor on Friday, 5th of March 1971. He was 83 years of age.

	LOUGHLIN	Kenneth	F/O	28.01.25	Removed

Upon his conviction by the Civil Power [LG 27 January 1925, issue 33015, page 596].

09178	OXLEY-BOYLE	Eric Hardy	S/Ldr	12.05.43	Resigned
	STALLARD	James	F/L	24.01.28	Resigned

My co-author reports that James Stallard, born born at Bodmin in Cornwall on 20th February 1897, was commissioned as a Lieutenant to the Devonshire Regiment in the Second World War. He died on Thursday, 29th December 1960, in Scotland at Stirling.

WALTER	Richard Slade	F/O	24.11.31	Relinquished

PILOT OFFICER

BAUGH	Robert Edward	F/O	16.04.24	Resigned

Appendix 3F - The Roll of Honour 1st January 1920 - 31st December 1920

Royal Air Force

AC2	BASS	Gerald Tipping	29 April 1920	230 Squadron
F/O	BOCKETT PUGH DFC	Henry Charles Edward	22 September 1920	84 Squadrpn
AC2	BRAITHWAITE	Percy	12 July 1920	24 Squadron
O/O	BYRNE	Brennan Claude Sydney	3 September 1920	47 Squadron
AC1	CARRO	Walter John	21 January 1920	47 Squadron
F/O	COURTENAY-DUNN Royal Engineers	Adrian Lancelot	21 March 1920	99 Squadron
F/O	DEANE MC 4/Norfolk Regiment	William	20 March 1920	20 Squadron
LAC	DELLOW	Leonard Alfred	18 September 1920	30 Squadron
/O	de PENCIER Canada	John Dartnell	17 May 1920	12 Squadron
F/O	ESSELL DFC	Robert Narcissus	9 December 1920	6 Squadron
F/O	FENWICK	Horace Edgar	4 November 1920	24 Squadron
F/O	FITZGERALD- New Zealand	Neale	14 June 1920	14 Squadron
F/O	FYFIELD	Albert John	29 April 1920	230 Squadron
AC1	GOODHILL	Arthur Leonard	29 November 1920	216 Squadron
F/O	GORDON DFC	Robert Bissett	20 March 1920	20 Squadron
F/O	HOLLAND	Horace Lloyd	21 February 1920	100 Squadron
F/O	HUTCHINSON	Harold	2 August 1920	6 Squadron
F/O	JAQUES MC AFC Durham Light Infantry	John Barclay	1 April 1920	216 Squadron
F/O	MACQUEEN	Alexander John	5 July 1920	12 Squadron
AC2	MARSHALL	Alexander Langton	1 November 1920	84 Squadron
F/O	McDONALD MC DFC. Ian Donald Roy		22 September 1920	84 Squadron
AC2	McINTOSH	J W	23 January 1920	58 Squadron
AC2	MELDRUM	Reginald Collin	1 April 1920	216 Squadron
S/Ldr	MOON DSO* Chevalier d'Honneur	Edwin Rowland	29 April 1920	230 Squadron
F/L	NUTTALL MC DFC AFC Frank Twice mentioned in a despatch New Zealand		18 September 1920	30 Squadron
AC2	OLIVER	Frank Cecil	28 June 1920	60 Squadron
F/O	PALMER DFC	Robert Daniel Cecil	2 August 1920	6 Squadron
F/O	PIPE	James	1 January 1920	31 Squadron
F/O	PITHEY DFC South Africa	Croye Rothes	21 February 1920	2 Squadron
F/O	PROUT AFC	Harold Oliver	4 November 1920	24 Squadron
F/O	PUGHE	Robert	16 April 1920	5 Squadron
F/O	REYNOLDS Hampshire Regiment	Victor Oliver	12 July 1920	24 Squadron
F/O	RIDLEY DSC	Cyril Burfield	17 May 1920	12 Squadron
F/O	RIGDEN	Cecil Osborne	29 November 1920	216 Squadron
P/O	SIBLEY	Desmond Wilkie	1 April 1920	216 Squadron
F/O	SIDEBOTTOM DFC William		8 December 1920	30 Squadron
F/O	SWANSTON DFC*	John Romilly	28 June 1920	60 Squadron
AC1	THACKER	Percy William James	14 June 1920	14 Squadron
Sgt	WADEY DFM	Edmund West	1 April 1920	216 Squadron
AC2	WALLWORK	Wallace	1 November 1920	84 Squadron
F/O	WALLER	Hardress de Warrenne	21 February 1920	2 Squadron

Army

Major	CHADS MC 2/Border Regiment	Harry Francis	28 August 1920	2 Squadron

Portuguese Navy

Sub-Lt	FONSECA	Guiltherine J d'A	29 April 1920	230 Squadron

Addendum

Air Chief Marshal Sir Ronald Ivelaw-Chapman who is profiled in Appendix E for 1919, was serving as a Flight Commander with 10 Squadron when the Armistice was signed in 1918. Upon hearing the news that the armistice would come into effect at 11 o'clock, Captain Ivelaw-Chapman managed to acquire a football from the squadron's mechanics and handing it to his observer took off in his FK.8 and, as recorded on pages 56 and 57 of *At The Eleventh Hour - Reflections, Hopes and Anxieties at the Closing of the Great War 1918* edited by Hugh Cecil and Peter H Liddle [Leo Cooper, 1998], *'Saw the last few minutes of the War. Our troops halted at 11.00.'* Flying over their heads his observer dropped the football and both officers were rewarded by seeing the soldiers having a good old kick-about; a pleasing sight, indeed.

Permanent Commissions.
LG 20 January 1920, issue 31743, page 837 appointed the following with seniority effective from 1st August 1919.

			FLIGHT LIEUTENANT			
	WATSON AM	Victor Albert		F/L	20.01.20	Cancelled
			FLYING OFFICER			
04044	HARRISON DFC	George Henry		G/Capt	18.03.46	Retirement**

LG 8 March 1921 issue 32250, page 1899

			FLIGHT LIEUTENANT			
	ROBARTS MC	Geoffrey Ward		W/Cdr	23.05.36	Retired list

At his own request [LG 2 June 1936, issue 34290, page 3526].

Aircraft Types Lost in Squadron Service

12th November 1918 – 31st December 1920

All images are sourced under Open Government Licence 2.0

Aircraft Manufacturing Company (Airco) DH4

Airco DH9

Airco DH9A

Airco DH10

Armstrong Whitworth FK.8

Avro 504

Bristol F2b fighters

Handley-Page O/400

Handley Page V/1500

Martinsyde G.100

Royal Aircraft Factory BE2E

Royal Aircraft Factory FE2B

Short Felixstowe F5 flying boats

Sopwith Camel

Sopwith Cuckoo

Sopwith Dolphin

Sopwith Pup

Sopwith Snipe

BV - #0050 - 251024 - C1 - 297/210/17 - PB - 9781911255574 - Gloss Lamination